HIDDEN®

Pacific Northwest

"An excellent guidebook that's been made even better in this updated and redesigned edition."
—*Seattle Times & Post-Intelligencer*

"Uncovers the true spirit of this unique region."
—*Tennessean*

"*Hidden Pacific Northwest* lives up to its name with its tips on finding attractions that are off the beaten path."
—*Edmonton Sun*

"Written with an eye for the off-beat, the book is the perfect companion for a jaunt up the Oregon coast, a camping trip on the Olympic Peninsula or even a visit to Vancouver. . . . Fun to read for both the casual visitor and the intrepid traveler."
—*Our World*

"*Hidden Pacific Northwest* spotlights traditional attractions and alternatives in Washington, Oregon and British Columbia. The authors avoid standard hotels and chain restaurants in favor of one-of-a-kind places and locally owned establishments."
—*Ashbury Park Press*

HIDDEN®

Pacific Northwest

Including Oregon, Washington, Vancouver, Victoria & Coastal British Columbia

EIGHTH EDITION

Ulysses Press®

BERKELEY, CALIFORNIA

Published by:
ULYSSES PRESS
P.O. Box 3440
Berkeley, CA 94703
www.ulyssespress.com

ISSN 1522-1172
ISBN10: 1-56975-576-0
ISBN13: 978-1-56975-576-1

Printed in Canada by Transcontinental Printing

20 19 18 17 16 15 14 13 12

AUTHORS: Eric Lucas, Richard Harris, Stephen Dolainski,
    John Gottberg
UPDATE AUTHOR: Nicky Leach
MANAGING EDITOR: Claire Chun
PROJECT DIRECTOR: Elyce Petker
COPY EDITORS: Lily Chou, Mark Woodworth
EDITORIAL ASSOCIATES: Ruth Marcus, Laurel Shane, Rebekah Morris
    Elizabeth Winter
TYPESETTERS: Lisa Kester, Matt Orendorff
CARTOGRAPHY: Pease Press
HIDDEN BOOKS DESIGN: Sarah Levin
INDEXER: Sayre Van Young
COVER PHOTOGRAPHY: courtesy of Washington State Tourism
ILLUSTRATOR: Catherine Rose Crowther

Distributed by Publishers Group West

The author and publisher have made every effort to ensure the
accuracy of information contained in *Hidden Pacific Northwest*,
but can accept no liability for any loss, injury or inconvenience
sustained by any traveler as a result of information or advice
contained in this guide.

For Sarah Levin,
who changed the face of the Pacific Northwest
and all the rest of the hidden world

Write to us!

If in your travels you discover a spot that captures the spirit of the Pacific Northwest, or if you live in the region and have a favorite place to share, or if you just feel like expressing your views, write to us and we'll pass your note along to the author.

We can't guarantee that the author will add your personal find to the next edition, but if the writer does use the suggestion, we'll acknowledge you in the credits and send you a free copy of the new edition.

ULYSSES PRESS
P.O. Box 3440
Berkeley, CA 94703
E-mail: readermail@hiddenguides.com

Acknowledgments

Ulysses Press would like to thank the following readers who took the time to write in with suggestions that were incorporated into this new edition of *Hidden Pacific Northwest*:

Terry and Paul Thierry of Seattle, WA, Vicci Rudin of Port Angeles, WA

What's Hidden?

At different points throughout this book, you'll find special listings marked with this symbol:

◄ *HIDDEN*

This means that you have come upon a place off the beaten tourist track, a spot that will carry you a step closer to the local people and natural environment of the Pacific Northwest.

The goal of this guide is to lead you beyond the realm of everyday tourist facilities. While we include traditional sightseeing listings and popular attractions, we also offer alternative sights and adventure activities. Instead of filling this guide with reviews of standard hotels and chain restaurants, we concentrate on one-of-a-kind places and locally owned establishments.

Our authors seek out locales that are popular with residents but usually overlooked by visitors. Some are more hidden than others (and are marked accordingly), but all the listings in this book are intended to help you discover the true nature of the Pacific Northwest and put you on the path of adventure.

Contents

Maps

OUTDOOR ADVENTURE SYMBOLS

The following symbols accompany national, state and regional park listings, as well as beach descriptions throughout the text.

Camping		Surfing	
Hiking		Waterskiing	
Biking		Windsurfing	
Horseback Riding		Canoeing or Kayaking	
Downhill Skiing		Boating	
Cross-country Skiing		Boat Ramps	
Swimming		Fishing	
Snorkeling or Scuba Diving			

ONE

The Pacific Northwest

The Pacific Northwest goes by many names, but perhaps "The Evergreen Playground" best captures its enchanting appeal. This is a land of intense beauty: gossamer mists on towering evergreens, icy summits that cast shadows on pastoral valleys and bustling cityscapes, wind-sculpted trees on wave-battered capes and inlets, warm breezes through juniper boughs. Powerful volcanoes, wondrous waterfalls, glistening waterways, even shifting desert sands.

The heavy rainfall for which the Pacific Northwest is famous is truly the heart that gives the region its majestic soul. The drizzle and clouds that blanket the coastal region during much of the winter and spring nourish the incredibly green landscape that grows thick and fast and softens the sharp edges of alpine peaks and jagged sea cliffs. But there's a flip side: Over half the region (meaning points east of the Cascade Range) is actually warm and dry through the year.

"The Evergreen Playground" fairly begs to be explored. While much of it remains undeveloped, vast expanses of wilderness are close by all metropolitan centers. Almost without exception, each city is surrounded by countless outdoor recreational opportunities, with mountains, lakes, streams and an ocean within easy reach. It's no surprise that residents and visitors tend to have a hardy, outdoorsy glow. After all, it is the proximity to nature that draws people here. That remains especially true in Oregon, where development of the land is allowed only in certain areas close to a city center within an "urban growth boundary." The areas outside the towns are protected from the ugly suburban sprawl that has spread throughout much of the West Coast.

Asian populations lend an exotic feel to the bustling commercial centers of Seattle, Portland and Vancouver, while the distinctly British aura of Victoria imparts an entirely different foreign appeal. A montage of tiny ghost towns, towering totem poles, aging wooden forts, Scandinavian and Bavarian communities, stage stops and gold-mining boomtowns, and old-time fishing villages adds a frontier feel to the Vancouver region.

This book will help you explore this wonderful area, tell of its history, introduce you to its flora and fauna. Besides taking you to countless popular spots, it will lead you to off-the-beaten-path locales. Each chapter will suggest places to eat, to stay, to sightsee, to shop and to enjoy the outdoors and nightlife, covering a range of tastes and budgets.

The book starts in Seattle, taking visitors in Chapter Two through this popular city and the surrounding communities spread along Southern Puget Sound. Chapter Three heads up the Sound, taking in some small and some not-so-small coastal towns and the San Juans, an archipelago of evergreen-clad islands. Chapter Four covers the moss-laden rainforests and historic port towns of Washington's Olympic Peninsula and southwestern coast while Chapter Five explores the numerous parks, forests, wildernesses and removed resort communities of the Washington Cascades.

Chapter Six heads to the arid plateau and desert region east of the Cascades in both Washington and Oregon. Portland, the "City of Roses," and the windy Columbia Gorge are the subject of Chapter Seven. Next we go on one of the nation's most scenic drives along the Oregon Coast in Chapter Eight and on to Mt. Hood, Mt. Bachelor, Crater Lake and other majestic peaks of the Oregon Cascades in Chapter Nine. Chapter Ten covers the cultural, learning and political centers lining the Heart of Oregon.

In Chapter Eleven we visit British Columbia, Canada's most westerly province, with stops in enticing Vancouver and the famous Whistler ski resort, followed by a motoring trip up the sleepy Sunshine Coast, an outdoors-lover's paradise. Chapter Twelve rounds out the book with a ferry trip to unspoiled Vancouver Island, its coasts lined with bucolic fishing villages, and to the very proper, very English Victoria, capital of the province.

What you choose to see and do is up to you, but don't delay; things are changing here. The Pacific Northwest is no longer the quiet backwater of a decade ago. Growth and expansion continue in the major population centers strung along the long, black ribbon of Route 5. While Northwesterners are vociferous advocates for preserving nature, rapidly increasing population and growing economic demands are taking a toll.

Sadly, it's becoming difficult to miss the horrid clear-cut swaths through the evergreen background, evidence of the logging industry that feeds the local economies. Salmon that once choked the many streams and rivers have dwindled in number, as have numerous forest creatures such as the spotted owl.

Tourism has also had an impact. As the beauty of the area has been "discovered" by travelers who've taken home tales of this don't-spread-it-around secret vacationland, it's become a hot destination, especially among international visitors. It's getting harder and harder to find those special hidden spots—go soon before "hidden" no longer applies.

▼▼▼▼▼▼▼▼▼▼

The Story of the Pacific Northwest

GEOLOGY

Between a billion and 200 million years ago, magma erupting from the earth's core led to spreading oceanic ridges in the Pacific and Atlantic oceans. As the oceans widened, the continents broke apart and what is now the Pacific Northwest made its first appearance. Washington and southern British Columbia grew again, beginning 100 million years ago, when island continents floating in the Pacific Ocean began to collide with North America and attach themselves to the mainland as microcontinents. Today, the North Cascades range, which spans the international boundary between northwestern Washington and British Columbia, is the best place to see the eroded remains of these nonvolcanic, island-formed terrains.

Washington and Oregon's ancestral volcanoes began to emerge 40 million years ago, but the modern Cascades appeared only about a million years ago with the pumice and lava erup-

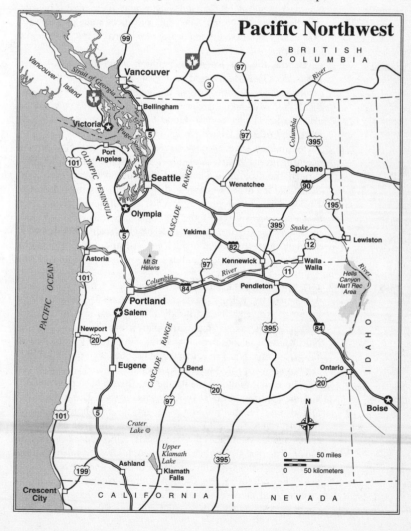

Pacific Northwest

tions that built Mount Rainier. Younger volcanoes like Mount St. Helens, the youngest and most active in the range, formed only 70,000 years ago and remain highly active today.

Unrelated to the volcanic Cascades, the Olympic Mountains began as lava flows along the continental shelf about 50 million years ago, mingling with ocean sediments and forming a thick offshore sedimentary delta. When the Cascades were pushed up by the subduction of the Pacific plate beneath the lighter North American plate, scientists think part of the oceanic plate, the Juan de Fuca plate, got hung up in the vicinity of Vancouver Island. The submerged offshore delta may have been forced to ride back to the North American continent and got rammed below lava basalts, forcing up a new nonvolcanic range: the Olympics.

During the last Ice Age, 2 million years ago, massive ice sheets from Canada covered the region, and glaciers sculpted the peaks, valleys and fjords of the distinctive Northwest landscape. By 10,000 years ago, the warmer climate had melted much of the ice, flooding Puget Sound, Hood Canal, the Strait of Juan de Fuca, and other glaciated troughs.

Six million years ago, the Columbia River was being pushed north from its course by mile-deep basaltic lava flows that formed the Columbia Plateau. Catastrophic floods—the most extensive in history—carved the Columbia Gorge between 19,000 and 12,000 years ago, when a 2000-foot-high ice dam that impounded glacial Lake Missoula failed. The Bretz Floods buzzed vertically through Cascade basalts, sculpting Channeled Scabland terraces, coulees (side canyons) and dry falls, and left boulders and gravel high and dry.

HISTORY   **THE FIRST PEOPLE** The first migrants may have come from Asia across the Bering Strait land bridge some 25,000 years ago. From the diverse background of those earliest inhabitants descended the many American Indian tribes that populated the North American continent. Kwakiutl, Haida, Bella Coola, Tlingit, Salish, Yakima, Nez Perce, Paiutes, Shoshone, Umpqua and Rogue are but a few of the Northwest tribes.

The verdant land of the Pacific Northwest both provided for and dictated the lifestyles of the various tribes. Those that lived inland east of the mountain ranges lived a hunter-gatherer lifestyle, harvesting wild foods throughout the year as they became available. When the Spaniards reintroduced horses to North America, Columbia Plateau people traveled farther afield, paddling up the Columbia to attend huge annual rendezvous near The Dalles to trade, socialize and intermarry.

The mild climate and abundant resources of the valley and coast led to a fairly sedentary lifestyle for the tribes that lived west of the mountain ranges. They constructed permanent vil-lages of communal red-cedar longhouses, fished the rich waters of the coast and mouths of rivers, and developed complex ritual arts, ceremonies and other cultural pursuits. Social status was recognized through the potlatch, a ceremony that emphasized eating, dancing and the redistribution of gifts, such as blankets and carved cedar boxes, by chiefs to prove their power and pres-tige.

Arrival of the white man brought many changes to the gen-erally peaceful natives. Introduction of the horse made life easier for a period, facilitating hunting and travel for the nomadic tribes. However, disease, drugs (namely alcohol) and distrust accompa-nied the newcomers and eventually added to the decline of the American Indian population. Land grabbing by European settlers forced the tribes onto ever-shrinking reservations.

Resurgence in American Indian arts and crafts is evident in galleries and museums throughout the Northwest. While most natives no longer live on the reservations but have integrated into white society, many have banded together to fight for change. Tribal organizations are now reclaiming lands and fishing rights; nations such as the Sechelt Band in British Columbia have won the legal right to independent self-government. There are even a growing number of native-owned-and-operated resorts such as Ka-Nee-Tah, a hot spring and golf retreat in central Oregon.

EARLY EXPLORATION   In terms of white exploration and settle-ment, the Pacific Northwest is one of the youngest regions on the continent. The Spanish began to arrive in the Northwest by sea as early as the mid-1500s; the Strait of Juan de Fuca, Heceta Head, Fidalgo Island, Cape Blanco, Quadra Island and other prominent landmarks bear witness to Spanish exploration and influence.

THE INFAMOUS PIG WAR

Tensions left over from the War of 1812 and the not-yet-forgotten American Revolution caused friction between the Americans and British in the North-west. The American/British Treaty of 1846 failed to define the border of the British territory, so the Americans and British agreed to use the 49th parallel. However, this latitude divided the San Juan Islands in two, leaving British and American soldiers staring each other down across the make-shift border. The entente was preserved until a lone British pig wandered into the garden of an American settler, who shot and killed the pig— the only bullet fired during the 13-year dispute, a diplomatic struggle for the islands that came to be called the "Pig War." Ultimately the islands were awarded to the United States by a German arbitrator in 1872.

Spanish interest waned when other pressing matters required the attention and money needed to chart the Northwest, and all claims to the area were dropped in 1819 as part of the negotiations regarding Florida.

The Russians also made their way into the region, beginning with the explorations of Vitus Dane in 1741. Soon afterward, Russian trappers trekked from Siberia down through Alaska and into the Northwest. As a result of losses brought on by the Napoleonic Wars, Russia renounced all claims to the area south of 54°40' in 1824.

Sir Francis Drake passed briefly along the Northwest Coast in 1579, but it was explorer Captain James Cook's expedition in 1778 in search of the legendary "Northwest Passage" that resulted in British claim to the region. When passing through China on their homeward-bound trip, he and his men discovered the high value of the pelts they carried, leading to an intense interest on the part of the British government in the profitable resources of the Northwest.

The government later commissioned Captain George Vancouver to chart the coastal area between 45° and 60° north latitude, which includes Oregon, Washington, British Columbia and Alaska. Mt. Baker, Whidbey Island, Puget Sound, Vancouver Island, Burrard Inlet and many other geographical features retain the names he gave them on his meticulously drawn maps completed between 1791 and 1795.

Captain Robert Gray was also plying Northwest waters at this time, making certain that the United States could lay claim to parts of the lucrative new territory. During his journey, he discovered the mighty Columbia River while searching for the same fabled waterway between the Pacific and Atlantic oceans.

Early explorers like Alexander McKenzie and Simon Fraser were actually the first Europeans to explore land routes, but it was not until Meriwether Lewis and William Clark explored and mapped overland passages, returning with stories of the area's beauty and natural bounty, that interest in settling the Northwest began in earnest.

THE NEWCOMERS   Trading posts were established to facilitate the fur enterprises; large firms like the Hudson's Bay Company and the North West Company vied for control of the profitable region. Settlements sprang up around these posts and continued to grow as the trickle of pioneers swelled into a wave with the opening of the Oregon Trail in the mid-1800s.

Tensions began to mount between American and British settlers who occupied the same territory and came to a head in the San Juan Islands in what's known as the bloodless "Pig War." An uneasy standoff between the nations held until successful negotiations divided American- and British-controlled territory in 1872.

Homesteading, fishing, logging, ranching and other opportunities kept the flow of settlers coming, as did a series of gold strikes. Stage routes were established, and river traffic grew steadily. There were enough residents to warrant separation of the Oregon Territory by the 1850s, and Washington and Oregon attained statehood by the turn of the 20th century. British Columbia was officially accepted as a Canadian province in 1871. Railroads pushed into the region, reaching Portland and Puget Sound by 1883 and British Columbia in 1885, ushering in the modern age.

> The land in the Pacific Northwest continues to shift slowly, as seen in the explosive powers of Mt. St. Helens and the creeping rise of the San Juan Islands from the Pacific.

Rapid industrial development came with the world wars, and the Northwest emerged as a major player in the shipbuilding and shipping industries. Expansion in lumber, agriculture and fishing continued apace. Growth industries today include banking, high technology and Pacific Rim trade. Modern residents are for the most part rugged individualists, fiercely proud of their natural setting and protective of the environment.

FLORA

While it's generally the coniferous trees that everyone equates with the Pacific Northwest, there is much more to the flora of the region than its abundance of redwoods, Western hemlock and white pine, red cedar and other evergreens. Each of the distinct geologic zones hosts its own particular ecosystem.

In the moist woodlands of the coastline, glossy madrone and immense Coast redwoods tower over Pacific trilliums and delicate ladyslippers. Bogs full of skunkcabbage thrive alongside fields of yellow Scotch broom and hardy rhododendrons in a riot of color. Unique to the region are pristine rainforests with thick carpets of moss and fern beneath sky-scraping canopies of fir, cedar and spruce.

In the lowland valleys, alders, oaks, maples and other deciduous trees provide brilliant displays of color against an evergreen backdrop each spring and fall. Daffodils and tulips light up the fields, as do azaleas, red clover and other grasses grown by the many nurseries and seed companies that prosper here. Wild berry bushes run rampant in this clime, bringing blackberries, huckleberries, currants and strawberries for the picking. Indian paintbrush, columbines, foxglove, buttercups and numerous other wildflowers are also abundant.

The verdant parks and forests of the mountain chains contain some of the biggest trees in the world, holding records in height and circumference, with fir, pine, hemlock and cedar generally topping the charts. Thick groves filter the sunlight, providing the perfect environment for mushrooms, lichens, ferns and mosses. The elegant tiger lily, beargrass, asters, fawnlily, phlox, columbine, valerian and a breathtaking array of alpine wildflowers thrive in high meadows and on sunny slopes.

With the dramatic decrease in rainfall in the plateaus and deserts zone comes a paralleling drop in the amount of plantlife, although it is still rich in pine, juniper, cottonwood and sagebrush. Flowers of the area include wild iris, foxglove, camas, balsam root and pearly everlasting.

FAUNA   It was actually the proliferation of wildlife that brought about white colonization of the Pacific Northwest, beginning with the trappers who came in droves in search of fur. It turns out that beaver and otter pelts were highly valued in China during the 1800s, so these creatures were heavily hunted. Nearly decimated colonies, now protected by law, are coming back strong. Playful otters are often spotted floating tummy up in coastal waters. Once endangered, bald eagles can be seen frequently wintering on the Skagit River and feeding on returning salmon.

Fish, especially salmon, were also a major factor in the economic development of the region, and remain so, though numbers of spawning salmon are dropping drastically. Nonetheless, fishing fanatics are still drawn here in search of the six varieties of Pacific salmon, along with flounder, ling cod, rockfish, trout, bass and other varieties of sportfish. Those who don't fish will still be fascinated by the seasonal spawning frenzy of salmon, easily observed at fish ladders in Washington, Oregon and British Columbia.

Watch for the Pacific giant salamander in fallen, rotting logs: it is the largest of its kind in the world, growing up to a foot in length and capable of eating small mice.

Among the more readily recognized creatures that reside in the Pacific Northwest are the orca, porpoises, dolphins, seals and sea lions often spotted cavorting in the waters just offshore. Twice-yearly migrations of gray whales on the trip between Alaska and California are much anticipated all along the coastline. Minke whales are more numerous, as are Dall's porpoises, often mistaken for baby orca because of their similar coloration and markings.

Of the varieties of bear living in the Northwest's remote forests, black bear are the most common in Oregon and southern Washington. Weighing upwards of 300 pounds and reaching six feet tall, they usually feed on berries, nuts and fish and avoid humans unless provoked by offers of food or danger to a cub. Grizzly bears are more prevalent farther north in the North Cascades range, which spans the international boundary between Washington and British Columbia. Big-game herds of deer, elk, antelope along with moose, cougar and mountain goats range the more mountainous areas. Scavengers such as chipmunks, squirrels, raccoons, opossums and skunks are abundant in the area as well.

Over 300 species of birds live in the Pacific Northwest for at least a portion of the year. Easily accessible mud flats and estuaries throughout the region provide refuge for tufted puffins, egrets, cormorants, loons and other migratory waterfowl making their way along the Pacific Flyway. Hundreds of pairs of bald eagles nest and hunt among the islands of Washington and British Columbia and winter along the Oregon coast, along with great blue herons and cormorants. You might also see red-tailed hawks and spotted owls if you venture quietly into the region's old-growth zones.

With a proliferation of protected refuges and preserves providing homes for great flocks of Canada and snow geese, trumpeter swans, great blue herons, kingfishers, cranes and other species, birdwatchers will be in seventh heaven in the Pacific Northwest, one of the fastest-growing birder destinations on the continent.

Twenty-three species of slug thrive in the 100-percent humidity of the Olympic rainforest and leave behind telltale viscous trails everywhere. The bane of gardeners, they are regarded as a mascot of the region, along with geoducks (pronounced gooeyducks), a type of razor clam found in Hood Canal. Souvenir shops stock plush toy replicas of slugs and gag cans of slug soup.

Where to Go

The number of tourists visiting the Pacific Northwest continues to grow as the secrets of its beauty and sunny summer and fall weather get out. Because the landscape is so widely varied, each area with its own appeal, here are brief descriptions of the regions presented in this book to help you decide where you want to go. To get the whole story, read the more detailed introductions to each chapter, then delve into the material that interests you most. We begin in Washington, head to Oregon, then up to cover British Columbia.

Seattle offers a comfortable mix of cultural sophistication and natural ruggedness. The clustered spires of its expanding skyline hint at the growth in this busy seaport, the shipping and transportation hub of the Northwest. Nearby communities stretched along Southern Puget Sound, including Tacoma, Olympia (the state's capital) and the Kitsap Peninsula, are also covered.

Northern Puget Sound and the San Juan Islands, regarded in this book as the coastal area stretched between Seattle and Blaine on the Canadian border, is completely enchanting, from sea-swept island chains to pastoral coastline. The entire region is punctuated by rich farming tracts, picturesque, forest-covered islands, quaint fishing villages and a shoreline of sloughs and estuaries. The arts are strong in the region, perhaps because of the preponderance of artists drawn by its natural beauty to live here.

American Indians were the first people to discover the beauty and bounty of the **Olympic Peninsula and Washington Coast**, with lush rainforests, stretches of driftwood-cluttered beach, tumbling rivers and snow-capped mountains. Several tribes still live in the area on the outskirts of the massive Olympic National Park alongside fishing villages such as Sequim and Port Angeles and the Victorian-style logging town of Port Townsend.

National parks, forests and wildernesses, including the North Cascades, Snoqualmie and Wenatchee national forests, Mt. Rainier National Park and the Mt. St. Helens National Volcanic Monument, make up the bulk of the spectacular **Cascades and Central Washington**. Fascinating Leavenworth, a Bavarian-style village, and several small resort towns are also important features here.

The majestic Cascade Range parallels the West Coast running through Oregon and Washington and up to British Columbia. Once past the slopes, you'll find sagebrush-filled high desert country with shoot-'em-up Western towns and quiet Indian reservations scattered through Washington and Oregon in the **East of the Cascades** zone. Commercial Spokane, pastoral Yakima and industrial Pendleton (home of the famous Pendleton Wools) are also described in this section.

Bounded by an evergreen forest, productive greenbelt and the mighty Columbia River, **Portland and the Columbia River Gorge** remain as close to nature as a growing metropolis can be. Portland, the "City of Roses," reflects a pleasant mix of historic buildings decorated in glazed terra cotta and modern structures

SO, WHO GIVES A HOOT?

Northern spotted owls are the fifth largest of the 19 owl species. They have been the center of controversy in recent years, the focus of the recurring nature-versus-commerce debate. As logging companies cut deeper into the old-growth forests, which have taken 150 years or more to grow, the habitat for this endangered owl grows smaller. (These nocturnal birds need thousands of acres per pair to support their indulgent eating habits.) The old-growth forests of the Pacific Northwest provide adequate nesting spots in the protected snags and broken branches of tall trees that shelter their flightless young. However, within the last hundred years, these glorious forests have been reduced to ten percent of their former range.

of smoked glass and brushed steel. These buildings lie in the downtown core intersected by the Willamette River and numerous parks. The sense of hustling enterprise falls away as you head east into Columbia River Gorge National Recreation Area, a particularly scenic 80-mile stretch of the Columbia River. Here you'll find gorgeous natural scenery such as Multnomah Falls and Beacon Rock; the charming town of Hood River, the Windsurfing Capital of the World; and The Dalles, a historically important town at the end of the gorge with an excellent museum.

The awe-inspiring beauty of the **Oregon Coast** includes 400 miles of rugged coastline dotted by small, artsy communities such as Yachats and Bandon and larger fishing villages such as Astoria, Newport and Coos Bay, all connected by Route 101, one of the most beautiful drives in the nation. Foresight on the part of the state legislature preserved the coast from crass commercial corruption, so great stretches remain untouched and entirely natural.

The **Oregon Cascades** hold a bevy of treasures including world-famous rivers like the Rogue and the Umpqua (fishing haunt of Zane Grey), the Mt. Hood and Mt. Bachelor ski resorts and the sapphire splendor of Crater Lake, the deepest lake in the country. As with the Washington Cascades, it is a region of national forests and wildernesses.

Cradled between the Coastal and Cascade mountain ranges is the **Heart of Oregon**, a pastoral valley of historic stage stops, gold-mining boomtowns and small farming communities. Sheep-covered meadows, cloud-shrouded bluffs and striped pastures line Route 5, the primary artery traversing the valley. Salem, the state capital, Eugene, home of the University of Oregon, and Ashland, site of the celebrated Shakespeare Festival, are included in this section.

Stretched above Washington and the United States border, British Columbia boasts delights that are hard to match. Extraordinary natural beauty surrounds **Vancouver and the Sunshine Coast,** seen in the caressing Pacific, soaring, protective mountains and vast tracts of forest. Bustling Vancouver sparkles and excites, with more than enough sightseeing, shopping, dining and entertainment opportunities to please one and all. The scenic Sunshine Coast entices with a broad range of recreational opportunities including hiking, biking, boating, camping, diving and fishing. The glacier-covered peaks of Garibaldi Provincial Park and alluring Whistler resort round out the territory.

Visitors to **Victoria and Vancouver Island** will find civility, gentility and a bit of pomp surrounded by one of the greatest outdoor vacation destinations around. Managing to retain the stately air of the British Empire outpost it once was, charming Victoria, the capital of British Columbia, rests at the southernmost tip of the island. Few roads connect the scattered seaport settlements and rugged provincial parks strewn across the remainder of the island, which is rather wild and wooly.

▼▼▼▼▼▼▼▼▼▼
When to Go

SEASONS

The Pacific Northwest isn't the rain-soaked, snow-covered tundra many imagine it to be. In fact, summer and fall days (June through September) are generally warm, dry and sunny. Overall temperatures range from the mid-30s in winter to the upper 80s in summer, except east of the Cascade range, where summer temperatures average in the mid-90s. There are distinct seasons in each of the primary zones, and the climate varies greatly with local topography.

The enormous mountain ranges play a major role in the weather, protecting most areas from the heavy rains generated over the Pacific and dumped on the coastline. Mountaintops are often covered in snow year-round at higher elevations, while the valleys, home to most of the cities, remain snow-free but wet during the winter months. East of the mountain ranges are temperature extremes and a distinct lack of rain. Travelers spend time at the rivers, lakes and streams during the hot, dry summers and frolic in the snow during the winter.

The mountainous zones are a bit rainy in spring but warm and dry in summer, when crowds file in for camping, hiking and other outdoor delights. Fall brings auto traffic attracted by the changing seasonal colors, while winter means snow at higher elevations, providing the perfect playground for cold-weather sports.

The coastal region is generally soggy and overcast during the mild winter and early spring, making this the low season for tourism. However, winter is high season among Northwesterners drawn to the coast to watch the fantastic storms that blow in across the Pacific. Be forewarned that these coastal mountain roads can be treacherous, especially in winter. When driving in snowpacked conditions, let someone know your itinerary and stick to it. Travel early in the day and keep simple signaling devices such as mirrors and whistles in the car. Summer offers easier travel and is typically warm and dry in the coastal valleys and along the crisp, windy coast, making it the prime season for travelers. And visitors *do* show up in droves, clogging smaller highways with recreational vehicles.

CALENDAR OF EVENTS

Festivals and events are a big part of life in the Northwest, especially when the rains disappear and everyone is ready to spend time outdoors enjoying the sunshine. Larger cities throughout the region average at least one major event per weekend during the summer and early fall. Below is a sampling of some of the biggest attractions. Check with local chambers of commerce (listed in the regional chapters of this book) to see what will be going on when you are in the area.

Seattle The **Seattle Print Fair** offers the chance to see and buy rare prints.

East of the Cascades In addition to catching a dog-sled ride, you'll hear carillon bells and perhaps munch wienerschnitzel at the **Bavarian Ice Fest** in Leavenworth.

Vancouver and the Sunshine Coast A quick plunge into frigid English Bay during the **Polar Bear Swim** on New Year's Day is said to bring good luck throughout the year.

Seattle The **Lunar New Year Celebration** is a day-long community event, with crafts, music, food and live entertainment. **Wintergrass** in Tacoma features bluegrass music and a street dance.

Olympic Peninsula and the Washington Coast The **Seafood and Wine Fest** in Newport, the oldest and largest wine fest in the Northwest, promises plenty of seafood, wine and live entertainment.

Oregon Coast Munch crustaceans to your heart's content at the annual **Crab Feed** in Charleston.

Vancouver and the Sunshine Coast **Chinese New Year** lights up Vancouver's Chinatown with fireworks, food and a boisterous dragon parade.

Seattle **St. Patrick's Day** is celebrated by the Irish Heritage Club with a parade, film festivals, lectures and music.

Washington Cascades There are world-class aerial ski jumpers and snowboarders, snow-castle and sculpture competitions, workshops and races at the **White Pass Winter Carnival**.

Portland and the Columbia River Gorge Collectors flock to the Portland Expo Center for **America's Largest Antique & Collectible Show**, where over seven acres of goods are on display.

Oregon Coast Events in Lincoln City and all along the coast celebrate the northward migration of gray whales during **Spring Whale Watch Week**.

Victoria and Vancouver Island All eyes are on the water during the **Pacific Rim Whale Festival** in Ucluelet and Tofino.

Seattle Enjoy some of the first blossoms of spring at the **Daffodil Festival Grand Floral Parade**, which passes through Tacoma, Puyallup and nearby communities.

Puget Sound and the San Juans If you'd rather catch those early-spring colors in all their natural glory, queue up for the drive through the rich farmlands of La Conner and Mount Vernon during the **Skagit Valley Tulip Festival**.

Washington Cascades   Enjoy over 40 different apple-oriented events during the **Washington State Apple Blossom Festival** held in Wenatchee.

Portland and the Columbia River Gorge   Delicate pink-and-white apple blossoms of the area orchards steal the show during the **Hood River Blossom Festival**.

Victoria and Vancouver Island   There's a lot of toe-tapping going on as top entertainers perform at the **Hot Jazz Jubilee** in Victoria.

MAY

Seattle   Bring your umbrella to watch contestants lure gulls in Port Orchard's **Seagull Calling Festival**. Running into June, the **Seattle International Film Festival** showcases a variety of screenings and a special focus on women in cinema.

Puget Sound and the San Juans   A salmon barbecue is held in conjunction with the 85-mile **Ski-To-Sea Relay Race** between Mt. Baker and Bellingham.

East of the Cascades   The ten-day **Spokane Lilac Festival** features a carnival, bed race, torchlight parade, food booths and more. There's also a **Hot Air Balloon Stampede** with over 50 balloons in Walla Walla. The **Maifest** in Leavenworth celebrates spring with Bavarian maypole dancing, a grand march and oompah bands.

Heart of Oregon   A hydroplane boat race, waterskiing show and parade are part of the fun at **Boatnik** in Grants Pass.

Vancouver and the Sunshine Coast   **Vancouver International Children's Fest**, with food and festivities geared to please the little ones, takes place in Vancouver. Vancouver's Granville Island hosts the **Vancouver New Play Festival**, which features experimental productions and new plays by Canadian playwrights.

Victoria and Vancouver Island   **Victoria Day** is the big event of the season, topped off by a grand parade in mid-May.

JUNE

Seattle   Live music and a beer garden are featured at the **Pike Place Market Festival**. You'll enjoy hearty servings of strawberry shortcake and performances by Norwegian dancers at the **Strawberry Festival** in Marysville.

Olympic Peninsula and the Washington Coast   Booths sell sausage, doughnuts, ice cream, baskets and dolls made of garlic at the **Northwest Garlic Festival** in Ocean Park (Long Beach Peninsula).

Portland and the Columbia River Gorge   Portland's biggest festival of the year, the **Rose Festival** is a month-long celebration with parties, pageants and a "Grand Floral Parade" second only to California's Rose Parade.

Oregon Coast   Participants from around the globe come to create a world of perishable marvels at the **Cannon Beach Sandcastle Contest**, ranked one of the top competitions in the world. The **Astoria Scandinavian Festival** celebrates the area's heritage. The **Summer Kite Festival** takes off in Lincoln City, the "Kite Capital of the World."

Oregon Cascades   The High Cascades play host to the **Sisters Rodeo** in Sisters.

Heart of Oregon   Outstanding jazz, bluegrass and gospel performances, as well as classical concerts, mark the month-long **Oregon Bach Festival** at the University of Oregon in Eugene. A similarly outstanding event is the **Peter Britt Music Festival** near Medford that features an array of music, dance and theatrical performances and runs through early September.

Vancouver and the Sunshine Coast   Vancouver pulls out all the stops in June with the colorful **Dragon Boat Races** on False Creek and the ten-day **International Jazz Festival** with performances by world-class musicians.

Victoria and Vancouver Island   Not to be outdone, Victoria has its fair share of summer events in June, including the **Oak Bay Tea Party** and the **Jazz Fest**.

Seattle   Get ready for alder-smoked salmon and live music at the **Ballard Seafoodfest**. Northwest talent is showcased in Bellevue at the **Pacific Northwest Arts and Crafts Fair**, host to over 300 artists, craftspeople and performers.

JULY

East of the Cascades   The **Sweet Onion Festival** is a celebration of Walla Walla's famous produce, with food booths, arts and crafts and onion contests. Cowboys and Indians turn out in force to take part in the rodeo and American Indian exhibition that are the centerpieces of the **Chief Joseph Days** in Joseph, Oregon.

Portland and the Columbia River Gorge   The **Robin Hood Festival** in Sherwood hosts a parade, live music and—what else?—an archery competition.

Oregon Coast   Coos Bay and North Bend join forces to present the **Oregon Coast Music Festival**.

Heart of Oregon   The **International Pinot Noir Celebration** attracts top winemakers from around the world to McMinnville.

Vancouver and the Sunshine Coast   Fort Vancouver Days, a citywide celebration with rodeo, chili cook-off and jazz concert, takes place in Vancouver, Washington. The first of the month brings **Canada Day Celebrations**, which take place throughout the country. The Sunshine Coast pulls out all the stops during July with the **Sea Cavalcade** in Gibsons, both good, old-fashioned fairs with booths, games, competitions and parades.

AUGUST   **Seattle**   Scottish roots are celebrated with pipe bands, athletic events and food at the **Pacific Northwest Highland Games and Clan Gathering.**

Puget Sound and the San Juans   Many of the Northwest's finest artists display their work at top local shows like the **Coupeville Arts and Crafts Festival** on Whidbey Island. Friday Harbor is the site of the **San Juan County Fair**, with arts and crafts, agricultural and animal exhibits, a carnival and food booths featuring the bounty of the islands.

Olympic Peninsula and the Washington Coast   Canoe races, traditional dancing and a street fair are just part of **Makah Days**, the largest American Indian celebration in Washington. World champions descend on Long Beach to compete in the **Washington State International Kite Festival.**

East of the Cascades   The **Steens Rim Ten-Kilometer Run** is followed by live music, kids' activities and fun at the **Frenchglen Jamboree**, both in Frenchglen, Oregon.

Portland and the Columbia River Gorge   The renowned **Mt. Hood Festival of Jazz** in Gresham is an eagerly awaited weekend of big-name musicians performing in the great outdoors.

Oregon Coast   Fresh blackberries and quality arts and crafts draw large crowds to the **Annual Blackberry Arts Festival** held in Coos Bay.

Heart of Oregon   A carnival, agriculture and craft exhibits, lots of entertainment and plenty of junk food await at the **Oregon State Fair** in Salem. Junction City's Danish roots are celebrated during the **Scandinavian Festival** with folk dancing, food and crafts.

Vancouver and the Sunshine Coast   The **Pacific National Exhibition**, a massive agricultural and industrial fair with everything from top-name entertainment to lumberjack contests, is a happening from mid-August through Labor Day in Vancouver. The Sunshine Coast also puts on **Roberts Creek Daze**, a fun-filled fair with games and booths.

Victoria and Vancouver Island   The **International Sandcastle Competition** takes the spotlight in Parksville.

SEPTEMBER **Seattle**   **Bumbershoot** brings music, plays, art exhibits and crafts to Seattle Center. "Do the Puyallup" is the catch phrase of the **Puyallup Fair**, one of the country's largest agricultural fairs. **Olympia Harbor Days**, one of the largest arts-and-crafts fairs in the Northwest, also offers a fascinating tugboat race.

Olympic Peninsula and the Washington Coast   Many of Port Townsend's grand Victorian homes are open to the public during the town's **Historic Homes Tour.**

East of the Cascades   Bronco busting awaits at the **Ellensburg Rodeo**, ranked among the top 25 rodeos in the nation. Tour the biergarten and German food circus at the **Odessa Deutchesfest**. See prize-winning livestock, produce and crafts, nibble cotton candy and enjoy a ride or two at the **Central Washington State Fair** in Yakima. In Oregon, the main event is the **Pendleton Roundup**, a major rodeo along with a historical parade of covered wagons and buggies and a pageant of American Indian culture. Leavenworth is ablaze during the **Washington State Autumn Leaf Festival**, complete with oompah bands and Bavarian costumes.

Portland and the Columbia River Gorge Portland's **Art in the Pearl** shakes up the city with dance, music, visual-art displays and theater performances.

Oregon Coast Vast quantities of salmon are slow-baked over an open alderwood fire at the **Indian Style Salmon Bake** in Depoe Bay. The **Bandon Cranberry Festival** in Bandon celebrates the autumn harvest with a cranberry foods fair, crafts and a parade.

Vancouver and the Sunshine Coast Alternative performance arts take center stage during the **Vancouver Fringe Festival**.

Victoria and Vancouver Island There's a flotilla of pre-1955 wooden boats in the **Classic Boat Festival** in Victoria's Inner Harbour. Salmon is king at the **Salmon Festival** in Port Alberni.

Seattle The **Issaquah Salmon Days Festival** features a salmon bake, races, live entertainment, arts and crafts, and a parade. Authors of all ethnicities converge for the **Rainbow Bookfest**, a literary extravaganza showcasing readings, book displays and fun children and teen areas celebrating writers of all backgrounds. **OCTOBER**

Olympic Peninsula and the Washington Coast There's plenty of seafood and entertainment along with a shucking contest at the **Oyster Fest** in Shelton.

Vancouver and the Sunshine Coast Celluloid delights brought from around the world are the focus of the **Vancouver International Film Festival**. Oktoberfest brews and oompah bands seem right at home in Whistler's Bavarian-style village.

Oregon Coast Artists, musicians, writers and craftspeople gather for the **Stormy Weather Arts Festival** in Cannon Beach. **NOVEMBER**

Vancouver and the Sunshine Coast **Cornucopia**, Whistler's wine and food celebration, features wine workshops, tastings, gourmet food events and live jazz.

Victoria and Vancouver Island Boat tours of local oyster farms, a costume ball and lots of oyster-inspired cuisine highlight Tofino's **Clayoquot Oyster Festival**.

Seattle **Zoolights** lends a festive spirit to Tacoma's famous Point Defiance Zoo from early December through Christmas. Seattle Center is all decked out with an ice-skating rink, Christmas train **DECEMBER**

display and a few arts-and-crafts booths during **Winterfest,** which runs through New Year's Eve.

East of the Cascades   The Bavarian village of Leavenworth looks like a scenic Christmas card during the **Christmas Lighting Festival.**

Heart of Oregon   Roseburg celebrates the holiday season with its **Umpqua Valley Festival of Lights,** which features Christmas lights formed into a variety of shapes, from Santa Claus to Mickey Mouse.

Vancouver and the Sunshine Coast   On December 31st there's the alcohol-free **First Night,** a New Year's Eve bash with entertainment on the village square at Whistler.

Victoria and Vancouver Island   **Butchart Gardens** puts on the holiday finery with Christmas light displays throughout the month.

▼▼▼▼▼▼▼▼▼▼▼▼
Before You Go

VISITORS CENTERS

For information on Washington log onto **Washington State Tourism's** website. ~ P.O. Box 42500, Olympia, WA 98504-2500; 360-725-5052, 800-544-1800; www.exp eriencewashington.com.

Travel Oregon Magazine is available from the **Oregon Tourism Commission.** ~ P.O. Box 14070, Portland, OR 97293; 800-547-7842; www.traveloregon.com.

Travel information and reservation services on British Columbia are available from **Tourism British Columbia.** ~ P.O. Box 9830, Station Provincial Government, Victoria, BC V8W 9W5; 800-435-5622; www.hellobc.com.

Both large cities and small towns throughout the region have chambers of commerce or visitor information centers; a number of them are listed in *Hidden Pacific Northwest* in the appropriate chapter.

For visitors arriving by automobile, Washington and Oregon provide numerous **Welcome Centers** at key points along the major highways where visitors can pull off for a stretch, grab a cup of coffee or juice and receive plenty of advice on what to see and do in the area. The centers are clearly marked and are usually open during daylight hours throughout the spring, summer and fall.

PACKING

Comfortable and casual are the norm for dress in the Northwest. You will want something dressier if you plan to catch a show, indulge in afternoon tea or spend your evenings in posh restaurants and clubs, but for the most part your topsiders and slacks are acceptable garb everywhere else.

Layers of clothing are your best bet since the weather changes so drastically depending on which part of the region you are visiting; shorts will be perfectly comfortable during the daytime in the hot, arid interior, but once you pass over the mountains and head for the coastline, you'll appreciate having packed a jacket to protect you from the nippy ocean breezes and damp chill, even on the warmest of days.

Wherever you're headed, during the summer bring some long-sleeve shirts, pants and lightweight sweaters and jackets along with your shorts, T-shirts and bathing suit; the evenings can be quite crisp. Bring along those warmer clothes—pants, sweaters, jackets, hats and gloves—in spring and fall, too, since days may be warm but it's rather chilly after sundown. Winter calls for thick sweaters, knitted hats, down jackets and snug ski clothes.

Special museums and exhibits throughout the coastal zone attest to the importance of whales, dolphins and other marine animals in the region.

It's not a bad idea to call ahead to check on weather conditions. Sturdy, comfortable walking shoes are a must for sightseeing. If you plan to explore tidal pools or go for long walks on the beach, bring a pair of lightweight canvas sneakers or waterproof river sandals that you don't mind getting wet.

Scuba divers will probably want to bring their own gear, though rentals are generally available in all popular dive areas. Many places also rent tubes for river floats and sailboards for windsurfing. Fishing gear is often available for rent as well. Campers will need to bring their own basic equipment.

Don't forget your camera for capturing the Pacific Northwest's glorious scenery and a pair of binoculars for watching the abundant wildlife that live here. Pack an umbrella and raincoat, just in case, and by all means don't forget your copy of *Hidden Pacific Northwest*!

LODGING

Lodging in the Northwest runs the gamut, from rustic cabins in the woods to sprawling resorts on the coastline. Chain motels line most major thoroughfares and mom-and-pop enterprises still vie successfully for lodgers in every region. Large hotels with names you'd know anywhere appear in most centers of any size.

Bed and breakfasts, small inns and cozy lodges where you can have breakfast with the handful of other guests are appearing throughout the region as these more personable forms of accommodation continue to grow in popularity. In fact, in areas like Ashland in southern Oregon and the San Juans in Washington, they are the norm rather than hotels and motels.

Whatever your preference and budget, you can probably find something to suit your taste with the help of the regional chapters in this book. Remember, rooms are scarce and prices rise in the high season, which is generally summer along the coastline and winter in the mountain ranges. Off-season rates are often drastically reduced in many places. Whatever you do, plan ahead and make reservations, especially in the prime tourist seasons.

Accommodations in this book are organized by region and classified by price. Rates referred to are for two people during high season, so if you are looking for low-season bargains, it's good to inquire. *Budget* lodgings are generally less than $60 per night and are satisfactory and clean but modest. *Moderate*-priced lodgings run from $60 to $110; what they have to offer in the way of luxury will depend on where they are located, but they often offer larger rooms and more attractive surroundings. At a *deluxe* hotel or resort you can expect to spend between $110 and $150 for a homey bed and breakfast or a double; you'll usually find spacious rooms, a fashionable lobby, a restaurant and a group of shops. *Ultra-deluxe* properties, priced above $150, are a region's finest, offering all the amenities of a deluxe hotel plus plenty of extras.

Whether you crave a room facing the surf or one looking out on the ski slopes, be sure to specify when making reservations. If you are trying to save money, keep in mind that lodgings a block or so from the waterfront or a mile or so from the ski lift are going to offer lower rates than those right on top of the area's major attractions.

DINING

Seafood is a staple in the Pacific Northwest, especially along the coast where salmon is king. Whether it's poached in herbs, glazed in teriyaki sauce, or grilled on a red-cedar plank, Indian-style, plan to treat yourself to this regional specialty often. While each area has its own favorite dishes, its ethnic influences and gourmet spots, Northwest cuisine as a whole tends to be hearty and is often crafted around organically grown local produce.

Within a particular chapter, restaurants are categorized geographically, with each entry describing the type of cuisine, general decor and price range. Lunch and dinner are served, except where noted. Dinner entrées at *budget* restaurants usually cost under $8. The ambience is informal, service usually speedy and the crowd a local one. *Moderate*-priced restaurants range between $8 and $16 at dinner; surroundings are casual but pleasant, the menu offers more variety and the pace is usually slower. *Deluxe* establishments tab their entrées from $16 to $25; cuisines may be simple or sophisticated, depending on the location, but the decor is plusher and the service more personalized. *Ultra-deluxe* dining rooms, where entrées begin at $25, are often gourmet places where the cooking and service have become an art form.

Some restaurants change hands often while others are closed in low seasons. Efforts have been made to include in this book places with established reputations for good eating. Breakfast and lunch menus vary less in price from restaurant to restaurant than evening dinners. If you are dining on a budget and still hope to experience the best of the bunch, visit at lunch when portions and prices are reduced.

The Pacific Northwest is a wonderful place to bring the kids. Besides the many museums, boutiques and festivals, the region also has hundreds of beaches and parks, and many nature sanctuaries sponsor children's activities, especially during the summer months. A few guidelines will help make travel with children a pleasure.

TRAVELING WITH CHILDREN

Many Northwest bed and breakfasts do not accept children, so be sure of the policy when you make reservations. If you need a crib or cot, arrange for it ahead of time. A travel agent can be of help here, as well as with most other travel plans.

If you're traveling by air, try to reserve bulkhead seats where there is plenty of room. Take along extras you may need, such as diapers, changes of clothing, snacks, toys and books. When traveling by car, be sure to carry the extras, along with plenty of juice and water. And always allow extra time for getting places, especially on rural roads.

A first-aid kit is a must for any trip. Along with adhesive bandages, antiseptic cream and something to stop itching, include any medicines your pediatrician might recommend to treat allergies, colds, diarrhea or any chronic problems your child may have.

It should be no surprise that Oregon's truly awesome peaks, some of which rise above 10,000 feet, are comprised mostly of volcanic rock.

When spending time at the beach or on the snow, take extra care the first few days. Children's skin is especially sensitive to sun, and severe sunburn can happen before you realize it, even on overcast days. Hats for the kids are a good idea, along with liberal applications of sunblock. Be sure to keep a constant eye on children who are near the water or on the slopes, and never leave children unattended in a car on a hot day.

Even the smallest towns usually have stores that carry diapers, baby food, snacks and other essentials, but these may close early in the evening. Larger urban areas usually have all-night grocery or convenience stores that stock these necessities.

Many towns, parks and attractions offer special activities designed for children. Consult local newspapers and/or phone the numbers in this guide to see what's happening where you're going.

Traveling solo grants an independence and freedom different from that of traveling with a partner, but single travelers are more vulnerable to crime and must take additional precautions.

WOMEN TRAVELING ALONE

It's unwise to hitchhike and probably best to avoid inexpensive accommodations on the outskirts of town; the money saved does not outweigh the risk. Bed and breakfasts, youth hostels and YWCAs are generally your safest bet for lodging, and they also foster an environment ideal for bonding with fellow travelers.

Keep all valuables well-hidden and clutch cameras and purses tightly. Avoid late-night treks or strolls through undesirable parts

Text continued on page 24.

High Adventure
in the Northwest

Whether you're an expert or a novice, a fanatic or simply curious, there's a sport here with your name written on it. Remember, the Pacific Northwest is known as "Evergreen Playground," not "Evergreen Couch Potato." So if what turns you on is dropping through the sky, paddling alongside whales or keeping your feet firmly on the ground, just do it!

For heart-stopping thrills, there's *bungee jumping*. Jumpers strapped into a full-body harness with three to five connecting bungee cords swan dive off a 191-foot-high bridge, the highest commercial bungee bridge in the Western Hemisphere. If this sounds great until you actually eyeball the 20-story drop, **Bungee.com** will refund the jump fee. Those who make the plunge are awarded membership in the Dangerous Sports Club. ~ P.O. Box 121, Fairview, OR 97024; 503-520-0303; www.bungee.com.

Heli-sports, from skiing untouched powder or blue glaciers to hiking spongy, moss-covered alpine fields, are currently all the rage in the high reaches of B.C. The helicopter ride to inaccessible areas is the highlight for many, while others appreciate the ease of having gear packed in for them. **Coast Range Heliskiing** offers daily tours out of Whistler. ~ P.O. Box 16, Pemberton, BC V0N 2L0; 604-894-1144, 800-701-8744; www.coastrangeheliskiing.com.

With so many majestic ranges in the Northwest, *mountaineering* abounds. Rock and ice climbing are big draws in both the Cascades and Rocky Mountains. Climbers should be familiar with cold-weather survival techniques before tackling Northwest heights, which are tricky at best. For climbers' guidelines and further information, turn to the **Outdoor Recreation and Information Center**. ~ REI Building, 222 Yale Avenue North, Seattle, WA 98174; 206-470-4060. The **Outdoor Recreation Council of B.C.** also has information. ~ 334-1367 West Broadway, Vancouver, BC V6H 4A9; 604-737-3058; www.orcbc.ca. Famous mountaineering clubs like **The Mountaineers** in Seattle and the **Mazamas** in Portland conduct classes and lead hiking and climbing trips to Northwest peaks. ~ The Mountaineers: 300 3rd Avenue West, Seattle, WA 98119, 206-284-6310, www.mountaineers.org; Mazamas: 909 Northwest 19th Avenue, Portland, OR 97209, 503-227-2345, www.mazamas.org.

Mountain bike descents—racing down alpine slopes on two wheels—is a growing sport in resort areas of British Columbia. Participants usually take high-performance mountain bikes on the gondola to the heights, then follow experienced guides down mountain faces that are the winter domain of skiers. **Whistler Blackcomb Resort** can tell you more. ~ 4545 Blackcomb Way, Whistler, BC V0N 1B4; 800-766-0449; www.whistler-blackcomb.com.

Rest assured: There are tamer outdoor adventures here. In fact, many swear that the best way to soak in the region's beauty is to travel slowly by bike or foot. Extensive guided *bicycling and walking tours* of the mountains, forests, coastline and islands last anywhere from two days to weeks. Top operators include **Backroads**. ~ 801 Cedar Street, Berkeley, CA 94710; 800-462-2848; www.backroads.com. The **Sierra Club** also leads tours. ~ Outing Department, 85 2nd Street, Second Floor, San Francisco, CA 94105; 415-977-5522; www.sierraclub.org.

In this realm of lakes, streams, rivers and ocean, it's no surprise that many of the top adventure sports are water-related. *Whitewater rafting* is one of the best-known adventure activities in the region, with challenging rapids on the Lewis, Snoqualmie and White rivers in Washington, the Rogue, Deschutes and McKenzie in Oregon and the Fraser and Green rivers in British Columbia. If you aren't acquainted with these rivers join a guided trip or chat with outfitters who know the treacherous spots to look out for. The **North West Rafters Association** is a good source for further information. ~ www.nwrafters.org.

Kayaking and canoeing are also popular ways to shoot the rapids. Paddlers ready to take on the open ocean gain access to spectacular places like the various marine parks in British Columbia (Desolation Sound and the Pacific Rim National Park) and Washington (numerous protected islands among the San Juans). Other placid bodies of water suitable for kayak and canoe exploration include the Hood Canal in Washington, the Willamette and Columbia rivers in Oregon and the Powell River Canoe Route on British Columbia's Sunshine Coast. The folks at **Ebb & Flow Paddlesports Limited** can tell you more about the waters and area outfitters. ~ 0604 Southwest Nebraska Street, Portland, OR 97201; 503-245-1756.

Squeezed between the border of Washington and Oregon, the breezy Columbia Gorge is reputed to be the *windsurfing* capital of the continent, with championship competitions held annually. English Bay in Vancouver and Washington's San Juan Islands are also popular destinations for the sport, with numerous outfits set up to teach would-be windsurfers or just rent the sailboards and wetsuits. The **Columbia Gorge Windsurfing Association** has information. ~ P.O. Box 182, Hood River, OR 97031; 541-386-9225; www.cgwa.net. The **United States Windsurfing Association** can put you in touch with top schools in the region. ~ www.uswindsurfing.org.

of town, but if you find yourself in this situation, continue walking with a confident air until you reach a safe haven. A fierce scowl never hurts.

These hints should by no means deter you from seeking out adventure. Wherever you go, stay alert, use your common sense and trust your instincts. If you are hassled or threatened in some way, never be afraid to yell for assistance. It's also a good idea to carry change for a phone call, or better yet, carry a cell phone, and know a number to call in case of emergency.

For more helpful hints, get a copy of *Safety and Security for Women Who Travel* (Travelers' Tales).

Women alone will usually feel safer in more conservative British Columbia, especially in the well-populated areas, but Vancouver and Victoria are major havens for drug addicts, so be cautious and stay alert in downtown areas. However, it's a good idea to remain cautious just the same.

Most major cities have hotlines for victims of rape and violent crime. In case of emergency in Seattle, contact **King County Sexual Resource Center**. ~ P.O. Box 300, Renton, WA 98057; 24-hour crisis line 800-825-7273; www.kcsarc.org. In Portland contact the **Portland Women's Crisis Line**. ~ 503-235-5333, 888-235-5333. The **Sexual Assault Support Services** offers assistance in Eugene. ~ 541-485-6700, 541-343-7227 (24-hour crisis line), 800-788-4727.

GAY & LESBIAN TRAVELERS   Information hotlines and social and support groups for gay and lesbians exist in several of the Northwest's larger cities and towns. Information on gay services and events in the Seattle area can be obtained from the **Gay City Health Project**. ~ 206-860-6969; www.gaycity.org. PFLAG **Information Referral Line** offers support and information in Spokane. ~ 509-489-2266.

❖❖

CRUISIN' THROUGH THE PACIFIC NORTHWEST

Nautical adventurers can embark on two week-long cruises through the Northwest offered by **Alaska Sightseeing Cruise West**. The Columbia and Snake Rivers voyage traces Lewis and Clark's search for the Northwest Passage. Departing from Portland, destinations on this scenic, wildlife-infused journey include Hells Canyon in Idaho, Washington's wine country and Hood River. The Canada's Inside Passage cruise follows Captain George Vancouver's expedition along the shore of the Pacific Northwest, taking in the fjords along the British Columbia coast, the towering granite mountains surrounding Princess Louisa Inlet, and the sights and sounds of Victoria and Vancouver. ~ 2401 4th Avenue, Suite 700, Seattle, WA 98121; 800-426-7702; www.cruisewest.com.

The Pacific Northwest is a hospitable place for senior citizens to visit, especially during the cool, sunny summer months that offer respite from hotter climes elsewhere in the country. Countless museums, historic sights and even restaurants and hotels offer senior discounts that can cut a substantial chunk off vacation costs. The national park system's Golden Age Passport, which must be applied for in person, allows free admission for anyone 62 and older to the many national parks and monuments in the region. They are available at any national park, ranger station, park office, or wildlife refuge. **SENIOR TRAVELERS**

The **American Association of Retired Persons** (AARP) offers membership to anyone age 50 or over. AARP's benefits include travel discounts with a number of firms and escorted tours with Gray Line buses. ~ 601 E Street Northwest, Washington, DC 20049; 800-424-3410; www.aarp.org, e-mail member@aarp.com.

Elderhostel offers reasonably priced, all-inclusive educational programs in a variety of Pacific Northwest locations throughout the year. ~ 11 Avenue de Lafayette, Boston, MA 02111; 877-426-8056, fax 617-426-0701; www.elderhostel.org.

Be extra careful about health matters. In addition to the medications you ordinarily use, it's a good idea to bring along the prescriptions for obtaining more. Consider carrying a medical record with you—including your medical history and current medical status, as well as your doctor's name, phone number and address. Make sure your insurance covers you while you are away from home.

Oregon, Washington and British Columbia are striving to make more destinations accessible for travelers with disabilities. For information on the areas you will be visiting, contact **Independent Living Resources**. ~ 2410 Southeast 11th Avenue, Portland, OR 97214; 503-232-7411 (ask for Kathe Coleman); www.ilr.org. **DISABLED TRAVELERS**

For more specific advice on traveling in the Pacific Northwest, turn to *B.C. Accommodations* from **Tourism British Columbia**, which lists many wheelchair-accessible lodgings in British Columbia. ~ P.O. Box 9830, Station Provincial Government, Victoria, BC V8W 9W5; 800-435-5622; www.hellobc.com.

The **Society for Accessible Travel & Hospitality** has general information regarding traveling with disabilities. ~ 347 5th Avenue, Suite 610, New York, NY 10016; 212-447-7284, fax 212-725-8253; www.sath.org. **Mobility International** USA provides more information and services for international exchange travel programs. ~ P.O. Box 10767, Eugene, OR 97440; 541-343-1284; www.miusa.org.

Flying Wheels Travel is a travel agency specifically for disabled people. ~ 143 West Bridge Street, Owatonna, MN 55060; 800-535-6790; e-mail thq@ll.net. Also providing assistance is

Travelin' Talk, a networking organization. ~ P.O. Box 1796, Wheat Ridge, CO 80034; 303-232-2979; www.travelintalk.net, e-mail info@travelintalk.net. **Access-Able Travel Source**, its sister organization, has worldwide information online. ~ 303-232-2979; www.access-able.com.

FOREIGN TRAVELERS

Passports and Visas   Entry into Canada and the U.S. calls for a valid passport, visa or visitor permit for all foreign visitors. U.S. visitors are not technically required to show a U.S. passport to gain entry to Canada—proof of citizenship (voter's registration, birth certificate, driver's license), including two pieces of photo identification, are all that's required—and may visit without a visa for up to 180 days. However, in 2007, tighter U.S. Department of Homeland Security regulations now mandate that all those traveling to the U.S. by air, including U.S. citizens, must show a valid passport to enter or reenter the U.S. This requirement will expand to include those entering by land and sea (including ferries) by January 2008. So, in a nutshell, everyone, including U.S. citizens, should now carry a valid passport at all times if they plan on visiting British Columbia and returning to the U.S.

Customs Requirements   Foreign travelers are allowed to bring in the following: 200 cigarettes (1 carton), 50 cigars or 2 kilograms (4.4 pounds) of smoking tobacco; one liter of alcohol for personal use only (you must be at least 21 years of age to bring in alcohol); and US$100 worth of duty-free gifts that can include an additional quantity of 100 cigars. You may bring in any amount of currency (amounts over US$10,000 require a form). Americans who have been in Canada over 48 hours may take out $400 worth of duty-free items ($25 worth of duty-free for visits under 48 hours). Carry any prescription drugs in clearly marked containers; you may have to provide a written prescription or doctor's statement to clear customs. Meat or meat products, seeds, plants, fruits and narcotics are not allowed to be brought into the United States. The same applies to Canada, with the addition of firearms.

Driving   If you plan to rent a car, an international driver's license should be obtained prior to arrival. United States driver's licenses are valid in Canada and vice versa. Some rental car companies require both a foreign license and an international driver's license along with a major credit card and require that the lessee be at least 25 years of age. Seat belts are mandatory for the driver and all passengers. Children under the age of 5 or 40 pounds should be in the back seat in approved child safety restraints.

Currency   American and Canadian money are based on the dollar. Bills in the United States come in six denominations: $1, $5, $10, $20, $50 and $100. Every dollar is divided into 100 cents; in Canada the $1 coin is generally used. Coins are the penny (1 cent), nickel (5 cents), dime (10 cents) and quarter (25 cents). Half-dollar and dollar coins are used infrequently. You may not use foreign currency to purchase goods and services in the United States and Canada. Consider buying traveler's checks in dollar amounts. You may also use credit cards affiliated with an American company such as Interbank, Barclay Card, VISA and American Express.

Electricity and Electronics   Electric outlets use currents of 110 volts, 60 cycles. For appliances made for other electrical systems, you need a transformer or adapter. Travelers who use laptop computers for telecommunication should be aware that modem configurations for U.S. telephone systems may be different from their European counterparts. Similarly, the U.S. format for videotapes and DVDs is different from that in Europe; U.S. Park Service visitors centers and other stores that sell souvenir videos often have them available in European format.

Weights and Measurements   The United States uses the English system of weights and measures. American units and their metric equivalents are as follows: 1 inch = 2.5 centimeters; 1 foot = 0.3 meter; 1 yard = 0.9 meter; 1 mile = 1.6 kilometers; 1 ounce = 28 grams; 1 pound = 0.45 kilogram; 1 quart (liquid) = 0.9 liter. British Columbia now uses metric measurements.

Outdoor Adventures

CAMPING

Parks in the lush Pacific Northwest rank among the top in North America as far as attendance goes, so plan ahead if you hope to do any camping during the busy summer months. Late spring and early fall present fewer crowds to deal with and the weather is still fine.

Though much of Washington's scenic coastline is privately owned, there are a few scattered parks along the shore and even more situated inland in the mountains. It is possible to reserve campsites at several state parks from Memorial Day through Labor Day; contact the **Washington State Parks and Recreation Commission** for details. ~ P.O. Box 42650, Olympia, WA 98504; 360-902-8844 (general information), 888-226-7688 (reservations only); www.parks.wa.gov.

You'll find a multitude of marvelous campsites along Oregon's protected coast and in its green mountain ranges. Some of the state parks with campgrounds are open year-round. Reservations are accepted at 46 parks and are essential if you hope to get a spot during July and August. The **Oregon Parks and Recreation Department** maintains **Reservations Northwest** (800-452-5687) to provide updated campsite availability. ~ 725 Summer Street Northeast, Suite C, Salem, OR 97301; 503-986-0707, 800-551-6949; www.oregonstateparks.org.

For information on camping in the various national parks and forests in the Puget Sound area, contact the **Outdoor Recreation Information Center**. Closed Monday in fall and winter. ~

REI Building, 222 Yale Avenue North, Seattle, WA 98174; 206-470-4060.

Many of British Columbia's prime wilderness areas, both marine and interior, are protected as provincial parks. Except for those that are day-use only areas, most parks are set up with some sort of camping facilities, from primitive sites with pit toilets to pull-through recreational vehicle pads (with nearby sani-stations but no electrical, water or sewage hook-ups). There is a minimal fee for use of the campsites available on a first-come, first-served basis year-round. For further information, contact **B.C. Parks**. ~ 1610 Mount Seymour Road, North Vancouver, BC V7G 2R9; 604-924-2200; www.gov.bc.ca/bcparks. Or try the **Outdoor Recreation Council of B.C.** ~ 1367 West Broadway, Suite 334, Vancouver, BC V6H 4A9; 604-737-3058; www.orcbc. ca, e-mail orc@intergate.ca.

For information on camping at the Pacific Rim National Park on Vancouver Island's western shore and other national parks in British Columbia, contact **Parks Canada West Region**. ~ 220 4th Avenue Southeast, Calgary, Alberta T2G 4X3; 403-292-4401; www.pch.gc.ca.

PERMITS   Wilderness camping is not permitted in the state parks of Oregon and Washington, but there are primitive sites available in most parks. Permits (available at trailheads) are required for wilderness camping in parts of the Alpine Lakes wilderness area of the Mt. Baker–Snoqualmie and Wenatchee national forests in Washington and in the Mt. Jefferson, Mt. Washington and Three Sisters wilderness areas of Oregon between May 24 and October 31; permits are available at the ranger stations. Campers should check with all other parks individually to see if permits are required.

Follow low-impact camping practices in wilderness areas; "leave only footprints, take only pictures." When backpacking and hiking, stick to marked trails or tread lightly in areas where no trail exists. Be prepared with map and compass since signs are limited to directional information and don't include mileage. Some guidelines on wilderness camping are available from the **Outdoor Recreation Information Center**. Closed Monday in fall and winter. ~ REI Building, 222 Yale Avenue North, Seattle, WA 98174; 206-470-4060. In British Columbia, wilderness camping is allowed in Garibaldi, Manning, Strathcona and Cape Scott provincial parks. No permit is required, but it's always best to check in with a ranger station to let someone know your plan before heading into the backcountry. A B.C. Parks regulation states that wilderness camping is permitted in any large provincial park provided that it is done one kilometer inland from any roadway and that campers leave no trace of their overnight stay. Contact **B.C. Parks** for further details. ~ 1610 Mount Seymour Road,

North Vancouver, BC V7G 2R9; 604-924-2200; www.
gov.bc.ca/bcparks.

Wilderness camping is also permitted in British Columbia's
national parks. Contact **Parks Canada—British Columbia** for
more information. ~ P.O. Box 129, Fort Langley, BC V1M 2RS;
604-513-4777; www.parcscanada.gc.ca.

BOATING

With miles of coastline and island-dotted straits to explore, it's no
wonder that boating is one of the most popular activities in the
Northwest. Many of the best attractions in the region, including
numerous pristine marine parks, are accessible only by water and
have facilities set aside for boaters.

Write, call or visit the website of the **Washington State Parks
and Recreation Commission** for a boater's guide to the Evergreen
State. ~ P.O. Box 42650, Olympia, WA 98504; 360-902-8844;
www.parks.wa.gov. The **Oregon State Marine
Board** will furnish information on boating
statewide. ~ P.O. Box 14145, Salem, OR 97309;
503-378-8587; www.osmb.state.or.us.

Boaters heading into B.C. waters from the U.S.
must clear customs at the first available port of entry;
Canada Customs can provide more information on
specific policies. ~ 604-666-5607; www.ccra-adrc.gc.ca.

> Oregon grows 99 percent
> of the entire U.S. com-
> mercial crop of hazel-
> nuts. (That's why the
> hazelnut coffee is so
> delicious here!)

There are several waterways suitable for extended canoeing and kayaking trips. The **American Canoe Association** can provide more information. ~ 7432 Alban Station
Boulevard, Suite B-232, Springfield, VA 22150; 703-451-0141;
www.acanet.org.

Whitewater rafting is particularly popular, especially on the
Rogue and Deschutes in Oregon and the Fraser River in British
Columbia where you will find outfitters renting equipment and
running tours throughout the summer months.

**WATER
SAFETY**

The watery region of the Pacific Northwest offers an incredible
array of water sports to choose from, be it on the ocean, a quiet
lake or stream or tumbling rapids. Swimming, diving, walking the
shore in search of clams or just basking in the sun are options
when you get to the shore, lake or river. Shallow lakes, rivers and
bays tend to be the most populated spots since they warm up
during the height of summer; otherwise, the waters of the Northwest are generally chilly. Whenever you swim, never do so alone,
and never take your eyes off of children in or near the water.

FISHING

With its multitude of rivers, streams, lakes and miles of protected
coastline, the Pacific Northwest affords some of the best fishing
in the world. The waters of British Columbia alone hold 74 known
species, 25 of those sportfish. Salmon is the main draw, but each

area features special treats for the fishing enthusiast that are described in the individual chapters of *Hidden Pacific Northwest*.

Fees and regulations vary, but licenses are required for salt- and freshwater fishing throughout the region and can be purchased at sporting-goods stores, bait-and-tackle shops and fishing lodges. You can also find leads on guides and charter services in these locations if you are interested in trying a kind of fishing that's new to you. Charter fishing is the most expensive way to go out to sea; party boats take a crowd but are less expensive and usually great fun. On rivers, lakes and streams, guides can show you the best place to throw a hook or skim a fly. Whatever your pleasure, in saltwater or fresh, a good guide will save you time and grief and will increase the likelihood of a full string or a handsome trophy.

For further information on fishing in Washington concerning shellfish, bottom fish, salmon, freshwater and saltwater sportfish, contact the **Washington Department of Fish and Wildlife**. ~ 600 North Capitol Way, Olympia, WA 98501-1091; 360-902-2200; wdfw.wa.gov.

The **Oregon Department of Fish and Wildlife** can supply information on fishing in the state. ~ 3406 Cherry Avenue Northeast, Salem, OR 97303; 503-947-6000; www.dfw.state.or.us.

For updated details and regulations for freshwater fishing in British Columbia, contact the **Fisheries Branch**. ~ Ministry of Water, Land and Air Protection, 10470 152nd Street, Surrey, BC B3R 043; 604-582-5222. Try the **Fisheries and Ocean Canada** for saltwater fishing. ~ Department of Fisheries and Oceans, 401 Burrard Street, Suite 200, Vancouver, BC V6C 354; 604-666-5835.

SKIING
As winter blankets the major mountain ranges of the Pacific Northwest, ski season heats up at numerous resorts. Ski enthusiasts head for Mt. Adams, Mt. Rainier and Mt. Baker in Washington, Mt. Hood, Mt. Bachelor and Mt. Ashland in Oregon and Mt. Seymour, Grouse Mountain and the Whistler/Blackcomb mountains in southwestern British Columbia. Specifics on the top resorts are listed in each regional chapter.

For additional information on skiing in Washington and Oregon, contact the **Pacific Northwest Ski Areas Association**. ~ P.O. 1720, Hood River, OR 97031; 541-386-9600; www.pnsaa.org. For information on skiing in British Columbia, obtain a copy of *Outdoor Adventure* from **Tourism British Columbia**. ~ 800-435-5622; www.hellobc.com.

TWO

Seattle and
Southern Puget Sound

Rain city? Not today. Last night's storm has washed the air clean, swept away yesterday's curtain of clouds to reveal Mt. Rainier in all its astonishing glory. From your hotel room window, you can see the Olympics rising like snow-tipped daggers beyond the blue gulf of Puget Sound. Below, downtown Seattle awakens to sunshine, espresso and the promise of a day brimming with discovery for the fortunate traveler.

The lesson here is twofold: Don't be daunted by Seattle's reputation for nasty weather, and don't limit yourself to anticipating its natural setting and magnificent greenery, awesome as they may be. For this jewel surrounded by water, earning it the nickname "The Emerald City," sparkles in ways too numerous to count after a decade or more of extraordinary growth.

Greater Seattle has changed dramatically. The city, squeezed into a lean, hour-glass shape between Elliott Bay and Lake Washington, covers only 84 square miles, and its population is still under 600,000. But the greater metropolitan area, reaching from Everett to Tacoma and east to the Cascade foothills, now boasts some 4 million.

While most newcomers have settled in the suburbs, Seattle's soaring skyline downtown is the visual focus of a region on the move. No longer the sleepy sovereign of Puget Sound, Seattle today is clearly the most muscular of the Northwest's three largest cities. Its urban energy is admired even by those who bemoan Seattle's freeway congestion, suburban sprawl, crime and worrisome air and water pollution. Growth has been the engine of change, and although the pace has slowed in the '90s, the challenges posed by too rapid an expansion remain persistent topics of discussion.

Seattle offered no hint of its future prominence when pioneers began arriving on Elliott Bay some 150 years ago. Like other settlements around Puget Sound, Seattle survived by farming, fishing, shipbuilding, logging and coal mining. For decades the community hardly grew at all. One whimsical theory has it that because the frontier sawmill town offered a better array of brothels to the region's loggers, miners and fishermen, capital tended to flow into Seattle to fund later investment and expansion.

Whatever the reason, the city quickly rebuilt after the disastrous "Great Fire" of 1889. But it would be another eight years before the discovery of gold in Alaska put Seattle on the map. On July 17, 1897, the ship *Portland* steamed into Elliott Bay from Alaska, bearing its legendary "ton of gold" (actually, nearly two tons), triggering the Klondike Gold Rush. Seattle immediately emerged as chief outfitter to thousands of would-be miners heading north to the gold fields.

Today, Seattle remains tied to its traditions. It's so close to the sea that 20-pound salmon are still hooked in Elliott Bay, at the feet of those gleaming, new skyscrapers. It's so near its waterfront that the boom of ferry horns resonates among its buildings and the cries of gulls still pierce the rumble of traffic. But the city's (and the state's) economy has grown beyond the old resource-based industries. International trade, tourism, agriculture and software giants like Microsoft now lead the way. The spotlight has passed from building ships to building airplanes, from wood chips to microchips, from mining coal to cultivating the fertile fields of tourism.

In the process, one of the nation's most vibrant economies has emerged. You can see that energy in Seattle's highrises, feel it in the buoyant street scene fueled in part by locals' infatuation with espresso. And there is fresh energy beneath your very feet. An "underground" of retail shops (as distinguished from the historic Pioneer Square Underground) has taken shape around the downtown Westlake stations in the Metro Transit Tunnel.

Civic energy has produced a glorious art museum downtown, a small but lively "people place" in Westlake Park, a spacious convention center and additions to Freeway Park. Private enterprise has added hotels, office towers with grand lobbies brimming with public art, shopping arcades, restaurants, nightclubs and bistros.

During the late '80s, as locals struggled with construction chaos, Seattle's downtown briefly suffered the nickname "little Beirut." Now, in the early years of the new millennium, downtown Seattle is once more under construction. But this time the atmosphere is one of urban revitalization, as the city has gained a new symphony hall, a plethora of condominiums and several upscale shopping and entertainment complexes. As vibrant as it is, downtown also exhibits the famed Seattle social courtesy and informality. Drivers on many downtown streets still stop to let waiting pedestrians cross, and it's not considered polite to honk your horn. Ask directions of anyone who looks like they know their way around; they'll almost always do their best to help. Only bankers and corporate executives wear suits to work, and not even all of those do. Casual wear is acceptable in almost every social situation; even the symphony and opera draw fans dressed in jeans. Historically, weather bureau statistics show that mid-July to mid-August brings the driest, sunniest, warmest weather—a sure bet for tourists, or so you'd suppose. But in the last decade or two, that midsummer guarantee all too often has been washed away by clouds or rain. What's the sun-seeking tourist to do?

Consider September. In recent years it has brought modestly reliable weather. Or, simply come prepared—spiritually and practically—for whatever mix of dreary and sublime days that fate delivers. An accepting attitude may be the best defense of all in a region once described in this way: "The mildest winter I ever spent was a summer on Puget Sound."

Have goofy weather, growth, gentrification of downtown neighborhoods and a tide of new immigrants eradicated the old Seattle? Not by a long shot. Pike Place Market's colorful maze is still there to beguile you. Ferry boats still glide like wedding cakes across a night-darkened Elliott Bay. The central waterfront is as clamorous, gritty and irresistible as ever. Pioneer Square and its catacomb-like underground still beckons. The soul of the city somehow endures even as the changes wrought by regional growth accumulate.

It is indeed the changing geography of the wider Puget Sound region that may appear more striking. What nature created here, partly by the grinding and gouging

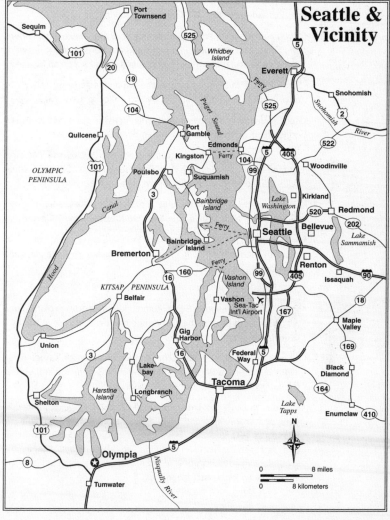

Seattle & Vicinity

Text continued on page 36.

Three-day Weekend

Seattle

Day 1
- Check in. It makes sense to stay downtown, where most of the key sights are located. Driving from other parts of this long, narrow city can be time consuming. If you *do* stay outside the downtown area, your best bet is to park at Seattle Center and ride the monorail instead of looking for downtown parking.

- If you haven't done so before starting your trip, make reservations for dinner and the theater tonight and the Underground Tour tomorrow. Seattle runs on reservations, and most locals plan far ahead.

- Stroll **Pike Place Market** and the **waterfront** (see the walking tour on pages 42) and visit the **Seattle Aquarium** (page 40).

- Rest your feet on a low-cost, scenic **Washington State Ferry** cruise from the Pier 52 terminal to Bremerton and back.

- On terra firma once more, climb the steep hill to the Westlake Center monorail terminal. Ride the **monorail** to Seattle Center. Take the elevator to the top of the **Space Needle** (page 56).

- Dine atop the Space Needle at the **Sky City Restaurant** (page 57) or, more affordably, at the **Seattle Center Food Court**.

- In the evening, enjoy your choice of Seattle Center performing-arts events, which may range from operas and ballets to stage plays and folk-dancing lessons.

Day 2
- Stroll down to **Pioneer Square** and take the **Underground Tour** (page 38) for a look at the abandoned city that lies hidden beneath downtown Seattle's streets.

- Above ground, ride the elevator to the top of **Smith Tower** (page 39) and imagine the long-ago time when this mini-skyscraper was the tallest building west of the Mississippi.

- Wander through the **International District** (page 39) and take your pick from the many small Asian restaurants along Main and Jackson streets for lunch. Feast your eyes on the exotic foodstuffs and fine Asian home furnishings at **Uwajimaya** (page 38). Complete your exploration of the district with a visit to the **Wing Luke Asian Museum** (page 39).

- For dinner this evening, why not enjoy Seattle's favorite food, alder-grilled salmon, at **Ivar's Salmon House** (page 69) on the Lake Union shoreline? Start driving up there early or take a cab; for a popular tourist restaurant, it's a little tricky to find.

- This could be the evening to check out the city's exceptionally lively nightclub scene. (If you don't feel like dyeing your hair green, simply wear your most authentically grungy camping clothes . . . .)

Day 3
- Is it raining? If not, this could be an ideal morning for sightseeing on attractive **Bainbridge Island** (page 74).

- If it *is* raining, check out the nearby **Museum of History and Industry** (page 66)—the name may sound boring, but the museum is fascinating.

- For lunch, try one of the interesting, affordable meals at the popular **Sound Food Cafe** (page 79).

- Sun still shining? How about a bike ride along **Alki Beach** (page 78) in West Seattle, with its old-time California atmosphere and its great views of the Seattle skyline across the bay?

- Still raining? The city has plenty of other good museums to stay dry in. One good bet is the Boeing's **Museum of Flight** (page 88), tracing the century-long history of the Seattle area's largest employer.

- Consider finishing up your Seattle spree with a big-splurge dinner at **Campagne** (page 52), one of the city's finest restaurants.

of massive lowland glaciers, is a complex mosaic. From the air, arriving visitors see a green-blue tapestry of meandering river valleys weaving between forested ridges, the rolling uplands dotted by lakes giving way to Cascade foothills and distant volcanoes, the intricate maze-way of Southern Puget Sound's island-studded inland sea.

From on high it seems almost pristine, but a closer look reveals a sobering overlay of manmade changes. Even as Seattle's downtown becomes "Manhattanized," the region is being "Los Angelesized" with the birth of a freeway commuter culture stretching from Olympia on the south to Everett on the north and beyond Issaquah on the east. Some commuters arrive by ferry from Bainbridge Island to the west. Farmlands and wetlands, forests and meadows, are giving way to often poorly planned, hastily built housing tracts, roads and shopping centers. And as the dense vegetation that once held the earth in place is scraped away, huge swathes of the metropolitan area are left naked and exposed to flooding, mudslides, rockfalls and other forms of damaging erosion.

For the traveler, such rapid growth means more traffic and longer lines for the ferry; more-crowded campgrounds, parks and public beaches; busier bikeways and foot trails; more folks fishing and boating and clam-digging. Downtown parking can be hard to find and expensive.

But despair not. The legendary Northwest may take a bit more effort to discover, but by almost any standard Seattle and its environs still offer an extraordinary blend of urban and outdoor pleasures close at hand. And growth seems only to have spurred a much richer cultural scene in Seattle—better restaurants serving original cuisines, more swank hotels, superb opera and a vital theater community, more art galleries and livelier shopping in a retail core sprinkled with public plazas that reach out to passersby with summer noon-hour concerts. In this chapter we will point you to familiar landmarks, help you discover some "hidden" treasures and find the best of what's new downtown as we look at a region that reaches from Olympia to Everett, Bremerton to Issaquah.

▼▼▼▼▼▼▼▼▼▼▼▼▼▼
Downtown Seattle

When you fly into Seattle, the central part of this lush region looks irresistible. From the air you'll be captivated by deep bays, harbors, gleaming skyscrapers, parks stretching for miles and hillside neighborhoods where waterskiing begins from the backyard. Central Seattle's neighborhoods offer a seemingly inexhaustible array of possibilities from the International District to Lake Union and the waterfront to Capitol Hill. Eminently walkable, this area can also be explored by monorail, boat and bike. From the lofty heights of the Space Needle to the city's underground tour, this is one of the Northwest's best bets.

SIGHTS   Downtown Seattle (Pioneer Square to Seattle Center, the waterfront to Route 5) is compact enough for walkers to tour on foot. Energetic folks can see the highlights on one grand loop tour, or you can sample smaller chunks on successive days. Since downtown is spread along a relatively narrow north–south axis, you can walk from one end to the other, then return by public transit via buses in the Metro Transit Tunnel or aboard the Waterfront Streetcar trolleys, each of which have stations in both Pioneer Square and the International District. The Monorail also runs north–south between Westlake Center and Seattle Center.

A good place to orient yourself is the Seattle Convention and Visitors Bureau's **Citywide Concierge Center**. Folks manning the desk will supply you with sightseeing advice, tickets for sports and the performing arts, and even book reservations for ground transportation and area restaurants. Closed Saturday and Sunday. ~ 701 Pike Street, Suite 800; 206-461-5840; www.seeseattle.org.

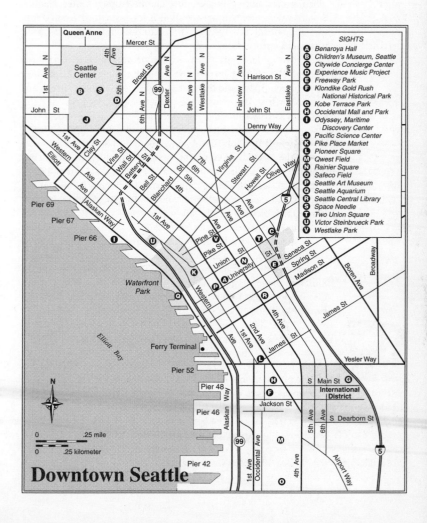

Downtown Seattle

Pioneer Square and its "old underground" remain one of Seattle's major fascinations. It was at this location that Seattle's first business district began. In 1889, a fire burned the woodframe city to the ground. The story of how the city rebuilt out of the ashes of the Great Fire remains intriguing to visitors and locals alike.

To learn exactly how the underground was created after the new city arose, then was forgotten, then rediscovered, you really need to take the one-and-a-half-hour **Underground Tour**. Several of these subterranean pilgrimages are offered daily to the dark and cobwebby bowels of the underground—actually the street-level floors of buildings that were sealed off and fell into disuse when streets and sidewalks were elevated shortly after Pioneer Square was rebuilt (in fire-resistant brick instead of wood). Admission. ~ 608 1st Avenue; 206-682-4646, fax 206-682-1511; www.undergroundtour.com.

Above ground, in sunshine and fresh air, you can stroll through 91 acres of mostly century-old architecture in the historic district (maps and directories to district businesses are available in most shops). Notable architecture includes gems like the **Grand Central Building**, 1st Avenue South and South Main Street, **Merrill Place**, 1st Avenue South and South Jackson Street, the **Maynard Building**, 1st Avenue South and South Washington Street, the cast-iron **Pergola** in Pioneer Square Park and facing buildings such as the **Mutual Life and Pioneer buildings**, 1st Avenue and Yesler Way. More than 30 art galleries are located in the Pioneer Square area. Here you can shop for American Indian art, handicrafts, paintings and pottery. (Incidentally, the Pioneer Building houses Seattle's first electric elevator.)

Yesler Way, located in the heart of the Pioneer Square area, itself originated as the steep "Skid Road" for logs cut on the hillsides above the harbor and bound for Henry Yesler's waterfront mill, and thence to growing cities like San Francisco. Later, as the district declined, Yesler Way attracted a variety of derelicts and became the prototype for every big city's bowery, alias "skid row."

AUTHOR FAVORITE

Pike Place Market is lots of fun, but I find it even more fascinating to wander up and down the food aisles of **Uwajimaya**, trying to identify the strange and exotic ingredients sold there—many of them bright pink. This retail store is not only the largest Asian grocery and gift store in the Northwest but also a worthwhile experience of Asian culture even if you're not shopping. ~ 600 5th Avenue South; 206-624-6248, 800-889-1928, fax 206-405-2996; www.uwajimaya.com.

The new city boomed during the Alaska Gold Rush in 1897-98. For a look back at extraordinary times, stop by the Seattle Unit of the **Klondike Gold Rush National Historical Park**, one of the tiniest National Park Service sites in the lower 48. In this historic red-brick building in downtown Seattle, you can see gold-panning demonstrations, a collection of artifacts, films and other memorabilia. Other units of the park are in Southeast Alaska. ~ 319 2nd Street South; 206-220-4240; www.nps.gov/klse.

The main pedestrian artery is **Occidental Mall and Park**, a tree-lined, cobbled promenade running south from Yesler Way to South Jackson Street allowing pleasant ambling between rows of shops and galleries (don't miss the oasis of **Waterfall Park** off Occidental on South Main Street).

For an overview of the whole district, ride the rattling old manually operated elevator to the observation level of the 42-story **Smith Tower**, built in 1914. Closed weekdays from November through March. ~ 2nd Avenue and Yesler Way; 206-662-4004, fax 206-622-9357; www.smithtower.com, e-mail info@smithtower.com.

Sharp ethnic diversity has always marked the **International District**, next door to Pioneer Square to the southeast. The polyglot community that emerged on the southern fringes of old Seattle always mixed its Asian cultures and continues doing so today, setting it apart from the homogeneous Chinatowns of San Francisco and Vancouver, across the border in British Columbia. ~ Yesler Way to South Dearborn Street, 4th Avenue South to Route 5.

Chinese began settling here in the 1860s, Japanese in the 1890s, and today the "I.D.," as it's commonly known, is also home to Koreans, Filipinos, Vietnamese and Cambodians. For all its diversity, the district clearly lacks the economic vitality, bustling street life and polished tourist appeal of other major Chinatowns. Yet some find the International District all the more genuine for its unhurried, even seedy, ambience.

A variety of mom-and-pop enterprises predominates in the I.D. —specialty-food and grocery stores, herbal-medicine shops, dim sum palaces and fortune-cookie factories.

Wing Luke Asian Museum offers a well-rounded look at the Northwest's Asian Pacific history and culture, representing ten groups of Asian Pacific immigrants. Presentations include historical photography and social commentary on the Asian-American experience. You may also see paintings, ceramics, prints, sculpture and other art. Closed Monday. Admission. ~ 407 7th Avenue South; 206-623-5124, fax 206-623-4559; www.wingluke.org, e-mail folks@wingluke.org.

Named after Seattle's sister city in Japan, **Kobe Terrace Park** offers pleasant strolling among Japanese pine and cherry blossom trees. An adjacent community garden is tended by local residents. ~ 221 6th Avenue South; 206-684-4075.

Hing Hay Park is the scene of frequent festivals—exhibitions of Japanese martial arts, Chinese folk dances, Vietnamese food fairs, Korean music and the like. It's colorful pavilion comes from Taipei, Taiwan. ~ South King Street and Maynard Avenue South.

The old **waterfront** beginning at the western edge of Pioneer Square remains one of the most colorful quarters of the city and what many consider Seattle's liveliest "people place." On sunny summer days, it is the most popular tourist draw in the city. The waterfront grows more interesting by the year, a beguiling jumble of fish bars and excursion-boat docks, ferries and fireboats, import emporiums and nautical shops, sway-backed old piers and barnacle-encrusted pilings that creak in the wash of wakes.

The action's concentrated between Piers 48 and 60, and again around Pier 70. Poking around by foot remains the favorite way to explore, but some folks prefer to hopscotch to specific sites aboard the **Waterfront Streetcar**, which runs from the International District to Pier 70. You also can climb into a horse-drawn carriage near Pier 60 for a narrated tour. Still another way to do it is via boat (see "Hey! The Water's Fine" at the end of this chapter). Here's a sampler of attractions: As you stroll south to north, you'll encounter a harbor-watch facility, a dozen historical plaques that trace major events, a public boat landing, the state-ferry terminal at Colman Dock and the waterfront fire station whose fireboats occasionally put on impressive, fountainlike displays on summer weekends. Ye Olde Curiosity Shop houses a collection of odd goods from around the world, Ivar's is the city's most famous fish bar, and cavernous shopping arcades include pier-end restaurants, outdoor picnic areas and public fishing. **Waterfront Park** is a crescent-shaped retreat from commercialism presenting sweeping views over the harbor.

Dating back to 1899, **Ye Olde Curiosity Shop** is a combination souvenir shop and museum that draws crowds with odd displays such as a Siamese twin calf, rare Eskimo walrus-tusk carvings and one of the world's largest collections of shrunken heads. The antique, coin-operated games are an easy way to get rid of pocket change. ~ 1001 Alaskan Way, Pier 54; 206-682-5844; www.yeolde curiosityshop.com.

The **Seattle Aquarium** allows you to descend to an underwater viewing dome for up-close looks at scores of Puget Sound fish. Other exhibits include a sea otter pool, a coral reef tank teeming with colorful tropical fish, and a giant Pacific octopus. Salmon are born at the aquarium and allowed to migrate to the open sea, returning later to spawn. Admission. ~ Pier 59 at Pike Street; 206-

386-4300, fax 206-386-4328; www.seattleaquarium.org, e-mail aquarium.programs@seattle.gov.

The Pike Hillclimb across Alaskan Way leads up—almost straight up, 155 steps' worth—past several decent restaurants and shops to the famed **Pike Place Market**. (There's an elevator for the walk-weary. You can also reach the north end of the Market from a stairway/elevator complex opposite the Pier 62/63 public wharf.) You'll also pass some piers whose sheds have been leveled to provide public access, the last vestiges of working waterfront on the central harbor—fish-company docks and such—as well as the Port of Seattle headquarters.

The venerable market, born in 1907, has proved itself one of the city's renewable treasures. Saved from the wrecking ball by citizen action in the early '70s, the market was later revitalized through long-term renovation. In August 2007, nine-acre Pike Place Market celebrates the centennial of its founding. **Pike Place Market National Historic District** and the surrounding neighborhood are, in many respects, better than ever. The main historic market, with its famous neon-lit clock, brass pig and fish-throwing vendors, now offers hundreds of different products in hundreds of categories, from clothing to different types of zucchini, even fresh crumpets. It currently has about 100 regular farmers, 200 craftspeople, 240 shops and restaurants, and 200 musicians and performers, and is visited by nearly 10 million visitors a year. In all, a market experience unparalleled in the nation! To learn more, visit the market's website or stop at the Info Booth at 1st Avenue and Pike Street. ~ Virginia Street to just south of Pike Street, 1st to Western avenues; 206-682-7453, fax 206-625-0646; www.pike placemarket.org, e-mail info@pikeplacemarket.org.

It costs less than a dollar to ride the Monorail, which zips between Seattle Center and Westlake Center in two minutes.

There are so many ways to enjoy the market that we can scarcely begin to list them. Come early for breakfast and wake up with the market (at least a dozen cafés open early). Come at noon for the ultimate experience of marketplace clamor amid legions of jostling shoppers, vendors hawking salmon and truck-farm produce, and street musicians vying for your contributions. Come to explore the market's lower level, often missed by tourists, a warrenlike collection of secondhand treasures, old books, magazines, posters and vintage clothing. Come to shop for the largest collection of handmade merchandise in the Northwest on handcraft tables at the market's north end. Come to browse all the "nonproduce" merchandise surrounding the main market—wines, exotic imported foods, French kitchenware, jewelry and avant-garde fashions.

Just a bit north is the Port of Seattle's **Pier 66**, the Bell Street Pier. With a small-craft marina, three restaurants, a museum, a

Seattle's Waterfront

Nowhere is the distinctive character of Seattle more visible than along the waterfront between Piers 52 and 70 and the adjacent Pike Place Market. (Of course, the waterfront contains many more piers south of this area, but they are used for industrial shipping and are inaccessible on foot. The best way to get a look is from a harbor tour boat.) This walking tour covers about two and a half miles. Although it can be completed in less than two hours, along the way you'll find enough points of interest to fill a whole day.

PIKE PLACE MARKET   Start at Pike Place Market, near the intersection of Pike Street and 1st Avenue on a steep hillside above the waterfront. (If you must park in this area, you're most likely to find a space beneath the Alaskan Way Viaduct downhill from the market. A better plan for drivers, though, is to park at one of the big lots around the Seattle Center and ride the monorail downtown. It lets you off just four blocks from the market.) On the street level are more than 100 food vendors' stalls where you'll find plenty of fresh fruits and veggies to snack on while you wander, free samples of tasty edible souvenirs, and fishmongers hawking fresh local seafood such as giant geoduck (pronounced "gooey duck") clams, along with arts-and-crafts stands. The lower level has small eateries and shops that sell exotica imported from such far-off lands as Egypt and India.

HARBOR STEPS PARK   From the south end of Pike Place Market, head south a short distance to Harbor Steps Park. (Here you're practically in front of the **Seattle Art Museum** (page 43); if time permits, it's well worth a visit either now or on the way back.) Walk down the broad 16,000-square-foot steps to Western Avenue. The waterfront promenade is just across the avenue. The steps take you down to Pier 59, site of the **Seattle Aquarium** (page 40). The aquarium is a must-see stop, where undersea attractions include jellyfish, migratory salmon and the

conference center and a skybridge leading up to the booming Belltown shopping/restaurant district along 1st Avenue, this recent development has become a popular stop for travelers.

At Pier 66 on the waterfront, **Odyssey, Maritime Discovery Center** contains four galleries of high-tech interactive exhibits for kids and adults that reveal how the industrial waterfront works, focusing on fishing, trade and boating. Children can steer a container ship into port, load a 20-ton cargo container onto a ship, and explore a scaled-down fishing boat. Other displays explain largest octopus in captivity. The aquarium is in the middle of the public waterfront area.

PIERS 62–70   If you walk north, you'll pass **Pier 62/63**, a bare-wood park serving as a 4000-seat municipal concert venue that has hosted such performers as Lyle Lovett, Jonny Lang, Judy Collins and Los Lobos. Between Anthony's Pier 66 Restaurant and the Edgewater Inn on Pier 67 is **Odyssey, Maritime Discovery Center** (page 42). Beyond the Edgewater Inn is the departure pier for the **Victoria Clipper** (high-speed ferry service to Victoria, B.C.; Pier 69). At the northern end of the waterfront is **Pier 70**, now home to offices and two restaurants but better known as the filming site for MTV's "The Real World: Seattle."

PIERS 55–57   If you walk south from the aquarium, you'll pass a large dining and shopping complex at **Pier 57**, where the central attraction for kids is a vintage carousel. **Pier 55** is the departure point for tour boats to **Tillicum Village** (206-933-8600, 800-426-1205), a replica Salish Indian village on a small island where trips include a traditional grilled salmon buffet. The pier is also home to **Argosy Cruises** (206-623-1445), offering daily boat tours of Seattle Harbor.

PIER 54   Pier 54 is the site of two venerable Seattle landmarks. **Ivar's Fish Bar** (206-467-8063), the original home of the clams and fish-and-chips restaurant that now has locations all over the Northwest, was started in 1938 by the late Ivar Haglund while he was director of Seattle's first aquarium next door. **Ye Olde Curiosity Shop** (page 40) is a combination souvenir shop and free museum.

PIER 52   Pier 52 is the terminal for the **Washington State Ferries** that run frequently to Bremerton, Bainbridge Island and Vashon Island. Taking any of these ferries as a foot passenger makes for a relaxing, low-cost scenic cruise and an introduction to the ferry system that will serve you well as you travel to other parts of the Puget Sound area.

PIONEER SQUARE   From the ferry terminal, you can either return the way you came, climbing back up the Harbor Steps, or go a few more blocks south to Pioneer Square, returning to central downtown along 2nd Avenue with its towering skyscrapers.

fishery management, the global economy, marine safety and environmental preservation. Closed Monday. Admission. ~ Pier 66, 2205 Alaskan Way; 206-374-4000, fax 206-374-4002; www.ody.org, e-mail info@ody.org.

South of Pike Place Market is the **Seattle Art Museum**, designed by the husband/wife architectural team of Robert Venturi and Denise Scott. The five-story, limestone-faced building highlighted with terra-cotta and marble has quickly become a regional, postmodern landmark. You'll enter the museum via a grand staircase, but to see the collections, you'll have to ascend by elevator to the galleries. Known for its Northwest Coast American Indian, Asian and African art, the museum also features Meso-American, modern and contemporary art, photography and European masters. Closed Monday. Admission. ~ 100 University Street; 206-654-3100, fax 206-654-3135; www.seattleartmuseum.org.

Located across the street from the Seattle Art Museum, the Seattle Symphony's massive **Benaroya Hall** gives the symphony its own dedicated concert facility after years of sharing space at Seattle Center with the opera and ballet. The grounds include a memorial garden dedicated to Washington residents who died in military conflicts from World War II to the present. ~ 200 University Street; 206-215-4700, 866-833-4747, fax 206-215-4701; www.seattlesymphony.org, e-mail info@seattlesymphony.org.

City center, or **Downtown,** has undergone a remarkable rejuvenation. It's a delightful place to stroll whether you're intent on shopping or not. Major downtown hotels are clustered in the retail core, allowing easy walks in any direction. Here's one way to sightsee:

Start at the south end of **Freeway Park,** which offers five-plus acres of lawns, gardens and fountains, and is the nation's first major park to be built over a freeway. The park's many waterfalls and pools create a splashy, burbling sound barrier to city noise. Beds of summer-blooming flowers, tall evergreens and leafy deciduous trees create a genuine park feeling, inspiring picnics by office workers on their noon-hour break. Amble north through the park, and take a short detour beneath a street overpass toward University Street (steps next to more waterfalls zigzag up to Capitol Hill and dramatic views of city architecture). ~ 6th Avenue and Seneca Street.

Continue north as the park merges with similarly landscaped grounds of the **Washington State Convention and Trade Center,** which offers occasional exhibits. Maps and information are on hand at the Visitor Concierge Center (206-461-5840), located on

COASTAL DWELLINGS

Offshore on Blake Island is **Tillicum Village,** a huge cedar longhouse styled after the dwellings of the Northwest Coast American Indians, situated on the edge of a 475-acre marine state park. The village presents traditional salmon bakes and performances by the Tillicum Village Dancers. Tillicum Village charters Argosy vessels from Pier 55 on Seattle's central waterfront year-round. ~ 206-933-8600, 800-426-1205, fax 206-933-9377; www.tillicumvillage.com.

the first level of the Convention Center. ~ 800 Convention Place; 206-694-5000, fax 206-694-5399; www.wsctc.com, e-mail info@wsctc.com.

Head west through linking landscaping that leads you past yet more waterfalls and flowers in the main plaza of **Two Union Square**. Cross 6th Avenue and enter the **US Bank Centre**, located on the corner of Union Street. This handsome building's lower levels contain the City Centre mall, featuring upscale shops and a theater complex, bold sculptures and stunning exhibits of colorful art glass. Wander and admire for a bit, stop for a meal or an espresso, then continue by leaving the building at the 5th Avenue and Pike Street exit. Cross 5th Avenue past what used to be the striking Coliseum Theater, now renovated and occupied by Banana Republic. Head west on Pike Street to 4th Avenue and turn right to enter triangular **Westlake Park** at 4th Avenue and Pine Street, which offers a leafy copse of trees and an intriguing pattern of bricks that replicate a Salish Indian basket-weave design best observed from the terraces on the adjoining Westlake Center.

Westlake Center is an enormously popular, multilevel shopping arcade, a people place offering espresso bars, flower vendors, handicrafts and access to what's been heralded as downtown's "new underground." The marbled, well-lighted, below-street-level arcades were created as part of the city's new downtown transit tunnel. Metro buses (propelled electrically while underground) rumble by on the lowest level. Just above it are mezzanines full of public art, with vendors and shops, and underground access to a string of department stores.

Walk south on 4th Avenue a few blocks to **Rainier Square**, between 4th and 5th avenues and University and Union streets, and discover another burgeoning underground of upscale enterprises. Follow its passageways eastward past a bakery, restaurants and access to the venerable **Fifth Avenue Theatre**. Continue east, up an escalator back to Two Union Square and Freeway Park.

Lodgings vary widely in style and price throughout the Seattle area. Downtown, there's a thick cluster of expensive luxury hotels interspersed with a few at moderate and even budget rates.

LODGING

◄ HIDDEN

The **Pioneer Square Hotel**, a Best Western property, combines a prime location with Four-Diamond historic charm. The essence of comfort is captured here by turn-of-the-20th-century decor and remarkably quiet rooms. Rates are quite reasonable by downtown standards. The Pioneer Square Historic District surrounding the hotel is a haven for fascinating restaurants, taverns, art galleries, shops and more. The ferry terminal and Seattle Art Museum are also within a few blocks. ~ 77 Yesler Way; 206-340-1234, 800-800-5514, fax 206-467-0707; www.pioneersquare.com, e-mail info@pioneersquare.com. DELUXE TO ULTRA-DELUXE.

The Edgewater has changed completely since the days when the Beatles used to fish for sand sharks from the windows, but the location—directly on the waterfront—is still hard to beat. The property began as a top-flight hotel on Pier 67, built in the 1960s for the World's Fair. It later slid into decay and was renovated in "mountain lodge" style—meaning stone fireplaces and natural-log furniture in the rooms. Half of the 223 rooms and suites have stunning views of Elliott Bay, West Seattle and the Olympic Peninsula. Rooms are comfortable, and the staff is accommodating. The restaurant has a fine water view. ~ 2411 Alaskan Way; 206-728-7000, 800-624-0670, fax 206-441-4119; www.edgewaterhotel.com, e-mail contactus@edgewaterhotel.com. ULTRA-DELUXE.

The **Alexis Hotel** is an elegant little haven two blocks from the waterfront and close to downtown stores and business centers. The 109 rooms have soft colors and contemporary furnishings mixed with a few antiques, all done in good taste. Some of the roomy suites have fireplaces. The service is unmatched in this renovated historic hotel. ~ 1007 1st Avenue; 206-624-4844, 866-356-8894, fax 206-621-9009; www.alexishotel.com, e-mail reservations@alexishotel.com. ULTRA-DELUXE.

Another luxury hotel, **The Inn at Harbor Steps** has perhaps the best possible location for exploring downtown Seattle on foot. Across the street from the Seattle Art Museum and two blocks from Pike Place Market, the 28-room inn occupies the lower floors of a condominium highrise overlooking the heart of the waterfront. Each spacious guest room features a king- or queen-size bed, a sitting area, a gas fireplace and an oversize bathtub; some have whirlpools. The rooms have high ceilings and floral print decor. ~ 1221 1st Avenue; 206-748-0973, 888-728-8910, fax 206-748-0533; www.innatharborsteps.com, e-mail inn@harborsteps.com. ULTRA-DELUXE.

HIDDEN ▶   The downtown location for the **Green Tortoise Hostel** is convenient to most central-Seattle attractions. With functional private and dorm rooms, 24-hour check-in, a common room and a fully equipped kitchen, it's much like a traditional hostel, with one extra advantage: a free breakfast. Many guest services, such as tours and discounts at local clubs, pubs and restaurants, add value as well. ~ 105 Pike Street; 206-340-1222, 888-424-6783, fax 206-623-3207; www.greentortoise.net, e-mail info@green tortoise.net. BUDGET.

Hostelling International—Seattle is a low-priced establishment on the edge of Pike Place Market. In addition to 125 sleeping units (including six private rooms for two), the bright, clean hostel has a kitchen, dining room, lounge, TV room and small library. Also available are bike storage and laundry facilities. ~ 84

Seattle's
Coffee Wars

*I*t doesn't take long for visitors to notice that Seattle's primary energy source is coffee. Coffee bars, the preferred business and social meeting spots, do a booming business, and it seems as if there's a drive-up espresso kiosk on every block. Conventional wisdom blames the weather for making the steamy, mood-lifting beverage more popular than Prozac, but on sunny summer days, you'll still see people waiting in line for iced lattes and granitas.

In 1971, "fresh coffee" still meant a new five-pound can of Folger's from the supermarket. Then Jim Stewart, with backing from his brother Dave, started Stewart Brothers Coffee, a small stand selling coffee beans in Pike Place Market. Jim first used a peanut roaster he'd bought from a vendor on a southern California beach but soon traveled to Italy to learn the art from master espresso roasters and purchased a real coffee-bean roaster. The unfamiliar smell of fresh roasted coffee wafted through the market and made his stand an instant hit. Later that same year, a second coffee-bean stand opened in Pike Place Market under the name Starbucks.

Soon the two rivals began buying coffee beans from different parts of the world, developing assorted distinctive blends and adding flavorings. In 1984 Starbucks started its first coffee bar at 4th and Spring streets in downtown Seattle. Meanwhile, Stewart Brothers began selling whole-bean coffee in bulk through supermarkets. Learning that there was another coffee wholesaler named Stewart, the brothers abbreviated the company's name to SBC Inc., which in turn inspired its trade name, Seattle's Best Coffee.

SBC grew to become the world's leading seller of specialty coffee beans, while Starbucks has expanded to nearly 4000 coffee bars, including locations in Tokyo, Beijing, Manila and Kuwait. Starbucks finally bought its in-city rival in 2003 but SBC retains an independent identity. The city now boasts 26 other retail and wholesale coffee-roasting companies as well as five green brokers (importers of unroasted coffee beans).

Union Street; 206-622-5443, 888-622-5443, fax 206-682-2179; www.hiseattle.org, e-mail reserve@hiseattle.org. BUDGET.

HIDDEN ►   **Pensione Nichols** offers European-style lodging within a block of Pike Place Market. Eight rooms on the third floor of a historic building share three baths and a large common space with a view of the bay, while two rooms share one bath on the second floor. The rooms are painted a cheerful yellow and have antique furnishings; some have windows, while others only have skylights. There are also two ultra-deluxe suites that sleep four and have views of the sound, fully equipped kitchens and private baths. A continental breakfast is served. ~ 1923 1st Avenue; phone/fax 206-441-7125, 800-440-7125; www.pensionenichols.com. DELUXE TO ULTRA-DELUXE.

A retreat from the throngs in Pike Place Market is **Inn at the Market**. The hotel, several shops and a restaurant are centered by a brick courtyard with a 50-year-old cherry tree. Light and airy and furnished in contemporary European style, the 70-room inn is one of Seattle's best. Guest rooms have views of the city, courtyard or water. ~ 86 Pine Street; 206-443-3600, 800-446-4484, fax 206-448-0631; www.innatthemarket.com, e-mail info@innatthemarket.com. ULTRA-DELUXE.

Hotel Monaco offers stylish, upscale accommodations in 189 funky, plush rooms and suites. The grand high-ceilinged lobby has columns and pilasters and a white stucco fireplace spotlighted by azure hues. Make sure to take advantage of their in-room pet goldfish adoption program. ~ 1101 4th Avenue; 206-621-1770, 800-715-6513, fax 206-261-7779; www.monaco-seattle.com. ULTRA-DELUXE.

A GRAND HOTEL

For grandeur and luxury check in to the **W Seattle**. This Italian Renaissance–style hotel was built in 1924 on land that was the site of the original University of Washington. Conveniently located in the heart of downtown close to Pike Place Market and the Seattle Art Museum, this grande dame is the ultimate statement of refined elegance. The 450 guest rooms are tastefully appointed, and modern conveniences combine gracefully with the classic furnishings. The public rooms, adorned with impressive floral arrangements and crystal chandeliers take you back to another era while the fantasy blown-glass arrangements in the main dining room bring you back to the 21st century. Add a health club with pool and huge jacuzzi and you need look no further. ~ 1112 4th Avenue; 206-264-6000, 877-946-8357, fax 206-264-6100; www.whotels.com, e-mail wseattle. whatwhen@whotels.com. ULTRA-DELUXE.

Considered a luxury hotel in the 1930s, the **Executive Hotel Pacific** is now a dignified, quiet downtown classic with 153 rooms. Though updated and decorated with modern furniture, it hasn't lost its old-fashioned flavor, with windows that open, ceiling fans and rather small rooms. The concierge is very helpful. ~ 400 Spring Street; 206-623-3900, 800-426-1165, fax 206-623-2059; www.pacificplazahotel.com, e-mail resehp@executivehotels.net. MODERATE TO DELUXE.

Located in a former 1920s apartment building, the **Hotel Andra** provides spacious guest rooms converted from studio apartments. Decorated in earth tones, the 119 rooms include sitting areas with love seats. There's also a fitness room. ~ 2000 4th Avenue; 206-448-8600, 877-448-8600, fax 206-441-7140; www.hotelandra.com, e-mail hotelandra@hotelandra.com. DELUXE TO ULTRA-DELUXE.

Between downtown and Seattle Center is **Sixth Avenue Inn**, a five-story motor inn with 167 rooms. The rooms are a cut above those in most motels. They contain brass beds, desks and large windows. Those on the north and in back are the quietest. There's a restaurant overlooking a small garden, a fitness facility and wireless internet. ~ 2000 6th Avenue; 206-441-8300, 888-627-8290, fax 206-441-9903; www.sixthavenueinn.com, e-mail sixth.avenue@starwoodhotels.com. DELUXE.

The **Sorrento Hotel** is known for its personal service and attention to detail. A historic building that has been remodeled, Sorrento is at the top of what is locally known as "Pill Hill" (for its proximity to the hospital), a few blocks from the downtown area to the north and the International District immediately south. Beyond the quiet, plush lobby are a notable restaurant and an inviting lounge with a piano bar that is a popular spot for a nightcap. The Sorrento has been called one of the most romantic hotels in Seattle. All 76 rooms and suites have a warm, traditional, European atmosphere. ~ 900 Madison Street; 206-622-6400, 800-426-1265, fax 206-343-6155; www.hotelsorrento.com, e-mail mail@hotelsorrento.com. ULTRA-DELUXE.

The **Inn at Virginia Mason** is an attractive, nine-story brick building owned by the medical center next door. On the eastern edge of downtown, it caters to hospital visitors and others looking for a convenient location and pleasant accommodations at reasonable prices. The 79 rooms have dark-wood furnishings and teal and maroon decor. Two suites have a fireplace and whirlpool tub. There's a small restaurant by a brick terrace. ~ 1006 Spring Street; 206-583-6453, 800-283-6453, fax 206-223-7545; www.innatvirginiamason.com. MODERATE TO DELUXE.

Villa Heidelberg is a bed and breakfast in a Craftsman-style home on a corner hillside. The inn has a wide wraparound porch that overlooks gardens of roses and rhododendrons. Inside, the atmosphere is comfortable and relaxed. The house features leaded glass windows, beamed ceilings and the original 1909 gaslight fixtures and embossed wall coverings. The six guest rooms are decorated in pastel florals and feature brass or oak beds and oak dressers. A full breakfast is served. ~ 4845 45th Avenue Southwest, West Seattle; 206-938-3658, 800-671-2942, fax 206-935-7077; www.villaheidelberg.com, e-mail info@villaheidelberg.com. MODERATE TO DELUXE.

DINING

The fine **al Boccalino** serves some of the city's best Italian dinners. Located in a brick building in Pioneer Square, the restaurant's atmosphere is unpretentious and intimate, the antipasti imaginative, and the entrées cooked and sauced to perfection. Saddle of lamb with brandy, tarragon and mustard is a favorite choice. There are daily specials for every course. No lunch on Saturday or Sunday. ~ 1 Yesler Way; 206-622-7688, fax 206-622-1798; e-mail alboccalino@aol.com. MODERATE TO DELUXE.

For a romantic dinner, try **Il Terrazzo Carmine** in the Merrill Place Building. For patio diners, a cascading reflecting pool drowns out some of the freeway noise. Entrées include roast duck with cherries or veal piccata with capers and lemon. The restaurant also features an extensive Italian wine list. No lunch on Saturday. Closed Sunday. ~ Pioneer Square, 411 1st Avenue South; 206-467-7797, fax 206-447-5716; www.ilterrazzocarmine.com. DELUXE.

HIDDEN ►

It's impossible not to get thoroughly filled at **Zaina**, a friendly, low-key Greek eatery in the midst of the lower downtown business district. The place is packed with office workers at lunch, but the crowd thins out after 1 p.m. The food is filling and flavorful. Closed Sunday. ~ 108 Cherry Street; 206-624-5687. BUDGET.

A favorite among downtowners is the **Botticelli Café**. The small café is known for its *panini*—little sandwiches made of toasted focaccia bread and topped with olive oil, herbs, cheeses, meats and vegetables. The espresso and ices are good, too. Breakfast and lunch only. Closed Saturday and Sunday. ~ 101 Stewart Street; 206-441-9235. BUDGET.

White-linen tablecloths, black-rattan furnishings and loads of plants await you at **L.A. Seafood Restaurant & Lounge**, an upscale Cantonese restaurant in the International District. In the foyer, the specials—such as hot and smoky crab in a spicy sauce, fresh fish with vegetables or clams in black-bean sauce—are posted on the blackboard. ~ 424 7th Avenue South; 206-622-8181. MODERATE TO DELUXE.

Shoppers and theatergoers love **Palomino** and its large, airy dining room, which lends itself to prime people watching. The food's good, too—this bustling downtown spot is best known for thin-crust pizzas that barely support the heap of toppings. Also on the menu is a variety of regional American and southern

European–inspired salads, pasta and roasted meat and poultry dishes. Though crowded, you can still count on fast and efficient service. ~ 1420 5th Avenue; 206-623-1300; www.palomino.com. MODERATE TO DELUXE.

Hidden away in the Pike Place Market is **Place Pigalle**. Wind your way past a seafood vendor and Rachel, the bronze pig (a popular market mascot), to this restaurant with spectacular views of Elliott Bay. The dark-wood trim, handsome bar and other touches make for a European-bistro atmosphere. The restaurant makes the most of fresh ingredients from the market's produce tables. Dine on fresh Penn Cove mussels with bacon, celery and shallots in balsamic vinaigrette, calamari in a dijon-ginger cream sauce, or one of the daily fresh salmon specials. The dishes are artfully presented. Patio dining available in summer. Closed Sunday. ~ 81 Pike Street; 206-624-1756. DELUXE.

Tucked into a hillside in Pike Place Market, **Il Bistro** is a cozy cellar spot with wide archways and oriental rugs on wooden floors. Light jazz, candlelight and well-prepared Italian food make it an inviting spot on a rainy evening. Several pastas are served; the entrées include rack of lamb, veal scallopine, fresh salmon and roasted half-chicken served with garlic mashed potatoes. Dinner only. ~ 93-A Pike Street; 206-682-3049, fax 206-223-0234; www.ilbistro.net. DELUXE TO ULTRA-DELUXE.

Across the cobbled street, you can observe the eclectic mix of shoppers and artists in the Pike Place Market at **Three Girls Bakery**, a popular hangout. This tiny lunch counter and bakery with just a few seats serves good sandwiches—the meatloaf sandwich is popular—and hearty soups, including chili and clam chowder. You have more than 50 kinds of bread to choose from. The sourdough and rye breads are recommended. If you don't have room for pastries, buy some to take home. You won't regret it. ~ 1514 Pike Place; 206-622-1045, fax 206-622-0245. BUDGET.

The food at **Oriental Mart** is a combination of Filipino and Asian—and it's very good and very inexpensive. Try the pork *adobo* if they have it that day; otherwise, any of the chicken prep-

◄ HIDDEN

AUTHOR FAVORITE

When I'm craving authentic Mexican food, I head to **El Puerco Lloron**. Every meal served here includes wonderfully fresh tortillas made by hand while hungry diners watch from the cafeteria line. The chiles rellenos compares with the best, and the tamales and taquitos are all authentic and recommended. There's a fiesta atmosphere in the warm, steamy room. ~ Pike Place Market Hillclimb, 1501 Western Avenue; 206-624-0541. BUDGET.

arations are excellent. There's no better place for lunch at the Market. The lunch counter is in back of the food-and-novelties store. ~ 1506 Pike Place Market; 206-622-8488. BUDGET.

In Post Alley, behind some of the market shops, you will find more than just a wee bit of Ireland at **Kells**. This traditional Irish restaurant and pub will lure you to the Emerald Isle with pictures and posters of splendid countryside. A limited menu includes Irish stew and meat pies. From the heavy, dark bar comes a host of domestic and imported beers. Irish musicians play live music seven days a week. ~ 1916 Post Alley; 206-728-1916, fax 206-441-9431; www.kellsirish.com/seattle. MODERATE

HIDDEN ►

Talk about hidden—this place doesn't even have a sign. You enter through the pink door off of Post Alley. **The Pink Door**, with its Italian kitsch decor, is lively and robust at lunchtime. Especially good are the *lasagna della porta rosa* and a delicious cioppino. In the evening, the pace slows, the light dims and it's a perfect setting for a romantic dinner. In the summer, rooftop dining offers views of the Sound. Closed Monday. ~ 1919 Post Alley; 206-443-3241, fax 206-443-3341; www.thepinkdoor.net. DELUXE.

Seattle was built on seven hills, though only six remain: the seventh hill, Denny, was scraped off and dumped into Puget Sound.

Off a brick courtyard above Pike Place Market, **Campagne** is one of the city's top restaurants. Diners enjoy French country cooking in an atmosphere both warm and elegant. The menu changes six times a year. Entrées may include rack of lamb brushed with puréed anchovy and garlic sauce or roasted sea bass with tarragon, lemon and tiny herb dumplings. The simply prepared dishes are usually the best: young chicken stuffed with ricotta, spinach and roasted herbs and served with sage-infused *jus* and rosemary roasted potatoes, for example. Dinner only. ~ 86 Pine Street; 206-728-2800, fax 206-448-7562; www.campagnerestaurant.com. DELUXE TO ULTRA-DELUXE.

The decor is spare and clean in **Wild Ginger**, and the menu is pan-Asian. Dark-wood booths fill the main dining room. There's also a satay bar where skewered chicken, beef, fish and vegetables are grilled, then served with peanut and other sauces. The wondrous Seven Elements Soup, an exotic blend of flavors, is a meal in itself. No lunch on Sunday. ~ 1401 3rd Avenue; 206-623-4450, fax 206-623-8265. MODERATE TO DELUXE.

Contemporary, international cuisine prepared with imagination is served at the **Dahlia Lounge** near the shops of Westlake Center. Bright red walls, a neon sign and paper-fish lampshades create a celebratory atmosphere. The chef draws upon numerous ethnic styles and uses Northwest products to develop such dishes as roasted mussels, spicy pork sausage and tomato fondue with aioli. ~ 2001 4th Avenue; 206-682-4142, fax 206-467-0568;

www.tomdouglas.com, e-mail admin@tomdouglas.com. DELUXE
TO ULTRA-DELUXE.

Just north of downtown, you'll find the thriving Belltown
shopping, dining and nightlife scene.

Dark and intimate, **Marco's Supperclub** is a little-known pur-   ◄ *HIDDEN*
veyor of fine, eclectic multiregional dishes; the deep-fried sage
leaves, an appetizer, are a true original. The staff is friendly and
experienced, the music is '30s and '40s jazz, and the filling meals
are reasonable by Belltown standards. Dinner only. Closed Sunday. ~ 2510 1st Avenue; 206-441-7801; www.marcossupperclub.
com. MODERATE TO DELUXE.

Scarlet walls, high-backed booths and dim lighting help **Belltown Pizza** stand apart from your average pizza joint. It helps,
too, that the pies here are damn tasty. Also on the menu is a small
selection of pasta, salads and focaccia sandwiches. But after 10
p.m. on weekends, expect a hip, lively crowd that's more interested in the bar than the food. Dinner only. ~ 2422 1st Avenue;
206-441-2653; www.belltownpizza.net, e-mail jimmyd09@com
cast.net. BUDGET TO MODERATE.

Artists and others without a lot of money for eats hang out
at **The Two Bells Bar & Grill**. Local artwork on the walls changes
every two months. This funky bar with 25 kinds of beer and a
host of inexpensive good food is a busy place. You can always find
good soups, sandwiches, burgers, salads and cold plates. Some
favorites are an Italian-sausage soup and the hot beer-sausage
sandwich. ~ 2313 4th Avenue; 206-441-3050, fax 206-448-9626.
MODERATE.

The oldest and loveliest structure in Pioneer Square is the Pioneer   **SHOPPING**
Building. In the basement, the **Pioneer Square Antique Mall** has
more than 6000 square feet of space devoted to antiques and collectibles and maintained by some 60 dealers. ~ 602 1st Avenue;
206-624-1164.

Grand Central Building houses 17 shops. Visitors can also
enjoy drinks and baked goods at lobby tables adjacent to a brick
fireplace. ~ 214 1st Avenue South; 206-623-7417.

Need a Morris Graves painting or a portrait of grunge legend Kurt Cobain? Several Pioneer Square galleries specialize in
local artists, including **Linda Hodges Gallery** (Closed Sunday
and Monday; 316 1st Avenue South; 206-624-3034; www.linda
hodgesgallery.com), **Davidson Galleries** (313 Occidental Avenue
South; 206-624-7684; www.davidsongalleries.com) and **Greg
Kucera Gallery** (212 3rd Avenue South; 206-624-0770; www.
gregkucera.com).

In the heart of the Pioneer Square district is the **Elliott Bay
Book Company**, featuring over 150,000 titles, including an out-

standing stock of Northwest books. You're bound to enjoy browsing, snacking in the on-premises café or listening in on frequently scheduled readings by renowned authors. ~ 101 South Main Street; 206-624-6600, 800-962-5311; www.elliottbaybook.com.

Seattle's connection with the Pacific Rim is legendary, and **Uwajimaya** demonstrates the tie with shoji screens and lamps, kanji clocks, goldimari ceramic pieces and Japanese, Chinese, Thai, Vietnamese, Filipino and American canned and frozen foods. ~ 600 5th Avenue South; 206-624-6248, fax 206-405-2996; www. uwajimaya.com.

Housed in the old Higo Variety Store building (a neighborhood institution from the 1920s), the KOBO **Gallery** showcases traditional Japanese handicrafts and contemporary Pacific Northwest. Handmade cedar bowls, lacquerware, vintage textiles, modern photography and ceramics are all available. Closed Sunday. ~ 604 South Jackson Street; 206-381-3000.

Along the waterfront, Piers 54 through 70 are shoppers' delights. You'll love **Ye Olde Curiosity Shop**, a Seattle landmark where the mummies "Sylvia," "Sylvester" and "Gloria" preside over souvenirs, American Indian totem poles and masks, Russian stacking dolls, lacquerware and Ukrainian eggs. ~ 1001 Alaskan Way, Pier 54; 206-682-5844; www.yeoldecuriosityshop.com.

Called the "Soul of Seattle," the **Pike Place Market** has been in business since 1907. Saved from the wrecking ball by citizen action in the early '70s, Pike Place is now a bustling bazaar with nearly 300 businesses (about 40 are eateries), 100 farmers (selling produce and flowers at tables and stalls) and 200 local artists and craftspeople. ~ 85 Pike Street; 206-682-7453; www.pike placemarket.org.

A notable establishment within the market is the **Pure Food Fish Market**, which ships fresh or smoked salmon anywhere in the U.S. ~ 1511 Pike Place; 206-622-5765; www.freshseafood.com.

HIDDEN ►
In the downtown area, 5th Avenue, Seattle's fashion street, is lined with shops displaying elegant finery and accessories. **Nancy Meyer** specializes in very fine European lingerie. Closed Sunday. ~ 1318 5th Avenue; 206-625-9200, 800-605-5098; www.nancymeyer.com. **Rainier Square** houses several prestigious retail establishments. ~ 1333 5th Avenue. **Turgeon Raine** is an exceptionally good, locally owned jewelry store. Closed Sunday. ~ 1407 5th Avenue; 206-447-9488, 800-678-0120; www.turgeonraine.com. Off 5th Avenue on Union is **Totally Michael's**, which has contemporary, upscale clothing. Closed Sunday. ~ 521 Union Street; 206-622-4920; www.totallymichaels.com.

At the **Westlake Center**, located at 4th Avenue and Pine Street, there's the **Fireworks Gallery** (206-682-6462; www.fireworks gallery.net) which takes its name from unusually fired sculptures.

Also offered are a variety of intriguing home accessories, gifts and jewelry. **Millstream** (206-233-9719) sells Northwest sculpture, prints, pottery and jewelry by local artisans. ~ 400 Pine Street. Fast foods, available on the third floor, include teriyaki, pizza, enchiladas and yogurt. Nearby, **Alhambra** offers high-end women's clothing, Indonesian furniture and a variety of jewelry. ~ 101 Pine Street; 206-621-9571; www.alhambranet.com.

NIGHTLIFE

Seattle's nightlife, music and club scene is astounding for a city its size. More than 50 clubs, lounges, restaurants and taverns feature live or deejay-spun music, and dozens more have occasional performances. The offerings run the gamut from folk to punk/metal; dance venues range from midnight raves in port district warehouses to salsa nights at Latin bars.

Unexpected Productions offers comedy performances and workshops in improvisational theater techniques. ~ The Market Theater, 1428 Post Alley, Pike Place Market; 206-325-6500; www.unexpectedproductions.org. And at **Comedy Underground**, comics entertain nightly. Cover. ~ 222 South Main Street; 206-628-0303; www.comedyunderground.com.

On Broadway, the public art will give you a free dance lesson—just follow the bronze "Dancing Feet" imbedded in the sidewalk.

There are many fine nightclubs in Pioneer Square, and on "joint-cover" nights, one charge admits you to nine places within a four-block radius. Among them is **Doc Maynard's**, heavy on rock-and-roll with live music on weekends. Cover. ~ 610 1st Avenue; 206-682-3705; www.docmaynards.com. The **New Orleans Creole Restaurant** offers live jazz and blues nightly along with Cajun Creole food in an eclectic, laidback atmosphere. Cover on weekends. ~ 114 1st Avenue South; 206-622-2563; www.neworleanscreolerestaurant.com. Over at **Trinity Night Club**, a mixed crowd enjoys deejay dance music. Cover. ~ 111 Yesler Way; 206-447-4140; www.trinitynightclub.com.

The Showbox nightclub features local, national and international live bands and all types of music and a full bar. Cover. ~ 1426 1st Avenue; 206-628-3151; www.showboxonline.com.

Belltown, near the Pike Place Market, has lots of activity after dark. **Crocodile Café**, one of Seattle's legendary spawning grounds for grunge, punk, rock and alternative bands, attracts a young crowd for live music. Closed Monday. Cover. ~ 2200 2nd Avenue; 206-441-5611; www.thecrocodile.com.

A venerable jazz outpost, **Tula's** provides scat lovers with live music every night, plus a full menu and bar. Cover. ~ 2214 2nd Avenue; 206-443-4221; www.tulas.com.

Dimitriou's Jazz Alley is a downtown dinner theater and premier jazz club with international acts. Closed Monday. Cover. ~ 2033 6th Avenue; 206-441-9729; www.jazzalley.com.

The **Seattle Symphony**'s large performance space, **Benaroya Hall**, has enabled it to vastly expand its schedule and repertoire. Noted especially for its attention to American composers, the symphony, under the direction of Gerard Schwarz, is one of the top recording orchestras in the United States. ~ 200 University Street; 206-215-4800, tickets 206-215-4747; www.seattlesymphony.org.

For satirical/comical revues on Friday, Saturday and some Wednesday nights, try the **Cabaret de Paris** dinner theater at the Crepe de Paris restaurant. Cover. ~ Rainier Square, 1333 5th Avenue; 206-623-4111.

The **Paramount Theatre**, the elaborate movie palace of the 1920s, now offers diverse events from Broadway musicals to political programs. ~ 9th Avenue and Pine Street; 206-467-5510; www.theparamount.com.

Video games, beer and pub food—sounds like a classic video arcade. But **Gameworks** is much more than that. With the latest in electronic games, virtual-reality games and adventures, this has become the highly successful (and highly publicized) prototype for what is now an international chain. ~ 1511 7th Avenue; 206-521-0952; www.gameworks.com.

Seattle Center–Queen Anne Area

Northwest of downtown a familiar landmark rises skyward—the Space Needle. This symbol of the city nestles comfortably among museums, cultural centers and a sports arena at the Seattle Center. Just north of the arts and entertainment complex sits the stunning Queen Anne area, a hilly neighborhood of fanciful homes and great views. This is the part of Seattle where the downtown bustle starts to give way to the more peaceful charms of the outlying neighborhoods.

SIGHTS

Seattle Center, once the site of the 1962 World's Fair, is now a 74-acre campus with more than a dozen buildings housing a variety of offices, convention rooms and theaters. Locals and visitors continue to flock to the **Space Needle** (admission; 206-905-2100; www.spaceneedle.com, e-mail info@spaceneedle.com) for the view or a meal, to summer carnival rides at the **Fun Forest**, to the **Center House**'s short-order ethnic eateries, to see nearby opera and live theater and to check out wide-ranging exhibits and demonstrations at the **Pacific Science Center** (admission; 206-443-2001, fax 206-443-3631; www.pacsci.org). The **Seattle Children's Theatre** (206-443-0807, fax 206-443-0442; www.sct.org, e-mail info@sct.org) has jovial performances geared to a young audience. The **Pacific Northwest Ballet** (tickets, 206-441-2424, fax 206-441-2420; information, 206-441-9411; www.pnb.org) has its offices and rehearsal space at the Phelps Center (where the public can watch the corps rehearse through a glass wall). ~ Seattle Center: Two miles north of the downtown core between Denny Way and Mercer Street; 206-684-7200, fax 206-684-7342; www.seattlecenter.com.

Kids will also enjoy visiting the **Children's Museum, Seattle** on the ground floor of Center House. The collection features a kid's-size neighborhood and multicultural global village, a two-story walk-through re-creation of a mountain forest and mechanically oriented displays. There is also a small lagoon for children and a drop-in art studio. Admission. ~ Seattle Center; 206-441-1768, fax 206-448-0910; www.thechildrensmuseum.org.

For an interactive history lesson on American rock-and-roll, stop by **Experience Music Project** (EMP), a must for music lovers of all stripes. Among the many highlights at this 140,000-square-foot space-age facility are a vintage guitar collection, a rock fashion exhibit and the Jimi Hendrix Gallery. Those with rock-star fantasies will get a kick out of the Sound Lab, where you can perform on stage. Closed Tuesday. Admission. ~ 325 5th Avenue North; 206-367-5483, 877-367-5483, fax 206-770-2727; www.emplive.org, e-mail experience@emplive.org.

LODGING

Conveniently located a block from Seattle Center, half of the **Best Western Executive Inn**'s rooms offer views of the Space Needle. In the lobby guests enjoy a fitness center with jacuzzi, a full-service restaurant and lounge. ~ 200 Taylor Avenue North; 206-448-9444, 800-351-9444, fax 206-441-7836. DELUXE.

On Lower Queen Anne Hill is the **Hampton Inn & Suites**. Standard rooms have either a king-size or two double beds, fireplaces and full kitchens. One- and two-room suites are also available. Full breakfast buffet included. ~ 700 5th Avenue North; 206-282-7700, 800-426-7866, fax 206-282-0899; www.hamptoninnseattle.com. DELUXE.

DINING

At the Space Needle's **Sky City Restaurant**, the entertainment— from 500 feet up—in either the restaurant or the observation deck is seeing metropolitan Seattle, its environs, Puget Sound, the Olympic Mountains and Mt. Rainier, the Queen of the Cascade Range, as you rotate in a 360° orbit. The restaurant serves vari-

DREAMWORKS

For a rewarding, spur-of-the-moment visit, drop by Seattle Center on a summer evening for a contemplative quarter-hour of gazing at the International Fountain. The combination of changing lights and waterworks synchronized to music during the first 15 minutes of every hour against a rose-tinted summer sunset can lull you into a dreamy state.

ous seafood, beef, pasta and poultry dishes, such as tea-smoked wild salmon and *sake* beef short ribs. Weekend brunch. ~ 400 Broad Street; 206-905-2100, fax 206-905-2211; www.spaceneedle.com/restaurant, e-mail skycitymanagers@spaceneedle.com. ULTRA-DELUXE.

HIDDEN ►

On the plaza at Five Point Square, next to the Chief Seattle statue, the **Five Point Cafe** is a distinctive Seattle landmark. With a sign on the door warning nonsmokers that smokers are welcome, and "Pinball Wizard" inevitably playing on the jukebox, it's a real joint. Why go? The food is good, no-nonsense and quite economical, and no one leaves hungry. Try the fish and chips or the meatloaf sandwich (yes, it's that kind of restaurant). ~ 415 Cedar Street; 206-448-9993. BUDGET.

For sublime breakfast pastries and delicious Mediterranean-inspired lunch items, head for **Macrina Bakery**, a cozy European-style bakery and café where the moss green walls are adorned with scrolls, ironwork, paintings and other work by local artists. Breakfast items include house-made coffee cakes, cereals and fruit pastries, while a changing lunch menu may offer such dishes as tartlet of roast chicken and goat cheese or cheese polenta with red chard. ~ 2408 1st Avenue; 206-448-4032, fax 206-374-1782; www.macrinabakery.com. MODERATE.

The 605-foot tall Space Needle, built to withstand wind velocities of up to 200 miles an hour, sways approximately one inch for every ten miles an hour of wind.

When Kaspar Donier moved his acclaimed restaurant to the Seattle Center area, he lost the old location's view atop an office building, but gained a nicer home and a different dinner crowd. Now, symphony, opera and ballet patrons flock to **Kaspar's** to feast on his intriguing contemporary Northwest cuisine. Kaspar's braised lamb shanks, for instance, may be the Northwest's best; his scallops are sumptuous and plentiful. Dinner only. Closed Sunday and Monday. ~ 19 West Harrison Street; 206-298-0123, fax 206-298-0146; www.kaspars.com, e-mail info@kaspars.com. DELUXE TO ULTRA-DELUXE.

Near Seattle Center, **Rice and Spice** serves authentic Thai cuisine in a friendly, comfortable setting. There are art objects from Thailand to look at while you wait for your order of Swimming Angel (chicken in a peanut-chili sauce over spinach) or another of the menu's 50-plus items. They vary in hotness and are rich with the flavors of coconut, curry, garlic, peanuts and peppers. No lunch on Saturday. Closed Sunday. ~ 101 John Street; 206-285-9000. BUDGET.

NIGHTLIFE   Home of the 1962 World's Fair, the **Seattle Center** still offers numerous nighttime diversions. ~ 305 Harrison Street; 206-684-8582.

The **Marion Oliver McCaw Hall for the Performing Arts** is the city's opera and ballet companies' glamorous concert hall. Founded in 1964, **Seattle Opera** is dedicated to producing theatrically compelling, musically accomplished opera. The leading Wagner company in America, the company stages five operas a year. ~ 321 Mercer Street; 206-389-7676, 800-426-1619; www.seattleopera.org.

Pacific Northwest Ballet's annual production of Tchaikovsky's *Nutcracker*, with fanciful sets designed by famed children's illustrator Maurice Sendak, is a perennial favorite. ~ 321 Mercer Street; 206-441-2424.

Music director Gerard Schwarz has led the **Seattle Symphony** to prominence by focusing on baroque and romantic classics and formerly little-known American composers such as Alan Hovhaness (a longtime Seattle resident), David Diamond and Howard Hanson. Masterpiece symphony concerts are Thursday and Saturday evenings and the occasional Sunday afternoon. The fact that symphony concerts rarely sell out offers visitors the chance to see one of the top orchestral ensembles in the United States. No shows mid-July to early September. ~ 206-215-4747; www.seattle symphony.org, e-mail info@seattlesymphony.org.

The **Seattle Repertory Theatre** plays an eclectic mix from musicals to classic dramas at the **Bagley Wright Theatre** and the **Leo K. Theatre**. ~ 155 Mercer Street between Warren Avenue and 2nd Avenue North; 206-443-2222, 877-900-9285; www.seattlerep.org. The nearby **Intiman Theatre** presents plays by the great dramatists, as well as new works. ~ 201 Mercer Street at 2nd Avenue North; 206-269-1900; www.intiman.org.

ACT Theatre in the old Eagles Auditorium next to the Convention Center specializes in works by new playwrights. ~ 7th and Union streets; 206-292-7676; www.acttheatre.org.

Capitol Hill

Seattle's sizable gay population and diverse array of gay inns, clubs and meeting places is one of the many reasons travelers are increasingly flocking to the city. While gay activities and nightlife are found throughout the city, the highest concentration is in Capitol Hill, one of Seattle's most cosmopolitan neighborhoods. Take a walk down Broadway in Capitol Hill, and you'll see one of the most vibrant gay communities in the country.

SIGHTS

Capitol Hill is a mixed neighborhood that is a fun place to browse. Within a block or two you can toss back an exotic wheatgrass drink at a vegetarian bar, slowly sip a double espresso at a sidewalk café, shop for radical literature at a leftist bookstore or hit a straight or gay nightclub. If you can't find it on Capitol Hill,

Seattle probably doesn't have it. Broadway Avenue is the heart of this region known for its boutiques, yuppie appliance stores and bead shops.

Home of some of the city's finest Victorians, this neighborhood also includes **Volunteer Park**. Be sure to head up to the top of the water tower for a great view of the region. ~ 15th Avenue East from East Prospect Street to East Galer Street.

The building that used to house the Seattle Art Museum is now the home of the **Seattle Asian Art Museum**. This Art Moderne building was a gift to the city in the 1930s by Dr. Richard Fuller, who was the museum's director for the next 40 years. The Japanese, Chinese and Korean collections are the largest, but the museum also has south and southeast Asian collections. Japanese folk textiles, Thai ceramics and Korean screen paintings are some of the highlights. One admission fee will get you into here and the Seattle Art Museum if you visit within the same week. Admission. ~ Volunteer Park, 1400 East Prospect Street; 206-654-3100, fax 206-654-3135; www.seattleartmuseum.org.

LODGING
The **Salisbury House Bed & Breakfast** is a quiet, dignified, gracious Capitol Hill home two blocks from Volunteer Park. The five crisp, clean rooms (all have private baths) are furnished with antiques and wicker. Fresh flowers, duvets on the beds, a full (meatless) breakfast and thoughtful innkeeper make this a well-done B&B. There are fireplaces in the living room and library and a refrigerator guests may use. A fully equipped 600-square-foot suite offers the lone television. ~ 750 16th Avenue East; 206-328-8682, fax 206-720-1019; www.salisburyhouse.com, e-mail sleep@salisburyhouse.com. DELUXE TO ULTRA-DELUXE.

Also in the popular, busy Capitol Hill area, **Gaslight Inn** is a bed and breakfast brimming with urban flair. The 1906 house is furnished with oak, maple and glass antiques. Various period styles have been effectively combined with modern amenities in the eight guest rooms. Most have private baths, and one boasts a fireplace. Gaslight has a heated, outdoor swimming pool (closed in winter) and an outdoor deck that overlooks the city. A continental buffet breakfast is served. ~ 1727 15th Avenue East; 206-325-3654, fax 206-328-4803; www.gaslight-inn.com, e-mail inn keepr@gaslight-inn.com. DELUXE.

On Capitol Hill near Volunteer Park in the Harvard-Belmont Historic District is the **Bacon Mansion**, a historic 1909 Tudor stucco home. In addition to the two-story carriage house, which has a living room, dining room and two guest rooms with a private bath in each, there are nine guest rooms in the main house, seven with private bath. The Capitol suite has a sun room with wet bar, fireplace, queen-size bed, view of the Space Needle and a big bathtub. ~ 959 Broadway East; 206-329-1864, 800-240-1864,

fax 206-860-9025; www.baconmansion.com, e-mail info@bacon
mansion.com. MODERATE TO ULTRA-DELUXE.

DINING

West of Broadway, on Pike and Pine streets, is a collection of bars
and restaurants catering to the hipster population. **611 Supreme**
is a cheery, comfy café specializing in crêpes both sweet and savory. Try the Gruyere and sautéed vegetables crêpe, or the citron
version. No lunch on weekdays. Weekend brunch. Closed
Monday. ~ 611 East Pine Street; 206-328-0292. BUDGET.

Ayutthaya is a corner restaurant in Capitol Hill renowned for
its Thai cookery. Small, clean-lined and pleasant in light wood,
Ayutthaya features plenty of chicken and seafood dishes along
with soups and noodles. Flavors blend deliciously in the curried
shrimp with green beans, coconut milk and basil. Or try the
chicken sautéed in peanut-chili sauce. No lunch on Sunday. ~
727 East Pike Street; 206-324-8833, fax 206-324-3135. BUDGET.

Café Septième is a re-creation of the small Parisian cafés that
cater to the literati and students. This full-service restaurant carries plenty of reading material and turns out cups of good coffee, lattes and light fare. Sandwiches and salads are standard, but
the real treat is the mouth-watering display table, loaded with
cakes, pies and cookies. Breakfast, lunch and dinner. ~ 214
Broadway East; 206-860-8858, fax 206-860-0760. MODERATE.

SHOPPING

The trendy boutiques of Capitol Hill draw shoppers looking for
the unusual, though there are many standard stores, too. You'll see
dozens of shops with new and vintage clothing, pop culture items,
and ethnic wear and artifacts, all interspersed with myriad cafés
and coffeehouses.

Yes, it's a sex shop. But **Toys in Babeland** isn't what you'd
expect. Plate-glass front windows, plenty of lighting and a comfy
bench have turned this purveyor of toys, books and body products into a neighborhood hangout. Come here to feel empow-
ered, admire the tasteful-albeit-pornographic glass art and meet

STARGAZING

Robert Redford's Sundance Festival may be more famous, but the **Seattle
International Film Festival** is actually the largest independent film event
in the country. Each spring, SIFF draws hundreds of thousands of cinema
lovers for its 25-day run, usually in Capitol Hill and downtown theaters,
and each year at least one of the SIFF favorites goes on to national
acclaim. Screenings, lectures and receptions abound at this large, well-
attended film festival. Admission. ~ 206-324-9996 (box office), 206-
464-5830; www.seattlefilm.com, e-mail info@seattlefilm.org.

more locals than at the corner café. ~ 707 East Pike Street; 206-328-2914; www.babeland.com.

Capitol Hill's **Broadway Market** is filled with popular shops like **Urban Outfitters**. Featuring casual urban wares, this shop offers new and vintage clothing, jewelry, housewares and shoes for the hip crowd. ~ 401 Broadway East; 206-322-1800.

Bailey/Coy Books is well-stocked with reading material, including gay and lesbian literature. ~ 414 Broadway East; 206-323-8842.

Chocoholics can get their fix in the Capitol Hill district at **Dilettante Chocolates**, a combination chocolatier and café. ~ 416 Broadway East; 206-329-6463, fax 206-325-2687; www.dilettante.com, e-mail barca@barcaseattle.com.

NIGHTLIFE In the "Pike-Pine corridor," west of Broadway, a string of stylish (and stylized) bars stretches toward downtown. East of Broadway, the clubs along Pike and Pine drop down a notch on the scene scale and gain in loungeability.

With its mohair booths and starry ceiling, the **Baltic Room** is a glamourous retro cocktail lounge. Music (both live and deejayed) ranges from jazz to hip-hop to Bollywood. Cover. ~ 1207 Pine Street; 206-625-4444; www.thebalticroom.com.

Barça is another slinky lounge, but less crowded and lacking in live music. Prime viewing is from the balcony. ~ 1510 11th Avenue; 206-325-8263; www.barcaseattle.com.

GAY SCENE Capitol Hill offers a number of popular gay and lesbian clubs and bars, including the following:

One of the biggest clubs in the area is **R Place Bar & Grill**. Depending on your mood, you can plunk down at the sports bar, throw darts, enjoy a music video, shoot pool, enjoy tunes from the jukebox or deejay, take advantage of the dancefloor or feast on quesadillas and taco salad. ~ 619 East Pine Street; 206-322-8828; www.rplaceseattle.com, e-mail rplace@qwest.net.

For a round of beers in a classic bar, head to the **Elite Tavern** for its busy pub atmosphere. ~ 622 Broadway; 206-324-4470.

Also popular is **Neighbours**, offering deejay dance music Friday and Saturday, including retro disco and Latin nights. Cover. ~ 1509 Broadway; 206-324-5358; www.neighboursonline.com.

Founded in 1985, the **Wild Rose** claims to be the oldest women's bar on the West Coast, offering food and drink, pool tables and video games as well as camaraderie. Occasional live music. ~ 1021 East Pike Street; 206-324-9210; www.thewildrosebar.com.

Vogue is the mecca of Seattle's leather/lace/latex enthusiasts. Partly gay and partly not, it features industrial and new-wave deejay music most nights. Themes vary—for instance, Tuesday is

talent show night while Sunday is fetish night. Cover. ~ 1516
11th Avenue; 206-324-5778; www.vogueseattle.com.

For a comprehensive list of gay Seattle's arts and entertainment scene, pick up a copy of the weekly *Seattle Gay News*. ~
www.sgn.org.

BOREN/INTERLAKEN PARKS   A secret greenway close to down-   **PARKS**
town is preserved by these neighboring parks on Capitol Hill; it's
just right for an afternoon or evening stroll. ~ Entry points are   ◀ HIDDEN
on 15th Avenue East across from the Lakeview cemetery and at
East Galer Street and East Interlaken Boulevard.

While downtown is the city's magnet,   ▼▼▼▼▼▼▼▼▼▼▼▼▼▼▼▼
some of Seattle's best parks, sightseeing   **Outlying Neighborhoods**
and nightlife can be found in its nearby
neighborhoods. Arboretums and science museums, lakeside dining and shopping worth a special trip are all in this region.

Few guidebooks look at the **Lake Washington Ship Canal** as a sin-   **SIGHTS**
gle unit. Yet it ties together a wondrous diversity of working waterfront and recreational shoreline along eight miles of bay, lake
and canal between Puget Sound and Lake Washington. Construction of the locks and canal began in 1911 and created a shipping
channel from Lake Washington to Lake Union to Puget Sound.
Along its banks today you can see perhaps the liveliest continuous boat parade in the West: tugs gingerly inching four-story-tall,
Alaska-bound barges through narrow locks; rowboats, kayaks,
sailboards and luxury yachts; gill-netters and trawlers in dry
dock; government-research vessels; aging houseboats listing at
their moorings; and seaplanes roaring overhead.

All in all, the ship canal presents a splendid overview of Seattle's rich maritime traditions. But you'll also discover plenty that's
new—rejuvenated neighborhoods like Fremont and south Lake
Union's upscale shoreline, a renovated Fisherman's Terminal and

LAKE UNION—SPEND THE DAY EXPLORING

The six miles or so of shoreline circling **Lake Union** present a varied mix
of boat works and nautical specialty shops, street-end pocket parks, boat-in
restaurants, seaplane docks, rental-boat concessions, ocean-research vessels, houseboats and flashy condos. You could spend a day exploring
funky old warehouses and oddball enterprises. The lake's south end offers extensive public access to the shore behind a cluster of restaurants, a wooden-boat center and new park.

a handful of trendy, waterside restaurants. Amid the hubbub of boat traffic and ship chandlers, you'll also encounter quiet, street-end parks for birdwatching, foot and bike paths, the best historical museum in the city and one of the West's renowned arboretums. Here's a summary, west to east.

Hiram M. Chittenden Locks in Ballard is where all boats heading east or west in the ship canal must pass and thus presents the quintessential floating boat show; it's one of the most-visited attractions in the city. Visitors crowd railings and jam footbridges to watch as harried lock-keepers scurry to get boats tied up properly before locks are either raised or lowered, depending on the boat's direction of passage. Terraced parks flanking the canal provide splendid picnic overlooks. An underwater fish-viewing window gives you astonishing looks at several species of salmon, steelhead and sea-going cutthroat trout on their spawning migrations (June to November). Lovely botanical gardens in a parklike setting offer yet more diversion. ~ 206-783-7059, fax 206-782-3192.

Fisherman's Terminal is home port to one of the world's biggest fishing fleets, some 700 vessels, most of which chug north into Alaskan waters for summer salmon fishing. But you'll always be able to see boats here—gill-netters, purse-seiners, trollers, factory ships—and working fishermen repairing nets, painting boats and the like. Here, too, are net-drying sheds, shops selling marine hardware and commercial fishing tackle. One café opens at 6:30 a.m. for working fishermen; there's a fish-and-chips window and one good seafood restaurant (Chinook's) overlooking the waterway. ~ On the south side of Salmon Bay about a mile east of the locks. ~ 206-728-3395, fax 206-728-3393.

The **Fremont District** is locally famous for the sculpture *Waiting for the Interurban*, whose collection of lifelike commuters is frequently seen adorned in funny hats, scarves and other cast-off clothing. Centered around Fremont Avenue North and North 34th Street at the northwest corner of Lake Union, the district is top-heavy with shops proffering the offbeat (handmade dulcimers, antiques and junk).

Gas Works Park occupies property that dangles like a giant green tonsil from Lake Union's north shore. Until 1956, the park's namesake "gas works" produced synthetic natural gas from coal and crude oil. Some of the rusting congeries of pipes, airy cat-walks, spiraling ladders, tall towers and stubby tanks were torn down during park construction, but enough remains (repainted in snappy colors) to fascinate youngsters and old-timers alike. ~ 2101 North Northlake Way.

On the south side of Union Bay, 230-acre **Washington Park** at Lake Washington Boulevard East and East Madison Street presents enough diversions indoors and out to fill a rich day of exploring in all sorts of weather. Most famous is the **Washington Park Arboretum** (which occupies most of the park with 10,000 plants), at its best in the spring when rhododendrons and azaleas—some 10 to 15 feet tall—and groves of spreading chestnuts, dogwoods, magnolias and other flowering trees leap into bloom. Short foot-paths beckon from the Visitors Center. But two in particular deserve mention—Azalea Way and Loderi Valley—which wend their way down avenues of pink, cream, yellow, crimson and white blooms. The arboretum's renowned Japanese Garden (admission) is especially rewarding in the spring months, and both arboretum and garden present splendid fall colors in October and early November. In the Winter Garden, everything is fragrant, and the Woodland Garden highlights the arboretum's acclaimed collection of Japanese maples. ~ Visitors Center: Arboretum Drive East; 206-543-8800, fax 206-325-8893; www.wparboretum.org, e-mail uwbg@u.washington.edu.

Miles of duff-covered footpaths lace the park. For naturalists, the premier experience will be found along the one-and-a-half-mile (each way) **Foster Island Trail** at the north end of the park on Foster Island behind the Museum of History and Industry (see later in this section). This footpath takes you on an intriguing bog-walk over low bridges and along boardwalks through marshy wet-lands teeming with ducks and wildfowl, fish and frogs and aquatic flora growing rank at the edge of Lake Washington.

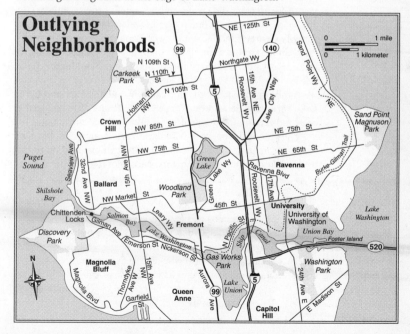

In summer, you can join the canoeists paddling the labyrinth of waterways around **Foster Island,** sunbathers and picnickers sprawling on lawns, anglers casting for catfish and trout and the swimmers cooling off on hot August afternoons. Canoes are for rent through the University of Washington.

On rainy days the **Museum of History and Industry** is a fitting retreat. It's the city's best early-day collection and pays special tribute to Puget Sound's rich maritime history, as befits any museum located next door to this vital waterway. Closed Monday. Admission. ~ 2700 24th Avenue East; 206-324-1126, fax 206-324-1346; www.seattlehistory.org, e-mail information@seattlehis tory.org.

University of Washington campus borders the canal north of Montlake Cut (part of the waterway) and is a haven for anyone who enjoys the simple pleasure of strolling across a college campus. It boggles the mind to think of what awaits you on its 693 acres—handsome old buildings in architectural styles from Romanesque to modern; Frosh Pond; the **Burke Memorial Museum of Natural History and Culture** (206-543-5590, fax 206-685-3039; www.burkemuseum.org) and its famous collection of Northwest Indian art; the **Henry Art Gallery** (closed Sunday and Monday; 206-543-2281, fax 206-685-3123; www. henryart.org) with its marvelous textiles and contemporary exhibits; red-brick quads and expanses of lawn and colorful summer gardens; canal-side trails on both sides of the Montlake Cut; access to the Burke-Gilman Trail; and a lakeside **Waterfront Activity Center** (206-543-9433) with canoe and rowboat rentals. Pick up a free walking tour map at the visitors center in Odegaard Undergraduate Library on George Washington Lane. ~ 206-543-9198.

A mile or so north of the ship canal, Woodland Park and Green Lake Park straddle Aurora Avenue North (Route 99) and together offer more than 400 acres of park, lake and zoo attractions.

The star of the parks is **Woodland Park Zoo,** which has won praise for its program of converting static exhibits into more natural, often outdoor environments. Most notable are the African

"U-DUB"

Exceptional architecture, a garden setting and easy access make a campus tour of the University of Washington (or U-dub, as locals call it) a highlight of a Seattle visit. The university began downtown in 1861; in 1895, it was moved to its present site. The Alaska–Yukon–Pacific Exposition of 1909 was held on the campus, and several of its fine buildings date from that event.

Savannah, Gorilla Exhibit, the Marsh and Swamp, the Jaguar Exhibit and the Elephant Forest. There's also a Tropical Rain Forest, heralded as a "journey through different levels of forest," and a seasonal contact yard and family farm. The Trail of Vines is an Asian rainforest where Indian pythons, lion-tailed macaques, orangutans, Malayan tapirs and siamangs live. Admission. ~ Fremont Avenue North and North 50th Street; 206-684-4800; www.zoo.org, e-mail webkeeper@zoo.org.

Green Lake Park, enormously popular with all ages and classes of Seattleites, is simply the best outdoor people-watching place in the city. Two loop trails circle the shore (the inner trail is 2 miles long, the outer 3.2 miles) and welcome all comers. On summer days, both paths are filled with strollers and race-walkers, joggers and skaters, bikers and nannies pushing prams. On the lake you will see anglers, canoeists, sailboarders, swimmers, birdwatchers and folks floating in inner tubes.

Seattle's neighborhoods offer several hotels and numerous bed-and-breakfast accommodations. A bed and breakfast can be a great value, offering a casual atmosphere, home-cooked food included in the room rate and personal contact with an innkeeper who usually knows the city well. Contact **Pacific Reservation Service**. Closed weekends. ~ 206-439-7677, 800-684-2932, fax 206-282-4354; www.seattlebedandbreakfast.com, e-mail informa tion@seattlebedandbreakfast.com.

LODGING

A favorite of visitors to the University of Washington, both gay and straight, the **Chambered Nautilus Bed and Breakfast Inn** is only four blocks from the campus. Breezily casual, the spacious home has a family atmosphere. Games and books, soft chairs by the fireplace and all-day tea and cookies add to the homeyness. Ten guest rooms on the second and third floors have antique furnishings. All have private baths and four feature private porches; two have gas fireplaces, and four offer kitchens. A business room with printer, computer and fax machine is always open. A full gourmet breakfast is served, sometimes on the sun porch. ~ 5005 22nd Avenue Northeast; 206-522-2536, 800-545-8459, fax 206-528-0898; www.chamberednautilus.com, e-mail stay@chambered nautilus.com. DELUXE TO ULTRA-DELUXE.

Also in the University District is the **Hotel Deca**, a 15-story tower with 155 corner rooms and three suites with balconies. All units have views of the mountains or the lake and cityscape. Standard hotel furnishings adorn the spacious rooms, decorated in art deco style. A handsome restaurant and lounge are on the floor below the lobby. ~ 4507 Brooklyn Avenue Northeast; 206-634-2000, 800-899-0251, fax 206-547-6029; www.hotel deca.com, e-mail hoteldeca@aol.com. MODERATE TO ULTRA-DELUXE.

DINING   **Ponti Seafood Grill** is near the Fremont Bridge on the Lake Washington ship canal. The Mediterranean-style restaurant offers spectacular views of the canal from flower filled patios. The menu has mostly seafood, though there are good pasta, steak and chicken dishes as well. Dinner only. ~ 3014 3rd Avenue North; 206-284-3000, fax 206-284-4768; www.pontiseafoodgrill.com, e-mail info@pontiseafoodgrill.com. DELUXE TO ULTRA-DELUXE.

When you're nostalgic for a neighborhood restaurant with an upbeat, casual flavor, head for **35th Street Bistro**. Set in the unpretentious Fremont District, it has high windows, a friendly atmosphere, music, and a seasonal southern European–inspired menu. Try the Napoleon Provençal or the grilled steak with horseradish and hand-cut french fries. Closed Monday. ~ 709 North 35th Street; 206-547-9850; www.35bistro.com, e-mail info@35bistro.com. MODERATE TO DELUXE.

You don't have to travel to the Deep South to get a taste of gourmet soul cookin', but expect to wait in line at the stylish **Kingfish Café**, where sepia-tinted family-album photos (including one of cousin Langston Hughes, the great African-American writer) adorn the walls. Big Daddy's Pickapeppa Steak is a menu favorite, along with the buttermilk fried chicken, the barbecued pork, and the crab and catfish cakes (served Benedict style at Sunday brunch). ~ 602 19th Avenue East; 206-320-8757; e-mail kingfishcafe@aol.com. MODERATE.

A restored Tudor-Victorian house is home to **Crush**, an intimate neighborhood bistro at the crest of the Madison Park neighborhood. Owner/chef Jason Wilson serves a continually changing seasonal menu that ranges from Gulf prawns to veal sweetbreads, and includes a good choice of vegetarian entrées, such as a roasted squash and marscapone ravioli. Dinner only. Closed Sunday and Monday. ~ 2310 East Madison Street; 206-302-7874; www.chefjasonwilson.com. MODERATE.

Rover's, in a small house surrounded by gardens, specializes in five-course meals of Northwest cuisine with a French accent and is just the place for those romantic occasions. Chef Thierry Rautureau creates the ever-changing menu based on locally available, fresh produce. In addition to seafood in imaginative sauces, entrées might include rabbit, venison, pheasant and quail. A good selection of Northwest and French wines is available. Service is friendly and helpful, and there is patio seating in summer. Dinner only. Closed Sunday and Monday. ~ 2808 East Madison Street; 206-325-7442, fax 206-325-1092; www.rovers-seattle.com. ULTRA-DELUXE.

A colorful and lively Spanish-eclectic restaurant in the Madison Park area, **Cactus** serves a cuisine representative of many different cultures, but mostly influenced by Southwestern food. Start with one of the most unusual items on the menu—a salad of baby field greens topped with beer-battered goat cheese, candied hazelnuts and a roasted-jalapeño-and-apple vinaigrette. One of the more unusual entrées is ancho-cinnamon chicken—marinated in ancho chile, cinnamon and Mexican chocolate and glazed with honey. No lunch on Sunday. ~ 4220 East Madison Street; 206-324-4140; www.cactusrestaurants.com. MODERATE.

Near the University of Washington, make a beeline for **Ebb n' Flow**. Upbeat and lively, this is the place to go for generous portions of well-prepared dishes with Southwestern and Northwest regional influences. The ever-changing menu may include *huevos rancheros* or grilled fresh fish. Breakfast is the most popular meal of the day. Closed Monday. ~ 2114 North 45th Street; 206-547-6313, fax 206-632-2127. MODERATE.

Touristy though it may be, the great view, alder-grilled fish and historic photos of native Salish people in old-time Seattle combine to make **Ivar's Salmon House** a great Seattle restaurant. The restaurant, done in Northwest American Indian longhouse–style architecture and decor, also features views of the kayak, canoe, tugboat, windsurfer and yacht activity on Lake Union. The menu includes Northwest American Indian–style alder-roasted salmon, pork loin and halibut. ~ 401 Northeast Northlake Way; 206-632-0767; www.ivars.net, e-mail webmail@keep clam.com. DELUXE.

Union Bay Café serves Northwest regional foods with an Asian and Italian influence. The seasonal entrées might include grilled sturgeon with roasted garlic, tomato and dill and hazelnut chicken on sautéed spinach with lemon butter. More unusual is the filet of ostrich grilled and served with Walla Walla sweet onions and a sauce of port wine, green peppercorn and sage. Lighter entrées are available in the simple, classic café. The appe-

AUTHOR FAVORITE

In 1992, a group of star chefs from some of Seattle's best-known restaurants got together to create a unique training program aimed at teaching commercial kitchen skills to the homeless. Since its inception, **FareStart** has trained over 1500 homeless and now prepares meals for local shelters and also serves daily lunch and Thursday-night dinners in their own Lake Union building. Most popular are the Guest Chef Dinners, where 200 lucky diners get to sample what the young trainees have been learning. An assortment of soups, salads and sandwiches are served. The meals are a frequent sellout, so book well in advance. ~ 7th Avenue and Virginia Street; 206-443-1233 ext. 6210; www.farestart.org, e-mail reservations@farestart.org. MODERATE.

tizer list is almost as long as the regular menu. Dinner only. Closed Monday. ~ 3515 Northeast 45th Street; 206-527-8364, fax 206-527-0436; www.unionbaycafe.com. DELUXE.

The **Santa Fe Cafe** is more upscale, offering a fussier version of Southwestern cuisine, more avocados and cilantro than beans and tortillas. Chile-flavored beer, anyone? Wags might call it Northwest/Southwest Contemporary cuisine; it's worth a visit after a trip to the Woodland Park Zoo. No lunch on weekends. ~ 5910 Phinney Avenue North; 206-783-9755. MODERATE.

SHOPPING   If you're in the market for a potato gun, would like to snack on Pez or are searching for a popping Martian, head on over to **Archie McPhee's** in Ballard. This novelty-and-toy store offers more than 10,000 exotic items from all over the world. ~ 2428 Northwest Market Street; 206-297-0240; www.mcphee.com.

At the **Washington Park Arboretum Visitor Center Gift Shop** are gardening books, cards, china, earrings, necklaces, serving trays and sweatshirts. You can also buy plants from the arboretum greenhouse. ~ 2300 Arboretum Drive East; 206-325-4510.

Dominated by the UW campus is the University District, a commercial neighborhood overflowing with a vast array of retail shops. One that attracts many tourists is **La Tienda/Folk Art Gallery**. Here you'll find handpicked craft items, jewelry and textiles from all over the world, including those made by 200 selected American artisans. Closed Sunday. ~ 2050 Northwest Market Street, 206-297-3605; www.latienda-folkart.com.

NIGHTLIFE   In Ballard, **Conor Byrne's** has live music, specializing in Irish, folk, bluegrass and blues. The Old World building has exposed bricks, high ceilings, original art and low light. Weekend cover. ~ 5140 Ballard Avenue Northwest; 206-784-3640; www.conorbyrnepub.com.

The **Tractor** tavern offers a mix of live rock, country, Celtic, jazz and alternative music. Cover. ~ 5213 Ballard Avenue Northwest; 206-789-3599; www.tractortavern.citysearch.com.

LIVE MUSIC AND LIVE ANIMALS

One of Seattle's most eagerly anticipated and fun summer events is the evening concert series, **Zoo Tunes**, held on the lawn at Woodland Park Zoo. Bring a lawn chair, a picnic and the whole family and enjoy great music by artists like the Indigo Girls, Little Feat, Leo Kottke, Shawn Colvin, David Wilcox and others (with a little bit of lions, tigers and bears, oh my! chorusing in the background). All proceeds benefit the zoo. ~ Fremont Avenue North and North 50th Street; 206-615-0076; www.zoo.org, e-mail concerts@zoo.org.

Near the University of Washington, you will find an array of clubs and places to park yourself at night.

There are cocktail service, full dinner and comedy shows Thursday through Sunday at **Giggles Comedy Club**. Cover on Friday and Saturday. ~ 5220 Roosevelt Way Northeast; 206-526-5653; www.gigglescomedyclub.com.

Located just barely off campus, the happening student hangout in the University District is the **Big Time Brewery & Alehouse**, which offers beer, pizza and a rowdy young crowd. Seattle's oldest brewpub (c. 1988), it has an antique bar, shuffleboard in the back room and a museum-like collection of beer bottles, cans, signs and memorabilia. ~ 4133 University Way Northeast; 206-545-4509; www.bigtimebrewery.com.

Nearby, **Tommy's Nightclub & Grill** features deejay dance music and live reggae and rock on alternating nights and some of the cheapest beer in town. ~ 4552 University Way Northeast; 206-634-3144; www.tommysnightclub.com.

BEACHES & PARKS

DISCOVERY PARK 🚶🚴 With two miles of beach trail and nine miles of footpaths winding through mixed forest and across open meadows, this bluff-top preserve (Seattle's largest at more than 534 acres) protects a remarkable "urban wilderness." Here are sweeping vistas, chances to watch birds (including nesting bald eagles) and study nature, the **Daybreak Star Indian Cultural Center** (206-285-4425, fax 206-282-3640) featuring art and cultural exhibits from various tribes, an interpretive center (closed Monday) with environmental displays and educational programs, four miles of road for bicycling and an 1881 lighthouse (oldest in the area). Fort Lawton Historic District includes Officers' Row and military buildings surviving from the park's days as an Army fort. There are areas suitable for picnics; restrooms and a visitor center are at the park's east gate. ~ Located a quarter-hour drive north of downtown in the Magnolia district. The main entrance is at 3801 West Government Way and 36th Avenue West; 206-386-4236, fax 206-684-0195.

CARKEEK PARK 🚶🚴 Tucked into a woodsy canyon reaching toward Puget Sound, this 216-acre wildland protects Piper's Creek and its resurrected runs of salmon and sea-going trout. Signs explain how citizens helped clean up the stream and bring the salmon back. Trails lead past spawning waters, to the top of the canyon and through a native-plant garden. You will find picnic areas, restrooms, play areas and beachcombing (as long as you take nothing home with you) and a pioneer orchard. ~ Take 3rd Avenue Northwest to 110th Street Northwest, turn and follow the signs; 206-684-0877, fax 206-364-4685.

SAND POINT MAGNUSON PARK 🚶 🚤 🛥 This 350-acre site carved from the Sand Point Naval Air Station presents generous access to Lake Washington and wide views across the lake. It's a favorite place to launch a boat, swim or toss a frisbee. You'll find picnic areas, restrooms, softball fields, tennis courts, swimming beaches with summer lifeguards, a community center and garden and a wheelchair-accessible wading pool. Adjacent to the park is the National Oceanic Atmospheric Administration's **Sound Garden**, which is full of sculptures that move and chime when the wind blows. The melodic garden gave the Seattle multiplatinum rock band its name. (Visitors who want to tour the garden must show picture ID at a checkpoint entrance at 77th Street and Sand Point Way.) ~ Located on Lake Washington, northeast of downtown Seattle, at Sand Point Way Northeast and 65th Avenue Northeast; 206-684-4075, fax 206-684-4853; e-mail parksinfo@seattle.gov.

HIDDEN ►

> Sand Point Magnuson Park's melodic Sound Garden gave the Seattle multiplatinum rock band its name.

SEWARD PARK 🏃 🚴 ⛵ 🚤 🎣 ⚓ On Bailey Peninsula, this 300-acre park jutting into Lake Washington encompasses Seattle's largest virgin forest. Walking through it on one of several footpaths is the prime attraction, but many come to swim and sunbathe, launch a small boat, fish or visit a fish hatchery. Seward Park offers a rare opportunity to see nesting bald eagles in an urban setting. The best introductory walk is the two-and-one-half-mile shoreline loop stroll; to see the large Douglas firs, add another mile along the center of the peninsula. The swimming beaches' gentle surf is ideal for children, and there are lifeguards in summer. You can fish from the pier for crappie and trout. There are tennis courts, picnic areas, restrooms and play areas. ~ Located on the west shore of Lake Washington, southeast of downtown, at Lake Washington Boulevard South and South Orcas Street; 206-684-4075, fax 206-684-4853; e-mail parksinfo@seattle.gov.

Seattle North

Heading north from Seattle, you'll cross the county line (into Snohomish County) toward the less urban and more maritime cities and villages lining Northern Puget Sound. You don't have to travel far to catch a glimpse of the region's past, before Seattlemania lured businesses and families to relocate here. North of Seattle you'll find a slower pace and strong reminders of Washington's history.

SIGHTS

North of Seattle, the long-time mill town of **Edmonds** has a lively charm and provides a link to the Olympic Peninsula. Ferries leave hourly from the Edmonds ferry landing, on a waterfront that has a recently redeveloped beach park, a long fishing pier and an underwater park that is popular with divers. The park teems with marine life that swims around sunken structures: boats, a dock, a bridge model and others. On shore, the **Edmonds Discovery Program** hosts summer beach walks. Closed Sunday. ~ 425-771-0230, fax 425-771-0253; www.ci.edmonds.wa.us, e-mail lider@ci.edmonds.wa.us.

The **Edmonds Chamber of Commerce** wins the prize for quaintness. Its information center is housed in a pioneer log cabin that looks like a storybook house. Closed weekends. ~ 121 5th Avenue North, Edmonds; 425-670-1496, fax 425-712-1808; www.edmondswa.com, e-mail chamberofcommerce@edmondswa.com.

A visit to the **Edmonds Historical Museum** with its working shingle-mill model, maritime heritage exhibits and collections of logging tools and household furnishings gives a better understanding of the pioneer heritage and industrial history of Edmonds. A walking tour takes you past the old shingle mills, Brackett's Landing (where the earliest pioneers settled), and numerous buildings constructed in the late 1800s and early 1900s. Closed Monday and Tuesday. ~ 118 5th Avenue North, Edmonds; 425-774-0900; www.historicedmonds.org.

LODGING

Rooms in the three-story **Travelodge** are comfortably decorated and clean, with dark blue carpets, curtains and bedspreads and cable television. There are even a few units with microwaves and fridges. Other amenities include hot tubs and continental breakfast. ~ 23825 Route 99, Edmonds; 425-771-8008, 800-578-7878, fax 425-771-0080; www.travelodge.com. BUDGET TO MODERATE.

DINING

If you venture up to Edmonds, try **La Galleria**. This small restaurant on the main drag doesn't look like much from the outside—thankfully the lace curtains block out most of the traffic view. But the traditional Italian fare is good; best choices include pollo *modena* (chicken breast sautéed with mushrooms in balsamic vinegar sauce) and penne with rock crab. Dinner only. Closed Monday. ~ 546 5th Avenue South, Edmonds; 425-771-7950; www.10000flavors.com. MODERATE.

For waterfront dining on the marina, **Anthony's HomePort Edmonds** fits the bill. This upscale eatery decked out in nautical decor is the place locals come to celebrate and sink their teeth into fresh, local seafood. Specialties include charbroiled yellowfin ahi in a ginger soy sauce and pineapple chutney, fishermen's cioppino, and Puget Sound oysters on the half shell. Come early on Sunday night for your share of the all-you-can-eat Dungeness crab extravaganza. **Anthony's Beach Café** on the ground level provides a more casual dining experience. Dinner and Sunday brunch only. ~ 456 Admiral Way, Edmonds; 425-771-4400, fax 425-771-2331; www.anthonys.com, e-mail edmonds@anthonys.com. MODERATE TO DELUXE.

SHOPPING   American Eagles is, simply, the largest hobby shop in the United States, with an inventory of more than 87,000 different items—one-fourth of them miniature soldiers. The specialty is plastic models and military books. Closed Sunday. ~ 12537 Lake City Way Northeast; 206-440-8448, fax 206-363-6569; www.ameri caneagleshobbies.com.

More than 150 dealers sell their wares at the **Aurora Antique Pavilion.** ~ 24111 Route 99, Edmonds; 425-744-0566.

▼▼▼▼▼▼▼▼▼▼
Seattle West

Seattle West offers some rare treasures such as a company town operating in the time-honored manner, a fascinating Indian cultural show, a marine-science center and inns that look like they were created for a James Herriott book. From the islands of Puget Sound west to Hood Canal, this is also a region rich in parks and natural areas. You'll also want to tour the Kitsap Peninsula, Bremerton's Naval Heritage and the parks of Southern Puget Sound.

SIGHTS   Since you can reach pastoral **Vashon Island** by state ferry from the Fauntleroy dock in West Seattle (a 15-minute crossing), we include it in this section of the book. However, Vashon stretches south for 13 miles toward Tacoma (accessible by another 15-minute ferry from Tahlequah), creating a lovely Seattle-to-Tacoma country-road alternative to Route 5. The ferry to Tacoma lands next to one of the city's highlights, splendid Point Defiance Park (see "Tacoma and Olympia" below).

HIDDEN ►

The Vashon Island Highway will take you fairly directly down the island, through the town of Vashon. Just south of town is the **Country Store and Gardens,** where you can peruse merchandise grown or produced on the island—fruit and syrups, berries and preserves, a nursery stocked with perennials and a variety of gardening tools, natural-fiber clothing, kitchenware and such. ~ 20211 Vashon Highway Southwest; 206-463-3655.

Side roads beckon from the highway to a handful of poorly marked state beaches and county parks. **Point Robinson County Park** on Maury Island (linked to Vashon via an isthmus at the hamlet of Portage) is easier to find and particularly interesting since it's next door to the Coast Guard's picturesque Point Robinson Lighthouse (not open to the public).

To the north, **Bainbridge Island** offers a much more attractive destination for most travelers, and you can see it on foot. The picturesque town is located on an island of the same name, just a 35-minute ferry ride from Coleman Dock. To see more than obvious attractions (restaurants, shops, a winetasting room), head for the mile-long waterfront footpath called **Walkabout** to the left of the ferry landing. Follow it along the shoreline, past shipyards and hauled-out sailboats under repair, to **Eagle Harbor**

Waterfront Park and its fishing pier and low-tide beach. Carry
on to a ship chandler and pair of marinas. Return as you came,
or through the town's business district.

Another interesting loop trip west of Seattle begins in the
Navy town of Bremerton. You can explore some of the region's
history, as well as the remote reaches of southern Puget Sound.

If you take the ferry or drive to Bremerton, you'll pass by the
Puget Sound Naval Shipyard. The best way to get here is the
Washington State Ferry (cars and walk-ons; one hour) or state

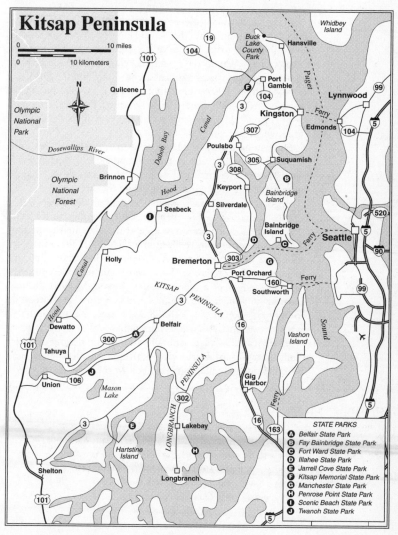

Kitsap Peninsula

STATE PARKS
A Belfair State Park
B Fay Bainbridge State Park
C Fort Ward State Park
D Illahee State Park
E Jarrell Cove State Park
F Kitsap Memorial State Park
G Manchester State Park
H Penrose Point State Park
I Scenic Beach State Park
J Twanoh State Park

foot-ferry (50 minutes) or the passenger-only fast ferry (35 minutes) from Seattle's Colman Dock (Pier 52) through Rich Passage to Bremerton. Although the shipyard is not open for public tours, it's an amazing sight even from a distance. ~ Burwell Street and Pacific Avenue, near the ferry dock, Bremerton; 360-476-7111, fax 360-476-0937; www.psns.navy.mil.

Bremerton Naval Museum looks back to the days of Jack Tar and square-riggers and includes a wood cannon from 1377. Closed Sunday. ~ 402 Pacific Avenue, a half-block north of the ferry dock, Bremerton. Closed Sunday.; 360-479-7447.

In the small town of Keyport, off Route 308 between Poulsbo and Silverdale, you'll find the **Naval Undersea Museum**. Historical exhibits here focus on the Navy's undersea activities from the Revolutionary War to the present. Diving and defense displays explore such subjects as nautical archaeology and the history of the submarine. There's also an interactive installation on the ocean environment. ~ 610 Dowell Street, Keyport; 360-396-4148; http://keyportmuseum.navy.mil, e-mail underseainfo@kpt.nuwc.navy.mil.

Only an hour from the heart of Seattle, the Kitsap Peninsula is framed on the east side by Puget Sound and the west by Hood Canal. Historic company towns, naval museums and remote parks make this area a fine retreat from the city.

HIDDEN ►   A good place to learn about the region's American Indian heritage is the town of **Suquamish**. Chief Seattle and the allied tribes he represented are showcased at the **Suquamish Museum**. There's an outstanding collection of photographs and relics, along with mock-ups of a typical American Indian dwelling and the interior of a longhouse. Two award-winning video presentations are shown in a small theater. Closed Monday through Thursday in winter. Admission. ~ 15838 Sandy Hook Road off Route 305, Suquamish; 360-598-3311 ext. 422, fax 360-598-6295; www.suquamish.nsn.us/museum.

Chief Seattle's Grave, set under a canopy of dugout canoes in a hillside graveyard overlooking Seattle (his namesake), is just a few miles down Suquamish Way. Follow the road signs.

◆◆◆

GARDEN ESTATE

If you enjoy gardens, don't miss a tour of the famous **Bloedel Reserve**. Once a private estate, the reserve has 150 acres of forest, meadows, ponds and a series of beautifully landscaped gardens. Reservations are required for a tour. Closed Monday and Tuesday. Admission. ~ 7571 Northeast Dolphin Drive, Bainbridge Island; 206-842-7631, fax 206-842-8970; www.bloedelreserve.org, e-mail email@bloedelreserve.org.

"Velkommen til Poulsbo" is an oft-repeated phrase in "Washington's Little Norway." Looking like a lane in faraway Scandinavia, the main street of **Poulsbo** is lined with wonderful galleries and boutiques. There are some wonderful samples of his-toric architecture on a **walking tour** of town; the **Greater Poulsbo Chamber of Commerce** can provide more information. ~ 19351 8th Avenue, Poulsbo; 360-779-4848, fax 360-799-3115; www. poulsbochamber.com, e-mail admin@poulsbochamber.com.

At the **Marine Science Center**, you can learn about the marine life that inhabit the waters of Southern Puget Sound; they even have touch tanks of friendly sea creatures. ~ 18743 Front Street Northeast, Poulsbo; 360-779-5549, fax 360-779-8960.

One of the West's last company towns, **Port Gamble** is a favored visitor stop. Situated on a bluff at the intersection of Admiralty Inlet and Gamble Bay, this century-old community is owned by the Pope and Talbot lumber firm.

◄ HIDDEN

The oldest running lumber mill in the United States (operating since 1853) was closed in 1995. Although all the sawmill workers were laid off, Pope and Talbot announced that they will keep the town running. The town had long been home to about 150 sawmill workers and their families, who rented homes by the company. Picturesque frame houses, towering elms and a church with Gothic windows and a needle spire give the community a New England look. Don't miss the mock-ups of Captain Talbot's cabin and A. J. Pope's office at the **Port Gamble Historic Museum**. Admission. ~ Route 3, Port Gamble; 360-297-8074, fax 360-297-7455; www.portgamble.com.

SOUTHERN PUGET SOUND   On a map, Southern Puget Sound looks like a fistful of bony fingers clawing at the earth. This maze of inlets, peninsulas and islands presents plentiful saltwater access and invites days of poking around. Here are three representative experiences in the area:

South of Bremerton is the **Longbranch Peninsula**, a showcase of Southern Puget Sound's outdoor treasures. Quiet coves and lonely forests, dairy farms, funky fishing villages with quiet cafés, shellfish beaches and oyster farmers, a salmon hatchery, fishing piers and wharves all await leisurely exploration. Take Route 16 to Route 302, proceeding west until you reach Key Center. The Key Peninsula Highway, running south from this community, is the main road bringing you to most attractions.

◄ HIDDEN

To visit the hamlet of **Lakebay** on Mayo Cove, turn east from Peninsula Highway three and a half miles south of Home (the town, not your Home Sweet) onto Cornwall Road and follow it to Delano Road. On the south side of the cove is **Penrose Point State Park** with 152 acres of forest, more than two miles of beaches, hiking trails, fishing, picnicking and camping. ~ 321 158th Avenue K.P.S., Lakebay; 253-884-2514, fax 360-753-1594.

At the end of the highway is another bayside village, **Long-branch,** on the shores of Filucy Bay, one of the prettiest anchorages in these waters.

HIDDEN ►   **Harstine Island** (northeast of Shelton via Route 3 and Pickering Road) is connected to the mainland by a bridge, providing auto access to a quintessential Southern Puget Sound island experience. Many of the island's public beaches are poorly indicated, but **Jarrell Cove State Park** and a marina on the other side of the cove are easily found at the island's north tip. You'll see plenty of boats from both sides of the cove, and at the park you can stroll docks, fish for perch, walk bits of beach or explore forest trails. Main roads loop the island's north end, or head for the far southern tip at Brisco Point near Peale Passage and Squaxin Island. ~ Foot of Wingert Road, off North Island Drive; 360-426-9226.

HIDDEN ►   The eastern shore of **Hood Canal** is located a mere mile or two from the western side of the channel, but in character it's worlds apart. Beach access is limited, but views across the canal to the Olympic Mountains are splendid, settlements few and quiet and back roads genuine byways—few tourists ever get here. This is also where the canal bends like a fishhook to the east, which has been nicknamed the "Great Bend."

To see the east shore in its entirety, begin at Belfair, leaving Route 3 for Route 300. At three miles, watch for Belfair State Park on the left. The road now narrows and traffic thins on the way to the modest resort town of Tahuya; shortly beyond, the canal makes its great bend. The road dives into dense forest, bringing you in about 11 miles to a T-junction; bear left, then left again to the ghost town of Dewatto. Take Dewatto Bay Road eastward out of town, then turn north and follow signs 12 miles to a left turn into the little town of **Holly,** or continue north 15 miles more to **Seabeck,** founded in 1856 as a sawmill town and popular today with anglers, scuba divers and boaters.

LODGING   Guest rooms at Poulsbo's **Holiday Inn Express** are modern and comfortably furnished with big beds, satellite television, individual air conditioning and other basic amenities; a few are equipped with kitchenette or jacuzzi. There is a seasonal outdoor pool and continental breakfast is included. ~ 19801 7th Avenue Northeast, Poulsbo; 360-697-4400, 800-465-4329, fax 360-697-2707; www.hiexpress.com/poulsbowa, e-mail psbwa@silverlink.net. MODERATE.

DINING   Spend a perfect summer day at Alki Beach in West Seattle, then take in dinner at the **Alki Café Beach Bistro,** where a well-rounded menu includes great salads (that change seasonally), seafood, meat, chicken and pasta dishes. Specials of the evening are listed in the dining area. ~ 2726 Alki Avenue Southwest; 206-935-0616; alkicafe.home.comcast.net. BUDGET TO MODERATE.

The **Alki Bakery** just down the street offers up a host of muffins and cinnamon rolls, scones, coffee, espressos and lattes. If you've overindulged, you can always take another stroll on the beach. ~ 2738 Alki Avenue Southwest; 206-935-1352, fax 206-935-1749; www.alkibakery.com. BUDGET.

Also in West Seattle, the **Cat's Eye Cafe** has great coffee, excellent muffins and super sandwiches . . . not to mention plenty of feline pictures and paraphernalia. Soup and sandwich for lunch is an excellent choice. Breakfast and lunch only. ~ 7301 Bainbridge Place Southwest; 206-935-2229, fax 206-935-1749; www.alkibakery.com. BUDGET.

The old island hangout is **Sound Food Cafe**. The restaurant is known for its casual atmosphere—windows overlooking the gardens and lots of wood inside. A variety of soups, salads and sandwiches of baked bread is available for lunch. Dinner entrées include pasta primavera, seafood dishes and a number of large salads. Desserts—sigh—come fresh from the bakery. Take your pick of lime curd French tart, raspberry apple pie, chocolate cream cake or any of the daily goodies. No dinner on Sunday and Monday. ~ 20312 Vashon Highway Southwest, Vashon Island; 206-463-0888. BUDGET.

The white-linen tablecloths and low lighting at the **Bistro Pleasant Beach** bespeak a comfortable island elegance. The chef specializes in Mediterranean seafood but includes a couple of succulent chicken dishes, pastas and aged beef entrées. The leg of lamb, served with roasted garlic, fresh herbs and shallot–rose cabernet sauce, comes recommended. Made-to-order pizzas are baked in the wood-fired oven. When the weather's nice, patio seating is available. Closed Monday. ~ 241 Winslow Way West, Bainbridge Island; 206-842-4347, fax 206-842-6997; www.bicom net.com/bistropb. MODERATE.

Exotic flavors and innovative sauces are what you'll find at the **Four Swallows**, an upscale Italian restaurant located in a spacious 1880s farmhouse. The kitchen staff, utilizing fresh Northwest ingredients, whips up gourmet, thin-crust pizzas and zesty pastas. The entrées show the chef's creativity, and include grilled

NORTHWEST CUISINE, SEATTLE STYLE

In the Northwest, regional cooking at its best emphasizes the bounty of fresh produce and seafood available; in Seattle, innovative chefs have turned it into a distinctive cuisine showcasing the dazzling variety of ingredients that pour in from farms and boats. Combined with fine wines from Washington's 200-plus wineries, it makes for meals that critics rave about.

veal chops with porcini-mushroom sauce and *brodetto*, a fresh fish-and-shellfish stew in a rustic saffron-tomato-fennel broth. Dinner only. Closed Sunday and Monday. ~ 481 Madison Avenue, Bainbridge Island; 206-842-3397; www.fourswallows.com. MODERATE TO DELUXE.

The family-run **Benson's** offers eclectic Northwest cuisine in a large but intimate dining room. The menu changes daily, focusing on local produce and fresh ingredients. ~ 18820 Front Street, Poulsbo; 360-697-3449, fax 360-697-9904; www.mormor bistro.com, e-mail info@mormorbistro.com. DELUXE.

Casa De Luna features fast and cheap traditional Mexican or Mexican-American fare. Diners are treated to colorful murals and sweet ballads while munching on tacos and burritos and sipping Negra Modelo. ~18830 Front Street Northeast, Poulsbo; 306-779-7676. BUDGET.

SHOPPING   In Poulsbo, you'll find paintings, pottery, weavings, cards, rosemaling, baskets, woodturnings, and even food products created by local artists at the **Verksted Co-operative Gallery**. ~ 18937 Front Street Northeast, Poulsbo; 360-697-4470; www.verksted gallery.com. The **Potlatch Gallery** carries a fine selection of prints, glasswork, pottery and jewelry by Northwest artists. ~ 18830-B Front Street Northeast, Poulsbo; 360-779-3377; www. potlatchgallery.com.

Get your fill of Norwegian strudels, bear claws, breads, pastries and cookies at **Sluys Bakery**. ~ 18924 Front Street Northeast, Poulsbo; 360-779-2798.

BEACHES & PARKS   MANCHESTER STATE PARK 🚶 🚵 ⛵ 🎣 🚣 🛶 This one-time fort overlooking Rich Passage includes abandoned torpedo warehouses and some interpretive displays explaining its role in guarding Bremerton Navy Base at the turn of the 20th century. The park is infamous for its poison oak—stay on the two miles of hiking trails, or try the 3400 feet of beach. The rocks off Middle Point attract divers. Fishing yields salmon and bottomfish. There are picnic areas, restrooms and showers. Day-use fee, $5. ~ Located at the east foot of East Hilldale Road off Beach Drive, east of Bremerton; 360-871-4065, fax 503-378-6308.

▲ There are 35 standard sites ($19 per night), 3 primitive walk-in sites ($14 per night), 15 RV hookup sites ($26 per night). Reservations: 888-226-7688.

FAY BAINBRIDGE STATE PARK 🚶 🎣 ⛵ 🚣 🛶 A small park (17 acres), it nevertheless curls itself around a long sandspit to present some 1400 feet of shoreline. The only campground on Bainbridge Island is here. Facilities include picnic areas, restrooms, showers, a play area, horseshoe pits and volleyball courts. Day-use fee, $5. ~ At Sunrise Drive Northeast and Lafayette Road about six miles north of the town of Bainbridge Island at the island's northeast tip; 206-842-3931, fax 360-753-1594.

▲ There are 10 standard sites ($19 per night), 26 RV hookups ($26 per night) and 13 primitive walk-in sites ($14 per night). Closed mid-October to mid-April.

BUCK LAKE COUNTY PARK 𝄞 🐎 🚣 🛶 🛥️ Near Hansville on the northern tip of the Kitsap Peninsula, picturesque Buck Lake is a good spot for quiet, contemplative fishing or a relaxing summer swim. Trout fishing is excellent on the lake or from the shore. Facilities include restrooms, picnic tables, a baseball diamond, a volleyball court, barbecue pits and a playground. ~ Buck Lake Road; take Route 104 from Kingston to Hansville Road and follow it north; 360-337-5350, fax 360-337-5385.

SALISBURY POINT 🚣 🎣 🛶 🛥️ 🚤 This tiny, six-acre park with a small stretch of saltwater beach is next to Hood Canal Floating Bridge and gives views of the Olympic Mountains across the canal. Shrimping is popular here. There are restrooms, picnic shelters and a playground. ~ North of Hood Canal Floating Bridge, turn left on Wheeler Road and follow the signs; 360-337-5350, fax 360-337-5385.

KITSAP MEMORIAL STATE PARK 𝄞 🎣 🛶 🚤 This 58-acre park four miles south of Hood Canal Floating Bridge has a quiet beach well suited for collecting oysters and clams. Between the canal, beach and playground facilities there's plenty to keep the troops entertained, making this a good choice for family camping. Restrooms, showers, a shelter, tables and stoves, boat moorage buoys, a playground and a volleyball court are available; some facilities are wheelchair accessible. Day-use fee, $5. ~ From Kingston take Route 104 (which turns into Bond Road) to Route 3, then follow it north until you reach the park; 360-779-3205, fax 360-779-3161.

▲ There are 21 standard sites ($17 per night); 18 sites with hookups ($26 per night); and a trailer dump ($5). A blufftop log cabin with full bedding, bath towels and a kitchenette (no stove) is also available; $135 per night in peak season.

◆◆

OLD MAN HOUSE STATE PARK

A day-use-only facility, **Old Man House State Park** was once the site of a longhouse. Check out the interpretive and historical displays. A small, sandy beach overlooks the heavy marine traffic that cruises through Agate Passage. You'll find pit toilet and picnic tables. Closed in winter. ~ On the Kitsap Peninsula north of Agate Pass off Route 305; 206-842-3931, fax 206-385-7248.

ILLAHEE STATE PARK 🚶 🚵 ⚓ ⛴ 🏖 🚤 🏊 🎣 Wooded uplands and 1700 feet of saltwater shoreline are separated by a 250-foot bluff at this site. A steep hiking trail connects the two park units. On the beach is a wheelchair-accessible fishing pier where anglers can cast for perch, bullhead and salmon; at the south end are tide flats for wading. Facilities include a picnic area, restrooms, showers, a baseball field, a play area and horseshoe pits. ~ Located at the east foot of Sylvan Way (Route 306) two miles east of Route 303 northeast of Bremerton; 360-478-6460, fax 360-792-6067.

▲ There are 24 standard sites (no hookups); $17 per night; one utility space ($24 per night).

TWANOH STATE PARK 🚶 🚲 ⚓ 🛶 ⛴ 🏖 🚤 🏊 🎣 With many amenities of a city park, Twanoh's 182 acres also include the forests, trails and camping of a more remote site. A two-mile hiking trail takes you through a thick forest of second-growth conifers next to Twanoh Creek; nearly a half-mile of saltwater beach attracts divers. Fishing yields cutthroat, salmon and trout. There are picnic areas, restrooms, showers, tennis, horseshoe pits and a concession stand. ~ Route 106, eight miles southwest of Belfair; 360-275-2222.

> Scenic State Beach offers glorious views across Hood Canal to the Olympics and north up Dabob Bay.

▲ There are 25 tent sites ($19 per night) and 22 full hookup sites ($26 per night). Closed in winter.

BELFAIR STATE PARK 🚶 🚵 ⚓ 🏖 Two creeks flow through this 63-acre park en route to Hood Canal, affording both fresh and saltwater shorelines. Along its 3720 feet of beachfront the saltwater warms quickly across shallow tide flats, but pollution makes swimming here risky; many instead swim in a lagoon with a bathhouse nearby. Shellfish are usually posted off-limits. There are picnic areas, restrooms and showers. ~ Route 300, three miles west of Belfair; 360-275-0668.

▲ There are 137 tent sites ($15 per night) and 47 full hookup sites ($21 per night); dump station ($5). Reservations: 888-226-7688.

SCENIC BEACH STATE PARK 🚶 ⚓ ⛴ 🏖 🚤 🎣 Nearly 1500 feet of cobblestone beach invites strolls; scuba divers also push off from here. Every year in May, 88 acres of native rhododendrons burst into bloom. Anglers try for salmon and bottom fish at the nearby artificial reef, and there's a boat launch less than a mile from the park. There are picnic areas, restrooms, showers, a play area, a horseshoe pit, a volleyball area and a community center. ~ Located just west of Seabeck on Miami Beach Road Northwest, about nine miles northwest of Bremerton; 360-830-5079, fax 360-830-2970.

▲ There are 52 standard sites ($19 per night); no hookups. Closed in winter. Reservations: 888-226-7688.

PENROSE POINT STATE PARK 🧍 🚲 ⛵ 🎣 🛶 🚤 🛥️ 🚣
With more than two miles of saltwater shoreline, this 152-acre park provides some of the most accessible public beaches on Southern Puget Sound. You can swim at the park's sandy, shallow-water beaches, hike along two miles of trail, launch a canoe or kayak, fish for bottomfish and salmon, picnic and camp. The entire park closes for the winter. Restrooms, showers, restaurant and grocery store are close by. Closed October through March. ~ Off Delano Road at the foot of 158th Avenue, near Lakebay on the Longbranch Peninsula; 253-884-2514, fax 253-884-2526.

▲ There are 82 standard sites ($19 per night). Reservations: 888-226-7688.

Seattle East, extending from the eastern shore of Lake Washington to the Cascade foothills, blends the urban and rural assets of this metropolitan region. Here you'll find wineries and archaeological sites, prime birdwatching areas and homey bed and breakfasts.

Seattle East

Renowned as Seattle's foremost suburb, Bellevue boasts a surprisingly diverse network of parks embedded within its neighborhoods. Getting there will most likely take you over **Evergreen Point Floating Bridge,** the world's longest floating bridge at 1.5 miles. **Mercer Slough Nature Park,** stretching north from Route 90 off Bellevue Way with the entrance at 2102 Bellevue Way Southeast, is the biggest and may be the best with some 300 acres of natural wetland habitat and four miles of trails. **Wilburton Hill Park,** between 128th Southeast and 118th Avenue on Main Street, is centered around the Bellevue Botanical Garden, filled with native and ornamental Northwest plants. The park covers over 100 acres and has more than three miles of hiking trails as well as softball and soccer fields. ~ 12001 Main Street off 116th Avenue Northeast; 425-452-2750; www.bellevuebotanical.org.

SIGHTS

To see what Bellevue used to be like before freeways, commuters and office towers, stroll the short stretch of shops along Main Street westward from Bellevue Way Northeast in **Old Bellevue.**

Seattle's rock legend Jimi Hendrix is buried south of Bellevue. A caretaker can show you the guitarist's grave at **Greenwood Memorial Park.** ~ 350 Monroe Avenue Northeast, Renton; 425-255-1511.

So bucolic is the setting for **A Big Red Barn,** it's hard to image that it's only five blocks from downtown Woodinville. Tucked amid lofty evergreens, green pastures and abundant orchards,

LODGING

this gothic dairy barn built in the late '30s houses a unique bed and breakfast. Its two rustic rooms feature wood-paneled walls, colorful quilts, and country-style decor. The centerpiece is the living room, with towering wood-beamed ceilings, floor-to-ceiling windows, a wood-burning fireplace, and a hand-carved, 24-foot table where guests gather for breakfast. Two-night minimum stay required on weekends. Reservations recommended. ~ 16560 140th Place Northeast, Woodinville; 425-806-4646, fax 425-488-7446; www.redbarncountryinn.com, e-mail innkeeper@abigredbarnbandb.com. DELUXE.

Set on three-plus acres, **A Cottage Creek Inn** has its own creek, pond and gazebo on the grounds. The English Tudor house features four rooms, one with a brass bed, one with an antique bed, all with their own bathrooms. There are full jacuzzis in the two larger rooms and a communal outdoor hut tub. There's a pleasant sitting room with a piano, which guests are encouraged to play. Full breakfast included. ~ 12525 Avondale Road Northeast, Redmond; phone/fax 425-881-5606; www.cottagecreekinn.com, e-mail innkeepers@cottagecreekinn.com. MODERATE TO DELUXE.

The **Woodmark Hotel on Lake Washington** is a handsome, four-story brick structure on Lake Washington's shore. Its small scale, residential-style lobby, and comfortable bar with a fireplace and shelves of books create the ambience of a welcoming, stylish home. The 100 rooms have all the amenities: mini-bars, televisions, robes and hair dryers. Ask for a room on the West side—they have lake views. ~ 1200 Carillon Point, Kirkland; 425-822-3700, 800-822-3700, fax 425-822-3699; www.thewoodmark.com, e-mail mail@thewoodmark.com. ULTRA-DELUXE.

HIDDEN ▶ In a quiet wooded area southeast of Seattle is the **Maple Valley Bed and Breakfast**. The two-story contemporary home has open-beamed ceilings, peeled-pole railings, cedar walls and detailed wood trim. Guests like to relax on the antique furniture in the

sights **AUTHOR FAVORITE**
I highly recommend a visit to the **Château Ste. Michelle** winery, even for teetotallers, because the spacious, parklike grounds surrounding the château are among the most beautiful places in the Seattle area for a relaxing stroll or a picnic. Located just south of Woodinville, Château Ste. Michelle is the state's largest winery with daily tasting and tours. Situated on a turn-of-the-20th-century estate, it also has duck and trout ponds, experimental vineyards and outdoor concerts on summer weekends. ~ 14111 145th Street Northeast, Woodinville; 425-415-3300, fax 425-415-3657; www.ste-michelle.com, e-mail info@ste-michelle.com.

sitting room. The two guest rooms are individually decorated and color coordinated with French doors that open onto a large deck. Both have log beds. On cool nights, heated, sand-filled pads ("hot babies") are used to warm the beds. A full breakfast is served on country-stencil pottery in a dining area that overlooks trees, wandering birds and ponds with ducks. ~ 20020 Southeast 228th Street, Maple Valley; 425-432-1409, 888-432-1409, fax 425-413-1459; www.seattlebestbandb.com/maplevalley, e-mail wild lifepond@hotmail.com. BUDGET TO MODERATE.

DINING

The open kitchen at **Andre's Eurasian Bistro** is as entertaining as the food. This restaurant offers a menu with Vietnamese specialties like spring rolls or chicken with lemongrass, as well as Continental selections, such as lamb with garlic. Vietnamese chef Andre Nguyen comes with experience from some of Seattle's best restaurants. No lunch on Saturday. Closed Sunday. ~ 14125 Northeast 20th Street, Bellevue; 425-747-6551, fax 425-747-4304; www.andresbistro.com. MODERATE.

You wouldn't expect to find a good restaurant in this little shopping strip, but here it is. At **Pogacha**, a Croatian version of pizza is the mainstay. The pizzas, crisp on the outside but moist inside, are baked in a clay oven. Because the saucing is nonexistent or very light, the flavor of the toppings—pesto and various cheeses, alone or over vegetables or meat—is more apparent. Other entrées include Adriatic-inspired grilled meats and seafood, salads and pastas. ~ 119 106th Avenue Northeast, Bellevue; 425-455-5670; www.pogacha.com. MODERATE.

One of the best Japanese restaurants in all of Puget Sound is hidden in the Totem Lake West shopping center in suburbia. **Izumi** features an excellent sushi bar. Entrées are fairly standard— beef, chicken sukiyaki and teriyaki and tempura—but the ingredients are especially fresh and carefully prepared. Service is friendly. No lunch on weekends. Closed Monday. ~ 12539 116th Avenue Northeast, Kirkland; 425-821-1959. MODERATE TO DELUXE.

◄ HIDDEN

A couple of local residents who grew up in Pakistan and Bangladesh have opened **Shamiana**. The food is cooled to an American palate but can be spiced to a full-blown, multistar *hot*. A buffet of four curries, salad, *nan* and *dal* is offered at lunch. Dinner is à la carte, and includes entrées such as lamb curry with rice *pulao* or chicken *tikka*. ~ 10724 Northeast 68th Street, Kirkland; 425-827-4902, fax 425-828-2765. MODERATE TO DELUXE.

SHOPPING

In Bellevue, **Bellevue Square** has 200 of the nation's finest shops, department stores and restaurants. ~ Northeast 8th Street and Bellevue Way Northeast; www.bellevuesquare.com.

One of the most elegant shops in Bellevue is **Alvin Goldfarb Jeweler**. Specializing in 18-carat platinum and gold pieces crafted by an in-house goldsmith who also works with precious and semi-precious gems, this is a mecca for discriminating people who desire a one-of-a-kind item. Closed Sunday. ~ 305 Bellevue Way Northeast, Bellevue; 425-454-9393; www.alvingoldfarbjeweler.com.

Hunters of antiques appreciate the **Kirkland Antique Gallery**. The mall has nearly 100 dealers selling antiques and collectibles. ~ 151 3rd Street, Kirkland; 425-827-7443.

Excellent Northwest ceramics, jewelry and blown glass make **Lakeshore Gallery** a fine place to stop even if you have no intention of buying. The carved woodwork is especially well done. ~ 107 Park Lane, Kirkland; 425-827-0606.

Refurbished farmhouses, a barn and a feed store are stocked with handicrafts and artful, designer clothing at Issaquah's **Gilman Village**. Among the 40-plus shops clustered in these historic structures is **The Revolutionary Gallery** (425-392-4982, www.revolution-gallery.com), an artists co-op featuring fun and functional artwork fashioned from recycled materials. ~ 317 Northwest Gilman Boulevard, Issaquah; www.gilmanvillage.com.

Hedges Family Estate is a Yakima Valley winery that has opened a full-fledged tasting room on the west side of the Cascades; some aging is done here. Hedges is known for its blends. ~ 195 Northeast Gilman Boulevard, Issaquah; 425-391-6056, 800-859-9463; www.hedgescellars.com.

NIGHTLIFE   Enjoy live blues tunes on Saturday at **Forecasters Public House at the Redhook Ale Brewery**. ~ 14300 Northeast 145th Street, Woodinville; 425-483-3232; www.redhook.com.

Daniel's Broiler has a live pianist playing contemporary hits seven nights a week. ~ Bellevue Place, 10500 Northeast 8th Avenue, 21st Floor, Bellevue; 425-462-4662.

There is live music Wednesday through Sunday nights at the **08 Seafood Grill and Twisted Cork Wine Bar**, located in the Hyatt Regency Bellevue. ~ 900 Bellevue Way Northeast, Bellevue; 425-462-1234.

With a welcoming fireplace and free appetizers Monday through Friday, the **Coast Bellevue Hotel** invites you into their lounge. ~ 625 116th Avenue Northeast, Bellevue; 425-455-9444.

◆◆

CANDYLAND

Satisfy your sweet tooth at **Boehm's Candies**, where hundreds of chocolates are hand-dipped every day. You can tour the factory (reservations are required; this is a popular spot) and watch the skilled workmanship that goes into making candies of this quality. ~ 255 Northeast Gilman Boulevard, Issaquah; 425-392-6652, fax 425-557-0560; www.boehms candies.com.

Good things come in small packages, and the **Village Theatre** proves it. The local casts here will tackle anything, be it Broadway musicals, dramas or comedy. ~ 303 Front Street North, Issaquah; 425-392-2202; www.villagetheatre.org.

MARYMOOR COUNTY PARK 🧍 🚴 🐎 This roomy, 640-acre preserve at the north end of Lake Sammamish in Redmond is a delightful mix of archaeology and history, river and lake, meadows and marshes, plus an assortment of athletic fields. A one-mile footpath leads to a lakeside observation deck, and there's access to the ten-mile Sammamish River Trail. The circa-1904 Clise Mansion, near a pioneer windmill, was built as a hunting lodge. Facilities include picnic areas, restrooms, play areas, baseball and soccer fields, tennis courts, a model-airplane airport, a bicycle velodrome with frequent races, a climbing wall and archaeological site. ~ Located on Westlake-Sammamish Parkway Northeast off Route 520, just south of Redmond city center; 206-205-3661, fax 206-296-1437.

BEACHES & PARKS

SAINT EDWARDS STATE PARK 🧍 🚴 🏊 🍴 This former Catholic seminary still exudes the peace and quiet of a theological retreat across its 316 heavily wooded acres and 3000 feet of Lake Washington shoreline. Except for a handful of former seminary buildings, the park is mostly natural, laced by miles of informal trails. To reach the beach, take the wide path just west of the main seminary building. It winds a half mile down to the shore, where you can wander left or right. Side trails climb up the bluff for the return loop. There's also a beach (no lifeguard) and year-round indoor pool (fee). You'll also find picnic areas, restrooms, a horseshoe pit, soccer and baseball fields, basketball, volleyball, badminton and a gymnasium (fee). ~ Located on Lake Washington's eastern shore, between Kenmore and Kirkland on Juanita Drive Northeast; 425-823-2992.

LUTHER BURBANK COUNTY PARK 🧍 🏊 🍴 At the northeast corner of Mercer Island in Lake Washington, this little jewel presents some 3000 feet of shoreline to explore along with marshes, meadows and woods. The entire 78-acre site is encircled by a loop walk. You can fish from the pier for salmon, steelhead, trout and bass, and in summer swim at the beach. Among the facilities are picnic areas, restrooms, a play area, tennis courts and an amphitheater with summer concerts. ~ Entrance is at 84th Avenue Southeast and Southeast 24th Street, via the Island Crest Way exit from Route 90 on Mercer Island, east of Seattle; 206-236-3545.

GENE COULON BEACH PARK 🏊 🚤 🍴 At the south tip of Lake Washington in Renton, this handsomely landscaped site is most notable for the loads of attractions within its 55 acres: one-and-a-half miles of lakeside path, the wildfowl-rich estuary of John's Creek and a "nature islet," a lagoon enclosed by the thousand-foot floating boardwalk of "Picnic Gallery," the famous seafood restaurant Ivar's, a fast-food restaurant, and interesting architecture reminiscent of old-time amusement parks. A logboom-protected shoreline includes a fishing pier. There's a boat harbor with an eight-lane boat launch, and good fishing from the pier for trout and salmon. The bathing beach is protected by a concrete walkabout with summer lifeguard. There are picnic grounds and floats, restrooms, play areas, and volleyball and tennis courts; there's a restaurant on park grounds and others nearby. ~ Bordered by Lake Washington Boulevard North in Renton, north of Route 405 via Exit 5 and Park Avenue North; 425-430-6700, fax 425-430-6603.

LAKE SAMMAMISH STATE PARK 🚶 🚴 ⛵ ⛴ 🛶 🚤 🛥️ A popular, 512-acre park at the southern tip of Lake Sammamish near Issaquah, it offers plenty to do, including swimming (no lifeguard), boating, picnicking, hiking and birdwatching along 6858 feet of lake shore and around the mouth of Issaquah Creek. Look for eagles, hawks, great-blue heron, red-wing blackbirds, northern flickers, grebes, kingfishers, killdeer, buffleheads, widgeon and Canada geese. Picnic areas, restrooms, showers, soccer fields and a jogging trail are the facilities here. ~ Located at East Lake Sammamish Parkway Southeast and Southeast 56th Street, two miles north of Route 90 in Issaquah (15 miles east of Seattle) via Exit 17; 425-649-4275.

▼▼▼▼▼▼▼▼▼
Seattle South

Meander from the heart of the city and you'll find one of the world's great aviation museums. Inviting saltwater beaches provide a convenient retreat from urban living. Seattle South serves as the city's back door to the wilderness.

SIGHTS

About ten miles to the south of downtown Seattle, off Route 5 at Boeing Field, you'll encounter the **Museum of Flight**. Centered in a traffic-stopping piece of architecture called the Great Gallery, the museum is a must. In the glass-and-steel gallery, 22 aircraft hang suspended from the ceiling, almost as if in flight. In all, more than 135 air- and spacecraft (many rare) trace the history of a century of aviation. You'll see the world's first fighter airplane, the first airliner to carry stewardesses, the first presidential jet Air Force One and the only existing M-21 Blackbird spyplane.

The 1909 **Red Barn** houses one wing of the museum. The so-called barn was originally a boat-building factory on the banks of the nearby Duwamish River. Later Bill Boeing bought it and turned it into the original headquarters for the Boeing Corporation. Relocated several times, the Red Barn now houses exhibits on Boeing's early days in the airplane business, a far cry from to-

Where Are
They Now?

Nearly 30,000 visitors each year make pilgrimages to Seattle to visit the gravesites of deceased superstars. The headstone of martial arts film hero **Bruce Lee** (1940–1973), engraved in English and Chinese, is found in Lake View Cemetery on Capitol Hill, just north of Volunteer Park. Alongside, another headstone marks the final resting place of his son, **Brandon Lee** (1965–1993), who died in a freak gunshot accident while filming *The Crow*. ~ 1554 15th Avenue East, Seattle; 206-322-1582.

Lake View Cemetery is also the final resting place of several Seattle historical figures—among them founding fathers Henry L. Yesler (1830–1892) and David "Doc" Maynard (1808–1873), and Chief Seattle's daughter Princess Angeline (1820?–1896).

Legendary guitarist **Jimi Hendrix** (1942–1970), who reigned as Seattle's most famous rock musician until his fatal drug overdose a year after his landmark appearance at Woodstock, is interred at Greenwood Memorial Park in suburban Renton. Because of the large number of fans who still visit the grave, a large open-air family mausoleum has been built on the site. ~ 350 Monroe Avenue Northeast, Renton; 425-255-1511.

Incidentally, Jimi Hendrix attended central Seattle's Garfield High School, where Bruce Lee met his future wife Linda Emery (class of '63) while he was giving a guest lecture on Chinese philosophy at Garfield High. Jimi and Bruce also shared the same birthday, November 27.

Don't look for the grave of Seattle's other deceased rock superstar, **Kurt Cobain** (1967–1994), lead singer and guitarist of the grunge group Nirvana. His remains were cremated and the ashes scattered in the Wishkah River near the south boundary of Olympic National Park. The river provides the water supply for the city of Aberdeen, Washington. If you can't make the pilgrimage out to Aberdeen, head for Seattle's Viretta Park instead. This tiny park, due south of Cobain's former home, has become an informal memorial site, complete with flowers, candles and graffiti left by fans. ~ 151 Lake Washington Boulevard East.

day's mammoth factories. Visitors can also tour the operating air traffic control tower. Admission. ~ 9404 East Marginal Way South; 206-764-5720, fax 206-764-5707; www.museumofflight. org, e-mail info@museumofflight.org.

Black Diamond (about 35 miles southeast of Seattle on Route 169) is an old coal-mining town with the odds and ends of its mining, logging and railroading history on display at the **Black Diamond Historical Society Museum**. This intriguing museum is housed in an 1884 railroad depot. Open Thursday and weekends or by appointment. ~ Baker Street and Railroad Avenue; 360-886-2142. But the real reason most folks stop here—on their way to Mt. Rainier, the Green River Gorge or winter ski slopes—is the famous **Black Diamond Bakery**. At last count, the bakery and its wood-fired ovens produced some 30 varieties of bread.

> Like Boeing, Seattle's other economic giant, Microsoft, also has its own museum, but it only exists in cyberspace. Look it up at www.microsoft.com/ mscorp/museum.

Green River Gorge is less than an hour from downtown Seattle but is worlds away from the big city. Just 300 feet deep, the steep-walled gorge nevertheless slices through solid rock (shale and sandstone) to reveal coal seams and fossil imprints and inspire a fine sense of remoteness. State and county parks flank the gorge (see "Parks" below).

LODGING   A stone's throw from Sea-Tac Airport, the **Seattle Marriott** is a wonderfully luxurious hotel featuring a 20,000-square-foot tropical atrium five stories high. Around it are 459 guest rooms. A restaurant, lounge, whirlpool, health club with massage therapy (by appointment) and gameroom round out the amenities. Airport shuttle is provided. ~ 3201 South 176th Street; 206-241-2000, 800-314-0925, fax 206-248-0789; www.marriott.com. DELUXE.

DINING   An excellent Thai restaurant convenient to Sea-Tac Airport is **Bai Tong**. Located in a former A&W drive-in, this eatery is known for its steamed curry salmon, grilled beef with Thai sauce and marinated chicken. The carpeted dining room is lush with potted plants, and the walls are adorned with photos of mouthwatering dishes. ~ 15859 Pacific Highway South, Sea-Tac; phone/fax 206-431-0893; www.baitongrestaurant.com. BUDGET.

For an unusual experience in low-priced dining, head west of the airport to the increasingly Latino suburb of Burien, where you'll find **El Trapiche Pupusería & Restaurant**. This homespun, unpretentious little restaurant serves authentic Salvadoran specialties such as *pollo asado* (a skinless, boneless chicken breast chargrilled in annatto-seed marinade), *pescado frito* (whole deep-fried tilapia), *pupusa de chicharrón* (cornmeal rounds stuffed with shredded pork and served with spicy slaw) and beef hoof soup (an acquired taste, to be sure). Practically the only Central American eatery in the greater Seattle area, El Trapiche's novelty draws a growing clientele from all parts of the city. ~ 127 Southwest 153rd Street, Burien; 206-244-5564, fax 206-242-2120. BUDGET TO MODERATE.

The **Green River Gorge Conservation Area** includes three state parks. Here we pick the two developed parks at the entrance and exit of the gorge and one nearby state park on a lake. ~ 253-931-3930, fax 253-931-6379.

PARKS

SEAHURST PARK 🧍 ⛵ 🎣 🛶 A well-designed, 152-acre site where landscaping divides 4000 feet of saltwater shoreline into individual chunks just right for private picnics and sunbathing. A nature trail and some three miles of primitive footpath explore woodsy uplands and the headwaters of two creeks. Other facilities include picnic areas, restrooms, and a marine laboratory with a small viewable fish ladder. ~ Located at Southwest 144th Street and 13th Avenue Southwest, via Exit 154B from Route 5, Burien; 206-988-3700.

FLAMING GEYSER STATE PARK 🧍 🚲 🛶 Once a resort, this 480-acre park downstream from the exit of Green River Gorge offers four miles of hiking trails and nearly five miles of riverbank. Originally, the flaming geyser area was a test site for coal samples, but miners found natural gas instead, which, when lit, produced a 20-foot flame. The "flaming geyser" is only eight inches high now, and can be seen off one of the trails. Pick up a trail map and brochure at the main office. Fish for rainbow trout and steelhead in season (check the posted regulations). There are picnic areas, restrooms, play areas, volleyball courts, a horseback riding area (but no stables) and horseshoe pits. ~ Green Valley Road, three miles west of Route 169, south of Black Diamond; 253-931-3930, fax 253-931-6379.

KANASKAT-PALMER STATE PARK 🧍 🚲 🛶 Lovely walking on riverside paths, especially in summer, is the hallmark of this 320-acre park upstream from the entrance to Green River Gorge. During fishing season, try for steelhead and trout (check posted regulations). Picnic areas, restrooms, showers, volleyball courts and horseshoe pits are the facilities here. ~ On Cumberland-Kanaskat Road off Southeast 308th Street, 11 miles north of Enumclaw and Route 410; 360-886-0148, fax 360-886-1715; e-mail kanaskat-palmer@parks.wa.gov.

▲ There are 31 standard sites ($19 per night) and 19 with partial hookups ($25 per night). Reservations: 888-226-7688.

NOLTE STATE PARK 🧍 🚲 ⛵ 🎣 🛶 Surrounding Deep Lake, 117-acre Nolte Park is famous for its huge Douglas firs, cedars and cottonwoods. A one-and-a-quarter-mile path circles the lake taking you around nearly 7200 feet of shoreline and past the big trees; a separate nature trail interprets the forest. You can swim at the lake (no lifeguards); motorboats are prohibited. The lake is open for fishing year round, offering trout, bass, crappie, catfish and silvers. There's a minimal picnic area. Closed October to mid-April. ~ On Veazie-Cumberland Road just south of Southeast 352nd Street, six miles north of Enumclaw and Route 410; 360-825-4646.

WEST HYLEBOS WETLANDS 🏃 A rare chunk of urban wetland tucked between industrialization and subdivisions, the 68-acre park offers examples of all sorts of wetland formations along a one-mile boardwalk trail—springs, streams, marshes, lakes, floating bogs and sinks. You'll also see remnants of ancient forest, plentiful waterfowl, more than a hundred species of birds and many mammals. Facilities are limited to portable toilets. ~ On South 348th Street at 4th Avenue South, just west of Route 99 and Exit 142; 253-835-6901, fax 253-835-6969.

Tacoma and Olympia

The Tacoma/Olympia region southwest of Seattle is rich in history, parks, waterfalls and cultural landmarks. Tacoma features numerous architectural gems; nearby villages like Gig Harbor are ideal for daytrippers. One of the nation's prettier capital cities (and here you may have thought Seattle was the capital of Washington!), Olympia is convenient to the wildlife refuges of Southern Puget Sound, as well as to American Indian monuments and petroglyphs.

Despite a lingering mill-town reputation, Tacoma, the city on Commencement Bay, has experienced a lively rejuvenation in recent years and offers visitors some first-rate attractions. Charles Wright, president of the Great Northern Railroad, chose it as the western terminus of his railroad, and he wanted more than a mill town at the end of his line. Some of the best architects of the day were commissioned to build hotels, theaters, schools and office buildings.

SIGHTS   Today, Tacoma is the state's "second city" with a population of 179,000. The city jealously protects its treasure trove of turn-of-the-20th-century architecture in a pair of historic districts overlooking the bay on both sides of Division Avenue. The 1893 **Old City Hall** at South 7th and Commerce streets was modeled after Renaissance Italian hill castles. The 1889 **Bostwick Hotel** at South 9th Street and Broadway is a classic triangular Victorian "flatiron."

The **Pantages Theater**, an exquisitely restored 1918 masterpiece of the vaudeville circuit, is the centerpiece of Tacoma's thriving theater district. A classic of the vaudeville circuit (W. C. Fields, Mae West, Will Rogers and Houdini all performed here), this theater offers dance, music and theater. The Pantages is worth visiting simply to gawk at its glittering grandeur. ~ Broadway Center, 901 Broadway, Tacoma; tickets, 253-591-5894, 800-291-

7593; tours and general information, 253-591-5890, fax 253-591-2013; www.broadwaycenter.org.

The **Tacoma Art Museum** hosts international-class shows, such as an exhibit featuring Picasso's ceramics and works on paper. The permanent collection focuses on the early works of Dale Chihuly. Closed Monday. Admission. ~ 1701 Pacific Avenue, Tacoma; 253-272-4258, fax 253-627-1898; www.tacoma artmuseum.org, e-mail info@tacomaartmuseum.org.

Union Station's 70-foot diameter rotunda dome rises 60 feet above ground level; the Beaux Arts neoclassical–style building dates from 1911. The rotunda holds one of the world's finest exhibits of glass art made entirely by Tacoma native Dale Chihuly, the renowned founder of the Pilchuck School of blown-glass art. ~ 1717 Pacific Avenue, Tacoma; 253-572-9310; www.chihuly. com/installations/unionstation.

The **Washington State History Museum** located next door offers a comprehensive view of the state's human cultures, from the original inhabitants dependent on salmon to the logging, fishing and farming that first brought settlers to the Northwest. Interactive exhibits allow visitors to sit in the driver's seat of a covered wagon, take a stab at separating wheat from chaff and experience a coal mine cave-in. Closed Monday. Admission. ~ 1911 Pacific Avenue, Tacoma; 253-272-9747, 888-238-4373, fax 253-272-9518; www.washingtonhistory.org.

The **Chihuly Bridge of Glass**, a tunnel of light and color created by the renowned Tacoma glass artist Dale Chihuly, connects the History Museum to the **Museum of Glass**. Dedicated to showcasing glass art from around the world, the museum also features contemporary painting, sculpture and mixed media pieces. Most exciting is the Hot Shop, a glass workshop where a resident team of glass blowers plies its trade. Closed Monday and Tuesday between Labor Day and Memorial Day. Admission. ~ 1801 East

THE BEST BOAT WATCHING GIG—HARBOR THAT IS

Gig Harbor, situated across the Tacoma Narrows off Route 16, is a classic Puget Sound small town. The community that arose around the harbor was founded as a fishing village by Croatians and Austrians. Today you're more likely to see every sort of pleasure craft here; it's one of the best boat-watching locales on Puget Sound. The tight harbor entrance funnels boats single-file past dockside taverns and cafés where you can watch the nautical parade. Or, rent a boat from Gig Harbor Rent-A-Boat and join the flotilla. ~ 8829 North Harborview Drive; 253-858-7341; www. gigharborrentaboat.com, e-mail gigharborrentaboat@comcast.net.

Dock Street; 253-284-4750, 866-468-7386, fax 253-396-1769; www.museumofglass.org, e-mail info@museumofglass.org.

The **Job Carr Cabin Museum** is a reconstruction of the first permanent settlers' log cabin that commemorates Tacoma's founding with original artifacts, photos and historical displays. Closed Sunday through Tuesday. ~ 2350 North 30th Street, Tacoma; 253-627-5405; www.jobcarrmuseum.org.

Without a doubt, Tacoma's prettiest garden spot is the **W. W. Seymour Botanical Conservatory**, a graceful Victorian domed conservatory constructed at the turn of the 20th century with over 12,000 panes of glass. Inside are exotic tropical plants, including birds of paradise, ornamental figs, cacti and bromeliads; seasonal displays of flowers; a collection of orchids; and a fish pond with waterfall. Closed Monday. ~ 316 South G Street, Tacoma; 253-591-5330, fax 253-627-2192; e-mail seymour@tacomaparks.com.

A treat for both kids and adults is **Point Defiance Park**, set on a sloping peninsula above the south Puget Sound shore. This 702-acre urban park has an outstanding zoo and aquarium with a Pacific Rim theme. You can watch the fish from above or through underwater viewing windows. You'll also see an outdoor logging museum with steam trains; Fort Nisqually, a reconstruction of the original 1850 Hudson's Bay Company post (closed Monday and Tuesday except in summer); rhododendron, rose, Japanese and native Northwest gardens; and numerous scenic overlooks (see "Beaches & Parks" below). ~ 5912 North Waterfront Drive, Tacoma off Pearl Street; 253-305-1000; www.metro parkstacoma.org.

HIDDEN ►

Steilacoom about five miles south of Tacoma is a quiet counterpoint to Gig Harbor's bustle. Founded by Yankee sea captains in the 1850s, it exudes a museum-like peacefulness and preserves a New England look among its fine collection of clapboard houses. Get a self-guiding brochure at **Steilacoom Historical Museum**. Open Friday through Sunday in February, November and December; open Wednesday through Sunday from March through October. Closed Monday and the month of January. ~ 1801 Ranier Street, Steilacoom; 253-584-4133; www.steilacoomhistorical.org.

Don't miss the **Pioneer Orchard**; it surrounds the **Nathaniel Orr Home**. Closed Monday through Thursday. ~ 1811 Rainier Avenue. At the 1895 **Bair Drug and Hardware Store**, you can order an old-fashioned float from the 1906 soda fountain. ~ 1617 Lafayette Street near Wilkes Street, Steilacoom; 253-588-9668, fax 253-588-0737; www.thebairrestaurant.com.

At the southern tip of Puget Sound, **Olympia**'s state capitol dome rises boldly as you approach on Route 5, a tempting landmark for travelers and an easy detour from the busy freeway. But this community of some 39,000 offers visitors more to peruse than government buildings and monuments. Nevertheless, the capitol campus may be the best place to begin your explorations.

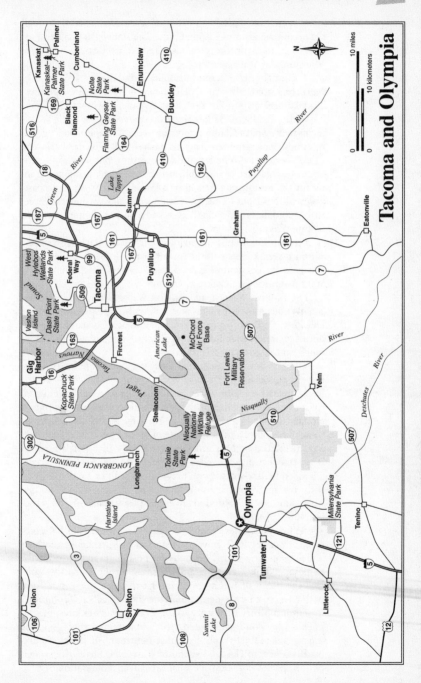

Tacoma and Olympia

You can take a daily guided tour seven days a week through the marbled halls of the Romanesque **Legislative Building** and see other buildings on the grounds—**Temple of Justice, Executive Mansion** and **State Library**.

The nearby **State Capitol Museum** includes a fine collection of Northwest Coast Indian artifacts. Closed Sunday through Tuesday. Admission. ~ 211 West 21st Avenue, Olympia; 360-753-2580, fax 360-586-8322; www.wshs.org/wscm.

Downtown, the handsomely restored **Old Capitol**, at 7th Avenue and Washington Street across from stately Sylvester Park, will catch your eye with its fanciful architecture. But most of downtown is a potpourri of disparate attractions—the **Washington Center for the Performing Arts** at 512 Washington Street Southeast, galleries, the **Capitol Theater** at 5th Avenue and Washington Street with its old films and local theater, and a bit of Bohemia along 4th Avenue West.

HIDDEN ►   **Percival Landing** is an inviting, harborside park with observation tower, kiosks with historical displays, picnic tables, cafés and boardwalks next to acres of pleasure craft. ~ At the foot of State Avenue at Water Street, Olympia.

For a longer walk, head south on Water Street, cross 4th and 5th avenues, then turn west and follow the sidewalk next to the Deschutes Parkway (or get in your car and drive) around the park-dotted shores of manmade **Capitol Lake**, which is two and a half miles from the town of Tumwater.

Tumwater marks the true end of Puget Sound. Before Capitol Lake was created, the sound was navigable all the way to the Deschutes River. **Tumwater Historical Park**, at the meeting of river and lake, is rich in both history and recreation. One of two pioneer houses here was built in 1860 by Nathaniel Crosby III (Bing Crosby's grandfather). Down by the river you can fish, have a picnic, explore fitness and hiking trails, watch birds in reedy marshes and see more historical exhibits. Across the river, a handsome, six-story, brick brew house built in 1906 marks an early enterprise that lives on in a 1933 brewery a few hundred yards south. ~ 777 Simmons Avenue, Tumwater; 360-754-4160, fax 360-754-4166.

Follow Deschutes Parkway south to **Tumwater Falls Park** (not to be confused with Tumwater Historical Park), a small park that's a nice spot for a picnic lunch and whose main attraction is the namesake "falls," twisting and churning through a rocky defile. Feel the throb of water reverberating through streamside footpaths. Listen to its sound, which the Indians called "Tumtum." You'll find plenty of history in the headquarters exhibit, including an American Indian petroglyph and a monument recounting the travails of the first permanent settlement north of the Columbia River here in 1845. ~ Deschutes Way and C Street, Tumwater; phone/fax 360-943-2550; e-mail otf@olytwnfoundation.org.

Ten miles south of Olympia are **Mima Mounds**, an unusual group of several hundred hillocks spread across 450 acres. Scientists think they could have been created by glacial deposits or, believe it or not, busy gophers. There is a self-guided interpretive trail offering a close look at this geologic oddity, as well as several miles of hiking trails. Wildflowers paint the mounds yellow, pink and blue from April through June. ~ Wadell Creek Road, Littlerock; 360-902-1004, fax 360-902-1775; www.dnr.wa.gov/nap.

No Cabbages Bed and Breakfast is a lovely home with a view of the water and access to the beach. It has three guest rooms with both private and shared bathrooms, and a suite with its own private entrance. The house is laden with eclectic, primitive folk art and interesting conversation. The grounds feature deer, fox, woodpeckers and a prayer labyrinth for introspection and walking meditation. The innkeeper serves an outstanding breakfast. ~ 10319 Sunrise Beach Drive Northwest, Gig Harbor; 253-858-7797; www.nocabbages.com, e-mail info@nocabbages.com. DELUXE.

LODGING

The **Lighthouse Bungalow** is a beautifully restored 1920s-era beachfront property with waterfront access to Bud Inlet on Puget Sound. The four-bedroom, four-bath upstairs unit sleeps ten and is furnished with mission-style antiques, hardwood floors, a full kitchen, a jacuzzi bath and views of the Sound and Olympic Mountains from its deck. The cozy one-bedroom, lower-level unit includes a sitting room and sleeps up to three. The owners lend bicycles, kayaks and a canoe. ~ 1215 East Bay Drive, Olympia; 360-754-0389, fax 360-754-7499; www.lighthousebungalow.com, e-mail info@lighthousebungalow.com. DELUXE TO ULTRA-DELUXE.

AUTHOR FAVORITE

Chocolates left on my pillow is but one of the reasons I have sweet dreams when I stay at **Chinaberry Hill**. This luxurious 1889 Victorian bed and breakfast offers three spacious romance suites with bay windows, double jacuzzis, private baths with showers and harbor views or a fireplace. The adjacent two-story carriage house, with its cabin atmosphere, is ideal for families featuring a queen-sized curved iron canopy bed, a double bed loft and a jacuzzi alcove. Appointed with period antiques and surrounded by gardens, the inn is an inviting retreat. ~ 302 Tacoma Avenue North, Tacoma; 253-272-1282, fax 253-272-1335; www.china berryhill.com, e-mail chinaberry@wa.net. DELUXE TO ULTRA-DELUXE.

DINING   If you've a hankering for barbecued ribs, fried chicken or catfish, try **Southern Kitchen**. This is no antebellum mansion, just a plain, well-lighted café with good food. Just as good as the entrées are the greens, grits, yams, fried okra, biscuits, homemade strawberry lemonade and melt-in-your-mouth corncakes served up alongside. The cooks are Southern stock themselves, so you can count on this fare being authentic. Breakfast is served all day. ~ 1716 6th Avenue, Tacoma; 253-627-4282. BUDGET.

One of the best views in Olympia is from **Falls Terrace**, through huge windows overlooking Tumwater Falls on the Deschutes River. A good way to start your meal is with some Olympia oysters. The menu features pasta dishes, an excellent bouillabaisse and an array of chicken and beef entrées. Reservations recommended. ~ 106 South Deschutes Way, Tumwater; 360-943-7830, fax 360-943-6899; www.fallsterrace.com. MODERATE TO DELUXE.

Gardner's Seafood and Pasta is no secret to locals, who flock to this small restaurant. While seafood is the specialty here, there are several pastas that are very good, too. Try the pasta primavera. The Dungeness crab casserole is rich with cream, chablis and several cheeses. Homemade ice cream and other desserts fill out the meal. Dinner only. Closed Sunday and Monday. ~ 111 West Thurston Street, Olympia; 360-786-8466. DELUXE.

Patrons don't usually go to a restaurant for the drinking water, but at **McMenamin's Spar Café Bar** it truly is exceptional because it comes from the eatery's own artesian well. Once a blue-collar café, the restaurant features large photographs of loggers felling giant Douglas firs. On the menu are thick milkshakes, giant sandwiches, prime rib and Willapa Bay oysters. ~ 114 East 4th Avenue, Olympia; 360-357-6444, fax 360-786-1716. MODERATE.

In downtown Olympia, the **Urban Onion** serves sizable breakfasts, good sandwiches and hamburgers and a hearty lentil soup. Dinners include chicken, seafood and *gado gado*—a spicy Indonesian dish of sautéed vegetables in tahini and peanut sauce, along with Mexican entrées. They also offer several vegetarian specials. The restaurant is part of a complex of shops in the former Olym-

AUTHOR FAVORITE

Do you enjoy good tempura? Then don't walk, run to **Fujiya** in downtown Tacoma. Masahiro Endo, owner and chef, is a great entertainer with his knife at the sushi bar. In addition, the chicken sukiyaki is delicious. ~ 1125 Court C, Tacoma; phone/fax 253-627-5319. MODERATE.

pian Hotel. ~ 116 Legion Way, Olympia; 360-943-9242, fax 360-754-2378. MODERATE.

The Olympia area isn't the place you'd expect gourmet French-Northwest cuisine, but chef Jean-Pierre Simon exceeds expectations at **Jean-Pierre's**. Located in a historic old home near the Olympia Brewery, Simon serves up luscious crêpes, pastas and fish entrées that meld French Provincial influences with local ingredients such as Dungeness crab. Reservations recommended. Closed Monday. ~ 316 Schmidt Place, Tumwater; 360-754-3702, fax 360-754-1352; www.jean-pierres.com. ULTRA-DELUXE.

In the Proctor District in north Tacoma you can find Northwest foods, gifts and clothing at the **Pacific Northwest Shop**. ~ 2702 North Proctor Street, Tacoma; 253-752-2242, 800-942-3523. Fine Irish imports are in stock at **The Harp & Shamrock**. ~ 2704 North Proctor Street, Tacoma; 253-752-5012. The **Old House Mercantile** offers gifts for the kitchen and garden as well as a selection of teapots and jewelry. ~ 2717-A North Proctor Street, Tacoma; 253-759-8850. Educational toys are found at **Teaching Toys**. ~ 2624 North Proctor Street, Tacoma; 253-759-9853. The **Northwest Museum Store** at the Washington State History Museum features American Indian gifts, jewelry and pottery. ~ 1911 Pacific Avenue, Tacoma; 253-798-5880.

SHOPPING

Near the Tacoma Dome downtown, **Freighthouse Square** is a thriving collection of shops and eateries in an old railroad warehouse. Dozens of shops offer local crafts, jewelry, ethnic gifts, flowers and food items. ~ 25th and East D streets, Tacoma; 253-305-0678; www.freighthousesquare.com.

For sportswear and outdoor gear in Tacoma, try **Sportco**. Shop warehouse-style for hunting, fishing, camping gear and guns. ~ 4602 East 20th Street, Tacoma; 253-922-2222; www.sportco.com. Or visit **Duffle Bag Army Navy Inc.** for camping, hunting and workwear. ~ 8207 South Tacoma Way, Tacoma; 253-588-4433, 800-588-4432; www.thedufflebag.com.

In Gig Harbor, **The Beach Basket** features, of course, baskets and other gifts. ~ 4102 Harborview Drive, Gig Harbor; 253-858-3008. Scandinavian utensils, books and gifts can be found at **Strictly Scandinavian**. ~ 7803 Pioneer Way, Gig Harbor; 253-851-5959. **Mostly Books** stocks books (you're kidding), bookmarks and postcards. ~ 3126 Harborview Drive, Gig Harbor; 253-851-3219.

In Olympia, contemporary women's clothing and accessories are found at **Juicy Fruits**. ~ 111 Market Street, Suite 103; 360-943-0572. **Olympic Outfitters** is housed in a restored, brick-and-metal building and is stocked with everything from bicycles to backpacking and cross-country ski gear. ~ 407 East 4th Avenue; 360-943-1114.

NIGHTLIFE For drinks and occasional music, a longtime favorite is **The Swiss Pub**, at the top of a flight of stairs connecting the State History Museum with the campus of the University of Washington—Tacoma. It's renowned for its collection of Chihuly glass, not a common thing for a college pub. ~ 1904 South Jefferson Avenue, Tacoma; 253-572-2821. **Katie Downs Tavern** is an adults-only pub overlooking Commencement Bay with a menu featuring local microbrews, seafood and pizza. ~ 3211 Ruston Way, Tacoma; 253-756-0771. Boasting one of the largest selections of draught beer in the state is the **Ale House Pub**. ~ 2122 Mildred Street West, Tacoma; 253-565-9367; www.alehousepub.com.

The **Tacoma Little Theatre** is a community theater producing five plays a year. ~ 210 North I Street, Tacoma; 253-272-2281; www.tacomalittletheatre.com.

South of Tacoma is **Happy Days Diner and Time Tunnel Lounge**, where deejays spin Top-40 nightly. Cover on Friday and Saturday. ~ 11521 Bridgeport Way Southwest, Lakewood; 253-582-1531.

The **Tides Tavern** in Gig Harbor features live bands on select weekends playing '50s and '60s rock and some rhythm-and-blues. Cover for live shows. ~ 2925 Harborview Drive, Gig Harbor; 253-858-3982; www.tidestavern.com.

BEACHES & PARKS **DASH POINT STATE PARK** 🚶 🚴 🏖 🏊 🛶 ⛴ Nearly 400 acres of forested wildland with 3300 feet of saltwater shoreline preserve a bit of solitude just barely outside the Tacoma city limits. Seven and a half miles of trail ramble through mixed forest of second-growth fir, maple and alder. The park's beach is one of the few places on Puget Sound where you'll find enjoyable saltwater swimming—shallow waters in tide flats are warmed by the summer sun. Tides retreat to expose a beachfront nearly a half-mile deep. There's fishing from the pier at Brown's Point Park south of Dash Point State Park, and swimming in tide flat shallows (no lifeguard). Facilities include picnic areas, restrooms and showers. ~ Located just northeast of Tacoma on Southwest Dash Point (Route 509); 253-661-4955, fax 253-661-4995.

▲ There are 114 developed sites ($19 per night) and 27 sites with hookups ($26 per night). Reservations: 888-226-7688.

POINT DEFIANCE PARK 🚶 🚴 🏕 🏊 🛶 ⛴ Jutting dramatically into Puget Sound, this 700-acre treasure is hailed by some as the finest saltwater park in the state, by others as the best city park in the Northwest. Here are primeval forests, some 50 miles of hiking trails, over three miles of public shoreline and enough other attractions to match almost any visitor's interests. Five Mile Drive loops around the park perimeter with access to trails, forest, beach, views, attractions and grand overlooks of Puget Sound. The park is also known for its zoo and aquarium, particularly the shark tank (fee). Popular with boaters, there's a fully equipped marina with boat rentals, a boathouse (253-591-5325) and a restaurant. You can fish from the pier or in a rented boat. You'll find picnic areas, restrooms, play areas, tennis courts and a snack bar at the boathouse. ~ The entrance is on North 54th and Pearl streets; 253-305-1000, fax 253-305-1098.

KOPACHUCK STATE PARK
Spectacular views across Carr Inlet toward the Olympic Mountains from a half-mile of shoreline gives Kopachuck much to boast about. Many car-top boaters launch from the beach near the park to fish for bottomfish and salmon or paddle out to Cutts Island Marine State Park a half-mile away. No lifeguard is on duty. There are picnic areas, restrooms and showers. ~ Located on Kopachuck Drive Northwest at Northwest 56th Street, about seven miles west of Gig Harbor and Route 16; 253-265-3606, fax 360-644-8112.

Before the Alaska Gold Rush thrust Seattle into prominence at the turn of the 20th century, Tacoma was Puget Sound's leading city.

▲ There are 41 sites for tents and RVs ($19 per night); no hookups are available. Closed October through April.

NISQUALLY NATIONAL WILDLIFE REFUGE This 3000-acre refuge's ecosystem is a diverse mix of conifer forest, deciduous woodlands, marshlands, grasslands and mud flats and the meandering Nisqually River (born in Mt. Rainier National Park). Here, the river mixes its fresh waters with the salt chuck of Puget Sound. The refuge is home to mink, otter, coyote and some 50 other species of mammals, over 200 kinds of birds and 125 species of fish. Trails thread the refuge; longest is the five-and-a-half-mile dike-top loop that circles a pioneer homestead long since abandoned. Fishing yields salmon, steelhead and cutthroat. Facilities include an education center and restrooms. Day-use fee, $3 per family. ~ Route 5 Exit 114, about 25 miles south of downtown Tacoma; 360-753-9467, fax 360-534-9302; www.fws.gov/nisqually.

TOLMIE STATE PARK A salt marsh with interpretive signs separates 1800 feet of tide flats from forested uplands overlooking Nisqually Reach. The sandy beach is fine for wading or swimming; at low tide you may find clams. A two-and-a-half-mile wheelchair-accessible perimeter hiking trail loops through the park's 106 acres. An artificial reef and three sunken barges 500 yards offshore and almost-nonexistent current make the underwater park here popular for divers. Fishing yields salmon and cod. You'll find picnic areas, restrooms and showers. ~ Hill Road Northeast, northeast of Olympia via Exit 111 from Route 5; phone/fax 360-456-6464.

MILLERSYLVANIA STATE PARK 🏃 🚲 ⛵ 🎣 ⛴ 🛶 ⛴
Some 842 acres of primeval conifer forest and miles of foot trail
are this park's big appeals. But visitors also come to enjoy its 3300
feet of shoreline along Deep Lake, where you can swim, launch a
small boat (no wake) or fish for trout, bass, perch and crappie.
Facilities include picnic areas and restrooms. ~ Exit 95 just east
of Route 5, ten miles south of Olympia; 360-753-1519, fax 360-
664-2180.

▲ There are 120 standard sites ($19 per night) and 48 sites
with hookups ($26 per night). No reservations necessary October
to May. Reservations: 888-226-7688; e-mail res.nw@state.or.us.

Outdoor Adventures

SPORT-FISHING

Salmon, of course, is the big draw for anglers
on Puget Sound. State hatchery programs see
to it that the anadromous fish are available
year-round, but the months from midsummer to midfall bring the
bulk of salmon—and anglers—to these waters. From mid-July to
late August, chinook salmon are king; by Labor Day coho take
over, until October. Then chum arrive, but since they tend to be
plankton eaters they don't bite. Pink salmon return in odd num-
bered years, in August, and are most plentiful in
the Sound north of Seattle, near Everett. Sockeye
can be found in Lake Washington as early as late
June until August.

Several charter companies operate fishing trips on
the Sound. The cost, which can range from $35 to $80
and up, usually includes everything except lunch and the
fishing license (which you can purchase through the charter
company).

Washington State fishers
catch more than 1.3 bil-
lion pounds of fish and
seafood annually, more
than half the nation's
total edible catch.

SEATTLE AREA Downtown, you can drop your line right into
Elliott Bay at **Waterfront Park** (Piers 57-61). But for the real deal,
head to Ballard, where the city's commercial fishing fleet is based
(at Fisherman's Terminal) and sportfishing tours can be chartered.
Adventure Charters offers full-day salmon-fishing trips year-round.
Afternoon tours are offered in summer, and all gear is provided.
~ 7001 Seaview Avenue Northwest, Shilshole Bay Marina; 206-
789-8245, 800-789-0448; www.seattlesalmoncharters.com.

SEATTLE NORTH All Seasons Charter Service operates two
boats for salmon or bottomfish. ~ Port of Edmonds; 425-743-
9590.

KAYAKING & SMALL BOATING

If your nautical knowhow extends no further than a good row
across a lake, then head for Lake Union, on the northern edge of
Seattle's downtown center. On a bright summer day, the waters
of Lake Union are dotted with kayaks, small wooden rowboats
and sailboats.

SEATTLE AREA To rent a single or double kayak, call **Northwest Outdoor Center** to reserve ahead. Kayaking on Lake Union is very popular, and it's not unusual for all the center's 100-plus kayaks to be rented on a nice day. Classes and guided trips from one day to five days are available. ~ 2100 Westlake Avenue North; 206-281-9694, 800-683-0637; www.nwoc.com. At the **Center for Wooden Boats**, not only can you rent one of several different kinds of classic wooden rowboats, you can also learn a bit about their history. There are also several small sailboats for rent, but only experienced boaters can rent one. The center is a nonprofit, hands-on museum that also offers sailing instruction and other heritage maritime skills such as knot-tying, navigation and boat building. ~ 1010 Valley Street; 206-382-2628, fax 206-382-2699; www.cwb.org. To rent a "kicker boat" for do-it-yourself sportfishing, you'll have to leave the lake.

TACOMA AND OLYMPIA Located near the tip of the peninsula in Point Defiance Park, the **Boathouse Marina** has 20 14-foot dinghies for rent. Most of the time they're rented by anglers, but you can take them out to explore the Sound if you prefer. Also for rent are motors to power the boats. ~ 253-591-5325.

SCUBA DIVING

Although the water temperature in Puget Sound averages a cool 45° to 55°, diving is quite popular, especially from October through April, when there's no plankton bloom because of reduced sunlight during those months. With several dive clubs in the Seattle-Tacoma area, there are usually many dives scheduled each weekend: a wall dive off Fox Island perhaps, or a shore dive at Three Tree Point (near Federal Way) or Sunrise Beach (near Gig Harbor). Southern Puget Sound and the area around Vashon Island are considered the best places to dive—you'll see starfish, crabs, ling cod, scallops and many more species. Be prepared, however: Currents are extremely strong south of Seattle so you'll need to check the tides and currents carefully before diving. The dive shops listed below can provide details about these hazards as well as information on local dive spots. If you're not an experienced diver, you can arrange lessons with these shops, although it takes several days to complete training for certification. With 11 locations between them, **Underwater Sports Inc.** (800-252-7177; www.underwatersports.com) and **Lighthouse Diving Centers** (800-777-3483; www.lighthousediving.com) are convenient to most Seattle-area locations. They offer lessons and trips, and they rent and repair equipment.

SEATTLE NORTH Underwater Sports Inc. has eight shops between Everett and Olympia. ~ Seattle: 10545 Aurora Avenue North; 206-362-3310, 800-252-7177. Edmonds: 264 Railroad Avenue; 425-771-6322. Everett: 205 East Casino Road #4; 425-355-3338; www.underwatersports.com.

Lighthouse Diving Centers offers outposts in Seattle and Lynnwood. ~ Seattle: 8215 Lake City Way Northeast; 206-524-1633. Lynnwood: 5421 196th Street Southwest #6; 425-771-2679.

SEATTLE SOUTH A full-service scuba shop, **Northwest Sports Divers Inc.** rents any equipment you might need. They also offer scuba certification classes. Closed Sunday. ~ 8030 Northeast Bothell Way, Suite B, Kenmore; 425-487-0624; www.nwsports divers.com.

SEATTLE EAST You'll find local branches of **Underwater Sports** in Bellevue and Kirkland. ~ Bellevue: 12003 Northeast 12th Street; 425-454-5168. Kirkland: 11743 124th Avenue Northeast; 425-821-7200; www.underwatersports.com.

In Bellevue, **Silent World** has classes, gear and rentals. There are beach dives on Sunday, as well as some one-day and two-day trips to the San Juans, Canada and tropical destinations. Closed Sunday. ~ 13600 Northeast 20th Street; 425-747-8842; www. silent-world.com.

TACOMA AND OLYMPIA In Tacoma, **Lighthouse Diving** takes divers to Canada, the Cayman Islands and other destinations for trips that range from one day to a week. Night dives are available. Lighthouse pros meet divers at designated locations. They use one tank per dive. ~ 2502 Pacific Avenue, Tacoma; 253-627-7617, fax 253-627-1877; www.lighthousediving.com. In Port Orchard, contact **Tagert's Dive Locker** for diving, camping trips and holiday dives, such as an Easter egg hunt underwater. Night dives are available. Trips are no more than a half day and use two to three tanks per dive. ~ 205 Bethel Avenue; 360-895-7860.

Underwater Sports Inc. offers shore and boat dives as well as dives abroad—both tropical and night dives. They repair gear. Dives are a day long and use two or three tanks. ~ Tacoma: 9606 40th Avenue Southwest; 253-588-6634. ~ Olympia: 1943 4th Avenue East; 360-493-0322; www.underwatersports.com.

With 11 locations between them, **Underwater Sports Inc.** (800-252-7177; www.underwatersports.com) and **Lighthouse Diving Centers** (800-777-3483; www.lighthousediving.com) are convenient to most Seattle-area locations. They offer lessons and trips, and they rent and repair equipment.

INLINE SKATING It takes about an hour to skate around Seattle's **Green Lake** on the paved multi-use trail. You can rent inline skates at **Gregg's Greenlake Cycle**. ~ 7007 Woodlawn Avenue Northeast; 206-523-1822; www.greggscycles.com.

GOLF Except when the occasional snowstorm closes them down, golf courses in the area are open year-round.

Hey! The Water's Fine

Even if you're a diehard landlubber, do not fail to go sightseeing here by boat at least once. Simply put, if you leave Seattle without plying its surrounding waters your trip will be incomplete. So don't hesitate: Head to the downtown central waterfront and make some waves.

On a clear day you can see forever, or so it would seem aboard one of the **Washington State Ferries**. Headquartered at Colman Dock, the ferries make frequent departures to Bremerton and to Bainbridge Island, both across Puget Sound to the west. From deck you'll be treated to grand views of Mount Rainier, Mount Baker and the Olympics Range, and you may even catch a glimpse of an orca (killer) whale. To Bremerton, you can ride the car-and-passenger ferry, the passenger-only boat or the high-speed ferry for pedestrians. At Pier 50 next door, you can board a passenger-only ferry to Vashon Island. ~ Pier 52; 206-464-6400; www.wsdot.wa.gov/ferries.

This is your captain speaking. That's just part of the show on **Argosy Cruises**, which offer at least two tours every day year-round. On the harbor spin you'll get grand mountain views and see boat traffic like you won't believe: freighters, tugboats, sailboats, ferries, you name it. The narrator spices up the trip. ~ Pier 55; 206-623-4252, 800-642-7816.

Argosy and **Gray Line Water Sightseeing** join forces for their "locks tour." The tour goes north to Shilshole Bay, eastward through the Hiram M. Chittenden Locks into the Lake Washington Ship Canal and then on to the south tip of Lake Union. You return to the waterfront by bus. Going through the locks is an experience in itself. And along the way you might even see salmon jumping. ~ Pier 55; 800-426-7505.

An American Indian performance is included in the **Tillicum Village-Blake Island** four-hour excursion to 475-acre Blake Island Marine State Park, which has tons of things to see and do. ~ Pier 55; 206-933-8600.

S.S. Virginia V is the last authentic operating steamboat of the legendary "Mosquito Fleet," the motley flotilla of steamboats that once carried foot passengers and cargo around Puget Sound before the coming of highways and autos. Recently renovated, the *Virginia V* is available for charter cruises. ~ 206-624-9119; www.virginiav.org.

A quieter, more peaceful way to see Elliott Bay is **Emerald City Charters'** sailboat tours. Pick a daytime or sunset tour and float gracefully past motorboats, ferries and tankers from May to mid-October. ~ Pier 54; 206-624-3931, 800-831-3274; www.sailingseattle.com.

SEATTLE NORTH Kayak Point Golf Course, about 30 miles north of Seattle, is hilly and overlooks the Olympic Mountains and Puget Sound. This public championship course with a double fairway is worth the drive. Amenities include an 18-hole putting course; shoes, clubs and carts for rent; and a restaurant in the same building. ~ 15711 Marine Drive Northeast, Stanwood; 360-652-9676.

The heart of Green River Gorge covers only some six miles on the map but is so twisted into oxbows that it takes kayakers 14 river miles to paddle through it.

SEATTLE EAST Bellevue Municipal Golf Course is one of the most active courses in the state, probably because it's a good walking course with moderate hills. This public course has 18 holes and cart rentals. ~ 5500 140th Avenue Northeast; 425-452-7250.

TACOMA AND OLYMPIA Lake Spanaway Golf Course in Pierce County Park. The 18-hole public course was cut out of a forest, so it's treelined but fairly open. It has a putting green and a pro shop and rents power and pull carts. ~ 15602 Pacific Avenue, Spanaway; 253-531-3660.

TENNIS Northwest precipitation practically turns tennis into an indoor sport. You'll have to call a few days in advance to reserve an indoor court at one of these public facilities.

SEATTLE SOUTH It helps to mention that you're an out-of-town visitor when you call—at least six days in advance—to reserve one of the ten hardtop indoor courts at the **Amy Yee Tennis Center**. The center also has four public outdoor courts. Tennis pros are available for lessons by appointment. ~ 2000 Martin Luther King Jr. Way South; 206-684-4764.

SEATTLE EAST The City of Bellevue operates the public courts at **Robinswood Tennis Center**. There are four indoor and four lighted outdoor courts; call six days in advance (start dialing at 8:30 a.m.). Pros are available for lessons. Fee. ~ 2400 151st Place Southeast at Southeast 22nd Street; 425-452-7690.

TACOMA AND OLYMPIA Call two or three days in advance to reserve one of the four public hardtop indoor courts (or five racquetball courts) at **Sprinker Recreation Center**. Professionals are available for lessons. Fee. ~ 14824 South C Street at Military Road, Tacoma; 253-798-4000.

RIDING STABLES Take off on a guided ride to the top of a mountain east of Seattle or a slow meander through a wooden tract near Tacoma.

SEATTLE EAST On a clear day, you can see more than 100 miles atop Tiger Mountain near Issaquah. **Tiger Mountain Outfitters** will get you there in a three-hour trail ride that will let you see Mt. Rainier 65 miles away in the distance and possibly black bear, deer and cougar within several yards. Call for reservations. ~ 24508 Southeast 133rd Street, Issaquah; 425-392-5090.

TACOMA AND OLYMPIA Su Dara Riding offers a "tranquil, peaceful" one-hour ride for up to seven people through woodland thick with firs and maples. On a clear day there are views of Mt. Rainier. Su herself says, "We ride rain or shine." ~ 8104 Canyon Road East, Puyallup; 253-531-1569; www.sudara.com.

It's no surprise to learn that Seattle has earned a nod from *Bicycling* magazine as one of the top bicycling cities in the country. Bicycle programs are administered by state, city and county transportation agencies, which has resulted in a network of bicycle lanes and trails throughout the region, many of them convenient for visitor recreational use.

BIKING

Helpful information, including bicycle route maps, is available from several agencies. The Washington Department of Transportation operates the **Bicycle Hotline** to request a route map and informative brochure. ~ P.O. Box 47393, Olympia, WA 98504; 360-705-7277; www.wsdot.wa.gov/bike. **The Seattle Bicycling Guide Map** is available from the Seattle Transportation Department and can usually be found in bike stores and public libraries, or ordered online at www.seattle.gov/transportation/bikemaps.htm. ~ 600 4th Avenue, Room 708, Seattle, WA 98104; 206-684-7583. **King County** publishes a bicycling guide map; it's distributed free at bike shops countywide and at Metro Transit centers, or online at www.metrokc.gov/bike.htm. Or call the King County Bike Hotline at 206-263-4700. The **Cascade Bicycle Club** serves as an all-purpose club, for riders of all skill levels. The club operates a hotline, which provides general information about bicycling in the area and club-sponsored weekend rides. ~ 206-522-3222; www.cascade.org.

SEATTLE AREA Although the central city is fairly hilly, especially if you're biking in an east–west direction, there are trails within Seattle that run near the water and on lower and flatter terrain that are ideal for recreational bicyclists. The most famous, of course, is the multi-use **Burke-Gilman Trail**, popular with bikers, walkers and joggers. It's flat, paved and, following an old railroad right of way, it extends from Gas Works Park on Lake Union, through the university campus, past lovely neighborhoods next to Lake Washington and on to Kenmore. In Kenmore, it links up with the **Sammamish River Trail**, which winds through Woodinville (and its wineries) and on to suburban Redmond. It's a lovely city-to-farmlands tour. In West Seattle, the **Alki Bike Route** (6 miles) offers miles of shoreline pedaling—half on separated bike paths—from Seacrest Park to Lincoln Park. Besides changing views of the city and Puget Sound, you should have great views of the Olympic Peninsula mountains.

TACOMA AND OLYMPIA When it comes to bicycling in Tacoma and Pierce County, "things are just getting going," according to one of the city's public works planners. The area does not yet have the extensive network of lanes and trails that they have up in Seattle, but continues to develop its bicycle and pedestrian plan. Meanwhile, the **Pierce County Department of Public Works** puts out a bike route map. ~ 2702 South 42nd Street, Suite 201, Tacoma; 253-798-7250. The **Tacoma Wheelmen's Bicycle Club** operates a recorded Ride Line. ~ 253-759-2800; www.twbc.org.

Among the more popular and convenient places to ride in the city is a two-mile lane along the **downtown waterfront**. Beginning at Schuster Parkway and McCarver Street, this multi-use lane (it's separated from traffic, however) extends to Waterview Street along Ruston Way and Point Defiance Park. Within **Point Defiance Park,** a shoulder lane of Five Mile Drive loops around the peninsula. Call the Metropolitan Park District for more information. ~ 253-305-1000; www.metroparkstacoma.org.

Bike Rentals For bike rentals, repairs, new bikes and accessories in Seattle, try **Gregg's Greenlake Cycle.** ~ 7007 Woodlawn Avenue Northeast; 206-523-1822; www.greggscycles.com. **The Bicycle Center of Seattle,** near the Burke-Gilman Trail, has mountain bikes, hybrids and tandems. ~ 4529 Sand Point Way Northeast; 206-523-8300; www.bicyclecenterseattle.com. The place to buy and repair a bike on Alki Beach is the **Alki Bike & Board Company.** ~ 2606 California Avenue Southwest, Seattle; 206-938-3322; www.alkibikeandboard.com.

HIKING Nearly every park mentioned in the "Beaches & Parks" sections of this chapter offers at least a few miles of hiking trail through forest or along a stream or beach. Some are outstanding, such as Nisqually National Wildlife Refuge, Green River Gorge, Point Defiance Park in Tacoma and Discovery Park in Seattle. All distances listed are one way unless otherwise noted.

DOWNTOWN SEATTLE For short strolls in downtown Seattle, try **Freeway Park** and the grounds of the adjoining Washington State Convention Center (.5 mile) and **Myrtle Edwards** and **Elliott Bay parks** (1.25 miles) at the north end of the downtown

AUTHOR FAVORITE

When I visit Seattle, I always make time for a bike ride along the **Burke-Gilman Trail** (see above). Full of walkers, joggers, skaters and bike commuters, this well-used corridor offers both urban and wooded stretches, highlighting why the Emerald City is one of the nation's top cycling cities.

waterfront. Just across Elliott Bay, West Seattle offers about four miles of public shoreline to walk around Duwamish Head and Alki Point.

SEATTLE NORTH   For a longer walk, the **Burke-Gilman Trail** (12 miles) extends from Gas Works Park in Seattle to Logboom Park in Kenmore and on to Redmond.

The **Shell Creek Nature Trail** (.5 mile), in Edmonds' Yost Park at 96th Avenue West and Bowdoin Way, is an easy walk along a stream. Contact Edmonds Parks and Recreation for a guide to the area. ~ Edmonds Parks Department: 700 Main Street; 425-771-0227.

SEATTLE WEST   Located southwest of Bremerton, **Gold Mountain Hike** (4 miles) is a moderate-to-strenuous climb with a 1200-foot elevation gain. You will survey the twisting waterways of Southern Puget Sound and Hood Canal from a 1761-foot point that also offers vistas from the Olympics to the Cascades and Edmonds to Olympia. The best access is from Holly Road at the trailhead called Wildcat.

SEATTLE EAST   Three foothills peaks nicknamed the "Issaquah Alps" (King County's Cougar Mountain Regional Wildland Park, Squak Mountain State Park and Tiger Mountain State Forest) south of Issaquah (about 15 miles east of Seattle) include miles and miles of trail and road open to hikers year-round. **Cougar Mountain Regional Wildland Park** (206-296-4145) is the best bet for visitors with resident deer, porcupines, bobcats, coyotes, black bears and four square miles of untouched land with trails. Call for trail maps. Another good resource is the **Issaquah Alps Trails Club** (www.issaquahalps.org), which publishes several hiking guidebooks and offers excursions, group hikes and general hiking information. One representative hike is the **West Tiger 3, 2, 1 Trail** (8–10 miles), which meanders to an elevation of 3000 feet at the summit of West Tiger 3 for stunning aerial views. Leave Route 90 at the High Point exit (the first exit east of Issaquah) and you will see the small parking lot where the trailhead is located.

SEATTLE SOUTH   The trail along **Big Soos Creek** (4.5 miles), now protected in two parks, is an inviting ramble on a blacktop path next to one of the few wetland streams still in public ownership hereabouts. The trail winds from Kent-Kangley Road to Gary Grant Park. In Kent, south of Seattle, follow signs off Route 516 (Kent-Kangley Road) at 150th Avenue Southeast.

TACOMA AND OLYMPIA   A wonderful river-delta walk, **Brown Farm Dike Trail** (5.5 miles), which starts on the Brown Farm Road, loops through the Nisqually National Wildlife Refuge. You may see bald eagles, coyotes, great blue heron, red-tail hawks and a variety of waterfowl such as wood, canvasback and greater scaup ducks, as well as mallards and pintails. Views stretch from Mt.

Rainier to the Olympics. You'll also see many of the islands in the south, Steilacoom and the Tacoma Narrows Bridge.

Transportation

CAR

Seattle lies along Puget Sound east of the Olympic Peninsula in the state of Washington. **Route 5** enters Seattle from Olympia and Tacoma to the south and from Everett from the north. **Route 90** from Eastern Washington goes near Snoqualmie and through Bellevue on its way into Seattle. **Route 405** serves the Eastside suburban communities of Bellevue, Kirkland and Redmond. **Route 169** leads from Route 405 southeast of Renton to Maple Valley, Black Diamond and Enumclaw.

AIR

About 20 miles south of downtown Seattle is **Seattle-Tacoma International Airport**, also called Sea-Tac, which is served by Aeroflot Russian Airlines, Air B.C., Alaska Airlines, America West Airlines, American Airlines, Asiana Airlines, ATA British Airways, Canadian Regional Airlines, Continental Airlines, Delta Air Lines, EVA Air, Frontier Airlines, Hawaiian Airlines, Horizon Air, JetBlue National Airlines, Northwest Airlines, Scandinavian Airlines, Shuttle by United, Southwest Airlines, Sun Country Airlines, TWA, United Airlines, US Airways and several smaller charter airlines. For general information, call 206-431-4444. There's a visitors information center on the baggage level of Sea-Tac International Airport (206-433-5218; www.portseattle.org/seatac).

FERRY

The **Washington State Ferry System** serves Seattle, Port Townsend, Tacoma, Southworth, Vashon Island, Bainbridge Island, Bremerton, Kingston, Edmonds, Mukilteo, Clinton, the San Juan Islands and Sidney, B.C. All are car ferries. ~ 206-464-6400; www.wsdot.wa.gov/ferries.

The **Victoria Clipper** passenger catamaran service operates daily trips (a two-and-a-half-hour trip) between Seattle and Victoria, B.C. ~ 206-448-5000, 800-888-2535; www.clippervacations.com.

BUS

Greyhound Bus Lines serves Seattle. The terminal is at 811 Stewart Street. ~ 800-231-2222; www.greyhound.com. **Gray Line of Seattle** provides inexpensive bus service from the airport to hotels and the downtown area. ~ 206-624-5077, 800-426-7532; www.graylineofseattle.com.

TRAIN

Rail service in and out of Seattle is provided by **Amtrak** on the "Empire Builder," "Coast Starlight" and "Amtrak Cascades." Call for more information on connections from around the country. ~ 800-872-7245; www.amtrak.com.

Most major car-rental businesses have offices at Seattle-Tacoma International Airport. Rental agencies include **Avis Rent A Car** (800-331-1212), **Budget Rent A Car** (800-527-0700), **Dollar Rent A Car** (800-800-4000), **Hertz Rent A Car** (800-654-3131) and **Thrifty Car Rental** (800-367-2277).

Bus transportation provided by **Metro Transit** is free in downtown Seattle. Metro Transit provides service throughout the Seattle-King County area. ~ 206-553-3000, 800-542-7876; www.transit. metrokc.gov.

Deemed transportation for the future, the **Monorail** was built for the 1962 World's Fair. It runs between downtown and the Seattle Center every ten minutes. ~ 206-905-2600; www.seattle monorail.com.

The downtown hub for both the monorail and the bus system is at Westlake Center, on Pine Street between 4th and 5th Avenues. The Monorail arrives on an elevated platform above the street-level mall, while buses load in an underground terminal. The buses are uniquely designed so they can switch from diesel to electric power when they enter the subterranean tunnels.

Waterfront Streetcar trolleys run from Seattle's historic Chinatown to Pier 70. ~ 206-553-3000; www.transit.metrokc.gov.

In the greater Seattle area are **Farwest Taxi** (206-622-1717), **North End Taxi** (206-363-3333) and **Yellow and Redtop Cab** (206-622-6500).

THREE

Northern Puget Sound and the San Juan Islands

"Every part of this land is sacred to my people. Every shining pine needle, every sandy shore, every mist in the dark woods, every clearing and humming insect is holy in the memory and experience of my people. . . . We are part of the earth and it is part of us. The perfumed flowers are our sisters; the deer, the horse, the great eagle, these are our brothers. The rocky crests, the juices in the meadows, the body heat of the pony, and man—all belong to the same family." This was part of Chief Seattle's poignant reply when, in 1854, the "Great White Chief" in Washington pressed to purchase some of the land around Puget Sound then occupied by several Northwest Indian tribes. And those sentiments still ring true today as the natural beauty and appeal of Northern Puget Sound and the San Juan Islands remain undiminished.

This awe-inspiring land supported the American Indians, providing for all their needs with verdant woods full of deer and berries and crystal waters full of salmon, letting them live in peaceful coexistence for hundreds of years. Even the weather was kind to them here in this "rain shadow," shielded by the Olympic and Vancouver mountain ranges.

Things slowly began to change for the Northwest Indian tribes and the land with the arrival of Juan de Fuca in 1592, who came to explore the coastline for the Spanish. The floodgates of exploration and exploitation weren't fully opened, however, until Captain George Vancouver came in 1792 to chart the region for the British, naming major landmarks such as Mt. Baker, Mt. Rainier, Whidbey Island and Puget Sound after his compatriots.

Establishment of trade with the American Indians and the seemingly inexhaustible quantity of animals to supply the lucrative fur trade drew many pioneers. Before long, industries such as logging, mining, shipping and fishing began to flourish, supporting the early settlers (and still supporting their descendants today).

Geologists who have studied the record say that a now long-disappeared continent moving eastward out of the Pacific Ocean eons ago collided with, or "docked" against, the Puget Sound mainland, laying the foundation for the multiplicity of land forms—islands, estuaries, mountains, coastlines—that characterize the northern Puget Sound region today.

The geographical layout of the 172 islands of the San Juan Archipelago made for watery back alleys and hidden coves perfect for piracy and smuggling, so the history of the area reflects an almost Barbary Coast–type of intrigue where a man could get a few drinks, a roll in the hay and be shanghaied all in one night. Chinese laborers were regularly brought in under cover of night to build up coastal cities and railroads in the 1800s. This big money "commodity" was replaced by opium and silk, and then booze during Prohibition.

Smuggling has since been curbed, and while things are changing as resources are diminished, logging and fishing are still major industries in the region. However, current booms in real estate and tourism are beginning to tilt the economic scale as more and more people discover the area's beauty.

The area referred to as Northern Puget Sound begins just beyond the far northern outskirts of Seattle, where most visitors first arrive, and extends northward up the coast to the Canadian border. Coastal communities such as Everett, Bellingham and Blaine tend to be more commercial in nature, heavily flavored by the logging and fishing industries, while other small towns such as La Conner and Mt. Vernon are still very pastoral, dependent on an agriculturally based economy. When heading east from Mt. Vernon, for every mile traveled toward the Cascade Mountains, the average annual rainfall increases by one inch. Consequently, springtime along this stretch of land is particularly lovely, especially in the Skagit Valley when the fields are ablaze in daffodils, iris and tulips. The world's biggest single grower of tulip bulbs—Washington Bulb Company—is based in the Skagit Valley.

Of the 172 named islands of the San Juans, we concentrate on the four most popular. These also are very pastoral, with rich soil and salubrious conditions perfectly suited to raising livestock or growing fruit. The major islands are connected to the mainland by bridges or reached by limited ferry service, an inhibiting factor that helps preserve the pristine nature here.

Although it's not considered part of the San Juans, serpentine Whidbey Island, with its thick southern tip reaching toward Seattle, is the largest island in Puget Sound. Situated at Whidbey's northern tip is Fidalgo Island, home of Anacortes and the ferry terminal gateway to the San Juans. Lopez is by far the friendliest and most rural of the islands, followed closely by San Juan, the largest and busiest. Shaw Island is one of the smaller islands, and lovely Orcas Island, named after Spanish explorer Don Juan Vincente de Guemes Pacheco y Padilla Orcasitees y Aguayo Conde de Revilla Gigedo (whew!) rather than orcas, is tallest, capped by 2400-foot Mt. Constitution.

The ferry system is severely overtaxed during the busy summer season when the San Juans are inundated with tourists, making it difficult to reach the islands at times and absolutely impossible to find accommodations if you haven't booked months in advance. The crowds drop off dramatically after Labor Day, a pleasant surprise since the weather in September and October is still lovely and the change of seasonal color against this beautiful backdrop is incredible.

▼▼▼▼▼▼▼▼▼▼▼▼▼▼▼▼
Northern Puget Sound

Stretched along the fertile coastline between the Canadian border and the outer reaches of Seattle, communities along Northern Puget Sound are dependent on agriculture, logging and fishing, so the distinct pastoral feel of the area is no surprise. Verdant parks and vista spots taking in the beauty of the many islands not far offshore head the list of sightseeing musts here. But islands and shorelines are just part of the scenic and geographic mix in this region, which also includes rivers and delta wetlands, forests and picturesque farmlands.

SIGHTS

As you drive north from Seattle along Route 5, you'll cross a series of major rivers issuing from the Cascade Mountains. In order, you'll pass the Snohomish River (at Everett), the Stillaguamish (not far from Stanwood), the Skagit (at Mt. Vernon/Burlington) and the Nooksack (Bellingham). The lower reaches of these streams offer wetlands and wildlife to see, fishing villages to poke around in, a vital agricultural heritage in the Skagit and Nooksack valleys, and small towns by the handful.

If you plan to catch the Mukilteo ferry to Clinton on Whidbey Island, be sure to allow enough time to visit the historic **Mukilteo Lighthouse** built in 1906. There are picnic tables above a small rocky beach cluttered with driftwood and a big grassy field for kite-flying adjacent to the lighthouse in little Mukilteo Lighthouse Park. A gift shop is located in the former assistant lighthouse-keeper's home. Open April through September, weekend and holiday afternoons only. ~ Mukilteo; 425-513-9602.

In Everett you'll find your best vantage point from the dock behind **Marina Village**, a sparkling complex of upscale shops, microbreweries and restaurants located in the second-largest marina on the West Coast. ~ 1728 West Marine View Drive, Everett.

In summer, a free boat ride will shuttle you from the 10th Street boat launch to picturesque **Jetty Island** for guided nature walks, birdwatching, campfires, a hands-on mudflat safari program to teach children about small marine animals and one of the only warm saltwater beaches on the Sound. For information, call 425-257-8300.

The **Firefighter's Museum** offers a storefront display of antique early-20th-century firefighting equipment. The collection is set up for 24-hour, through-the-window viewing. ~ 13th Street Dock, Everett.

The **Everett Area Chamber of Commerce** can provide you with more information. Closed Saturday and Sunday. ~ 2000 Hewitt Avenue, Suite 205, Everett; 425-257-3222, fax 425-257-2074; www.everettchamber.com, e-mail info@everettchamber.com.

On the hillside above the marina, ornate **mansions** of the lumber barons that once ruled the economy here line Grand and

Rucker streets from 16th Street north. None are open to tour, but a slow drive up and down these avenues will give you a feel for the history of the city.

Everett is the home of the **Boeing Company's** largest aircraft assembly plant—in fact, the largest building in the world by volume at 472 million cubic feet. As the largest aerospace business in the U.S., Boeing employs nearly 80,000 people in the Puget Sound area alone. Begin a visit at the **Future of Flight Aviation Center**, located at the western edge of Paine Field 30 miles north of Seattle. Hourly tours of the assembly plant are available (reservations recommended). The factory visit begins with a video of how airplanes are built, then leads past assembly lines for the 747, 767 and 777—and soon the 787—in various stages of assembly, manufacture and flight testing. Children must be four feet tall to take factory tours. Closed Thanksgiving, Christ-

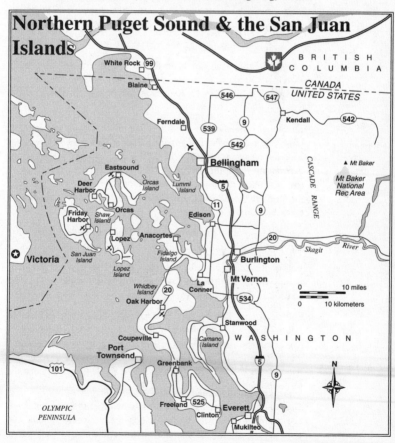

Northern Puget Sound & the San Juan Islands

Text continued on page 118.

Island-Hopping to the San Juans

The trip through the San Juan Islands is the longest and most beautiful cruise the Washington State Ferries network has to offer. It's not expensive, but in recent years, as both tourism and population in the Puget Sound area have grown enormously, the San Juan ferries have become so overburdened that even island residents have a hard time getting home during the summer months and on sunny weekends. If visiting during the off-season is out of the question, the best strategy is to arrive in Anacortes the afternoon before, sleep early and get in line for the ferry by dawn. The ferry schedule changes seasonally so obtain a current one at any ferry terminal or toll booth. Study the San Juan Island schedule carefully—it's complicated.

Day 1
- Leaving Seattle, head north on Route 5 to **Edmonds** (Exit 189), where a 30-minute ferry trip will take you to **Kingston** on the Olympic Peninsula (16 to 20 sailings daily from 5:50 a.m. to 11:45 p.m.).

- Drive eight miles north on Route 104 for a look at picturesque, New England–like **Port Gamble** (Chapter Two, page 77). Another 25 miles north via Routes 104, 19 and 20 brings you to **Port Townsend** (Chapter Four, page 168), a quaintly Victorian village on the northwest tip of the peninsula. Along the way, you might stop for lunch at the **Chimacum Café** (page 172), or you can catch a quick bite on the ferry.

- Take the ferry across to Keystone on **Whidbey Island** (page 130), a 30-minute trip (ten sailings daily from 6:30 a.m. to 8:30 p.m.).

- Follow Route 20 for 40 miles up the northern half of Whidbey Island, visiting **Coupeville** (page 131), yet another picture-perfect historic town, along the way.

- Before crossing **Deception Pass** from Whidbey Island to **Fidalgo Island** (page 137), be sure to walk out on the bridge for a magnificent seascape view. You've almost reached today's destination, so if you have time and feel like stretching your legs, the beaches and hiking trails of **Deception Pass State Park** (page 137) are the place to do it.

- Crossing the bridge, drive another six miles to the town of **Anacortes** (page 137); check into your lodging for the evening. Dine out, then go to bed early so you can catch the dawn ferry well rested.

Day 2
- Be at the Anacortes ferry dock no later than (yawn!) 5 a.m. to catch the first ferry of the day to **Orcas Island** (page 147). Otherwise you can expect to wait in line for *at least* three hours to get on another one. The trip to Orcas Island takes about one hour with intermediate stops at Lopez and Shaw islands; there are 10 to 12 sailings daily from 5:35 a.m. to 9:30 p.m. or later; vehicles for Orcas load 20 minutes before sailing.

- Have breakfast on the ferry or upon arrival on Orcas Island.

- Check into your accommodations and buy food for a picnic lunch.

- Head for **Moran State Park** (page 150), the largest and finest park in the Washington State Parks system. Take in the view from the top of Mount Constitution, the highest point in the San Juans. Then take your pick of many hiking possibilities.

- By mid-afternoon you may be ready for a nap.

- For dinner this evening, try a seafood feast at the **Restaurant at the Deer Harbor Inn** (page 149).

Day 3
- It's not quite as critical to catch the first ferry from Orcas to **San Juan Island** (page 142) because any of the ferries, which run from 7:20 a.m. to 9:45 p.m., is likely to unload as many vehicles at Orcas as are waiting to load. The trip to Friday Harbor takes about 30 minutes.

- Visit the **Whale Museum** (page 156).

- Take a driving tour around San Juan Island. On opposite sides of the island you'll find the sites of two historic forts of **San Juan Island National Historical Park** (page 142), where U.S. and British armies faced off in the anticlimactic "Pig War" over control of the San Juans. Several coastal beaches and parks along the way offer opportunities for picnicking and wildlife viewing. You may even see bald eagles or orca whales.

- As evening nears, catch a ferry back to Anacortes. The trip takes one to one and a half hours, depending on whether the ferry makes intermediate stops, and there are 10 or 12 sailings daily from 7:20 a.m. to 9:05 p.m.

- Back in Anacortes, you're less than an hour away from Seattle via Route 5.

mas and New Year's Day. Admission. ~ 8415 Paine Field Boulevard, Mukilteo; 425-438-8100, 888-467-4777, fax 425-265-9808; 360-756-0086 (factory tours), 800-464-1476; www.future offlight.org.

HIDDEN ►   Visitors to **Biringer Farm** can not only pick fresh strawberries and raspberries (in summer) and pumpkins (in fall), they can also participate in fun farm activities. Seasonal events include wandering a giant corn maze and visiting the "Not So Scary Boo Barn." Kids can ride the barrel-train and the whole family can take a tractor-drawn trolley to the fields. But the prime reason to visit remains the incomparable fresh berries. Watch carefully for direction signs off Route 529 north of downtown Everett. ~ 4625 40th Place, Everett; 425-259-0255; www.biringerfarm.com, e-mail farm-info@biringerfarm.com.

Mt. Vernon, situated on the broad banks of the Skagit River, has done little to capitalize on its superior riverside location. But it does claim the liveliest "main street" in the valley. The true main street is signed as 1st Street here; it is lined with a variety of vintage architecture in both brick and wood dating to the turn of the century. Preservation or recycling of old buildings is in full swing.

Each spring, the fields of the Skagit Valley are alive with color as the tulips and daffodils begin to appear. **The Skagit Valley Tulip Festival Office** provides a guide to the festival that runs the entire month of April; the guide lists events and includes a tour map of the fields, children's activities and display gardens. ~ 100 East Montgomery Street, Suite 250, Mt. Vernon; 360-428-5959, fax 360-428-6753; www.tulipfestival.org, e-mail info@tulipfestival.org.

There are interesting gardens to view year-round. The prettiest is **RoozenGaarde** with display gardens and a great little gift shop. ~ 15867 Beaver Marsh Road, Mt. Vernon; 360-424-8531, fax 360-424-4920; www.tulips.com, e-mail info@tulips.com.

West of Mount Vernon, across the channel from the Swinomish Indian Reservation, **La Conner** (see "Walking Tour" on page 120) is in the running for the title of quaintest little seaside town in the Puget Sound area.

Bay View, **Edison** and the town of **Bow**, a trio of country hamlets (located in the northern valley across Route 20), are treasures of the old way of life and are rarely discovered by the average tourist. Here, you'll see century-old farmhouses rising behind white picket fences, boatworks (some still active) that once turned out fishing boats, country taverns alive with the rustic merriment of farmers, loggers, truck drivers and dairymen. Here, too, are a smattering of art galleries, antique shops, country cafés and upscale eateries.

Located just north of Bay View, **Padilla Bay National Estuarine Research Reserve** is the place to find bald eagles, great blue herons and dozens of other species of waterfowl and raptors. The interpretive center offers exhibits on the region's natural and maritime history. The center is closed Monday and Tuesday. ~ 10441 Bay View–Edison Road, Mount Vernon; 360-428-1558, fax 360-428-1491; www.padillabay.gov, e-mail alex@padillabay.gov.

Early growth in **Bellingham** centered around the industries of mining and logging. To this day, the city retains an industrial nature with thriving ports that are home to a large fishing fleet and, more recently, the Alaska Marine Highway Ferry System terminal, tempered by a firm agricultural base. Perhaps it is because of this outward appearance that visitors are often amazed at the array of cultural arts and international dining experiences to be enjoyed here.

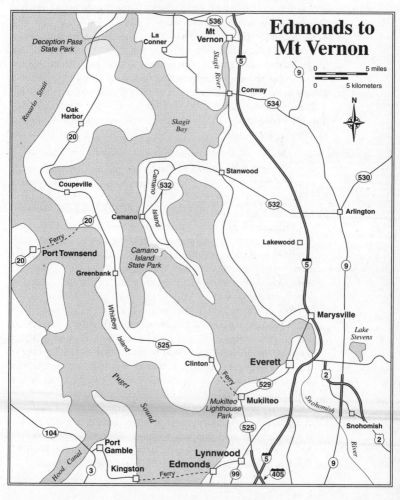

Edmonds to Mt Vernon

WALKING TOUR
La Conner

Built on pilings above the bank of Swinomish Channel, La Conner got its start in the 1880s as a market center for farmers in the Skagit Flats. Now a historic district, this small village of fewer than 800 people is easy to explore on foot and, with its many well-preserved homes and buildings, offers a glimpse of turn-of-the-20th-century life.

SKAGIT COUNTY HISTORICAL MUSEUM Park your car at the **La Conner Chamber of Commerce**. ~ 606 Morris Street; 360-466-4778, 888-642-9284, fax 360-466-0204; www.laconnerchamber.com. Walk a short distance up 4th Street to the top of the hill to visit the Skagit County Historical Museum, where you'll find a collection of farm and fishing equipment, vintage clothing, household furnishings, dolls and photographs. The museum also has a video theater and a section for temporary exhibits. Closed Monday. Admission. ~ 501 4th Street; 360-466-3365, fax 360-466-1611; www.skagitcounty.net/museum, e-mail museum@co.skagit.wa.us.

GACHES MANSION From the museum, head south along 4th Street, which turns a corner and becomes Calhoun Street. Follow Calhoun downhill toward the channel for two blocks to the Gaches Mansion. This grand

Bellingham has two noteworthy museums. The first is the **Whatcom Children's Museum**, which has several hands-on exhibitions to delight the kids (ages 2–10). Closed Monday. Admission. ~ 227 Prospect Street, Bellingham; 360-733-8769, fax 360-738-7409; www.whatcommuseum.org, e-mail museuminfo@cob.org.

Just down the street, the red-brick Victorian architecture of the **Whatcom Museum** is as interesting as the fine collections of contemporary American art, Northwest art and regional history featured inside. It's also a good point to start a walking tour of the many outdoor sculptures scattered around downtown. Closed Monday. Admission for special shows. ~ 121 Prospect Street, Bellingham; 360-676-6981, fax 360-738-7409; www.whatcommuseum.org, e-mail museuminfo@cob.org.

A Sculpture Walk route guide is available at the museum or from **Bellingham/Whatcom County Tourism**. ~ 904 Potter Street, Bellingham; 360-671-3990, 800-487-2032, fax 360-647-7873; www.bellingham.org, e-mail tourism@bellingham.org.

Victorian home was built in 1891 by a local merchant who wanted the finest house in town. The mansion houses the **La Conner Quilt Museum**, the Pacific Northwest's only quilt museum. Closed Monday and Tuesday, and the first two weeks of January. Open weekends only in December. Admission. ~ 703 South 2nd Street; phone/fax 360-466-4288; www.laconnerquilts.com, e-mail lacquiltm@aol.com.

MAGNUS ANDERSON CABIN   Stroll a block south of the Gaches Mansion to see the Magnus Anderson Cabin next to city hall. The oldest structure in Skagit County, the 1869 cabin was moved here from a solitary location on the north fork of the Skagit River to save it from decay. ~ 2nd and Douglas streets.

MUSEUM OF NORTHWEST ART   Walk one more block west to 1st Street, then proceed north. This time-capsule waterfront street has been gentrified with boutiques, galleries and restaurants yet still retains a palpable air of history. Two longish blocks up the street you'll find the Museum of Northwest Art, which exhibits the works of regional artists, presenting a cohesive look at the distinctive school of visual arts that has developed in the Pacific Northwest—an often surrealistic blend of Northwest Coast Indian and Asian motifs. Admission. ~ 121 South 1st Street; 360-466-4446, fax 360-466-7431; www.museumofnwart.org. Walking three blocks up Washington Street and five blocks south on 3rd Street will bring you back to the chamber of commerce and your car.

At the **Maritime Heritage Park** you can observe outdoor hatchery tanks, watch fish make their way up the ladder (recommended in October and November), learn about the life cycle of salmon, or just toss a line (with the proper license and only in October) into the abutting creek for steelhead or chinook salmon. ~ 1600 C Street, Bellingham; 360-676-6985.

No visit to Bellingham is complete without a trip to the **Big Rock Garden**, a serene Japanese garden with plantings, a patio and deck areas overlooking Lake Whatcom where visitors can sit and take it all in. ~ 2900 Sylvan Street, Bellingham; 360-676-6985, fax 360-647-6367; www.cob.org.

◄ HIDDEN

Don't miss the opportunity to stroll through the grounds of **Western Washington University** on the Western Sculpture Tour to enjoy the many fountains, sculptures and rich variety of architecture on this green campus. Brochures are available at the visitors information center on campus or at the Western Gallery. ~ McDonald Parkway, Bellingham; 360-650-3900; westerngallery.wwu.edu/sculpture.

Immediately adjacent to the campus is **Sehome Hill Arboretum**, 180 acres laced with six miles of hiking trails and fern-lined footpaths under a cool green canopy of moss covered trees; only the hum of traffic and the view from the observation tower remind you that you are in the city rather than some forest primeval. ~ 25th Street at Bill McDonald Parkway, Bellingham; 360-676-6985, fax 360-647-6367.

North of Bellingham in Ferndale, **Hovander Homestead Park** features a 19th-century farmhouse alive with cows, goats and even peacocks that is also a handsome Victorian residence (open April to October). Laced by the Nooksack River, the 720-acre park also includes **Tennant Lake**, where you'll find a boardwalk leading out over the swamp and marsh habitats that border the edge of the lake, and a fragrance garden with braille signs. There's also an interpretive center. Admission. ~ 5299 Nielsen Avenue, Ferndale; 360-384-3444.

To see the largest collection of original log homes in the state, stop by **Pioneer Park**. Each of the 12 buildings is a minimuseum. You'll see a post office, a stagecoach inn, a granary, a veteran's museum, a schoolhouse and a residence. Look for the little log church. Closed Monday and from October through April. ~ 2004 Cherry Street, Ferndale; 360-384-6461.

Another site in the Northern Puget Sound area worth taking in is **Peace Arch State Park**. The large white arch, flanked by American and Canadian flags, is surrounded by bountiful formal gardens with sculptures throughout and symbolizes the ongoing friendship between the two neighboring countries. The park is meticulously groomed, and spills across the international boundary. ~ Follow the signs to the park off Route 5, Exit 276, Blaine; 360-332-8221; www.peacearchpark.org, e-mail peacearch@parks.wa.gov.

SCENIC SKAGIT VALLEY

The Skagit Valley has become a year-round retreat for city visitors, as nourishing to the soul in winter as it is inspiring to the adventurous spirit in summer. Indeed, artists and writers have been gathering in the Skagit for decades, including members of the famed "Northwest School" beginning in the 1930s— Mark Tobey, Morris Graves, Kenneth Callahan, Clayton James, Guy Anderson and many others. They were drawn by the Skagit's enchanting blend of meandering river levees and farm fields, bayous and bays, nearby islands and distant misty mountains, along with the extraordinary quality of the valley's ever-changing light.

The Hotel Planter, originally built in 1907, is right in the thick
of things when it comes to shopping and dining in downtown La
Conner. The 12 rooms have skylights, light paint and carpeting,
floral chintz comforters and pine furnishings. There's also a jacuzzi under the gazebo on the garden terrace out back. ~ 715 1st
Street, La Conner; 360-466-4710, 800-488-5409, fax 360-466-
1320; www.hotelplanter.com, e-mail hotelplanter@aol.com.
MODERATE TO DELUXE.

Built in 1914, the **Benson Farmstead Bed and Breakfast** is a
four-room charmer in the heart of "the Skagit Valley" farms.
Some guests come for the big farm breakfasts and cozy rooms
full of country antiques, each with a private bath and queen bed.
Others come for the chance to stay on a working crop farm that's
been in operation for more than eight decades. Still others stay
for the proximity to some of the state's best country bicycling.
Or perhaps they seek the English garden and the garden of flowers filled with antique machinery. There is also the barn cottage,
which can sleep up to ten people. Closed in the winter except to
groups. ~ 10113 Avon-Allen Road, Bow; 360-757-0578, 800-441-
9814; www.bbhost.com/bensonbnb, e-mail bensonfarmstead@
hotmail.com. MODERATE.

As you might guess from the name, **Schnauzer Crossing** is ◄ HIDDEN
presided over by a delightful group of schnauzers. Choose from
a spacious garden suite with fireplace, garden sitting room,
jacuzzi tub and double shower, a smaller lakeview room done in
iris motif or a cottage perfect for families or couples seeking romantic seclusion. Well-thought-out amenities in each room include thick terry robes for the trip to the hot tub in the Japanese
garden. An outdoor aviary allows guests to view finches up close.
Gourmet breakfast included. Two-night minimum stay during
the weekend and holidays. ~ 4421 Lakeway Drive, Bellingham;
360-733-0055, 800-562-2808, fax 360-734-2808; www.schnau
zercrossing.com, e-mail schnauzerx@aol.com. ULTRA-DELUXE.

Housed in the old Blaine Air Force Base a few miles from the
Canadian border and Birch Bay State Park, the **Birch Bay Hostel**
provides 37 beds in bare shared or private rooms. From
November to April the hostel is open for groups only. ~ 7467
Gemini Street, Blaine; 360-371-2180; biz.birchbay.net/hostel.
BUDGET.

There is something for everyone at the sumptuous **Semiahmoo
Resort-Golf-Spa,** located on the tip of the sandy spit stretched
between Semiahmoo Bay and Drayton Harbor. History buffs will
enjoy browsing through the resort's collection of early photography, romantics will delight in a walk on the beach or a leisurely
sunset meal in one of the restaurants or lounges, and sports fanatics will flip over the array of activities, including tennis, golf at

two of the top-rated courses, and biking and hiking throughout an 1100-acre wildlife preserve. Treat yourself to a massage at the full-service European spa. The guest rooms are spacious and nicely appointed; some rooms have decks or patios, and others have woodburning fireplaces. ~ 9565 Semiahmoo Parkway, Blaine; 360-371-2000, 800-770-7992, fax 360-371-5490; www.semiahmoo.com, e-mail info@semiahmoo.com. ULTRA-DELUXE.

DINING

Anthony's Home Port is the spot for seafood when it comes to waterfront dining in Everett. Prime picks on the seasonal menu include Whidbey Island mussels, ginger-sesame steak, Dungeness crab cakes, roasted garlic prawns sprinkled with gremolatta and a variety of fresh oysters. Their four-course Sunset Dinner (served Monday through Friday from 4:30 to 6 p.m.) is a bargain and includes everything from appetizer to dessert. You can dine alfresco on the deck or pick a spot in the considerably less breezy dining room or lounge. ~ 1726 West Marine View Drive, Everett; 425-252-3333, fax 425-252-7847. MODERATE TO ULTRA-DELUXE.

Best bet for breakfast or lunch in La Conner is the **Calico Cupboard** at the south end of the main drag, where they serve hearty and wholesome baked goods, soups, salads, sandwiches and vegetarian fare as good for the heart as for the taste buds. Don't be surprised if there is a line to get into this modest café. No dinner. ~ 720 1st Street South, La Conner; 360-466-4451, fax 360-466-2181; www.calicocupboardcafe.com. BUDGET.

The **Farmhouse Restaurant**, a large eatery with country decor dominated by heavy oak tables and chairs, believes in serving solid, old-country-style portions of meat and potato classics—yankee pot roast, roast turkey with garlic mashed potatoes and gravy, New York steaks and baked potatoes— along with a hearty selection of daily baked goods like their famous pies thrown in for good measure. The lunch buffet and kids' menu are great bargains. Breakfast, lunch and dinner. ~ 13724 La Conner–Whitney Road, outside of Mt. Vernon; 360-466-4411, fax 360-466-4413; www.thefarmhouserestaurant.net. MODERATE.

Locals rave about the excellent dining at the light-filled **Pacific Cafe** in Bellingham, next to the Mt. Baker Theater. This attractive bistro has been serving up Asian- and European-inspired Northwest dishes since 1985, and has fans from as far away as Seattle. Among the most popular appetizers are seasonal fried oysters and Dungeness crab cakes with ginger apricot sauce, and fried calamari with aioli sauce. The wild-caught salmon here is justly famous, even in salmon-savvy Washington, as are the Gulf prawns in lemon passionfruit sauce. No dinner Sunday or Monday. ~ 100 North Commercial Street, Bellingham; 360-647-

0800; www.thepacificcafe.com, e-mail info@thepacificcafe.com. MODERATE TO DELUXE.

In addition to coffees and teas, **Harris Avenue Cafe**, serves up fresh daily soups, salads, sandwiches and pastries to an eclectic crowd of regulars. It's almost too bohemian, but the cocoa mocha makes it worth the trip. Breakfast and lunch only. ~ 1101 Harris Avenue, Bellingham; 360-738-0802. BUDGET.

The tables at **Café Toulouse** are always full, a testament to the quality breakfast, lunch and dessert selections served here.

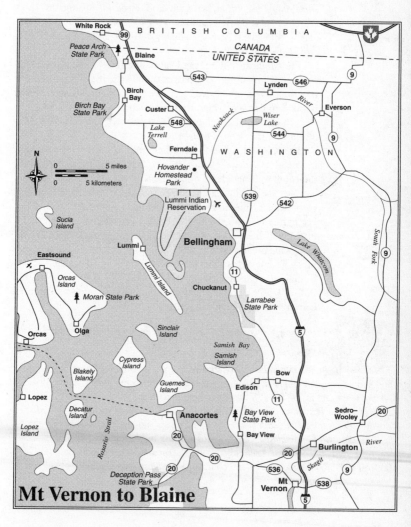

Mt Vernon to Blaine

Favorites include fresh fruit pancakes, curried chicken salad, roast pork with mint jelly or smoked turkey with cranberry-apple cream-cheese sandwiches. You will also find pizzas and calzones from their wood-fire stove, and many selections from the fresh daily dessert board accompanied by piping espresso or latte to finish the meal. ~ 114 West Magnolia Street, Crown Plaza Building, #102, Bellingham; 360-733-8996. BUDGET.

Dutch Mother's Restaurant is *the* place in Lynden for traditional (that's to say, hearty) Dutch cuisine such as pot roast, meatloaf, beef cutlet, sausage and pirogies. Waitresses sport Dutch dress and often can be overheard speaking Dutch with locals. ~ 405 Front Street, Lynden; 360-354-2174, fax 360-354-2987. MODERATE.

For Mexican dining, try **Chihuahua**. Decorated with Mexican murals, paintings and parrot sculptures, the dining room offers booth and table seating. There's also dining in an enclosed patio. Popular specialties are fajitas, *carne asada* and a wide variety of combination plates. ~ 5694 3rd Avenue, Ferndale; 360-384-5820, fax 360-384-0644. BUDGET TO MODERATE.

For romantic waterfront dining, it's hard to beat the Semiahmoo Resort's elegant dining room, **Stars**. Soft piano music fills the room as diners feast on mixed seafood plank roast (salmon, halibut, sea scallops, red potatoes and vegetables), Dungeness crabcakes, parmesan-crusted sea scallops and other rich entrées. For lighter fare, try the livelier, budget-priced **Packers Oyster Bar** just down the corridor for chilled garden gazpacho soup, a salmon sandwich, shrimp caesar salad or homestyle burgers. No lunch at Stars; closed Sunday and Monday in off-season. ~ 9565 Semiahmoo Parkway, Blaine; 360-371-2000, 800-770-7992, fax 360-371-5490; www.semiahmoo.com, e-mail info@semiahmoo.com. DELUXE TO ULTRA-DELUXE.

AUTHOR FAVORITE

At the **Boundary Bay Brewery**, bare woodplank floors and simple wooden tables and chairs create an unpretentious setting for "Northwest pub fusion food." What's that, you ask? In this case, it means eclectic offerings such as olive tapenade and yam-ale *chilades*. Wash it all down with a sampler of small glasses of all six beers and ales they make in plain sight on the premises. Watch a movie in the beer garden while enjoying your meal. ~ 1107 Railroad Avenue, Bellingham; 360-647-5593, fax 360-671-5897; www.bbaybrewery.com, e-mail bbaybrewery@bbay brewery.com. MODERATE.

Antique hounds will want to make the quick 15-minute trip east **SHOPPING** of Everett to Snohomish, home to **Star Center Antique Mall**, a five-level mall with over 200 dealers and dozens of other antique shops to browse through. ~ 829 2nd Street, Snohomish; 360-568-2131; www.myantiquemall.com, e-mail starmall@myantique mall.com.

In Everett, the **Everett Public Market** is the prime browsing spot for antiques as well as Northwest arts and crafts. The market also houses a natural foods co-op that offers organically grown fruits and vegetables. ~ 2804 Grand Avenue, Everett; 425-304-1000; www.everettpublicmarket.com.

Shopping is a major drawing card of little La Conner, with most of the boutiques and galleries concentrated along 1st and Morris streets. Focus on **Earthenworks** for fine art. ~ 713 1st Street, La Conner; 360-466-4422; www.earthenworksgallery.com. **The Scott Collection** also has a selection of fine art. ~ Pier 7 Building on 1st Street, La Conner; 360-466-3691; wwwscottcol lection.com. Stop by **Bunnies by the Bay** for collectibles and unique gifts. ~ 617 East Morris Street, La Conner; 360-293-8037; www.bunniesbythebay.com.

Rosabella's Garden Bakery is the perfect place to pick up unique vintage gifts as well as supplies for a picnic. The shop, located on a working farm and 50 acres of fruit orchards, sells apples, baked goods, wine and lunches. Their five-pound apple pies and homemade hard cider are not to be missed. Closed in winter. ~ 8933 Farm to Market Road, Bow; 360-766-6360, fax 360-766-6365; e-mail rmerritt@wavecable.com.

The best shops and galleries in Bellingham are generally located in the Fairhaven District.

Artwood is a co-op gallery of fine woodworking by Northwest artists. ~ 1000 Harris Avenue, Bellingham; 360-647-1628; www.artwoodgallery.com. Try **Inside Passage** for gifts made in Pacific Northwest. ~ 355 Harris Street, inside the Bellingham cruise terminal, Bellingham; 360-734-1790.

Dutch Village Mall is a collection of 12 shops specializing in imported Dutch lace, foodstuffs, wooden shoes and the like. The "mall" is built around a 150-foot-long canal to re-create a typical Dutch street scene. ~ 655 Front Street, Lynden; 360-354-4440.

Everett's **Club Broadway Big Apple** has both a large sports bar **NIGHTLIFE** and a danceclub. Cover. ~ 1611 Everett Avenue, Everett; 425-259-3551; www.clubbroadway.com. Things are jumping at **Anthony's Home Port**, with great happy-hour prices and a nice sheltered deck overlooking the marina. Outdoor seating is only available during the warm months. ~ 1725 West Marine View Drive, Everett; 425-252-3333; www.anthonys.com.

The **La Conner Pub and Eatery,** housed in a waterfront structure that was at one time Brewster's Cigar Store, is the primary watering hole in La Conner and does a booming business through the wee hours of the morning. There are always at least six microbrews on tap. ~ 702 1st Street, La Conner; 360-466-9932.

There are a half-dozen other country taverns scattered across the Skagit Valley, well known to locals but nearly unknown to tourists, which also serve up terrific burgers, microbrewery ales and bitters and weekend jazz and dancing. The **Conway Pub and Eatery** is best for burgers. ~ 18611 Main Street, Conway; 360-445-4733. The **Old Edison Inn** is also very popular. ~ 5829 Cains Court, Bow; 360-766-6266.

You'll find great happy-hour specials and the best sunset views in the little bar of **The Black Cat.** ~ 1200 Harris Avenue, Sycamore Square, Suite 310, Fairhaven; 360-733-6136.

HIDDEN ▶

BEACHES & PARKS

MUKILTEO LIGHTHOUSE PARK 🛥 🚤 ⏝ A swath of beach adjacent to the Whidbey Island–Mukilteo Ferry facilities on Puget Sound, Mukilteo Lighthouse Park is a day-use-only facility known primarily as a prime salmon-fishing spot with seasonal public boat launch (fee). Noble little Elliott Point Lighthouse, also known as Mukilteo Lighthouse, on the tip will keep shutterbugs happy; it's also a fine spot for beachcombing or picnicking while waiting for the ferry to Whidbey Island. There are restrooms, picnic grounds and seasonal floats. Boat launch parking fee. ~ Take the Mukilteo exit off Route 5 and follow the signs to the ferry; 425-355-4141, fax 425-347-4544.

BAY VIEW STATE PARK 🚶 🚲 ⏝ ⛵ ⚓ ⏝ 🐟 🦀 This tiny park on the north side of the town of Bay View overlooks the **Padilla Bay National Estuarine Research Reserve,** an ecological pocket with over 11,000 acres of marsh and tidelands tucked between the north Skagit Valley at Bay View and March Point. The Breazeale Padilla Bay Interpretive Center, half a mile north on Bay View–Edison Road, is a good place to get better acquainted with the many forms of wildlife that inhabit the area. A nature trail winds through parts of the wildlife habitat area just beyond the center. Restrooms, showers (fee), fireplaces, picnic tables and shelter, and a kitchen are some of the facilities here. Day-use fee, $5. ~ Exit 230 off Route 5 in Burlington, follow Route 20 west to Bayview–Edison Road. Turn right, then follow the signs to the park; 360-757-0227, fax 360-757-1967.

▲ There are 46 standard sites ($19 per night), 30 RV hookup sites ($25 to $27 per night) and 3 primitive sites ($10 per night). Reservations: 888-226-7688.

LARRABEE STATE PARK 🚶 🚲 🐴 ⏝ ⛵ 🛥 ⏝ This 2683-acre park on Samish Bay offers 14 miles of hiking trails, including two steep trails to small mountain lakes (Fragrance and Lost lakes), and a one-and-a-half-mile stretch of beach with numerous tidepools for views of the local marine life. There's good freshwater fishing for trout in either of the mountain lakes and crabbing (with a license), clamming and saltwater fishing in Chuckanut and Samish bays and newly acquired Clayton Beach. You'll find restrooms, showers, picnic tables and shelters, a playground, barbecue grills and kitchens. ~ On scenic Chuckanut Drive (Route 11), seven miles south of Bellingham; 360-676-2093, fax 360-676-2061.

▲ There are 51 standard sites ($16 per night), and 26 RV hookup sites ($22 per night) and 8 primitive sites ($10 per night). Reservations: 888-226-7688.

TEDDY BEAR COVE ⌇ This secluded, narrow stretch of white   ◄ HIDDEN
sand bordered by thick trees just south of the Bellingham city limits is a public beach that lacks facilities—and the water is very cold in case you're thinking of swimming. The beach area curves out around the shallow cove, like a thumb jutting out toward Chuckanut Bay. ~ There's a well-signed parking lot along Chuckanut Drive, Route 11, at the inter-section of California Street. The trail to the beach is marked with signs at the parking lot and mean-ders down a steep bank for 100 yards or so from the road; 360-733-2900, fax 360-676-1180.

> The Skagit Valley's farm-lands, estuaries and tide flats attract several species of hawks and is one of the best places in all of North America to go "hawkwatching."

BIRCH BAY STATE PARK 🚶 ⌇ ⌇ 🚻 ⌇ The highlight of this 192-acre park with 6000 feet of shoreline is the warm, shallow bay, which is suitable for wading up to half a mile out in some spots. The bay is bordered by a mile-long stretch of driftwood and shell-strewn beach edged by grassland. Swimming, clamming and crabbing are popular here. The camping area is inland in a stand of cedar and Douglas fir; nestled in the lush greenery it's hard to tell that the park sits in the shadow of BP's Cherry Point Refinery. Birdwatchers frequent the park to visit the marshy estuary at the south border that at-tracts over 100 varieties of birds. Facilities include restrooms, fire-places, picnic tables, shelters and trails; some facilities for the dis-abled. ~ Eight miles south of Blaine off Birch Bay; 360-371-2800, fax 360-371-0455.

▲ There are 147 standard sites ($16 per night), and 20 RV hookup sites ($22 per night) and 2 primitive hike- or bike-in sites ($10 per night). Reservations: 888-226-7688.

SEMIAHMOO PARK 🚲 ⌇ This long, slender spit dividing Semiahmoo Bay and Drayton Harbor is a favorite among beach lovers, who can stroll sandy, narrow beaches on both sides of the spit, and of birdwatchers who come here to observe bald eagles, loons, herons and others supported by this protected, nutrient-rich habitat. Kite flying is also ideal here. The spit has been an important site for native peoples of the United States and Canada. It was also the site of a fish cannery, the history of which is reviewed in the park's museum. Restrooms, picnic tables, and a bike path are found here. ~ Located near Blaine. Take the Birch Bay–Lynden Road exit west off Route 5, turn north onto Harbor View Road then west onto Lincoln Road, which becomes Semiahmoo Parkway and leads into the park; 360-733-2900, fax 360-676-1180.

▼▼▼▼▼▼▼▼▼ Whidbey Island

Whidbey Island, stretching north to south along the mainland, is the longest island in the continental United States aside from Long Island. This slender, serpentine bit of land is covered in a rolling patchwork of loganberry farms, pasturelands, sprawling state parks, hidden heritage sites and historic small towns. The artistic hamlet of Langley near Whidbey's southern tip is a current hotspot for weekend escapes from Seattle.

SIGHTS

Most of the sights in **Langley** are concentrated along 1st and 2nd streets, where falsefront shops house small galleries, boutiques and restaurants. There's a lovely stretch of public beach flanked by a concrete wall adorned in Northwest Indian motifs just below **Seawall Park** (look for the totem pole on 1st Street), and a wonderful bronze statue by local artist Georgia Gerber above a second stairwell leading down to the beach.

In the spring months, you'll find a colorful tulip display at **Holland Gardens.** During the balance of the year come to see the beautiful floral displays that make this small garden a local favorite. ~ Corner of Southeast 6th and Ely streets, Oak Harbor.

Beautiful greenery typifies Whidbey Island, and one Greenbank area establishment offers visitors a close look at cultivating the landscape. The famous **Meerkerk Rhododendron Gardens** feature hundreds of varieties of these showy bushes—with 2000 types spread across 53 acres—which find Whidbey's climate one of the

AUTHOR FAVORITE

sights

Spanning the "Grand Canyon of Puget Sound," **Deception Pass Bridge** links Whidbey with Fidalgo Island. Most visitors just drive slowly by, taking in the sights. But if you want a little more excitement, stroll out onto the bridge for vertigo-inducing views—straight down into the swift, churning currents of Deception Pass. You can also walk down to the shore on the footpaths of Pass Island to watch the streaming waters up close and personal.

best on earth. Magnolia, maple and cherry trees add to the beauty of this spot, which is also a test garden. April and May are the peak months for blooms, with daffodils providing additional color. The nursery has rhodies for sale on weekends from the end of March through May. Admission. ~ Just off Route 525 south of Greenbank; 360-678-1912; www.meerkerkgardens.org, e-mail meerkerk@ whidbey.net.

Only a few wine grapes ripen in Puget Sound's cool climate; **Whidbey Island Vineyard & Winery** specializes in clean, crisp vintages, such as Madeleine Angevine and Siegerrebe, that are rarely grown elsewhere. Closed Tuesday in summer, and Monday and Tuesday the rest of the year. ~ 5237 South Langley Road; 360-221-2040, fax 360-221-4941; www.whidbeyislandwinery.com, e-mail winery@whidbeyislandwinery.com.

Ebey's Landing National Historical Reserve, set aside as the first such reserve in the country in 1978, lies midway up Whidbey Island. The reserve protects 17,400 acres of beaches, uplands, woods and prairies; historic pioneer farms homesteaded under the Donation Land Law of 1850; Fort Ebey and Fort Casey state parks; Penn Cove, long used by the Skagit Indians from across Puget Sound; and the historic town of **Coupeville**, where falsefront buildings line Front Street above the wharf. Here you'll find Alexander Blockhouse (Alexander and Front streets) and Davis Blockhouse (Sunnyside Cemetery Road), built by early settlers for protection against possible Indian attacks, and a good collection of pioneer agricultural artifacts and historical displays in the **Island County Historical Museum** (908 Northwest Alexander Street, Coupeville; 360-678-3310). Reduced hours in winter. Admission. ~ Ebey's Landing National Historical Reserve, P.O. Box 774, Coupeville, WA 98239; 360-678-6084; www. nps.gov/ebla.

Built in 1903, **Admiralty Head Lighthouse** at Fort Casey State Park features an interpretive center offering history on the region's military past. You'll also enjoy excellent views of Admiralty Inlet and the Olympic Mountains. Hours vary; call ahead. ~ 1280 Engle Road, Coupeville; 360-240-5584; www.ad miraltyhead.wsu.edu, e-mail gloria@wsu.edu.

LODGING

There are some 11 hotels on the island, all motel-style and clustered around Oak Harbor. But the big draw on Whidbey has always been bed-and-breakfast inns, over 80 of them at last count. Your choices run the gamut from log cabins in the forest to beach cabins and posh retreats. For a comprehensive list, contact the **South Whidbey Visitor Information and Lodging Referral Service**. Closed Sunday in winter. ~ P.O. Box 403, 208 Anthes Avenue, Langley, WA 98260; 360-221-6765, fax 360-221-6468; www.visitlangley.com, e-mail langley@whidbey.com.

HIDDEN ►   The beautiful **Inn at Langley** has perfected the fine art of hospitality at a polished property worthy of its magnificent waterfront setting. With a decorator's color palette taken directly from the beach, guest rooms in zen-like shades of gray, cream, tan and brown accented by lots of natural wood are elegant, presenting a delicate balance of modern art and furnishings, and are decked out with every possible amenity (fireplace, jacuzzi, Krups coffee set, wi-fi and large deck to take advantage of the 180° view). A serene oriental garden set in front of the grand dining room is an added touch. If you can afford the tariff, this is the most luxurious selection available on the island. Buffet breakfast. ~ 400 1st Street, Langley; 360-221-3033, fax 360-221-3033; www.innat langley.com, e-mail info@innatlangley.com. ULTRA-DELUXE.

Cliff House is an architecturally stunning two-story structure of wood and sweeping panes of glass set on a wooded bluff overlooking Puget Sound. Guests have the run of the two-bedroom house, with its open central atrium, wonderful gourmet kitchen, sunken sitting area with fireplace and wraparound cedar deck with large jacuzzi. A stairway leads down to miles of empty beach. There is also a separate small cottage with one bedroom. ~ 727 Windmill Drive, Freeland; 360-331-1566, 800-297-4118; www.cliffhouse.net, e-mail wink@whidbey.com. ULTRA-DELUXE.

The **Captain Whidbey Inn**, a well-preserved and maintained log inn on Penn Cove, is a fine example of the type of Northwest retreat all the rage years ago and now coming back into fashion. This walk into the past offers several cozy, antique furnished rooms that share two baths and waterfront views; two rows of spacious, pine-paneled rooms with baths and a few private cottages with fireplaces. This is one of only a handful of waterside accommodations in the region. ~ 2072 West Captain Whidbey Inn Road, Coupeville; 360-678-4097, 800-366-4097, fax 360-678-4110; www.captainwhidbey.com, e-mail captain@whidbey.net. MODERATE TO ULTRA-DELUXE.

The **Auld Holland Inn** is a reasonably priced roadside motel with flair, from the flowering window boxes on the European exterior to the immaculately clean, antique-filled rooms. Some rooms have fireplaces and princess canopied beds. For those seeking budget prices, there are 24 mobile home units with two or three bedrooms tucked behind the full-sized windmill housing the motel's office. If you're looking for more luxury, there are six deluxe-priced units furnished with jacuzzis and fireplaces. Continental breakfast. ~ 33575 Route 20, Oak Harbor; 360-675-2288, 800-228-0148, fax 360-675-2817; www.auldhollandinn.com, e-mail dutchvillage@oakharbor.net. MODERATE TO DELUXE.

DINING   Since 1989, **Cafe Langley** has served Mediterranean favorites such as spanikopita, moussaka, dolmas and lamb shish kabobs along

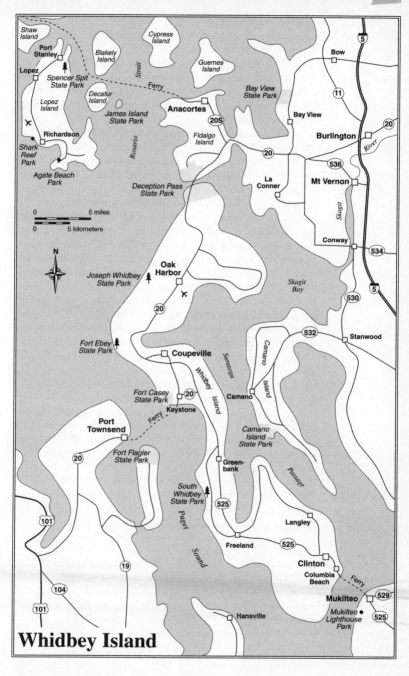

Shaw
Island
Port
Stanley
Lopez
Blakely
Island
Cypress
Island
Guemes
Island
Bow
Spencer Spit
State Park
Decatur
Island
Ferry
Bay View
State Park
Lopez
Island
James Island
State Park
Anacortes
Bay View
Burlington
Richardson
Strait
Rosario
Fidalgo
Island
20S
20
Shark
Reef
Park
River
Agate Beach
Park
Deception Pass
State Park
La
Conner
Mt Vernon
536
0   5 miles
0   5 kilometers
Skagit
Conway
534
N
Oak
Harbor
Joseph Whidbey
State Park
Skagit
Bay
530
20
532
Fort Ebey
State Park
Coupeville
Stanwood
Saratoga
Camano
Island
Fort Casey
State Park
20
Keystone
Ferry
Camano
Whidbey
Island
Port
Townsend
Camano
Island
State Park
Fort Flagler
State Park
20
Green-
bank
Passage
South
Whidbey
State Park
Puget
525
101
Langley
19
Freeland
525
Sound
Clinton
Columbia
Beach
104
Ferry
529
101
Hansville
Mukilteo
Mukilteo
Lighthouse
Park
525

Whidbey Island

with fresh seafood (Penn Cove mussels, grilled salmon and hali-but), pastas and steaks. The atmosphere here is airy Mediterran-ean, with stucco-like walls, exposed beams and an assortment of exotic fish etched on a glass partition. There are often people waiting in the park across the street for a table in this popular café. Closed Tuesday during winter. ~ 113 1st Street, Langley; 360-221-3090, fax 360-221-8542; www.langley-wa.com/cl. MODERATE TO DELUXE.

The **Doghouse Tavern** is the place to go for burgers, fish-and-chips and chowder. A totem on the side of this waterfront build-ing points the way to their separate family dining room in case you've got the kids along. ~ 230 1st Street, Langley; 360-221-4595. BUDGET TO MODERATE.

Seafood lovers flock to the **Fish Bowl Restaurant**, which has become known as one of Whidbey Island's finest seafood restau-rants. Chef David Bagley's menu offers a choice between small bites and full entrées, including a bouillabaisse of fish and shell-fish simmered in lobster stock; pan-seared scallops on linguine with a hazelnut cream; crab cakes with asparagus risotto; and halibut with a mushroom-and-walnut caramel sauce. The at-mosphere is elegant yet casual, with an outdoor patio. Dinner only. Closed Monday from October to May. ~ 317 2nd Street, Langley; 360-221-6511, fax 360-221-6424; www.fishbowlrestau rant.com, e-mail fishbowl@whidbey.com. DELUXE.

Christopher's Front Street Cafe specializes in "creative con-temporary cuisine" with a menu that changes seasonally. The emphasis is on fresh, local fare, especially seafood, and runs the gamut from superb Penn Cove mussels, to beef and chicken, veg-etarian dishes, and pasta; regional wines and microbrews are also available. Closed Sunday from Labor Day to Memorial Day. ~ 103 Northwest Coveland Street, Coupeville; 360-678-5480; www.christophersonwhidbey.com, e-mail info@christopherson whidbey.com. BUDGET TO DELUXE.

SHOPPING   There's plenty to keep shoppers and browsers busy on Whidbey Island, especially in artsy Langley and historic Coupeville. The

AUTHOR FAVORITE

Toby's Tavern serves up a cheeseburger that was rated tops by actress Kathleen Turner, who starred in the film *War of the Roses*, which was filmed partly in and around Coupeville in 1989. Good fish-and-chips, Penn Cove steamed mussels and an upscale atmosphere add a touch of class to this waterfront watering hole. ~ 8 Northwest Front Street, Coupeville; 360-678-4222; www.tobysuds.com. MODERATE.

best art galleries are concentrated in Langley. **Museo** specializes in art glass made by local Whidbey Island artists. ~ 215 1st Street, Langley; 360-221-7737; www.museo.cc. The **Gaskill/Olson Gallery** showcases bronzes, paintings, sculpture and pottery. ~ 302 1st Street, Langley; 360-221-2978; www.gaskillolson.com. **Soleil** carries double-sided aluminum-alloy pieces by Arthur Court, silver, bone, pewter and glass jewelry, candles, stationery, photo albums and soaps. ~ 308 1st Street, Langley; 360-221-0383. The **Hellebore Glass Gallery** has fine handblown glass created on the premises. ~ 308 1st Street, Langley; 360-221-2067.

Another noteworthy shop in town is **The Star Store**, a modern mercantile selling fun clothing and housewares. ~ 201 1st Street, Langley; 360-221-5222; www.starstorewhidbey.com. You can also browse the two shops of **Whidbey Island Antiques**. ~ 2nd Street and Anthes Avenue, Langley; 360-221-2393; www.whidbeyislandantiques.com.

There's an array of charming shops in the revitalized waterfront district of Coupeville. In addition to numerous private art galleries and studios, you'll want to drop by the **Penn Cove Gallery**, a cooperative where contemporary paintings, sculpture, watercolors, photography, jewelry, ceramics, glass and wood work will be shown to you by the artists who created the work. ~ 9 Northwest Front Street, Coupeville; 360-678-1176; www.penncovegallery.com, e-mail info@penncovegallery.com.

If it's sunny out and a picnic is in order, stock up at **Bayleaf** for imported cheeses, cold cuts, olives, wines and rustic, fresh-baked bread. Closed Monday and Tuesday. ~ 101 Coveland Street, Coupeville; 360-678-6603; www.bayleaf.us.

Hong Kong Gardens has a pool table and karaoke every Friday and Saturday night. The occasional band plays on Saturday nights. ~ 9324 State Route 525, Clinton; 360-341-2828.   **NIGHTLIFE**

Or drop by **Toby's Tavern**, where they filmed the bar scene from the movie *War of the Roses*. ~ 8 Northwest Front Street, Coupeville; 360-678-4222; www.tobysuds.com.

SOUTH WHIDBEY STATE PARK There are 347 acres with 4500 feet of rocky shoreline to explore in this lovely state park. Hikers here will enjoy the one-and-a-quarter-mile loop trail through an old-growth stand of fir and cedar. Anglers seek silver salmon, and climbing is popular. Black-tailed deer, herons and osprey are among the many creatures here. Only the hardy will venture into the cold waters of Admiralty Inlet for a dip. There are restrooms, showers, picnic tables, shelter and firepits. Day-use fee, $5. ~ Take Route 525 nine miles north of Clinton to Bush Point Road, which after six miles becomes Smuggler's Cove Road; 360-902-8844, fax 360-331-5202.   **BEACHES & PARKS**

▲ There are 46 standard sites ($19 per night) and 8 RV hookup sites ($25 per night). Closed December and January. Reservations: 888-226-7688.

FORT CASEY STATE PARK 🏃 🛶 🛶 🚤 🛥 🚤 🛤 History buffs and children will enjoy exploring the military fortification of this 137-acre park. While most of the big guns are gone, you'll still find panoramic views of the Olympic Mountains across the Strait of Juan de Fuca from the top of the concrete bunkers built into the escarpment. Wild roses and other flowers line the paths to the museum housed in pretty Admiralty Head Lighthouse and the beachside campground that overlooks the Keystone Harbor ferry terminal. Scuba enthusiasts swarm to the underwater trail through the park's marine wildlife sanctuary off Keystone Harbor, and anglers try for salmon and steelhead. Facilities include restrooms, showers, picnic tables, fireplaces and an underwater marine park. ~ At Coupeville turn south off Route 20 onto Engle Road and follow the Keystone Ferry signs to the park; 360-678-4519, fax 360-428-1094.

▲ There are 35 standard sites ($18 per night) and 3 primitive sites ($10 per night). Reservations: 888-226-7688.

FORT EBEY STATE PARK 🏃 🚲 🏃 🛶 🛤 The massive guns are long gone from this coastal World War II fortification, but there are still bunker tunnels and pillboxes to be explored. The picturesque beach at Partridge Point is the hands-down favorite of the islanders; at low tide it's possible to walk the five-mile beach stretch to Fort Casey. Anglers cast a rod for bass on Lake Pondilla. There are restrooms, showers, picnic tables, fireplaces and nature trails. ~ From Route 20 turn west onto Libbey Road, then south onto Hill Valley Drive and follow the signs; 360-678-4636, fax 360-678-5136.

▲ There are 38 standard sites ($19 to $22 per night), 11 RV hookup sites ($22 to $25 per night) and 3 primitive sites ($14 per night). The secluded campsites under a canopy of Douglas fir are much nicer than the crowded sites at nearby Fort Casey. Reservations: 888-226-7688.

OAK HARBOR WINDJAMMER PARK 🏃 🚲 🏊 ⛵ 🛶 🚤 🚤 🛤 A full-scale windmill and an A-6 Prowler, first used in Vietnam and donated by the Navy, are just two of the features of this day-use park on Oak Harbor Bay next to the sewage processing plant (not a deterrent, believe it or not). A sandy beach slopes down from the lighted walking path bordering expansive green fields suitable for flying kites or playing frisbee. Anglers will find salmon, bottomfish and bass. There are two wading pools in summer and a protected swimming area. There are bathhouses, picnic tables, ball fields, tennis and volleyball courts and a playground. ~ Located in downtown Oak Harbor off Pioneer Parkway, east of Route 20; watch for the windmill; 360-679-5551, fax 360-679-3902.

▲ An RV park with 56 full hookups and hot showers can be accessed at Beeksma Drive or City Beach Street ($20 per night). An overflow area has campsites with no hookups.

DECEPTION PASS STATE PARK 🏃 🚴 🚣 🛥 🚢 🚢 🚢
🛏 The most popular state park in Washington, it encompasses over 4100 acres laced with 35 miles of hiking trails through forested hills and wetland areas and along rocky headlands. There are several delightful sandy stretches for picnics or beach-combing. Breathtaking views from the 976-foot steel bridge spanning the pass attract photographers from around the world. There's swimming in Cranberry Lake in the summer and flyfishing for trout on Pass Lake. Facilities include restrooms, showers, bathhouses, picnic tables, kitchens, shelters, fireplaces, a concession stand, a retreat center and an underwater park. ~ Take the Mukilteo ferry to Whidbey Island and follow Route 525 and Route 20, or take Route 5 to Exit 230 and follow Route 20 West to the park on the northern tip of the island; 360-675-2417, fax 360-675-8991; www.deceptionpassfoundation.org, e-mail deception.pass@parks.wa.gov.

In Deception Pass State Park, you'll find beaver dams and muskrats at Cranberry Lake's south shore.

▲ There are 163 standard sites ($16 per night), 14 RV hookup sites ($22 per night) and 5 primitive sites ($10 per night). Reservations: 888-226-7688.

A two-hour drive northwest of Seattle, Anacortes on Fidalgo Island is a good place to enjoy folk art, ride a charming excursion train and see impressive murals. Quiet inns and waterfront restaurants make this town a pleasant retreat.

Fidalgo Island

But Anacortes is only the beginning of adventures on this charming island. Often called the first of the San Juans, Fidalgo is actually linked to the mainland by the Route 20 bridge over Swinomish Channel in the Skagit Valley, and to Whidbey Island by another bridge. Access is easy. Nevertheless, you can still find quiet beaches and parks to explore. Lonely trails wind through an enormous forest reserve to superb viewpoints. A mini "Lake District" clusters more than half a dozen splendid lakes. And a marvelous resort complex—Scimitar Ridge Ranch—combines a working Northwest horse ranch and a deluxe campground that includes covered wagons outfitted for camping.

Because of its ferry terminal, **Anacortes** is known as "the gateway to the San Juans," but don't just zip on through because there's plenty to see and do here. One of the best ways to get acquainted with the city and its history is to take a walking tour of downtown

SIGHTS

to view over 100 life-size murals attached to many of the historical buildings. As part of the **Anacortes Mural Project,** these murals are reproductions of early-20th-century photographs depicting everyday scenes and early pioneers of the town. A tour map of the murals is available from the **Anacortes Chamber of Commerce.** ~ 819 Commercial Avenue, Anacortes; 360-293-3832, fax 360-293-1595; www.anacortes.org, e-mail info@anacortes.org.

In the late 1800s, the bustling city of Anacortes was also referred to as the "Magic City," "Liverpool of the West" and "New York of the West."

Another reminder of earlier days is the **W. T. Preston,** a drydocked sternwheeler that once plied the waters of the Sound breaking up log jams. Closed weekdays in April, May and September, and from October through March. Admission. ~ 7th Street and R Avenue, Anacortes; 360-293-1916; www.anacorteshistorymuseum.org, e-mail coa.museum@cityofanacortes.org.

At the **Anacortes Museum,** you'll find an entertaining collection of memorabilia from Anacortes, Fidalgo and Guemes islands, as well as exhibits detailing the history of the islands. In front of the museum there's a highly amusing (but non-functional) drinking fountain with varying levels suited for dogs, cats, horses and humans, which was donated to the city by the Women's Temperance Union. Closed Tuesday and Wednesday. ~ 1305 8th Street, Anacortes; 360-293-1915, fax 360-293-1929; http://museum.cityofanacortes.org.

LODGING

At the **Holiday Motel,** one of the only motels that keeps its prices low even during high season, you get what you pay for. Aging rooms are very basic but tidy, with nicked furnishings in both the cramped bedroom and separate sitting room. ~ 2903 Commercial Avenue, Anacortes; 360-293-6511. BUDGET.

The **Anaco Bay Inn** is a step up, with 18 spacious, well-appointed rooms, all featuring a cozy fireplace. Some rooms have kitchens while others offer jetted tubs—the Honeymoon Suite, of course, has both. Rooms without kitchens have microwaves and mini-fridges. Four two-bedroom suites are also available. A public jacuzzi, a library and laundry facilities round out the amenities. An expanded continental breakfast is included. ~ 916 33rd Street, Anacortes; 360-299-3320, 877-299-3320; www.anacobayinn.com, e-mail anacobay@fidalgo.net. MODERATE.

The **Ship House Inn** is an attractive high-waterfront property facing the San Juan Islands. Handcrafted by the owner in knotty cedar, accommodations are in three pleasant cabins, with nautical bunk-style beds, fridges, microwaves, TVs and private decks. Continental breakfast included. Closed November to mid-April. ~ 12876 Marine Drive, Anacortes; 360-293-1093; www.ship

houseinn.com, e-mail info@shiphouseinn.com. MODERATE TO
DELUXE.

The **Deception Cafe & Grill** serves traditional hand-breaded oys-   **DINING**
ters and prawns, grilled burgers and mouth-watering, homemade
desserts. Look for this unpretentious roadside establishment on
the hill four miles north of Deception Pass. Breakfast, lunch and
dinner. ~ 5596 Route 20, Anacortes; 360-293-9250. MODERATE.

Potted plants, taped light jazz and tablecloths soften the rough
edges of **Charlie's**, a hash house overlooking the ferry terminal and
water. Captive diners, here during the long wait for the ferry, choose
from soups, salads, sandwiches and seafood at lunch and pasta,
steak and seafood for dinner. ~ 5407 Ferry Terminal Road, Anacortes; 360-293-7377; www.charliesrestaurant.com. MODERATE TO
DELUXE.

Most of the great shops on Fidalgo Island are scattered along   **SHOPPING**
Anacortes' Commercial Avenue. **Left Bank Antiques**, housed in
two floors of a renovated barn, absolutely bulges with American   ◀ *HIDDEN*
and European antiques and architectural items. ~ 1904 Commercial Avenue, Anacortes; 360-293-3022, fax 360-299-8888; www.
leftbankantiques.com.

The historic **Marine Supply and Hardware** is packed to the
rafters with nautical antiques and memorabilia. Closed Sunday. ~
202 Commercial Avenue, Anacortes; 360-293-3014; www.ma
rinesupplyandhardware.com.

Resist the temptation to buy smoked salmon to take home until you visit **SeaBear Smokehouse**, which has been producing authentic smoked salmons since 1957. Not only does the smokehouse sell smoked salmon, smokehouse chili and smoked salmon
chowder, it also offers tours Monday through Friday. Pose with a
salmon, learn to fillet, or just taste the goods. ~ 605 30th Street,
Anacortes. Take 22nd Street east toward the Anacortes Marina,
turn right onto T Avenue and you'll find the warehouse in an industrial complex a block down on the right; 360-293-4661, 800-
645-3474; www.seabear.com.

Life on pastoral Lopez Island is slow and amiable; resi-   ▼▼▼▼▼▼▼▼▼▼
dents wave to everyone and are truly disappointed if you   **Lopez Island**
don't wave back. Lopez didn't earn its nickname as the
"Friendly Island" for nothing. Even better, it remains much less
developed than San Juan and Orcas islands.

The history of the island is well mapped out at the **Lopez Island**   **SIGHTS**
Historical Museum with its exhibit of pioneer farming and fishing
implements, stone, bone and antler artifacts and fairly large maritime collection. While you're here, pick up a historical landmark

tour guide to the many fine examples of Early American architecture scattered around the island. Closed Monday and Tuesday, and October through April. ~ 28 Washburn Place, Lopez Village; 360-468-2049; www.rockisland.com, e-mail lopezmuseum@rockis land.com.

Stroll out to **Agate Beach Park** on MacKaye Harbor Road to watch the sunset. Another good sunset view spot is **Shark Reef Park** on Shark Reef Road, where you might see some harbor seals, heron and, if you're lucky, a whale or two.

Shaw Island is one of only four of the San Juan Islands that can be reached by ferry, but most visitors to the San Juans miss it. You need to stay on the ferry from Anacortes and get off at Shaw, one stop beyond Lopez Island. Those who do make the trip are in for a treat. Stop by the general store near the ferry landing for picnic supplies before heading out to **South Beach County Park** on Squaw Bay Road, two miles to the south.

Afterward, continue east along Squaw Bay Road, turn north on Hoffman Cove Road and make your way to the picturesque little red schoolhouse. Park by the school and cross the street to see the **Shaw Island Library and Historical Society**, a tiny log cabin housing a hodgepodge of pioneer memorabilia. Open limited hours on Tuesday, Thursday and Saturday. ~ Schoolhouse Corner; 360-468-4068.

LODGING   The **Lopez Islander Bay Resort**, once a dog-eared motel, has turned upscale. All of the 26 rooms and two suites have been refurbished. All rooms have decks overlooking Fisherman's Bay, perfect for a view of the sunset. Rental houses on the bay are also available. The marina has been upgraded (new floats and piers, a seaplane dock). An ambitious outings program for guests includes opportunities to bike, kayak and fish. Laundry and fitness facilities are included. ~ 2864 Fisherman Bay Road, Lopez Village; 360-468-2233, 800-736-2864, fax 360-468-3382; www.lopezislander.com, e-mail li@rockisland.com. MODERATE TO DELUXE.

Edenwild, a welcome addition to the scant list of lodgings on the island, is a two-story Victorian. The eight guest rooms are pretty, with carpeted floors and clawfoot tubs; three rooms have romantic fireplaces, one is handicapped accessible and four have views of Fisherman's Bay or San Juan Channel. Included in the room rates is breakfast, served in the sunny dining nook or on the delightful garden terrace. Apéritifs and truffles are served in the rooms. ~ Lopez Village; 360-468-3238, 800-606-0662, fax 360-468-4080; www.edenwildinn.com, e-mail edenwild@rockisland.com. ULTRA-DELUXE.

The **Lopez Lodge** in the village has two no-frills, motel-like rooms that share a bath. One studio has a private bath and full kitchen. ~ 35 Weeks Point Road, Lopez Village; 360-468-2816; www.lopezlodge.com. BUDGET TO DELUXE.

The **Bay Cafe** has an imaginative menu featuring fresh Northwest products. There are always daily specials to choose from, and regular entrées may include duck confit, handmade vegetable ravioli and filet of beef tenderloin. Check out the surprising garlic cheesecake. Reservations are essential, especially during summer. Closed Monday and Tuesday in the winter. ~ Lopez Village Road, Lopez Village; 360-468-3700, fax 360-468-4000; www.bay-cafe.com, e-mail thebaycafe@aol.com. DELUXE TO ULTRA-DELUXE.

DINING

Both the general store and ferry landing on Shaw Island are operated by Franciscan nuns.

Set off to one side within the **Lopez Island Pharmacy** is an old-fashioned, red, white and black soda fountain, the best spot for lunch on Lopez. Grab a booth or a stool at the bar and order a sandwich, bowl of soup or slice of pie to go with your phosphate, malt, float or other fountain treat. No dinner. Closed Sunday. ~ 157 Lopez Village Road, Lopez Village; 360-468-4511, fax 360-468-3825; www.lopezislandpharmacy. com, e-mail biz@lopezislandpharmacy.com. BUDGET.

The **Lopez Islander Restaurant** is a true waterfront restaurant, looking west across Fisherman Bay to spectacular evening sunsets. In summer, ask for a table on the outdoor dining patio. Specialties of the house include an award-winning clam chowder and a daily fresh sheet of local seafood—salmon and halibut, for example. The resort's tiki bar stays open later with a limited menu. ~ Fisherman Bay Road, Lopez Village; 360-468-2233, fax 360-468-3382; www.lopezislander.com. MODERATE TO DELUXE.

For the most part, shopping here is limited to establishments in Lopez Village. **Archipelago** sells cotton T-shirts and women's casual apparel. Limited hours during the off-season. ~ 360-468-3222. **Islehaven Books and Borzoi** stocks an admirable selection of new books and regional music. ~ 360-468-2132. For fine art, visit **Chimera Gallery**, the cooperative showcase for prints, paintings, weaving, pottery, handblown glass and jewelry produced by local artists. Closed Monday through Thursday. ~ 360-468-3265.

SHOPPING

SPENCER SPIT STATE PARK 🚶 🚲 ⚓ 🐟 🦪 ⛵ This long stretch of silky sand on Lopez Island encloses an intriguing saltwater lagoon. The mile-long beach invites clamming, crabbing, shrimping, bottom fishing, wading and swimming during warm summer months. Facilities include restrooms, beach firepits and picnic shelters. Day use fee, $5. ~ Take the ferry from Anacortes to Lopez Island, then follow the five-mile route to the park on the eastern shore of the island; 360-902-8844.

BEACHES & PARKS

▲ There are 37 standard sites ($19 per night) and 7 primitive sites ($14 per night). Closed November through February. Reservations: 888-226-7688.

San Juan Island

San Juan Island, the namesake of the archipelago, is a popular resort destination centered around the town of Friday Harbor. This 20-mile-long island has a colorful past stemming from a boundary dispute between the United States and Great Britain. The tension over who was entitled to the islands was embodied in American and British farmers whose warring over, get this, a pig, nearly sent the two countries to the battlefield. When an American farmer shot a British homesteader's pig caught rooting in his garden, ill feelings quickly escalated. Fortunately, cooler heads prevailed so that what is now referred to as the "Pig War" of 1859 only resulted in one casualty: the pig.

SIGHTS

The history of this little-known incident is chronicled through interpretive centers in the **San Juan Island National Historical Park**, which is composed of English Camp and American Camp. Located on West Valley Road at the north end of the island is **English Camp**, which features barracks, a formal garden, cemetery, guardhouse, hospital and commissary. **American Camp**, on Cattle Point Road at the south end of the island, is where the officers and laundress' quarters, and the Hudson Bay Company's Bellevue Sheep Farm remain. ~ 360-378-2240, fax 360-378-2615; www.nps.gov/sajh.

San Juan Historical Museum is located on the 1891 James King farmstead. The museum complex consists of the original farmhouse, milk house and carriage house, as well as the original county jail. A variety of memorabilia is displayed throughout, including American Indian baskets and stone implements, an antique diving suit, period furniture and clothing. A great place to learn about the region's maritime history, the museum also features an excellent collection highlighting the region's proud past. Hours vary seasonally, so call ahead. ~ 405 Price Street, Friday Harbor; phone/fax 360-378-3949; www.sjmuseum.org, e-mail curator@sjmuseum.org.

HIDDEN ►

Oyster lovers and birdwatchers should make the trip down the dusty road to **Westcott Bay Sea Farms**, where they'll find saltwater bins of live oysters, mussels and clams (available in spring and summer only) and an array of birds attracted to the oyster beds that stretch out into the bay. Closed weekends in winter. ~ 904 Westcott Drive, Friday Harbor; 360-378-2489, fax 360-378-6388; www.westcottbay.com, e-mail kathleen@westcottbay.com.

The lavender fields at **Pelindaba Lavender Farm** are awash with color in the summertime, the best time to visit this working organic farm. An old farmhouse serves as the general store here, offering all things lavender, from soaps and essential oils to honey, pepper and even vinegar. Self-guided tours and signage explain the farming and distilling operations. Closed Monday and Tuesday from October to December; closed January to April. ~ 33 Hawthorne Lane, Friday Harbor; 360-378-4248, 866-819-1911, fax 360-378-8946; www.pelindaba.com, e-mail admin@pelindaba.com.

Afterglow Vista is the mausoleum of one of the region's wealthy families. The structure itself is fascinating; an open, Grecian-style columned complex surrounds six inscribed chairs, each containing the ashes of a family member, set before a round table of limestone. A seventh chair and column have obviously been removed, some say as part of Masonic ritual, others believe because a member of the family was disinherited or because the seventh member considered life unending. ~ Roche Harbor Resort, 4950 Reuben Tarte Memorial Drive, Roche Harbor.

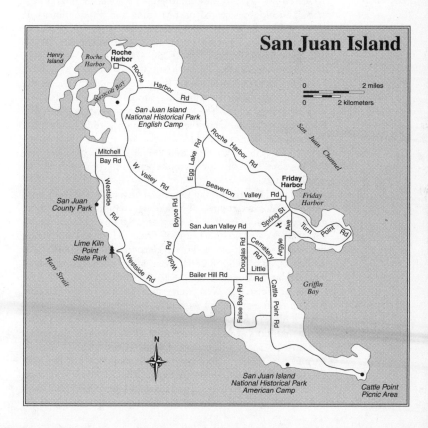

LODGING   Named for its view, **Olympic Lights** is a remodeled 1895 farm-house set on five grassy, breeze-tossed acres overlooking the Olympic Peninsula across the Strait of Juan de Fuca. Guests kick off their shoes before heading up to the cream-carpeted second floor with three comfortably appointed, pastel-shaded rooms; a fourth room on the ground floor is also available. You'll find no frilly, Victoriana clutter here, just a peaceful night snuggled under down comforters topped off by a farm-fresh breakfast. ~ 146 Starlight Way, Friday Harbor; 360-378-3186, 888-211-6195, fax 360-378-2097; www.olympic lights.com, e-mail olympiclights@rockisland.com. DELUXE.

Believe it or not, Friday Harbor was named after an early 1800s settler named Joe Friday.

The **Tower House Bed & Breakfast** is a romantic Queen Anne–style B&B located on ten acres overlooking the San Juan Valley. It features two large suites with private baths and sitting rooms. Its crown jewel is the tower room with a tufted window seat and stained-glass window. Popular with honeymooners, the Tower House strives to cater to its guests every need. A large vegetarian breakfast is served on fine china and antique linens. If given notice, the owners will accommodate vegans. Of course, no inn would be complete without a couple of friendly cats. ~ 392 Little Road, Friday Harbor; 360-378-5464, 800-858-4276; www.san-juan-islands.com. ULTRA-DELUXE.

If you've dreamed of life on the water, you'll appreciate the **Wharfside Bed and Breakfast,** a 60-foot, two-masted sailboat with two guest rooms. The forward stateroom with a queen and bunkbeds feels cozy, while the aft stateroom with queen bed is a little roomier. The rates include a cruise in summer. ~ Port of Friday Harbor; 360-378-5661, 800-899-3030; www.fridayharbor lodging.com, e-mail slowseason@rockisland.com. DELUXE TO ULTRA-DELUXE.

Friday's Historic Inn is a renovated historic inn with 15 individually decorated rooms, all with down comforters and wildlife art. Several rooms have private jacuzzis. All this romance is conveniently located in the heart of Friday Harbor. Continental breakfast. ~ 35 1st Street, Friday Harbor; 360-378-5848, 800-352-2632, fax 360-378-2881; www.friday-harbor.com, e-mail stay@friday-harbor.com. DELUXE TO ULTRA-DELUXE.

Set in the rolling West Valley near English Camp National Park and surrounded by a working ranch, **States Inn & Ranch** is a bit of Sleepy Hollow in San Juan. Each of the ten rooms has a decor that hints at its namesake state—tiny Rhode Island comes closest, with shells and brass dolphins on the fireplace mantle, various renditions of ships on the walls and copies of the New England publication *Yankee* to peruse. The friendly and informative innkeepers and the multicourse country breakfasts with prize-winning dishes make up for the slight sulphur odor of the tap water. The inn is also disabled-accessible (hard to find in the islands), and menus can be arranged for special diets. Full breakfast. ~ 2687 West Valley Road, Friday Harbor; 360-378-6240, 866-602-2737; www.statesinn.com, e-mail ranch@statesinn.com. MODERATE TO ULTRA-DELUXE.

Roche Harbor has something for everyone. You can check in to the 1886 Hotel de Haro, where gingerbread trim, parlor beds, antiques and a roaring fireplace bring back memories of the good old days. In addition to this three-story, 20-room establishment, nine former workers' cottages have been converted into two-bedroom units, ideal for families. The cottages are convenient to the swimming pool. Also available are the McMillin Suites, newly constructed carriage houses for families or larger groups, and four luxury guest suites in the recently remodeled McMillin Family Home. Each suite has a king-size bed, two TVs, a fireplace in the sitting room, a clawfoot iron bathtub, and lovely views of the harbor. For contemporary lodging, choose one- to three-room harbor-view condominiums. ~ 248 Reuben Memorial Drive, Roche Harbor; 360-378-2155, 800-451-8910, fax 360-378-6809; www.rocheharbor.com, e-mail roche@rocheharbor.com. MODERATE TO ULTRA-DELUXE.

DINING

The Blue Dolphin is an unpretentious diner serving hearty portions of home-cooked breakfast favorites like biscuits and gravy, eggs Benedict, blueberry pancakes and chicken-fried steak. No dinner. ~ 185 1st Street, Friday Harbor; 360-378-6116. BUDGET.

Among the best restaurants on the island, the rustic look and rural setting of the Duck Soup Inn hardly hints at the creative bill of fare. Several seafood and beef options are available, but why not try the inn's namesake—duck stew seasoned with chipotle chiles, lime and cilantro or perhaps with african spices and lemon-zest dumplings? For starters, there are appetizers such as Westcott Bay home-smoked oysters or sea scallop ceviche; as well as fine Northwestern and European wines. Dinner only. Closed November through March. Call for hours. ~ 50 Duck Soup Lane, Friday Harbor; 360-378-4878; www.ducksoupinn.com. ULTRA-DELUXE.

SHOPPING

Most of the shops are located within blocks of Friday Harbor, giving you plenty to do while waiting for the ferry. Near Sunshine Alley, Dolphin Art (360-378-3531) sells original screenprint art on cotton sportswear. ~ 165 1st Street, Friday Harbor.

Art lovers visiting Friday Harbor will want to stop by several galleries. Waterworks Gallery features a collection of contemporary eclectic Northwest art in media such as glass, sculpture, oil and watercolor. ~ 315 Spring Street, Friday Harbor; 360-378-3060; www.waterworksgallery.com, e-mail info@waterworksgallery.com.

The Garuda & I carries an amazing selection of ethnic arts, beads, crafts, musical instruments as well as jewelry from local artisans. ~ 60 1st Street, Friday Harbor; 360-378-3733; www.thegaruda andi.com.

NIGHTLIFE   On San Juan Island, **Herb's Tavern** is the local sidle-up-to-the-bar joint with pool tables. ~ 80 1st Street, Friday Harbor; 360-378-7076. To watch the game on several TVs visit at **Haley's Bait Shop**, a smoke-free sports bar and grill. ~ 175 Spring Street, Friday Harbor; 360-378-4434. The **Roche Harbor Resort Lounge** has weekend dancing to live music in the summer. ~ 248 Reuben Memorial Drive, Roche Harbor; 360-378-2155.

BEACHES & PARKS   **SAN JUAN COUNTY PARK** 🏊 🛶 🎣 ⛴ 🚤 ⚓ Orca whales frequently pass by the rocky shoreline of this 12-acre park on the western edge of San Juan Island. Swimming is good in the shallow, protected bay; fishing is fair for bottomfish, rock-fish, salmon and crab. There are restrooms, picnic tables and fire pits. ~ On Westside Road just north of Lime Kiln Point State Park; 360-378-8420, fax 360-378-2075; www.co.san-juan.wa.us/parks, e-mail parks@co.san-juan.wa.us.

Because of its location on Smallpox Bay, San Juan County Park is a haven for kayakers and scuba divers who enjoy the easy waters in the shallow bay or the more challenging shelf that drops steeply off about 80 feet out.

▲ There are 18 standard sites ($25 per night), two mooring buoys ($8 per night) and one premium site ($34 per night). Group camping sites for up to 30 people are available. Reservations: 360-378-1842.

LIME KILN POINT STATE PARK 🏃 Situated on a rocky bluff overlooking Haro Strait, the park is named for an early lime kiln operation, with remnants of old structures still visible to the north of the lighthouse. The bluff is the prime whale-watching spot on San Juan Island. A footpath takes you to picturesque Lime Kiln Lighthouse, listed on the National Register of Historic Places. Restrooms, picnic tables and interpretive displays are found here. There is no drinking water for the public. ~ Off Westside Road on the western shore of San Juan Island; 360-378-2044.

CATTLE POINT NATURAL AREA 🏃 🛶 Though it takes a precarious scramble down a rocky ledge to reach it and picnic tables on the bluff above lend little privacy, this gravelly half-moon is arguably the prettiest public beach on San Juan Island. Anglers will find bottomfish and salmon. Facilities include picnic tables, shelter, restrooms, interpretive signs and a nature trail. ~ Follow Cattle Point Road through American Camp and on to the southern tip of the island. ~ 360-856-3500, fax 360-856-2150.

FOURTH OF JULY BEACH 🚶 🛥 This secluded, gravelly crescent is where the locals head when they're looking for privacy. There are often bald eagles nesting in the nearby trees, a poignant sign of this aptly named stretch. The shallow, little bay area extends out a long way and is suitable for wading on hot days. Anglers can try for bottomfish and salmon. There are pit toilets, picnic tables and a fenced grassy area off the parking lot suitable for frisbee. Large groups should call for a permit. ~ Located on the northeastern edge of American Camp; 360-378-2902, fax 360-378-2996.

Trendy, artsy-craftsy and lovely to look at, Orcas Island is a resort that caters to everyone from backpackers to the well-to-do. A nature sanctuary pocketed with charming towns, the island also boasts more sun than some of its neighbors.

▼▼▼▼▼▼▼▼▼▼

Orcas Island

One of Orcas Island's leading landmarks is **Rosario Resort & Spa.** Even if you're not planning to stay here during your trip, make sure to visit the original mansion here for a fantastic evening show that includes music performed on a 1910 Steinway grand piano and an amazing pipe organ along with entertaining narration and slides of life on the island in the early 1900s. Call ahead for show schedule. ~ 1400 Rosario Road, Eastsound; 360-376-2222, fax 360-376-2289; www.rosarioresort.com.

SIGHTS

◀ *HIDDEN*

Of the many small historical museums in the San Juans, the **Orcas Island Historical Museum** is our favorite. Six interconnected log cabins of prominent early settlers house a fine assemblage of artifacts representing the culture of the Coast Salish and area homesteaders. Island industry, home and social life, farming and oral histories comprise some of the featured exhibits. Closed Monday and from October through May. Admission. ~ 184 North Beach Road, Eastsound; 360-376-4849; www.orcasisland.org/~history, e-mail orcasmuseum@rockisland.com.

Madrona Point, a pretty madrone tree–dotted waterside park saved from condo development by the Lummi Indians and local residents, is a fine spot for a picnic. It's at the end of the unmarked road just past Christina's Restaurant in Eastsound. No dogs are allowed.

◀ *HIDDEN*

One of Orcas Island's best-kept secrets is Doug and Jeri Smart's **Little House on the Farm,** a no-host home for rent that looks so homey passersby just assume the Smarts live in it. The Victorian house nicely accommodates four people who have the run of it, from the two bedrooms with queen-size beds to the reading room, full kitchen, stone fireplace in the living room and jacuzzi. Decorated with Victorian country furnishings, the house sits on 25 acres of fenced pastures, ponds and woodlands complete with

LODGING

◀ *HIDDEN*

grazing horses. Carriages and sleighs are on display in the yard. ~ Eastsound; 360-376-5306; www.walkinghorsefarm.com, e-mail stay@walkinghorsefarm.com. ULTRA-DELUXE.

It's not unusual to find semi-tame deer roaming around the ample grounds of **Rosario Resort,** tucked away on Cascade Bay on the east side of the horseshoe of Orcas Island. The motel-style rooms scattered along the waterfront or perched on the hillside overlooking the bay are spacious and comfortable, and some feature fireplaces, jacuzzis and private balconies. Three pools, a fitness room and sauna round out the amenities. A marina is available for guests who want to arrive by boat. ~ 1400 Rosario Road, Eastsound; 360-376-2222, 800-562-8820, fax 360-376-2289; www.rosarioresort.com. ULTRA-DELUXE.

Expect a wide variety of accommodations at the funky **Doe Bay Resort & Retreat,** including hostel beds, camping, yurts and cabins, some of which are fully equipped. There are shared central bathrooms, a community kitchen and a small seasonal café on the grounds of this large retreat along with a splendid three-tiered sauna and three mineral baths perched on a covered deck. Be aware of the strict seven-day, advance-notice cancellation policy. Closed Sunday through Thursday from October through April. ~ 107 Doe Bay Road, Olga; 360-376-2291, fax 360-376-5809; www.doebay.com, e-mail contact@doebay.com. BUDGET TO ULTRA-DELUXE.

DINING

Bilbo's Festivo specializes in Southwestern fare. A margarita or *cerveza* on the tiled garden patio surrounded by adobe walls is a great way to relax. Bilbo's serves dinner only, but opens **La Taqueria,** a lunch outlet in the courtyard, during the summer months.

AUTHOR FAVORITE

A stay at **Turtleback Farm Inn** is like stepping into the much-loved story *The Wind in the Willows,* surrounded as it is by acres of forest and farm tracts full of animals as far as the eye can see. Rooms in this lovely, late-19th-century farmhouse vary in size and setup, but all 11 rooms have a charming mix of contemporary and antique furniture, cozy quilts and antique fixtures in private baths. The newer Orchard House offers four spacious rooms with king-sized beds, a sofa sitting area, a gas fireplace, a dining corner, refrigerators and large decks overlooking the valley. Full breakfast. ~ 1981 Crow Valley Road, Eastsound; 360-376-4914, 800-376-4914, fax 360-376-5329; www.turtlebackinn.com, e-mail info@turtlebackinn.com. DELUXE TO ULTRA-DELUXE.

~ North Beach Road, Eastsound; 360-376-4728. BUDGET TO MOD-ERATE.

The Restaurant at the Deer Harbor Inn, is tucked away in an expanse of orchard grove peering out over Deer Harbor and the Olympic Range and is where locals come for that special night out. The daily menu is chalked on the board; rock cod, coho salmon and choice steaks are prime picks. For diners on the deck, this is a great spot to watch the sunset. Dinner only; reservations recommended. ~ 33 Inn Lane, Deer Harbor; 360-376-4110, 877-377-4110, fax 360-376-2237; www.deerharborinn.com, e-mail stay@deerharborinn.com. DELUXE TO ULTRA-DELUXE.

SHOPPING

You'll find several interesting shops in Eastsound. **Darvill's Gallery** carries antique maps, etchings and fine prints and has a connected bookstore. Closed Tuesday and Wednesday. ~ 296 Main Street, Eastsound; 360-376-2351; www.darvillsrareprints.com.

An 1866 cabin houses **Crow Valley Pottery & Gallery**, a long-established studio that got its start making ceramic wind bells in-spired by Northwest tribal arts. It has expanded to represent nu-merous island artists and craftspeople working in art glass, metal sculpture, watercolors, jewelry, pastels and more. ~ 2274 Orcas Road, Eastsound; 360-376-4260, fax 360-376-6495; www.crow valleypottery.com, e-mail pottery@crowvalley.com.

◄ HIDDEN

Don't spend all your time and money in Eastsound proper be-cause you won't want to miss **Orcas Island Pottery**, the oldest ex-isting craft studio on Orcas. You can watch potters at work through the windows of the studio. ~ 338 Old Pottery Road, off West Beach Road, Eastsound; 360-376-2813; www.orcasisland pottery.com, e-mail orcaspots@rockisland.com.

Sallie Bell Designs carries a curious selection of boutique items—jewelry and clothing, both elegant and casual. ~ 140 Sedum Hill Road, Orcas; 360-376-2275, 800-273-4055; www.monkeypuzzle.com.

The Right Place has pottery strewn about the garden and in the showroom. In the summertime you can try using the wheel yourself. ~ 2915 Enchanted Forest Road, Eastsound; 360-376-4023; www.rightplacepottery.com.

◄ HIDDEN

At a bend in Horseshoe Highway as you reach Olga is **Orcas Island Artworks**, the cooperative art gallery showcasing fine arts, handicrafts and furniture all produced by local hands. Closed January to mid-February. ~ 360-376-4408; www.orcasis land.com/artworks.

NIGHTLIFE

Moran Lounge is the place to go for live entertainment through-out the year. ~ Rosario Resort, 1400 Rosario Road, Eastsound; 360-376-2222.

For convivial pub action, step into the **Lower Tavern** and amuse yourself with darts and pool. Beer and wine only. ~ Prune Alley and Main Street, Eastsound; 360-376-4848.

HIDDEN ▶

Or hang out in **The Living Room**, a yoga studio/community arts center that hosts concerts, poetry readings, storytelling and stand-up comedy. ~ 474 North Beach Road, Eastsound; e-mail thelivingroom@orcasonline.com.

BEACHES & PARKS

MORAN STATE PARK 🏃 🚲 ⛵ 🏊 ⚓ 🛶 🐎 Washington's fifth-largest park consists of 5252 verdant acres dotted with five freshwater lakes and crowned by sweeping Mt. Constitution. There are 38 miles of forest trails connecting the four mountain lakes, numerous waterfalls and five campgrounds. There is fishing for rainbow, cutthroat and kokanee trout on several lakes, with boat rentals available seasonally. Facilities include restrooms, showers, kitchen shelters and picnic tables. ~ Located near Eastsound, accessible by state ferry from Anacortes; 360-376-2326, fax 360-376-2360.

▲ There are 136 standard sites ($16 per night) and 15 primitive sites ($10 per night). Reservations: 888-226-7688.

HIDDEN ▶

OBSTRUCTION PASS STATE PARK 🏃 🏊 🛶 This primitive, heavily forested locale located on the southeastern tip of Orcas Island is tricky to get to, so the crowds are kept to a minimum, a reward for those who care to search it out.

The area has a hiking trail, ten campsites (no potable water) and a beach with cold water for brave swimmers. Anglers will find bottomfish and rockfish. There are vault toilets, picnic tables, three mooring buoys and trails. ~ From the town of Olga follow Point Lawrence Road east, turn right on Obstruction Pass Road and keep right on Trailhead Road until you hit the parking area. From there it's a half-mile hike to the campground; 360-376-2326, fax 360-376-2360.

The view from Moran State Park's stone tower at the peak of Mt. Constitution takes in the San Juans, Mt. Baker and Vancouver, B.C.

▲ There are 10 primitive sites ($10 per night); hike-in only.

OTHER PARKS Many of the smaller islands are preserved as state parks including **Doe, Jones, Clark, Sucia, Stuart, Posey, Blind, James, Matia, Patos** and **Turn.** They are accessible by boat only and in most cases have a few primitive campsites, nature trails, a dock or mooring buoys off secluded beaches, but no water (except Jones, Stuart and Sucia, in season) or facilities except for composting toilets. Costs are $10 for mooring buoys, $12 for camping, $10 plus $.50 per foot for boats to dock overnight. Washington watertrail sites cost $12 per night and must be reached by a beachable human-powered watercraft. For more inguise Aleutian hunters and, acting like a hearing aid, collected sound. ~ West Beach; 360-376-3677; www.ospreytours.com, e-mail info@ospreytours.com. For lessons or tours contact **Shear-water Sea Kayak Tours**, which offers half- and full-day tours. Custom overnight trips can also be arranged. Shearwater has also sold accessories and clothing since 1982, making it the oldest outfitter on the islands. ~ P.O. Box 787, Eastsound, WA 98245; 360-376-4699; www.shearwaterkayaks.com, e-mail info@shearwaterkayaks.com.

SCUBA DIVING

The protected waters of Puget Sound hold untold treasures for the diver: Craggy rock walls, ledges and caves of this sunken mountain range and enormous forests of bull kelp provide homes for a multitude of marine life. Giant Pacific octopus thrive in these waters, as do sea anemones and hundreds of species of fish. "Within 15 minutes of Friday Harbor on San Juan Island, there are hundreds of great dive spots," says one local diver who grew up in the area. The west side of San Juan Island and the south side of Lopez Island are particular favorites, largely because the absence of silt means the water is cleaner and therefore clearer. There are also lots of ledges along these rocky coasts, which abound with exceptional wall-dive spots. Acres of bull kelp forests, with their teeming marine life, are also popular dive spots. But just as these waters hold great beauty, they can also be treacherous with tremendous tidal changes and strong currents.

NORTHERN PUGET SOUND **Washington Divers, Inc.** offers complete rental and diving services, including a full schedule of diving activities year-round, from one-day trips to two-week-long international excursions. A one-day dive charter to the San Juan Islands is the most popular trip. In the summer, extended daylight hours make it possible to make up to two dives during the six-to seven-hour trip. The shop also runs night dives and a free "come along" beach dive at least two weekend days a month. Scuba certification classes (open water) are also available. ~ 903 North State Street, Bellingham; 360-676-8029, fax 360-647-5028; www.washingtondivers.com.

WHIDBEY ISLAND Besides air fills, diving lessons and rental of wetsuits and other equipment, **Whidbey Island Dive Center** offers half- to full-day dive charters using two tanks per dive. One popular spot for experienced divers is under the bridge at Deception Pass State Park, where currents reach seven knots—"a diver's rush." For the less experienced, the charter to the diving sanctuary off Keystone Jetty is an excellent spot to view marine life. The Dive Center also teaches all types of certification. ~ Northeast 7th Avenue #1, Oak Harbor; 360-675-1112, 679-2247; www.whidbeydive.com.

formation, contact Washington State Parks: 360-902-8844, e-mail infocent@parks.wa.gov.

Outdoor Adventures

Spending time on the water is a part of daily life here, and certainly something that visitors should not miss. In fact, many of the 100-plus islands of the San Juans are accessible only by boat. Rental options are numerous; on the mainland, contact **Fairhaven Boatworks** for kayaks, rowboats and sailboats. Closed Monday, as well as weekdays in winter. ~ 501 Harris Avenue, Bellingham; 360-714-8891; www.whatcomboatworks.org.

BOATING

In the islands, try **North Isle Sailing**, which offers sea cruises around Whidbey, the San Juans and Canada. Trips last from a half day to a week. ~ 2250 North Swantown Road, Oak Harbor; 360-675-8360, 800-580-8360; www.northislesailing.com.

Captain Bob Plank of **Viking Cruises** has been leading tours since 1979 aboard his wooden-hulled custom-built boat, which holds 49 people. Choose from a wide variety of trips including a three-hour Skagit Bay float and crabfeast. In winter, consider taking a birdwatching tour to see the more than 200 species that flock to the islands. ~ 109 North 1st Street, La Conner; 360-466-2639; www.vikingcruises.com.

SPORT-FISHING

Catching some salmon is the hoped-for reward when you head out on a fishing charter through Northern Puget Sound and the San Juan Islands. As a bonus, you're also likely to encounter seals, eagles and whales as you sail past islands wooded with red-bark madrone trees.

In winter, of course, the temperature on the water can get chilly and the water a bit choppy. All the charter fishing services listed here provide boats with heated, enclosed cabins to keep you comfortable. Charter fees include bait and tackle, but do not include a fishing license or food and drink.

NORTHERN PUGET SOUND **Jim's Salmon Charter** specializes in arranging full-day trips to fisheries in the San Juan and Canadian islands for groups of no more than six people. Jim has more than three decades of experience. Bait and tackle are included. ~ Marine Drive, Blaine Marina; 360-332-6724.

In Everett, Gary Krein is president of the Charter Boat Association of Puget Sound and owner of **All Star Fishing Charters**. He operates a 28-foot fiberglass-bottom boat that can carry up to six people each, and encourages "angler participation" on his full-day trips (two daily in summer, one in winter). The boat comes fully equipped with electronic fishfinding equipment that seeks out the salmon and bottomfish. Bait and tackle are included. ~ Port of Everett; 425-252-4188, 800-214-1595; www.allstarfishing.com, e-mail gary@allstarfishing.com.

Mike Dunnigan is the skipper of **Sea Hawk Salmon Charters**. He runs year-round, exclusive eight-hour charters for up to four people to fish for salmon, bottomfish and halibut. Bait and tackle are included. ~ Skyland Marina, Anacortes; 360-424-1350; www.seahawksalmoncharters.com.

SAN JUAN ISLANDS **Trophy Charters** will pick anglers up from the other islands before heading out on a four- to six-hour fishing trip seeking salmon and bottomfish in a 29-foot sportfisher that holds six. Captain Monty runs a fast boat (up to 30 mph), so travel time is reduced. ~ Friday Harbor; 360-378-2110; www.fishthesanjuans.com.

RIVER FISHING
Several rivers in the area—the Snohomish, Skykomish, Skagit and Sauk, for example—provide year-round catches, notably steelhead and all species of salmon except sockeye (it's not permitted to take this fish from rivers). **All Rivers Guide Service** offers customized, seven- to nine-hour fly-fishing trips in a 16-foot heated drift boat. All bait and tackle are included, and the knowledgeable professional guides also offer instruction in fishing. ~ 425-736-8920; www.allriversguideservice.com, e-mail mark@allriversguideservice.com. **Pacific Northwest Sportfishing** specializes in full-day fishing trips on a 16-foot heated drift boat, raft or a 23-foot jetboat for up to six people. Bait and tackle are included. ~ Bellingham; 360-676-1321; www.pacific-northwest-sportfishing.com, e-mail info@pacific-northwest-sportfishing.com.

KAYAKING
For nonadventurers who want an outdoor experience that's a lot of fun but not extremely challenging, a guided water excursion in a sea kayak may be just the thing. No previous kayaking ex-perience is necessary to join one of these groups for a paddling tour on the gentle waters of Chuckanut Bay, with its sandstone formations near Bellingham; of sea caves around Deception Pass State Park on Whidbey Island; or off San Juan Island, where you are likely to see whales, seals and other marine wildlife. Unless noted, the operators listed here generally offer a regular schedule of excursions from April–May to September–October. Cost for a sea kayak excursion ranges from $30 to $60. Most operators can also arrange overnight or longer trips.

NORTHERN PUGET SOUND **Moondance Sea Kayaking Adventures** leads half-day to five-day trips to nearby locations such as Chuckanut Bay, Cypress Island and Clark's Point (where you'll see a fossil of the entire trunk of a palm tree). A slightly longer trip to sea caves occasionally heads down to Deception Pass State Park where the wave action is rougher. ~ Bellingham; 360-738-76 www.moondancekayak.com.

LOPEZ ISLAND **Lopez Kayaks** offers morning and after sea-kayaking tours in double kayaks for eight peo MacKaye Harbor, which is also popular with seals. If y experience, you can also rent a kayak for your own use joining a tour or buy your own vessel, accessories books. Open May through October. ~ 2845 Fish Road; 360-468-2847; www.lopezkayaks.com.

SAN JUAN ISLAND Since the waters just off the we Juan Island are in the main whale-migration corrido of seeing whales are good. If not, there's plenty to view, notably seals and bald eagles. (The h bald-eagle nestings in the lower 48 states is Islands.) There are also kelp forests, jutting rocky outcroppings. A biologist or scientist excursions led by **Sea Quest Kayak Expe** four to twelve. There are also camping tr five days that go through primary orca Harbor; 360-378-5767; www.sea-quest **Kayaking** escorts up to ten people on set excursions. You can also arrange two to six days. Paddlers will see Friday Harbor; 360-378-4223, seas.com.

ORCAS ISLAND **Osprey Tours** to half-day and full-day sea-ka kan Eskimo tradition, owner frame kayaks with bifurcate split the water and provide gives each kayaker an Ale conical visor that resemb

SAN JUAN ISLAND Island Dive & Water Sports is a full-service dive shop, retail and rental. It specializes in daily half-day charters, guaranteeing you at least two dives using one tank per dive, in different locations during the trip. One might be a vertical wall dive, another may be in a grotto filled with marine life. Its vessels can accommodate up to 18 divers. Openwater certification classes are also available. Closed Wednesday and Thursday. ~ 2-A Spring Street Landing, Friday Harbor; 360-378-2772, 800-303-8386; www.divesanjuan.com. **Underwater Sports Inc.** offers full-day chartered trips to the islands, night dives, rentals, open-water certification, classes and air fills. ~ 205 East Casino Road, Everett; 425-355-3338; www.underwatersports.com.

In 1996, San Juan County outlawed jet skis. Locals complained that the serenity of the San Juans was disrupted by the incessant buzzing of cityfolk zipping around on their waterfront.

Saddle up for a gentle, leisurely ride around an 85-acre ranch or take in the scenic beauty of the San Juan Islands.

RIDING STABLES

NORTHERN PUGET SOUND A year-round operation, **Lang's Pony and Horse Farm** takes up to 14 riders on a leisurely guided trail ride (half-hour to two hours) around the hilly and wooded ranch, which is about 30 miles south of Bellingham. The farm also offers a Mom's Camp so mothers can ride in tranquility, as well as summer camps and riding lessons. Call for reservations. ~ 21463 Little Mountain Road, Mt. Vernon; 360-424-7630; www.comeride.com.

WHIDBEY ISLAND Put on jeans and a pair of sturdy leather shoes (leave your Birkenstocks and sneakers at home) for a guided trail ride through the hilly, wooded **Madrona Ridge Ranch**. Please call ahead (evenings are best) to arrange a one-and-a-half-hour ride; groups are limited to up to two people at a time. Riding lessons are available for all ages, but the trail rides are for teens and adults only. Nonriders can enjoy nature walks and the nearby beach. ~ Madrona Way, Coupeville; 360-678-4124.

Award-winning design, lush scenery and the Northwest's only par-5 to an island green are among the distinctions of golf courses in this part of the state.

GOLF

NORTHERN PUGET SOUND **Dakota Creek** was named one of the most challenging 18-hole courses by the Pacific Northwest Golf Association. This public course, carved out of a mountain, is quiet, well maintained and hilly. ~ 3258 Haynie Road, Custer; 360-366-3131; www.dakotacreekgolf.com.

The 18th hole at **Homestead Farms Golf Course** is the Northwest's only par-5 on an island green. The public course is

Text continued on page 158.

Whale Watching in the San Juan Islands

Here in the waters of the San Juan archipelago there are three resident pods, or extended families, of *Orcinus Orca*, otherwise known as "killer" whales. Because they are so frequently and easily spotted in the protected waters, these gentle black and white giants have been carefully studied by scientists since 1976.

Their research is documented at the **Whale Museum**, where you can learn more about whales. A photo collection with names and pod numbers will help you identify some of the 90 resident orcas, distinguished by their grayish saddle patches and nicks, scars or tears in the dorsal fins. There are displays of full-sized skeletons, videos and models of local marine mammals. Call ahead for winter hours. Admission. ~ 62 1st Street North, Friday Harbor; 360-378-4710, 800-946-7227, fax 360-378-5790; www.whalemuseum.org.

The Whale Museum also has an orca adoption program set up to help fund the ongoing research and all sorts of whale-related educational material, art and souvenirs available in their gift shop. They operate a 24-hour hotline (Washington only, 800-562-8832) for whale sightings and marine mammal strandings as well.

From May to September you can often see the whales from shore when they range closest to the islands to feed on migrating salmon. The best shoreline viewing spots are **Lime Kiln Point** on San Juan Island or **Shark Reef Park** on Lopez Island. Sightings drop dramatically in the winter as the pods disperse from the core area in search of prey.

If you want to get a closer look, put on your parka and sunglasses, grab your binoculars and camera and climb aboard one of the **wildlife cruises** that ply the waters between the islands. Even if you don't see any orca during the trip, you will almost certainly spot other interesting forms of wildlife such as sleek, gray minke whales, Dall's porpoises (which look like miniature orca), splotchy brown harbor seals, bald eagles, great blue heron, cormorants or tufted puffin.

Deer Harbor Charters offers four-hour whale-watching tours from April to October on a 36-foot boat that carries 20 people from Rosario Resort or on a 47-foot boat that carries 30 people from Deer Harbor Marina. Both boats have a naturalist guide. ~ P.O. Box 303, Deer Harbor, WA 98243; 360-376-5989, 800-544-5758; www.deerharborcharters.com.

Island Mariner Cruises boasts a high success rate for spotting whales. It's no wonder: the naturalist has worked there for years and they use more spotting services—including a plane—than any other on the island. Enjoy day-long nature and whale-watching expeditions with commentary on the history, flora and fauna of the San Juans as you cruise through the islands on a boat designed for whale watching that holds over 100 people. ~ 5 Harbor Loop, Bellingham; 360-734-8866, 877-734-8866; www.orcawatch.com, e-mail mariner@orcawatch.com.

Western Prince Cruises has similar naturalist-accompanied wildlife tours on a half-day basis. Boats normally carry fewer than 30 people and the environmentally friendly *Western Prince II* is powered by biodiesel. ~ Friday Harbor; 360-378-5315, 800-757-6722; www.orcawhalewatch.com. **Viking Cruises** offer three-hour nature tours to Deception Pass from La Conner. Their three-day excursion to Rosario Resort in Eastsound combines a crabfeast and pipe-organ concert with whale-watching trips. The captain claims an 80 percent success rate for spotting whales. ~ 109 North 1st Street, La Conner; 360-466-2639, 888-207-2333; www.viking cruises.com. You can also try **San Juan Boat Tours Inc.** for a three-and-a-half-hour whale-sighting excursion aboard a 100-foot tour vessel. ~ Friday Harbor; 360-378-3499, 800-232-6722; www.whaletour.com.

Happy spotting!

flat, but has lots of water. ~ 115 East Homestead Boulevard, Lynden; 360-354-1196.

A good choice is the **Walter E. Hall Memorial Golf Course,** an 18-hole public facility with well-kept grounds, a restaurant and cart rentals. ~ 1226 West Casino Road, Everett; 425-353-4653; www.walterhallgolf.com. The 18-hole **Kayak Point Golf Course** has an 18-hole putting course, a driving range, a full-service restaurant and lounge, and cart, shoe and club rentals. ~ 15711 Marine Drive, Stanwood; 360-652-9676. **Overlook Golf Course,** a nine-hole public course with a view of Big Lake, offers club and cart rentals. ~ 17523 State Route 9, Mt. Vernon; 360-422-6444.

> The greatest concentration of wintering bald eagles can be found at the Skagit River Bald Eagle Natural Area, 7800 acres located between Marblemount and Rockport.

There's a hilly front nine at **Lake Padden Municipal Golf Course,** located in Lake Padden Park. It's a tight, densely treed public course. ~ 4882 Samish Way, Bellingham; 360-738-7400; www.lakepaddengolf.com. **Sudden Valley Golf and Country Club** is an 18-hole semiprivate course that sits on a lake. There are cart rentals, a driving range and a snack shop. ~ 4 Club House Circle, Bellingham; 360-734-6435; www.sudden valleygolfclub.com.

The most expensive course (up to $65 greens fees) in the area is the semiprivate **Semiahmoo Golf and Country Club.** It's ranked as one of nation's best resort courses and was designated as a sectional qualifying course for the 1997 U.S. Open. The 18-hole, par-72 course was designed by Arnold Palmer; hole number 4 has a scenic view of Mt. Baker and the valley beyond. ~ 8720 Semiahmoo Parkway, Blaine; 360-371-7005.

The **Avalon Golf Club** has the hottest new links around the Sound. The 27-hole public course will keep you busy for a while. You can rent pull-carts, too. ~ 19345 Kelleher Road, Burlington; 360-757-1900; www.avalonlinks.com.

SAN JUAN ISLAND It's only nine holes, but the **San Juan Golf and Country Club** "plays like 18." Private, but open to the public, the course is set on a wooded, rolling tract next to Griffin Bay. Cart rentals are available. ~ 806 Golf Course Road, Friday Harbor; 360-378-2254; www.sanjuangolf.com.

TENNIS   No need to leave your racquet at home with so many public courts to take advantage of. In Everett, you'll find six first-come, first-served lighted courts at **Clark Park.** ~ 2400 Lombard Street. Or try the courts at **Fairhaven Park** in Bellingham. ~ 107 Chuckanut Drive; 360-676-6985.

On Whidbey Island, you can use the four lighted courts at **Coupeville High School** at South Main Street or the four clay courts at **Oak Harbor City Park** at 1501 City Beach Street. On Fidalgo Island, try the six courts at **Anacortes High School** facility. ~ 20th Street and J Avenue. On San Juan, try the four courts at the **Friday Harbor High School** at Guard Street or head out to the **Roche Harbor Resort** at Roche Harbor Road.

For bicycling in the Bellingham area, the best map is "Bicycling in Bellingham and Whatcom County," which outlines trails according to traffic volume, surface status (gravel, paved, etc.) and hill difficulty; it also categorizes trails as City Ride, City Trail or Country Ride. The map is available in many bicycle stores and during the summer from the **Bellingham/Whatcom County Convention and Visitors Bureau.** ~ 904 Potter Street, Bellingham; 360-671-3990, 800-487-2032; www.bellingham.org.

BIKING

If you plan to bike on the San Juan Islands, it's important to remember that the islands' narrow roads don't have special lanes or other provisions for cyclists. Lopez Island is probably the best bet for the occasional bicyclist: you'll be able to bike long, flat country roads, rather than the steeper, twisting roads of some of the other islands. You can rent a bike on the island or in Anacortes before ferrying over for the day.

The hardy cyclist might prefer a 20-mile hilly and winding route around San Juan Island or 16 miles of steep, twisting roads beginning at the ferry landing on Orcas Island.

For bike trails here and in other parts of the state, contact the **Washington Department of Transportation** to request a route map and informative brochure, or call 360-705-7277 for the Bicycle Hotline. ~ P.O. Box 47300, Olympia, WA 98504.

NORTHERN PUGET SOUND Bellingham offers several bike routes, some arduous, some easy, all highlighting the scenery and history of the area. One is the moderate **Interurban Trail** (also known as the Chuckanut Trail). The seven-mile trail, which follows an old trolley route, begins at the Fairhaven Parkway and ends at Larrabee State Park. The best of the bunch is the fairly easy, 45-minute **Lake Padden Loop** in Lake Padden Park. It connects to a series of trails on **Mt. Galbraith**, a local hot spot for mountain biking.

WHIDBEY ISLAND Those looking for a long-distance ride will enjoy the 50-mile Island County Tour, which begins at Columbia Beach on Whidbey Island and continues on to Deception Pass at the northern tip of the island. This trip is moderately strenuous, with high traffic on a good portion of the ride, but the spectacular views of the Strait of Juan de Fuca and the Saratoga Passage are reward enough.

SAN JUAN ISLAND The slightly difficult, 30-mile **San Juan Island Loop** leads along hilly, winding roads through Friday Harbor, Roche Harbor, San Juan Island National Historical Park and along the San Juan Channel.

ORCAS ISLAND The **Horseshoe Route** is by far the most difficult island bike route, with 16 miles of steep, twisting roads beginning at the ferry landing in Orcas, continuing through Eastsound, then on to Olga. An alternative route for the very hardy starts in Olga, passes through Moran State Park and ends in Doe Bay, with a possible challenging 3.5-mile sidetrip up and back down Mt. Constitution.

Bike Rentals For mountain-bike sales and repairs in the Northern Puget Sound region, contact **The Bicycle Center**. ~ 4707 Evergreen Way, Everett; 425-252-1441. For year-round mountain-bike rentals, sales and repairs in the Bellingham area, try **Fairhaven Bike & Mountain Sports**. ~ 1108 11th Street, Bellingham; 360-733-4433.

Located just off Route 20, the main drag into Anacortes, the **Skagit Cycle Center** rents bikes (and helmets) by the week. The center's location is ideal for cyclists heading to the San Juans ferry or just pedaling around nearby Skagit Valley. ~ 1620 Commercial Avenue, Anacortes; 360-588-8776.

Lopez Bicycle Works rents, repairs and sells mountain bikes, touring bikes and hybrids and will let you drop off the bike at the ferry landing when you leave for the day. Closed October through April. ~ Fisherman's Bay Road, Lopez Island; 360-468-2847; www.lopezbicycleworks.com.

For bike rentals on San Juan Island, contact **Island Bicycles**, which offers hybrids and road bikes, as well as bike sales, repairs and friendly advice. Limited winter hours. ~ 380 Argyle Avenue, Friday Harbor; 360-378-4941; www.islandbicycles.com.

Rent, buy or repair mountain bikes and hybrids on Orcas Island at **Dolphin Bay**, which also offers custom tours for 10 to 30 people. ~ Ferry Landing; 360-376-4157. Mountain bikes, road bikes, tandems, bike trailers and trail-a-bikes can be found for sale or rent at **Wildlife Cycles**, which also does repairs and offers off-road tours. ~ 350 North Beach Road, Eastsound; 360-376-4708; www.wildlifecycles.com.

HIKING

All distances listed for hiking trails are one way unless otherwise noted.

NORTHERN PUGET SOUND On the **Langus Riverfront Park Nature Trail** (2.5 miles) in Everett, hikers are likely to spot red-tailed hawk or gray heron as they make their way through towering spruce, red cedar and dogwood trees along the banks of the Snohomish River, past Union Slough and on toward Spencer Island, a protected haven for nesting ducks.

The Padilla Bay National Estuarine Reserve (360-428-1558) in the tiny community of Bay View (about six miles west of Burlington) offers the best hikes in the area. The **Padilla Bay Shore Trail** (2.3 miles) is a bicycle/pedestrian path with views of the estuary, mudflat, sloughs and tidal marsh. The Breazeale Interpretive Center is one mile north of the Shore Trail. Binoculars and trail guides can be checked out at the center to aid your exploration of the forest and meadow along the **Upland Trail** (.8 mile).

There are several good choices for hikes in Bellingham. The **Interurban Trail** (6 miles) begins near the entrance to Larrabee State Park and hugs the crest above Chuckanut Drive overlooking the bay and the San Juan Islands. Chuckanut Drive passes the rose gardens of Fairhaven Park on its way into the revitalized Fairhaven District of the city.

There are 5.9 miles of rolling trails through the lush **Sehome Hill Arboretum**, crowned by views of Mt. Baker and the San Juans from the observation tower at the summit. Since no motorized boats are allowed on **Lake Padden**, the path (3 miles) around the glistening lake and through some of the park's 1008 acres is both peaceful and rejuvenating.

In Birch Bay State Park in Blaine, the gently sloping **Terrell Marsh Trail** (.5 mile) winds through a thickly wooded area of birch, maple, red cedar, hemlock and fir, home to pileated woodpeckers, bald eagle, ruffed grouse, blue heron, muskrats and squirrels, and on to Terrell Marsh, the halfway point on the loop, before passing back through the forest to the trailhead.

WHIDBEY ISLAND   The most picturesque hikes on Whidbey Island are found in and around Fort Ebey State Park. The **Ebey's Landing Loop Trail** (3.5 miles) has some steep sections on the bluff above the beach, but carry your camera anyway to capture the views of pastoral Ebey's Prairie in one direction and Mt. Rainier and the Olympic Mountains framed by wind-sculpted pines and fir in the other. Trimmed in wild roses, the trail swings around Perego's Lagoon and back along the driftwood-strewn beach. Be aware that the trail passes over some private property.

The **Partridge Point Trail** (3.5 miles) in Fort Ebey State Park climbs through a mix of coastal wildflowers on a windswept bluff rising 150 feet above the water with wide views of Port Townsend, Admiralty Inlet, Protection Island and Discovery Bay. A

AUTHOR FAVORITE

On Lopez Island, the easiest and most popular bike route here is the **Lopez Island Perimeter Loop**, 32 miles of gently rolling hills and narrow, paved roads passing by Fisherman's Bay, Shark Reef Park, MacKaye Harbor and Agate Beach on the west side of the island and Mud Bay, Lopez Sound and Shoal Bay on the east side.

fenced path at the southern end drops down the headland to the cobbly beach below.

There are numerous trails to choose from in Deception Pass State Park. Locals prefer **Rosario Head Trail** (.3 mile) on the Fidalgo Island side, stretching over the very steep promontory between Rosario Bay and Bowman Bay with sweeping views of San Juans, Rosario Strait and the Strait of Juan de Fuca; the **Lighthouse Point Trail** (1.5 miles), near Bowman Bay. On the Whidbey Island side of the bridge, climb the steep switchback on **Goose Rock Perimeter Trail** (3.5 miles) and you might see great blue heron on Cornet Bay, then follow the path down under the bridge next to the swirling waters of the pass and on to quiet North Beach. Heartier hikers might want to tackle the **Goose Rock Summit Trail** (.5 mile), with an altitude gain of some 450 feet for an unparalleled view of Deception Pass and the Cascades.

FIDALGO ISLAND   In Anacortes, your best bet is to head for the **Washington Park Loop Road** (3 miles), located on Fidalgo Head at the end of Sunset Avenue four miles west of downtown. Rewarding views on this easy, paved path with a few moderate slopes include incredible glimpses of the San Juan Islands, Burrows Pass and Burrows Island. You'll also find quiet, cool stretches through dense woods and access to beaches and romantic, hidden outcroppings suitable for a glass of champagne to toast the breathtaking sunsets.

LOPEZ ISLAND   On Lopez, ideal hiking choices include the **Shark Reef Park Trail** (.5 mile), a mossy path that meanders through a fragrant forest area and along a rock promontory looking out over tidal pools, a large kelp bed, a jutting haul out spot for seals and across the channel to San Juan Island. Spencer Spit State Park's **Beach Trail** (2 miles) travels down the spit and around the salt marsh lagoon alive with migratory birds; at the end of the spit is a reproduction of a historic log cabin built by early settlers, a fine spot for a picnic or brief rest stop with a nice view of the tiny islands offshore.

SAN JUAN ISLAND   Two of the best hiking alternatives on San Juan are the established hiking trails of the San Juan Island National Historical Park. The **Lagoon Trail** (.5 mile) in American Camp is actually two trails intertwined, starting from a parking area above Old Town (referred to on maps as First) Lagoon and passing through a dense stand of Douglas fir connecting the lovely, protected cove beaches of Jakle's Lagoon and Third Lagoon. The highlight of the short but steep **Mt. Young Trail** (.75 mile) in English Camp are the plates identifying the many islands dotting the waters as far as the eye can see. If you want a closer view of the water, you can take the flat, easy **Bell Point Trail** (2 miles), also in English Camp, which runs along the edge of the coast.

ORCAS ISLAND Unless you plan to spend an extended period of time here, there's little chance of covering the many hiking trails that twist through Moran State Park on Orcas Island connecting view spots, mountain lakes, waterfalls and campgrounds. The **Mountain Loop** (3.9 miles) is fairly easy and takes in sights such as log cabins and a dam and footbridge at the south end of Mountain Lake. For a little more challenge, try a section of the two-part **Twin Lakes Trail**: one part (2.2 miles) heads up the valley at the north end of Mountain Lake; the other (3.7 miles) takes you from the summit of Mt. Constitution along a rocky ledge to Twin Lakes and the Mountain Lake Campground, with occasional views through the thick trees. If you're a waterfall lover, take the **Cascade Creek Trail** (4.3 miles) from the south end of Mountain Lake past Cascade and Rustic falls and on to Cascade Lake.

▼ ▼ ▼ ▼ ▼ ▼ ▼ ▼ ▼ ▼

Transportation

Route 5, also known as the Pacific Highway, parallels the Northern Puget Sound coastline all the way up to the Canadian border. **Route 20** from Burlington takes you into Anacortes, the main jump-off point for ferry service to the San Juan Islands. **Route 16** leads from Tacoma across The Narrows and onto the Kitsap Peninsula where it connects to **Route 3** skirting the Sinclair Inlet and continuing north to Port Gamble.

CAR

AIR

Visitors flying into the Northern Puget Sound area usually arrive at either **Bellingham International Airport** (360-671-5674) or the much larger and busier **Seattle-Tacoma International Airport** (see Chapter Two for further information). Carriers serving the Bellingham airport include Casino Express, EliteAir, Horizon Airlines and San Juan Airline.

Charter and regularly scheduled commuter flights are available into the tiny **Friday Harbor Airport** through Northwest Sea Planes, Island Air and San Juan Airline. ~ 360-378-4724. Small commuter airports with limited scheduled service include **Anacortes Airport, Eastsound Airport** and **Lopez Airport**; all are served by San Juan Airline.

> Close to five million vehicles a year cross the U.S./Canada border at Blaine, Washington, making this the West Coast's busiest northern border station.

FERRY

Washington State Ferries, which are part of the state highway system, provide transportation to the main islands of the San Juans —Lopez, Orcas, Shaw and Friday Harbor on San Juan—departing from the Anacortes Ferry Terminal (Ferry Terminal Road; 888-808-7977 in Washington). Schedules change several times per year, with added service in the summer to take care of the heavy influx of tourists. The system is burdened during peak summer months, so arrive at the terminal early and be prepared to wait patiently (sometimes three hours or more) in very long lines if you plan to take your car along; walk-on passengers seldom wait long. ~ 206-464-6400.

BUS

Greyhound Bus Lines (800-231-2222; www.greyhound.com) provides regular service into Bellingham, Everett and Mt. Vernon. Stations are in Bellingham at 401 Harris Avenue in Fairhaven Station, 360-733-5251; in Everett at 3201 Smith Avenue, 425-252-2143; and in Mt. Vernon at 105 Kincaid Street, Suite 100, 360-336-5111.

The **Bellingham/SeaTac Airporter** provides express shuttle service between Bellingham, Mt. Vernon, Stanwood, Anacortes, Marysville, Oak Harbor and the SeaTac airport. ~ 360-380-8800, 866-235-5247.

TRAIN

Amtrak offers service into Everett on the Puget Sound shoreline via the "Empire Builder," which originates in Chicago and makes its final stop in Seattle before retracing its route. West Coast connections through Seattle on the "Coast Starlight" are also available. ~ 3201 Smith Avenue, Everett; 800-872-7245; www.amtrak.com.

CAR RENTALS

At the Bellingham International Airport, you'll find **Avis Rent A Car** (800-331-1212), **Budget Rent A Car** (800-527-0700) and **Hertz Rent A Car** (800-654-3131).

A less expensive local rental agency is **U-Save Auto Rental** (360-293-8686) in Anacortes.

PUBLIC TRANSIT

Whatcom Transportation Authority provides public transit in Lynden, Bellingham, Blaine, Birch Bay, Ferndale and Gooseberry Point. ~ 360-676-7433; www.ridewta.com. **Skagit Transit** services the Mt. Vernon, Sedro Woolley, Anacortes and Burlington areas. ~ 360-757-4433; www.skagittransit.org. In Everett you can get just about anywhere for 50 cents via **Everett Transit**. ~ 425-257-7777. **Island Transit** covers Whidbey Island, with scheduled stops at Deception Pass, Oak Harbor, Coupeville, the Keystone Ferry, Greenbank, Freeland, Langley and the Clinton Ferry. ~ 360-678-7771; www.islandtransit.org. In smaller towns like La Conner and Mt. Vernon and on most of the islands there are no public transportation systems set up; check the Yellow Pages for taxi service.

TAXIS

A cab company serving the Bellingham International Airport is **City Cab, Inc./Yellow Cab** (360-733-8294). For service from the Friday Harbor Airport contact **Bob's Taxi Service** (360-378-3550). **Triangle Taxi** (360-293-3979) serves the Anacortes Airport.

FOUR

Olympic Peninsula and Washington Coast

One of the most spectacular sights for many Pacific Northwest visitors is sitting on the dock of the bay (Seattle's Elliott Bay, that is) watching the sun set behind the stark profile of the Olympic Mountains. The area is even more memorable looking from the inside out.

The Olympic Peninsula is a vast promontory bounded on the east by Puget Sound, the west by the Pacific Ocean and the north by the Strait of Juan de Fuca. With no major city—the largest town is Port Angeles, a community of only 19,000 people—it retains a feeling of country living on the edge of wilderness, which indeed it is. Remote it may be but the Olympic Peninsula is where much of the seattle Metropolitan area comes to play. Be sure to make reservations when possible at lodges, motels and campgrounds or arrive very early to get a spot, especially on weekends.

Olympic National Park, which dominates the peninsula, is a primeval place where eternal glaciers drop suddenly off sheer rock faces into nearly impenetrable rainforest, where America's largest herd of Roosevelt elk roams unseen by all but the most intrepid human eyes, where an impossibly rocky, protected coastline (at 73 miles the longest wilderness beach in the Lower 48) cradles primitive marine life forms as it has done for millions of years. No fewer than five Indian reservations speckle sections of a coast famed as much for its shipwrecks as for its salmon fishing.

South of the national park, the Washington coast extends down the Northwest's finest sand beaches and around two enormous river estuaries, to the mouth of the Columbia River and the state of Oregon. In this region, two towns have become major resort centers: Ocean Shores and Long Beach.

The Washington coast is known for its heavy rainfall, and justifiably so. Although the Olympics are not high by many standards—its tallest peaks are under 8000 feet—they catch huge amounts of precipitation blowing in from the Pacific Ocean. So much snow falls that more than 60 glaciers survive at elevations as low as 4500 feet. Even greater amounts fall on the windward slopes: 120 to 167 inches

165

a year and more in the Forks area. Not only does this foster the rapid growth of mushrooms and slugs, but it has also led to the creation of North America's greatest rainforest in the soggy Hoh River valley. Yet a mere 40 miles away as the raven flies, Sequim—in the Olympic rain shadow—is a comparative desert with only about 15 inches of rain per year.

The first residents of the peninsula and coast were tribes like the Makah, Ozette and Quileute, whose descendants still inhabit the area today. A seafaring people noted for their woodcarving, they lived in a series of longhouses facing the sea and are known to have inhabited this region for as long as 2500 years.

Their first contact with Europeans came in 1775, when they massacred a Spanish landing party. Three years later, the ubiquitous British captain James Cook sailed the coast and traded for sea otter furs with Vancouver Island natives; his report opened the gates to the maritime fur trade.

American entrepreneur John Jacob Astor established a fort at the mouth of the Columbia River in 1803, and two years later Meriwether Lewis and William Clark led a cross-country expedition that arrived at Cape Disappointment, on the Washington side of the Columbia, in the winter of 1805. White settlement was at first slow, but by the mid-19th century Port Townsend had established itself as Puget Sound's premier lumber-shipping port, and other communities sprang up soon after.

Olympic National Park was annexed to the national park system in 1938. But long before that, Washingtonians had discovered its natural wonders. A fledgling tourism industry grew, with lodges constructed at several strategic locations around the park, including lakes Crescent and Quinault, Sol Duc Hot Springs and Kalaloch, overlooking the Pacific. Coastal communities were also building a visitor infrastructure, and quiet beach resorts soon emerged.

Today, typical Olympic Peninsula visitors start their tour in Port Townsend, having traveled by ferry and car from Seattle or Whidbey Island, and use Route 101 as their artery of exploration. Port Townsend is considered the most authentic Victorian seacoast town in the United States north of San Francisco, and its plethora of well-preserved 19th-century buildings, many of them now bed and breakfasts, charms all visitors. Less than an hour's drive west, the seven-mile Dungeness Spit (a national wildlife refuge) is the largest natural sand hook in the United States and is famed for the delectable crabs that share its name. Port Angeles, in the center of the north coast, is home to the headquarters of Olympic National Park and is its primary gateway. The bustling international port town also has a direct ferry link to Victoria, Canada, across the Strait of Juan de Fuca.

Neah Bay, the northwesternmost community in the continental United States, is the home of the Makah Indian Museum and Cultural Center and an important marina for deep-sea fishing charters. Clallam Bay, to its east, and La Push, south down the coast, are other sportfishing centers. The logging town of Forks is the portal for visitors to the national park's Hoh Rainforest.

Route 101 emerges from the damp Olympic forests to slightly less moist Grays Harbor, with its twin lumber port towns of Aberdeen and Hoquiam. Though these towns combined have a population of over 25,000, they have limited appeal to travelers, who typically head over the north shore of Grays Harbor to the hotels

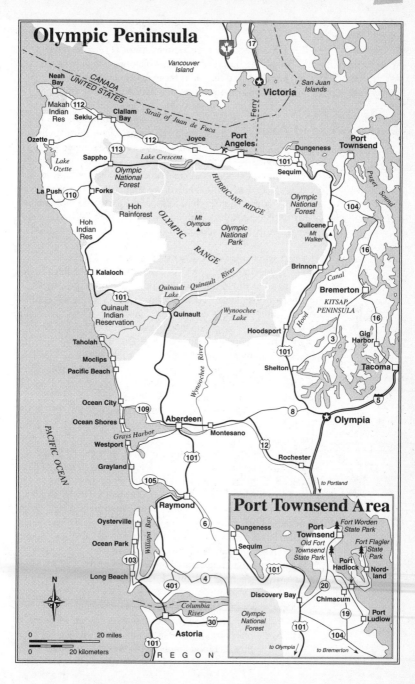

Olympic Peninsula

Vancouver
Island

17

Neah
Bay

UNITED STATES
CANADA

Victoria

San Juan
Islands

Ferry

Makah
Indian
Res

112

Clallam
Bay

Sekiu

Strait of Juan de Fuca

Ozette

113

112

Joyce

Port
Angeles

Dungeness

Port
Townsend

Sappho

Lake Crescent

101

Sequim

Lake
Ozette

Olympic
National
Forest

HURRICANE RIDGE

Puget Sound

La Push

110

Forks

Olympic
National
Forest

104

Hoh
Rainforest

OLYMPIC

Mt
Olympus

Olympic
National
Park

Quilcene

Mt
Walker

Hoh
Indian
Res

RANGE

16

Kalaloch

Quinault River

Brinnon

Canal

Quinault
Lake

Quinault River

Bremerton

101

Quinault
Indian
Reservation

Quinault

Wynoochee
Lake

KITSAP
PENINSULA

Hood

Hoodsport

16

Taholah

3

Gig
Harbor

Moclips

101

Tacoma

Pacific Beach

Wynoochee River

Shelton

Ocean City

109

Aberdeen

8

Olympia

5

Ocean Shores

PACIFIC OCEAN

Grays Harbor

Montesano

12

Westport

Grayland

101

Rochester

105

to Portland

Raymond

6

Port Townsend Area

Oysterville

Willapa Bay

Dungeness

Port
Townsend

Fort Worden
State Park

Ocean Park

103

Sequim

Old Fort
Townsend
State Park

Fort Flagler
State
Park

101

Port
Hadlock

Nord-
land

Long Beach

401

4

Discovery Bay

20

Chimacum

19

Port
Ludlow

N

Columbia River

30

Olympic
National
Forest

101

104

0   20 miles

Astoria

101

to Olympia

to Bremerton

0   20 kilometers

O R E G O N

of Ocean Shores, or down the south shore of the harbor to the quaint fishing village of Westport.

Serene Willapa Bay is another huge river estuary south of Grays Harbor. The resort strip of 28-mile-long Long Beach Peninsula, which provides a seaward dike for the bay, is older and less contrived than the Ocean Shores area. Wildlife refuges, oyster farms and cranberry bogs lend it a sort of 1950s Cape Cod ambience.

▾ ▾ ▾ ▾ ▾ ▾ ▾ ▾ ▾ ▾ ▾ ▾ ▾ ▾
Port Townsend Area

Before either Seattle or Tacoma were so much as a tug on a fisherman's line, Port Townsend was a thriving lumber port. Founded in 1851, it has retained its Victorian seacoast ambience better than any other community north of San Francisco. Much of the city has been designated a National Historic Landmark district, with more than 70 Victorian houses, buildings, forts, parks and monuments. Many of the handsomely gabled homes are open for tours and/or offer bed-and-breakfast accommodations.

SIGHTS   The best way to see **Port Townsend** is on foot. When you drive into town on Route 20, you'll first want to stop at the **Port Townsend Chamber of Commerce** visitors center for maps, brochures and event information. Then continue east on Route 20 as it becomes Water Street. ~ 2437 East Sims Way, Port Townsend; 360-385-2722; www.ptguide.com, e-mail info@ptchamber.org.

In Port Townsend's restored 1892 **City Hall**, you'll find the **Jefferson County Historical Society Museum**, featuring Victorian antiques and artifacts. Thousands of photos from Port Townsend's early days are housed in the museum's archives office (13694 Airport Cutoff Road/Route 19; 360-379-6673). Admission. ~ 548 Water Street, Port Townsend; 360-385-1003, fax 360-385-1042; www.jchsmuseum.org, e-mail jchsmuseum@olympus.net.

Heading west on Water Street by foot, note the elegant stone and wood-frame buildings on either side of the street, most of them dating from the 1880s and 1890s. Turn right on Adams Street; halfway up the block on the right is the **Enoch S. Fowler Building**, built in 1874, the oldest two-story stone structure in Washington. A former county courthouse, it now houses the weekly newspaper.

Turn left at Washington Street and five blocks farther, on your left, you'll see the **James House**, built in 1889. It has five chimneys and a commanding view of the harbor—and in 1973 became the Northwest's first bed and breakfast. ~ 1238 Washington Street, Port Townsend; 360-385-1238, 800-385-1238, fax 360-379-5551; www.jameshouse.com, e-mail info@jameshouse.com.

Turn right up Harrison Street, then right again at Franklin Street. Two blocks farther, at Franklin and Polk streets, the **Captain Enoch S. Fowler Home**, built in 1860, is the oldest surviving house in Port Townsend and is typical of New England–style homes.

Two more blocks ahead, you will encounter the **Rothschild House**, built in 1868 by an early Port Townsend merchant. Notable for its outstanding interior woodwork, it's maintained by the State Parks Commission for public tours. Closed October through April. Admission. ~ Franklin and Taylor streets, Port Townsend; 360-385-1003; www.jchsmuseum.org.

A block north, **Trinity Methodist Church** (1871) is the state's oldest standing Methodist church. Its small museum contains the Bible of the church's first minister. ~ Taylor and Clay streets, Port Townsend; 360-385-0484.

A block east, the 1889 **Ann Starrett Victorian Boutique Hotel Mansion**, now an inn, offers public tours from noon until three during the months of July and August. Admission. ~ 744 Clay Street, Port Townsend; 360-385-3205, 800-321-0644; www.star rettmansion.com, e-mail info@starrettmansion.com.

The **Lucinda Hastings Home** was the most expensive house ever built in Port Townsend when it was erected in 1889 at a cost of $14,000. ~ Clay and Monroe streets, Port Townsend.

Turn right here, and return down Monroe to Water Street and your starting point at City Hall. Get back in your car and drive north on Monroe Street. (The arterial staggers a half-block right at Roosevelt Street onto Jackson Street, then turns right onto Walnut Street.) All roads flow into W Street, the south boundary of **Fort Worden State Park Conference Center**. If the fort looks familiar, it could be because it was used in the filming of the Richard Gere–Debra Winger classic, *An Officer and a Gentleman*. Authorized in 1896, it includes officers' row and a refurbished **Commanding Officer's House** (admission), the **248th Coast Artillery Museum** (admission), gun emplacements, a concert pavilion, marine interpretive center and **Point Wilson Lighthouse**. Fort Worden offers stretches of beach that command impressive views of the Cascades and nearby islands. ~ Port Townsend; 360-344-4400, fax 360-385-7248; www.fortworden.org.

LEISURELY LISTENING

Chamber music doesn't come much more idyllic than the annual summer **Olympic Music Festival**, held on a farm near Port Townsend between late June and early September. Founded by members of the Philadelphia String Quartet in 1984, the much-loved weekend Concerts in the Barn now attract 12,000 people a year for a relaxed afternoon of professionally played chamber music, strolls in grassy meadows, and picnics. Concerts are held rain or shine on Saturday and Sunday. ~ 206-527-8839; www.olympicmusicfestival.org, e-mail info@olympicmusicfestival.org.

On the dock at Fort Worden is the **Port Townsend Marine Science Center**. Of special interest are its four large touch tanks, representing different intertidal habitats, where creatures like starfish, anemones and sea cucumbers can be handled by curious visitors. Daily guided walks as well as a birding boat trip around Protection Island National Wildlife Refuge are offered in the summer. Hours vary seasonally; call ahead. Admission. ~ Port Townsend; 360-385-5582, 800-566-3932; www.ptmsc.org, e-mail info@ptmsc.org.

Visitors driving to Port Townsend typically cross the one-and-a-half-mile **Hood Canal Floating Bridge** on Route 104 from the Kitsap Peninsula. Located 30 miles southeast of Port Townsend, it is the world's only floating bridge erected over tidal waters and one of the longest of its kind anywhere. Constructed in 1961, the bridge was washed away during a fierce storm in February 1979, but was rebuilt in 1982.

Traveling south from Port Townsend, Route 20 joins Route 101 at Discovery Bay. Twelve miles south of the junction is the town of **Quilcene** on the Hood Canal, a serpentine finger of Puget Sound. The town is especially noted for its oyster farming and processing and is the location of a state shellfish research laboratory (not open to the public). The **Mount Walker Observation Point**—five miles south on Route 101, then another five miles on a gravel road that starts at Walker Pass—offers a spectacular view of the Hood Canal and surrounding area. On a clear day, you can see Seattle and the Space Needle.

LODGING   The **James House** claims to have been the Pacific Northwest's first bed and breakfast. Just a few steps from shops and restaurants at the foot of the bluff that stands behind lower downtown, it dates from 1889, though it's only been a bed and breakfast since 1973. The house is unmistakable for its five chimneys; inside, the floors are all parquet. All rooms have private baths. There is a fireplace and a library, and a full breakfast is served. Save a few moments to enjoy the English gardens with an impressive view of the water. Two bungalow-style units, adjacent to the James House, are also available. Kids over 12 are welcome. ~ 1238 Washington Street, Port Townsend; 360-385-1238, 800-385-1238, fax 360-379-5551; www.jameshouse.com, e-mail info@jameshouse.com. DELUXE TO ULTRA-DELUXE.

For those less than enthralled with bed and breakfasts, the **Palace Hotel** provides historic accommodation in a former seafarers' bordello. Though nicely renovated, this is a bit rustic: After checking in at the main lobby you must climb a long flight of stairs (or two) to your room. There are 15 guest chambers, each with antiques recalling the red-light flavor of the past. Three of the rooms, including the madam's former room, even have kitchenettes. ~

1004 Water Street, Port Townsend; 360-385-0773, 800-962-0741, fax 360-385-0780; www.palacehotelpt.com, e-mail palace@olympus.net. MODERATE TO ULTRA-DELUXE.

The renowned **Ann Starrett Victorian Boutique Hotel Mansion**, a National Historic Landmark built in 1889, is a classic mansion in Victorian style. High on a bluff overlooking downtown Port Townsend and Puget Sound, it combines diverse architectural elements—frescoed ceilings, a free-hung spiral staircase, an eight-sided dome painted as a solar calendar, the requisite gables and dormer window—into a charming whole. The 11 guest rooms all have private baths and are furnished with antiques, of course. Five-night minimum from November through Christmas. ~ 744 Clay Street, Port Townsend; 360-385-3205, 800-321-0644; www.starrettmansion.com, e-mail info@starrettmansion.com. DELUXE TO ULTRA-DELUXE.

With so many heritage choices, few visitors actually opt for a motel stay. If you do, check out **The Tides Inn**, along the waterfront at the south end of town. Among the 45 rooms are five efficiencies and nine with hot tubs; most units have balconies overlooking the bay. ~ 1807 Water Street, Port Townsend; 360-385-0595, 800-822-8696, fax 360-379-1115; www.tides-inn.com, e-mail tidesinn@cablespeed.com. BUDGET TO ULTRA-DELUXE.

The Dungeness crab was the first commercially harvested shellfish on the Olympic coast.

Built in 1936 for use by pilots guiding ships through the Strait of Juan de Fuca, the two-bedroom, weathered-shingle **Pilot's Cottage** exudes oodles of simple rustic charm and atmosphere from its quiet waterfront location overlooking Point Hudson Harbor. Amenities include a kitchen, living room and wood-burning stove. The cottage can be rented by the night, week or longer and sleeps four total; no smoking or pets. It's walking distance to downtown. ~ 327 Jackson Street, Port Townsend; 360-379-3811; www.pilotscottage.com. DELUXE.

For students and backpackers, the **Olympic Hostel at Fort Worden State Park** offers some of the least expensive accommodations on the Olympic Peninsula. Housed in a former World War II barracks building, it has 30 beds in men's and women's dormitories, along with private rooms for couples and families. ~ 272 Battery Way, Port Townsend; 360-385-0655, 800-909-4776; www.olympichostel.org, e-mail olympichostel@olympus.net. BUDGET.

South of town about 20 miles, **The Resort at Port Ludlow** is one of the Northwest's premier family resorts. It boasts a championship golf course, tennis courts, swimming pools, a marina, hiking and biking trails and 1500 acres of land. There are 37 guest rooms with fireplaces, six condominiums and one beach house. Other amenities include oversized jetted tubs and decks, and a restaurant with marvelous views of water and mountains.

~ 1 Heron Road, Port Ludlow; 360-437-7000, 800-732-1239, fax 360-437-7410; www.portludlowresort.com, e-mail info@port ludlowresort.com. ULTRA-DELUXE.

DINING

For an evening of fine dining, it would be hard to top the **Manresa Castle**. Located in an 1892 hilltop inn that overlooks the town and bay like a German castle on the Rhine River, it combines an elegant restaurant and an Edwardian pub. The menu offers regional and seasonal specialties, everything from curry chicken and bouillabaisse to tiger prawns. Sunday brunch is also served. Closed seasonally; call ahead. ~ 7th and Sheridan streets, Port Townsend; 360-385-5750, fax 360-385-5883; www.manresacastle.com, e-mail info@manresacastle.com. DELUXE.

Breakfasts draw full houses at the **Salal Cafe**. Huge omelettes and various seafood and vegetarian recipes get *oohs* and *ahs*, as do the burgers and meat dishes. Lunch features gourmet home-style cooking, along with crêpes and sandwiches. No dinner. ~ 634 Water Street, Port Townsend; 360-385-6532. BUDGET.

Some say the **Shanghai Restaurant** serves the best Chinese food this side of Vancouver's Chinatown. Forget the view of the RV park across the street, and enjoy the spicy Szechuan and northern Chinese cuisine. ~ Point Hudson, Port Townsend; 360-385-4810, fax 360-385-0660. BUDGET TO MODERATE.

HIDDEN ▶

The **Chimacum Café**, nine miles south of Port Townsend, is a local institution. This is food like grandma should have made—country-fried chicken dinners, baked ham and so forth, followed, of course, by homemade pies brimming with fresh fruit. Breakfast, lunch and dinner are served. ~ 9253 Rhody Drive, Chimacum; 360-732-4631. BUDGET TO MODERATE.

SHOPPING

Port Townsend offers the most interesting shopping on the peninsula with its array of galleries, antique and gift shops, bookstores, gourmet dining and all-purpose emporiums. Proprietors have paid particular attention to historical accuracy in restoring

AUTHOR FAVORITE

Ask locals where to eat, and chances are they'll recommend the **Fountain Café**. You'll probably have to stand in line for a seat, but the wait will be worth it. Occupying the ground floor of a historic building (is there anything else in downtown Port Townsend?), the Fountain serves outstanding seafood and pasta dishes, including oysters as you like 'em. Soups and desserts are homemade. The decor is eclectic and showcases young local artists. ~ 920 Washington Street, Port Townsend; 360-385-1364. MODERATE.

commercial buildings. Many of the shops feature the work of talented local painters, sculptors, weavers, potters, poets and writers.

If you're looking for antiques, try the **Port Townsend Antique Mall** or any of the many other shops along the 600 through 1200 blocks of Water or Washington streets. ~ Antique Mall: 802 Washington Street, Port Townsend; 360-379-8069.

Live blues, jazz, opera and folk music accompany dinner at **Lanza's Ristorante** on the weekend. Closed Sunday and Monday. ~ 1020 Lawrence Street, Port Townsend; 360-379-1900.

NIGHTLIFE

BEACHES & PARKS

FORT WORDEN STATE PARK A 434-acre estate right in Port Townsend, this turn-of-the-20th-century fort includes restored Victorian officers houses, barracks, theater, parade grounds and artillery bunkers. A beach and a boat launch are on Admiralty Inlet, at the head of Puget Sound. Try the dock or beach for salmon fishing. Restrooms, picnic areas, tennis courts and lodging are found here. ~ The entrance is located on W Street at Cherry Street, at the northern city limits of Port Townsend; 360-344-4400, fax 360-385-7248; www.fortworden.org, e-mail fwcamping@parks.wa.gov.

▲ There are 80 RV hookup sites ($25 to $31 per night). Primitive sites are also available ($14 per night). Reservations, by mail, by fax or via the internet, are strongly recommended year-round. Reservations: 200 Battery Way, Port Townsend, WA 98368.

KAH TAI LAGOON NATURE PARK This midtown park, which features 15 acres of wetlands and 40 acres of grasslands and woodlands, is a great place for birdwatching: more than 50 species have been identified here. There are two and a half miles of trails, a play area for kids, interpretive displays, restrooms and picnic areas. ~ 12th Street near Sims Way, Port Townsend.

OLD FORT TOWNSEND STATE PARK Decommissioned in 1895 when Indian attacks on Port Townsend (the town) were no longer a threat, the fort site has six and a half miles of trails and a beach on Port Townsend (the inlet). You can fish from the shore. You'll find restrooms and picnic areas. Closed October through May. Day-use fee, $5. ~ Old Fort Townsend Road, two miles south of the town of Port Townsend off Route 20; 360-385-3595 or 360-385-3595, fax 360-385-7248; www.fortworden.org/oft.html, e-mail fwoftd@parks.wa.gov.

▲ There are 40 standard sites ($13 per night) and 4 primitive sites ($10 per night). Closed early November to mid-April.

FORT FLAGLER STATE PARK Fort buildings dating from 1898 are a major attraction here. In addition, the saltwater beach on Admiralty Inlet is popular for clamming, beachcombing and fishing for salmon, halibut, sole, crab and shellfish. There are also a boat launch, hiking trails, restrooms, picnic areas and lodging. ~ Off Route 116, on the north tip of Marrowstone Island, eight miles northeast of Hadlock; 360-385-1259, 888-226-7688, fax 360-379-1746.

▲ There are 101 standard sites ($16 to $19 per night) and 12 RV hookup sites ($22 per night). No camping November through February. Reservations: 888-226-7688.

DOSEWALLIPS STATE PARK 🚶 🚴 ⚓ ⛵ At the mouth of the Dosewallips River on the Hood Canal, a long, serpentine arm of Puget Sound, this 425-acre park is especially popular among clam diggers and oyster hunters during shellfish season. You'll find a beach of oyster shells and cobble, hiking trails, restrooms, showers and picnic areas. ~ Route 101, in Brinnon, 37 miles south of Port Townsend; 360-796-4415, fax 360-796-3242.

▲ There are 100 standard sites ($16 per night) and 40 RV hookup sites ($22 per night). Reservations: 888-226-7688.

OLYMPIC NATIONAL FOREST 🚶 🚴 🐎 ⛵ ⚓ ⛵ ⛵ Surrounding Olympic National Park on its east, south and northwest sides, this national forest provides ample recreational opportunities, including good fishing for trout and, in some areas, for rock cod and salmon in the forest's many lakes and rivers. It includes five wilderness areas on the fringe of the park. There are restrooms and picnic areas. Dogs and hunting are allowed in the national forest, but not in Olympic National Park. Some areas of the park and some campgrounds close seasonally due to weather. ~ Numerous access roads branch off Route 101, especially south of Sequim, and between Quilcene and Hoodsport, on the east side of the Olympic Peninsula; 360-956-2400, fax 360-956-2330; www.fs.fed.us/r6/olympic, e-mail mailroom-r6_olympic@fs.fed.us.

▲ There are 23 campgrounds throughout the forest. Camping costs range from free to $15 per night. Three cabins, sleeping four to six people, rent for $30 to $40 per night.

Port Angeles Area

The northern gateway to Olympic National Park as well as a major terminal for ferries to British Columbia, the Port Angeles area is one of northwest Washington's main crossroads. Sequim on Route 101, 31 miles west of Port Townsend, and nearby Port Angeles are two of the peninsula's more intriguing towns.

SIGHTS
The town of **Sequim** (pronounced "Squim") is graced with a climate that's unusually dry and mild for the Northwest: it sits in the Olympic rain shadow. A major attraction just north of town is the

Olympic Game Farm, whose animals—lions, tigers, bears, buffalo and many others—are trained for film roles. Driving tours of the farm are available year-round; walking tours, including a studio barn, are offered during the summer. Admission. ~ 1423 Ward Road, Sequim; 360-683-4295, fax 360-681-4443; www.oly gamefarm.com, e-mail gamefarm@olympus.net.

In the Sequim–Dungeness Valley area, the **Museum and Art Center** preserves the native and pioneer farming heritage of Sequim and showcases the work of local artists. Closed Sunday and Monday. ~ 175 West Cedar Street, Sequim; 360-683-8110; www.se quimmuseum.org.

For visitor information, contact the **Sequim–Dungeness Chamber of Commerce Visitors Center**. ~ 1190 West Washington Street, Sequim; 360-683-6197, 800-737-8462; www.cityofse quim.com, e-mail info@cityofsequim.com.

North off Route 101, the Dungeness Valley is dotted with lavender, strawberry and raspberry fields. Weathered barns left over from the area's dairy farming days are still visible. Pay a visit to the **Cedarbrook Lavender & Herb Farm**, where 300 different varieties of lavender and herbs fill the air with a marvelous (but indefinable!) aroma and inspire many a gourmet chef to go on a culinary buying spree. Closed Monday in winter; closed in January. ~ 1345 Sequim Avenue South, Sequim; 360-683-7733, 800-470-8423, 800-471-8423; www.cedarbrook herbfarm.com, e-mail marcella@cedarbrookherb farm.com.

> On the Strait of Juan de Fuca at the foot of the Olympic Mountains, this region often may be dry when it's pouring rain just a few miles south.

Opposite the mouth of the Dungeness River is one of the Olympic Peninsula's most remarkable natural features: the **Dungeness Spit**, almost seven miles long and the largest natural sand hook in the United States. A short trail within the adjacent **Dungeness Recreation Area** provides access to this national wildlife refuge. At the end of the spit, the **New Dungeness Lighthouse** rises 63 feet above the sea. Established in 1857, the lighthouse is now on the National Register of Historic Places. Visitors who brave the five-and-a-half-mile walk out along the spit will be rewarded with an in-depth tour of the facilities. ~ 360-683-9166; www.newdungenesslighthouse.com, e-mail light keepers@newdungenesslighthouse.com.

Seventeen miles west of Sequim on Route 101 is the fishing and logging port of **Port Angeles**, the Olympic Peninsula's largest town. A major attraction here is the **City Pier**. Adjacent to the ferry terminal, it boasts an observation tower, promenade decks and a picnic area. ~ Port Angeles; 360-452-2363.

The **Arthur D. Feiro Marine Life Center**, where visitors can observe and even touch samples of local marine life, is also found at the City Pier. Call for hours. Admission. ~ Port Angeles; 360-417-6254; www.olypen.com/feirolab, e-mail feirolab@olypen.com.

As the gateway to Olympic National Park, Port Angeles is home to national park headquarters. At the **Olympic National Park Visitor Center**, you'll find an excellent video and exhibits on the natural and human history of the park. Usually open daily in the summer; varying hours the rest of the year. ~ 3002 Mt. Angeles Road, Port Angeles; 360-565-3130; www.nps.gov/olym.

Nestled in the shadow of Olympic National Park, award-winning **Port Angeles Fine Art Center** is located in a leafy five-acre sculpture park and hosts changing mixed-media exhibitions, lectures and concerts, and the Strait of Juan de Fuca Festival of Fine Arts every Memorial Day weekend. Closed Monday through Wednesday. ~ Take Route 101 westbound to Race Street and the Olympic National Park Hurricane Ridge turnoff. Turn left (south) and proceed 1 mile towards Hurricane Ridge. Turn left (east) on Lauridsen Boulevard and proceed .25 mile to PAFAC parking adjacent to a domed water silo; 360-417-4590; www.portangelesartcenter.com, e-mail info@pafac.org.

The **Museum at the Carnegie** has county archival and genealogical records, as well as exhibits like period clothing and old photos. Winter hours are Wednesday through Saturday, or by appointment. Call for summer hours. ~ 207 South Lincoln Street, Port Angeles; 360-452-2662; www.clallamhistoricalsociety.com, e-mail artifact@olypen.com.

For tourist information, contact the **North Olympic Peninsula Visitor & Convention Bureau**. ~ 338 West 1st Street, Port Angeles; 360-452-8552, 800-942-4042; www.olympicpeninsula.org, e-mail info@olympicpeninsula.org.

LODGING You'll feel good right down to your cockles—as well as your steamer clams and horse clams—after shellfishing on the saltwater beach outside the **Sequim Bay Resort**. The eight fully equipped housekeeping cottages here are suitable for vacationing families and shoreline lovers. There are no pets allowed in the cottages. There are also guest laundry facilities and hookups for RVs. Two-night minimum stay required. ~ 2634 West Sequim Bay Road, Sequim; 360-681-3853, fax 360-681-3854; www.sequimbayresort.com, e-mail sequimbayresort@yahoo.com. BUDGET TO MODERATE.

Just a spit from the Spit—Dungeness, that is—is the **Groveland Cottage**, by the coast north of Sequim. The early-20th-century building has four carpeted rooms with art, antique decor and private baths; some boast jacuzzis and fireplaces. There is also a private cottage with a queen-size bed and private bath. The rooms may be simple, but service is not: coffee is delivered to your room in anticipation of the gourmet breakfast. Wi-fi is available in all

rooms. The accent overall is on comfort. They also rent 32 vacation cottages in the area. ~ 4861 Sequim-Dungeness Way, Dungeness; 360-683-3565, 800-879-8859, fax 360-683-5181; www. sequimvalley.com, e-mail simone@olypen.com. MODERATE.

Perhaps the nicest motel-style accommodation in these port communities is the **Red Lion Hotel**. A modern building that extends along the Strait of Juan de Fuca opposite the ferry dock, it offers rooms with private balconies overlooking the water. A strand of beach and swimming pool beckon bathers. ~ 221 North Lincoln Street, Port Angeles; 360-452-9215, 800-733-5466, fax 360-452-4734; www.redlionportangeles.com, e-mail pa.front desk@redlion.com. DELUXE.

Victoria, across the strait on Vancouver Island, is said to be "more British than the British"—but the same slogan could almost apply to **The Tudor Inn**. The host serves a traditional English breakfast and afternoon refreshment in the restored Tudor-style home. Most of their antique collection is Old English, and the well-stocked library will steer you to books on a wide variety of subjects. All five bedrooms have private baths; one has a gas fireplace and small balcony. ~ 1108 South Oak Street, Port Angeles; 360-452-3138, 866-286-2224, fax 360-457-9360; www.tudor inn.com, e-mail info@tudorinn.com. DELUXE.

El Cazador is a casual, family-run restaurant with festive murals. What sets it apart is its use of fresh seafood in traditional Mexican dishes that consistently win local "best of" awards. The burrito à la Veracruz stuffed with baby shrimp is especially good. ~ 531 West Washington Street, Sequim; 360-683-4788, fax 360-683-2203; www.el-cazador.com. BUDGET.

DINING

AUTHOR FAVORITE

Situated on the water with beautiful gardens and spectacular views of the San Juan Islands, the **Domaine Madeleine Bed and Breakfast** excels in both comfort and hospitality. There are five rooms at this charming inn, including a honeymoon cottage. There's the Renoir Suite, with a 14-foot-high basalt fireplace and impressionist art, and the Ming Room, with antiques, a jacuzzi and a large private balcony. All rooms have fireplaces, feather beds and French perfumes. Four rooms have jacuzzis for two. Relax in the cozy coffee nook or try your hand at the antique organ. The full gourmet breakfast is elegantly presented—don't miss it. Gay-friendly. ~ 146 Wildflower Lane, Port Angeles; 360-457-4174, 888-811-8376, fax 360-457-3037; www.domainemadeleine.com, e-mail romance@domaine madeleine.com. ULTRA-DELUXE.

A delightful surprise in the bucolic Dungeness Valley is **Cedar Creek Cuisine**, which occupies a rustic two-story, 1896 country physician's home and office. Menus, inspired both by Pacific Northwest and southern French cuisine, make excellent use of such local foods as Dungeness crab and seasonal wild mushrooms. Seafood *arabbiata* is a standout. ~ 665 North 5th Avenue, Sequim; 360-683-3983; www.cedarcreekcuisine.com. DELUXE.

The undisputed winner in the northern Olympic Peninsula fine-dining sweepstakes is **C'est Si Bon**. The decor is modern and dramatic, with handsome oil paintings and full picture windows allowing panoramas of the Olympic Range. The cuisine, on the other hand, is classical French: quails stuffed with mushrooms, veal, pork and chicken, coquilles St. Jacques, filet mignon with dungeness crab. There are French wines and desserts, too. Dinner only. Closed Monday. ~ 23 Cedar Park Road, four miles east of Port Angeles; 360-452-8888; www.cestsibon-frenchcuisine.com. ULTRA-DELUXE.

> The Dungeness Spit and the surrounding bay and estuary are teeming with wildlife, including seabirds, seals, fish, crabs and clams.

A New England reader raved about the clam linguine at the charming **Bella Italia**. Indeed, this restaurant is a destination in itself for many Puget Sound–area foodies. In addition to a variety of pasta, this intimate, candlelit eatery whips up Tuscan steak, cioppino and veal Marsala. It also has an extensive wine selection. Dinner only. ~ 118-E East 1st Street, Port Angeles; 360-457-5442, fax 360-457-6112; www.bellaitaliapa.com, e-mail bella@olypen.com. MODERATE TO DELUXE.

Port Angeles Crabhouse, located in the Red Lion Hotel, offers sweeping waterfront views in a casually elegant decor of etched glass and tapestry-covered booth seating. Simple and straightforward seafood dishes such as cracked Dungeness crab and grilled salmon are the specialties. ~ 221 North Lincoln Street, Port Angeles; 360-457-0424, fax 360-452-4734. MODERATE TO ULTRA-DELUXE.

Practically next door is the **First Street Haven**, one of the best places around for quick and tasty breakfasts and lunches. Have a homemade quiche and salad, along with baked goods and the house coffee, and you'll be set for the day. Breakfast and lunch only, but no lunch on Sunday. ~ 107 East 1st Street, Port Angeles; 360-457-0352, fax 360-452-8502. BUDGET.

SHOPPING Mad Maggi Salon Boutique is a women's clothing shop that doubles as a hair salon. ~ 131 East Washington Street, Sequim; 360-683-5733.

NIGHTLIFE You didn't come to this part of the state for its nightlife, and that's good. What little there is usually exists only on Friday and Saturday nights.

The **Port Angeles Crabhouse Lounge** in the Red Lion Hotel features daily drink specials. ~ 221 North Lincoln Street, Port Angeles; 360-457-0424.

SEQUIM BAY STATE PARK **BEACHES & PARKS**
Shellfish (clams, oysters and crabs) as well as fishing for salmon and halibut are the main attractions at this park on Sequim Bay, sheltered from rough seas by two spits at its mouth and from heavy rains by the Olympic rain shadow. There's a beach; you'll also find restrooms and picnic areas. ~ Route 101, four miles east of Sequim; 360-683-4235, fax 360-681-5054.

▲ There are 63 standard sites ($16 per night), 16 RV hook-up sites ($22 per night) and 3 hike- or bike-in primitive sites ($10 per night). Reservations: 888-226-7688.

DUNGENESS RECREATION AREA The Dungeness Spit is a national wildlife refuge, but a recreation area trail provides access. Marine birds, bald eagles and seals are among the impressive wildlife to be seen; the Dungeness crab is internationally famous as a fine food. There are restrooms, showers and picnic areas. ~ Located at the base of the Dungeness Spit, five miles west of Sequim on Route 101, then four miles north on Kitchen-Dick Road; phone/fax 360-683-5847.

▲ There are 67 sites (no hookups); $14 per night. Closed October through January.

SALT CREEK RECREATION AREA ◄HIDDEN
One of the finest tidepool sanctuaries on the Olympic Peninsula is this three-mile stretch of rocky beach. Starfish, sea urchins, anemones, mussels, barnacles and other invertebrate life can be observed . . . but not removed. Anglers will find rockfish. Restrooms, picnic areas, playground and hiking trails are all here. ~ Located three miles north from Joyce (or 15 miles west from Port Angeles) on Route 112, then another three miles north on Camp Hayden Road; 360-928-3441, fax 360-417-2395, www.clallam.net/countyparks, e-mail ccps@olypen.com.

▲ There are 52 standard sites ($14 to $16 per night) and 39 RV sites ($20 to $22 per night).

The Olympic Peninsula's main attraction—in fact, the reason most tourists come here at all—is Olympic National Park. Rugged,

Olympic National Park

glaciated mountains dominate the 1442-square-mile park, with rushing rivers tumbling from their slopes. The rainier western slopes harbor an extraordinary rainforest, and a separate 57-mile-long coastal strip preserves remarkable tidepools and marvelous ocean scenery. Wildlife in the park includes the rare Roosevelt elk, as well as deer, black bears, cougars, bobcats, a great many smaller mammals and scores of bird species. Besides the main part of the park, which encompasses the entire mountain wilderness in the center of the peninsula and can be entered from the north or west, Olympic National Park includes a separate Coastal Unit spanning 73 miles of Pacific headlands and beaches.

SIGHTS   There is no lack of facilities throughout the park: picnic areas, hotels, restaurants and groceries. For general information on the park, call the **Olympic National Park Visitor Center**. ~ 360-565-3130; www.nps.gov/olym.

The most direct route into the park from Port Angeles is the Heart of the Hills/Hurricane Ridge Road. It climbs 5200 feet in just 17 miles to the **Hurricane Ridge Lodge**, where there are breathtaking views to 7965-foot Mt. Olympus, the highest peak in the Olympic Range, and other glacier-shrouded mountains. Visitors to Hurricane Ridge can dine in the day lodge, picnic, enjoy nature walks or take longer hikes. In winter, enjoy the small downhill ski area here and many cross-country trails. ~ 360-565-3131.

Olympic National Park was originally set aside to protect the largest unmanaged herd of Roosevelt elk in the country and was almost named Elk National Park.

Twenty miles west of Port Angeles on Route 101 is **Lake Crescent**, one of three large lakes within park boundaries. Carved during the last Ice Age 10,000 years ago, it is nestled between steep forested hillsides. A unique subspecies of trout lures many anglers to its deep waters. There are several resorts, restaurants, campgrounds and picnic areas around the lake's shoreline. From National Park Service–administered Lake Crescent Lodge, on the southeast shore, a three-fourth-mile trail leads up Barnes Creek to the beautiful **Marymere Falls**. ~ 360-928-3211, fax 360-928-3253; www.lakecrescentlodge.com, e-mail lclodge@olypen.com.

West of Lake Crescent, the Sol Duc River Road turns south to **Sol Duc Hot Springs**, 12 miles off of Route 101. Long known to the Indians, the therapeutic mineral waters were discovered by a pioneer in 1880 and like everything else the white man touched, soon boasted an opulent resort. But the original burned to the ground in 1916 and today's refurbished resort, nestled in a valley of old-growth Douglas fir, is more rustic than elegant. The springs remain an attraction. Sol Duc is a major trailhead for backpacking trips into Olympic National Park; also located here is a ranger station. Closed November through mid-March. ~ 866-476-5382, fax 360-327-3593; www.visitsolduc.com, e-mail info@visitsolduc.com.

The main population center on the Olympic Coast, and the nearest to the Hoh Rainforest, is the lumber town of **Forks**. With over 3000 people, it is the largest town between Port Angeles and Hoquiam. (It's also Washington's rainiest town, with well over 100 inches a year.) Steelhead fishing, river rafting and mushroom gathering are major activities here, but the one most evident to visitors is the timber industry. Some days, in fact, there seem to be more log trucks on the roads than passenger cars.

The **Forks Timber Museum** is filled with exhibits of old-time logging equipment and historical photos, as well as pioneer and Indian artifacts. Interpretive trails, gardens and a logger memorial are next to the visitors center. Open April through October and by appointment in winter. ~ Route 101 South, Forks; 360-374-9663, fax 360-374-9253; www.forkswa.com.

On the coast 14 miles west of Forks is the 800-year-old Indian fishing village of **La Push**, center of the **Quileute Indian Reservation**. Sportfishing, camping and beach walking are popular year-round. An abandoned Coast Guard station and lighthouse here are used as a school for resident children. ~ 360-374-6163, fax 360-374-6311.

A national park road eight miles west of Forks branches off the La Push Road and follows the north shore of the Quileute River five miles to **Rialto Beach**, where spectacular piles of driftwood often accumulate. There are picnic areas and campgrounds here, and a trailhead for hikes north up the beach toward Cape Alava.

On the west side of the national park are three more major points of entry. The **Hoh Rainforest** is 19 miles east of Route 101 via the Hoh River Road, 13 miles south of Forks. For national

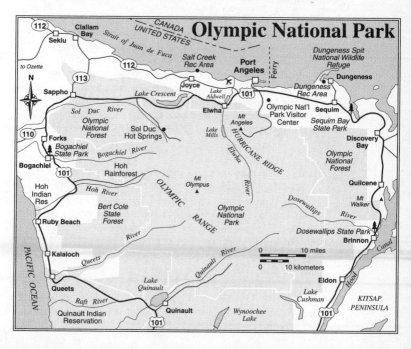

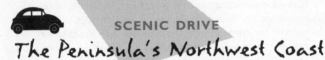

The Peninsula's Northwest Coast

Much less traveled than Route 101, Route 112 runs from near Port Angeles to Neah Bay on the northwest tip of the Olympic Peninsula. The drive takes about one and a half hours each way. Allow an additional one and a half to two hours to see the Makah Cultural and Research Center. You may wish to make this an all-day excursion by adding a side trip to Lake Ozette, one of the most hidden spots you can reach by road in Olympic National Park.

THE NORTHWEST COAST   From Port Angeles, follow Route 101 west for five miles, then turn off to the right on Route 112. For much of its length, this narrow two-lane highway runs within sight of the Strait of Juan de Fuca and partly traces the water's edge. Travel 46 miles to the sister communities of **Clallam Bay** and **Sekiu** (pronounced "C-Q"). These are prime sportfishing grounds for salmon and huge bottomfish, especially halibut. Check out the wonderful tidepools north of Clallam Bay at **Slip Point**. Just west of Sekiu, at the mouth of the Hoko River, visitors can view the remains of a 2500-year-old Makah Indian fishing village at the **Hoko Archaeological Site**.

NEAH BAY   Continue for 18 more miles past Sekiu to the highway's end at Neah Bay, the administrative center of the Makah Indian Reservation. This rather bleak little village has a few motels and a commercial fishing fleet, and visitors can book charter-fishing excursions from the harbor. Beyond the town, roads continue to stormswept beaches on Cape Flattery, strewn with driftwood and shipwrecks. Neah Bay's touristic centerpiece, the **Makah Cultural and Research Center** houses finds from the Ozette Dig at Cape Alava, about 20 miles down the Pacific coast, inter-

park information here, call the **Forks Ranger Station** (360-374-7566). There's a less well-known rainforest at the end of the gravel, 19-mile **Queets River Road**, 14 miles off Route 101, 17 miles west of Quinault. Finally, **Lake Quinault**, on Route 101 at the southwestern corner of Olympic National Park, is the site of several resorts and campgrounds, including the venerable Lake Quinault Lodge. Water sports of all kinds are popular at this glacier-fed lake, surrounded by old-growth forest.

The **Hoh Indian Reservation** is 25 miles south of Forks, off Route 101. Of more interest to most visitors is the **Kalaloch Lodge**, 35 miles south of Forks on Route 101. A major national preted through the eyes of the Makah themselves. Few relics remain from the ancient culture of the Northwest Coast tribes because their wooden structures and implements rotted away quickly in the damp climate. Ozette, however, was buried 500 years ago by a mudslide that preserved it from the elements until archaeologists discovered it in the 1970s. The artifacts exhibited in an atmospheric longhouse setting at the cultural center include baskets, log canoes, clothing, wood carvings and whaling harpoons. Closed Monday and Tuesday from September through May. Admission. ~ 1880 Bay View Avenue; 360-645-2711, fax 360-645-2656; www.makah.com, e-mail makahmuseum@centurytel.net.

LAKE OZETTE   Returning from Neah Bay on Route 112, two miles before you reach Sekiu a paved secondary road turns off to the south (right) and goes 20 miles to Lake Ozette, the northernmost part of Olympic National Park's Coastal Unit. The largest of the park's three lakes, it is separated from the ocean by a strip of land just three miles wide. Several trails lead from here to the sea, including the Indian Village Trail, which leads to the Ozette Dig (no longer open) at Cape Alava, and the Ozette Loop Trail, which weaves past 56 petroglyphs that depict various aspects of historic Makah life. Backcountry permits are required for all overnight trips in the park.

SAPPHO   Back on Route 112, six miles east of Clallam Bay Route 113 turns off to the south (right) and goes nine miles through the forest to join Route 101 at Sappho. Here you face a choice: If you turn east (left), you'll return to Port Angeles, a distance of 45 miles through Olympic National Forest and Olympic National Park, passing **Lake Crescent** and **Marymere Falls** (page 180) and the road to **Sol Duc Hot Springs** (page 180). If you turn west (right), Route 101 will take you through Forks to the turnoff for the **Hoh Rainforest** (page 181) and past that to the beaches of the **Olympic National Park Coastal Unit** (below), a total distance of 53 miles.

park facility, it affords spectacular ocean views at the southernmost end of the park's coastal strip. ~ Kalaloch Lodge: 157151 Route 101; 360-962-2271, 866-525-2562, fax 360-962-3391; www.visitkalaloch.com, e-mail info@visitkalaloch.com.

The **Olympic National Park Coastal Unit** includes some 3300 square miles of designated marine sanctuary both above and below water level. Although most of the 73-mile seacoast is unreachable by road, trails lead down to six diverse beaches from Route 101 between Kalaloch and Ruby Beach. Here you'll find broad, log-strewn expanses of sand, gravel stretches great for beachcombing, and rocky tidepools teeming with tiny marine life.

LODGING   Set on the south shore of gorgeous Lake Crescent, the 1916 **Lake Crescent Lodge** provides a variety of rooms and cottages with lake or mountain views. Units in the historic main building share bathrooms. Of the 17 cottages, 4 have fireplaces; if you don't opt for one of these, you can relax in front of the lobby's stone fireplace or in the sunroom. Amenities include an on-site restaurant and lounge, as well as rowboat rentals. Pets are accepted with a daily charge. The main lodge in closed mid-October through April; the four fireplace cottages are open weekends only during this period. ~ 416 Lake Crescent Road, 20 miles west of Port Angeles; 360-928-3211, fax 360-928-3253; www.lakecrescent-lodge.com, e-mail lclodge@olypen.com. MODERATE TO DELUXE.

The rustic **Log Cabin Resort** is a historic landmark also on the shores of Lake Crescent along Route 101. Budget-watchers can stay in the main lodge; more upscale are the lakeshore chalets and cabins. There is also an RV park with full hookups on Log Cabin Creek. The handsome log lodge has a restaurant and a gift shop; all manner of boats are rented at the marina. Closed November through April. ~ 3183 East Beach Road, 21 miles west of Port Angeles; 360-928-3325, fax 360-928-2088; www.logcabinresort.net, e-mail logcabin@logcabinresort.net. MODERATE TO DELUXE.

The **Sol Duc Hot Springs Resort** is another historic property, originally built in 1910 around a series of hot sulphur pools 12 miles south of Route 101. The 32 cabins (six with kitchens) were rebuilt in the mid-1980s and now have indoor plumbing! The River Suite is a three-bedroom cabin that sleeps ten. The best plunge, however, after a day of hiking or fishing, remains the water in three ceramic natural mineral spring pools, kept between 98° and 104°F and cleaned nightly. There is also a full-size swimming pool. Camping sites and RV hookups are available. The resort is closed November to mid-March. ~ Sol Duc Hot Springs Road, 40 miles west of Port Angeles; 360-327-3583, 866-476-

◆◆◆

IN MEMORIAM

Much of the Olympic coastline remains undeveloped. Hikers can wander along the high-water mark or on primitive trails, some wood-planked and raised above the forest floor. Offshore reefs have taken many lives over the centuries since European exploration began, and two memorials to shipwreck victims are good destinations for intrepid hikers. Nine miles south of Ozette, the **Norwegian Memorial** remembers seamen who died in an early-20th-century shipwreck. Six miles farther south, and about three miles north of Rialto Beach opposite La Push, the **Chilean Memorial** marks the grave of 20 South American sailors who died in a 1920 wreck.

5382, fax 360-327-3593; www.visitsolduc.com, e-mail info@sol-duc.com. DELUXE.

The hamlet of Sekiu flanks Route 112 on the protected shore of Clallam Bay, on the Strait of Juan de Fuca. The lone waterfront hotel here is **Van Riper's Resort**. Family owned and operated, it's a cozy getaway spot. More than half of the 16 rooms have great views of the boats on the picturesque strait. ~ 280 Front Street, Sekiu; 360-963-2334, 888-462-0803, fax 360-963-2776; www.anripersresort.com. BUDGET TO DELUXE.

The Cape Motel and RV park has eight motel rooms and two cottages; five have kitchens. Six months of the year, an RV park with restrooms is also open. ~ 1510 Bayview Avenue, Neah Bay; phone/fax 360-645-2250, 866-744-9944. BUDGET.

Among several low-priced bed and breakfasts in Forks is the **River Inn B&B**, an A-frame chalet on the banks of the Bogachiel River two-and-a-half miles from town. Two bedrooms share a bath and sundecks; one has a private bathroom and stairs leading to the hot tub. You can fish from the shore or relax in the hot tub while keeping your eyes open for elk, deer and river otter. Full breakfast. Closed in September. ~ 2596 West Bogachiel Way, Forks; 360-374-6526, fax 360-374-6590; www.jeffwoodwardsportfishing.com, e-mail laura.riverinn@yahoo.com. MODERATE.

The **Kalaloch Lodge** is perched on a bluff high above the crashing surf. Accommodations here (which may disappoint some) include 10 lodge units, 10 motel units, 20 log cabins with kitchenettes (but no utensils provided) and 18 units atop the bluff, 7 of which are duplexes. The lodge has a dining room overlooking the Pacific Ocean, as well as a general store, gas station and gift shop. ~ 157151 Route 101, 35 miles south of Forks; 360-962-2271, 866-525-2562, fax 360-962-3391; www.visitkalaloch.com, e-mail info@visitkalaloch.com. ULTRA-DELUXE.

Forks also has a youth hostel, complete with the cosmopolitan atmosphere one would expect. The **Rain Forest Hostel**, like other lodgings of its ilk, offers dorm bunks and community bathrooms and kitchen. The common room is a bonus with its fireplace and library. There is also one room for a couple and one room for a family as well as land for camping. ~ 169312 Route 101 North, 23 miles south of Forks; 360-374-2270; www.rainforesthostel.com, e-mail go2hostel@centurytel.net. BUDGET.

If you're planning a stay in the corner of Olympic National Park that includes beauteous Lake Quinault, consider the **Lake Quinault Lodge**—especially if you can get a lakefront room in the historic cedar-shingled lodge itself. The huge building arcs around the shoreline, a totem-pole design on its massive chimney facing the water. Antiques and oversized leather furniture adorn the main lobby, constructed in the 1920s. There is also a sun porch, recently renovated dining room and bar. There are fireplace and lakeside units available. You can rent boats in the summer, hike year-round or relax in the pool or sauna. ~ 345 South Shore Road, Quinault; 360-288-2900, 800-562-6672, fax 360-288-2901; www.visitlakequinault.com, e-mail info@visitlakequinault.com. DELUXE.

DINING   The best choice for dining in the park is the **Log Cabin Resort.** Enjoy the view of beautiful Lake Crescent, where anglers dip their lines for the unique crescenti trout, a subspecies of rainbow trout. Dishes range from Cajun chicken quesadillas to clams and mussels sautéed in vermouth. ~ 3183 East Beach Road, 21 miles west of Port Angeles; 360-928-3325, fax 360-928-2088. MODERATE.

There's a dining room at the **Sol Duc Hot Springs Resort,** just behind the hot sulphur springs. The food is solid Northwest fare, including some vegetarian dishes. Closed November to mid-March. ~ Sol Duc Hot Springs Road, 40 miles west of Port Angeles; 360-327-3583, 866-476-5382, fax 360-327-3593; www.visitsolduc.com, e-mail info@solduc.com. MODERATE TO DELUXE.

A mile high in the Olympic Range, 17 miles south of Port Angeles, the **Hurricane Ridge Visitors Center** frames glaciers in the picture windows upstairs from its coffee shop. Come for the view, but the standard American snacks served here aren't half-bad, either. Open January through May, weather permitting. ~ Hurricane Ridge Road; 360-565-3131. BUDGET.

Sunsets from the **Kalaloch Lodge,** high on a bluff overlooking the ocean in the national park's coastal strip, can make even the most ordinary food taste good. Fortunately, the fresh salmon and halibut served here don't need the view for their rich flavor. Breakfast, lunch and dinner. ~ 157151 Route 101, 35 miles south of Forks; 360-962-2271, 866-525-2562, fax 360-962-3391; www.visitkalaloch.com. MODERATE TO DELUXE.

The restaurant at the park's **Lake Quinault Lodge** faces another gorgeous lake surrounded by lush cedar forests. As you've come to expect along this coast, the seafood is excellent. Breakfast and dinner year-round. ~ 345 South Shore Road, Quinault; 800-562-6672, fax 360-288-2901; www.visitlakequinault.com, e-mail info@visitlakequinault.com. DELUXE.

Other than the national park lodges, pickings are slim in the restaurant department along this stretch of highway. A mile north of Forks, the **Smoke House Restaurant** serves standard American fare that should stave off hunger pangs if nothing else. ~ 193161 Route 101 North at La Push Road; 360-374-6258. MODERATE.

SHOPPING   For authentic Northwest Indian crafts, you won't do better than the gift shop at the **Makah Cultural and Research Center** on the Makah Indian Reservation near Cape Flattery at the end of Route

The Hoh Rainforest

No matter where you go on this earth, there's only one Hoh Rainforest. It's said to be one of the only coniferous rainforests in the world. Spared the logger's blade after a long-running battle between locals and conservationists, it's been undisturbed since time began. In other words, it's a natural wonder to be cherished.

Reached by traveling 13 miles south from Forks on Route 101, then 19 miles east on Hoh River Road, this is the wettest spot in the contiguous 48 states. In fact, wet isn't the word: even the air drips like a saturated sponge, producing over 30 inches of fog drip in the summer. The average annual precipitation due to rainfall is 145 inches, more than 100 inches of which fall between October and March. But temperatures at this elevation, between 500 and 1000 feet, rarely fall below 40° in winter or rise above 85° in summer. The legacy of this mild climate is dense, layered canopies of foliage.

The forest floor is as soft and thick as a shag carpet, cloaked with mosses, bracken ferns, huge fungi and seedlings. Hovering over the lush rug are vine maple, alder and black cottonwood, some hung with moss, stretching wiry branches to taste any slivers of sunlight that may steal through the canopy. Above them, Douglas fir, Sitka spruce, Western hemlock, Western red cedar and other gigantic conifers rise 200 to 300 feet, putting a lid on the forest. In all, over 300 plant species live here, not counting 70 epiphytes (mosses, lichens and such).

Some compare this environment to a cathedral. Indeed, the soft light is like sun filtered through stained glass, and the arching branches could pass for a vaulted apse. To others, it's simply mystical. The ancient coastal Indians would have agreed.

Though there are similar rainforests in Washington, the rainforest ecology is most conveniently studied at the **Hoh Rainforest Visitor Center** and on the nature trails that surround it. ~ 360-565-3130; www.nps.gov/olym. The **Hoh River Trail** extends for 17.5 miles to the river's source in Blue Glacier, on the flank of Mt. Olympus, but the rainforest can be appreciated by most visitors on one of two loop hikes that are both about a mile long. About three-fourths of a mile in, you'll see enormous old-growth Douglas fir, spruce and hemlock, some over nine feet in girth and at least 500 years old. At about one mile, the trail drops down to Big Flat, the first of several grassy open areas. The winter grazing of Roosevelt elk, whose survival was a major reason for the creation of Olympic National Park, has opened up the forest floor. Keep your eyes open, too, for wildlife. Besides the elk, you may spot river otter or weasel. Black bears and cougars also inhabit these forests. Bald eagles and great blue heron feed on the salmon that spawn seasonally in the Hoh.

112. ~ 1880 Bay View Avenue, Neah Bay; 360-645-2711; e-mail makah@centurytel.net.

BEACHES & PARKS

OLYMPIC NATIONAL PARK 🚶 🚴 🐎 🎣 ⛵ 🏕 🛶 ⛷ 🎿 🏊 🚣 ⛴ 🛥 🚤 ⛵ This spectacular national park, 922,651 acres in area and ranging in elevation from sea level to nearly 8000 feet, contains everything from permanent alpine glaciers to America's lushest rainforest (the Hoh) to rocky tidepools rich in marine life. Wildlife includes deer in the mountains, elk in the rainforest, steelhead and salmon in the rivers and colorful birds everywhere. Three large lakes—Crescent (near Port Angeles), Ozette (on the coast) and Quinault (on the southwestern edge)—are especially popular visitor destinations. There are restrooms, picnic areas, hotels, restaurants and groceries. ~ Route 101 circles the park. The numerous access roads are well marked; 360-565-3000, fax 360-565-3015 (Port Angeles); ranger stations in Forks (360-374-5877) and Sol Duc (360-327-3534); www.nps.gov/olym.

▲ There are 16 campgrounds; $10 to $18 per night.

BOGACHIEL STATE PARK 🚶 🚤 Not far from the Hoh Rainforest, this eternally damp park sits on the Bogachiel River, famous for its salmon and steelhead runs. Hiking and hunting in the adjacent forest are popular activities, although this park is more of a campsite than a day-use area. Facilities include restrooms, showers and limited picnic areas. Day-use fee, $5. ~ Route 101, six miles south of Forks; 360-374-6356.

▲ There are 36 standard sites ($17 per night), 6 RV hookup sites ($24 per night) and 2 primitive sites ($12 per night).

▼▼▼▼▼▼▼▼▼▼
Ocean Shores–Pacific Beach

A six-mile-long, 6000-acre peninsula, Ocean Shores was a cattle ranch when a group of investors bought it for $1 million in 1960. A decade later, its assessed value had risen to $35 million. Today, it would be hard to put a dollar figure on this strip of condominium-style hotels and second homes, many of them on a series of canals. The main tourist beach destination on the Grays Harbor County coastline, it's located along Route 115, three miles south of its junction with Route 109.

SIGHTS

Folks come to **Ocean Shores** for oceanside rest and recreation, not for sightseeing. One of the few "attractions" is the **Ocean Shores Interpretive Center** four miles south of the town center near the Ocean Shores Marina, which has exhibits describing the peninsula's geological formation and human development. Open daily from April through September; open the rest of the year by appointment only. ~ 1033 Catala Avenue Southeast, Ocean Shores;

360-289-4617, fax 360-289-0189; www.oceanshoresinterpretive center.com.

The 22-mile beach that parallels Routes 115 and 109 north to Moclips is an attraction in its own right. Beyond Moclips, however, the coastline gets more rugged. Eight miles past Moclips, the **Quinault Indian National Tribal Headquarters** in the village of Taholah, on the Quinault Indian Reservation, offers guided fishing trips on reservation land and tribal gifts in a small shop and museum. ~ 1214 Aalis Drive, Taholah; 360-276-8215, 888-616-8211, fax 360-276-4191; www.quinaultindiannation.com.

LODGING

The nearest ocean beach area to the Seattle-Tacoma metropolitan area, Ocean Shores' condominiums and motels are frequently booked solid during the summer and on holiday weekends, even though prices can be high. At other times, it can be downright quiet . . . and inexpensive.

Like almost every other lodging on this stretch of shoreline, **The Polynesian Resort** is as close to the water as you can get—a short quarter-mile trek across the dunes to the high-tide mark. The four-story building has 69 guest rooms ranging from motel units to three-bedroom penthouse suites. It has a restaurant, lively lounge, indoor pool and spa, outdoor games area and indoor game room popular with families. ~ 615 Ocean Shores Boulevard Northwest, Ocean Shores; 360-289-3361, 800-562-4836, fax 360-289-0294; www.thepolynesian.com, e-mail thepoly@techline.com. ULTRA-DELUXE.

Guesthouse Inn and Suites has 65 units and all the amenities of a larger resort, including a golf course and a heated outdoor pool, as well as oceanside views. Rooms are equipped with microwaves, refrigerators, coffeemakers and TVs. Complimentary breakfast included. ~ 648 Ocean Shores Boulevard, Ocean Shores; 360-289- 3323, 800-448-2433, fax 360-289-3320; www.guesthouseoceanshores.com, e-mail info@guesthouseoceanshores.com. MODERATE.

AUTHOR FAVORITE

sights A winding, scenic coastal drive to the end of Route 112 climaxes at **Cape Flattery**, the northwesternmost corner of the contiguous United States. The road at times runs within feet of the water, providing spectacular blufftop views of the Strait of Juan de Fuca and Tatoosh Island—a great location for whale watching between March and May. A short trail leads to the shore. Beach hikers can find some of the last wilderness coast in Washington south of here.

Neighboring units at **The Grey Gull** are fewer in number (37), but they're all studios or suites with fireplaces, microwaves, VCRs and private decks or balconies. The Gull has an outdoor pool and jacuzzi guarded by a wind fence. Dogs are welcome in selected rooms. ~ 651 Ocean Shores Boulevard, Ocean Shores; 360-289-3381, 800-562-9712, fax 360-289-3673; www.thegreygull.com, e-mail greygull@thegreygull.com. DELUXE.

The **Caroline Inn** offers four bi-level townhouse suites with great views, just steps from the water. The decor follows a *Gone With the Wind* theme in soft rose colors. The rooms are furnished with sleigh beds and other antiques. Each suite offers all the comforts of home and then some: fireplaces, jacuzzis, complete kitchens and living areas with entertainment centers. ~ 1341 Ocean Shores Boulevard, Ocean Shores; 360-289-0450, 800-303-4297, fax 360-289-5149; www.oceanshoreswashington.com. DELUXE.

One of few accommodations away from "the strip" is the **Discovery Inn**, a condo motel close to the Ocean Shores Marina near the cape's southeast tip, five miles from downtown. Rooms are built around a central courtyard with a seasonal pool. There is an indoor jacuzzi and family game room. A private dock on Ocean Shores' grand canal encourages boating and fishing. ~ 1031 Discovery Avenue Southeast, Ocean Shores; 360-289-3371, 800-882-8821. BUDGET TO MODERATE.

North up the coast from frenetic Ocean Shores are numerous quiet resort communities and accommodations. At Ocean City, four miles north, the **Pacific Sands Motel** is one of the top economy choices on the coast. There are just nine units, but they're well kept; seven have kitchens and three have fireplaces. The extensive grounds include a nice swimming pool, playground, picnic tables and direct beach access across a suspension bridge. ~ 2687 State Route 109, Ocean City; 360-289-3588; www.pacific-sands.net, e-mail info@pacific-sands.net. BUDGET.

HIDDEN ▶

The **Iron Springs Resort** has 28 units in 25 cottages built up a wooded hill and around a handsome cove at the mouth of Boon Creek. The beach here is popular for razor clamming, crabbing and surf fishing; the cottages are equally popular for their spaciousness and panoramic views. All have kitchens and fireplaces. There are an indoor pool and playground. ~ 3707 Route 109, Copalis Beach; 360-276-4230, fax 360-276-4378; www.ironspringsresort.com, e-mail reservations@ironspringsresort.com. MODERATE TO DELUXE.

Ocean Crest Resort may be the most memorable accommodation on this entire stretch of beach. It's built atop a bluff, so getting to the beach involves a 132-step descent down a staircase through a wooded ravine. But the views from the rooms' private balconies are remarkable, and all but the smallest rooms have fireplaces and refrigerators. There are exercise facilities with a

swimming pool, jacuzzi and weight room open to all guests free
of charge. ~ Sunset Beach, Route 109, Moclips; 360-276-4465,
800-684-8439, fax 360-276-4149; www.oceancrestresort.com,
e-mail info@oceancrestresort.com. DELUXE.

DINING

Mariah's provides a spacious, relaxing cedar dining room with a
domed ceiling and skylights. Offerings include fresh seafood,
steaks, prime rib and pasta. Dinner only and Sunday breakfast
buffet. ~ 615 Ocean Shores Boulevard, Ocean Shores; 360-289-
3315, 800-562-4836, fax 360-289-0294; www.thepolynesian.
com, e-mail thepoly@techline.com. BUDGET TO DELUXE.

The **Home Port Restaurant** is appointed like the private garden of a sea captain home from the waves. Steaks, seafood and
pasta dominate the menu. ~ 857 Point Brown Avenue opposite
Shoal Street, Ocean Shores; 360-289-2600, fax 360-289-0558;
e-mail homeport3@coastaccess.com. MODERATE TO DELUXE.

No trip to the Washington coast would be complete without
having at least one meal that includes seafood. **Mike's Seafood** is
a casual eatery that can adequately oblige. Offering a fresh assortment of Pacific Northwest seafood, Mike's is particularly
popular with the locals during the winter Dungeness crab season.
~ 830 Point Brown Avenue, Ocean Shores; 360-289-0532.
BUDGET TO MODERATE.

The **Sand Castle Drive-in** is the in-spot for hamburgers, with interesting variations such as the oyster burger and the clam burger.
~ 788 Point Brown Avenue, Ocean Shores; 360-289-2777. BUDGET.

A bit of Manzanillo on the Washington coast, **Las Maracas**
feels like the tropics with its bright tropical colors and profusion
of plants. All the usual Mexican specialties are on the menu, but
the best bets are the fajitas, crab and prawn enchiladas and seafood chimichangas. ~ 729 Point Brown Avenue, Ocean Shores;
360-289-2054, fax 360-289-2054. MODERATE.

AUTHOR FAVORITE

For a gourmet Continental dinner in spectacular surroundings,
check out the **Ocean Crest Resort**. Attentive service and superb meals
(with a focus on seafood and Northwest regional cuisine), amid an atmosphere of Northwest Indian tribal art, only add to the enjoyment of the
main reason to dine here: the view from a bluff, through a wooded
ravine, to Sunset Beach. Breakfast, lunch and dinner. ~ Sunset Beach,
Route 109, Moclips; 360-276-4465, 800-684-8439, fax 360-276-4149;
www.oceancrestresort.com, e-mail info@oceancrestresort.com.
DELUXE TO ULTRA-DELUXE.

Authentic Irish pub fare is dished up at **Galway Bay Irish Restaurant and Pub**, where you can ward off the coastal chill with Irish stew, beef sautéed in Guinness, and chicken and mushroom pasties. The pub decor is authentic, with wainscoted walls adorned with Irish prints and memorabilia. Breakfast, lunch and dinner. ~ 880 Point Brown Avenue Northeast, Ocean Shores; 360-289-2300; www.galwaybayirishpub.com, e-mail bgibbons@galwaybayirishpub.com. MODERATE.

SHOPPING   The most interesting galleries in Grays Harbor County are, not surprisingly, in the beach communities. For oil paintings, watercolors, hand-made jewelry and textile crafts, make sure to seek out **The Cove Gallery**. ~ Route 109, Iron Springs; phone/fax 360-276-4360. The **Gallery Marjuli** exhibits recent works by Pacific Northwest artists. ~ 865 Point Brown Avenue Northwest, Ocean Shores; 360-289-2858.

NIGHTLIFE   In Ocean Shores, at the Polynesian Hotel, **Mariah's** is a nice place to enjoy a nightcap. ~ 615 Ocean Shores Boulevard, Ocean Shores; 360-289-3315, 800-562-4836; www.thepolynesian.com.

Along with a convivial atmosphere nightly, **Galway Bay Irish Restaurant** hosts live music on Friday and Saturday nights. ~ 880 Point Brown Avenue Northeast, Ocean Shores; 360-289-2300; www.galwaybayirishpub.com.

BEACHES & PARKS   **OCEAN CITY STATE PARK** 🏃 🚲 🐎 🏊 🛶 ⛺ 🚗 ⛵ This North Beach park, stretching for several miles along the Pacific coastline, offers a dozen access points. There are clamming and surf fishing (in season), horseback riding on the beach (but not on the dunes or soft sand), surf kayaking in summer, kite flying when the wind blows, birdwatching especially during migratory periods, and beachcombing year-round. Swimming is not recommended because of undertow and riptides. This flat, sandy beach is the same broad expanse that stretches 22 miles north to Pacific Beach. You can drive on some sections of the beach! You'll find restrooms and picnic areas. ~ Off Route 115 and Route 109 north of Ocean Shores; campground is two miles north of Ocean Shores on Route 115; 360-289-3553, fax 360-289-9405.

▲ There are 149 standard sites ($16 per night) and 29 RV hookup sites ($22 per night). Reservations: 888-226-7688.

PACIFIC BEACH STATE PARK 🏃 🛶 ⛵ Broad, flat and sandy North Beach, extending 22 miles from Moclips (just north of Pacific Beach) to the north jetty of Grays Harbor at Ocean Shores, is the *raison d'être* of the entire park. Beachcombing, kite flying, jogging and (in season) surf-perchfishing and razor-clam digging are popular activities. Swimming is not recommended because of undertow and riptides. Facilities are limited to restrooms and picnic areas. ~ Located along Route 109 in Pacific Beach; 360-276-4297, fax 360-276-4537.

▲ There are 23 standard sites ($15 per night) and 41 RV hookup sites ($21 per night). Reservations: 888-226-7688.

Industrial towns are not often places of tourist interest. The twin cities of Aberdeen and Hoquiam, on the northeastern shore of the broad

Grays Harbor Area

Grays Harbor estuary, are an exception. A historic seaport, a rich assortment of bird life and numerous handsome mansions built by old timber money make it worthwhile to pause in this corner of Washington.

Aberdeen has about 16,000 people, Hoquiam around 9000, and the metropolitan area includes some 33,000. Wood-products industries provide the economic base; in fact, more trees are harvested in Grays Harbor County than in any other county in the United States. Boat building and fisheries, both more important in past decades, remain key businesses.

For information on the region, check with the **Grays Harbor Chamber of Commerce.** ~ 506 Duffy Street at Route 101, Aberdeen; 360-532-1924, 800-321-1924; www.graysharbor.org.

SIGHTS

If you're coming down Route 101 from the north during the summer, it's wise to follow the signs and make your first stop a guided tour of **Hoquiam's Castle.** A stately, 28-room hillside

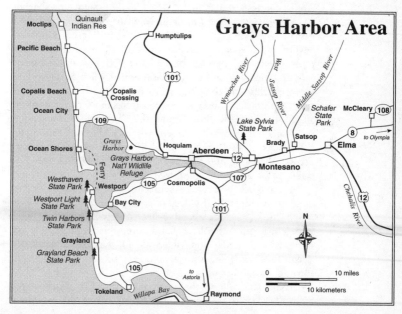

mansion built in 1897 by a millionaire lumber baron, it has been fully restored with elegant antiques like Tiffany lamps, grandfather clocks and a 600-piece, cut-crystal chandelier. With its round turret and bright red color, the house is unmistakable. It is now a bed-and-breakfast inn. Open for tours by appointment. Admission. ~ 515 Chenault Avenue, Hoquiam; 360-533-2005, fax 360-533-9814; www.hoquiamcastle.com, e-mail info@hoquiam castle.com.

Also in Hoquiam is the **Polson Museum**. Built in the early 1920s by a pioneer timber family and furnished with pieces donated by Hoquiam and Grays Harbor County residents, the 26-room home represents the history of the area. It is surrounded by native trees and the Burton Ross Memorial Rose Gardens. Open Wednesday through Sunday from April through December; open weekends only from January through March. Admission. ~ 1611 Riverside Avenue at Route 101, Hoquiam; phone/fax 360-533-5862; www.polsonmuseum.org.

A couple miles west of Hoquiam on Route 109, at Bowerman Basin on Grays Harbor, next to Bowerman Airfield, is the **Grays Harbor National Wildlife Refuge**, one of four major staging areas for migratory shorebirds in North America. Although this basin represents just two percent of the intertidal habitat of the estuary, fully half of the one million shorebirds that visit each spring make their stop here. April and early May are the best times to visit. An annual shorebird festival occurs the last weekend in April. ~ 360-753-9467, fax 360-534-9302; fws.gov/graysharbor.

A major attraction in neighboring Aberdeen, just four miles east of Hoquiam on Route 101, is the **Grays Harbor Historical Seaport**. Craftspersons at this working 18th-century shipyard have constructed a replica of the *Lady Washington*, the brigantine in which Captain Robert Gray sailed when he discovered Grays Harbor and the Columbia River in 1783. There are also two 18th-century longboat reproductions and a companion tall ship to the *Lady Washington*, the *Tall Chieftain*. Visitors can go for a sail on the *Lady Washington* when the ship isn't touring the West Coast. Call 24 hours ahead for schedules. ~ 712 Hagara Street, Aberdeen; 360-532-8611, 800-200-5239, fax 360-533-9384; www.ladywashington.org.

A few blocks west, the **Aberdeen Museum of History** offers exhibits, dioramas and videos of regional history in a 1922 armory. Displays include several re-created early-20th-century buildings: a one-room school, a general store, a blacksmith's shop and more. Closed Sunday and Monday. ~ 111 East 3rd Street, Aberdeen; 360-533-1976; www.aberdeen-musuem.org, e-mail museum@aberdeen-museum.org.

Route 105 follows the south shore of Grays Harbor west from Aberdeen to the atmospheric fishing village of **Westport**, at the estuary's south head. Perhaps the most interesting of several small museums here is the **Westport Maritime Museum**, housed in a Nantucket-style Coast Guard station commissioned in 1939 but decommissioned in the 1970s. Historic photos, artifacts and memorabilia help tell the story of a sailor's life. The museum also has exhibits of skeletons of marine mammals (including whales), a beachcombing exhibit, a children's discovery room and tours of the Grays Harbor lighthouse. Closed Tuesday, Wednesday and Thursday in winter. Admission. ~ 2201 Westhaven Drive, Westport; 360-268-0078, fax 360-268-1288; www.westportwa.com/museum, e-mail westport.maritime@comcast.net.

There's considerable character at **Hoquiam's Castle Bed & Breakfast**, a three-story Victorian hillside mansion. Each of the four guest rooms, all with private bath, are individually decorated with antiques. A full breakfast is served in the hand-carved oak dining room. Museum-quality period furnishings fill the house, which is open for tours by appointment. ~ 515 Chenault Avenue, Hoquiam; 360-533-2005, fax 306-533-9814; www.hoquiamcastle.com, e-mail info@hoquiamcastle.com. DELUXE TO ULTRA-DELUXE.

LODGING

It's a comfort to know that Grays Harbor has a few memorable restaurants to go with its memorable accommodations.

The twin cities of Aberdeen and Hoquiam have a strip of look-alike motels along Route 101. Though it's hard to choose one above another, the **Olympic Inn Motel** is notable for its modern, spacious rooms. Decor in the 56 units is simple but pleasant. ~ 616 West Heron Street, Aberdeen; 360-533-4200, 800-562-8618, fax 360-533-6223. MODERATE.

Just southeast of Aberdeen, the **Cooney Mansion** is located in a secluded wooded area on a golf course with an adjoining tennis court and park. A National Historic Landmark built in 1908 by a lumber baron, its interior was designed to show off local woods. Now a B&B, it has nine bedrooms, five with private baths, as well as a jacuzzi, sauna, sundeck and exercise room. Full lumber baron's breakfast included. Call for availability during winter. ~ 1705 5th Street, Cosmopolis; 360-533-0602, 800-977-7823; www.cooneymansion.com, e-mail cooney@techline.com. MODERATE TO ULTRA-DELUXE.

East of Aberdeen in the county seat of Montesano is the **Abel House**. This stately 1908 home has five bedrooms, two with private baths. There are also a game room and reading room and an exquisite English garden. A full breakfast, afternoon tea and dessert are included in the room rate. ~ 117 Fleet Street South, Montesano; 360-249-6002; www.abelhouse.com, e-mail abelhouse@reachone.com. MODERATE.

Farther east—halfway from Montesano to Olympia, in fact, but still in Grays Harbor County—**The McCleary Hotel** maintains antique-laden rooms that seem to be especially popular with touring bicyclists. ~ 42 Summit Road, McCleary; 360-495-3678. BUDGET.

In Westport, at the mouth of Grays Harbor, the largest motel is the **Château Westport**. Many of the 108 units have balconies and fireplaces, and a third are efficiency studios with kitchenettes. The upper floors of the four-story property, easily identified by its gray mansard roof, have excellent ocean views to enjoy with your complimentary continental breakfast. Dip into the indoor pool and hot tub. ~ 710 West Hancock Avenue, Westport; 360-268-9101, 800-255-9101, fax 360-268-1646; www.chateauwestport.com, e-mail chateau@tss.net. MODERATE TO ULTRA-DELUXE.

For value-hunters, **The Islander Resort** offers 32 simple but clean and spacious motel units. Forty-seven RV spaces are also available, some overlooking the harbor. ~ 421 East Neddie Rose Drive, Westport; 360-268-9166, 800-322-1740, fax 360-268-0902; www.westport-islander.com, e-mail info@westport-islander.com. MODERATE.

You can catch a fish, clean it and cook it for dinner all without straying from the **Grayland Motel and Cottages**, located on the beach south of Westport. The grounds offer a fish- and clam-cleaning shed, children's play area, motel units and self-contained cottages with tiled kitchens, pine furnishings and small living/dining areas. ~ 2013 State Route 105, Grayland; 360-267-2395, 800-292-0845; www.westportwa.com/grayland motel. BUDGET.

DINING

Bridges Restaurant is a handsome, garden-style restaurant with one dining room and a banquet room that's actually a greenhouse. As the size of its parking lot attests, it's very popular locally, for its lounge as well as its cuisine. Local seafood, steaks, chicken and pasta highlight the menu. No lunch on Sunday. ~ 112 North G Street, Aberdeen; 360-532-6563, fax 360-532-5490. MODERATE TO DELUXE.

For historic flavor, you needn't look further than **Billy's Bar and Grill**. Named for an early-20th-century ne'er-do-well notorious for mugging loggers and shanghaiing sailors, Billy's boasts an ornate century-old ceiling and a huge antique bar. This is the place to start the day with a hearty breakfast, or settle back with a burger and a beer and soak up the past. ~ 322 East Heron Street, Aberdeen; 360-533-7144, fax 360-533-7508. BUDGET TO MODERATE.

Elsewhere in the area, the **Hong Kong Restaurant** is surprisingly authentic for a town so far removed from China. It has chop suey and egg foo yung, yes, but it also has egg flower soup, *moo goo gai pan* and other tastes from the old country. Closed Monday. ~ 1212 East 1st Street, Cosmopolis; 360-533-7594. BUDGET.

There aren't many restaurant choices in McCleary, but if you appreciate a good old-fashioned hamburger, head for **Bear's Den**. An authentic 1950s burger stand with drive-up service and a tiny inside dining area, the Den makes burgers to order with heated buns, homemade fries, quality beef and a variety of toppings. Some other specialties are fresh salads and soda fountain treats. ~ 301 Simpson Avenue, McCleary; 360-495-3822. BUDGET.

SHOPPING

Browse vintage nautical baubles such as old ship lanterns and stern wheels at **Salt Box Gifts and Antiques**, housed in an old '20s schoolhouse. Closed Monday and Tuesday. ~ 1628 State Route 105, Grayland; 360-267-1044.

NIGHTLIFE

Folks in the Grays Harbor area show a predilection for **Sidney's Casino**, which features a Harley bar. ~ 512 West Heron Street, Aberdeen; 360-533-6635 or 360-533-0296 (bar).

Also check out the Victorian bar at **Billy's Bar and Grill**. ~ 322 East Heron Street, Aberdeen; 360-533-7144. The posh lounge at **Bridges Restaurant** is also a happenin' spot for drinks. ~ 112 North G Street, Aberdeen; 360-532-6563.

BEACHES & PARKS

LAKE SYLVIA STATE PARK 🚶 🚵 ⛱ 🛶 🛥 🎣 Visitors can circumambulate this narrow, forest-enshrouded lake on a two-mile hiking trail. Also here are trout fishing (from a non-motorized boat or from shore), a swimming beach and boat rentals in season. There are restrooms, picnic areas and groceries. ~ Off Route 12, via North 3rd Street, two miles north of Montesano; 360-249-3621, 888-226-7688, fax 360-249-5571.

▲ There are 35 standard sites ($17 per night). Closed early October to early April.

> Grays Harbor National Wildlife Refuge is the last place to be flooded at high tide and the first to have its mudflats exposed, giving the avians extra feeding time.

SCHAFER STATE PARK 🚶 🏊 🎣 Once a family park for employees of the Schafer Logging Company, this tranquil 119-acre site on the East Fork of the Satsop River is still popular with families. This heavily forested park is ideal for picnics, hikes and fishing. You can fish for rainbow trout, cutthroat trout, salmon and steelhead in the river. Swimmers may find the water too cold. You'll find restrooms and picnic areas. ~ West 1365 Schafer Park Road, 12 miles north of Elma, off Route 12 via Brady; 360-482-3852, fax 360-586-4272.

▲ There are 43 standard sites ($17 per night), 6 RV hookup sites ($24 per night) and 2 primitive sites ($12 per night). Closed in winter.

WYNOOCHEE LAKE RECREATION AREA 🚶 🚵 🏇 🛶 🎣 🏊 🛥 🎣 Originally an Army Corps of Engineers project, now run by Tacoma Power, this four-and-a-half-mile-long lake was created in 1972 by a water-supply and flood-control dam on the Wynoochee River. A ten-mile trail winds around the lake, past a beach and designated swimming area. Trout fishing, waterskiing, swimming (the water is cold, though), horseback riding and wild-life watching are also popular. Restrooms and picnic areas are the only facilities. ~ Off Route 12, about 35 miles north of Montesano on Wynochee Valley Road. Take a left on Forest Service Road 22 and a right on Forest Service Road 2294; 360-956-2402.

▲ There are 46 developed sites and 10 primitive sites ($10 to $12 per night) in the Coho campground. Closed October through April.

WESTHAVEN & WESTPORT LIGHT STATE PARKS 🧍 🚴 🐎
🦭 🐦 🏄 🥾 🛶 🚤 🛷 Westhaven State Park, which occupies the southern headland at the mouth of Grays Harbor, is a great place for watching birds and wildlife, including harbor seals and whales during migratory periods. Surfing is excellent here (try the jetty) and there are yearly competitions. Surfers and swimmers should be very careful of riptides. Westhaven is adjacent to Westport Light State Park, from which you can see a historic lighthouse that's warned coastal ships of the entrance to Grays Harbor since 1897. There's a multi-use paved trail connecting the two parks that's open for hiking, bicycling, inline skating and other nonmotorized forms of transportation. You can fish for sal-mon, ocean perch, codfish and Dungeness crab from the shores of both parks or the jetty of Westhaven. There are restrooms and pic-nic areas. ~ Both parks are close to downtown Westport; West-haven is about one and a half miles from downtown on East Year-out Drive; Westport Light is a half mile from downtown at the end of Ocean Avenue; 360-268-9717, fax 360-268-0372.

TWIN HARBORS STATE PARK 🧍 🚴 🏄 🛷 The Washington
coast's largest campground dominates this 172-acre park. It also includes the Shifting Sands Nature Trail with interpretive signs for dunes explorers. Beachcombing, kite flying and clamming are pop-ular activities on the broad, sandy beach. There's fishing in the surf or from a boat (which you can charter at Westport) for cod, sal-mon, ocean perch and Dungeness crab, but swimming is not rec-ommended because of riptides. You'll find restrooms and picnic areas. ~ Located along Route 105, four miles south of Westport and four miles north of Grayland; 360-268-9717, fax 360-268-0372.

▲ There are 250 standard sites ($19 per night) and 49 RV hookup sites ($26 per night). Reservations (May 15 to September 15): 888-226-7688.

GRAYLAND BEACH STATE PARK 🧍 🛷 This 400-acre park is
broad and flat and ideal for surf fishing, clam digging, beachcomb-ing, kite flying and other seaside diversions. Swimming is discour-aged due to riptides. You'll find restrooms, groceries and restau-

rants in Grayland. ~ Route 105, one mile south of Grayland; 360-267-4301, fax 360-267-0461.

▲ There are 98 RV hookup sites ($26 to $30 per night) and 14 yurts (call for yurt prices). Reservations: 888-226-7688.

Long Beach–Willapa Bay

This region is the largest "unpopulated" estuary in the continental United States. Its pristine condition makes it one of the world's best places for farming oysters. From Tokeland to Bay Center to Oysterville, tiny villages that derive their sole income from the shelled creatures display mountains of empty shells as evidence of their success. Begin your visit on Route 105 south from Westport, then head east along the northern shore of Willapa Bay.

SIGHTS

Thirty-three miles from Westport, Route 105 rejoins Route 101 at **Raymond**. This town of 3000, and its smaller sister community of **South Bend** four miles south on Route 101, are lumber ports on the lower Willapa River.

You'll find murals—43 of them, to be exact—on walls from Ocean Shores to the Columbia River, Elma to Ilwaco. Chambers of commerce and other visitor information centers have guide pam-

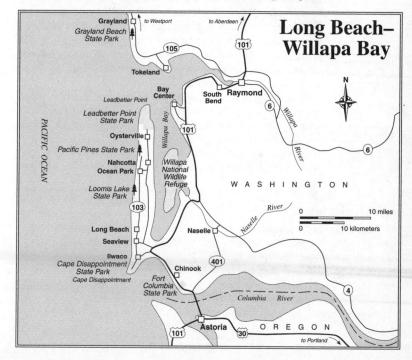

phlets. But no mural is larger than the 85-foot-wide painting of an early logger on the **Dennis Company Building**. ~ 5th Street, Raymond.

Attractions in South Bend include the **Pacific County Museum**, with pioneer artifacts from the turn of the 20th century. ~ 1008 West Robert Bush Drive, South Bend; 360-875-5224; www.pacificcohistory.org, e-mail museum@willapabay.org.

Also have a look at South Bend's 1910 **Pacific County Courthouse**, noted for its art-glass dome and historic foyer wall paintings. ~ 300 Memorial Drive off Route 101, South Bend; 360-874-9334.

The **Long Beach Peninsula**, reached via Route 101 from South Bend (43 miles), has had a significant flow of vacationing Northwest urbanites for over a century. But its economy is more strongly founded in fishing and cranberry growing. Information is available from the **Long Beach Peninsula Visitor Bureau**. ~ 3914 Pacific Highway at the intersection of Routes 101 and 103, Seaview; 360-642-2400, 800-451-2542; www.funbeach.com, e-mail ask@funbeach.com.

Route 103, which runs north–south up the 28-mile-long, two-mile-wide peninsula, is intersected by Route 101 at **Seaview**. The town of **Long Beach** is just a mile north of the junction.

Long Beach's principal attraction is a 2300-foot-long wooden **boardwalk**, South 10th to Bolstad streets, elevated above the dunes, enabling folks to make an easy trek to the high-tide mark. The beach, incidentally, is open to driving on the hard upper sand, and to surf fishing, clamming (in season), beachcombing, kite flying and picnicking everywhere.

Kite flying is a big thing on the Washington coast, so it's no accident that the **World Kite Museum and Hall of Fame** is in Long Beach. The museum has rotating exhibits of kites from around the world—Japanese, Chinese, Thai and so on—with displays of stunt kites, advertising kites and more. Open daily May through September; call for hours from October to April.

CATCH THE WAVE

In October and early November, the cranberry harvest takes precedence over all else on the peninsula. Most fields are owned by local farmers who sell much of their crop to Ocean Spray. The **Pacific Coast Cranberry Research Foundation** offers free self-guided tours of the cranberry bogs during harvest, and other times by appointment. Closed in winter. ~ 2907 Pioneer Road, Long Beach; 360-642-5553; www.cranberrymuseum.org, e-mail cranberries@willapabay.org.

Admission. ~ 303 Sid Snyder Drive South off Route 103, Long Beach; 360-642-4020; www.worldkitemuseum.com, e-mail info@worldkitemuseum.com.

The **Pacific Coast Cranberry Museum** provides a historic view of the West Coast cranberry industry. Exhibits include hand tools, cranberry boxes, labels, pickers, sorters and separators. Closed mid-December through March. ~ 2907 Pioneer Road, Long Beach; 360-642-5553; www.cranberrymuseum.org, e-mail cranberries@willapabay.org.

North of Long Beach ten miles is **Ocean Park,** the commercial hub of the central and northern Long Beach Peninsula. Developed as a Methodist camp in 1883, it evolved into a small resort town.

Older yet is **Oysterville,** another three miles north via Sandridge Road. Founded in 1854, this National Historic District boasts the oldest continuously operating post office in Washington (since 1858) and 17 other designated historic sites. Get a walking-tour pamphlet from the **Old Church** beside the Village Green. ~ Territory Road, Oysterville.

South of Seaview just two miles on Route 103 is **Ilwaco,** spanning the isthmus between the Columbia River and the Pacific.

Local history is featured at the impressive **Ilwaco Heritage Museum.** A series of galleries depicts the development of southwestern Washington from early Indian culture to European voyages of discovery, from pioneer settlement to the early 20th century. Admission. ~ 115 Southeast Lake Street, Ilwaco; 360-642-3446, fax 360-642-4615; www.ilwacoheritagemuseum.org, e-mail ihm@ilwacoheritagemuseum.org.

About eight miles southeast, a short distance before Route 101 crosses the Columbia River to Astoria, Oregon, **Fort Columbia State Park** is a highly recommended stop for history buffs. Two buildings at the site are museums: the **Fort Columbia Interpretive Center,** exhibiting artifacts of early-20th-century military life in a former coastal artillery post, and the **Columbia House,** which the Daughters of the American Revolution have restored to depict the everyday lifestyle of a military officer of the time. ~ Route 101, Chinook; 360-777-8221.

LODGING

Possibly the most delightful accommodation anywhere on the Washington coast is the **Shelburne Country Inn.** The oldest continually operating hotel in the state, it opened in 1896 and is still going strong. Fifteen guest rooms are furnished with Victorian antiques and fresh flowers. All have private baths and most have decks. A hearty country breakfast is served in the morning, as well as freshly baked cookies upon arrival. ~ 4415 Pacific Way, Seaview; 360-642-2442, 800-466-1896, fax 360-642-8904; www.theshelburneinn.com, e-mail innkeeper@theshelburneinn.com. DELUXE TO ULTRA-DELUXE.

HIDDEN ►   Another one-of-a-kinder, but for very different reasons, is **The Historic Sou'wester Lodge, Cabins Tch! Tch! & RV Park**. It's a place much beloved by youth hostelers who, well, grew up. Proprietors Leonard and Miriam Atkins have intentionally kept the accommodation simple and weathered. They advertise it as a B&(MYOD)B—"bed and (make your own damn) breakfast." Common areas include the living room and library. Sleeping options include rooms in the historic lodge, cedar-shingled housekeeping cabins, a dozen-or-so vintage TCH! TCH! RVs and mobile homes ("Trailer Classics Hodgepodge") and an area for RVs and tent campers. Almost every option includes kitchen facilities. The historic lodge draws an artistic clientele and often hosts cultural events such as poetry readings or evenings of chamber music and theater. It also is the closest lodging to the ocean in Seaview, separated from the water only by protected wetlands. ~ Beach Access Road, 38th Place, Seaview; 360-642-2542; www.souwester lodge.com, e-mail info@souwesterlodge.com. BUDGET TO DELUXE.

The Whale's Tale Motel in downtown Long Beach offers amazingly economical one- and two-bedroom suites with living rooms and full kitchens. Though the accommodations are plain and a little frayed around the edges, guests enjoy the use of a recreation hall with a Ping-Pong table, pool table, hot tub, sauna and exercise equipment, as well as free use of a rubber boat, freshwater fishing gear and metal detector during the summer season only. ~ 620 South Pacific Avenue, Long Beach; 360-642-3455, 800-559-4253; www.thewhalestale.com, e-mail whalesta@ willapabay.org. BUDGET TO MODERATE.

Numerous beachfront cabin communities speckle the shoreline of the Long Beach Peninsula north from the towns of Ilwaco and Seaview. One of the best is the **Klipsan Beach Cottages**. Each of the ten cottages, in a lovely garden setting, has a kitchen and fireplace or wood-burning stove (with free firewood). There is also a two-bedroom and a three-bedroom unit. Closed in early January. ~ 22617 Pacific Highway, Ocean Park; 360-665-4888, fax 360-665-3580; www.klipsanbeachcottages.com, e-mail d&m@ klipsanbeachcottages.com. MODERATE TO ULTRA-DELUXE.

Shakti Cove is just five minutes from the water. Ten rustic cabins have full kitchens and sleep up to four guests. The units are furnished with queen-size beds, couches and feature eclectic decor. Pets are welcome. Gay-friendly. ~ 25301 Park Avenue, Ocean Park; 360-665-4000, fax 360-665-6000; www.shakticove. com, e-mail covekeepers@shakticove.com. MODERATE.

Willapa Bay oyster lovers frequent the beds near the north end of the Long Beach Peninsula, and this is where they'll find

HIDDEN ►   the **Moby Dick Hotel**. An eight-room bed-and-breakfast inn that first opened its doors in 1930, it maintains a country nautical atmosphere, with rambling grounds, its own organic vegetable garden and oyster farm. A fireplace, bayside pavilion sauna and piano beckon on rainy days. A new 24-foot yurt with heated bamboo floor, skylight and circular space accommodates up to 30 people for retreats, meditations and workshops. ~ 25814 Sandridge Road, Nahcotta; 360-665-4543, 800-673-6145, fax 360-665-6887; www.mobydickhotel.com, e-mail mobydickhotel@willapabay.org. MODERATE TO DELUXE.

Housed in the oldest hotel in Washington, the **Tokeland Hotel and Restaurant** pairs delicious local foods with panoramic views of Willapa Bay. Homecooked meals may include dishes ranging from pasta, salmon and crab Louie to steak and a nightly chicken special; breakfast involves blueberry pancakes, and crab and cheddar grilled on sourdough. Every Sunday the Tokeland offers a much sought-after cranberry pot roast. ~ 100 Hotel Road, Tokeland; 360-267-7006; www.tokelandhotel.com, e-mail scott@tokelandhotel.com. MODERATE.

DINING

For a unique dining experience, visit the **Dock of the Bay**, on an off-the-beaten-track peninsula that juts into Willapa Bay 12 miles south of South Bend just off Route 101. Oysters, of course, are a specialty at this café/tavern; they even serve them for breakfast, along with other seafood omelettes. The fish market here also sells fresh crab and smoked salmon. ~ Bay Center Road at 2nd and Bridge streets, Bay Center; 360-875-5130. MODERATE.

◄ HIDDEN

Opposite the Shoalwater Restaurant entrance is **The Heron & Beaver Pub**, with light meals produced by the same kitchen as the Shoalwater Restaurant. ~ Shelburne Country Inn, 4415 Pacific Way, Seaview; 360-642-4142; www.shoalwater.com, e-mail info@shoalwater.com. MODERATE.

AUTHOR FAVORITE

I've seen Willapa Bay oysters on the menus at gourmet restaurants throughout the Northwest. The best place to try them is at the source—the highly acclaimed **Shoalwater Restaurant**, located in the historic Shelburne Country Inn, Washington's oldest continuously operated hotel. Expensive, but worth it. Everything is exquisite. From the Dungeness crab and shrimp cakes to the mussel and clam chowder, the roast duck breast to the pan-fried Willapa Bay oysters with a spicy Creole mayonnaise, and the creative preparations of the day's fresh catches, a meal here is one to savor. The turn-of-the-20th-century ambience adds an element of comfort. ~ Shelburne Inn, 4415 Pacific Way, Seaview; 360-642-4142; www.shoalwater.com, e-mail info@shoalwater.com. DELUXE.

Owned and operated by the former chef and manager of the renowned Shoalwater Restaurant, the **42nd Street Café** is fast making its own reputation. Hand-cut ravioli sautéed in a cider glaze with apples and red onions, iron skillet fried chicken, pot roast with vegetables and other down-home fare are prepared with a gourmet hand. The café is located in a converted army barracks. The dining room is bright and casual with blue and green cloth napery, candles and fresh flowers; in the off season the chef plays her harp for guests on Sunday nights. Breakfast, lunch and dinner. ~ 4201 Pacific Way, Seaview; 360-642-2323, fax 360-642-3439; www.42ndstreetcafe.com, e-mail blaine@42nd streetcafe.com. MODERATE TO DELUXE.

HIDDEN ▶

The **Corral Drive In** claims its Tsunami is the world's largest hamburger—and who's to argue with a five-pounder on a 16-and-a-half-inch bun? Not only is it huge (the drive-in needs 24-hour notice—better have the whole family along), it's actually quite good. The place also has regular burgers, fries, milkshakes and such. ~ North Pacific Highway and 95th Street North, Long Beach; 360-642-2774. BUDGET.

Mountains of oyster shells surround **The Ark Restaurant and Bakery**, located near the north end of the Long Beach Peninsula on oyster-rich Willapa Bay. In fact, the casual, relaxed restaurant has its own oyster beds—as well as an herb and edible-flower garden and a busy bakery. Nearby are cranberry bogs and forests of wild mushrooms. All these go into the preparation of creative dishes like Scotch salmon, sturgeon Szechuan and oysters Italian, and the Ark oyster feed, a decades-old tradition. Dinner Tuesday through Sunday; Sunday brunch. Call for winter hours. ~ 3310 273rd Street and Sandridge Road, Nahcotta; 360-665-4133, fax 360-665-5043; www.arkrestaurant.com, e-mail dine@arkrestau rant.com. MODERATE TO DELUXE.

SHOPPING

There's wonderful bric-a-brac at **Marsh's Free Museum**, from world-famous Jake the Alligator Man, an authentic shrunken head and freaks-of-nature stuffed animals to antique dishes and saltwater taffy. ~ 409 South Pacific Avenue, Long Beach; 360-642-2188, fax 360-642-8177; www.marshsfreemuseum.com, e-mail jake@marshsfreemuseum.com.

The souvenir most typical of beach recreation here, perhaps, would be a colorful kite. Look for them in Long Beach at **Above It All Kites.** ~ 312 Pacific Boulevard South, Long Beach; 360-642-3541; www.aboveitallkites.com.

Noted watercolorist Eric Wiegardt displays his work at the **Wiegardt Studio Gallery.** Open Monday through Saturday in July and August, Friday and Saturday the rest of the year. ~ 2607 Bay Avenue between Route 103 and Sandridge Road, Ocean Park; 360-665-5976; www.ericwiegardt.com.

The **Lightship Restaurant** has the Long Beach Peninsula's only ~ **NIGHTLIFE**
ocean-view restaurant from its third-story loft; come for a sun-
set drink. ~ Edgewater Inn, 409 Southwest Sid Snyder Drive,
Long Beach; 360-642-3252. Quiet beers are best quaffed at **The
Heron & Beaver Pub** in the Shelburne Inn. ~ 4415 Pacific Way,
Seaview; 360-642-4142.

LOOMIS LAKE STATE PARK 🚶 ⬛ Situated south of Klipsan ~ **BEACHES
Beach, this day-use park offers ocean beach access with good ~ & PARKS**
fishing from the shore and good clamming on the beach. Swimming is not recommended. Facilities include restrooms and picnic areas. ~ Park Road off Route 103 (Pacific Way), four miles
south of Ocean Park; 360-642-3078, fax 360-642-4216.

PACIFIC PINES STATE PARK 🚶 ⬛ This day-use
park offers beach access for various activities, like
beachcombing, kite flying, jogging, surf fishing and
razor clam digging in season. The coastal dune environment bristles with foxglove, lupine and a variety of
ferns; keep your eye out for hummingbirds, rabbits, deer
and raccoons. There are restrooms and picnic areas. ~ At
274th Place off Park Avenue, a mile north of Ocean Park;
360-642-3078, fax 360-642-4216.

> Leadbetter Point State
> Park was originally
> named Low Point in
> 1788; it was re-
> named in 1852.

LEADBETTER POINT STATE PARK 🚶 🚲 ⬛ Shifting dunes and
mudflats, ponds and marshes, grasslands and forests make this
northern tip of the Long Beach Peninsula an ideal place for those
who like to observe nature. As many as 100 species of migratory
birds stop over here. There are numerous hiking trails. Surf fishing is popular, but riptides discourage swimming. You'll find pit
toilets, restrooms and picnic areas. ~ Stackpole Road, via Route
103 and Sandridge Road, three miles north of Oysterville;
360-642-3078, fax 360-642-4216.

CAPE DISAPPOINTMENT STATE PARK 🚶 🚲 ⛴ 🚤 🎣 ⬛
The point where the Columbia River meets the Pacific Ocean has
been a crossroads of history for two centuries. The Lewis and
Clark expedition arrived at this dramatic headland in 1805 after
18 months on the trail. Two 19th-century lighthouses—at North
Head on the Pacific and at Cape Disappointment on a Columbia
sandbar—have limited the number of shipwrecks to a mere 200
through 1994. The fort was occupied from the Civil War through
World War II. Today, the 1800-acre park contains the Lewis and
Clark Interpretive Center, numerous forest, beach and clifftop
trails, a boat launch, a swimming beach, fishing (in the surf, from
the jetty or from a boat), summer interpretive programs, an interpretive center open year-round, lighthouse tours, restrooms,
picnic areas and groceries. ~ Route 101, two and a half miles
southwest of Ilwaco; 360-642-3078, fax 360-642-4216.

▲ There are 152 standard sites ($19 per night), 83 RV hook-up sites ($24 per night), and yurts and cabins ($40 per night). Reservations: 888-226-7688.

▼▼▼▼▼▼▼▼▼▼▼▼▼▼
Outdoor Adventures

SPORT-FISHING

Despite charter operators' complaints that government restrictions hinder their operations, the Strait of Juan de Fuca is still one of the nation's great salmon grounds, with chinook, coho and other species running the waters during the summer months. From April to September, halibut is also big in these waters—literally: one local operator holds the state record, 268 pounds. Bottomfish like ling cod, true cod, red snapper and black bass round out the angling possibilities.

OLYMPIC COAST When **Big Salmon Fishing Resort** isn't breaking state records for halibut (288 pounds), it runs half-day charters for salmon and bottomfish. The store also sells bait and rents tackle. Closed October to March. ~ 1251 Bay View Avenue (or Front Street), Neah Bay; 360-645-2374, 866-787-1900; www.bigsalmonresort.com.

Olson's Resort & Marina runs year-round charters out of Neah Bay and Sekiu for halibut, bottomfish and salmon (in season). ~ Sekiu; 360-963-2311; www.olsonsresort.com.

GRAYS HARBOR AREA **Deep Sea Charters** operates seven boats for one-day bottomfish and overnight tuna charters. Bait and tackle included. ~ Across from Float 6, Westport; 360-268-9300, 800-562-0151; www.deepseacharters.biz.

Angler Charters runs one-day trips for salmon, bottomfish and halibut. Bait and tackle is provided. ~ 401 Westhaven Drive, Westport, across from Float 14; 360-268-1030, 800-422-0425; www.anglercharters.net.

LONG BEACH–WILLAPA BAY At the mouth of the Columbia River, Ilwaco is another center for deep-sea fishing. Salmon and sturgeon are caught near the river mouth, while tuna, rockfish, cod and sole are in deeper waters. **Seabreeze Charters** arranges day charters, operating seven boats, most of which carry up to 16 people. Large engines cut down run times for deep-bottom trips. ~ 185 Howerton Way Southeast, Ilwaco; 360-642-2300, 800-204-9125; www.seabreezecharters.net.

RIVER FISHING

It's not just the fish—salmon, steelhead, trout—that attract anglers to the mountain streams flowing from the Olympic Mountains. Spectacular scenery and glimpses of eagles, deer, elk and other wildlife sweeten the deal.

PORT ANGELES AREA An hour or two away are several destinations for river fishing: the Sol Duc, Bogachiel, Hoh, Queets and Calawah rivers.

Return of the Monster Slayers

Makah, the tribal name of Neah Bay's native people, means "generous food"—and no wonder! For 2000 years, the main protein in the Makah diet was the meat of the gray whale. Men of the tribe would chase one of the 35-ton leviathans in canoes, harpoon it, and kill it by stabbing it repeatedly with spears as it towed them through the open ocean. So vital was whaling to the Makah culture that in their 1855 treaty the U.S. government guaranteed their right to hunt whales forever—the only treaty ever made by the United States that contains such a guarantee. Thereafter, the tribe also sold whale oil to non-Indian settlers and became the wealthiest Indians in the Northwest. (They are now among the poorest.) They had to stop in the 1920s after the whales nearly disappeared from coastal waters due to industrial whaling.

In recent years, since the California gray whale population has recovered and the whales have been removed from the endangered species list, the Makah intend to hold new whale hunts on a limited scale, still in traditional hand-carved log canoes but using a specially designed rifle—hopefully a single carefully aimed shot at the same instant the harpoon is thrown— as a more humane alternative to spears. Meat from the whales would be divided among the 1800 tribal members, storing any excess in tribal freezers. Under the supervision of the National Marine Fisheries Service, the tribe is allowed to take up to 20 migrating adult whales without calves in a five-year period. After nearly five years of planning the hunt and practicing the use of the harpoon and rifle, and a year of ceremonial purification, tribal hunters killed their first whale in May 1999.

Makah whaling is the subject of one of the biggest animal rights controversies in the Northwest. Opponents interpret the language of the Makah treaty as allowing whaling only as long as non-Indians were also hunting whales, before the present international ban. They also fear that despite federal prohibitions the tribe might find the Japanese importers' $1 million offer for a single whale an irresistible temptation. Tribal leaders say whaling is a matter of cultural preservation, discipline and pride. They claim that many of the tribe's health problems may come from the loss of their traditional whale meat diet and point out that the indigenous Chukotki people of Russia's Pacific coast have been "harvesting" about 165 gray whales a year for the last 40 years, yet the whale population continues to grow. Escalating with each whale hunt, the dispute is unlikely to be resolved soon.

OLYMPIC NATIONAL PARK   The lower Quinault River is not "overpacked" with fishermen—yet—partly because nontribal people may not fish rivers on the reservation without a Quinault guide. Contact the **Quinault Indian Nation Department of Natural Resources** to receive information about available guides for drift boat or walk-in fishing. ~ 1214 Aalis Street, Taholah; 360-276-8211 ext. 374, 888-616-8211; www.quinaultindianna-tion.com. **Three Rivers Resort & Guide Service** operates four 16-foot drift boats for two anglers on the Sol Duc, Bogachiel and Hoh rivers (another "quiet" spot). The eight-hour trips are for salmon and steelhead. Tackle, continental breakfast, and lunch are provided. ~ 7764 La Push Road, Forks; 360-374-5300; www.forks-web.com/threerivers.

SHELL-FISHING   Before you start digging up clams or other shellfish, please remember that just like other forms of fishing, a license is required for this activity. You can pick one up at tackle shops and other locations that sell fishing licenses. Recreational harvesting of shellfish is permitted on public beaches, but you should double-check, because much of the state's tideland is privately owned. Generally, shellfishing is permitted year round; razor clams and oyster harvests are restricted by season and location. Call the **Washington State Department of Fish and Wildlife** for information. ~ 360-902-2700, www.wa.gov. You can also call the **Shellfish Regulation** hotline. ~ 866-880-5431; www.wa.gov/wdfw/fish/shellfish/beachreg. You must also check with the Health Department's **Recreational Marine Biotoxin Hotline** to find out which waters are unhealthy for shellfish harvesting. ~ 800-562-5632; www.doh.wa.gov.

RIVER RUNNING   The Elwha River flows from the Olympic Mountains into the Strait of Juan de Fuca. Along the way, there are some Class II white-water rapids—not quite a thrill ride, but enough excitement for good family fun (it's the only commercially rafted whitewater on the peninsula). Besides that, there's plenty of wildlife to see—elk,

DIGGIN' IN

Folks who like to shellfish will be happy in Washington. There are clams (littleneck, butter, Manila and razor), scallops, oysters (Willapa Bay is famous for its oysters), mussels and crab (Dungeness Spit, north of Sequim, is the home of the renowned Dungeness crab). Then, of course, there's that Northwest oddity, the geoduck (say "gooey-duck"), whose huge foot cannot fit within its shell. See "Shellfishing" for information on this popular activity.

osprey, bald eagles, deer, harlequin ducks—as well as a view of a glacier. **Olympic Raft and Kayak** runs multiple trips daily, each lasting about two and a half hours. The trips down the Class II+ Elwha and Class II Hoh rivers are on rafts. Both beginning and experienced rafters can partake. ~ 123 Lake Aldwell Road, Port Angeles; 360-452-1443, 888-452-1443; www.raftandkayak.com.

KAYAKING

Experienced or novice, kayakers who paddle around a mountain lake, through coastal marshlands or under sea cliffs will be rewarded not only with good exercise but also with the opportunity to observe abundant wildlife in a wilderness setting. Companies offering guided tours generally operate during the warmer months (May through September). But think about this: Many kayakers swear the best time to paddle is in the rain.

PORT TOWNSEND AREA Port Townsend is a sea-kayaking center; call **Sport Townsend**, where you can buy backpacks and kayaks. ~ 1044 Water Street, Port Townsend; 360-379-9711; www.sporttownsend.com. For rentals, lessons and private nature tours guided by well-known kayaker Richard Roshon, contact **Kayak Center at PT Outdoors**. Closed in winter. ~ 1017 Water Street; 360-379-3608, 888-754-8598; www.ptoutdoors.com. **Olympic Outdoor Center** offers private, sunset and overnight kayaking tours in the spring and summer. The center also rents kayaks and offers classes. ~ 18971 Front Street, Poulsbo; 360-697-6095, 800-592-5983; www.kayakproshop.com.

PORT ANGELES AREA For kayak rentals and sales in Port Angeles, try **Sound Bikes and Kayaks**. ~ 120 East Front Street, Port Angeles; 360-457-1240; www.soundbikeskayaks.com.

You may have Lake Aldwell all to yourself, aside from the waterfowl nesting along its shores, when you join a two-hour guided tour of this clear blue lake. **Olympic Raft and Kayak** uses the more stable sea kayaks for these lake tours. The service also offers a four-hour trip in the saltwater Freshwater Bay just west of Port Angeles, which teems with bald eagles, otters and endangered marbled murrelets. ~ 123 Lake Aldwell Road, Port Angeles; 360-452-1443, 888-452-1443; www.raftandkayak.com.

KITE FLYING

Several miles of wide, flat beach make the beaches at Ocean Shores and Long Beach ideal kite-flying spots. A nationally sanctioned kite-flying festival in June brings some of the sport's best fliers to Ocean Shores; the same month, competing stunt kites fill the sky over Long Beach. In August, Long Beach hosts the weeklong Washington State International Kite Festival, said to be the biggest kite festival in the country (about 100,000 people attend). You don't have to be up to championship standards, though, to buy a kite and fly it or to visit a museum about kite flying.

OCEAN SHORES–PACIFIC BEACH   Pick up a kite and some tips on how to fly it at **Ocean Shores Kites**. Besides dozens of different kites, the store sells windsocks and other wind toys (Frisbees, etc.). ~ Shores Mall, 172 Chance a la Mer, Ocean Shores; 360-289-4103, fax 360-289-0517; www.oceanshoreskites.com.

LONG BEACH–WILLAPA BAY   In Long Beach is the **World Kite Museum and Hall of Fame**, which has probably the largest collection of Chinese and Japanese kites outside Asia. Open Friday through Tuesday from October through April, daily the rest of the year. Admission. ~ 303 West Sid Snyder Drive, Long Beach; 360-642-4020; www.worldkitemuseum.com.

WHALE WATCHING   California gray whales and humpbacks head back up to Alaskan waters between March and May. Orcas, or killer whales, are frequently seen in the waters of the Strait of Juan de Fuca, and we land-based mammals can't seem to get enough of the spectacle. Many fishing charter operators convert to whale-watching cruises during these months.

GRAYS HARBOR AREA   Two-and-a-half-hour cruises generally head offshore toward the whales' migration path, but occasionally the whales wander into Grays Harbor and the boats never get out to sea. In Westport, contact **Ocean Charters** for whale-watching trips. ~ Across from Float 6; 360-268-9144, 800-562-0105; www.oceanchartersinc.com. In the same harbor, **Deep Sea Charters** offers more of the same from March to mid-October. ~ Across from Float 6; 360-268-9300, 800-562-0151; www.deep seacharters.biz. From Westport, there's a number of specialty whale-cruise operators.

SKIING   The only skiing on the Olympic Peninsula is **Hurricane Ridge Ski Area**, 17 miles south of Port Angeles, in Olympic National Park. Here skiers will find a few downhill runs and several cross-country trails starting from the visitors center. There are two rope tows and a T-bar lift on site. The Hurricane Hill Road cross-country trail (1.5 miles one way) is probably the easiest of the area's six trails; the most challenging is the Hurricane Ridge Trail to Mt. Angeles, a steep three-mile route that's often icy. Rentals of downhill, cross-country and snowshoeing equipment are also available. Open April through October, weekends and weather permitting only. Contact the **Olympic National Park Visitor Center**. ~ 3002 Mt. Angeles Road, Port Angeles; 360-565-3130, for road conditions 360-565-3131; www.portangeles.org.

RIDING STABLES   On the Olympic Peninsula, it's possible to saddle up for a guided mountain ride through forests of towering trees or a ride along the beach at sunset.

OCEAN SHORES–PACIFIC BEACH   **Nan-Sea Stables** teaches natural horsemanship in Western or English style. A three-hour day camp in summer and Saturdays in winter provides grooming, saddling, riding lessons and a trail ride that is great for kids and beginners, ages seven and up. ~ 255 State Route 115, Ocean Shores; 360-289-0194, fax 360-289-3918; www.horseplanet. com, e-mail nansea@horseplanet.com.

GOLF

Bay views, ocean views, mountain views—take your pick. They're part and parcel with the courses in this region, all of which rent power carts, push carts and clubs.

PORT TOWNSEND AREA   The public 18-hole **Discovery Bay Golf Club** is set in the woods above Discovery Bay. It is a fairly flat course, although it can get a bit mushy after winter rains. ~ 7401 Cape George Road, Port Townsend; 360-385-0704. The public, double-teed, nine-hole **Port Townsend Golf Club** is located in town. It's considered the driest winter course in the area (it gets only 17 inches of rain), with rolling terrain, small greens and a driving range. ~ 1948 Blaine Street, Port Townsend; 360-385-4547. *Golf Digest* has named the semiprivate 27-hole **Port Ludlow Golf Course** designed by Robert Muir Graves one of the best in the country. Although housing flanks one section, the spectacular views of Ludlow Bay and abundant wildlife prompt comments like "Amazing" and "It's like golfing in a national park" from local duffers. ~ 751 Highland Drive, Port Ludlow; 360-437-0272.

For biking, hiking, canoeing and country life, you can't beat Puget Island, a bucolic retreat just minutes from Cathlamet connecting Washington to Oregon via ferry.

PORT ANGELES AREA   Although the 18-hole private **Sunland Golf and Country Club** goes through a housing development, it's well treed and fairly flat. Call for reciprocal play times. ~ 109 Hilltop Drive, Sequim; 360-683-6800. **Dungeness Golf Course** offers a semiprivate, 18-hole course. The number-three hole, called "Old Crabbie," has ten contracts guarding the crab-shaped green. ~ 1965 Woodcock Road, Sequim; 360-683-6344.

OCEAN SHORES–PACIFIC BEACH   The front nine of the municipal **Ocean Shores Golf Course** has a links-like layout in the dunes; the back nine wanders into the trees. ~ 500 Canal Drive Northeast at Albatross Street, Ocean Shores; 360-289-3357.

GRAYS HARBOR AREA   An old farming tract turned into a public 18-hole golf course in the early 1920s, **Oaksridge Golf Course** is very flat. It's pretty wet in the winter, but drains fast. The front nine is long. ~ 1052 Monte–Elma Road, Elma; 360-482-3511.

BIKING

Except along the southwestern shore areas, bicycling this part of Washington requires strength and stamina. There's spectacular beauty here, but there's also lots of rain and challenging terrain.

PORT TOWNSEND AREA Recreational bicyclists will probably enjoy a ride through **Fort Worden State Park**, which overlooks the Strait of Juan de Fuca, in Port Townsend.

OLYMPIC COAST A recommended road tour is the 85-mile **Upper Peninsula Tour** from Sequim to Neah Bay. The 55-mile trip down Route 101 from **Port Angeles to Forks** is also recommended. A paved six-mile trail loops the Port Angeles waterfront. The trail is flat, mostly following the shoreline, with picnic tables and other stopping spots along the way. On a clear day, you can see across the strait to Victoria.

OCEAN SHORES–PACIFIC BEACH One of the area's gentlest biking opportunities is the 14-mile **Ocean Shores Loop** from North Beach Park. For a map, call the Ocean Shores Chamber of Commerce, 360-289-2451; www.oceanshores.org.

GRAYS HARBOR AREA Worthy of a long ride is the 69-mile **Aberdeen-Raymond-Westport** loop on Routes 101 and 105. A new paved trail has been built in Westport along the beach. It runs for a mile and a half between two small state parks.

LONG BEACH–WILLAPA BAY The 42-mile **Seaview-Naselle** loop in Pacific County is popular.

Bike Rentals In Port Townsend, rent mountain bikes, tandems, running strollers, bike trailers and road bikes at **Port Townsend Cyclery**. ~ 252 Tyler Street, Port Townsend; 360-385-6470; www.ptcyclery.com. **Sound Bikes and Kayaks** rents hybrids and mountain bikes. ~ 120 East Front Street, Port Angeles; 360-457-1240; www.soundbikeskayaks.com.

HIKING

All distances listed for hiking trails are one way unless otherwise noted.

PORT TOWNSEND AREA **Mount Walker Trail** (2 miles) ascends the Olympics' easternmost peak (2804 feet) through a rhododendron forest. The view from the summit, across Hood Canal and the Kitsap Peninsula to Seattle and the Cascades, is unforgettable. The trailhead is one-fifth mile off Route 101 at Walker Pass, five miles south of Quilcene.

AUTHOR FAVORITE

One of the most unforgettable hikes I've experienced is the **Hoh River Trail** (17.5 miles), which wanders through lush, primeval rainforest teeming with deer from the Hoh Ranger Station to Glacier Meadows, at the base of the Blue Glacier on 7965-foot Mt. Olympus, the park's highest point. (Afterwards, I felt like a very tired Greek god.)

PORT ANGELES AREA Dungeness Spit Trail (5.5 miles) extends down the outside of the longest natural sandspit in the United States, and back the inside. The spit is a national wildlife refuge with a lighthouse at its seaward end. The trail begins and ends at the Dungeness Recreation Area.

OLYMPIC NATIONAL PARK Olympic National Park and adjacent areas of Olympic National Forest are rich in backpacking opportunities. Most trails follow rivers into the high country, with its peaks and alpine lakes. **Obstruction Point Trail** (7.4 miles) leads from the Deer Park Campground to Obstruction Point, following a 6500-foot ridgeline.

The easy **Spruce Railroad Trail** (2 miles) begins near North Shore Picnic Area or the west side of Log Cabin Resort on Lake Crescent. It follows the railroad bed of the historic Spruce Railroad and offers spectacular views of glacial Lake Crescent and surrounding mountains. No elevation gain.

Seven Lakes Basin Loop (22.5 miles) has several trail options, starting and ending at Sol Duc Hot Springs.

Coastal areas of the Olympic Peninsula have hiking trails as well. **Cape Alava Loop** (9 miles) crosses from the Ozette Ranger Station to Cape Alava; follows the shoreline south to Sand Point, from which there is beach access to shipwreck memorials farther south; and returns northeast to the ranger station. Prehistoric petroglyphs and an ancient Indian village can be seen en route.

GRAYS HARBOR AREA Wynoochee Lake Shore Trail (12 miles) circles this manmade reservoir in Olympic National Forest north of Montesano.

Shifting Sands Nature Trail (.5 mile) teaches visitors to Twin Harbors State Park, south of Westport, about plant and animal life in the seaside dunes.

LONG BEACH–WILLAPA BAY Along the southwestern Washington coast there are few inland trails, but the long stretches of flat beach appeal to many walkers. **Leadbetter Point Loop Trail** (2.5 miles) weaves through the forests and dunes, and past the ponds, mudflats and marshes, of the wildlife sanctuary/state park at the northern tip of the Long Beach Peninsula. Accessible from Oysterville, it's of special interest to birdwatchers.

The Trail of the Ancient Cedars (3.2 miles) goes through an important grove of old-growth red cedar, some as large as 11 feet wide and 150 feet tall, on Long Island, and be sure there is at least a six-foot tide. You must find your own boat access to Long Island. The Willapa Bay National Wildlife Refuge provides interpretive brochures at its headquarters. ~ Milepost 24, Route 101; 360-484-3482.

▼ ▼ ▼ ▼ ▼ ▼ ▼ ▼ ▼ ▼ ▼ ▼
Transportation

CAR

Route 101 is the main artery of the Olympic Peninsula and Washington coastal region, virtually encircling the entire land mass. Branching off Route 5 in Olympia, at the foot of Puget Sound, it runs north to Discovery Bay, where **Route 20** turns off to Port Townsend; west through Port Angeles to Sappho; then zigzags to Astoria, Oregon, and points south. Remarkably, when you reach Aberdeen, 292 miles after you start traveling on 101, you're just 36 miles from where you started!

Traveling from Seattle, most Olympic Peninsula visitors take either the Seattle–Winslow ferry (to Route 305) or the Edmonds–Kingston ferry (to Route 104), joining 101 just south of Discovery Bay. From Tacoma, the practical route is **Route 16** across the Narrows Bridge. From the north, the Keystone ferry to Port Townsend has its eastern terminus midway down lanky Whidbey Island, off Route 20. Northbound travelers can reach the area either through Astoria, on Route 101, or via several routes that branch off Route 5 north of Portland.

AIR

William R. Fairchild International Airport, near Port Angeles, links the northern Olympic Peninsula with Seattle and western Canada via Kenmore Air and Rite Bros. Aviation charter flights. ~ 360-417-3433.

FERRY

Washington State Ferries serves the Olympic Peninsula directly from Whidbey Island to Port Townsend and indirectly across Puget Sound (via the Kitsap Peninsula) from Seattle and Edmonds. ~ 206-464-6400, 888-808-7977; www.wsdot.wa.gov/ferries. The **Black Ball Transport** offers direct daily service between Port Angeles and Victoria, B.C. ~ 360-457-4491; www.ferrytovictor ia.com. **Victoria Express** provides foot-passenger service. ~ 360-452-8088; www.victoriaexpress.com. Some smaller cruise lines may make stops in Port Angeles.

CAR RENTALS

In Port Angeles, **Budget Car and Truck Rental** can be found in town. ~ 800-527-0700.

PUBLIC TRANSIT

For local bus service in the northern Olympic Peninsula, including Port Angeles and Sequim, contact **Clallam Transit System** in Port Angeles. ~ 360-452-4511, 800-858-3747; www.clallamtransit. com. Port Townsend, Sequim and eastern Jefferson County are served by **Jefferson Transit**. ~ 360-385-4777, 800-371-0497; www.jeffersontransit.com. The **Grays Harbor Transportation Authority** offers bus service to Aberdeen, Ocean Shores and the surrounding region. ~ 360-532-2770, 800-562-9730; www.ghtr ansit.com.

Bus service between Raymond, Long Beach and Astoria, Oregon, is provided by the **Pacific Transit System**. ~ 360-642-9418, 800-833-6388; www.pacifictransit.org.

FIVE

The Cascades and Central Washington

Perhaps without even realizing it, many Americans have a burning image of this region. For it was here, in the Cascade Range, that Mt. St. Helens blew its top in 1980. But the area has a lot more going for it than one hyperactive mountaintop. Indeed, think of the Cascades and Central Washington as one wild place for anyone who loves the outdoors.

The Cascade Range contains some of the most beautiful mountain scenery in the United States, much of it preserved by two major national parks, several national recreation areas and numerous wilderness areas that make this a major sports haven. There are also glaciers galore; 316 are in the North Cascades National Park Service Complex alone. Thousands of miles of trails and logging roads lace the Cascades, leading to mountaintop lookout towers, old gold mines, lakes, streams and gorgeous sights.

The hand of man has done little to alter the Cascades. When the North Cascades Highway (Route 20) was finally completed in 1972, it was with the understanding that it would be closed during the heavy snows, usually from November until April. Thus, most of the Cascades are still wild and remote, seen and experienced by humans but not transformed by them.

The range, about 700 miles long, begins at the Fraser River in southern British Columbia and extends southward through Washington and Oregon and into California just beyond Lassen Peak. The most dominant features of the Cascades are its 15 volcanoes. Washington lays claim to five, with Mt. Rainier the granddaddy at 14,411 feet. Most peaks are under 10,000 feet, and Harts Pass, the highest pass in the state, is only 6197 feet.

Although the range is not a comparatively high one, it served as an effective barrier to exploration and development until well into the 20th century. The pioneers who came over the Oregon Trail avoided it, choosing instead to go down the Columbia River to the Cowlitz River, travel up to present-day Toledo, then move overland to Puget Sound at Tumwater and Olympia.

Mining has always been part of the Cascades story. Although no major gold strikes have been found, several smaller ones have kept the interest alive, and there's probably never been a day since the mid-1870s when someone wasn't panning or sluicing in the mountains.

The range supports a wide variety of plants and wildlife because it has so many climatic zones. Naturalists have given names to eight distinct ones: Coastal Forest Zone, Silver Fir Zone, Sierran Mixed-Conifer Zone, Red Fir Zone, Subalpine Zone, Alpine Zone, Interior Fir Zone and Ponderosa Pine Zone. Each zone has its own community of plants, animals and birds.

Although most of the range is under the stewardship of the Forest Service, which by law has to practice multiple-use policies, most people think of the Cascades as their very own. It is used by mushroom hunters, hikers, runners, birdwatchers, anglers, hunters, photographers, painters, skiers, horse riders, loggers and miners. Whichever of these apply to you, enjoy.

North Cascades

Extending from the Canadian border south into the Mt. Baker–Snoqualmie National Forest, the North Cascades region has over 300 glaciers, valleys famous for their spring tulip fields and some of the best skiing in the Pacific Northwest. Backroads wind through old logging towns past mountain lakes to unspoiled wilderness areas. The North Cascades National Park Service Complex forms the core of this realm that includes Rainy and Washington passes, two of the Cascades' grandest viewpoints.

SIGHTS

Beginning at the northernmost approach, **Route 542** enters the Cascades from Bellingham, a pleasant, two-lane, blacktop highway that is shared by loggers, skiers, anglers and hikers. Much of the route runs through dense forest beside fast streams and with only rare glimpses of the surrounding mountains. The road deadends a few miles beyond the Mt. Baker day-use lodge for skiers, at a lookout called Artist Point. In clear weather you will see 9127-foot **Mt. Shuksan**, one of the most beautiful peaks in the Cascades. It can't be seen from any other part of the range, but it probably appears on more calendars and postcards than its neighbor Mt. Baker or even Mt. Rainier.

The **Mt. Baker** ski slopes usually open in November and run all the way into April, making for the longest ski season of any area in Washington. During summer the mountain is popular with day hikers and backpackers. Several hiking trails wind through high alpine meadows dotted with wildflowers in the Heather Meadows area. ~ Mt. Baker Ranger District; 360-856-5700, fax 360-856-1934.

Mt. Baker was named by George Vancouver in May 1792, in honor of Joseph Baker, a lieutenant on his ship. It was first climbed on August 17, 1868, by a party of four led by an experienced alpinist named Edmund T. Coleman. Although it is listed as

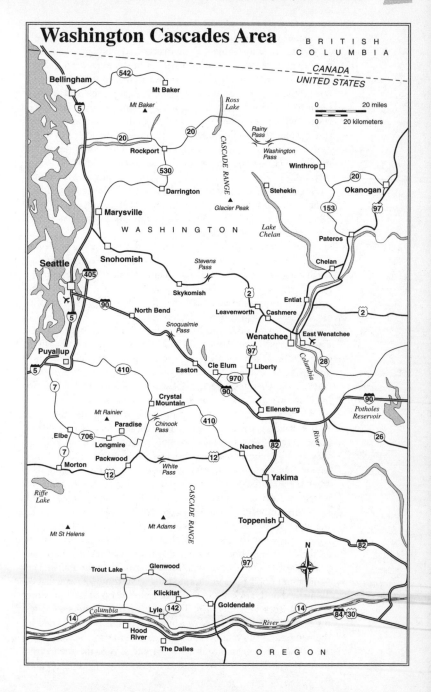

Washington Cascades Area

BRITISH COLUMBIA

CANADA
UNITED STATES

Bellingham
542
Mt Baker
Mt Baker ▲

Ross Lake

0   20 miles
0   20 kilometers

20
Rockport
20
CASCADE RANGE
Rainy Pass
Washington Pass
Winthrop
20

530
Darrington
Stehekin
Okanogan
153
97

Marysville
Glacier Peak ▲
Lake Chelan
Pateros

WASHINGTON

Seattle
405
Snohomish
Stevens Pass
Chelan

Skykomish
2
Entiat

90
North Bend
Leavenworth
Cashmere
2

5
Snoqualmie Pass
Wenatchee
East Wenatchee

Puyallup
Columbia
28

5
410
Easton
Cle Elum
Liberty
97
970
90

7
Crystal Mountain
Ellensburg
90
Potholes Reservoir

Mt Rainier ▲
Paradise
Chinook Pass
410

Elbe
706
26

7
Longmire
Naches
82

Morton
Packwood
12
12
River

White Pass
Yakima

Riffe Lake
CASCADE RANGE

Mt St Helens ▲
Mt Adams ▲
Toppenish
82

N

Trout Lake
Glenwood
97

Klickitat
Lyle
142
Goldendale

14
Columbia
Hood River
River
14
84
30

The Dalles

OREGON

an active volcano and occasionally steam is seen rising from it, Mt. Baker hasn't erupted since 1880.

Route 20, one of America's premier scenic routes, goes through the North Cascades National Park Service Complex and along the way provides hiking trails, roadside parks, boat launches and one of the more unusual tours in the Cascades, the **Seattle City Light Skagit Tours** offers a unique opportunity to experience the rugged wilderness. The two-and-a-half-hour Diablo Lake Adventure travels across Diablo Dam. It includes a scenic cruise (with dinner on Monday and Thursday in July and August) deep into the Skagit Gorge and across Diablo Lake. Often compared to the Swiss Alps, the North Cascades offer snow-capped mountains peaks, alpine valleys and glaciers. Reservations are recommended. Tours run seasonally June through September. Admission. ~ 206-684-3030, fax 206-233-1642; www.skagittours.com, e-mail skagit tours.reservations@seattle.gov.

Because the highway is enclosed by the Ross Lake National Recreation Area, new development is virtually nonexistent, and the small company towns of Newhalem and Diablo look frozen in the pre–World War II days. **Ross Lake**, created by the hydroelectric project, is a fjordlike lake between steep mountains that eventually crosses over into British Columbia.

When driving on Route 20, be forewarned: No gasoline is available between Marblemount and Mazama, a distance of more than 70 miles, and there are few places to buy groceries. Fill your tank and bring your lunch. Also, the highway at Milepost 134, just west of the Cascade Crest, is closed by mid-November due to heavy snows and doesn't open again until April.

Three historic hydroelectric power plants and dams on the Skagit River generate 25 percent of Seattle's electricity. Ross Lake on the Skagit River was formed by Ross Dam. Diablo Dam was built a short distance downstream, creating the much smaller Diablo Lake. Stairstepped below Diablo is Gorge Lake, created by Gorge Dam. Ross Lake is an international body of water because its backwaters cross the border into Canada, and when the timber was being cleared before the lake was formed, the work was done via a road in from British Columbia.

Another way to reach Route 20 is over what is locally known as the **Mountain Loop Highway**, a favorite weekend drive for years before Route 20 was completed across the mountains. The Mountain Loop begins in Granite Falls with Route 92, which goes along the South Fork of the Stillaguamish River past the one-store towns of Robe and Silverton. The road is crooked and slow driving because it follows the river route closely. It is always closed in the winter and sometimes landslides close it for much of the summer. Near the old mining town of Monte Cristo, the road turns north along the Sauk River and emerges in the logging town of

Darrington. Here you can drive due north to catch Route 20 at Rockport or turn west on Route 530 and return to Route 5.

Route 20 plunges into the Cascades and goes over two passes— **Rainy Pass**, 4860 feet, and **Washington Pass**, 5477 feet—before descending into the Methow Valley. Stop at each viewpoint and turnout for stunning views of the region. One viewpoint above Ross Lake shows miles of the long, narrow lake, and another just beyond Washington Pass gives a grandstand view of the jagged mountains behind the pass.

The only way to visit the resort town of **Stehekin**, at the tip of Lake Chelan, is by boat, plane or hiking. Most visitors take the trip up the lake on the **Lady of the Lake**, the tour-mail-supply boat for Stehekin and points between. The schedule allows you up to seven hours in Stehekin, and you can buy lunch at the Stehekin landing. Bike and bus tours coordinated with the ferry schedule are available. Reservations suggested. Admission. ~ 509-682-4584, fax 509-682-8206; www.ladyofthelake.com.

If you'd like to fly into Stehekin, contact **Chelan Airways**. ~ 1328 West Woodin Avenue (one mile west of Chelan on Route 97A); 509-682-5555, fax 509-682-5065 (call first); www.chelan airways.com, e-mail info@chelanairways.com.

LODGING

The **Glacier Creek Lodge** is a rustic motel with nine units and thirteen blue-and-white cabins. The cabins are one or two bed-

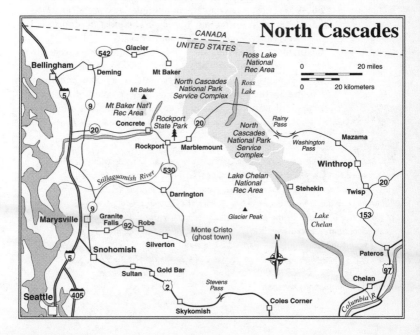

North Cascades

rooms, with bath, double bed, bedside table and tired furniture. The motel units are so small there's no room for a table. In addition to a hot tub, there is a large lobby where continental breakfast is served. ~ 10036 Mt. Baker Highway, Glacier; 360-599-2991, 800-719-1414, fax 360-599-1048; www.glaciercreeklodge.com, e-mail glaciercrklodge@aol.com. BUDGET TO ULTRA-DELUXE.

One of the larger lakeside resorts is **Baker Lake Resort**, 20 miles north of Concrete on Baker Lake Road. It is a mixture of RV sites and nine rustic cabins on the lake. Four of the cabins have bathrooms, showers and a refrigerator, but guests must bring their own cookware, utensils, linen and towels. Boating and fishing are popular on the lake; boat rentals are available. Closed early October to late May. ~ 46110 East Main Street, Concrete; 360-853-8341, 888-711-3033, fax 425-462-3118; e-mail bakerlake recpse@puget.com. BUDGET TO MODERATE.

A lodge with bed-and-breakfast ambience, the **Cascade Mountain Lodge** is a vintage Northwest cedar-shake hostelry with an adjoining restaurant and lounge. There are 13 refurbished rooms, some with antique and hand-carved furnishings. All rooms come with modern comforts such as microwaves, refrigerators and TVs. Guests can have breakfast, lunch or dinner in the restaurant or on an adjoining outdoor patio adorned by a three-tiered fountain and dozens of hanging flower baskets. ~ 44628 Route 20, Concrete; 360-853-8870, 800-251-3054, fax 360-853-7123; www.cascademountainlodge.com. MODERATE.

Rustic reigns in remote Stehekin. The most outdoorsy is the **Stehekin Valley Ranch**, owned and operated by the Courtneys, the major family in the valley. The ranch is nine miles from town, up the Stehekin River Valley. Guests are housed in tent cabins with wooden walls and canvas-covered roofs. Showers and toilets are in the main building. Five newer cabins have private baths. All meals are included and served in the dining room,

AUTHOR FAVORITE

The best way to get to Stehekin is also an incomparably scenic way to see Lake Chelan and its surroundings. **Chelan Airways** has been flying the lake for more than a half-century, and its experienced floatplane pilots not only give passengers the best views, they know every nook and cranny of the lake and all the stories that accompany them. Round-trip passage is not too expensive, but it's worth a flight just to see the sights even if you don't stay "uplake." Closed November through March. ~ 1328 West Woodin Avenue (one mile west of Chelan on Route 97A); 509-682-5555, fax 509-682-5065 (call first); www.chelanairways.com, e-mail info@chelanairways.com.

which has split logs for tables and seats. Horseback rides, river rafting and kayaking trips are offered. Closed October to mid-June. ~ P.O. Box 36, Stehekin, WA 98852; 509-682-4677, 800-536-0745; www.stehekin.biz, e-mail ranch@courtneycountry. com. MODERATE.

The fanciest Stehekin lodging is **Silver Bay Inn**, at the head of the Stehekin River a short distance from the village. In the owners' home there is a room with a kitchenette and private bath. Also on the property are three spacious, well-appointed cabins that will sleep six and are complete with kitchens, dishwashers and decks. Bikes, kayaks and canoes are available for guests, as is the riverside hot tub. ~ 10 Silver Bay Road, Stehekin; 254-377-3912, 800-555-7781, fax 509-687-3142; www.silverbayinn.com, e-mail stehekin@silverbayinn.com. ULTRA-DELUXE.

DINING

A popular place along the Mt. Baker Highway is **Milano's Market and Deli**, a combination small restaurant and deli offering a hearty supply of soups, salads, fresh pasta dishes and homemade bread and desserts. This is a good place to have a picnic lunch made up. If the weather is right, the deck is open for outside dining. ~ 9990 Mt. Baker Highway, Glacier; 360-599-2863. BUDGET.

A big, airy place decorated with family memorabilia dating back to the 1800s, **The Eatery Restaurant** at the Skagit River Resort specializes in downhome fare. Breakfast features biscuits and gravy, while lunch touts eight different burgers and dinner means steaks, chops and fish. Don't miss the housemade pies and milkshakes. ~ Route 20, Marblemount; 360-873-2041, fax 360-873-4077; www.northcascades.com. BUDGET TO MODERATE.

On the western edge of Concrete, **Cascade Mountain Lodge** has established a local reputation for good, plain American food (steaks, chops, burgers) and delicious pie (made by a local woman especially for the restaurant). The interior is decorated with antique furnishings and decorations. There's also a full-service bar. ~ 44628 Route 20, Concrete; 360-853-8771, 800-251-3054; www.cascademountainlodge.com. BUDGET.

SHOPPING

If you're in Concrete on Saturday from mid-May through August, hit the **Saturday Market** in the **Concrete Senior Center** for arts and crafts and baked goods. ~ 45821 Railway Avenue.

Potter Stephen Murray is known for his wood-fired ceramic dinnerware that comes in a variety of lustrous glazes. He also works with stoneware and porcelain. Individual pieces are sold at his **Sauk Mountain Pottery** store east of Concrete. ~ 50303 Route 20, Concrete; 360-853-8689.

NIGHTLIFE

The Cascades isn't the place to go for stellar nightlife. After a day traipsing around in the mountains, most people return to town tired and only want to eat and go to bed. Consequently, only the busiest areas even have live music.

PARKS

MT. BAKER–SNOQUALMIE NATIONAL FOREST 🚶 🚲 🐎 🛷 🎣 ⚓ 🏕️ 🚣 🏊 🛶 This 1.7-million-acre forest begins at the Canadian border and goes south along the western slopes of the Cascades to Mt. Rainier National Park. It is dominated on the north by the inactive volcano, 10,778-foot Mt. Baker. Another inactive volcano, 10,568-foot Glacier Peak, lies in the middle of the forest. The Forest Service controls the land for the ski areas at Crystal Mountain, Mt. Baker, Stevens Pass and Snoqualmie Pass. Its best-known wilderness area is Alpine Lakes Wilderness, but it also includes the Glacier Peak, Noisy Diobsud, Boulder River, Henry M. Jackson, Clearwater, Norse Peak and Mt. Baker Wilderness areas. Within the forest is excellent fishing for rainbow trout · in Baker Lake and many other streams and lakes. There are picnic areas, restrooms and showers. Parking permit, $5 per day or $30 for an annual pass. ~ Four east–west highways cross the national forest: Routes 90, 20, 2 and 410; 425-775-9702, fax 425-744-3255; www.fs.fed.us/r6/mbs.

▲ Camping is permitted (unless otherwise posted) along the highways, trails and the Pacific Crest Trail, as well as at established campsites. Most of the 40-plus campgrounds are primitive with pit toilets and vary from walk-in to drive-in sites (RV sites are available); $10 to $16 per night. Roughly 60 percent of sites are available for reservation: 877-444-6777.

ROCKPORT STATE PARK 🚶 🚲 🏊 🚣 This park is essentially a large campground in a grove of old-growth Douglas fir. Most of the camping areas are shielded from one another by thick undergrowth. It is near the fish-laden Skagit River, which makes it popular with steelheaders. There are picnic areas, restrooms, showers and five miles of footpaths. In winter, open weekends and holidays for day-use only. ~ Route 20, one mile west of Rockport; phone/fax 360-853-8461.

▲ There are 50 RV sites ($26 per night), 8 walk-in sites ($19 per night) and 4 three-sided Adirondack shelters ($25 per night).

HOWARD MILLER STEELHEAD COUNTY PARK 🚶 🚲 🏕️ 🏊 🚤 ⚓ 🚣 One of the most popular parks on the Skagit River for steelheaders and travelers alike, this county park covers 97 acres and has exhibits of a historic cabin, an old river ferry and dugout canoe. Anglers will find salmon and trout, and birders will enjoy bald-eagle watching from December to February. Facilities include picnic areas, a playground, a clubhouse, restrooms, showers and a trailer dump. ~ Located in the middle of Rockport at the junction of Routes 20 and 530; 360-853-8808, fax 360-853-7315.

▲ There are both tent and RV sites available ($18 to $20 per night). Call the park for more information and reservations.

NORTH CASCADES NATIONAL PARK SERVICE COMPLEX

Covering 684,313 acres in the north central part of the state, this park is divided into two units. The northern unit runs from the Canadian border to **Ross Lake National Recreation Area.** The southern unit continues on to the **Lake Chelan National Recreation Area.** Much of its eastern boundary is the summit of the Cascade Range, and the western boundary is the Mt. Baker–Snoqualmie National Forest. It is the most rugged and remote of the national parks in Washington and has the fewest roads. All visitor facilities and most roads in the northern portion are inside the Ross Lake National Recreation Area. On the southern end, the Lake Chelan National Recreation Area covers the heavy-use area on the north end of the lake, including the village of Stehekin. Try for rainbow trout in Ross Lake, steelhead in the Skagit River downstream from Newhalem and rainbow and eastern brook trout in high lakes. There are visitors centers in Newhalem and Stehekin, and rangers sometimes lead nature walks. Picnic areas, restrooms and nature walks are located here. ~ Only Route 20 goes through Ross Lake National Recreation Area, and in winter the road closes after the visitors center. 360-856-5700, fax 360-856-1934; www.nps.gov/noca, e-mail noca_information@nps.gov.

> The town of Concrete, home to the Portland Cement Company, was formerly known as "Minnehaha," "Baker" and, most appropriately, "Cement City."

▲ There are over 350 campsites at four campgrounds. You can camp year-round at Goodell Creek, which has potable water in summer and vault toilets; $10 per night. Colonial Creek and Newhalem Creek campgrounds have potable water, flush toilets and dump stations; $12 per night. Gorge Lake sites are free, but you'll have to bring in your own drinking water. The adjacent Okanogan Forest has more sites, including the popular Lone Fir and Early Winters campgrounds. Reservations: 877-444-6777.

Methow Valley

The scenery changes quickly and dramatically once you have crossed Washington Pass into the Methow Valley. Located along Route 20 between Mazama and Pateros, this region includes the tourist center of Chelan, gateway to one of the state's most popular lake-resort areas.

SIGHTS

As you descend the east slope of the Cascades, the thick, fir forest gives way to smaller pine with almost no underbrush. The mountains become bare, and you can see for miles. And by the time you arrive in **Winthrop**, you will wonder if you are in Colorado or Wyoming because the small town is all falsefronts, saloon doors, hitching rails and wooden porches. Winthrop adopted a Wild West theme years ago, and it has revitalized the sawmill town and surrounding area into one of the state's most popular destinations. Winthrop is named after Theodore Winthrop, a 19th-century Yale graduate and adventurer/traveler who wrote *The Canoe and the Saddle* and other novels about his excursions in the Pacific Northwest.

The **Shafer Museum** is a collection of early-1900s buildings, including the cabin built by town founder Guy Waring in 1897. Exhibits include a stagecoach, antique automobiles and the largest collection of mining artifacts in the Pacific Northwest. Closed Tuesday and Wednesday, and from late September to late May. ~ One block up the hill off Route 20, Winthrop; 509-996-2712; www.winthropwashington.com/winthrop/shafer, e-mail shafer-museum@winthropwashington.com.

HIDDEN ▶ There are several areas around Winthrop worth driving to, including 6197-foot **Harts Pass** a short distance from town. This is the highest point to which you can drive in Washington and is only an hour's drive on a gravel Forest Service road. The views from the summit are spectacular.

Not long after driving south on Route 153, the last of the timbered mountains are left behind, and the Methow Valley flattens into a series of irrigated ranches with broad hayfields. The valley is gaining popularity with people from Puget Sound looking for more space, so houses are beginning to line the low hills on both sides.

When you reach the **Columbia River** at Pateros, the landscape is one of basaltic cliffs on both sides of the river. Instead of a fast-flowing river there is a chain of lakes behind dams all the way past Wenatchee. Route 97 hugs the west side of the Columbia, then splits off onto 97A at Chelan Falls and swings away from the river to go through the resort town of Chelan, which sits at the end of **Lake Chelan**. The two highways meet again at Wenatchee.

The lake is a remnant of the Ice Ages. Scoured out of the mountains by glaciers, it is one of the deepest lakes in the region, more than 1500 feet deep in at least one area, which places its bed at 400 feet below sea level. It is 50 miles long but quite narrow, and the mountains rising from its shores give it the appearance of a Norwegian fjord.

Chelan is a small town that has been given over almost entirely to apples and tourism. Woodin Avenue is the main drag and the lakefront is lined with resorts, but the small-town atmosphere remains intact, so a farmer can come to town and still buy a two-by-four or a cotter pin.

The **Lake Chelan Historical Society Museum** displays American Indian artifacts and early farming equipment. One room depicts a miner's cabin, and another shows a typical country kitchen.

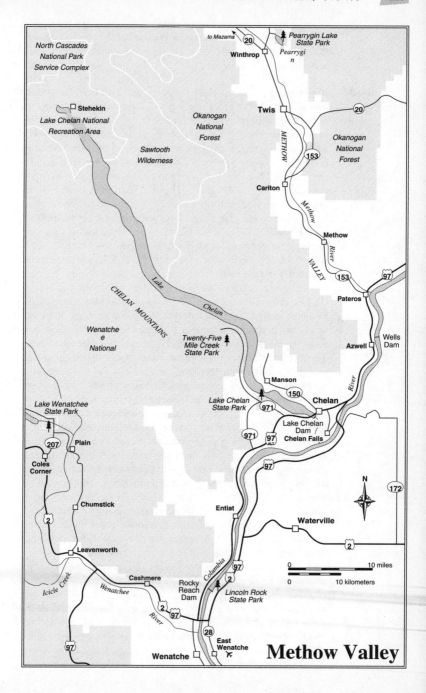

Methow Valley

Limited hours October through May. Closed Sunday from June through September. ~ Woodin Avenue and Emerson Street, Chelan; 509-682-5644; www.chelanvalley.com/history, e-mail historical@chelanvalley.com.

LODGING   If you want to get up close and personal with the North Cascades, head for the **Freestone Inn and Cabins**. The 15 cabins sit across the highway from the Forest Service/National Park Service information center at the foot of the mountains. Varying in size and widely spaced, each cabin is heated with a propane fireplace; the bathrooms are heated. All cooking utensils are provided. In the inn, all 21 rooms have fireplaces. The inn has one hot tub, the cabins have another. The Recreation Center offers cross-country ski rentals in the winter and mountain-bike rentals in the summer for adventurers who want to explore the Methow Valley Nordic Ski Trails—a 175-kilometer network of trails that intersect the property. ~ 31 Early Winters Drive, Mazama; 509-996-3906, 800-639-3809, fax 509-996-3907; www.freestone inn.com, e-mail info@freestoneinn.com. ULTRA-DELUXE.

The most elaborate place in the Methow Valley, and one of the best resorts in the Pacific Northwest, is **Sun Mountain Lodge**. Built at the 3000-foot level atop a small mountain, this low-rise, stone-and-timber resort gives a 360-degree view of the Cascades, Pasayten Wilderness, Okanogan Highlands and Methow Valley. The 112 units are spread over three buildings atop the mountain and down the road in 16 rustic, cozy cabins. The resort has just about everything: several miles of hiking trails that become cross-country ski trails in the winter, two pools, two hot tubs, an exercise room, a full-service spa, saddle-and-pack horses, mountain-bike rentals, canoe and sailing on the lake, heli-skiing and tennis. It also has a great restaurant. Rooms feature bentwood furniture, a fireplace (only the suites have real-wood fireplaces), coffee, the thickest and softest towels and robes you can hope for and no television. ~ 604 Patterson Lake Road, Winthrop; 509-996-2211, 800-572-0493, fax 509-996-3133; www.sunmoun tainlodge.com, e-mail sunmtn@methow.com. ULTRA-DELUXE.

Hotel Rio Vista has a facade that looks like it was made out of matchsticks. The 29 bright and airy rooms all overlook the Methow River and have mini-fridges and private decks. A hot tub and quaint riverside picnic area round out the amenities. Located on the south side of town, this lodging is within walking distance of downtown's eateries. It also runs a fully equipped Aspen loft cabin, ten miles west of town, which has a fireplace and sleeps six. ~ 285 Riverside Avenue, Winthrop; 509-996-3535, 800-398-0911; www.hotelriovista.com, e-mail info@hotelriovista.com. MODERATE TO DELUXE.

On the south edge of Winthrop is the **Virginian Resort**. Located on the high bank of the Methow River, the riverfront rooms in this 32-unit motel have balconies. There are also seven cabins, which are a bit more expensive, but several have wood stoves and room enough for four. Kitchens are equipped with microwaves. Offsite, the resort also rents the **Westar Lodge**, which sleeps 30 and includes a full-service kitchen and a couple of secluded acres on the Chewuch River. Also available is a two-bedroom cottage that sleeps five and has a full kitchen. ~ 808 North Cascades Highway, Winthrop; 509-996-2535, 800-854-2834, fax 509-996-2483; www.virgin ian-resort.com, e-mail info@virginian-resort.com. BUDGET TO MODERATE.

Winthrop's town hall was originally the Duck Brand Saloon, built in 1891.

The oldest and most reliable resort in Chelan is **Campbell's Resort**, which has been in business since 1901. With 170 rooms, it is still growing along the lakeshore in the heart of town. It has two heated pools, an outdoor jacuzzi, a day spa, a good beach and boat moorage. The larger rooms have kitchenettes and one king or two queen beds, and are decorated in soft pastels or earth tones. ~ 104 West Woodin Avenue, Chelan; 509-682-2561, 800-553-8225, fax 509-682-2177; www.campbellsresort.com, e-mail info@campbellsresort.com. ULTRA-DELUXE.

One of the most complete resorts inside the Chelan city limits is **Darnell's Lake Resort**, a few blocks southwest of the city center on Route 150. It has a heated pool and hot tub, putting greens, lighted tennis courts, swimming beach, waterskiing, volleyball, badminton and game rooms. The resort is divided into two three-story buildings. All rooms have balconies with views of the lake. All units are suites; some have two bedrooms. The penthouse suites have two fireplaces and private jacuzzi. Closed mid-October through March. ~ 901 Spader Bay Road, Chelan; 509-682-2015, 800-967-8149, fax 509-682-8736; www.darnells resort.com, e-mail info@darnellsresort.com. ULTRA-DELUXE.

On the eastern edge of Chelan is the clean and comfortable **Apple Inn Motel** with white stucco walls and black wood trim. The 41 rooms are small and clean; some have kitchenettes, all have microwaves; coffeemakers and TVs. The heated outdoor pool is open in the summer, and a hot tub is open year-round. ~ 1002 East Woodin Avenue, Chelan; 509-682-4044, 800-276-3229, fax 509-682-3330; www.appleinnmotel.com, e-mail info@appleinnmotel.com. MODERATE.

The dramatic **Sun Mountain Lodge Dining Room** garners statewide attention. The room is cantilevered with views down into the Methow Valley and Winthrop 1000 feet below. All seats here

DINING

have a view. The food is wonderful. The menu features seafood and creatively prepared grilled or roasted meats. ~ Sun Mountain Lodge, Patterson Lake Road, Winthrop; 509-996-2211, 800-572-0493, fax 509-996-3133; www.sunmountainlodge.com, e-mail sunmtn@methow.com. ULTRA-DELUXE.

One of Winthrop's most trendy restaurants is the oddly named **Duck Brand Cantina** in the hotel of the same name. The menu reflects an effort to please several palates, including Mexican, Continental and American. The restaurant is divided into two areas: a dining room filled with antiques and old photographs, and a deck overlooking Winthrop's sole street. Breakfast, lunch and dinner. ~ 248 Riverside Avenue, Winthrop; 509-996-2192, 800-996-2192, fax 509-996-2001; www.methownet.com/duck, e-mail duckbrand@methow.com. DELUXE.

Decorated in rustic Western style with wooden tables, hardwood floors, and elk heads mounted on the walls, **Three Fingered Jack's Saloon and Restaurant** offers fresh meats and vegetables, homemade soups, salads and desserts. The New York steaks are cut in-house in this family-run establishment. Vegetarians might try the fettuccine with garlic parmesan sauce. ~ 176 Riverside Avenue, Winthrop; phone/fax 509-996-2411; www.3fingered jacks.com. MODERATE.

Although Campbell's Resort is so large it overwhelms some people, it is hard to find a better place in the area for a good meal than the resort's **Campbell's House Cafe**. The large room seats about 130 and is pleasantly decorated in early American furnishings with walls covered with an eclectic collection of prints, documents and paintings. The menu is large: prime rib, medallions of pork, Asian-style jumbo prawns, the catch of the day and a variety of pasta. In summer, open daily for all three meals; no breakfast on weekdays in winter. ~ 104 West Woodin Avenue, Chelan; 509-682-2561, 800-553-8225, fax 509-682-2177; www.campbellsresort.com, e-mail info@campbellsresort.com. MODERATE.

A few doors down from Campbell's on the lakefront is **J.R.'s Bar and Grill**. It has two floors—with open-air seating on the top level—and specializes in lunches of sandwiches (some are purely vegetarian), soups and salads. Dinner offers a series of specials throughout the week, seafood, steak and several pastas. ~ 116 East Woodin Avenue, Chelan; 509-682-1031. BUDGET TO MODERATE.

SHOPPING Art is popular, and quite often very good, in Winthrop, especially at **Hildabob's Gallery**, where you will find paintings, sculpture and handknit apparel. Closed January to mid-April. ~ 231 Riverside Avenue, Winthrop; 509-996-2094. Art by local artists is available in the gift shop. **Sun Mountain Lodge**. ~ Patterson Lake Road, Winthrop; 509-996-4716.

Art is also a growth industry in the Chelan area. **Main Street Gallery** features watercolors, oils, pottery, glass and sculpture by local artists, as well as textiles and clothing. ~ 208 East Woodin Avenue, Chelan; 509-682-9262; www.mainstreetgallery chelan.com.

However, the apple is king in Chelan, and the **Harvest Tree** is a mail-order store with more than 1500 apple gift items, packaged apples and other Northwest-produced foods. ~ 109 East Woodin Avenue, Chelan; 509-682-3618, 800-568-6062; www. theapplestore.net.

NIGHTLIFE

In Winthrop the **Winthrop Palace** offers live rock and rhythm-and-blues music most nights during summer. Cover on occasion. ~ 918 Riverside Avenue, Winthrop; 509-996-2245; www.win throppalace.com.

Not much happens in Chelan after dark, which may be fine if you're planning to wake up in time to catch the *Lady of the Lake* cruise in the morning. If you simply must go out, your best bet may be the **Ruby Theatre**, a small but historic pink theater that presents double-feature movies and weekend matinees. ~ 135 East Woodin Avenue, Chelan; 509-682-5016; www.rubytheatre.com.

Seven miles west of Chelan, the Colville Indian Reservation operates the **Mill Bay Casino**, with blackjack, roulette, craps and slot machines. ~ 455 Wapato Lake Road, Manson; 509-687-2102, 800-648-2946; www.colvillecasinos.com.

Also in Manson, the **Sports Bar at Uncle Tim's** has live entertainment and dancing in summer, and karaoke Friday and Saturday in winter. ~ 76 West Wapato Way, Manson; 509-687-3035.

PARKS

PEARRYGIN LAKE STATE PARK This 696-acre park is popular for travelers in RVs because it is close to Winthrop and has a sandy beach on a small lake surrounded by mountains. Anglers will find rainbow trout off the fishing dock. Facilities include picnic areas, barbecue pits, restrooms and showers. Closed November through March. ~ Bear Creek Road, four miles northeast of Winthrop; 509-996-2370.

ORCHARDS, ORCHARDS EVERYWHERE

Chelan has some of the best orchards along the eastern slopes of the Cascades. If you take a drive northwest of town on Route 150 to Manson, you will see thousands of acres of apple orchards climbing up the sun-baked hills from the lake.

▲ There are 92 standard sites ($19 to $26 per night), two primitive sites ($14 per night) and 71 RV hookup sites ($22 to $27 per night). Reservations: 888-226-7688.

LAKE CHELAN STATE PARK 🏃 🚴 🏕 🏊 🐟 🎣 🚣 🛶
🚤 ⚓ This is a favorite park for youths yearning for sunshine, and in July and August the shoreline looks more like California than Washington with its broad, sandy beach (great swimming) and play area. Because it has docks and launching areas for skiers, it is equally popular with powerboaters and waterskiers. Anglers fish for rainbow trout, kokanee salmon, burbot, lake trout and bass as far away from the powerboats as possible. There are picnic tables, restrooms, a concession stand and showers. ~ Route 971, nine miles west of Chelan; 509-687-3710.

▲ There are 109 standard sites ($19 per night) and 35 RV hookup sites ($26 per night). Reservations highly recommended for summer: 888-226-7688.

TWENTY-FIVE MILE CREEK STATE PARK 🏃 🚴 🏊 🐟 🎣
🎣 🚣 🚤 ⚓ More remote than Lake Chelan State Park but popular with those more interested in mountain scenery than body scenery, this park is quiet, with the Chelan Mountains behind and the jagged peaks of the Sawtooth Wilderness across the lake. The small beach is mostly for wading, though boaters fish in the lake. There are picnic areas, restrooms, showers and moorage at the marina; a concession stand offers snacks, groceries and fishing supplies. Closed October through March. ~ Route 971, 20 miles up-lake from Chelan; 509-687-3610.

▲ There are 46 standard sites ($17 per night) and 21 RV hookup sites ($24 per night). Closed in winter. Reservations: 888-226-7688.

LINCOLN ROCK STATE PARK 🚴 🏕 🏊 🎣 🚣 🚤 ⚓ ⚓ Named for a rock outcropping that resembles Abraham Lincoln's profile, this state park in the Columbia River canyon is a short distance north of Wenatchee. There is swimming, fishing for trout and salmon, and boating. Several species of wildlife reside in the park, including marmots, rabbits, deer, beaver, nighthawks and swallows. Facilities include picnic shelters, restrooms, showers, volleyball courts, a playfield and play equipment for children. Closed mid-October to early March. ~ Route 97/2, six miles north of East Wenatchee; 509-884-8702, fax 509-886-1704.

▲ There are 27 standard sites ($19 per night) and 67 RV hookup sites ($26 per night). Reservations: 888-226-7688.

▼▼▼▼▼▼▼▼▼▼▼▼▼
Wenatchee Area

Famous for its apple orchards, the sunny Wenatchee Area is located in the heart of Washington. Popular with rafters and gold panners, this region is also home to one of the state's most picturesque gardens.

You have a choice of two highways when leaving Chelan: You can
continue along Route 97A, which cuts through the Cascade foothills back to the Columbia River and south to Wenatchee, or cross
the Columbia at Chelan Falls, hardly more than a junction, and
follow Route 97 south through the orchard town of Orando to
East Wenatchee. Stop at **Rocky Reach Dam** to visit the Fish
Viewing Room where healthy numbers of migratory salmon and
steelhead swim past the windows. The dam also has a museum
showing the natural and human history of the Columbia River,
along with a Nez Perce Indian portrait collection and other rotating exhibits. ~ Located 28 miles south of Chelan; 509-663-
7522, fax 509-661-8149; www.chelanpud.org.

SIGHTS

Wenatchee is the largest town in this region and directed more
toward orchards than tourists, although you will certainly feel
welcome. On the northern edge of town, overlooking the Columbia River, Wenatchee and Rocky Reach Dam, is **Ohme Gardens**.
You will find nine acres of alpine gardens developed by the Ohme
family on the steep, rocky outcroppings at the edge of their property overlooking the Columbia River. Closed mid-October to
mid-April. Admission. ~ 3327 Ohme Road, Wenatchee; 509-662-
5785, fax 509-662-6805; www.ohmegardens.com.

Downtown, the **Wenatchee Valley Museum & Cultural Center**
has several permanent exhibits including a 1919 Wurlitzer theater pipe organ and an apple-packing shed featuring an apple
wiper, sizing machine and a 1924 orchard truck. In the gift shop
area is an original WPA mural by Peggy Strong depicting the
change of the postal service from its pioneer days to a modern,

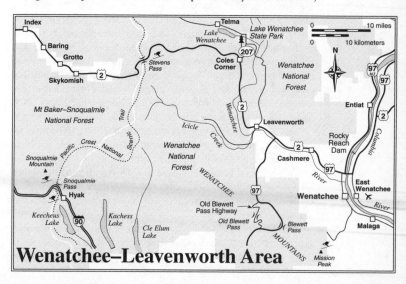

Wenatchee–Leavenworth Area

organized unit. Closed Sunday and Monday. Admission. ~ 127 South Mission Street, Wenatchee; 509-664-3340, fax 509-664-3356; www.wenatcheevalleymuseum.com, e-mail wvmcc@wen atcheevalleymuseum.com.

Ten miles west via Routes 2 and 97, **Cashmere**, so-named because it reminded a pioneer of Kashmir, India, has an early American theme to its downtown buildings. The **Cashmere Pioneer Village and Museum** has almost two dozen original structures from Chelan and Douglas counties assembled to recreate a pioneer village, including a blacksmith shop, school, gold mine and hotel. Closed weekdays from November to late December; closed completely from late December through February. ~ 600 Cotlets Way, Cashmere; 509-782-3230, fax 509-782-3219.

From Cashmere, Routes 2 and 97 follow the swift Wenatchee River into the Cascades. Shortly before reaching Leavenworth, Route 97 turns south toward the Route 90 Corridor towns of Cle Elum and Ellensburg by going over 4101-foot **Blewett Pass**. An alternative route, in the summer only, is to follow the **Old Blewett Pass Highway**, which has been preserved by the Wenatchee National Forest. The old highway is a series of switchbacks with sweeping views of the Cascades. No services are available until you reach Cle Elum and Ellensburg, other than a small grocery store at **Liberty**, a gold-mining town just off the highway that is making a comeback as people move into its modest cabins along the main street.

LODGING   Most hotels in Wenatchee are along North Wenatchee Avenue. The largest hotel in this part of the state is the **Coast Wenatchee Center Hotel,** at nine stories one of the tallest buildings along the eastern edge of the Cascades. The 147 rooms are newly remodeled and larger than those at most other hotels in town, and suites have desks, armoires and potted plants. A large lobby has a baby grand piano. There's a restaurant, an indoor-outdoor pool and jacuzzi and a fitness center. ~ 201 North Wenatchee Avenue, Wenatchee; 509-662-1234, 877-964-1234, fax 509-662-0782; www.coasthotels.com. DELUXE.

For a low-priced place, try the **Super 8**. It has 103 rooms on three floors decorated with subtly flowered bedspreads, unobtrusive furniture and wallhangings. There is a heated pool and hot tub. Continental breakfast included. ~ 1401 North Miller Street, Wenatchee; 509-662-3443, 800-800-8000, fax 509-665-0715; www.super8wenatchee.com, e-mail super8@nwi.com. MODERATE TO DELUXE.

The **Village Inn Motel** is in the heart of town. The white-and-green motel has 21 units, six with refrigerators. A bit impersonal, but it's clean, quiet and reasonably priced. ~ 229 Cottage Avenue,

Cashmere; 509-782-3522, 800-793-3522, fax 509-782-8190; www.cashmerevillageinn.com. BUDGET.

DINING

Want Italian? Try **Visconti's Italian Restaurant**. Both Southern and Northern Italian dishes are offered in a family-friendly atmosphere. Their wood-fired oven is used to "broil-roast" seafood and prime cuts of meat. ~ 1737 North Wenatchee Avenue, Wenatchee; 509-662-5013, fax 509-667-9543; www.viscontis.com, e-mail wenatchee@viscontis.com. MODERATE TO DELUXE.

A top-notch steakhouse is **The Windmill**. It's a down-to-earth place, with waitresses who have been there for years. A blackboard keeps a running total of the number of steaks sold there since 1962. Prime rib and lobster are now offered in addition to a wide selection of meat and seafood dishes. Fresh-baked pies round out the meals. Dinner only. ~ 1501 North Wenatchee Avenue, Wenatchee; 509-665-9529, fax 509-662-5030; www.the windmillrestaurant.com, e-mail greatsteaks@thewindmillrestaurant.com. MODERATE TO ULTRA-DELUXE.

As a reflection of Central Washington's growing Hispanic population, **Tequila's** is owned by former residents of Mexico. The refried beans are homemade, and the salsa is as tangy as you'd get in Guadalajara. ~ 800 North Wenatchee Avenue, Wenatchee; 509-662-7239. MODERATE.

SHOPPING

A wide range of Washington souvenirs and products, everything from jam to smoked salmon, can be found at **Pak It Rite**. Closed Sunday. ~ 126 North Wenatchee Avenue, Wenatchee; 509-663-1072, 800-666-2730; www.pakitrite.com.

Victorian Village is a small mall constructed in the best of the Victorian Carpenter Gothic style—round towers, falsefronts and steeples. You will find a hair salon, an equestrian shop and, inter-

AUTHOR FAVORITE

Cashmere is the place to shop for a wide range of apple-based food products and gifts. Especially tempting is **Liberty Orchards**, which has been making fruit confections since 1920. Known for their Aplets and Cotlets, fruit-and-nut concoctions sprinkled with powdered sugar, Liberty Orchards also sells a wide variety of apple-themed gifts. Tours of the candy factory are offered on weekdays, and the company store is open weekends during the summer. ~ 117 Mission Street, Cashmere; 509-782-2191; www.libertyorchards.com, e-mail service@libertyorchards.com.

estingly for a Victorian theme, a Mexican restaurant. ~ 611 South
Mission Street, Wenatchee.

For cider tastings and gifts with an apple theme, check out
the **Washington Apple Country Gift Shop**, located at the Cashmere Cider Mill. Open Monday through Friday from May
through October; limited hours through February. ~ 5420 Wood-
ring Canyon Road, Cashmere; 866-459-9614; www.washington
applecountry.com.

NIGHTLIFE   Although Wenatchee is the largest town in the Cascades, the nightlife choice is slim. Your best bet may be the lounges in some of
the chain motor inns, but don't expect much.

PARKS   **OKANOGAN-WENATCHEE NATIONAL FORESTS**   At 4 million acres, this is one of the
largest national forests in the United States. It encompasses eight
wilderness areas, hundreds of lakes, downhill-ski areas and more
than 4000 miles of trails for hiking, riding and biking (including
the Pacific Crest National Scenic Trail). Salmon, steelhead, searun
cutthroat trout, bull trout, bass, crappie, walleye and sturgeon
are among the fish found in streams and lakes. There are picnic
areas and restrooms. ~ The forest is crossed by Routes 12, 97/2
and 90; 509-664-9200, fax 509-644-9280.

▲ There are more than 120 campgrounds; RVs accommodated in some campgrounds (no hookups); prices range from free
to $18. Most campgrounds do not take reservations; the five that
do can be reached at 877-444-6777.

Leavenworth Area   Think Bavarian! If you like cuckoo clocks, fancy
woodwork, beer steins and alpenhorns, you'll love
making a stop in Leavenworth.

SIGHTS   One of the major tourist spots in the Cascades, **Leavenworth** welcomes visitors with oompah bands, specialty stores and impressive
alpine scenery. Almost everything here—architecture, hotels, restaurants, annual events—is centered around the Bavarian theme.
Mountains are on three sides, and a river rushes through town.
During most of the summer, free concerts and dancing exhibitions are given in the City Park, and outdoor art exhibits are held
on weekends.

Just west of Leavenworth, Route 2 enters **Tumwater Canyon**,
which follows the Wenatchee River some 20 miles. It is marked
by sheer canyon walls, plunging river rapids and deciduous trees
along the riverbank that turn into brilliant colors in autumn.

Route 2 continues over **Stevens Pass**, a popular ski area and
where the **Pacific Crest National Scenic Trail** (see "Hiking" at the
end of this chapter) crosses the highway. Soon after crossing the

summit and passing Skykomish, the **Skykomish River** parallels the highway. This is one of Western Washington's most popular white-water rivers. Most trips originate in the small alpine village of **Index,** a short distance off the highway. The sheer-faced, 5979-foot **Mt. Index** looms behind the town. From there, the river rumbles down past the small towns of Gold Bar and Sultan, then flattens out onto the Puget Sound lowlands.

One of the most pleasant spots in Leavenworth is the **Hotel-Pension Anna.** It has 16 rooms with furniture and decor imported from Austria. Heavy wooden bed frames and cupboards are used throughout, along with feather beds and down comforters. Three suites come with fireplace and jacuzzi, and all rooms have private baths. Breakfast is included. ~ 926 Commercial Street, Leavenworth; 509-548-6273, 800-509-2662, fax 509-548-4656; www.pensionanna.com, e-mail info@pensionanna.com. MODERATE TO ULTRA-DELUXE.

LODGING

A Bavarian wood carver was imported to fashion the rails and ceiling beams of the **Enzian Inn,** and the entire 105-room motel with its turret and chalet-styled roofs shows similar touches. The eight suites have king-size beds, spas and fireplaces. It has indoor and outdoor pools and hot tubs. During the winter, free cross-country ski equipment is available to guests; in summer, guests get a free round of putting at Enzian Falls Championship Putting Course. The complimentary buffet breakfast is served in the big solarium on the fourth floor. ~ 590 Route 2, Leavenworth; phone/fax 509-548-5269, 800-223-8511; www.enzianinn.com, e-mail info@enzianinn.com. DELUXE.

sights

AUTHOR FAVORITE

The only museum in the country devoted exclusively to nutcrackers, the **Leavenworth Nutcracker Museum** displays artifacts from as early as the 14th century up to modern times. The collection consists of more than 5000 nutcrackers from around the world, including Italy, Germany, Turkey, the U.S. and India. You'll see the popular soldier nutcracker, as well as nutcrackers in the shape of dragons, dogs and rams. Moses, Abraham Lincoln, Bugs Bunny, Thomas Edison and Shakespeare have all been immortalized as, you guessed it, nutcrackers in the museum's gift shop. Open daily 2 p.m. to 5 p.m. from May through October; open weekends only November through April. Admission. ~ 735 Front Street, Leavenworth; 509-548-4573, 509-548-4708, fax 509-548-4760; www.nutcrackermuseum.com, e-mail curator@nutcrackermuseum.com.

For a change of pace, try renting one of the townhouses at the **Linderhof Inn**, next door to the Enzian Inn. The 11 townhouses are divided into one- and two-bedroom units that sleep six and eight respectively. They have cathedral ceilings with balcony bedrooms and full kitchens with all appliances. There are 22 additional units, some with fireplaces and spas, all with handcrafted furniture. There is an outdoor pool and hot tub. Continental breakfast is included, and there's wireless internet throughout the property. ~ 690 Route 2, Leavenworth; 509-548-5283, 800-828-5680, fax 509-548-6705; www.linderhof.com, e-mail info@linderhof.com. MODERATE.

More and more bed and breakfasts and inns are opening outside town. One is **Run of the River Inn & Refuge**, a mile east of Icicle River from Route 2. The building is made of logs and has cathedral ceilings with pine walls and handmade log furniture. The six rooms come with private baths and cable television, as well as jacuzzis, river-rock fireplaces and private decks. A private lodge sleeps two. Stay here, kick back and just contemplate the beautiful setting. There are complimentary mountain bikes for exploring the many surrounding trails and backroads and complimentary snowshoes in winter. Breakfasts are country-style. The inn accepts nonsmoking adults only. ~ 9308 East Leavenworth Road, Leavenworth; 509-548-7171, 800-288-6491, fax 509-548-7547; www.runoftheriver.com, e-mail info@runoftheriver.com. ULTRA-DELUXE.

Located in a wooded setting on the banks of the Wenatchee River, the **All Seasons River Inn** offers spacious rooms and suites overlooking the river, all with jacuzzis and most with fireplaces and private decks. The inn provides full breakfasts and bicycles for touring the nearby Icicle Loop. Nonsmoking; no children or pets. ~ 8751 Icicle Road, Leavenworth; 509-548-1425, 800-254-0555; www.allseasonsriverinn.com, e-mail info@allseasonsriverinn.com. ULTRA-DELUXE.

Farther down the mountain you'll find the **Dutch Cup Motel**, which is popular with skiers. The two-story motel has 20 units with refrigerators, microwaves and cable television. Small, quiet, supervised pets are welcome. ~ 918 Main Street, Sultan; 360-793-2215, 800-844-0488, fax 360-793-2216; www.dutchcup.com, e-mail dutchcup@mac.com. BUDGET TO MODERATE.

DINING Café Mozart Restaurant's wall sconces, gold chandeliers, floral carpeted floors and candlelit tables create an intimate baroque-style atmosphere in each of the four dining rooms. The German-born chef prepares Central European favorites such as beef goulash soup and smoked half duck glazed with orange-raspberry confiture. You might also find almond-crusted halibut with champagne-orange hollandaise sauce. If you have room for dessert or if you stop by between meals, treat yourself to Mozart's chocolate torte (seven layers of rich marzipan wine crème covered with dark chocolate). Reservations recommended. Open daily for lunch and dinner from June through October; no lunch Monday through Thursday from November through May. ~ 829 Front Street, Leavenworth; 509-548-0600; www.cafemozartrestau rant.com, e-mail mozart@crcwnet.com. MODERATE TO DELUXE.

The **Gingerbread Factory** is a delight for children and parents alike, with decorated cookies and gingerbread houses. The café sells pastries, quiches, sandwiches, soups, salads, espresso and all sorts of gifts related to gingerbread. Lunch only; although coffee and pastries are available for breakfast. Closed Wednesday and another weekday in winter; call for hours. ~ 828 Commercial Street, Leavenworth; 509-548-6592; www.gin gerbreadfactory.com, e-mail sales@gingerbreadfactory. com. BUDGET.

> Leavenworth has the best selection of specialty shops in the Cascades; about 80 are crammed into a two-block area.

The **Dutch Cup Restaurant** is one of the most popular restaurants on the Stevens Pass route. It opens at 7 a.m. to catch the ski crowd as they head up the highway and stays open until 10 p.m. to get them on the way home. The home-cooking menu includes country breakfasts, burgers, soups and sandwiches for lunch, and offers steaks, prime rib and chicken for dinner. ~ 927 Route 2, Sultan; 360-793-1864, fax 360-793-3447. MODERATE.

The **Index Café** offers breakfast and lunch to travelers heading up and down Route 2. Stop in for fish and chips, pot roast sandwiches and chicken with artichokes. ~ 49315 Route 2, Index; 360-799-1133. BUDGET.

SHOPPING

A **Book for All Seasons** offers a wide variety of books, cards and author readings. ~ 703 Route 2, Leavenworth; 509-548-1451.

NIGHTLIFE

Andreas Keller German Restaurant offers live accordian music on weekends in winter and spring, nightly in summer and fall. ~ 829 Front Street, Leavenworth; 509-548-6000; www.and reaskellerrestaurant.com. For live rock and blues in the summer, try **Uncle Uli's Pub** on weekends. ~ 901 Front Street, Leavenworth; 509-548-7262.

Leavenworth's major sports bar is the **Old Post Office Tavern**, with TVs, pool tables and karaoke on Friday and Saturday nights. ~ 213 9th Street, Leavenworth; 509-548-7488.

PARKS

LAKE WENATCHEE STATE PARK 🚶 🚴 🐎 ⛺ 🏕 🛶 🎣 ⛷ 🚣 🛥 The lake is tucked away near Stevens Pass and is popular in summer for canoeing, kayaking, sailing, swimming and fishing (kokanee and whitefish) and in the winter for cross-country skiing. The secluded, wooded campsites are great.

Picnic areas, restrooms and showers are found here, and in July and August there are interpretive programs on Saturdays. ~ Route 207, 18 miles northwest of Leavenworth and four miles off Route 2; 509-763-3101.

▲ There are 155 standard sites ($17 per night) and about 42 RV hookup sites ($24 per night). Reservations: 888-226-7688.

▼▼▼▼▼▼▼▼▼▼▼▼▼
Route 90 Corridor

This pristine area remains one of America's scenic icons. From snow-capped peaks to dramatic waterfalls, the corridor is one of the Northwest's hidden treasures. It extends from Snoqualmie across the Cascades to Ellensburg and the Kittitas Valley. Fasten your seat belts for a breathtaking ride past volcanic peaks, fir forests and rivers where you're likely to land tonight's dinner.

SIGHTS
The Cascades begin rising only a half-hour's drive east of Seattle. The town of **Snoqualmie** has an ornate, old railroad depot that is the oldest continually operating train station in the country. It's also home to the **Snoqualmie Valley Railroad**, which makes a five-mile trip through the Snoqualmie Valley on weekends (April through September) and runs a special Christmas train. Admission. ~ 38625 Southeast King Street, Snoqualmie; 425-888-3030; www.trainmuseum.org; e-mail info@trainmuseum.org.

Nearby is **Snoqualmie Falls**, a thundering cataract with a small park, observation platform and trails leading to the river below the 270-foot falls.

The town of **North Bend** has adopted an alpine theme for its downtown buildings, but it hasn't caught on with the vigor of Winthrop and Leavenworth. Not to be confused with the Oregon coastal town of the same name, this hamlet sits snugly in the shadow of the looming Mt. Si. The **North Bend Ranger District Forest Service Station** offers maps, books and other outdoor-recreation information. Open Monday through Friday. ~ 42404 Southeast North Bend Way, North Bend; 425-888-1421.

The Summit at Snoqualmie Pass has four major ski areas, for downhill and snowboarding, and one cross-country ski area with more than 35 miles of groomed trails. ~ 1001 State Route 906, Snoqualmie Pass; 425-434-7669; www.summitatsnoqualmie.com. **Snoqualmie Pass Visitor Center** offers maps and books. Closed Monday through Thursday. ~ Exit 52 off Route 90 on State Route 906; on Snoqualmie Pass; 425-434-6111.

In **Cle Elum**, an American Indian name meaning "swift water," you will find the unusual **Cle Elum Historical Telephone Museum**, which commemorates and explains (through exhibits of ethnic costumes, old switchboards and railroad, logging and mining items) why Cle Elum was the last U.S. town to switch over from a manual long-distance switchboard. (Twenty-seven dialects were commonly heard during the town's early days as a mining center.) Open by appointment or call for hours. ~ 221 East 1st Street, Cle Elum; 509-674-5939; www.nkcmuseums.org, e-mail nkchs@yahoo.com.

At the foot of 4th Street is the access point for the 113-mile-long **Iron Horse State Park,** a section of the former railroad right of way with the rails and ties removed and the roadbed smoothed over for walking, jogging, cross-country skiing and biking. It is part of the **John Wayne Pioneer Trail** that will eventually run the width of the state.

Three miles away from Cle Elum is the tiny town of **Roslyn,** used as the set for TV's quirky "Northern Exposure." It was formerly a coal-mining town with a large population of Italian, Croatian and Austrian immigrants who worked in the mines. There are separate cemeteries—23 in fact—for these nationalities.

As you drive through the Kittitas Valley to Ellensburg, notice that the prevailing wind off the Cascades gives trees a permanent lean toward the east. When you reach Ellensburg, you're out of the Cascades and entering the arid climate that characterizes most of the eastern side of Washington. **Ellensburg** is perhaps best known for its rodeo each Labor Day weekend, and in keeping with the Western legacy, the Western Art Association has its headquarters there and holds an annual show and auction each May.

The **Clymer Museum of Art** displays work by the famous Western artist, John Ford Clymer, who lived in Ellensburg. Closed Sunday from January through April. ~ 416 North Pearl Street, Ellensburg; 509-962-6416, fax 509-962-6424; www.clymermuseum.com, e-mail clymermuseum@charter.net.

The **Kittitas County Historical Museum** displays American Indian and pioneer artifacts and has extensive rock and doll collections. Closed Sunday. ~ 114 East 3rd Avenue, Ellensburg; 509-925-3778; www.kchm.org, e-mail kchm@kchm.org.

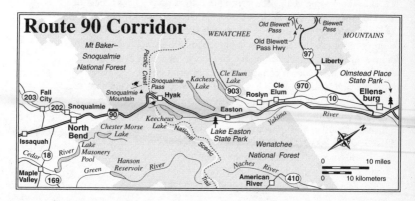

Four miles east of town is the **Olmstead Place State Park,** a working farm that uses pioneer equipment. The 217-acre farm and all its buildings were deeded to the state. Restrooms and picnic tables are available, and weekend tours are offered from Memorial Day to Labor Day. ~ 921 North Ferguson Road, Ellensburg; 509-925-1943.

LODGING   **The Edgewick Inn,** located two miles east of town, is a straightforward motel with 42 clean and quiet units and two suites with jacuzzis. ~ 14600 468th Avenue Southeast, North Bend; 425-888-9000, fax 425-888-9400; www.edgewickinn.com. MODERATE.

About the only place to stay at Snoqualmie Summit is the **Summit Lodge at Snoqualmie Pass.** Outfitted for skiers, its 81 rooms come with king-size or two queen-size beds, and it has a complimentary ski-storage area and coin-operated laundry. Tired guests also enjoy the indoor sauna, jacuzzi and heated outdoor pool. The large lobby is stocked with comfortable leather sofas set around the native-stone fireplace. ~ P.O. Box 163, Snoqualmie Pass, WA 98068; 425-434-6300, 800-557-7829, fax 425-434-6396. DELUXE.

A former Milwaukee Railroad crew house and recognized in the National Historic Register, **Iron Horse Inn** has been converted into one of the state's best inns. The 12 rooms, half with shared baths, are named for former occupants. All are decorated in turn-of-the-20th-century antiques—with an emphasis, not surprisingly, on railroad trinkets and tools. Four remodeled cabooses sport queen-size beds, refrigerators and sundecks with hot tub. A third caboose and the deluxe honeymoon suite has a jacuzzi; an outdoor hot tub serves everyone else. The Iron Horse

AUTHOR FAVORITE

When I want to spend a pricey night in the lap of luxury, I can't think of a more dramatic setting to do it in than the clifftop **Salish Lodge and Spa at Snoqualmie Falls,** perched on the cliff overlooking the spectacular falls. Visitors might recognize it as the backdrop for the eerie David Lynch TV drama *Twin Peaks.* The 89 rooms and suites are decorated in an upscale-country motif with down comforters, wicker furniture, woodburning fireplaces and jacuzzis. Only a few rooms have views of the falls, but the interiors are so well done that most visitors console themselves by watching the falls from the lounge or observation deck. There is also a full-service spa. ~ 6501 Railroad Avenue Southeast, Snoqualmie; 425-888-2556, 800-272-5474, fax 425-888-2420; www.salishlodge.com, e-mail reservations@salishlodge.com. ULTRA-DELUXE.

is adjacent to the Iron Horse State Park Trail, where cross-country skiing, bicycling, horseback riding and walking are popular. Full breakfast is included in the rate. ~ 526 Marie Avenue, South Cle Elum; 509-674-5939, 800-228-9246; www.ironhorseinnbb. com, e-mail maryp@ironhorseinnbb.com. MODERATE TO DELUXE.

For more impersonal lodgings, the **TimberLodge Inn**, on the western edge of town, has 35 bright, clean rooms and one deluxe suite with fridge, microwave and wi-fi, far enough off the street to deaden the noise of the busy main drag. Amenities include a hot tub. There is a daily breakfast bar. ~ 301 West 1st Street, Cle Elum; 509-674-5966, 800-584-1133, fax 509-674-2737. MODERATE.

A restored Victorian home located near the Central Washington University campus in downtown Ellensburg, the **Ellensburg Guest House** has two guest suites furnished with antiques and private baths. ~ 606 North Main Street, Ellensburg; 509-962-3706. DELUXE.

DINING

The **Salish Lodge & Spa at Snoqualmie Falls** offers spectacular views over the falls and canyon below, and the food is first rate. The menu leans toward what has become known as Northwest cuisine: lots of seafood, fresh fruits and vegetables, and game. The restaurant boasts the largest wine list in the state and a dessert list almost as long. ~ 6501 Railroad Avenue, Snoqualmie; 425-888-2556, 800-272-5474; www.salishlodge.com, e-mail reservations@salishlodge.com. ULTRA-DELUXE.

Twede's Café, which served as the model for the diner in television's *Twin Peaks*, has faux gas lamps, wood paneling and neon across the ceiling. Stay for a cup of "damn good coffee" and their infamous cherry pie. ~ 137 West North Bend Way, North Bend; 425-831-5511. BUDGET.

Cle Elum is better known for its inns and small hotels, but it has at least one good restaurant, **Mama Vallone's Steak House**, where you never have to wait for someone to replenish your water or bring more bread. A specialty is *bagna cauda*, a fondue-style mixture of olive oil, anchovy and garlic served with dipping strips of steak or seafood. Lunch served only in summer on weekends. ~ 302 West 1st Street, Cle Elum; 509-674-5174. MODERATE TO DELUXE.

The **Starlight Lounge** offers updates on comfort food such as pan-fried chicken, cinnamon-crusted pork chops and the classic martini. Weekend brunch, too. ~ 402 North Pearl Street, Ellensburg; 509-962-6100. MODERATE TO DELUXE.

A short walk away is **The Valley Café**. Food is American with a Northwest flair. Fish (frequently salmon) and chicken dominate the dinner menu. There are also lamb, steak, pasta and vegetarian options on the menu. ~ 105 West 3rd Avenue, Ellensburg; 509-925-3050. MODERATE.

SHOPPING   Antique hunters will enjoy Ellensburg, which has at least half a dozen antique stores in a three-block area, including a mall. The **Showplace Antique Mall** is a restored art deco theater with up to 40 antique dealers displaying at a time. ~ 103 East 3rd Avenue, Ellensburg; 509-962-9331.

NIGHTLIFE   Cle Elum has almost nothing in nightlife other than taverns with jukeboxes, although occasionally **Iron Horse Inn** guests will bring their own instruments to the piano in the lobby area for a sing-along. ~ 526 Marie Avenue, Cle Elum; 509-674-5939.

In Ellensburg between the rodeos there is little entertainment.

PARKS   **LAKE EASTON STATE PARK** 🚶 🚲 🏊 🛶 ⛵ 🚤 🚣
On Route 90, near the summit at Snoqualmie Pass, this lakeside park with forested trails is used as a base for skiers and snow-mobilers in winter, as a lunch stop for travelers in spring and fall, and for hiking, swimming and trout fishing in the summer. Facilities include picnic areas, a swimming beach and restrooms. ~ Route 90, a mile west of Easton; 509-656-2230.

▲ There are 95 standard sites ($19 per night) near the Yakima River and 45 RV hookup sites ($26 per night) near the lake. Reservations: 888-226-7688.

▼▼▼▼▼▼▼▼▼▼▼▼
Mt. Rainier Area
It is always a dramatic moment when Mt. Rainier suddenly appears ahead of you (in the Northwest it is often just called The Mountain). You could spend weeks in this area and only sample a small portion of its recreational possibilities. Whether you approach from the east or the west, the forest gets thicker and thicker and the roadside rivers get swifter and swifter. The national park is almost surrounded with national forest wilderness areas as buffer zones against clear-cut logging. Located southeast of Seattle, this peak is the site of the aptly named town of Paradise. *Note: Mount Ranier is currently closed due to massive flooding in November 2006 and severe damage to visitors services and trails throughout the park. Some areas are expected to be cleared by April 2007, and there is limited entry to Paradise via a shuttle at Longmire, but the superintendent states it may take two years to recover and reopen.*

SIGHTS   Coming from Route 5 down Route 7 toward Mt. Rainier, right before the town of Elbe is a turnoff that will take you north on Route 161 to **Northwest Trek Wildlife Park**. A free-roaming animal park owned by the Tacoma Metro Parks Department, it provides a rare opportunity to see native wildlife of the Pacific Northwest up close. The highlight is a 55-minute tram ride around a 435-acre expanse of forest and meadows inhabited by hundreds of large grazing animals, including bison, caribou, bighorn sheep, mountain goats, Roosevelt elk and a few elusive moose. Migratory sandhill cranes and geese also live in the park. There is often a wait of an hour or more for the tram ride. In the meantime, you can walk around the more conventionally zoolike area near the tour station and see predators such as wolves, bears, cougars, owls and eagles as well as smaller animals like beavers, raccoons and badgers that would be hard to spot in a free-roaming setting. There's also a network of paved and unpaved nature trails that can take an hour or more to explore fully, plus a hands-on discovery center for kids. The gift shop features animal-motif gift items made by regional artisans, and the café has a full lunch menu as well as an outdoor picnic area. If you're planning to visit Mt. Rainier, Northwest Trek is right on the way. Closed Monday through Thursday from November to mid-February. Admission. ~ 11610 Trek Drive East (off Route 161), Eatonville; 360-832-6117, fax 360-832-6118; www.nwtrek.org.

If you arrive via Route 706 you will have to go through Elbe on Route 7 which has the **Mt. Rainier Scenic Railroad,** a steam-powered train that makes a 14-mile trip through the lush forest and across high bridges to Mineral Lake. It runs daily in July and August and on Saturday and Sunday in June, September and December. A four-hour dinner train is offered Friday through Sunday in the summer. ~ P.O. Box 921, Elbe, WA 98330; 360-569-2588, 888-783-2611; www.mrsr.com.

Once inside the park you may be almost overwhelmed by the scenery. **Mt. Rainier** is so monstrous (14,410 feet) that it makes everything around it seem trivial. In fact, Mt. Rainier is the tallest mountain in the Northwest and has more glaciers—25—than any other mountain in the contiguous 48 states. **Mt. Rainier National Park** has numerous visitor centers and interpretive exhibits along winding roads. For park information, contact the National Park Service in the Longmire Museum at 360-569-2211 ext. 3314; www.nps.gov/mora.

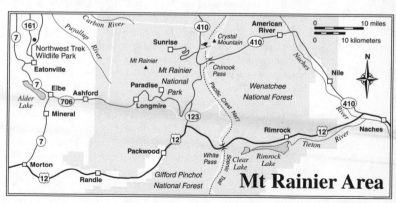

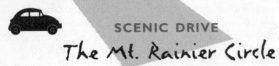

The Mt. Rainier Circle

Mt. Rainier, the huge landmark mountain visible (on clear days) from everywhere in the Puget Sound area, makes for a spectacularly scenic all-day trip from Seattle. Heading south from the city on Route 5, take Exit 149, drive two miles to Kent, and turn south on Route 167, another wide, fast, divided highway. Go seven miles to Puyallup, turn off on Route 161, and suddenly you're off the freeway and on your way through the forests and farmlands of Pierce County.

NORTHWEST TREK WILDLIFE PARK   Located about 17 miles south of Puyallup is Northwest Trek Wildlife Park (page 242), Washington's premier animal park, where you can take an hour-long tram tour for an up-close look at large animals native to the Pacific Northwest roaming in a 435-acre natural habitat. There's usually a wait, so expect to spend two to three hours here.

PARADISE   Ten miles south of Northwest Trek, Route 161 meets Route 7. Turn south (left) and go nine miles to Elbe, where Route 706, the well-marked road to **Mt. Rainier National Park** (page 243), turns off to the east (left). Passing Alder Lake, it's about 15 miles to the park's Nisqually Entrance, where on sunny weekends you may have to wait in a long line to pay the $10-per-vehicle entrance fee. As you drive through

In **Paradise**, head to the **Henry M. Jackson Visitor Center**, which has several exhibits and audiovisual shows. Paradise is one of the most beautiful places in the park, and the visitors center is one of the busiest. It has a snack bar and gift shop. Closed weekdays (except holidays) between October and April. *Note: The visitors center also contains the Guide Center for those wishing to arrange a climb to the summit. This visitors center will close permanently in fall 2008 and be replaced by the smaller but more energy-efficient new Paradise Visitor Center, which is under construction nearby.* ~ Paradise, WA; 360-569-2211 ext. 2328.

The **Longmire Museum** emphasizes the natural history of the park with rock, flora and fauna exhibits as well as with exhibits on the human history of the area. Its old historic buildings have stood since the 1880s when the Longmire family lived there. The museum also has information for hikers, and next door at the National Park Inn you can rent cross-country skis or snowshoes. ~ Longmire, WA; 360-569-2211 ext. 3314.

lofty primeval forest at the base of the mountain, you'll see signs of a vast mudslide that occurred when the sleeping volcanic giant stirred and melted part of the glacier that caps its summit. About 15 miles into the park, a turnoff on the left takes you up to timberline at Paradise, where the busy visitors center has a cafeteria, trails that wend through alpine meadows, and exhibits about climbing the mountain.

SUNRISE   Beyond the Paradise turnoff, Route 706 is closed in the winter but stunning in the summer as it traverses Backbone Ridge, offering panoramic views of the jagged Catamount Range to the southeast. In about 15 miles you'll join Route 123 northbound. Another ten miles brings you to the summit of 4675-foot Cayuse Pass. Four miles farther on is the turnoff on the left that winds by switchbacks up the east slope of the mountain to **Sunrise Visitor Center**, a 16-mile climb to the highest point in the park that you can reach by car. Another network of alpine hiking trails starts here, and it's usually much less crowded than Paradise.

HOMEWARD   When you descend from Sunrise, turn north (left) on Route 123 and you're on your way out of the park. The highway takes you 38 miles through **Mt. Baker–Snoqualmie National Forest** (page 222) to Enumclaw. Angle to the right on Route 164, drive 15 miles to Auburn, and hop onto divided four-lane Route 18 westbound. Three quick miles and you're back on Route 5, just 20 miles south of downtown Seattle. Allow one and a half hours for the return trip from Mt. Rainier to Seattle.

The **Ohanapecosh Visitor Center**, located down in the southeast corner near a grove of giant, ancient cedar trees, has history and nature exhibits. Closed mid-October through May. ~ 360-569-6046.

The **Sunrise Visitor Center** has geological displays and at 6400 feet is the closest you can drive to the peak. Numerous trails fan out from the center for day hikes, but be aware that even into July, there is often snow on the trails. ~ 360-663-2425.

Nearby, at the intersection of Routes 410 and 12 east of the mountain, you can watch elk and bighorn sheep being fed by game officials during the middle of winter at the **Oak Creek Wildlife Recreation Area**, which is accessible only from Route 12.

Two inns are located inside Mt. Rainier National Park, and several other places to stay are around the park in Ashford, Packwood, Elbe, Crystal Mountain, Morton and the White Pass area.

LODGING

The most popular is **Paradise Inn**. Nineteen miles into the park, this nonsmoking inn has 126 rooms and a lobby that boasts exposed beams, peeled-log posts, wooden furniture, Indian-made rugs and two huge fireplaces. The views from outside are grand, but the rooms are ordinary. The inn is closed for renovations until May 2008. ~ Paradise, WA 98398; 360-569-2275, fax 360-569-2770. MODERATE.

The other in-park hotel is the **National Park Inn**, six miles from the Nisqually entrance. Built in 1916, the inn offers much of the rustic charm of the Paradise Inn, yet is much smaller with only 25 rooms, 18 with private baths. Some rooms have views of the mountain. In keeping with the rustic theme, there are no telephones or televisions. The lobby has an enormous stone fireplace. ~ Longmire, WA 98397; 360-569-2275, fax 360-569-2770; www.ranierguestservices.com. MODERATE TO DELUXE.

Equally popular with lovers of old inns is **Alexander's Country Inn & Restaurant**. This inn was built in 1912 as a small hotel designed to look like a manor with turret rooms and grand entrance hall. It retains the Old World look while adding modern conveniences such as a hot tub in a backyard gazebo. A full-course country breakfast is included, as is wine in the evening. ~ 37515 Route 706 East, Ashford; 360-569-2300, 800-654-7615, fax 360-569-2323; www.alexanderscountryinn.com, e-mail info@alexanderscountryinn.com. MODERATE TO DELUXE.

In Packwood on the southern flank of the national park is the **Cowlitz River Lodge**. It is notable for clean, brightly decorated rooms and views of the mountains, although not "The Mountain." It is set back from the busy Route 12 far enough for the logging trucks to be a distant hum rather than an immediate roar. ~ 13069 Route 12, Packwood; 360-494-4444, 888-305-2185, fax 360-494-2075; www.escapetothemountains.com, e-mail cowlitz000@centurytel.com. MODERATE.

On the northeast boundary of the park is **Crystal Mountain Resort**, a year-round resort that is best known for its skiing. Visitors can choose from a number of places to stay, ranging from

OLD-FASHIONED PEACE OF MIND

Peace and quiet are the overwhelming virtues of the **Apple Country B&B**. With four antique-furnished bedrooms in a 1911 house and a small cottage on a working farm, hard-working hostess Shirley Robert wants her guests to feel as serene as the setting suggests. Sit outside your antique-furnished rooms overlooking the back yard and orchards beyond, sipping lemonade, and peace prevails. ~ 4561 Old Naches Highway, Naches; 509-965-0344, 877-788-9963, fax 509-965-1591; www.applecountryinnbb.com, e-mail apple@applecountryinnbb.com. MODERATE.

condominiums to inexpensive hotels, all of which are nonsmoking. Don't expect much charm because skiing, not hotel amenities, is the focus. Typical is **Silver Skis Lodge and Crystal Chalets**, which has a cluster of one- and two-bedroom units, some with fireplaces and views. All have kitchens and televisions and can sleep from four to eight people. They are decorated in the traditional rental-condo manner of wood furniture and durable fabrics. ~ Crystal Mountain Lodging, 33000 Crystal Mountain Boulevard, Crystal Mountain; 360-663-2558, 888-668-4368, fax 360-663-0145; www.crystalmtlodging-wa.com. MODERATE TO ULTRA-DELUXE.

A bit farther east toward Yakima is the White Pass ski area with **The White Pass Village Inn**. The complex has 50 rental units designed for large groups, up to eight in many units, and they have a bit of variation in decor since all are privately owned. Some have fireplaces and sleeping lofts, while all have full kitchen facilities. ~ P.O. Box 3035, White Pass, WA 98937; 509-672-3131, fax 509-672-3133; www.whitepassvillageinn.com, e-mail info@whitepassvillageinn.com. DELUXE.

Good restaurants are hard to find around Mt. Rainier but there are a few worth mentioning.

DINING

Set on three wooded acres, which also include log cabins and an RV park, the **Gateway Inn** offers a wood-paneled coffee shop–style restaurant serving breakfast, lunch and dinner. The standard road fare of burgers, steaks and omelettes is enhanced by local trout and freshly baked breads and fruit pies. Closed Monday through Thursday from late December through March. ~ 38820 Route 706 East, Ashford; 360-569-2506. BUDGET TO MODERATE.

One of the most popular restaurants between Mt. Rainier and Mt. St. Helens is **Peters Inn**, a large, old-fashioned place where they serve burgers, steaks, veal and some seafood. In busy seasons, they have a large salad bar. Pies and cinnamon rolls are made locally. ~ 13051 Route 12, Packwood; 360-494-4000. MODERATE.

The **Whistlin' Jack Lodge** is a rustic lodge 20 miles east of Mt. Rainier National Park that offers a sophisticated level of dining unusual in these parts. Panfried rainbow trout boned tableside and a signature appetizer of crab-stuffed artichoke hearts served with garlic toast points are among the specialties. Prime rib, lobster and "bubbleberry" pie (a blend of apples, cherries, raspberries and huckleberries) round out the menu. Breakfasts are also exceptional, with items such as huckleberry coffee cake. The spacious dining area is set with white linen napery and the lounge features a huge fireplace built from local river rock. Picture windows overlook the Naches River. ~ 20800 State Route 410, Naches; 509-658-2433, 800-827-2299. MODERATE TO ULTRA-DELUXE.

PARKS

MT. RAINIER NATIONAL PARK 🚶🚲🐎🎿🏕️⚓ One of the most heavily used national parks in Washington, Mt. Rainier is everybody's favorite because the mountain can be approached from so many directions and the area around it is glorious no matter the time of year. The mountain is open for climbing for individuals or groups, and may be done under the leadership of Rainier Mountaineering Inc. (360-569-2227; www.rmiguides.com, e-mail info@rmiguides.com), or by direct registration with the climbing rangers, for experienced mountaineers. The park charges a climbing fee per person, per climb above 10,000 feet. Otherwise, you can hike the lower stretches of the mountain. The lower elevations are notable for the great views of vast meadows covered with wildflowers from July until August, and for dramatic fall colors in September and October. Numerous trails lead day hikers to viewpoints, and backpackers can register on a permit system for backcountry campsites. A backcountry fee may be charged for a reservation for overnight trips during the summer months. The park is open year-round with special areas set aside for winter sports at Paradise. Fishing is permitted in designated waters without a state license. Check with a ranger for regulations. You will find picnic areas, restrooms, four information centers, museums and self-guided nature trails. Day-use fee, $15 per vehicle (good for seven days). ~ Entrances to the park are located on Route 410 on the northeast, Route 706 on the southwest and Route 123 on the southeast; 360-569-2211 ext. 3314.

Mt. Rainier last erupted around 1845, and the mountain has been quiet since. However, steam vents on the summit are still active, and geologists warn another eruption is inevitable—someday.

▲ There are four car campgrounds, one walk-in campground, and one campground accessible only to high-clearance vehicles. Overnight hike-in backcountry areas are first-come, first-served, though you can reserve a spot ($20 reservation fee). RVs are allowed (no hookups). Fees range from free to $15 per night. Information about making reservations for two campgrounds during the summer months can be found at www.nps.gov/mora.

Mt. St. Helens Area

There are few certitudes in travel writing, but here's one: Don't miss Mt. St. Helens. At the southern end of the Washington Cascades an hour north of Portland, this peak might best be described as a cross between a geology lesson and a bombing range. East of this landmark is Gifford Pinchot National Forest and Mt. Adams Wilderness, the heart of a popular recreation area ideal for rafting and fishing.

On May 18, 1980, Mt. St. Helens, dormant for 123 years, blew some 1300 feet off its top and killed 57 persons, causing one of the largest natural disasters in recorded North American history.

Today, access to the volcano remains limited because the blast and resulting mudslides and floods erased the roads that formerly entered the area.

SIGHTS

A major sightseeing destination, **Mt. St. Helens Visitor Center** is on Route 504 at Silver Lake, five miles east of Route 5. The center is elaborate and includes a walk-in model of the inside of the volcano and other volcanoes in the Cascades. Two short films about the eruption play almost continuously. ~ 3029 Spirit Lake Highway, Castle Rock; 360-274-0962, fax 360-274-9285. There is also the **Coldwater Ridge Visitor Center**, 38 miles farther east on Route 504. It is located eight miles from the mountain at milepost 43 and offers ranger-led programs. Good for one day, the Monument Pass allows you to visit these two visitors centers and also the Johnston Ridge Observatory (closed November to May; 360-274-2140). ~ 360-274-2114, fax 360-274-2151; www. fs.fed.us/gpnf/mshnvm.

Windy Ridge is the closest you can get to the volcano, and it is reached by driving south from Randle on a series of Forest

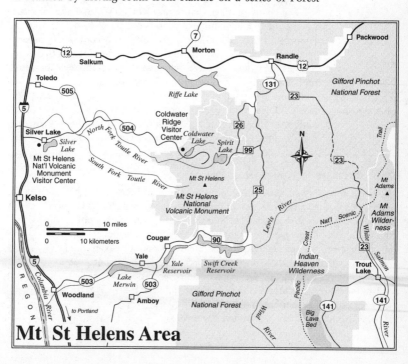

Mt St Helens Area

Service roads. Hourly talks are given by rangers in the amphitheater there in summer. **Meta Lake Walk** is on the way to Windy Ridge, and rangers tell how wildlife survived the blast. A 30-minute talk is given in **Ape Cave** on the southern end of the monument. It includes a walk into the 1900-year-old lava tube that got its name from the first group of people who mapped and explored the cave, a boy scout group called St. Helens Apes.

East of Mt. St. Helens, continue south through **Gifford Pinchot National Forest** on paved national forest roads. First, buy a copy of the national forest map at the forest headquarters visitors centers, or from a ranger station. You can drive to the edge of **Indian Heaven Wilderness Area** and hike through peaceful meadows and acres of huckleberry bushes, or continue east to the edge of the **Mt. Adams Wilderness Area** with views of that mountain reflected in lakes. Day and overnight permits are required to enter wilderness areas in the Gifford Pinchot National Forest. This whole area is known for wild huckleberries, and there are two seasons for them; in the lower elevations, they ripen in July and into August, then a week or two later the higher-elevation berries ripen. For more information, call the Gifford Pinchot National Forest Headquarters. ~ 360-891-5001, fax 360-891-5045; www. fs.fed.us/gpnf.

The roads will eventually take you to **Trout Lake**, a small town close to a wetland area of the same name near Mt. Adams. Here you'll find all services and a Forest Service Ranger Station. Just west of town is a vast lava flow called the **Big Lava Beds** and a lava tube called **Ice Cave**, which is chilly all through the summer. Both are reached on Forest Service roads.

HIDDEN ► From Trout Lake, drive east 16 miles to the small cowboy town of **Glenwood**. There's not much more than a country tavern and post office to the town, but in the Shade Tree Inn tavern you can get directions to some of the more unusual sights in the area,

THE DAY THE MOUNTAIN BLEW

At 8:32 a.m. on May 18, 1980, the growing bulge that had been forming in the past weeks pushed a small section of rock down the slope of Mt. St. Helens, and suddenly the mountain exploded with the force of 500 atomic bombs the size of the one dropped on Hiroshima. It powdered the mountainside and blew it into the atmosphere at about 500 miles per hour. Simultaneously, practically the whole north flank lurched down the mountain at about 200 miles per hour. By evening, ash had covered a quarter-million square miles in three states and the silhouette of Mt. St. Helens was left standing with a huge bite taken out of its north slope—1300 feet shorter than its 9677-foot stature the day before.

such as 300-foot-high basalt columns and what is locally called "volcano pits," a series of small craters left behind by cinder cones.

From Glenwood, take the Glenwood-Goldendale Road to the junction with Route 142 and drive back southwest to Klickitat and the Columbia Gorge at Lyle. This takes you through the deep, winding Klickitat River Canyon with views of the river, a steelheaders' favorite. Mt. Adams often frames the scene.

The **Seasons Motel**, about halfway between Mt. Rainier and Mt. St. Helens, has 49 recently renovated rooms in a slate-blue, two-story, frame building at the intersection of Routes 12 and 7. All beds are queen-size. A free continental breakfast is available. ~ 200 Westlake Avenue, Morton; 360-496-6835, 877-496-6835, fax 360-496-5127; www.whitepasstravel.com, e-mail reservations@whitepasstravel.com. MODERATE.

LODGING

Located 17 miles west of Morton in the tiny town of Salkum, **The Shepherd's Inn** is about 45 minutes away from Mt. Rainier and one hour away from Mt. St. Helens. The inn's five rooms offer country Victorian furnishings and brass beds. If you have the urge to tickle the ivories, you may do so on the grand piano. There's also a double jacuzzi. Full breakfast includes wild huckleberry crêpes. ~ 168 Autumn Heights Drive, Salkum; 360-985-2434, 800-985-2434; www.theshepherdsinn.com, e-mail shepherd@theshepherdsinn.com. MODERATE.

◀ HIDDEN

The Farm Bed and Breakfast is on six acres in Trout Lake, close to Mt. Adams. Two rooms decorated in antiques with cozy quilts are available in this three-story 1890 farmhouse. Surrounding the B&B are perennial gardens, a barn and a vegetable garden. Hosts Rosie and Dean Hostetter serve a full breakfast with fresh raspberries and strawberries in season. ~ 490 Sunnyside Road, Trout Lake; 509-395-2488, fax 509-395-2127; www.thefarmbnb.com, e-mail innkeeper@thefarmbnb.com. MODERATE.

Also on the southeastern edge of Mt. Adams is the outdoor-oriented **Flying L Ranch**. Originally a working ranch, since 1960 the Flying L has been a guest ranch but now without horses. Hiking and photography are popular here. Bikes are available free of charge to get around the mostly flat roads in the area. In the winter, cross-country skiing and snowshoeing access is nearby. The main lodge has six rooms, five with private baths; a two-story guesthouse has five rooms with private baths, and three separate cabins sleep four to six. The main lodge has a large common kitchen where guests can prepare their own lunches and dinners. Closed November to December 26. ~ 25 Flying L Lane, Glenwood; 509-364-3488, 888-682-3267; www.mt-adams.com, e-mail flyingl@mt-adams.com. MODERATE TO DELUXE.

◀ HIDDEN

The **Wheel Café** has long been a local fixture in downtown Morton, with its all-pine paneling. Breakfast specialties include blue-

DINING

berry or strawberry pancakes, while dinner choices are a large salad bar, steaks, prime rib, burgers, fish and chips and house-made pies. There is also an adjoining bar area with dart boards, pool table and pull tabs. ~ 185 Main Street, Morton; 360-496-3240. BUDGET TO MODERATE.

Plaza Jalisco offers classic Mexican fare, with daily specials such as *pollo loco*. ~ 200 Westlake Avenue, Morton; 360-496-6660. MODERATE.

PARKS

MT. ST. HELENS NATIONAL VOLCANIC MONUMENT The monument covers 110,000 acres and was created to preserve and interpret the area that was devastated by the 1980 eruption. Interpretive centers and overlooks along Route 504 show vast mud flows and the forests that were flattened by the blast. Access to the east side of the monument is limited to a few Forest Service roads, most of which are closed in the winter. Fishing is excellent for bass and trout in nearby Silver Lake and good for trout in lakes behind dams on the Lewis River, south of the monument. Facilities include interpretive centers, picnic areas, scenic overlooks and self-guided nature walks; viewpoints on the east side are closed during the winter. ~ From the west, Route 504 (Exit 49 from Route 5) leads to the Mt. St. Helens Visitor Center on the shores of Silver Lake, as well as the Coldwater Ridge Observatory (Milepost 43) and the Johnson Ridge Observatory (Milepost 52); Southside attractions are along Route 503 (Exit 21 from Route 5). The eastside blast area, including Windy Ridge, is located on Route 99, accessible from the north via Route 12 to Forest Road 25 and from the south via Route 503 to Forest Road 25; 360-449-7800, fax 360-449-7801.

GIFFORD PINCHOT NATIONAL FOREST This 1.37-million-acre forest covers most of the southern Cascades to the Columbia River, marked by the Mt. St. Helens Volcanic National Monument on the west and Mt. Adams on the east. Enclosing seven wilderness areas, the forest is well-accessed by a network of roads and trails used for a variety of recreational uses. Of particular interest are the **Big Lava Beds**, 14 miles west of Trout Lake, where unusual formations of basalt are found, and the **Ice Cave**, six miles southwest of Trout Lake, a lava tube where ice remains until late summer. Rivers and frequently stocked lakes offer excellent fishing. In late summer, huckleberry picking is very popular. You'll find picnic areas and restrooms. Parking fee, $5. ~ The easiest way to reach the forest is by Route 12 from the north. There is also access on smaller roads such as State Route 14, State Route 503 off Route 5 at Woodland, and Route 504 off Route 5 at Castle Rock; 360-891-5000, fax 360-891-5010.

▲ There are 24 campgrounds ($10 to $91 per night), 21 primitive campgrounds and 10 horse camps. Reservations: 877-444-6777; www.fs.fed.us/gpnf.

▼▼▼▼▼▼▼▼▼▼▼▼▼▼

Outdoor Adventures

Winter steelhead, Dolly Varden, rainbow trout, eastern brook trout, walleye, sturgeon, catfish, bass, perch and crappie all can be caught in the interior and along the flanks of the Cascade Range. Fishing is typically done from the banks or on private boats, but most resorts on lakes and rivers have boats and fishing tackle for rent.

FISHING

The other Cascade rivers, such as the Methow, Wenatchee, Yakima, Snake and Klickitat, drain into the Columbia River. All have good trout, walleye and steelhead fishing.

The Klickitat River has an excellent summer steelhead run as does the Columbia. As their numbers continue to dwindle, fewer and fewer salmon can be caught upstream from the Bonneville Lock and Dam, the first of 14 dams on the river.

During salmon runs, American Indians still fish with their traditional dip nets from the Fisher Hill Bridge near Klickitat.

You'll need a Washington State Fishing License to fish in most places, although not in all national parks. You can buy one at most bait shops.

NORTH CASCADES Several rivers in the area—Skykomish, Snohomish, Sauk and Skagit for example—provide year-round catches, notably steelhead and all species of salmon except sockeye (it's not permitted to take this fish from rivers). **John's Guide Service** offers fishing trips for small groups throughout the North Cascades region. ~ Concrete; 360-853-9801; www.johns-guide-service.com, e-mail johnsguidesvc@hotmail.com.

"Mild to wild"—that's how one outfitter describes the range of whitewater-rafting experiences in the Cascades. From the easy Class I and II rapids on the Skagit, to the steady Class II and III staircase rapids on the Suiattle, to the Tieton's Class IV and the Skykomish's Class IV-plus rapids, whitewater-rafting trips are fun and popular throughout the Cascades. In the Wenatchee–Leavenworth area, the Wenatchee River, which has a relatively easy Class III rapid, makes a great trip for families with children. Depending on the river, outfitters generally operate April through October. From mid-December through January, the Skagit is the place for float trips to observe bald eagles, who migrate to the area to feed on salmon from the river. A caveat, though: One guide warns that classifications can be misleading, and inexperienced rafters may think they can handle rapids beyond their skill.

RIVER RUNNING

NORTH CASCADES **Downstream River Runners** rafts the Skagit, Sauk and Suiattle rivers in the North Cascades region, as well as several others elsewhere in the state. They do trips at all lev-

Text continued on page 256.

Snow
Bound

It's all downhill from here: Yes, friends, we are going to take you skiing. Whether you are into slopes or cross-country, the best ski areas in Washington are stretched along the Cascades from Mt. Baker to Mt. Rainier.

Beginning at the northernmost ski area and working south toward the Columbia River, **Mt. Baker** is 56 miles east of Bellingham and has an elevation range of 3500 to 5090 feet. Receiving the highest amount of average snowfall of any ski area in North America, Mt. Baker's ski park has two options, one all natural, including their half pipe, and a six-acre manmade area. Seven lifts and two rope tows take you up to over 38 trails. ~ Route 542; 360-734-6771, snowline 360-671-0211; www.mtbaker.us, e-mail snow@mtbaker.us. The state's only helicopter skiing is **North Cascade Heli-Skiing**, which operates out of the Freestone Inn in Mazama. ~ 509-996-3272; 800-494-4354; www.heli-ski.com, e-mail info@heli-ski.com.

Some skiers prefer **Stevens Pass**, located on Route 2 about 65 miles east of Everett, because at times it has more powdery snow than spots at the summit of Snoqualmie Pass. ~ 206-812-4510; www.stevenspass.com, e-mail info@stevenspass.com. One of the area's smaller mountains is **Leavenworth Winter Sports Club**, a mile north of Leavenworth with a 400-foot vertical drop and a network of cross-country trails. ~ 509-548-5115; www.skileavenworth.com.

Probably the best powder snow at a large ski area is at **Mission Ridge**, 13 miles southwest of Wenatchee. Its base elevation is 4570 feet (the highest base area in the state of Washington), with a 2200-foot vertical rise and views of Mt. Rainier and the Columbia River. Closed Tuesday and Wednesday during non-holiday weeks. ~ On Mission Ridge Road, up Squilchuck Canyon; 509-663-6543, snowline 509-663-3200; www.mission ridge.com, e-mail info@missionridge.com. But the largest operation of all is **The Summit at Snoqualmie Pass**, 47 miles east of Seattle. Four major ski areas are to be found in a space of two miles: **Alpental, Summit East, Summit West** and **Summit Central**. The average summit elevation is 4100 feet and the average base is 2900 feet. The Summit at Snoqualmie offers the largest night-skiing operation in the country, as well as a tubing center, a lodge and a Nordic center where you can cross-country ski, telemark and snowshoe. ~ 425-434-7669, snow conditions 206-236-1600, road conditions 800-695-7623, information 206-236-7277; www.summitatsnoqualmie.com.

Way up in the sky is **Crystal Mountain**. Forty miles east of Enumclaw just off Route 410 and in the shadow of Mt. Rainier, the summit has an elevation of 7012 feet. Crystal has 2300 acres including 1000 acres of backcountry terrain. The vertical drop is 3100 feet, and there are 50 trails, 13 percent of which are beginner, 57 percent of which are intermediate and 30 percent of which are advanced. ~ 360-663-2265, 888-754-6199; www.skicrystal.com, e-mail comments@skicrystal.com. In the same general area, **White Pass** is 20 miles east of Packwood on Route 12 southeast of Mt. Rainier. A family-oriented ski area, this place is rarely crowded. Five lifts and a rope tow serve 32 runs. Their 18-kilometer cross-country trail system is double tracked with a skating lane. ~ 509-672-3101, snowline 509-672-3100; www.skiwhitepass.com.

Cross-country skiing is particularly popular on the eastern slopes of the mountains. Some of the best is in the Methow Valley, where 90 miles of trails are marked, the majority of which are groomed. The **Methow Valley Sport Trails Association** has a hotline for ski-touring information (509-996-3860) and a brochure showing the major trails. ~ P.O. Box 147, Winthrop, WA 98862; 509-996-3287; www.mvsta.com.

Echo Valley offers downhill and cross-country skiing as well as rope tows, one lift, 14 miles of trails and a six-foot-wide skating lane for freestyle cross-country skating. A full-service rental shop stocks ski gear, and a school offers both downhill and cross-country lessons. In summer, there's a mountain-biking/hiking center. Echo Valley is seven miles northwest of Chelan on a dirt road off Route 150 and has elevations of 3000 feet. ~ 509-687-3167. The Leavenworth area maintains several ski trails, including the **Icicle River Trail** (7.5 kilometers), kid-friendly **Ski Hill** (5 kilometers) and **Leavenworth Golf Course** (8 kilometers). You can actually ski from your hotel in downtown Leavenworth to the golf course trails (2 kilometers). ~ 509-548-7267; www.echovalley.org, e-mail info@echovalley.com.

Leavenworth Outfitters, located a half mile from five snow parks in the Lake Wenatchee area, offers cross-country ski lessons, and the store rents 120 pairs of cross-country skis, snowshoes and sleds. ~ 325 Division, Leavenworth; 509-548-0368.

els of difficulty (rivers range from Class I to Class V). Eagle-viewing trips are offered in December and January. Downstream doesn't rent boats, but it offers many years of experience. ~ Monroe; 206-906-9227; www.riverpeople.com, e-mail rafting@river people.com.

WENATCHEE AREA Besides whitewater trips, **All Adventures Rafting** offers eagle-viewing and scenic floats (accompanied by a naturalist) on rafts or inflatable kayaks on three rivers in Washington and one in Oregon. They can arrange rafting trips of all levels of experience, and for individuals using wheelchairs or with other special needs. ~ BZ Corner; 509-493-3926, 800-743-5628; www.alladventures.net, e-mail driver@gorge.net.

LEAVENWORTH AREA **Alpine Adventures' Wild and Scenic River Tours** concentrates its operation on rivers found within the Cascade Loop (the Route 2–Route 20 driving loop), including the Skykomish, Sauk, Nooksack, Wenatchee, Methow and Skagit. They also run trips on the Tieton River in September. Alpine's trips range from scenic floats to all classes of whitewater rafting, last from one hour to several days, and can accommodate from six to 200 people. ~ Seattle; 206-323-1220, 800-723-8386; www. alpineadventures.com. Experienced guides at **Leavenworth Outfitters** lead rafting trips on the Wenatchee River. They arrange trips or provide gear for snow-shoeing, kayaking and cross-country skiing. ~ 21312 Route 207, Leavenworth; 509-548-0368; www. leavenworthoutfitters.com.

SKIING

In the winter, the Cascades turn into a wonderland for all types of skiing—cross-country, downhill and snowboarding. See the "Snow Bound" feature for more information. For skiing conditions call the Forest Service's Avalanche Center at 206-526-6677.

GOLF

It seems that nearly every community in the foothills has a golf course. And the courses are as varied as the individual communities that host them.

METHOW VALLEY Along the eastern slopes of the North Cascades, in the Methow Valley, the public **Lake Chelan Golf Course** is fairly challenging, with small elevated greens and a tenth-hole canyon to hit over. This 18-hole course is open March through November, weather permitting, and has golf lessons, a driving range and full-service restaurant and bar. ~ 1501 Golf Course Road, Chelan; 509-682-8026, 800-246-5361. The privately owned, public **Bear Creek Golf Course** has 18 holes and two sets of tees. Designed by Herman Court, the course is scenic with valleys, hills and mountains. Closed in winter. ~ 8-A Bear Creek Golf Course Road, Winthrop; 509-996-2284.

WENATCHEE AREA **Three Lakes Golf Course** is a pretty tough par-69, 18-hole public course, set on rolling terrain with a few water hazards. It includes a driving range, snack shop and restaurant. Weather permitting, it's open year-round. ~ 2695 Golf Drive, Malaga; 509-663-5448.

LEAVENWORTH AREA The Wenatchee River runs around the **Leavenworth Golf Club**, a semiprivate golf course that is closed to the public for a few hours each week. The spectacular mountain valley setting makes it worth the effort to get a tee time at this short, tight 18-hole course. The club, designed by members, is open April through October. ~ 9101 Icicle Road, Leavenworth; 509-548-7267.

ROUTE 90 CORRIDOR The 18-hole public **Mt. Si Golf Course** has breathtaking views of its namesake. ~ 9010 Boalch Avenue Southeast, Snoqualmie; 425-888-1541. **Tall Chief Public Golf Course** has 12 easy holes. ~ 1313 West Snoqualmie River Road South East, Fall City; 425-222-5911. Although it's relatively flat, **Cascade Golf Course**, with good drainage, is probably the best winter course in the area. The public nine-hole course, designed by Emmett Jackson, has three sets of tees and easy access from Route 90. ~ 14303 436th Avenue Southeast, North Bend; 425-888-0227. **Sun Country Golf Course**, a public nine-hole course, is equipped with RV spots for golfers who want to stay. Closed in winter. ~ 841 St. Andrews Drive, Cle Elum; 509-674-2226. The semiprivate **Ellensburg Golf Club**, designed by the Elks Club in the 1930s, has a nine-hole course available to the public. The Yakima River runs alongside the course. ~ 3231 Thorp Highway South, Ellensburg; 509-962-2984.

Besides guided rides, some outfitters also schedule pack trips that last overnight or longer. Always call ahead to make arrangements.

Seen from atop a horse, the Cascades wilderness areas—deep mountain valleys, alpine meadows ablaze with wildflowers, heavily forested slopes and high peaks—take on new beauty. Winter weather limits horseback riding to the warmer months, from mid-April through October.

RIDING STABLES

NORTH CASCADES For a two-and-one-half-hour "nose-to-tail" guided ride—six riders maximum—through a pine forest to Coon Lake, which is in the North Cascades Wilderness Park, contact **Stehekin Valley Ranch**. ~ Stehekin; 509-682-4677, 800-536-0745; www.courtneycountry.com.

METHOW VALLEY Guided rides at **Sun Mountain Lodge** are open to the public. The lodge's stable of 35 horses is one of the largest in the Cascades. The 90-minute ride is perfect for beginners; a four-hour trip through the aspen, pine and fir trees of the valley up to a lookout ridge is popular with more experienced riders. Private rides are also available, as are winter sleigh rides. ~ Patterson Lake Road, Winthrop; 509-996-4735, 800-572-0493; www.sunmountainlodge.com.

LEAVENWORTH AREA At **Eagle Creek Ranch,** a guided ride into Wenatchee National Forest follows a trail through alpine meadows blooming with dozens of varieties of wildflowers before reaching a lookout peak for a spectacular view of the Cascades. The ranch also offers horse-drawn sleigh rides in the winter. ~ 7951 Eagle Creek Road, Leavenworth; 509-548-7798, 800-221-7433; www.eaglecreek.ws, e-mail ranch@eaglecreek.ws. Located in Lake Wenatchee State Park, **Icicle Outfitters and Guides** has seasonal hourly guided rides, sleigh rides, day trips and summer pack trips that take two to ten people through timber past Nason Creek. ~ P.O. Box 322, Leavenworth, WA 98826; 509-763-3647, 800-497-3912; www.icicleoutfitters.com.

BIKING

For the most part, bicycling in the Cascades is not for the faint of heart or inexperienced. Besides that, unless you bring your own bike, it's hard to find bikes to rent. One exception is the Leavenworth area, where a relatively easy seven-mile loop will take you along the river and through town. You can pick up a free map at the **Leavenworth Chamber of Commerce.** ~ 940 Route 2, Leavenworth; 509-548-5807; www.leavenworth.org.

HIKING

The Cascades are a backpacker's paradise laced with thousands of miles of maintained trails. All distances listed are one way unless otherwise noted.

NORTH CASCADES The **Pacific Crest National Scenic Trail** (480 miles) has its northern terminus just north of Washington at the Canadian border. It is a hard hike in many places but can be broken into easier chunks, such as from Stevens Pass to Snoqualmie Pass. Contact the **Outdoor Recreation Information Center** for further details. Closed Monday in winter. ~ REI building, 222 Yale Avenue North, Seattle; 206-470-4060.

The **Heliotrope Ridge Trail** (2.7 miles) leads to a precipice where you can look down on Coleman Glacier. This popular hike has three hazardous stream crossings and can be accessed from Road 39 at Heliotrope Ridge, just east of the town of Glacier. Purchase a one-day trail parking pass ($5) before parking at the trailhead. Contact the visitors center for more information (360-856-5700, 360-599-2714; www.fs.fed.us/r6/mbs).

In Ross Lake Recreation Area, try the hike up Desolation Peak on the **East Bank Trail** (19.3 miles from the highway). The views of the surrounding mountains and Ross Lake are spectacular.

Perhaps the most historic route in the North Cascades is **Cascade Pass Trail** (3.5 miles), the American Indians' route across the mountains for centuries. It is also a route from Marblemount to Stehekin (9 miles), if you want to really make a trip of it.

All along **Route 20** are signs for trailheads—all are worth exploring. The signs show the destination and distance of each trail.

For a long trip—allow three or four days—**Image Lake** (16 miles) is considered one of the most beautiful in the Central Cascades. The lake mirrors Glacier Peak, the most remote and inaccessible of the Washington volcanoes.

METHOW VALLEY   Goat Peak Trail (2.5 miles) leads to a 7001-foot summit that has a staffed lookout tower. The fairly steep trail starts from a Forest Service road near Mazama; it is hikeable only from July through September. Contact the Methow Valley Visitors Center (509-996-4000) for information or, in winter, the Methow Ranger Station (509-996-4003; www.fs.fed.us/r6/oka).

> Beat writer Jack Kerouac spent a summer at the lookout tower atop Desolation Peak.

LEAVENWORTH AREA   Icicle Gorge Trail (3.5 miles roundtrip) is an interpretive loop trail a short distance west of Leavenworth.

Enchantment Lakes (15 miles) is Washington's most beloved backpacking trip because the lakes are so otherworldly. They are approached from Icicle Creek near Leavenworth. The hike is a hard one, and permits ($5) must be obtained through the Leavenworth Ranger Station (509-548-6977; www.fs.fed.us/r6/wenatchee).

ROUTE 90 CORRIDOR   Iron Horse Trail State Park (113 miles) is a former railroad right-of-way that is used by hikers, horse riders, cross-country skiers and bicyclists. No motorized vehicles are allowed on the trail, which goes from North Bend over Snoqualmie Pass to Vantage.

MT. RAINIER AREA   Wonderland Trail (93 miles) goes entirely around Mt. Rainier and can be made in stages ranging from the 6.5-mile section between Longmire and Paradise to the 39-mile section from Carbon River to Longmire.

Northern Loop Trail (34 miles roundtrip) runs through the wilderness with frequent views of the mountain between Carbon River and Sunrise.

MT. ST. HELENS AREA   Klickitat Trail (17 miles) takes you through a remote part of the Gifford Pinchot National Forest and is part of an old American Indian trail network. For more information contact Randle Ranger Station (one mile east of Randle on Route 12; 360-497-1100), or the Klickitat Trail Conservancy (www.klickitat-trail.org).

Willard Springs Trail (3 miles roundtrip) winds through the **Conboy Lake National Wildlife Refuge** just south of Glenwood. It skirts the lake, which is dry in summer, and passes back through Ponderosa pines.

Indian Heaven (13 miles) is a beautiful section of the Pacific Crest National Scenic Trail that people return to again and again. It is near Trout Lake and goes past numerous lakes reflecting the surrounding mountains.

Transportation

CAR

Route 542 travels east from Bellingham through Glacier to dead-end at Mt. Baker Lodge. Route 20, also known as the North Cascades Highway, is one of the state's most popular highways and goes east from Route 5 at Burlington to the Methow Valley. Route 2, one of the last intercontinental, two-lane, blacktop highways, runs from Everett to Maine and is called the Stevens Pass Highway in Washington. From Seattle, Route 90 goes over Snoqualmie Pass to Cle Elum and Ellensburg.

AIR

Only one airport, Pangborn Memorial Airport in Wenatchee, serves this large area, and only one carrier, Alaskan Airlines/Horizon Air, offers scheduled service. ~ 509-884-2494; www.pangbornairport.com. The roadless Lake Chelan area is served by Chelan Airways, which makes scheduled and charter flights between Chelan and Stehekin. ~ 509-682-5555; www.chelanairways.com.

FERRY

The Lady of the Lake provides daily transportation between Chelan, Manson, Fields Point, Prince Creek, Lucerne, Moore, Moore Point and Stehekin. You can also catch the smaller Lady Express, which has fewer stops but faster service and runs in the winter (except on Tuesday, Thursday and Saturday). ~ 1418 West Woodin Avenue, Chelan; 509-682-4584; www.ladyofthelake.com, e-mail info@ladyofthelake.com.

BUS

Greyhound Bus Lines (800-231-2222; www.greyhound.com) offers service to Leavenworth and Wenatchee and a stop in Cashmere. The Wenatchee station is at 300 South Columbia Street, 509-662-2183; while the Centralia/Chehalis Station is at 1232 Mellen Street, Centralia, 360-736-9811.

Link Transit serves Cashmere, Chelan, Dryden, East Wenatchee, Entiat, Leavenworth, Malaga, Manson, Monitor, Orondo, Peshastin, Rock Island, Waterville and Wenatchee. ~ 509-662-1155; www.linktransit.com.

TRAIN

Amtrak travels from Seattle, Portland and Spokane to Wenatchee via the "Empire Builder." ~ 800-872-7245; www.amtrak.com.

CAR RENTAL

At the Wenatchee airport are Budget Rent A Car (800-527-0700) and Hertz Rent A Car (800-654-3131). In Wenatchee is John Clark Motors (509-663-0587, 800-972-2298). Ellensburg has Budget Rent A Car (800-527-0700).

SIX

East of the Cascades

If state boundaries were determined by similar geography, customs and attitude, Washington and Oregon as we know them would simply not exist. Instead, they'd be split into two more states using the crest of the Cascades as the dividing line or would run vertically from California on the south to Canada on the north with one state taking either side of the mountain range.

Well, who ever said life was perfect? So what we have are two states whose eastern and western halves bear almost no resemblance to each other. From the Cascades west, the land is damp, the forests thick and the climate temperate. The eastern side of the range is almost exactly the opposite: Very little rain falls and most crops are irrigated by water from the Columbia Basin Project created by Grand Coulee Dam, or by water from deep wells. Here, the winters are cold and the summers are hot.

Even the people are as different as east and west. While those in the western halves tend to be liberal and innovative, the eastern residents are more conservative and content with the status quo. And since we're in a status-quo frame of mind now, we take you through both eastern Washington and Oregon in this chapter. Other chapters look at the western sides of the states. So buckle up!

In contrast, only bits and pieces of eastern Oregon are irrigated because it has not been blessed with any large rivers other than the Snake. It remains mostly arid, the northern reaches of the Great American Desert that runs north from Mexico through Arizona, California and Nevada. It is land more suitable for cattle grazing than growing crops, although in some valleys ranchers have drilled wells or dammed small streams to enable them to irrigate meadows. This kind of open and sparsely populated countryside doesn't appeal to all travelers, so you tend to see more recreational vehicles and truck stops than hotels and restaurants.

If urban amenities such as hotels, finer restaurants, theater and shopping centers are what you're after, head to Washington's larger cities—Spokane, Walla Walla, the Tri-Cities and Yakima. Elsewhere you'll find RV parks and inexpensive but clean motels. On the lakes and streams are rustic resorts, some with log cabins.

Away from the cities, hunting and fishing abound. Many streams and lakes are stocked regularly with trout, and a few sturgeon are still caught in the Snake and Columbia rivers. Deer, elk and an occasional black bear are popular quarry, as are waterfowl, pheasant, grouse and quail. Don't be startled while driving along a mountain road during hunting season if you spot someone in camouflage clothing carrying a rifle emerge from the forest.

Some of the most interesting geology in North America can be found in this region due to its tortured creation by volcanoes, lava flows through vast fissures and floods gigantic beyond imagining. Throughout the two states' eastern sides you will find vivid reminders of this creation process. In Oregon it is shown by hundreds if not thousands of dead volcanoes and cinder cones, the lava flows that have not yet been covered by windblown soil, the brilliantly colored volcanic ash deposits, and sheer canyons whose basalt walls were created by these lava flows. In Washington it is the dramatic Coulee Country along the Columbia River and the beautiful Palouse Country with its steep, rolling hills.

The forests are mainly pine with very little underbrush. Along some parts of the eastern slope of the Cascades you will find larch, the only species of coniferous trees that are deciduous. They are brilliantly colored in the fall and stand out as vividly as sumac and maples in the dark green forest.

One stretch of landscape of unusual origin is the Channeled Scablands south and west of Spokane, which was created by floods from a lake formed at the end of the Ice Age in the valley around Missoula, Montana.

In Oregon you will find the painted hills of the John Day Fossil Beds National Monument, the dramatic canyons of the Owyhee River and the vast Alvord Desert, barren of vegetation and flat as an airport. In both states east of the mountains is another treasure: peace and quiet. There are lonesome roads undulating off into the distance, small rivers stocked with trout, open pine forests, vast lakes made by man, working cowboys and mornings so tranquil you can hear a door slam.

As is true elsewhere in America, the general rule is the smaller the town the friendlier the people, so don't be surprised if folks stop to talk about anything or nothing in particular. Also, nearly everything is less expensive than along the coast.

Traveling these remote areas you will have a continual sense of discovery as you visit places barely large enough to get themselves onto state maps. And you will find small towns that don't bother opening tourist bureaus but have a clean motel, a good café, friendly people to talk to and a small city park for your picnic.

While the Indian wars had less bloodshed than in other parts of the West, one campaign has become almost legendary for the skill with which the Nez Perce tribe eluded the white army, and for the "humane" manner in which the war was fought. This was the running battle of 1877, when Chief Joseph led his band of a few warriors and a lot of women, children and elderly people on a brilliant retreat from their ancestral home in the Wallowa Valley 1400 miles across Idaho and Montana, only to be captured a few miles south of their goal, the Canadian border.

A few remnants of the pioneer years still remain standing in eastern Oregon and Washington. Here and there you'll see the remains of a cabin with the tall tripod of a windmill where a homesteader tried but failed to "prove up" the land given him by the Homestead Act. You'll also see remains of ghost towns (although some have been rediscovered and are peopled again). Most of these towns were built at or near mines and abandoned when the mines began coughing up only rocks and sand.

For your own exploration of this fascinating region, this chapter is divided into six sections:

The Okanogan Highlands, often called the Okanogan Country or simply the Okanogan, has boundaries that are fairly easy to determine: Route 97 to the west, the Canadian border to the north, the Columbia River on the east and the Colville Indian Reservation on the south.

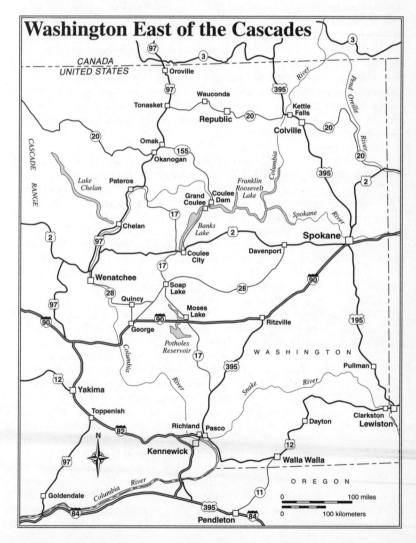

Washington East of the Cascades

Grand Coulee Area includes all the Columbia River system from where it swings west at the southern end of the Colville Indian Reservation and follows past Grand Coulee Dam south to the Vantage–Wanapum Dam area, where the Columbia enters the Hanford Nuclear Reservation.

The Spokane Area covers the only true metropolitan center east of the Cascades.

Southeastern Washington encompasses the famed Palouse Hills between Spokane and Pullman; the Snake River town of Clarkston; Walla Walla; the Tri-Cities of Pasco, Kennewick and Richland; and Yakima and the agricultural and wine-producing valley of the same name.

Northeastern Oregon covers the Pendleton and La Grande areas, the Blue Mountains, the beautiful Enterprise and Joseph area on the edge of the Eagle Cap Wilderness, and across the Wallowa Mountains to the few entrances to Hells Canyon on the Snake River. The centerpiece of this region is the Wallowas, a broad valley in the Enterprise and Joseph area where Wallowa Lake, one of the most beautiful in America, reflects the mountains of the Eagle Cap Wilderness.

Southeastern Oregon is the largest area covered and the least populated. It includes the cowboy country of the vast high desert that occupies most of the region, as well as the lava wasteland near La Pine and the multicolored John Day Fossil Beds National Monument.

▼▼▼▼▼▼▼▼▼▼▼▼▼ Okanogan Highlands

One of the pleasures of touring the Okanogan Country is simply driving down country roads to see where they lead. A number of ghost towns, some no more than a decaying log cabin today, dot the map.

Most visitors enter the Okanogan Country from Route 97, the north–south corridor that runs up the Columbia River Valley to Bridgeport, then follows the Okanogan River Valley north toward Canada. This is desertlike country with irrigated orchards on either side of the highway and open range climbing back up the mountains.

SIGHTS   First, contact the **Omak Visitor Information Center** for brochures and maps. Closed weekends in winter. ~ 401 Omak Avenue, Omak; 509-826-4218, 800-225-6625, fax 509-826-6201; www.omakchronicle.com/omakvic, e-mail omakvic@northcascades.net.

The **Okanogan County Historical Museum**, also headquarters for the county historical society, has a collection of pioneer farm and ranch implements and historical photos. This is also a good place to start your travels because members of the volunteer staff have lived in the region for many years and know where everything is, including skeletons in the county's closets. Open from Memorial Day to Labor Day. Admission. ~ 1410 2nd Avenue North, Okanogan; 509-422-4272; e-mail ochs@ncidata.com.

Northwest of Omak is a region that was a silver mining area in the 1880s. Here, adventurers will find the remote town site for the short-lived **Ruby**. Named for either the type of silver prospec-

HIDDEN ►

tors hoped to find there or for a prospector's girlfriend or prostitute, the site has no structures left, only foundations and wagon roads. ~ Salmon Creek Road, 10 to 15 miles northwest of Omak.

West of Oroville, is **Nighthawk**, which was a ghost town until recently. The paved county road, which heads west from Route 97 near the Canadian border, curves along the Similkameen River Valley, then swings south into a valley between the mountains of the Pasayten Wilderness of the North Cascades National Park and a series of steep ridges to the east. This area is dotted with old mines, some still worked from time to time, but most of the land along the valley floor and stretching up the hillsides a few hundred feet has been turned into orchards or expanses of alfalfa with grazing cattle. Nighthawk now has two permanent residences, but mostly consists of a historic old store, post office, hotel and pink house from the few-year boom when prospectors found precious metals there in the 1890s. **Loomis**, the other mining town farther south on this loop drive, is no longer a ghost town. The highway passes Palmer Lake and Spectacle Lake, both of which have public beaches, before rejoining Route 97.

One of the most interesting drives is to **Molson**, a ghost town   ◄ HIDDEN
15 miles east of Oroville off Route 97 near the Canadian border. Molson was founded when a nearby mine was attracting hundreds of prospectors and workers. Owing to a land-claim mix-up, a farmer took over the whole town, so a new one had to be built and it was named New Molson. The two towns, less than a mile apart, fought over everything except education for their children. They built a school halfway between the towns, and it became Center Molson. Today **Old Molson** is an outdoor museum with one historic building, two homesteads, sheds, early 1900s

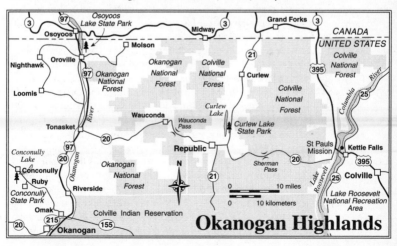

Okanogan Highlands

machinery, a steam engine and more. The **Center Molson school building** has three stories of artifacts and a tea room. Open Memorial Day weekend to Labor Day weekend. ~ Information, 509-485-3292 (ask for Mary Louise Lowe).

Route 20 is one of Washington's best highways for leisurely rural driving, especially as it traverses the Okanogan Country on its way to the Idaho border. It comes in from the Cascades to Omak-Okanogan, joins Route 97 north to Tonasket, swings east across the heart of the highlands through Wauconda and Republic, crosses the Columbia River at Kettle Falls and continues on to Tiger, where it follows the Pend Oreille River south to the Idaho border at Newport. There it disappears. The highway follows the path of least resistance beside streams and along valleys where ranches stretch off across rolling hills that disappear in pine forests. ~ Main Street, Okanogan.

Heading east from Tonasket, the first notable town you'll come to is **Republic**. Created by a gold rush in the late 1890s, Republic still hosts one last operative gold mine, the Kinross Gold mine, a short distance outside town. The **Stonerose Interpretive Center** lets visitors dig for fossils on a hillside on the edge of Republic. The site is named for family rose fossils found there. Closed November through April; closed Monday and Tuesday from May through October. Admission to the fossil dig site. ~ 509-775-2295; www.stonerosefossil.org, e-mail srfossils@rca bletv.com.

HIDDEN ►

Continue eastward and you'll reach a historical site called **St. Paul's Mission** where Route 395 crosses the Columbia River. It was built as a chapel for American Indians in 1845 and operated until the 1870s. A modest museum is also here. ~ Route 395, Kettle Falls.

In **Colville**, ten miles east of Kettle Falls, several buildings make up the **Keller Historical Park**. Sponsored by the Stevens County Historical Society, the complex has a museum, a fire lookout tower, Colville's first schoolhouse, a trapper's cabin, a blacksmith shop, mine, a farmstead cabin, a machine shop, a sawmill and the 1910 home of the pioneer Keller family complete with original furniture. Open to the public May through September and by appointment the rest of the year. Admission to museum and house. ~ 700 North Wynne Street, Colville; 509-684-5968; www.stevenscounty historicalmuseum.org, e-mail schs@ultraplix.com.

LODGING

The most modern motel in Okanogan is the **Okanogan Inn**. It has 77 rooms (including two suites and four rooms with kitchenettes), an unpretentious dining room, lounge and a seasonally heated swimming pool. ~ 1 Appleway Street and Route 97, Okanogan; 509-422-6431, 877-422-7070, fax 509-422-4214; www. okanoganinn.com, e-mail inn@okanoganinn.com. MODERATE.

A cheaper Okanogan motel is the 25-room **Ponderosa Motor Lodge** downtown, a clean one-story motel of basic design with a pool. Two-bedroom suites with kitchens are available. ~ 1034 South 2nd Avenue, Okanogan; 509-422-0400, 800-732-6702, fax 509-422-4206; www.ponderosamotorlodge.com, e-mail pond@communitynet.org. BUDGET.

The **U and I Motel** has nine small "cabinettes" with rustic paneling; each unit has a microwave and refrigerator. They come with deck chairs, so you can sit and look across a lawn and flower garden to the Okanogan River. You can also fish from one of the benches along the river. ~ 838 2nd Avenue, Okanogan; 509-422-2920; e-mail pacos19@hotmail.com. BUDGET.

In Omak are several small, inexpensive motels including the **Rodeway Inn & Suites**, which has rooms with refrigerators and microwaves. ~ 122 North Main Street, Omak; 509-826-0400, 888-700-6625, fax 509-826-5635. BUDGET.

Several small resorts are scattered along lakes in the area. Among them is the **Bonaparte Lake Resort**. This resort, 26 miles from both Republic and Tonasket, has ten airy and clean log cabins along the lake shore. Three have bathrooms and kitchens; the "Penthouse" also comes with linens. There are public showers and a bathroom. A general store and lakeside café round out the amenities. Closed in winter. ~ 695 Bonaparte Lake Road, Tonasket; 509-486-2828, fax 509-486-1987; www.bonapartelakeresort.com, e-mail bonaparte@nvinet.com. BUDGET.

Farther east, near Republic, the **K Diamond K Ranch** offers total immersion in ranch living: sleeping in a group lodge, riding lessons, eating with the ranch owners, relaxing with campfire sing-alongs and hayrides. Guests can also hike, bike, fish, explore old mines and pan for gold. A working ranch, the K Diamond K is open year-round. ~ 15661 Route 21 South, Republic; 509-775-3536, 888-345-5355, fax 509-775-3520; www.kdiamondk.com, e-mail kdiamond@televar.com. DELUXE.

AUTHOR FAVORITE

For a trip back to the Old West, head to the **Hidden Hills Country Inn**, a rustic-style bed and breakfast surrounded by fields of wildflowers and pine trees. The eight guest rooms, most of which offer mountain views, have a turn-of-the-20th-century feel with floral wallpaper, pedestal sinks, brass beds and gleaming woodwork. Full breakfast. ~ 104 Hidden Hills Lane, Tonasket; 509-486-1895, 800-468-1890, fax 509-486-8264; www.hiddenhillsresort.com, e-mail information@hiddenhillsresort.com. MODERATE.

Farther east is **Dominion Mountain Retreat,** a Craftsman-style bungalow in the foothills of Old Dominion Mountain, six and a half miles from Colville. The loft cabin can sleep up to four people (a fifth on the window seat) and has a fully equipped kitchen stocked with breakfast foods, a woodstove, private tiled bath, two decks (one of them rooftop) and a covered porch. Hot tub shared with owner. Access by four-wheel drive only in winter. Fresh cookies on arrival. No credit cards. ~ 694 Mosby Road, Colville; 509-684-6878; www.dominionmountainretreat.com, e-mail lwaters@plix.com. MODERATE.

DINING   Basic, standard fare is pretty much the order of the day here. For starters, there is the **Sun Valley Restaurant and Lounge,** which serves adequate, straightforward lunches and dinners and farmer-sized breakfasts. ~ Appleway Street and Route 97, Okanogan; 509-422-2070, fax 509-422-4214. BUDGET TO DELUXE.

The choices are few in Omak, but one café and bakery that rates high is the antique-decorated **Breadline Cafe,** where lunch features big sandwiches on fresh-baked, whole-grain breads and dinner includes shrimp Creole, jambalaya, pepper steak, portobello and eggplant marinara over pasta, and apple maple–glazed pork loin. Closed Sunday and Monday. ~ 102 South Ash Street, Omak; 509-826-5836; www.breadlinecafe.com; e-mail info@breadlinecafe.com. MODERATE.

Omak's **North Country Pub** serves nothing fancy—burgers, steaks, tacos and barbecue—but it's solid, filling food. The lunch specials are usually pretty good, and if you're there on a Thursday night, the steak special is a bargain. ~ 15 South Main, Omak; 509-826-4271. BUDGET TO MODERATE.

One of the few deluxe dining choices in the region is provided by **Hidden Hills Country Inn.** This contemporary hotel has created a dining room built to resemble an 1890s mansion. The large room overlooks a pond and is handsomely decorated with cherry and maple furnishings, China cabinets and fringed lamps. The menu offers just one multicourse dinner selection that changes every night. Steaks and chicken breast are among the possibilities. ~ 104 Hidden Hills Lane, Tonasket; 509-486-1895, 800-468-1890, fax 509-486-8264; www.hiddenhillsresort.com, e-mail information@hiddenhillsresort.com. ULTRA-DELUXE.

One of the more interesting places to stop for a snack or down-home American meal is **Wauconda,** the one-store town on Route 20 east of Tonasket. A breakfast and lunch counter to the left of the door is between the cash register and a large dining room overlooking a valley and low mountains beyond. The food is uncomplicated and hearty, and the portions are generous. No dinner Sunday. ~ 2360 Route 20, Wauconda; 509-486-4010. MODERATE.

Downtown Oroville sports a few restaurants, including **Fat Boys Diner**, a classic joint specializing in burgers, steaks and barbecued ribs, with a few pasta dishes on the side. Breakfast is served daily. ~ 1518 Main Street, Oroville; 509-476-4100. BUDGET.

SHOPPING

Omak's Main Street provides a few good browsing spots such as **Mustard Seed Gallery & Gifts**, which features handmade Polish pottery, plus crafts, jewelry and collectibles. ~ 21 North Main Street, Omak; 509-826-2463.

Check out the Omak Stampede, an annual rodeo held in August.

Western wear of all kinds plus handcrafted silver jewelry, Pendleton blankets and saddles are stock and trade at the **Detros Western Store**, a few miles north of Omak in Riverside. Closed Saturday. ~ 107 Main Street, Riverside; 509-826-2200.

You don't have many retail options in the small town of Oroville. However, **Prince's Center** may be all you need (or find). Half of Prince's is devoted to groceries; the other side carries general merchandise—everything from footwear and apparel to toys and garden tools. ~ 1000 23rd Avenue, Oroville; 509-476-3651.

NIGHTLIFE

Most nightlife in this cowboy and fruit-picking area is limited to taverns, a few of which have live bands on weekends.

Big-screen TV, pool, darts, karaoke on weekends and beer on tap are provided by **Shorthorn Tavern** in downtown Omak. ~ 3 North Main Street, Omak; 509-826-0338.

PARKS

CONCONULLY STATE PARK Strung along the edge of the town of the same name, this site is popular with boaters, swimmers, families and anglers seeking kokonee, large- and smallmouth bass, rainbow trout, German brown trout and Eastern brook trout. For hikers, there is a nature trail. Other facilities here include picnic areas, restrooms, a children's play area and a wading pool. ~ Located 22 miles north of Omak on Conconully-Okanogan Highway; 509-826-7408.

▲ There are 82 standard sites ($17 per night) and 2 primitive sites ($12 per night). Closed weekdays in winter except holidays or by appointment.

OSOYOOS LAKE STATE PARK This lakeshore park is one quarter mile north of Oroville and stretches along the southern end of Osoyoos Lake. It has some of the few trees in the area for shade while picnicking and camping and is the most popular state park in the area. It is heavily used by Canadians and Americans alike since it is almost on the Canadian border. For nature lovers, the lake is a prime nesting area for Canadian geese; for anglers, this is a year-round spot for bass and salmon. Facilities are limited to picnic areas and restrooms. Closed weekdays (except holidays) in winter. ~ Route 97, on the northern end of Oroville; 509-476-3321.

▲ There are 86 standard sites ($17 per night) that accommodate RVs (no hookups) and 6 primitive sites ($12 per night). Reservations: 888-226-7688.

CURLEW LAKE STATE PARK 🚶 🚲 ⛵ ⚓ 🎣 🛶 🚤 ⚓
This 128-acre setting is on the southeastern shore of a lake in a pine forest with several islands. Remnants of homesteaders' cabins can be seen near the park, and a large variety of animals, including chipmunks, squirrels and deer, lives in the area. Several species of birds also can be seen. The park is bordered on the south by Colville National Forest. Picnic area and restrooms are the facilities here. Closed late November to April. ~ Route 21, ten miles north of Republic; 509-775-3592.

▲ There are 57 standard sites ($15 per night), 25 RV hookup sites ($21 per night), and 2 primitive sites ($11 per night). First-come, first-served.

Grand Coulee Area

The centerpiece of the Grand Coulee Area, not surprisingly, is Grand Coulee Dam with its spectacular laser light shows during the summer months. The sheer mass of the dam is almost overwhelming and for decades was the largest concrete structure in the world.

Also of interest are the many lakes created by the dam that have become some of the Northwest's most popular recreation areas. The backwaters of the dam itself, named in honor of President Franklin D. Roosevelt, reach far north nearly to the Canadian border and east into the Spokane River system. A chain of lakes and some smaller dams were built to hold irrigation water for distribution south and east of the dam. These include Banks Lake and the Potholes Reservoir, known as the Winchester Wasteway. These lakes continue south to the Crab Creek Valley before re-entering the Columbia River below Vantage.

SIGHTS   **Grand Coulee Dam** was built in the 1930s and memorialized by the songs of Woody Guthrie. The area that became known as the Columbia Basin was so barren before the dam that locals liked to say you had to prime yourself to spit and that jackrabbits crossing the basin had to carry canteens. The dam was the largest concrete pour in the world for many decades after its completion at the beginning of World War II. It stands 550 feet above bedrock, as tall as a 46-story building, and at 5223 feet is nearly a mile long. While its 12 million cubic yards of concrete may be difficult to imagine, the Bureau of Reclamation points out that this is enough to build a standard six-foot-wide sidewalk around the world at the equator.

In addition to powering the hydroelectric system with the 151-mile-long Lake Roosevelt, the dam serves the additional purpose of irrigating more than 500,000 acres. Water is pumped 280 feet up the canyon wall to fill Banks Lake's reservoir, from which the water is moved through canals and pipes to the area's farmland.

Visitors are welcome at the dam and can go on guided tours. One of the most popular events is the nightly **laser show**, a free, 40-minute demonstration that uses the spillway of the dam for its screen. It is shown nightly from Memorial Day through September. ~ 509-633-9265; www.grandcouleedam.org, e-mail chamber@grandcouleedam.org.

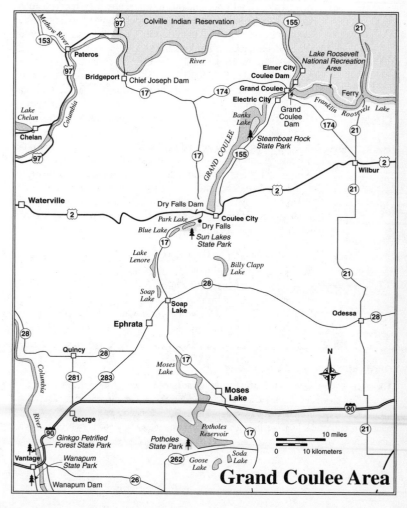

Grand Coulee Area

The **Colville Tribal Museum, Gallery and Gift Shop** displays authentic village and fishing scenes, coins and metals dating from the 1800s and many ancient artifacts. The gift shop sells local beadwork and other artwork by tribal members. Closed December through April. ~ 512 Mead Way, Coulee Dam; 509-633-0751.

The best way to appreciate the stark beauty of the Grand Coulee Area is to drive south from the dam on Route 155 along **Banks Lake**. The artificial lake is used for all water sports, and its color and character change dramatically with the time of day and weather.

At Coulee City you come to the **Dry Falls Dam**, which holds Banks Lake water and sends it on south into a system of canals. Pinto Ridge Road heads due south from Coulee City and passes **Summer Lake**, a favorite picnic spot. The falls are created by the irrigation water from Banks Lake.

The main route out of Coulee City is across Dry Falls Dam, then south on Route 17 past Dry Falls and Sun Lakes State Park, along a series of smaller lakes in the coulees—Park Lake, Blue Lake, Lake Lenore (where you can see the form of a small rhinoceros that was trapped in a prehistoric lava flow) and finally to Soap Lake.

Soap Lake was so named because the water used to foam before the ground water rose. The water is rich in minerals—sodium, chloride, carbonate, sulfate, bicarbonate and plenty of others—and matches the contents of water in the Baden Baden Spa in Germany. It has attracted a number of motels that pump water for use in the rooms or into spas where people go to soak themselves seeking comfort for a variety of skin, muscle and bone afflictions.

South of Soap Lake the coulees flatten out, and the landscape away from the Columbia River becomes the gently rolling wheat-growing region. **Moses Lake** in the center of the Columbia Basin, is better known as a hub for farmers of the basin than as a tourist destination. The lake for which the town is named joins the Potholes Reservoir to the south.

COULEE CAN BE CONFUSING

This area is frequently baffling to visitors because of the similarity of place names. The towns of Coulee Dam and Grand Coulee are at the site of Grand Coulee Dam itself, while Coulee City is 30 miles away at the southern end of Banks Lake. In the same area are still two more small towns with names that often get confused: Elmer City and Electric City.

If you want a room with a view, there are two good places near **LODGING**
the dam. The **Columbia River Inn** is right across the street from
Grand Coulee Dam. Most rooms have a view of the spillway,
and nightly laser light shows are across the street in the summer.
The motel has 35 rooms, a sauna, an exercise facility, an outdoor
pool and a hot tub. Two rooms have jacuzzis. ~ 10 Lincoln
Street, Coulee Dam; 509-633-2100, 800-633-6421, fax 509-
633-2633; www.columbiariverinn.com, e-mail info@columbia
riverinn.com. MODERATE.

The other is **Coulee House Motel**, which is up a hill and provides a top-notch view. It has clean, unremarkable rooms and a
swimming pool and hot tub. Free internet is available. ~ 110
Roosevelt Way, Coulee Dam; 509-633-1101, 800-715-7767, fax
509-633-1416; www.couleehouse.com, e-mail info@coulee
house.com. MODERATE.

Several budget-priced motels and resorts are located near
Banks Lake and Lake Roosevelt. **Ala Cozy**, a mile and a half
from the marina at the end of Banks Lake, offers 14 motel-style
units with private bathrooms and refrigerators. There's a pool on
the premises. ~ 9988 Route 2 East, Coulee City; 509-632-5703,
877-678-2918, fax 509-632-5383; alacozymotel.com, e-mail ala
cozy@hotmail.com. BUDGET TO MODERATE.

In Soap Lake, **Notaras Lodge** is the best-known and one of
the most modern motels in town. The four-building complex
plus restaurant has 15 rooms, 7 of which have jacuzzis. The
rooms boast unusual decor, with names like the "Old Mexico"
room—with a red roof, stucco walls and wrought-iron balcony—and the "bunk house," complete with a wooden pack
horse saddle and a 1900 cistern pump that turns the water on for
the copper kettle sink. The accommodations are spacious and
equipped with microwave ovens, refrigerators and coffee makers. Massages, whirlpool therapy and mineral baths in Soap Lake
water are available. ~ 236 Main Street, Soap Lake; 509-246-
0462, fax 509-246-1054; www.notaraslodge.com, e-mail nota
ras@televar.com. MODERATE TO DELUXE.

Moses Lake is one of the most popular RV destinations in the
central part of the state because several lakes are in the immediate vicinity, and hot, sunny weather is almost guaranteed. Several
motels are also along the Route 90 corridor and the lake, including the **Best Western Lake Inn**, which has 159 fully renovated
units, some on Moses Lake. In addition to boating and waterskiing, right off the dock, the motel has a heated pool, a sauna,
and a restaurant and lounge. ~ 3000 West Marina Drive, Moses
Lake; 509-765-9211, 800-235-4255, fax 509-766-0493; www.
lakeinnparadise.com, e-mail chart@lakeinnparadise.com. MOD-
ERATE TO DELUXE.

The **Lakeshore Resort Motel** is also on the lake, where a marina and waterskiing are available. The motel has 24 units, nine housekeeping cabins and a heated pool. ~ 3206 West Lakeshore Court, Moses Lake; 509-765-9201, fax 509-765-1800; www.lakeshoreresortmotel.com, e-mail hapnravi@yahoo.com. BUDGET.

DINING   A well-known eatery in this region is the **Melody Restaurant & Lounge**. With views of the Grand Coulee Dam and its summer laser light show, the Melody offers standard American fare, seafood and pasta. Breakfast, lunch and dinner. ~ 512 River Drive, Coulee Dam; 509-633-1151, fax 509-633-2925. BUDGET TO MODERATE.

If you want Asian food, **Siam Palace** will have it. Thai, Chinese and American dishes are served. Closed Sunday and Monday. ~ 213 Main Street, Grand Coulee; 509-633-2921. BUDGET.

A light-filled, contemporary restaurant built of native stone, **Michael's on the Lake** offers both indoor and outdoor dining. A spacious deck overlooks Moses Lake. Prime rib, hamburgers, oriental chicken salad and home-style desserts like cobblers are especially popular here. ~ 910 West Broadway, Moses Lake; 509-765-1611, fax 509-766-2804; www.michaelsonthelake.com, e-mail michaels@michaelsonthelake.com. MODERATE TO DELUXE.

SHOPPING   The **Colville Tribal Museum, Gallery and Gift Shop** sells local beadwork and other items crafted by the tribal members. Closed December through April. ~ 512 Mead Way, Coulee Dam; 509-633-0751.

NIGHTLIFE   **Moses Lake** has a series of free concerts, all beginning at 8 p.m., on most Saturdays from July to September, in its 5000-capacity outdoor amphitheater on the lakeshore. Nationally known musicians perform here. ~ Located 49 miles south of Coulee City; 509-765-7888, 800-992-6234.

PARKS   **LAKE ROOSEVELT NATIONAL RECREATION AREA**   This area stretches 151 miles along the entire length of Lake Roosevelt, including parts of the Spokane and Kettle rivers. Owing to the arid climate, the lake has miles and miles of sandy beaches and outcroppings of dramatic rocks. Only when you get close to the Spokane River do trees begin appearing along the shoreline. It is a particular favorite for waterskiers. Sailing and windsurfing are also popular activities. More than 30 species of fish are found here, including walleye, rainbow trout, sturgeon, yellow perch and kokanee, the land-locked salmon. There are only picnic areas. ~ The lake can be accessed from Grand Coulee and Davenport in the South and Kettle Falls to the north; 509-633-9441, 800-824-4916 for lake levels, fax 509-633-9332; www.nps.gov/laro.

▲ There are 27 campgrounds with over 600 sites; $10 per night from May through September, $5 per night from October to April.

STEAMBOAT ROCK STATE PARK 🧍 🐎 ⛺🔱🛶 ⛵ This is one of Washington's most popular state parks and thus is one of the many parks where camping-space reservations are a necessity. The park is on the shores of Banks Lake at the foot of the butte by the same name. The ship-shaped butte rises 800 feet above the lake and has a good trail to the 640-acre flat top. Fishing for bass, walleye, trout, crappie, kokanee and perch is good year-round, and it's a popular place to ice fish. You'll find picnic tables, playground equipment, a bathhouse and a seasonal snack bar. ~ Route 155, 12 miles south of Grand Coulee; 509-633-1304, fax 509-633-1294.

▲ There are 26 standard sites ($16 per night), 100 RV hookup sites ($27 per night) and 92 primitive sites ($10 per night). Reservations: 888-226-7688.

SUN LAKES STATE PARK 🧍 🐎 ⛺ 🚤 This park is located on the floor of the coulee that was scoured out when the Columbia River's normal course was blocked by ice and debris at the end of the Ice Age. The river, three and a half miles wide, flowed over nearby 400-foot-high Dry Falls, which was the original name of the state park but was changed because of the lakes and recreation. It is now home to boating, riding, jetskiing, hiking and golfing. Picnic areas and restrooms are here. Included in the park is 76-person Camp Delaney, an environmental learning center. ~ Route 17, seven miles southwest of Coulee City.

▲ There are 152 sites and 39 with RV hookups; $17 to $24 per night. Note: A private concessionaire (Sun Lakes Park Resort, 34228 Park Lake Road Northeast, Coulee City, WA 99115; 509-632-5291; www.sunlakesparkresort.com) operates a portion of the park and offers 50 cabins ($65 to $93 per night for three to four people, $119 to $149 for lake views), 10 mobile homes ($99

WHERE WATER WORKS

You may think of Washington as a rainy place, but without Grand Coulee Dam and the string of smaller dams that came along later to turn the Columbia and Snake rivers into a series of lakes, eastern Washington would be barren. Instead, in this part of the state one of the most common scenes is an irrigation sprinkler going about its business of turning the sand into a rich soil that grows wheat, wine grapes, fruit, soybeans, barley, oats, rape, grass seed, corn, alfalfa, potatoes, peas and a host of other crops.

to $129 per night for up to six people) and 112 full hookups ($20 to $33 per night). There's a general store, a snack bar, a heated swimming pool, boat rentals and marina, laundry, an 18-hole mini-golf course and a nine-hole golf course.

POTHOLES STATE PARK The potholes were created when water from the Columbia Basin Project seeped in to fill depressions around the coarse sand dunes in the area. Now the dunes stand above the water level and are used for campsites, bird blinds and picnic areas. The area supports a large population of waterfowl and other birds, including blue herons, white pelicans, sand-hill cranes, hawks and eagles. A lawn and shade trees, tables and stoves are beside the lake. Rainbow trout, bass, perch, crappie, bluegill and walleye are found in the park. There are restrooms and showers. ~ Route 262, 17 miles southwest of Moses Lake; 509-346-2759, fax 360-664-8112.

▲ There are 60 RV hookup sites ($22 per night) and 61 primitive sites ($10 per night). Reservations: 888-226-7688.

GINKGO PETRIFIED FOREST STATE PARK More than 200 species of fossilized trees have been identified in this area of barren hillsides and lava flows, making it one of the largest fossil forests in the world. The park has an interpretive center overlooking the Columbia River with a wide selection of petrified wood and also has a one-mile interpretive hiking trail. No camping, fishing or swimming are permitted at Ginkgo, but you can head four and a half miles south on the Columbia River to **Wanapum State Park**. It has hiking trails and swimming. Fishing is popular and boat ramps are available. There are picnic areas and restrooms. ~ Located on the edge of Vantage, a tiny town on Route 90 where it crosses the Columbia River; 509-856-2700, fax 509-856-2294.

> Don't be put off by the Winchester Wasteway's name—wasteway refers to the water that has been used for irrigation and has seeped along bedrock to emerge again ready for reuse.

▲ Wanapum has 50 RV hookup sites ($22 per night). Open weekends only in winter. Reservations: 888-226-7688.

Spokane

The northeastern corner of Washington is an area of pine forests, sparkling lakes, sprawling wheat farms and urban pleasures in a rural setting. Spokane is where the Midas-rich miners from Idaho came to live in the late 19th century, so the city has an abundance of historic homes, museums, bed and breakfasts and inns, and one of the most beautiful city park systems in the West.

SIGHTS The best way to become acquainted with Spokane is to take the self-guided "City Drive Tour" outlined in a brochure from the city that is available in all hotels and at the **Spokane Convention and Visitors Bureau.** ~ 201 West Main Avenue; 509-747-3230, 888-776-5263; www.visitspokane.com.

Another useful brochure is the self-guided tour of historic architecture in downtown Spokane. The "City Drive Tour" takes you along Cliff Drive where many of the finest old homes stand and through **Manito Park**, one of the city's largest parks. Manito Park includes the Japanese Garden built by Spokane's sister city in Japan and the **Duncan Formal Gardens,** whose lush scenery looks like something out of a movie set in 18th-century Europe. ~ Grand Avenue between 17th and 25th avenues.

The tour continues past **Coeur d'Alene Park**, off 2nd Avenue, and the stately **Patsy Clark Mansion** at 2nd Avenue and Hemlock Street. It goes on to the **Northwest Museum of Arts & Culture** with its major collection of regional history and fine art. Closed Monday. Admission. ~ 2316 West 1st Avenue; 509-456-3931, fax 509-363-5303; www.northwestmuseum.org.

Next is **John A. Finch Arboretum**, which features an extensive collection of deciduous and evergreen trees from all over the world. From there the tour leads you back to the downtown area. ~ 3404 West Woodland Boulevard, off Sunset Boulevard; 509-363-5455, fax 509-363-5454.

The city is most proud of its **Riverfront Park**, located in the heart of downtown and known for the natural beauty of its waterfall and island. A glorious addition to Spokane built for the 1974 World's Fair, the park has the restored 1909 Looff Carrousel and various other rides and food concessions, plus an IMAX Theater (admission). The Spokane Falls Skyride offers aerial views of the waterfall. It also has footpaths, natural amphitheaters, lawns and hills, and always the roar of the waterfall for a backdrop. ~ 507 North Howard Street; 509-625-6600, 800-336-7275, fax 509-625-6630; www.spokane riverfrontpark.com.

Another must see is the château-style **Spokane County Courthouse** across the river from downtown. Oddly enough, it was designed in the 1890s by a young man whose only formal training in architecture came from a correspondence course. It is a magnificent conglomeration of towers and turrets, sculpture, iron and brickwork in the French Renaissance manner. ~ Broadway just off Monroe Avenue.

Spokane has several wineries with sales and tasting rooms. On a bluff overlooking the Spokane River, **Arbor Crest Wine Cellars** is in a building designated as a National Historic Site. ~ 4705 North Fruithill Road; 509-927-9463, fax 509-927-0574; www.arborcrest.com, e-mail info@arborcrest.com.

Latah Creek Wine Cellars has a Spanish-style building with a large courtyard and a tasting room decorated with oak. ~ 13030

East Indiana Avenue; 509-926-0164, fax 509-926-0710; www. latahcreek.com, e-mail info@latahcreek.com.

LODGING Spokane has some pleasant hotels that don't carry big-city rates like those found in Seattle and Portland. You won't find deluxe or luxury accommodations here, but the down-home hospitality of the hotel staffs more than makes up for it.

Two of the largest offer perhaps the best rooms and service. The **Ridpath Hotel** is a renovated establishment downtown divided into two buildings across the street from each other with a second-story skywalk connecting them. The second building has the larger rooms, which all look inside to the courtyard and large swimming pool. The lobby is small, but the staff is cheerful. There are two restaurants and a weight room. ~ 515 West Sprague Avenue; 509-838-2711, fax 509-747-6970; www.theridpath hotel.com. MODERATE.

The **Doubletree Hotel Spokane City Center** was built for Spokane's 1974 World's Fair and has the best location, right along the Spokane River and on Riverfront Park. The lobby is impressive, and most rooms have good views of the river, park or downtown. It also has two restaurants. ~ 322 North Spokane Falls Court; 509-455-9600, 800-222-8733, fax 509-455-6285; www.doubletree.com. MODERATE TO DELUXE.

The **Spokane House Travelodge** is a favorite of many who visit Spokane frequently. Built on a hill west of town, it is roughly halfway between the airport and downtown, is quiet and affords good views of the city's growing skyline. ~ 4301 West Sunset Highway; 509-838-1471, 800-550-7635, fax 509-838-1705. MODERATE.

The **Davenport Hotel**, housed in a restored building in downtown Spokane, is the region's classiest place to stay. The 1914 building has 283 rooms outfitted with hand-carved mahogany furniture and suites with whirlpool tubs. Be sure to check out the Hall of the Doges, a ballroom decorated in Venetian palatial style, and the stained-glass ceiling of the Peacock Room. Amenities include a spa and health club, as well as a restaurant, café and lounge. The Davenport Tower is a new extension of the hotel just across the street. ~ 10 South Post Street; 509-455-8888, 800-899-1482, fax 509-624-4455; www.thedavenporthotel.com, e-mail info@thedavenporthotel.com. ULTRA-DELUXE.

The **Fotheringham House** is Spokane's best bed and breakfast, and, for that matter, one of the best in the state. The fully restored Fotheringham House is in the Browne's Addition, Spokane's equivalent of San Francisco's Nob Hill, where many of the mining barons built their homes. There are four guest rooms with Victorian furnishings in keeping with the architecture. Full breakfast. ~ 2128 West 2nd Avenue; 509-838-1891, fax 509-

275-1898; www.fotheringhamhouse.com, e-mail info@fothering
hamhouse.com. MODERATE TO DELUXE.

DINING

Spokane's most popular Asian cuisine comes from one of several
Mustard Seed Asian Cafés. The menu offers specialties from several provinces in China, as well as Japanese dishes. Sample traditional fare such as sweet-and-sour shrimp, or check out fusion
dishes like Asian tacos with curry chicken. ~ Northtown Mall,
4750 North Division Street; 509-483-1500, fax 509-483-1599;
and 9806 East Sprague Avenue, 509-924-3194, fax 509-924-
7288; www.mustardseedweb.com. MODERATE.

A favorite lunch and dinner spot is **The Onion.** Occupying
a vintage downtown building, The Onion has a 1904 mahogany
bar, 1890s prints and brass accents. A wide menu of appetizers
and entrées includes onion rings, deep-fried mozzarella, burgers,
caesar and taco salads, vegetable stir-fries and baby back ribs. ~
302 West Riverside Street; 509-747-3852, fax 509-624-9965.
MODERATE.

Located in the opulent Davenport Hotel, the **Palm Court Grill**
serves up a winning mixture of big-city elegance and small-town
informality. Lunches and dinners are unabashedly gourmet, featuring artfully arranged plates. Dishes include crabcakes with yellow cherry tomato vinaigrette, salmon with huckleberry sauce
and papaya salad, and fresh papardelle pasta. Breakfasts and the
celebrated champagne Sunday brunch are more traditional, but

Spokane

with a twist: omelettes made with crab and avocado, french toast made with baguettes, and fresh pastries. Reservations recommended. ~ 10 South Post Street; 509-789-6848; www.thedaven porthotel.com, e-mail info@thedavenporthotel.com.

SHOPPING   The Skywalk in the downtown core, a series of weatherproof bridges that connects 15 blocks on the second level, makes downtown shopping pleasant year-round. It leads to the major downtown department stores such as **Nordstrom** at Lincoln Street and Main Avenue (509-455-6111) and **Macy's** at Wall Street and Main Avenue (509-626-6015), several specialty shops, restaurants and art galleries.

With more and more Canadians driving just over a hundred miles to Spokane, where nearly all goods are less expensive, the city has had a surge of discount stores, from national chain stores to the West Coast warehouse stores. Shopping centers have sprung up on the north and northeast edges of town. Covered shopping areas include **Northtown Mall** at Division Street and Wellesley Avenue, **Franklin Park Mall** at Division Street and Rowan Avenue and **University City** at Sprague Avenue and University Street.

The **Flour Mill** is one of the more charming places to shop. It was built as a flour mill but was turned into a specialty shopping center in 1974 with more than a dozen shops, including gift stores, cafés and restaurants. ~ 621 West Mallon Avenue; 509-755-7551, fax 509-458-4014; www.spokaneflourmill.com.

NIGHTLIFE   **Dempsey's Brass Rail** is a popular gay and lesbian nightspot with a dancefloor and drag shows. Cover on Friday and Saturday. ~ West 909 1st Street; 509-747-5362.

The **Spokane Jazz Orchestra**, the oldest continually performing professional community jazz orchestra in the country, performs big band–style concerts as well as Latin, jazz, blues and more throughout the year at various venues around town. ~ P.O. Box 174, Spokane, WA 99210; 509-838-2671, fax 509-747-3739; www.spokanejazz.com, e-mail sales@spokanejazz.com.

The **Spokane Symphony Orchestra** performs more than 60 orchestral concerts per year, including 10 concert classic performances, six superpops shows and three pairs of chamber orchestra concerts. ~ Ticket office, 818 West Riverside Avenue, Suite 100; 509-624-1200, fax 509-326-3921; www.spokanesymphony.org.

The **Spokane Civic Theatre** presents musicals, comedies and dramas from late September through June. ~ 1020 North Howard Street; 509-325-1413; www.spokanecivictheatre.com.

PARKS   **RIVERSIDE STATE PARK** 🏃 🚴 ⚓ 🚤 🚣 ⛵ On the edge of Spokane, this 10,000-acre park includes nearly eight miles of

Spokane River shoreline (perfect for rainbow trout fishing), odd basaltic formations in the river and Indian paintings on rocks. It houses the Spokane House interpretive center (open weekends), which tells the history of the oldest trading post in Washington. Canoes and kayaks area available for rent and interpretive hikes and tours are available for an additional fee. Facilities include a 600-acre off-road vehicle park, picnic areas with shelters, restrooms, hot showers and horse trails; wheelchair accessible. ~ Located six miles northwest of Spokane at 9711 West Charles Road, Nine Mile Falls; 509-465-5064, fax 509-465-5571; www.riverside statepark.org, e-mail riverside@parks.wa.gov.

Idaho, Montana, Canada and much of Washington can be seen from the summit of Mt. Spokane.

▲ There are 16 standard campsites ($16 per night) and 14 RV hookup sites ($22 per night).

MT. SPOKANE STATE PARK This 5881-foot mountain is used as much or more in the winter as it is in summer, but warm-weather visitors find its views spectacular. It is especially pretty during the spring when its slopes are blanketed with flowers and in the fall when the fields are brown and the leaves have turned. For those into winter sports, there are skiing (downhill and cross-country) and snowmobiling. During warm weather, the park has some of the best mountain biking in Washington. There are picnic areas and restrooms. ~ Located at the end of Route 206, 30 miles northeast of Spokane; 509-238-4258, fax 509-238-4078.

▲ There are 8 standard sites ($15 per night). Closed in winter.

TURNBULL NATIONAL WILDLIFE REFUGE One of the most popular natural places for day trips in the Spokane area, the refuge was established in 1937 primarily for waterfowl. It has several lakes and wooded areas and a marked, self-guided auto-tour route. You will also find hiking trails, cross-country skiing areas and restrooms. Day-use fee March through October. ~ Cheney Plaza Highway, five miles south of Cheney; 509-235-4723, fax 509-235-4703.

Southeastern Washington

The drive from Spokane south into Oregon is one of unusual beauty, especially early or late in the day, or in the spring and fall. The entire region between the wooded hills around Spokane to the Blue Mountains is known as the Palouse Country. Here the barren hills are low but steep, and wheat is grown on nearly every acre. In fact, it is acknowledged as the best wheat-growing land in the world.

SIGHTS   Proceeding south from Spokane along Route 195, you'll find that the two best places to view the Palouse Hills are **Steptoe Butte State Park** (see "Parks" below) and **Kamiak Butte County Park**. Kamiak Butte stands 3360 feet high and offers bird's-eye views of the Palouse Hills. The park has picnic areas, a hiking trail and, unlike Steptoe Butte, a fringe of trees on its crest and over 100 kinds of vegetation, including the Douglas fir more common to the damp, coastal climate. Kamiak Butte is 18 miles east of Colfax and 15 miles north of Pullman just off Route 27.

The town of **Pullman** is almost entirely a product of Washington State University, although a few agricultural businesses operate on the edge of town. Continuing south from this campus town, Route 195 gains elevation through the small farming communities of Colton and Uniontown, then crosses over into the edge of Idaho just in time to disappear into Route 95 and then take a dizzying plunge down the steep Lewiston Hill, where you drop 2000 feet in a very short time over a twisting highway. The old highway with its hairpin turns is still passable and is exciting driving if your brakes and nerves are in good condition.

Clarkston, Washington, and Lewiston, Idaho, are separated by the Snake River, which flows almost due north through Hells Canyon before taking a sudden westward turn where Idaho's Clearwater River enters in Lewiston. Boat operators will take you up to the Snake River—you can't drive there. Most of the Snake River boat operators are headquartered in these two towns. For more information, contact the **Clarkston Chamber of Commerce**. ~ 502 Bridge Street, Clarkston; 509-758-7712, 800-933-2128, fax 509-751-8767; www.clarkstonchamber.org, e-mail info@clarkstonchamber.org.

The population has followed the Snake on its way west to join with the Columbia, but it is a tamed river now, a series of slackwater pools in deep canyons behind a series of dams: Lower Gran-

AUTHOR FAVORITE

A life-size diorama that fires my imagination is the **Yakama Nation Cultural Heritage Center**'s depiction of the Yakama catching salmon by hand at Celilo Falls. Imagining is all one can do since the falls vanished when The Dalles Dam was constructed and the Yakama turned to growing asparagus and hops. The history of the tribe is told in dioramas and writings by and about the tribe preserved in a large library. The center also has a theater for films and concerts and a restaurant that serves traditional dishes. Admission (to museum). ~ Route 97, 100 Spilyay Loop, Toppenish; 509-865-2800, fax 509-865-5749; www.yakimamuseum.com, e-mail inquiries@yakima.com.

ite, Little Goose, Lower Monumental and Ice Harbor. The main highway doesn't follow the Snake River because of the deep canyon it carved, so from Clarkston you follow Route 12 west through the farming communities of Pomeroy and Dayton to Walla Walla, then on to the Tri-Cities area around Richland, where the Snake enters the Columbia River. Along the way is Dayton, an agricultural town with over 117 buildings listed on the National Register of Historic Places. Most impressive is the beautiful 1881 **Dayton Depot**, a classic Victorian building that had an upper floor for the stationmaster's quarters. Closed Sunday in summer and Monday year-round. ~ 222 East Commercial Street, Dayton; 509-382-2026; dayton.bmi.net.

Walla Walla looks much like a New England town that was packed up and moved to the rolling hills of Eastern Washington, weeping willows, oak and maple trees included. Best known for its colleges, Whitman and Walla Walla College, the town with a double name has many ivy-covered buildings, quiet streets lined with old frame houses, enormous shade trees and, rather incongruously amid this Norman Rockwellian beauty, the state penitentiary.

To see more of the city by foot, stop by the **Chamber of Commerce** for four different historic walking trail guides, including the *Historic Homes Trail Guide*. ~ 29 East Sumach Street, Walla Walla; 509-525-0850, 877-998-4748, fax 509-522-2038; www.wwchamber.com, e-mail info@wwchamber.com.

At **Whitman Mission National Historic Site**, one of the Northwest's worst tragedies occurred because of a basic misunderstanding of American Indian values by an American missionary, Marcus Whitman. He and his wife, Narcissa, founded a mission among the Cayuse Indians in 1836 to convert the Cayuse to Christianity. As traffic increased on the Oregon Trail, the mission became an important stop for weary travelers. Eleven years later the Cayuse felt betrayed by Whitman because his religion hadn't protected them from a measles epidemic that killed half the tribe. On November 29, 1847, the Cayuse killed both Whitmans and 11 others and ransomed 50 to the Hudson's Bay Company. The site is run by the National Park Service. There's a visitors center, a memorial monument, a millpond and walking paths to sites where various buildings once stood. None of the original buildings remain. Admission. ~ Route 12, seven miles west of Walla Walla; 509-529-2761, fax 509-522-6355; www.nps.gov/whmi.

The **Columbia River** runs free for about 60 miles through the Hanford Reservation, but when it swings through the Tri-Cities (Richland, Pasco and Kennewick) it becomes Lake Wallula, thanks to McNary Dam. Several city parks with picnic and boating facilities are along the river, such as **Columbia Park**. ~ Off Route 240, between Edison and Columbia Center Boulevard, Kennewick.

The Tri-Cities are best known for the nuclear-power plant and research center in nearby Hanford. It was here that the components for the first atomic bombs were assembled. A nuclear-related visitors center tells the nuclear story. The **Columbia River Exhibition of History, Science and Technology** features exhibits and historical displays that focus on people's interaction with the environment, such as hydroelectric power, nuclear energy and environmental restoration. Closed Sunday. Admission. ~ 95 Lee Boulevard, Richland; 509-943-9000, fax 509-943-1770; www.crehst.org, e-mail crehstmuseum@crehst.org.

From the Tri-Cities, the population follows the Yakima River, which flows into the Columbia at the Tri-Cities. The **Yakima Valley** is the state's richest in terms of agriculture: Yakima County ranks first nationally in the number of fruit trees, first in the production of apples, mint and hops and fifth in the value of all fruits grown. It is also the wine center of the state: Some 40 wineries have been built between Walla Walla and Yakima, and they have helped create a visitor industry that has encouraged the growth of country inns and bed and breakfasts. Brochures listing the wineries and locations are available in visitors centers and many convenience stores, and once you're off Route 82, signs mark routes to the wineries.

Fort Simcoe State Park is probably the best-preserved frontier army post in the West and was one of the few forts where no shots were fired in anger. It was used in the late 1850s during the conflict with the local American Indian people. There's a museum/interpretive center (closed Monday and Tuesday from April to September; closed October through March). Five of the original buildings are still standing, including the commanding officer's home. Closed weekdays from October through March. ~ Located at the end of Fort Simcoe Road, about 35 miles south of Yakima; 509-874-2372, fax 509-874-2351.

The **Central Washington Agricultural Museum** has a large collection of early farm machinery including a working windmill, a blacksmith shop, a furnished log cabin and a tool and artifact collection. Closed Monday and Tuesday in summer, Monday through Wednesday in winter. ~ 4508 Main Street, Union Gap; 509-457-8735.

The **Yakima Valley Museum** has a comprehensive collection of horse-drawn vehicles, a re-creation of the office of the late Supreme Court Justice William O. Douglas and a unique collection of neon signs. There is also an interactive children's museum and an operating ice cream soda fountain. Closed Monday from November to March. Admission. ~ 2105 Tieton Drive, Yakima; 509-248-0747, fax 509-453-4890; www.yakimavalleymuseum.org, e-mail info@yakimavalleymuseum.org.

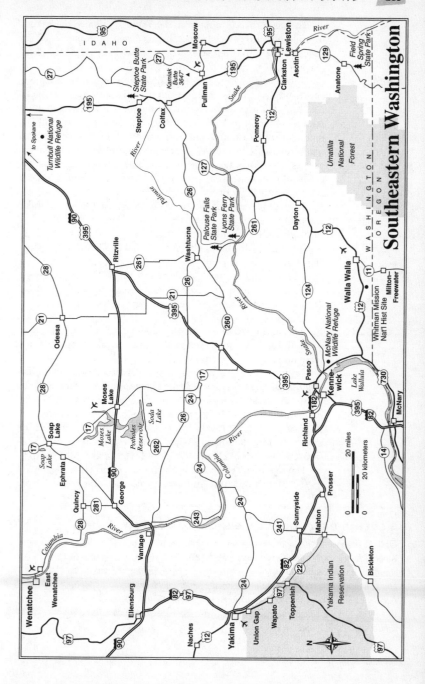

The main road leading from the Yakima Valley to the beautiful Columbia River Gorge (see Chapter Seven) is Route 97, which runs south from Toppenish, crosses Satus Pass (3107 feet) and reaches the Gorge just past Goldendale. An alternate route from

HIDDEN ►

the Yakima Valley down to the Columbia River is the **Mabton-Bickleton Road**, which heads south from the small town of Mabton through the even smaller Bickleton. An unincorporated town with a scattering of Victorian houses and falsefront store buildings, Bickleton's claim to fame is hundreds of houses for (are you ready for this?) bluebirds. Maintained by residents, the houses are on fence posts along the highway and country lanes and literally all over town. The one in front of the community church is a miniature copy of the church itself.

Twelve miles outside Bickleton sits the funky **Whoop-N-Holler Ranch and Museum**. The owners showcase a vast array of turn-of-the-20th-century pioneer memorabilia, much of which was handed down through their families. Highlights are the large classic auto collection and various horse-drawn vehicles, including an antique hearse on sled runners. Closed Monday through Thursday from May to October. Admission. ~ 1 Whitmore Road at East Road; 509-896-2344; e-mail whpnhllr@starband.net.

LODGING

It's difficult to find anything other than your basic, cookie-cutter motel in southeastern Washington, although Yakima shows some imagination.

Pullman has about half a dozen motels, none particularly distinguished. The best view is at the **Hawthorn Inn & Suites**. ~ 928 Olson Street at Davis Way, Pullman; 509-332-0928, 800-333-8400, fax 509-334-5275; www.hawthorn.com, e-mail hawthorn@pullman.com. The **Quality Inn** is near both the campus and the airport. ~ 1400 Southeast Bishop Boulevard, Pullman; 509-332-0500, 800-669-3212, fax 509-334-4271. MODERATE TO DELUXE.

Dayton seems to be out in the middle of nowhere—gateway to the Blue Mountains and an agricultural center. The **Purple**

◆◆

A SCENIC DRIVE DOWN A CROOKED HIGHWAY

Only in the late 1980s was the highway completely paved between the Snake River Canyon and the Wallowas in Oregon. But now you can take one of the prettiest mountain drives in the Northwest by following **Route 129** south from Clarkston in the southeastern corner of Washington through Anatone, then down into the Grande Ronde River valley over probably the most crooked highway in the Northwest. Be sure your brakes (and fortitude) are in good condition.

House B&B is thus an unexpected pleasure. This elegant inn, on the National Register of Historic Places, is housed in an 1882 Queen Anne mansion that was built by a pioneer physician. Two upstairs bedrooms share a bath; the master suite downstairs has a private bath. All rooms are furnished in period antiques; there's a library and heated outdoor pool. A separate carriage house has full amenities and a private bath. The full breakfast is cooked to order. Small pets are welcome. ~ 415 East Clay Street, Dayton; phone/fax 509-382-3159, 800-486-2574. MODERATE TO DELUXE.

Walla Walla has about ten motels, most of them in the budget to moderate range. The **Budget Inn** offers a continental breakfast. ~ 305 North 2nd Street, Walla Walla; 509-529-4410, 888-529-4161, fax 509-525-5777. BUDGET.

The Tri-Cities area has several fair-size motels, many with meeting rooms since the Hanford Nuclear Center is nearby. One of the largest is the **Clover Island Inn**, built on an island in the Columbia River. Half of the rooms have views of the river. The complex has a pool, hot tub, restaurant and lounge. ~ 435 Clover Island, Kennewick; 509-586-0541, 866-586-0542, fax 509-586-6956; www.cloverislandinn.com, e-mail cloverisland.inn@verizon.net. MODERATE.

Yakima does a lively convention business, and one of the best places to stay is next door to the convention center. **Red Lion Yakima Center Hotel** has 153 large, comfortable rooms with colorful furnishings and spacious bathrooms, two heated pools, a dining room and a lounge. ~ 607 Yakima Avenue East, Yakima; 509-248-5900, 800-733-5466, fax 509-575-8975. MODERATE.

The **Hilltop Restaurant** shares the steep hill with the Hawthorn Inn & Suites, looking down on the city of Pullman. It caters to the local trade with thick steaks, fresh seafood and a full-service lounge. No lunch Saturday and Sunday. ~ 920 Olson Street at Davis Way, Pullman; 509-334-2555, fax 509-334-5275; www.hilltoprestaurant.com, e-mail hilltop@pullman.com. MODERATE.

DINING

If you're good at what you do, so goes the saying, the world will beat a path to your door. This could be the slogan for **Patit Creek Restaurant**. It has been in business since 1978 and has built a national reputation for excellent dishes in what is most accurately described as French country cuisine. Meat is the specialty—beef and lamb. Most of the food is grown locally, some by the staff, and since some of the luxurious plants inside and around the outside are herbs, they may one day season your food. No lunch Saturday through Tuesday. Closed Sunday through Tuesday. ~ 725 East Dayton Avenue, Dayton; 509-382-2625. ULTRA-DELUXE.

Text continued on page 290.

Washington Wine

For a long time, Washington's liquor laws were so restrictive that it was illegal to bring wine into the state; you had to buy it from the state-run stores. The best Washington wine in those days was made by an Italian immigrant, Angelo Pelligrini, who taught Shakespeare at the University of Washington and made wine in his basement—illegally.

That has changed completely. Over 300 wineries are spread across the state, most in Eastern Washington, and many of those in the Puget Sound region own vineyards in Eastern Washington or buy their grapes there. The soil and climate are excellent for wine grapes, and the **Washington Wine Commission** likes to remind us that Eastern Washington is on the same latitude as some of France's great winegrowing regions. ~ 1000 2nd Avenue, Suite 1700, Seattle; 206-667-9463, fax 206-583-0573; www.washingtonwine.org.

Washington has four viticultural regions: Columbia Valley, which extends southward from the Okanogan Country into Oregon and east to Idaho; Yakima Valley, which runs from the foothills of the Cascades east to the Kiona Hills near Richland and is bisected by Interstate 82, making it the most convenient for visits; the Walla Walla Valley region, which straddles the Oregon–Washington border, taking in some vineyards in the Milton-Freewater area; and the Puget Sound region, which covers areas from Olympia in the south to Bellingham in the north, and includes various Puget Sound and San Juan Islands in between.

In keeping with the French adage that the best grape vines "like to be in sight of the water but don't want to get their feet wet," some of the best vineyards in Eastern Washington are on south-facing slopes above the Columbia, Yakima and Snake rivers, where they get as much as 16 hours of sunlight a day and fresh irrigation water on well-drained soil. As with all wine-producing areas, many wineries have been built in palatial settings.

One of the most dramatic is the **Columbia Crest Winery**. Built on a hillside overlooking the Columbia River, it produces more than a million gallons of wine annually and has a reflecting pool, fountain and courtyard, a luxurious lobby and tasting-and-sales room. ~ Route 221, Paterson; 509-875-2061, 800-309-9463, fax 509-875-2568; www.columbia-crest.com.

Running a close second is **Château Ste. Michelle**. This is the state's oldest continuously operating winery. ~ 14111 145th Street Northeast, Woodinville; 425-415-3300, fax 425-415-3657; www.chateau-ste-michelle.com.

Featuring syrah and bordeaux varieties, **White Heron Cellars** emphasizes a natural winemaking process, leaving as much of the ecosystem undisturbed as possible. It also features a concert venue showcasing jazz and blues with a spectacular view. ~ 10035 Stuhlmiller Road, Quincy; 509-797-9463; www.whiteheronwine.com, e-mail info@whiteheronwine.com.

A wine that keeps gaining new fans is the **Silver Lake** label. The tasting room stands on a hill overlooking the winery's acres of grapes. They have three tasting rooms in the area. ~ 1500 Vintage Road, Zillah, 509-829-6235; 715 Front Street, Suite A1, Leavenworth, 509-548-5788; 15029 Woodinville-Redmond Road, Woodinville, 425-485-2437; www.silverlakewinery.com.

The Puryear family, Gail and Shirley, call **Bonair Winery** a "hobby that got out of hand." The winery not only offers a versatile range of wines, including fine chardonnays and cabernets, its gallery features exhibits of local artwork and photography. The setting, on a curve of land inside one of the valley's main irrigation canals, is inviting. ~ 500 South Bonair Road South, Zillah; 509-829-6027, fax 509-829-6410; www.bonairwine.com, e-mail shirley@bonairwine.com.

The quirky **L'Ecole N° 41** got its name from the retired schoolhouse near Walla Walla in which it was built. ~ 41 Lowden School Road, Lowden; 509-525-0940, fax 509-525-2775; www.lecole.com; e-mail info@lecole.com.

Joel Tefft focuses on very limited bottlings of fine handcrafted wines at **Tefft Cellars** outside Sunnyside. Aside from cabernet sauvignon and lush, velvety merlot, the Teffts make unique, light, dry sparkling wines and ports, a rarity in Washington. ~ 1320 Independence Road, Outlook; 509-837-7651, 888-549-7244, fax 509-839-7337; www.tefftcellars.com.

The most homey of the wineries is probably **Kiona Vineyards**. It is a family operation, with a tasting room, winery and the Kiona Vineyard at the home of John and Ann Williams. The winery was one of the originals to produce lemberger. ~ 44612 North Sunset Road, Benton City; 509-588-6716, fax 509-588-3219; www.kionawine.com, e-mail kiona1wine@aol.com.

Sagelands Vineyards is located in a French-country building set on a rolling hillside above the Yakima River. The tasting room features a stone fireplace and cathedral ceilings. ~ 71 Gangl Road, Wapato; 509-877-2112, 800-967-8115, fax 509-877-3377; www.sagelandsvineyard.com, e-mail sagelands.info@sagelandsvineyard.com.

Pontin del Roza came into being because the Pontin family's Italian heritage included a love of wine. They decided to add wine grapes to the crops they had been growing on their Prosser farm for two decades and produce both reds and whites. ~ 35502 North Hinzerling Road, Prosser; 509-786-4449; e-mail pontindelroza@msn.com.

Founded in 1982 with a planting of riesling grapes, **Hogue Cellars**, located in the Columbia Valley, is known for grapes with intense fruit flavor and natural acidity. ~ 2800 Lee Country Road, Prosser; 509-786-4557, 800-565-9779, fax 509-786-4580; www.hoguecellars.com, e-mail info@hoguecellars.com.

Cheers!

If you're feeling nostalgic for New York delis, **Merchants Ltd.** will help. It has a wide choice of foods and a sidewalk café ideal for Walla Walla's mostly sunny weather. Closed Sunday. ~ 21 Main Street East, Walla Walla; 509-525-0900, fax 509-522-3065; www.merchantsdeli.com. BUDGET TO MODERATE.

The Cedars is one of the Tri-Cities' most striking restaurants. It is cantilevered over the Columbia River with boat-docking facilities. The specialties are steaks, seafood and prime rib. Favorites include the *biergarten* steak and the daily fresh fish specials. Dinner only. ~ 355 Clover Island, Kennewick; 509-582-2143, fax 509-582-2144; www.cedarsrest.com. MODERATE TO DELUXE.

Emerald of Siam serves authentic Thai food in a former drugstore. A buffet lunch is served on weekdays, or you may order from the menu. Closed Sunday. ~ 1314 Jadwin Avenue, Richland; 509-946-9328. BUDGET.

Prosser is a farm town, pure and simple. But what better place for fine, gourmet country cuisine? At **The Blue Goose**, local wine and produce form the basis for a Tuscan/Northwest menu that ranges from veal marsala to chicken-fried steak (well, it is a country restaurant). The wine list features more than 50 local wines, some of them superb vintages, at prices you'll never see in any urban restaurant. ~ 306 7th Street, Prosser; 509-786-1774, fax 509-786-7557. MODERATE TO DELUXE.

Over the years, **Birchfield Manor** has won more magazine awards than any other Washington restaurant outside the Puget

THE OLDEST MAN IN WASHINGTON

The Tri-Cities area was the site of the 1996 discovery of the controversial Kennewick Man, one of the oldest human skeletons ever found in North America, radiocarbon-dated to between 8400 and 9200 years old. Because the skull was much different from those of modern American Indians, the find was first thought to suggest the presence of Caucasians in archaic America but is now believed to be "proto-Mongolian," with possible genetic links both Russian Europeans and to native peoples' Asian ancestors. The Colville, Yakima, Umatilla and Nez Perce tribes each claim Kennewick Man as an ancestor, demanding reburial rights under the Native American Graves Protection Act. The ancient bones were locked up at the University of Washington's Burke Museum until 2005, when a court cleared the way for scientists to study the skeleton. Preliminary findings suggest that he was indeed American Indian, about 45 years old, 5 feet 9 inches, and may have been a hunter when the climate was cooler and wetter.

Sound region. The owners restored an old farmhouse and filled it with antiques, then opened the restaurant with a menu of seven entrées including fresh salmon in puff pastry, filet mignon, rack of lamb and lobster linguini. Local fruit and vegetables are used, and the fixed menu includes an appetizer, a salad and a home-made chocolate treat. Closed Sunday through Wednesday except for large groups. ~ 2018 Birchfield Road, Yakima; 509-452-1960, 800-375-3420, fax 509-452-2334; www.birchfieldmanor.com, e-mail reservations@birchfiledmanor.com. ULTRA-DELUXE.

SHOPPING

Yakima offers several intriguing shopping areas. One is the **North Front Street Historical District**, where the city's oldest buildings, some of them made of rough-hewn local rock, now house an assortment of boutiques, restaurants and brew pubs.

Yesterday's Village is a collection of shops in the former Fruit Exchange Building. The remodeled building houses some 75 shops that sell antiques, glassware, collectibles, furniture and jewelry. ~ 15 West Yakima Avenue, Yakima; 509-457-4981.

NIGHTLIFE

Yakima has one of the widest selections of nightlife in southeastern Washington, ranging from cultural events to country-and-western taverns. **Warehouse Pub** serves traditional food and occasionally offers live music. ~ 5110 Tieton Drive, Yakima; 509-972-2075; www.warehousepub.com.

In addition, Yakima has frequent concerts put on by the **Yakima Symphony Orchestra**. Season runs October through April. ~ 32 North 3rd Street #333, Yakima; 509-248-1414; www.yakimasymphony.org.

Square dancing is very popular in the Yakima Valley, and numerous clubs welcome travelers to their dances. Dances are held Thursday and Saturday nights at the Yakima Square and Round Dance Center. ~ 207 East Charron Road, Moxee; 509-452-6438.

PARKS

STEPTOE BUTTE STATE PARK This park consists of the butte, a picnic area and primitive toilets at the base and summit. The reason for the park's existence is the butte itself, which rises to an elevation of 3612 feet out of the rolling Palouse Hills with panoramic views that are popular with photographers. The butte is actually the top of a granite mountain that stands above the lava flows that covered all the other peaks. The word "steptoe" has entered the international geological vocabulary to represent any similar remnant of an earlier geological feature standing out from the newer feature. There are seven picnic sites at the foot of the butte; no water. ~ Off Route 195, roughly 50 miles south of Spokane; 509-646-9218, fax 509-646-9288; e-mail cpt.central@parks.wa.gov.

FIELD SPRING STATE PARK 🚶 🚴 ⛷ This 792-acre park is in forested land on the eastern slope of the Blue Mountains. It is just below Puffer Butte, a 4500-foot mountain that overlooks the Grand Ronde River Canyon. For hikers, there are a one-mile trail to the summit of Puffer Butte and ten miles of hiking paths. Winter brings cross-country skiing, snowshoeing and tubing. There are restrooms and showers. ~ Route 129, four miles south of Anatone; 509-256-3332.

▲ There are 20 standard sites ($16 per night) and 2 primitive sites ($10 per night). A teepee for eight people is $20 per night.

FORT WALLA WALLA PARK AND MUSEUM 🚶 🚴 This collection of pioneer buildings is located on a 208-acre former Army fort and cemetery containing victims from both sides of the first conflicts with the Indians. It also has 20 buildings, some authentic and others replicas, of pioneer homes, schools and public buildings. One of the largest collections of horse-drawn farm equipment in the Northwest is also owned by the museum (admission; closed November through March; 755 Myra Road, Walla Walla; 509-525-7703; www.fortwallawallamuseum.org, e-mail info@fortwallawallamuseum.org). There are also nature and bicycle trails in the park. Other facilities include picnic areas, a skate park and BMX track, restrooms, play equipment and volleyball courts. ~ Located on the southeast side of Walla Walla on Dalles Military Road at Myra; 509-527-4527.

PALOUSE FALLS/LYONS FERRY PARK 🚶 ⚓ 🏖 🚤 🐟 ⚙ This two-part, remote park is out in the rugged Channeled Scablands. The Lyons Ferry section consists of a pleasant, grassy area with boat ramps at the confluence of the Snake and Palouse rivers. About seven to eight miles up the Palouse River is the Palouse Falls section, with a dramatic picnic area and viewpoint overlooking the thundering 200-foot-tall Palouse Falls. There are picnic areas and restrooms; a wheelchair-accessible hiking trail there and at Lyons Ferry, as well as a boat launch ramp, concessionaire, hiking areas and a restaurant, are nearby. ~ Route 261, 23 miles southeast of Washtucna; Lyon's Ferry 509-399-2223 ext. 262; Palouse 509-646-9218.

▲ Palouse Falls has 10 tent sites ($17 per night); Lyons Ferry has 52 standard sites ($17 per night). Both close in winter.

McNARY NATIONAL WILDLIFE REFUGE 🚶 ⚙ This is one of the major resting areas in the Pacific Flyway for migratory waterfowl, especially Canada geese, American widgeon, mallards, pintails and white pelicans. The population peaks in November, and the few summer migratory birds, such as the pelicans and long-billed curlews, arrive in the spring and summer. The refuge covers over 15,000 acres that stretch along the confluence of the

Snake River downstream into the mouth of the Walla Walla River. Hunters look for waterfowl and upland birds, while anglers cast a rod for largemouth black bass, catfish and crappie. Self-guided wildlife trail through the marsh and croplands. ~ 500 East Maple Street, southeast of Pasco just off Route 395 on the Snake River; 509-547-4942, fax 509-544-9047.

For the most part, northeastern Oregon remains the parched land so inhospitable to settlers nearly two centuries ago. Nowadays,

Northeastern Oregon

towns are still few and far between, leaving plenty of room for viewing the wagon ruts left by the original pioneers. Also a part of the northeastern Oregon experience are the vividly colored earthscapes at the John Day Fossil Beds National Monument and the whitewater rafting opportunities in the Snake River along the Idaho border. Capping it off in the state's northeastern corner is a surprisingly lush area surrounding the Wallowa Mountains that reminds many visitors of the Swiss Alps.

Northeastern Oregon

John Day Country

The fascinating fossils and fantastic scenery of John Day Fossil Beds National Monument are a long way from any populated area—and that's part of what makes this trip special. This trip is hard to complete in a single day, so plan to spend the night at a motel in John Day or Mitchell. From Portland, drive 108 fast miles east on Route 84 and turn south on Route 97 at Biggs, on the Columbia River just below John Day Dam. (Just about everything in this part of the state is named John Day, after an early explorer for John Jacob Astor's fur-trading company. Robbed by Indians and left afoot in this vast wasteland, Day eventually made it back to his base camp on the coast but never regained his sanity.)

SHANIKO AND ANTELOPE   Driving 57 miles south on two-lane Route 97 will bring you to the semi-ghost town of Shaniko (page 428), where well-preserved wooden buildings and old wagons create an open-air museum. Another eight miles bring you to the equally unpopulated ranch town of Antelope, which was overwhelmed in the 1980s when cult leader Bhagwan Shree Rajneesh and 500 followers established an ashram here (to the horror of the locals), and voted to change the town's name to Rajneesh. (Later, the guru left the country due to IRS

SIGHTS   At the Oregon–Washington border, Route 129 heading south from Clarkston, Washington, changes to Route 3 and runs along high ridges and through ponderosa-pine forests until it enters the **Wallowa River Valley**. This valley is postcard-perfect with the jagged Wallowa Mountains providing an ideal backdrop to the broad valley with the lush farms and ranches, rail fences, ranch buildings and the small, winding Wallowa River. Once you've seen it you'll understand why it is becoming a haven for artists and writers.

The twin towns of **Enterprise** and **Joseph** can be used as a base for exploratory trips around Wallowa Lake and backpacking into the Eagle Cap Wilderness. Joseph is named after the revered Chief Joseph, head of the Nez Perce tribe last century. It is well worth exploring for its array of art galleries and for an introduction to the history of the region. Stop by first at the **Wallowa County Museum** to see exhibits depicting the worlds of the white pioneers and the Nez Perce Indians. The building, dating from 1888 and serving at various times as a newspaper office, hospital, meeting hall and bank, is of interest itself. Closed from the third weekend in September to Memorial Day. ~ 110 South Main Street, Joseph; 541-432-6095.

trouble, his followers moved away, and the 90 remaining residents changed the name back.)

CLARNO   At Antelope, turn east on Route 218. A 22-mile drive through drab brown hills lead to the Clarno Unit of John Day Fossil Beds. The least colorful of the national monument's several units, it has a hillside trail among the petrified logs of a prehistoric forest and exhibits of fossilized seeds and nuts. Twenty more miles east lead to the tiny town of **Fossil**, where a homespun local museum displays not only fossils but also such oddities as an antique poker table and a two-headed calf.

SHEEP ROCK   Sixty-five miles south of Fossil on Route 19, the highlight of the Sheep Rock Unit of John Day Fossil Beds is the **Basin Trail**, a colorful hike through blue and green painted desert with replica skeletons of prehistoric rhinoceroses and saber-tooth cats in the spots where the originals were found. The nearby visitors center has historical displays and a lab full of paleontologists at work.

PAINTED HILLS   Turn west (left) on Route 26 and drive 32 miles, then take the well-marked three-mile access road to the national monument's Painted Hills Unit. Though the fossilized leaves found here may be of interest mainly to paleobotanists, the hike through the brilliant yellow, white and scarlet landscape is unforgettable. From here, the shortest route back to civilization is to continue west on Route 26, a distance of 194 miles back to Portland, traversing the south slope of Mt. Hood along the way.

A gravel road takes you another 25 miles to **Hat Point** for a view across one of the most rugged stretches of Hells Canyon.

The last miles of the **Oregon Trail**, which began in St. Joseph, Missouri, run along the same general route taken by Route 84 from the city of Ontario northwest through Baker City, La Grande, Pendleton and along the Columbia River until hitting the rapids in the Cascades. Several sites have been set aside that show ruts made by the wagons along the trail. You can see them at Vail, west of Ontario, and along the route near Baker City in Burnt River Canyon, Gold Hill, Durkee, Pleasant Valley and Baker Valley.

Don't miss the **National Historic Oregon Trail Interpretive Center** on top of Flagstaff Hill on Route 86 east of Baker City. The center looks rather like a prairie schooner from a distance and has a permanent collection of artifacts found along the trail, a theater for stage productions and outdoor exhibits showing a wagon-train encampment and mine operation. Admission. ~ 541-523-1843, fax 541-523-1834; oregontrail.blm.gov.

You also can visit a number of **ghost towns**, all visible records of the boom-and-bust nature of the mining industry—with broken windmills, abandoned shacks and fireplaces surrounded by ashes from burned houses that bear witness to failed homesteads. Some of these towns are making a comeback. Neighboring Baker City are such falsefronted old-timers as Greenhorn, Sumpter, Granite, Whitney, Bourne, Sparta and Cornucopia, which have colorful remains of the original towns and mining equipment standing among the summer homes that have taken root. Most of these towns are along Route 7 or on Forest Service roads leading off it.

Route 7 leads from Baker City southwest to Route 26, which you can stay on heading west to **John Day** and **Canyon City**, twin towns that look very much like the Old West. In fact, twice a year the main street of John Day is closed to vehicular traffic so that a local rancher can drive his cattle through town to and from their summer range.

The best-known museum in these parts was a store owned for decades by two Chinese immigrants, Ing Hay and Lung On. The **Kam Wah Chung & Co. Museum**, next to the city park in the center of John Day, began as a trading post on the military road that ran through the area. Then the Chinese laborers in the mines bought the building for a community center, general store and an herbal doctor's office. The museum has thousands of artifacts related to the building's history and more than a thousand herbs, some from China and others from the immediate area. Closed until summer 2007; call for hours. ~ Ing Hay Way, John Day; 541-575-2800.

The **John Day Fossil Beds National Monument** is a three-part monument that attracts serious and amateur photographers from all over the world to capture the vivid colors of the volcanic-ash deposits and the fossils of plants and animals. See "Scenic Drive" for more information. ~ 32651 Route 19, Kimberly; 541-987-2333, fax 541-987-2336; www.nps.gov/joda, e-mail joda_interp retation@nps.gov.

LODGING   One of the best hotels in Pendleton is the 170-room **Red Lion Hotel**, just off Route 84 on a hill above the city. Newly remodeled rooms have picture windows and balconies overlooking the wheat fields rolling off to the north and west. The hotel has a formal dining room with a window wall, a coffee shop, a lounge and a pool. ~ 304 Southeast Nye Avenue, Pendleton; 541-276-6111, 800-733-5466, fax 541-278-2413; www.redlion.com. MODERATE TO DELUXE.

Most of the hotels in the Enterprise–Joseph area are in the moderate category. The lone exception is **Wallowa Lake Lodge**, a lodge under continual renovation located on the lakeshore with adjoining cabins (with kitchens) and rooms that are simply but pleasantly decorated. ~ 60060 Wallowa Lake Highway, Joseph; 541-432-9821, fax 541-432-4885; www.wallowalake.com, e-mail information@wallowalake.com. MODERATE TO ULTRA-DELUXE.

An alpine look was adopted by builders of the **Chandler's Inn,** which has five simply furnished rooms. Three rooms at the top of a log staircase have private baths and the two downstairs share one and a half baths off of a common sitting room and game room. ~ 700 South Main Street, Joseph; 541-432-9765; www.josephbed andbreakfast.com, e-mail cbbti700@eoni.com. MODERATE.

In Enterprise, the **Wilderness Inn** is a basic motel: clean and uncomplicated. ~ 301 West North Street; 541-426-4535. BUDGET TO MODERATE. Or try the **Country Inn.** ~ 402 West North Street, Enterprise; 541-426-4022. BUDGET.

The selection is thin in the area of John Day Fossil Beds National Monument. The town of John Day has several motels in the low range. For instance, the **Best Western John Day Inn** has 39 units. ~ 315 Main Street, John Day; 541-575-1700, 800-243-2628, fax 541-575-1558; www.bestwestern.com. MODERATE. You can also try the similar but smaller **Little Pine Inn** whose 13 rooms include microwaves and refrigerators. ~ 250 East Main Street, John Day; 541-575-2100; e-mail littlepineinn@century tel.net. BUDGET.

DINING

Red meat is almost required eating in cowboy towns, but in Pendleton you can find a wider variety at **Raphael's Restaurant and Catering,** a restaurant and cocktail lounge that displays the work of local American Indian artists. The menu has beef (of course), but monthly featured entrées may include crab, lobster or wild game. Closed Sunday and Monday. ~ 233 Southeast 4th Street, Pendleton; 541-276-8500, 888-944-2433; www.raphaelsrestaur ant.com. DELUXE.

Good food is making inroads in the Wallowa Valley, and one of the first notable eateries was **Vali's Alpine Delicatessen and**

HAUNTED HOTEL

Heading south, you'll find the landmark **Geiser Grand Hotel,** which was built by the Geiser family in 1889, during Baker City's gold-rush era. The current owners have painstakingly restored the grand staircase and the wrought-iron-and-mahogany balustrade, as well as the crystal chandeliers and ten-foot-high windows. I can attest to the haunted reputation of this hotel. While staying in the ornate Cupola Suite, I was kept awake all night by the sound of running bathwater in my bathroom, partying noises in a nonexistent upstairs room and the sensation of someone getting into bed with me. I was later told that working girls once occupied this room when the hotel was a brothel. ~ 316 Main Street, Baker City; 541- 523-1889, 888-434-7374; www.geisergrand.com, e-mail info@ geisergrand.com. DELUXE.

Restaurant. German-Hungarian dishes such as goulash, chicken paprikas and wienerschnitzel are served, but for the nonadventurous there is also plain old American fare. The decor is also German-Hungarian. Open for continental breakfast (on Saturday and Sunday) and dinner only. Between Memorial Day and Labor Day, open every day except Monday and Tuesday; otherwise, open only Saturday and Sunday. ~ 59811 Wallowa Lake Highway, Joseph; 541-432-5691; e-mail vali@uci.net. MODERATE.

SHOPPING   Offering a fine selection of books on regional history and travel is **Armchair Books.** Closed Friday through Sunday. ~ 39 Southwest Dorion Street, Pendleton; 541-276-7323. Elsewhere in town, **Collectors Gallery** also highlights books of local interest and is a good source for Umatilla Indian artwork. Closed Sunday. ~ 223 Southeast Court Street, Pendleton; 541-276-6697.

Baker City has become an antiques mecca. You'll find items dating back to the pioneer years of the town, including oak furniture bought at estate sales, glass, rock collections, kitchen utensils and tools. **Memory House Antiques** specializes in Depression glass and furniture. Closed Sunday and Monday in winter, Sunday in summer. ~ 1780 Main Street, Baker City; 541-523-6227.

NIGHTLIFE   Live music is hard to come by except on special occasions, such as rodeos and patriotic holidays. An exception is in Pendleton. **Crabby's Underground Saloon and Dance Hall** has deejay music on Thursday, Friday and Saturday night. It's located in a basement beneath several small shops, and in addition to the music and dancefloor has poker and pool tables. Closed Sunday. ~ 220 Southwest 1st Street, Pendleton; 541-276-8118.

PARKS   **WALLOWA LAKE STATE PARK** 🏃 ⚓ 🛶 🎣 🚤 ⛴ ⛵ On the southern end of the lake with large playground areas surrounded by trees, this park stretches from the lakeshore well back into the pine and spruce timber. Hiking trails are nearby. Good rainbow trout fishing can be found north of the park. There are day-use areas, a marina, a boat dock and a concessionaire. ~ Located at the southern end of Wallowa Lake on Route 82; 541-432-4185.

▲ There are 89 tent sites ($13 to $17 per night) and 121 RV hookup sites ($17 to $21 per night), two yurts ($29 per night) and one cabin ($58 to $80 per night).

HELLS CANYON NATIONAL RECREATION AREA 🏃 ⚓ 🚤 ⛵ This 652,488-acre monument protects the Snake River Gorge, a canyon that has an average depth of 6000 feet, the deepest river gorge in the world. It is one of the most popular whitewater-rafting trips in the United States. Rafts can be launched from Hells

SOUTHEASTERN OREGON   299

Canyon Dam in Oregon and Pittsburg Landing on the Idaho side
of the river. The Snake River is very swift, and swimming is allowed only in certain spots. There's fishing access from 18 sites;
smallmouth bass, catfish and crappie are
best. There is also sturgeon (catch-and-release only). Facilities include day-use picnic
areas, scenic overlooks, a visitors center
(closed Saturday and Sunday from Labor Day
to Memorial Day) and restrooms. Higher elevations in the park are closed in winter. ~ You
can reach the area two ways: by taking Route 86
from Baker City through Halfway to Forest Service
Road 39; or by heading east on Route 350 from the
town of Joseph south to Forest Service Road 39; 541-
426-5546; www.fs.fed.us/hellscanyon.com.

Hells Canyon was well known
to prehistoric American Indians
and early white settlers alike,
as evidenced by 8000-year-
old petroglyphs, artifacts
from Chief Joseph's Nez
Perce, remnants of
1860s gold mines and
1890s homesteads.

▲ There are numerous campgrounds. Indian Crossing (14
tent sites, $6 to $10 per night) is the starting point for some of
the area's horseback riding and hiking trails, making it an ideal
place to set up camp. Ollokot Campground (12 campsites, $8 to
$10 per night) is also popular. Both campgrounds are only open in
summer. There is also primitive camping along the river for rafters
and backpackers.

If you thought northeastern Oregon seemed
lonely, you probably haven't yet experienced southeastern Oregon. To travel in this

Southeastern Oregon

part of the state you need a sturdy, reliable car, a cooler for cold
drinks and snacks, and it might not be a bad idea to take along
camping equipment because hotels/motels are few and far between.

Harney County is the largest county in the United States, larger
in fact than many northeastern states, but this part of the country
is really wide open. Harney is the largest of the three counties in
southeastern Oregon at 10,228 square miles and has the smallest
population, just over 7500. One town, Wagontire on Route 395,
has a population that hovers around seven. Some say it depends
on how many children are home for the holidays.

Few roads run through this area: Route 395 from California
and Route 95 from Nevada are the main north–south corridors.
Route 20 goes across the center from Idaho to the Cascades, and
Route 140 runs across the bottom from northern Nevada through
Lakeview to Klamath Falls. In Malheur County you will find evidence of its diverse culture as Basque shepherds, Mexican cowboys
and laborers, Japanese-American laborers and various Europeans
came through and left their marks.

In Harney County are wildlife refuges around Malheur Lake
and Steens Mountain. The only real population center is Burns.

Crane, a tiny town southeast of Burns on Route 78, has the only public boarding school in the country.

SIGHTS   Northeast of Lakeview on Route 395 is **Abert Rim**, at 30 miles the largest exposed fault in North America. The massive fault juts up into the desert sky like a continuous cliff on the east side of Route 395, while on the west side of the highway is the talcum-white wasteland around **Lake Abert**.

Northwest of Lakeview just off Route 31 on county roads in Christmas Valley is **Hole in the Ground**, a 700-foot-deep crack caused by an earthquake. In the same area, **Fort Rock** is the remnant of a volcano crater and ocean shoreline that looks like one side of a destroyed fort. Indian sandals found there were carbon-dated and found to be 10,000 years old.

About 25 miles northeast of Christmas Valley is **Lost Forest**, a 9000-acre ponderosa-pine forest that has managed to survive in the middle of the harsh desert. The forest is surrounded by shifting sand dunes, which are popular with the all-terrain-vehicle set.

Oregon's longest lake, manmade **Lake Owyhee**, has miles of striking desert topography along its shores. It is reached by taking Route 201 south from Nyssa to the small town of Owyhee, then a county road that dead-ends at the lake. Farther down in the desert where the Owyhee River still runs free is some of the state's best whitewater for river runners.

LODGING   Down in the desert, Burns has four or five motels, including the **Days Inn Ponderosa Motel**. It has 52 ordinary but clean rooms that don't smell of disinfectant, and a swimming pool. ~ 577 West Monroe Street, Burns; 541-573-2047; www.daysinn.com. BUDGET.

The **Silver Spur Motel** offers 26 cozy and simple guest rooms with cable television, microwaves, refrigerators and coffee makers. Pine furnishings, floral linens and wallpaper create a more pleasant, homey feel than the average motel. Guests have free access to a nearby health club. There is also a golf course nearby. ~ 789 North Broadway Avenue, Burns; 541-573-2077, 800-400-2077, fax 541-573-3921; www.silverspurmotel.net, e-mail silver spurmotel@yahoo.com. BUDGET.

HIDDEN ▶   **Hotel Diamond** is located 54 miles southeast of Burns. Built in 1898 as a hotel, the wood structure serves as a point of departure for Malheur National Wildlife Refuge, Diamond Craters and the Pete French Round Barn Historical site. The hotel has five small, wood-trimmed rooms with shared baths and three rooms with private baths. Full breakfast included. Closed November to April. ~ 49130 Main Street, Diamond; 541-493-1898; www.cen tral-oregon.com/hoteldiamond. MODERATE.

There are just a few places to stay in the area around Steens Mountain, Alvord Desert and Malheur and Harney lakes, so reservations are strongly recommended. A historic place is the 1924 **Frenchglen Hotel**, a classic ranch house with screened porch. Frenchglen has eight rooms decorated with rustic pine and patchwork quilts and has two shared baths. A newly built addition provides five more rooms, all with private baths. Breakfast, lunch and a family-style dinner are available. Closed November to mid-March. ~ 39184 Route 205, Frenchglen; 541-493-2825, fax 541-493-2828; e-mail fghotel@centurytel.net. MODERATE.

Two miles north of Lakeview is **Hunter's Hot Springs Resort**, which has Oregon's only geyser. Named Old Perpetual, it shoots water and steam 60 feet into the air every 90 seconds. The resort has a thermal pool, and the hot water is reputed to have healing powers. The 19 units are simply decorated in what the owner calls country style. The resort also offers a racquetball court. ~ Route 395 North, Lakeview; 541-947-4142, 800-858-8266, fax 541-947-2800; www.huntershotspringresort.com. BUDGET TO MODERATE.

For a real cowpoke experience, head to **Willow Springs Guest Ranch**, a 2500-acre working cattle ranch in Lakeview. Guests can enjoy a comfortable overnight bed-and-breakfast experience or saddle up with the ranch hands and learn something about the

ranching lifestyle. Activities include horseback riding, bicycling, hiking and campfire cookouts. Rustic Western cabins are duplex style and include a queen bed, private bath, pedestal fireplace, art by famous Western artists such as Frederic Remington, and a long covered porch with rockers. There is a wood-fired hot tub. The ranch generates all its electricity from wind and solar power and generators (lanterns are provided for night owls). No pets or children under 12. ~ 34064 Clover Flat Road, Lakeview; 541-947-5499; www.willowspringsguestranch.com, e-mail info@will owspringsguestranch.com. DELUXE TO ULTRA-DELUXE.

DINING   For a casual lunch or picnic fixings, a good bet is **Broadway Delicatessen Co.**, a bright, cheerful deli inside a historic quarried-rock storefront. The menu features made-to-order sandwiches on a choice of seven breads, pasta and potato salads, tossed green salads, a full espresso bar and daily soup specials. There are also house-made cheesecakes, bread pudding and other tempting desserts. Breakfast and lunch only. ~ 530 North Broadway, Burns; 541-573-7020. BUDGET.

SHOPPING   Unless you're a rockhound, souvenir shopping is likely to prove challenging in these parts. Perhaps your best bet is the gift shop at Ontario's **Four Rivers Cultural Center**, where you'll find artworks and handmade gift items from the four cultures represented in the museum, as well as a large selection of adults' and children's books on Western history, American Indian and Japanese cultures, Japanese gardening and koi ponds. ~ 676 Southwest 5th Avenue, Ontario; 541-889-8191.

PARKS   **MALHEUR NATIONAL WILDLIFE REFUGE** At 187,000 acres, Malheur covers an interesting and diverse wildlife population and geological features. Malheur Lake is a major resting area for migratory birds on the Pacific Flyway. Fishing is permitted at Krumbo Reservoir. Malheur Field Station (541-493-2629) has dormitory and family housing and meals available. ~ Located 32 miles southeast of Burns on Route 205, then 6 miles on Princeton-Narrows Road; 541-493-2612; www.fws.gov/malheur.

HART MOUNTAIN NATIONAL ANTELOPE REFUGE This 275,000-acre refuge 65 miles northeast of Lakeview protects a large population of antelope, bighorn sheep, mule deer, coyotes, a variety of smaller animals and a bird population. Hart Mountain, the centerpiece of the refuge, rises to 8065 feet and has deep gorges, ridges and cliffs on the west side. The east side of the mountain climbs more gradually. For rockhounds, collections are limited to seven pounds per person. Fishing is permitted in Rock and Guano creeks depending on conditions. Restrooms and a visitors center are the only facilities. ~ Located 65 miles northeast of

Lakeview on county roads off Routes 395 and 140; 541-947-3315; www.fws.gov/sheldonhartmtn, e-mail sheldon-hart@fws.gov.

▲ Hot Springs Campground has 30 primitive sites (no fee).

Although eastern Washington is not, as one local guide puts it, "blue ribbon" fishing territory for most of the year, the region has its moments: come August, some big salmon show up in the Klickitat River; September starts the steelhead run in the Snake River; and trout in June and July make the Yakima River the most popular flyfishing stream in the Northwest. Some outfitters can also arrange hunting trips for game like elk, deer and bighorn sheep.

▼▼▼▼▼▼▼▼▼▼▼▼▼▼

Outdoor Adventures

FISHING

GRAND COULEE AREA For information on fishing in Banks and Roosevelt lakes, contact **Coulee Playland**. ~ P.O. Box 457, Electric City, WA 99123; 509-633-2671; www.couleeplayland. com. In winter, Banks Lake, near Grand Coulee, is a popular place to ice fish.

SPOKANE AREA G. L. Britton of **Double Spey Outfitters** has been flyfishing since he was a boy; he now guides visiting anglers for half-day walk-and-wade flyfishing trips for trout on the Spokane during August and September, and full-day steelhead trips on a driftboat on the Snake and Grande Rhonde rivers in October and November. The rest of the year, Britton will take you out to one of the local lakes for a full day of fishing that's more "teach-you" than "trophy." Flies, rods and leaders are provided. ~ West 11254 Meadowview Lane, Nine Mile Falls; 509-466-4635; e-mail deanriver@aol.com.

◆◆◆◆◆◆◆◆◆◆◆◆◆◆◆◆◆◆◆

In winter, Banks Lakes, near Grand Coulee, is a popular place to fish.

SOUTHEASTERN WASHINGTON If you'd "rather be fishing," then call Dan Little at **RBF Excursions** to arrange a day of flyfishing for steelhead or guided summer salmon and steelhead trips to the Klickitat River, about 65 miles away; for part of the year, Dan guides on Olympic Peninsula Rainforest rivers as well. ~ P.O. Box 271, Klickitat, WA 98628; 541-993-1351; www.rbf-excursions.com, e-mail rbfexcursions@hotmail.com.

Fishing excursions on the Snake River between the Idaho/Washington border are offered by **Beamer's Hells Canyon Tours**. Spring and summer half-day to four-days trips on a fishing sled seek bass, trout and sturgeon; in fall, it's steelhead. Bait and tackle provided. ~ 1451 Bridge Street, Clarkston; 509-758-4800, 800-522-6966, fax 509-758-3643; www.hellscanyontours.com, e-mail beamerstours@bhct.net. **Snake River Adventures** provides day tours as well as single or multiday guided trips for steelhead, sturgeon, bass and trout on the Snake, Salmon and Clearwater rivers. ~ 4832 Hells Gate Road, Lewiston, ID; 208-746-6276, 800-262-8874, fax 208-746-9906; www.snakeriveradventures. com, e-mail sra@lewistondsl.com.

RIVER RUNNING

In September on the Tieton River, in southeastern Washington, water is released from the dam that controls the flow, creating Class III and some Class IV rapids and drawing ever-increasing crowds of rafters. It may not be a "hidden" spot, but it's still a thrill. Whitewater thrills come on the Snake River in Northeastern Oregon, where it cuts through walls of black basalt, forming Hells Canyon, the deepest gorge in the country. Spring is the best time to hit good whitewater, but be forewarned: classifications are arbitrary and the hard classes aren't necessarily the best. Watch water levels more closely than class.

SOUTHEASTERN WASHINGTON Chinook Expeditions has been leading guided trips and wildlife-watching tours since 1974. Rivers rafted include the Skagit, Snohomish, Skykomish, Toutle and Queets. Guide Shane Turnbull says all trips are very interpretive. All river and camping gear is included. ~ P.O. Box 256, Index, WA 98256; 360-793-3451, 800-241-3451; www.chinook expeditions.com, e-mail sturnbull@earthlink.net. **Rivers, Inc.** offers full-day guided trips on paddle rafts down the Wenatchee, Methow, Suiattle and Tieton rivers in the summer. ~ P.O. Box 2092, Kirkland, WA 98083; 425-822-5296. **Idaho Afloat** leads one- to six-day rafting trips down Class II to Class IV rivers. ~ P.O. Box 542, Grangeville, ID 83530; 208-983-2414, 800-700-2414; www.idahoafloat.com.

Snake Dancer Excursions provides full- and half-day jet boat tours down the Snake River and through Hells Canyon, with a stop at Kirkwood Ranch. Trips cover 85 sets of rapids that rate as high as Class IV. ~ 1550 Port Drive, Suite B, Clarkston; 509-758-8927, 800-234-1941, fax 509-758-8925; www.snakedancer excursions.com, e-mail sdexcursions@qwest.net.

Another popular location for rafting is the Snake River between the Washington and Idaho border. Contact **O.A.R.S.**

IT'S ALL RECENT HISTORY

Compared with the rest of the country, the Northwest's history is both recent and benign. The Northwest is so new that East Coast visitors look askance when they find that the major cities weren't founded until the latter part of the last century. Very little recorded history goes back before 1800; the Lewis and Clark Expedition of 1804–1806 was the first overland crossing between the original 13 states and the Pacific Coast, and they were the first to describe the lower Snake River.

Dories for guided tours on rafts, dories and inflatable kayaks on Class III and Class IV rivers. Trips on the Snake River last three to five days; Salmon River expeditions are four to seventeen days. ~ P.O. Box 67, 2687 South Route 49, Angels Camp, CA 95222; 209-736-4677, 800-346-6277, fax 209-736-2902; www.oars.com, e-mail info@oars.com.

NORTHEASTERN OREGON Some of the most challenging whitewater rapids anywhere can be found on the Owyhee River in southeastern Oregon's Malheur County. Among the outfitters offering raft and kayak trips on the Owyhee from April through May is **Oregon River Experiences**. ~ 18074 South Boone Court, Beavercreek; 503-632-6836, 800-827-1358; www.oregonriver.com. **Oregon Whitewater Adventures** offers five-day trips on the Owyhee. ~ 39620 Deerhorn Road, Springfield; 541-746-5422, 800-820-7238; www.oregonwhitewater.com.

For a list of other outfitters licensed to operate raft or float trips in Hells Canyon, write or call the **Wallowa Visitors Center**. ~ 88401 Route 82, Enterprise, OR 97828; 541-426-4978; www.fs.fed.us/r6/w-w.

Mountain valleys and high desert vistas give golfers satisfying course options, and greens fees that are lower than in urban areas sweeten the deal. Winter weather closes many courses for two to five months.

GOLF

OKANOGAN HIGHLANDS Hilly terrain makes a cart rental highly recommended at the nine-hole **Oroville Golf Club**. The scenic semiprivate course runs beside a river. Closed Thursday afternoon. ~ 3468-A Nighthawk Road, two miles west of Oroville; 509-476-2390, fax 509-476-2408. Between Omak and Okanogan is the **Okanogan Valley Golf Club**. This public course is surrounded by hills on one side and orchards on the other. Closed in winter. ~ 105 Danker Cutoff, off the Okanogan–Conconully Route; 509-826-6937; www.okanoganvalleygolf.com.

GRAND COULEE AREA **Banks Lake Golf and Country Club** offers 18 holes for golf enthusiasts. The public course is next to Banks Lake, and offers a few canyons and wide fairways. Closed in winter. ~ 19849 Lundolph Road Northeast, one mile south of Electric City; 509-633-0163.

SPOKANE AREA If you've seen San Francisco's Lincoln Park Municipal Golf Course with its view across the city skyline, Spokane's **Indian Canyon Golf Course** will seem familiar. Set on a hillside that undulates downward toward Spokane, the public 18-hole course is well known throughout the region. Closed in winter. ~ West 4304 West Drive; 509-747-5353, fax 509-747-0622.

SOUTHEASTERN WASHINGTON In Yakima the public, 18-hole **Suntides Golf Course** is fairly flat, so it's very walkable, making it popular with seniors and junior golfers. There's water on 13 of the holes. You'll find a restaurant on the premises. ~ 231 Pence Road, Yakima; 509-966-9065, fax 509-966-2742; www.sun tidesgolf.com. The 17th hole at public **Apple Tree Golf Course** is called Apple Island, and is shaped like an apple and surrounded by water (this is apple country, after all). ~ 8804 Occidental Road, Yakima; 509-966-5877.

Sun Willows Golf Course is a public, 18-hole course that's very playable for all handicaps. It's fairly flat, but has several lakes. Carts are available for rent. ~ 2535 North 20th Avenue, Pasco; 509-545-3440. A canyon runs through **Canyon Lakes Golf Course**, which makes for plenty of interesting shots on this 18-hole public course. Rated one of the top ten courses in the Northwest, Canyon Lakes also has a champion putting course and full practice facilities. ~ 3700 West Canyon Lakes Drive, Kennewick; 509-582-3736.

NORTHEASTERN OREGON   Courses are scarce in eastern Oregon simply because there aren't that many people around. The nine-hole **Echo Hills Golf Course** is par 36 and rather challenging, with hills and gullies. It's 23 miles northwest of Pendleton. ~ Take the Echo exit off Route 84; 541-376-8244. For18 holes, try the fairly flat but attractive course at **Pendleton Country Club**. ~ 69772 Route 395 South, Pendleton; 541-443-4653; www. pendletoncc.com.

South of Pendleton, the public, 18-hole **Baker City Golf Course** is a fairly easy course. ~ 2801 Indiana Avenue; 541-523-2358. Near Hells Canyon is the laidback, nine-hole **Alpine Meadows**. The par-72 course is surrounded by beautiful mountains. ~ 66098 Golf Course Road, Enterprise; 541-426-3246. **John Day Golf** is a challenging nine-hole course with hills and a sand-trap. ~ 27631 Golf Club Road, John Day; 541-575-0170.

SKIING   Ski areas in this part of the state, particularly the southeast part, are little farther away from the hustle and bustle of the larger, more popular spots elsewhere. The full-service resorts all offer equip-

PACK IT UP

Several outfitters are licensed to lead overnight horse pack trips into the Hells Canyon National Recreation Area and Eagle Cap Wilderness. A few offer day rides and llama pack trips. For a list, contact park headquarters. ~ Wallowa Mountains Visitor Center, 88401 Route 82, Enterprise, OR 97828; 541-426-5546, fax 541-426-5522; www.fs.fed.us/hellscanyon.

ment rentals for downhill skiing, cross-country skiing and snow-boarding. In addition, lessons are available for all levels.

OKANOGAN HIGHLANDS Downhill and cross-country skiing are both popular in this region, particularly the latter because there is so much open country and powdery snow. Cross-country trails are maintained at most downhill areas, but any country road, most golf courses and parks may be used by skiers. **Loup Loup Ski Area** has a 1240-foot vertical drop for downhill skiing and snowboarding. Its four lifts serve over a dozen runs. There is a small half-pipe for snowboarders, and 25 kilometers of groomed trails for cross-country skiers. Closed Monday, Tuesday and Thursday, and April to mid-December. ~ Route 20, between Twisp and Okanogan; 509-826-2720, fax 509-826-5469; www.skitheloup.com, e-mail info@skitheloup.com.

Sitzmark Ski Lodge has a base elevation of 4950 feet and a modest 650-foot drop. There is a chair lift, a rope tow and runs for snowboarders. The majority of runs are intermediate (60 percent). Closed mid-March to mid-December. ~ Located 20 miles northeast of Tonasket on Havillan Road; 509-485-3323; www.skisitzmark.com. **49° North** has six chairlifts on 1900 feet as well as a snowboard park and 380 miles of groomed trails. Closed mid-April to mid-November. ~ Located ten miles east of Chewelah; 509-935-6649, 866-376-4949; www.ski49n.com.

SOUTHEASTERN WASHINGTON Ski Bluewood, 22 miles southeast of Dayton at the end of a Forest Service road, has 1125 vertical feet of downhill skiing. There are two triple-chair lifts and one surface lift, as well as a snowboard terrain park. Closed Monday and Tuesday, and from mid-April to mid-November. ~ 262 East Main Street; 509-382-4725, fax 590-382-4726; www. bluewood.com, e-mail info@bluewood.com.

BIKING

For the most part, automobile traffic is sparse in these regions, so bicyclists have little trouble finding long stretches of road that are practically deserted, and scenically beautiful. But they're also challenging and attract avid cross-country bicyclists, especially along Routes 3 and 86 in the Wallowa National Forest near Hells Canyon. Recreational bicyclists, however, have a couple of options. Along the bank of the Spokane River, the paved **Centennial Trail** extends from Riverside State Park to the Washington–Idaho state line (37 miles) and continues on to Coeur d'Alene, Idaho, 25 miles farther. The trail is a relatively flat, easy ride with a few hills in the park (and nobody says you have to go the full distance; you might just want to go as far as Plante's Ferry Park, where you'll find some interesting basalt rock formations in the water). Just west of Spokane is the forested Riverside State Park, which has several gravel trails for mountain biking. Mt. Spokane, which rises some 5800 feet, is another recommended destination.

In the Yakima area, besides an easy five-mile multi-use route along the **Yakima Greenway**, which meanders along the river, there are several possible routes through the local wine country. The **Yakima Valley Visitors and Convention Bureau** has information and maps. ~ 10 North 8th Street; 509-575-6062, 800-221-0751; www.yakimacenter.com.

The **Snake River Bikeway** runs six miles between Clarkston and Asotin along both the Clearwater and Snake rivers. Access it from Beachview Park at the corner of Beachview and Chestnut in Clarkston. Also, a 24-mile tour from **Palouse** leads south on Route 27 to Clear Creek Road to Route 272 back to Palouse.

In some cities, you'll find some bicycle routes that double as hiking trails (see "Hiking," below).

Bike Rentals & Tours   There are three bike shops along Spokane's main street. Rent or repair a mountain bike or buy equipment at **North Division Bicycle Shop**. ~ 10503 North Division Street, Spokane; 509-467-2453, 888-222-2453; www.northdivision.com. **Spoke 'N Sport** rents and sells mountain bikes, racks and trailers. There's also a full-service bike shop. ~ 212 North Division Street, Spokane; 509-838-8842.

In the Yakima area, contact the **Yakima Valley and Convention Bureau** for a map of bike routes through the local wine country. ~ 10 North 8th Street; 509-575-6062, 800-221-0751. Mountain-bike sales and repairs are available through **Valley Cycling and Fitness**. ~ 1802 West Nob Hill Boulevard, Yakima; 509-453-6699; www.valleycyclingandfitness.com.

For a variety of scheduled rides in the Yakima area, check out **Mount Adams Cycling**. ~ P.O. Box 745, Yakima, WA 98907; www.mountadamscycling.org.

HIKING   All distances listed for hiking trails are one way unless otherwise noted.

OKANOGAN HIGHLANDS   Backpackers and day hikers alike enjoy this area because the weather is often clear and dry. A number of established hiking trails are shown on Forest Service maps and in free brochures given out at the ranger station in Okanogan. ~ 1240 South 2nd Avenue; 509-826-3275, fax 509-826-3789.

A good walk for a family with small children is the one-mile trail leading from Bonaparte Campground just north of the one-store town of Wauconda to the viewpoint overlooking the lake. Another easy one is the **Big Tree Trail** (1 mile) loop from Lost Lake Campground, which is only a short distance north of Bonaparte. This one goes through a signed botanical area.

One of the most ambitious highlands trails is the southern segment of the **Kettle Crest Trail** (15 miles). The trek begins at the summit of Sherman Pass on Route 20 and winds southward past

Sherman Peak and four other major mountains, the highest peak measuring 7135 feet. The trail is through mostly open terrain, and you'll have great views of the mountains and Columbia River Valley. ~ 509-684-7000.

GRAND COULEE AREA A system of paths and trails connects the four towns clustered around Grand Coulee Dam. The Bureau of Reclamation built a paved route about two miles long called the **Community Trail**, which connects Coulee Dam and Grand Coulee. An informal system of unpaved paths connects these two towns to Elmer City and Electric City.

> Forest areas in the Okanogan Highlands are more open than in the Cascades and Olympics, making it a favorite among hikers.

The newest is the walking/biking trail called the **Down River Trail** (6.5 miles). It runs north along the Columbia River from Grand Coulee, beginning in the Coulee Dam Shopping Center. Some access points are accessible for wheelchairs. ~ 509-633-9503.

Bunchgrass Prairie Nature Trail (.5-mile roundtrip) begins in the Spring Canyon Campground, which is three miles up Lake Roosevelt by water and two miles from Grand Coulee. This loop trail starts in the campground and goes through one of the few remaining bunchgrass environments here. ~ 509-633-9441.

SOUTHEASTERN WASHINGTON Cowiche Canyon (3 miles) starts five miles from Yakima. The trail is actually an old railroad bed that ran through the steep canyon. The canyon has unusual rock formations, and you can expect to see some wildlife.

Noel Pathway (4.6 miles) is a trail inside the city limits of Yakima that follows the Yakima River. The pathway is used by bicyclists, as well.

Transportation

CAR

Eastern Washington and Oregon is served by a network of roads that range from interstates to logging roads that have been paved by the Forest Service. **Route 97** serves as the north–south dividing line between the Cascade Mountains and the arid, rolling hills that undulate to the eastern boundaries of the states.

Route 90 runs through the center of the Washington, from Spokane southwest through Moses Lake, George and across the Columbia River at Vantage, where the highway turns almost due west for its final run to Puget Sound.

Route 5 bisects Portland, Oregon, and provides access from the north via Vancouver, Washington. This highway is also the main line from points south like the Willamette Valley and California.

Route 82 begins near Hermiston, Oregon, crosses the Columbia River to the Tri-Cities (Richland, Kennewick and Pasco) and runs on up the Yakima Valley to join Route 90 at Ellensburg. **Route 84** runs almost the entire length of the Columbia River

Gorge in Oregon before swinging southeast at Hermiston and connecting Pendleton, La Grande and Baker City with Ontario on the Idaho border.

Other major highways are **Route 395**, starting south of Lakeview, Oregon, and continuing into Washington at the Tri-Cities to Ritzville. It joins with Route 90 at Ritzville only to emerge again at Spokane, where it continues north into British Columbia. Smaller but important highways include **Route 12** between Clarkston and Walla Walla, and **Route 195** running between Spokane and the Clarkston–Lewiston area.

Perhaps the most beautiful of all the highways in Washington is **Route 20**, which starts at Whidbey Island and continues to the North Cascades, through the Methow Valley, then straight through the Okanogan Highlands to Kettle Falls, where it merges with Route 395. It becomes Route 20 again at Colville, and continues southeast to Newport on the Idaho border.

AIR

Spokane International Airport is by far the busiest in Eastern Washington with ten airlines serving the area: Alaska Airlines, America West, Delta Airlines, Frontier, Horizon Air, Northwest Airlines, Skywest, Southwest Airlines, United Airlines and United Express ~ www.spokaneairports.net.

Other airports with scheduled service in Washington are **Moses Lake, Pullman, Wenatchee, Yakima**, the **Tri-Cities** and **Walla Walla**. All of these smaller cities are served by either Horizon Air or United Express, or both. In addition, Delta Airlines serves the Tri-Cities. Empire Airlines serves the Tri-Cities and Yakima.

BUS

Three bus lines operate in the region. From the Spokane terminal at 221 West 1st Avenue are **Greyhound Bus Lines** (509-624-5251, 800-231-2222; www.greyhound.com) and **Northwestern Trailways** (509-838-5262). Greyhound also serves Yakima at the depot at 602 East Yakima Avenue (509-457-5131).

Operating from Medical Lake (just southwest of Spokane) is **Alpha Omega Tours and Charters**. ~ 419 North Jefferson Street; 509-299-5545, 800-351-1060; www.alphaomegatoursandchar ters.com.

TRAIN

Washington is one of the few states to have two **Amtrak** routes. Both start in Spokane. The first route runs from Spokane due west with stops in Ephrata, Wenatchee, Everett and Edmonds before arriving in Seattle. The other route runs southwest from Spokane to the Columbia River Gorge with stops in Pasco, Bingen and Vancouver, and ultimately goes to Portland, Oregon. ~ 800-872-7245; www.amtrak.com.

Car-rental agencies in Spokane include the following: **Budget Car and Truck Rental** (800-527-0700) and **Thrifty Car Rental** (800-367-2277).

Agencies in the Tri-Cities include **Avis Rent A Car** (800-331-1212), **Budget Rent A Car** (800-527-0700) and **Hertz Rent A Car** (800-654-3131). Walla Walla is served by **Budget Rent A Car** (800-527-0700).

The Tri-Cities area has **Ben Franklin Transit**. ~ 509-735-5100; www.bft.org. **Valley Transit** serves Walla Walla and College Place. ~ 509-525-9140; www.valleytransit.com. Pullman has **Pullman Transit**. ~ 509-332-6535; www.pullmantransit.com. Yakima has **Yakima Transit**. ~ 509-575-6175.

Major taxi companies in the area are **Valley Cab** (509-535-7007) and **Spokane Cab** (509-568-8000).

SEVEN

Portland and the Columbia River Gorge

But for the flip of a coin, Portland could have been called Boston. Our story begins with two pioneers, Asa Lovejoy of Massachusetts and Francis Pettygrove of Maine, hitting the Oregon Trail in search of the American Dream. On a fall 1843 canoe journey up the Willamette River from Fort Vancouver to Oregon City, Tennessee drifter William Overton (traveling with Lovejoy) thought the land was perfect for a settlement. Lacking the 25-cent filing fee, he split the claim with Lovejoy in return for the money. Overton soon grew tired of working the land, and sold his half to Francis W. Pettygrove.

Soon, Lovejoy found himself partners with Pettygrove at "The Clearing," what native guides called the area. Lovejoy wanted to call the new town Boston, but Pettygrove preferred to appropriate the name of Maine's Portland. True gentlemen, they settled the matter with a coin toss at Oregon City's Francis Ermatinger House.

Pettygrove won, but it was years before Portland began to rival Oregon City, the immigrant hub at the end of the overland trail. Even today, with a metropolitan population of more than 2 million, many visitors wonder how this city emerged as Oregon's centerpiece. Unlike the largest cities of the Pacific Northwest or California, it is not located on a major coast or sound. Although it is midway between the equator and the North Pole, Portland is not central to the geography of its own state. Yet from the arts and winter recreation to architecture and vineyards, this city is an admirable metropolis, one that merits inclusion on any Northwest itinerary.

The community boasts a rich cultural life, has a popular National Basketball Association franchise, is blessed with some of the prettiest urban streets in the Northwest, is a veritable haven for antique lovers, runners, cyclists and garden aficionados and has an impressive array of jazz clubs, bistros and offbeat museums.

And yet the legacy of "The Clearing" is very much intact as the city remains intimately connected to the great outdoors. Near the entrance to the fabled Columbia River Gorge, Portland is just 65 miles from the nearest glacier and 110 miles from the ocean. Riverfront greenspace, the 5000-acre Forest Park and the wonderful wetlands of Sauvie Island all demonstrate why this city has been named "best" on the Green Index, a study of pollution, public health and environmental policy.

When the weather turns very wet, as it does in the winter months, residents head for the powder-packed slopes of Mt. Hood or start gearing up for a bit of steel-heading on the nearby coastal rivers. Winter is also the height of the cultural season, enjoyed at the Portland Center for the Performing Arts and dozens of other venues around town.

Portland's emergence as a major city owes much to emigrant New England ship captains who decided, in the mid-19th century, that the town's deep riverfront harbor was preferable to the shallows of Oregon City. Easy ocean access via the Columbia made the new port a convenient link to the emerging agrarian economy of the Willamette Valley, as well as the region's up-and-coming lumber mills. Like San Francisco, Portland flourished as an international shipping hub and as a gateway for the 1852 gold rush that began in the Jacksonville region.

As the Northwest's leading port and economic center, the town soon attracted the state's new gentry, the lumber barons, shipping titans, traders, mercantilists and agribusiness pioneers. They drew heavily on the architectural legacy of the Northeast and Europe, erecting Cape Cod–style homes, Victorian mansions, villas and French Renaissance–style mini-châteaus complete with Italian marble and virgin-redwood interiors.

A city that started out in life as a kind of New England–style village crafted out of native fir was made over with brick office blocks sporting cast-iron facades. Florentine, Italianate, gothic, even Baroque architecture began to emerge along the main drags. City fathers worked hard to upgrade the town's agrarian image, often with mixed results.

To unify the community, planners added a 25-block-long promenade through the heart of town. Lined with churches, office blocks, apartments and homes, these "Park Blocks" offered a grassy median ideal for contemplating the passing scene. Like a Parisian boulevard, this was the place where one might come for the hour and stay for the day. Brass water fountains, known as Benson Bubblers and left on 24 hours a day, brought the pure waters of the Cascades to street level.

While the city's New England quality made Bostonians feel right at home, Portland also attracted a significant Chinese community that labored long and hard d railroad lines and in salmon factories. Badly persecuted, they were just one of ma victims of intolerance in this city that became a Ku Klux Klan center. Blacks, Je and Catholics were also victimized at various times. But as Portland grew, this plorable bigotry was replaced by a new egalitarianism. The city's intellectual flourished thanks to the arrival of several major universities and prestigious eral arts colleges.

As Portland modernized, it developed into a manufacturing center famo everything from swimsuits to footwear. But as the city flourished as a cent high-tech industry, it did not forget its roots. Visitors eager to discover the I west flock here and to the Columbia River Gorge in pursuit of outdoor ac from windsurfing to birding. An ideal home base, this city has also draw famous artists, musicians and writers from larger, more congested and ex communities like New York and Los Angeles.

Although much of Portland's best is within easy walking distance c town, the city's outer reaches are also well worth your time. The touch great urban centers—science museums, zoos, children's museums and craft

are all found here. Amid its multiple museums and theater companies, as well as countless other amenities, Portland also offers many pleasant surprises such as a strong used book–seller community, the sole extinct volcano within the limits of a continental U.S. city and the world's smallest park.

Careful restoration of the downtown core and historic old town, a beautiful riverfront area and thriving nightlife make Portland a winner. Neighborhoods such as Nob Hill, Hawthorne and Sellwood all invite leisurely exploration. And when it comes to parks you can choose from more than 80 spanning 37,000 acres.

In this chapter we have divided the city into three geographic regions. The Central Portland region encompasses downtown, the Skidmore Old Town District and the Yamhill Historic District. Portland West covers the balance of the city and metropolitan region west of the Willamette River. Portland East explores the metro area east of the Willamette River including Lloyd Center, Burnside, Sellwood and southerly destinations like Oregon City.

Because of its proximity to Portland, we have included the Columbia River Gorge region in this chapter. Even if you only have a couple of hours to cruise up to Multnomah Falls, by all means go. The Columbia River Gorge National Recreation Area is 292,500 acres in size and includes 80 miles of the most scenic part of the Columbia River Gorge corridor. It extends beyond Hood River and White Salmon, as far as The Dalles. The main historic drive ends at Multnomah Falls, but the other side of Cascade Locks takes visitors to the Rowena Plateau past orchards to The Dalles. This area includes part of the journey west for many Oregon pioneers; imagine how it felt for them to glide through this verdant, waterfall-lined canyon after 2000 miles of hardscrabble, blazing desert and treacherous mountain passes. This fir-clad valley really was Valhalla, the light at the end of the tunnel some people call the American Dream. We think you'll enjoy it as much as they did.

Central Portland

The urban renaissance is clearly a success in Portland. A walkable city with perpetually flowing drinking fountains, this riverfront town is a place where commerce, history, classic architecture and the arts flourish side by side. Even when the weather is foul, Portland is an inviting place.

Downtown Portland *does* have its sleek towers, but it also contains plenty of low-lying delights as well. It's easy to tell that the city has spent a lot of time and money on parks and public art projects—Portland, after all, is the city whose mayor dreamed up the "Expose Yourself to Art" campaign in the 1970s (and that was mayor Bud Clark himself clad in an open trench coat on the famous poster).

A city that focuses so much on user-friendly public spaces certainly is welcoming to visitors. Whether you're taking a slow stroll along Park Avenue or shopping the markets of Portland's Chinatown (once the West Coast's largest Chinese community), Central Portland will impress you as much more than just the place where the populace clocks in from 9 to 5.

Text continued on page 318.

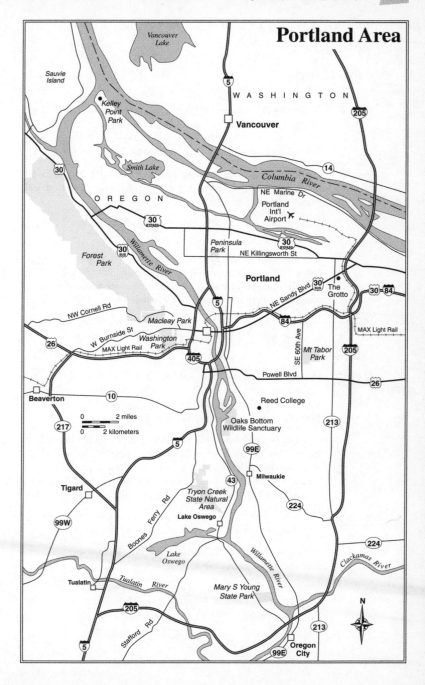

Portland Area

Vancouver Lake

Sauvie Island

WASHINGTON

Vancouver

Kelley Point Park

Smith Lake

30

Columbia River

14

OREGON

NE Marine Dr

Portland Int'l Airport

30 BYPASS

Peninsula Park

30 BYPASS

Forest Park

30 BUS

Willamette River

NE Killingsworth St

Portland

NE Sandy Blvd

30 BUS

The Grotto

30 — 84

5

NW Cornell Rd

Macleay Park

84

MAX Light Rail

26

W. Burnside St

Washington Park

MAX Light Rail

405

SE 60th Ave

Mt Tabor Park

205

Powell Blvd

26

Beaverton

10

Reed College

0   2 miles

0   2 kilometers

217

5

Oaks Bottom Wildlife Sanctuary

213

99E

43

Milwaukie

Tigard

Tryon Creek State Natural Area

224

99W

Boones Ferry Rd

Lake Oswego

Lake Oswego

224

Clackamas River

Tualatin

Tualatin River

Willamette River

Mary S Young State Park

N

205

213

5

Stafford Rd

99E

Oregon City

Three-day Weekend

Portland

Day 1
- Spend the day downtown. Start with a walking tour, admiring (or at least chuckling at) Portland's quirky architecture and statuary such as the **Portland Building** (page 319) and *Portlandia* (page 319), as well as the **Ira Keller Memorial Fountain** (page 319).

- Try **Alexis** (page 325) or **Jake's Famous Crawfish** (page 325) for lunch. Eat well before or after the noon hour, when both landmark restaurants are packed.

- Don't miss **Powell's City of Books** (page 326), the world's largest bookstore.

- If it's not raining, continue your walking tour through the **Yamhill** (page 320) and **Skidmore/Old Town** (page 320) historic districts and **Chinatown** (page 322). If it *is* raining, get your intercultural experience at the **Portland Art Museum** (page 318).

- The place for dinner is **Harborside Restaurant** (page 325), with its wildly eclectic menu and great waterfront view.

Day 2
- Stroll or drive through the Nob Hill district to **Washington Park** (page 336), where it's easy to while away the whole day. Begin by surrounding yourself with beauty at the **International Rose Test Garden** and the **Japanese Garden Society**.

- You may (or may not) wish to learn about Oregon's logging heritage at the **World Forest Discovery Museum** (page 338). Or, rejecting the notion that the only good tree is a dead tree, stroll through **Hoyt Arboretum** (page 338) for proof that absolutely everything grows tall in Portland's misty climate.

- Give equal time to the animal kingdom at the **Oregon Zoo** (page 337), with its wonderful open-space African habitats.

- For dinner, check out **Bluehour** (page 340), where Northwest cuisine gets a Mediterranean kick.

- Later on, one nightlife option is to go to the movies at the historic **McMenamins Mission Theater** (page 344), where you can watch from a comfy sofa while sipping your favorite libation.

Day 3   • Today's the day to take in two great sightseeing experiences just past the city's outskirts. Head east on Route 84 to Troutdale and turn off to drive the **Historic Columbia River Highway** (page 348). Take your time—you can easily visit every scenic stop and wish there were more. (Actually, there is, but you have to hike to the upper rim to see it.)

• Finish your visit with lunch at **Multnomah Falls Lodge** (page 356).

• Driving back toward Portland via Route 84, veer south on Route 205 to **Oregon City** (pages 342-43). Starting at the **End of the Oregon Trail Interpretive Center and Historic Site**, tour the 19th-century museum houses of the historic district.

• Take a sunset ride on the **Oregon City Municipal Elevator.**

• Heading back to downtown Portland, put the crowning touch on your visit with an elegant dinner at **Typhoon! on Broadway** (page 324), arguably the city's best Thai restaurant.

SIGHTS   A good place to orient yourself is the **Portland Oregon Informa-tion Center**. Here you can pick up helpful maps and brochures. Closed Sunday. ~ Pioneer Courthouse Square, 701 Southwest 6th Avenue; 503-275-8355, 877-678-5263; www.travelportland.com.

Pioneer Courthouse Square is a popular gathering point. A waterfall and more than 71,000 red bricks inscribed with the names of local residents who donated money for the square's con-struction are all here. Named for adjacent **Pioneer Courthouse**, the oldest public building in Oregon (completed in 1873), which you may want to explore, the square offers a variety of special events including concerts and, at Christmastime, a ceremonial Christmas-tree lighting. The **Visitor Information Center** is a great place to pick up maps and brochures for a walking tour of the area. ~ 701 Southwest 6th Avenue; 503-223-1613, fax 503-222-7425; www.pioneercourthousesquare.org, e-mail liz@pioneer courthousesquare.org.

Head west on Yamhill Street for one block then south on Park Avenue to the **Oregon Historical Society**, the place to learn the story of the region's American Indians, the arrival of the Euro-peans and the westward migration. Permanent exhibits include a maritime gallery, a Northwest art gallery and a comprehensive Oregon history exhibit. You'll also find a museum store and re-search library. Closed Sunday. Admission. ~ 1200 Southwest Park Avenue; 503-222-1741, fax 503-221-2035; www.ohs.org, e-mail orhist@ohs.org.

Adjacent to the Oregon Historical Society is the **First Congre-gational Church**, dating from 1895. This Venetian gothic–style basalt structure, modeled on Boston's Old South Church and crowned by a 175-foot tower, is at its best in the fall. Elms shade the street in front of the church, making this one of the prettiest cor-ners in Portland. ~ 1126 Southwest Park Avenue; 503-228-7219, fax 503-228-6522.

Directly across the street is the **Portland Art Museum**, known for its collection of Asian and European art as well as 20th-cen-

AUTHOR FAVORITE

The open-air **Portland Saturday Market**, held on weekends from March to Christmas Eve, offers a wonderful slice of local life. Ankeny Park and the district beneath the Burnside Bridge is a great place to shop for arts and crafts, sample savory specialties served up by vendors and enjoy performances by musicians, street performers and clowns. A per-manent store showcases arts and crafts during the week. ~ 108 West Burnside Street; 503-222-6072, fax 503-222-0254; www.saturdaymarket. org, e-mail info@saturdaymarket.org.

tury American sculpture. The vast collection of American Indian art and artifacts showcases excellent tribal masks and wood sculptures. The pre-Columbian pieces, box drums, potlatch dishes and cones are all notable. Don't miss the skylit sculpture courtyard. The Silver gallery has more than 100 rare objects on display. Closed Monday. ~ 1219 Southwest Park Avenue; 503-226-2811, fax 503-226-4842; www.portlandartmuseum.org, e-mail info@pam.org.

Head east to 11th Avenue and then turn south to **The Old Church**. Built in 1883, this gothic classic is one of the city's oldest and best-loved buildings. Noon concerts are held Wednesday. Closed weekends. ~ 1422 Southwest 11th Avenue; 503-222-2031, fax 503-222-2981; www.oldchurch.org, e-mail staff@old church.org.

Head east on Columbia Street to Southwest 5th Avenue. Take 5th Avenue north to the **Portland Building**, a postmodern office landmark opened in 1982. Above the entrance is *Portlandia*, the world's second-largest hammered-bronze sculpture. Designed by Michael Graves, this whimsical skyscraper represents the Northwest with an American Indian motif, making extensive use of turquoise and earth tones. ~ 1120 Southwest 5th Avenue; 503-823-4000, fax 503-823-3050.

On the Portland Building's second floor is the **Metropolitan Center for Public Art**. Here you'll find a portion of the *Portlandia* mold and renderings of the building, as well as pieces from the *Visual Chronicle of Portland*, a continually evolving series of works on paper meant to represent how the city views itself. The center is unstaffed—it's more an exhibition space than a museum—but it has assembled a walking-tour book that is available at the information desk on the first floor of the Portland Building. Open during regular business hours (when the building is open). ~ 1120 Southwest 5th Avenue; 503-823-5111, fax 503-823-5432; www.racc.org, e-mail info@racc.org.

Walk east on Main Street to Justice Center and learn about the history of local law enforcement at the **Portland Police Historical Museum**. Closed Saturday through Monday. ~ Room 1682, 1111 Southwest 2nd Avenue; 503-823-0019; www.port landpolicemuseum.com.

When you're ready to take a break, head south to the **Ira Keller Memorial Fountain**, located across from the Civic Auditorium. Situated in a pretty little park, this is a lovely spot to rest your weary feet. ~ Clay Street between 3rd and 4th avenues.

Farther south, past the Hawthorne Bridge on Harbor Way, you'll come to the sloped-roof buildings of **RiverPlace**, a popular shopping, hotel, restaurant and nightclub complex on the water. A promenade overlooks the Willamette River and the marina's many plush yachts.

Then return north to **Salmon Springs Fountain**, a synchronized fountain that is a favorite meeting place. Kids and dogs love to play in its cool water on hot days. ~ Salmon Street at Front Avenue.

A block away is **Mill Ends Park**, located in the median at Southwest Front Avenue and Taylor Street. Just two feet wide, this is the smallest official city park in the world, according to the *Guinness Book of World Records*.

Proceed northward to **Tom McCall Waterfront Park**, which is notable for being the green river frontage that in the 1970s replaced a busy, ugly stretch of freeway blocking the Willamette. You'll get a great view of Portland's skyline here. ~ Front Avenue.

Bounded by the Willamette River, Southwest 2nd Avenue, and Morrison and Taylor streets is the **Yamhill Historic District**. This area, on the National Register of Historic Places, boasts 19th-century cast-iron architecture favoring the Italianate style.

Walk west on Yamhill to the shops and cafés of **Yamhill Marketplace**. ~ 110 Southwest Yamhill Street; 503-224-3450, fax 503-224-3450.

Then stroll back to the waterfront and walk north on Front to the **Oregon Maritime Museum**. Here's your chance to learn Northwestern maritime history and see models of early ships, historical photographs and interpretive displays, all aboard the steam sternwheeler *Portland*. Closed Monday and Tuesday. Admission. ~ River Wall, between Morrison and Burnside bridges at the foot of Pine Street; 503-224-7724, fax 503-224-7767; www.oregonmaritimemuseum.org, e-mail info@oregonmaritime museum.org.

To fully experience the Portland waterfront consider boarding an excursion boat. **Sternwheeler Rose** departs from the Oregon Museum of Science and Industry and offers scenic Willamette River cruises. ~ 503-286-7673, fax 503-286-9661; www.stern wheelerrose.com, e-mail staff@sternwheelerrose.com. Another possibility is Portland's cruise ship **Portland Spirit**, which has year-round lunch, brunch, and Saturday-night dinner cruises. The *Portland Spirit* leaves from Salmon Street Springs Fountain in Tom McCall Waterfront Park. ~ 503-224-3900, 800-224-3901, fax 503-231-9089; www.portlandspirit.com.

The **Skidmore/Old Town** area illustrates Portland's commitment to adaptive reuse. This area between Front and 3rd streets both north and south of Burnside Street boomed in the later 19th century when the harbor was bustling. The look of the buildings from that era derives from Florentine civic palaces: broad, strong, imposing facades constructed of brick and cast iron. Eventually this became the rowdy part of town where sailors caroused, and polite society began to keep away as the buildings fell into disrepair. But interest has grown in the waterfront over the past 30

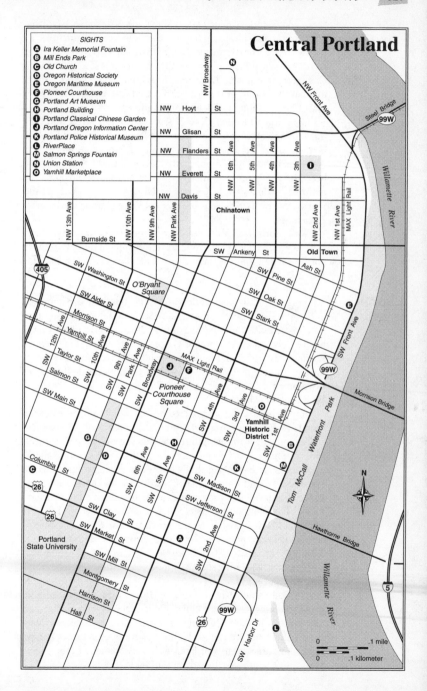

Central Portland

SIGHTS
- Ⓐ Ira Keller Memorial Fountain
- Ⓑ Mill Ends Park
- Ⓒ Old Church
- Ⓓ Oregon Historical Society
- Ⓔ Oregon Maritime Museum
- Ⓕ Pioneer Courthouse
- Ⓖ Portland Art Museum
- Ⓗ Portland Building
- Ⓘ Portland Classical Chinese Garden
- Ⓙ Portland Oregon Information Center
- Ⓚ Portland Police Historical Museum
- Ⓛ RiverPlace
- Ⓜ Salmon Springs Fountain
- Ⓝ Union Station
- Ⓞ Yamhill Marketplace

years, and historic commercial buildings and warehouses have been reborn as trendy shops, galleries, restaurants and nightclubs.

Next, head north through **Chinatown** on 4th Avenue. Not as large as it was at the turn of the 20th century, it is still packed with Chinese restaurants and markets. The ornate entry gate to Chinatown at the corner of Burnside Street and 4th Avenue looks a bit out of place among the neighboring adult bookstores.

Continue north on 4th to Northwest Everett Street and turn right. In one block you'll arrive at the **Portland Classical Chinese Garden**, a walled oasis of plants, ponds, stone sculptures and pavilions linked by winding pathways. The traditional teahouse here provides a serene setting for a light snack after strolling the premises. Admission. ~ Corner of Northwest 3rd Avenue and Northwest Everett Street; 503-228-8131; www.portlandchinese garden.org.

Walk north on Northwest 3rd Avenue; at Glisan Street head west to 6th Avenue. Then walk north to **Union Station**, Portland's marble-walled Amtrak Station. ~ 800 Northwest 6th Avenue; 503-273-4866.

LODGING   Lodgings in tightly packed downtown Portland are concentrated in large, historic hotels similar to those you'll find in cosmopolitan eastern cities like New York or Boston. As a result of the hustle for space, the majority of quality hotels in Central Portland are priced in the deluxe or ultra-deluxe range. If you're looking to save money, you may want to stay outside the downtown area (see "Lodging" in the "Portland East" and "Portland West" sections below).

A grand hotel and a registered historic landmark, **The Benson Hotel** offers casual fireside elegance in the lobby and 287 comfortably large guest rooms with understated gray decor, oak furniture, armoires and Early American prints. Like a good English club, the walnut-paneled lobby court contains easy chairs, comfortable sofas and a mirrored bar. Marbled halls, chandeliers, brass fixtures, a grand staircase and grandfather clock add an elegant touch. The stamped-tin ceiling, a common architectural feature in the late 19th and early 20th centuries, is one of the finest we've seen. Amenities include a health club and two restaurants. ~ 309 Southwest Broadway; 503-228-2000, 888-523-6766, fax 503-471-3920; www.bensonhotel.com, e-mail reservations@bensonhotel. com. ULTRA-DELUXE.

A good value is the 127-room **Hotel Lucia**, conveniently located to shops, cafés and clubs. Contemporary in feel, the cozy guest rooms have mostly king- or queen-sized beds covered with down comforters and plush bathrooms for guests' use. A lounge, restaurant, fitness center and business center round out the amenities. ~ 400 Southwest Broadway; 503-225-1717, 877-225-1717,

fax 503-205-2051; www.hotellucia.com, e-mail info@hotel
lucia.com. DELUXE.

Boutique hotels are one of the fastest-growing trends in the
lodging industry and Portland has one of its own, **Hotel Vintage
Plaza**. A remake of the historic Wells Building, this hotel features
a ten-story atrium. Each of the 107 guest rooms and expansive
suites is named for a local winery. Rooms with burgundy and
green color schemes come with cherry-wood armoires, neoclassical furniture, columned headboards, black-granite nightstands
and Empire-style column bedside lamps. On the top floor are
some "Starlight" rooms, with light-sand beach motifs and one-
way solarium windows for stargazers. Local fine wines can be
sampled at the complimentary tasting held each evening in front
of the fireplace in the lobby. ~ 422 Southwest Broadway; 503-
228-1212, 800-263-2305, fax 503-228-3598; www.vintageplaza.
com, e-mail reservations@vintageplaza.com. ULTRA-DELUXE.

An excellent value, **Four Points by Sheraton Downtown** is the
place to enjoy views of boat traffic on the Willamette. The rooms
have a contemporary feel, with oak furniture and earth-toned
decor. Enjoy the sunset from the comfort of your deck. The
140-room inn is within walking distance of Portland's business
and shopping district. A fitness center, café and bar are also here.
~ 50 Southwest Morrison Street; 503-221-0711, fax 503-484-
1417; e-mail fourpoints.fppdx@fourpoints.com. MODERATE.

Enjoying one of the best locations in town, **RiverPlace Hotel**
offers 84 rooms, suites and condos, many with views of the Willamette. In the midst of the Esplanade area featuring bookstores,
antique shops and restaurants, this establishment is a short walk
from the downtown business district. Wing-back chairs, teak tables, writing desks, fireplaces and pastel decor make the rooms

AUTHOR FAVORITE

When the inevitable Portland rain begins to fall, I like to sneak off to the library
at **The Heathman Hotel**, where many of the books are signed by authors
who've stayed here. Later I'll mosey down to the lounge for an evening of soft
jazz or have dinner in the lively restaurant. These are just the everyday delights offered by this landmark hotel. How far does The Heathman go to
make its guests happy? When Luciano Pavarotti wanted to sleep in after a
late arrival, the hotel manager asked a contractor across the street to
postpone the start of noisy construction from 7 to 10 a.m. They agreed
and the tenor slept soundly. ~ 1001 Southwest Broadway at Salmon
Street; 503-241-4100, 800-551-0011, fax 503-790-7111; www.heath
manhotel.com, e-mail info@heathmanhotel.com. ULTRA-DELUXE.

inviting. A sauna, whirlpool, 24-hour room service and a business center are all available. ~ 1510 Southwest Harbor Way; 503-228-3233, 800-227-1333, fax 503-295-6161; www.riverplacehotel. com, e-mail reservations@riverplacehotel.com. ULTRA-DELUXE.

For reasonably priced rooms and suites head for the **Hotel Deluxe**. This recently renovated 130-unit establishment built in 1912 has a mirrored lobby, leaded skylights and a chandelier. The eclectic rooms here come with down bedding, oak furniture, contemporary couches and flat-screen TVs. There is also a classy dining room with marble pillars supporting the embossed gold-leaf ceiling. ~ 729 Southwest 15th Avenue; 503-219-2094, 866-895-2094; www.hoteldeluxeportland.com, e-mail sales@hotelde luxeportland.com. MODERATE TO DELUXE.

DINING

Thai native Bo Kline re-invents the complex flavors of her home country at **Typhoon! on Broadway**, a downtown restaurant crowded with satisfied diners. Artfully presented dishes include superwild shrimp in hot chili garlic sauce, pineapple fried rice and stir-fry ginger beef. If you have room for dessert, there's homemade coconut ice cream or espresso crème brûlée. ~ Hotel Lucia, 410 Southwest Broadway; 503-224-8285, fax 503-224-3468; www.typhoonrestaurants.com. MODERATE.

The interior of **Saucebox** is mesmerizing, with glowing lanterns, a gleaming bar and two huge original paintings. The food is equally stunning, a pan-Asian and regional Hawaiian menu featuring Javanese salmon, Korean-style baby back ribs and seared ahi. The bar is known for its expansive repertoire of fabulous drinks—try a coconut-lime Rickey, a ginger cosmopolitan or wild ginseng martini. Dinner only. Closed Sunday and Monday. ~ 214 Southwest Broadway; 503-241-3393, fax 503-243-3251; www. saucebox.com, e-mail info@saucebox.com. MODERATE.

A favorite in Portland is **The Heathman Restaurant**. The menu, which changes seasonally, transforms traditional French

AUTHOR FAVORITE

With fresh flowers and big red chairs, **Wilf's Restaurant and Bar** is one of the most elaborate dining rooms in Portland. In this elegant setting along the tracks you can enjoy a menu emphasizing organic and sustainably produced ingredients in dishes like Northwest salmon filet with an apricot glaze, veal lafayette or rack of lamb. Since they specialize in tableside cooking, entrées such as steak Diane and prawns flambé, and desserts like bananas Foster or crêpes Suzette are works of performance and culinary art. No lunch on Saturday. Closed Sunday. ~ 800 Northwest 6th Avenue; 503-223-0070, fax 503-223-1386; www.wilf restaurant.com. DELUXE.

dishes with Northwest ingredients, seafood and game meats. Some specialties include grilled lightly smoked salmon, seared ahi tuna wrapped in prosciutto, and roast rack of lamb. This spacious dining room and adjacent brass and marble bar is a great place to watch the passing scene on Broadway. The walls are graced with a classy collection of contemporary art. The Heathman also has an extensive breakfast menu. ~ 1001 Southwest Broadway at Salmon Street; 503-790-7752, fax 503-790-7112; www.heathmanhotel. com, e-mail info@heathmanhotel.com. MODERATE TO DELUXE.

The brick pizza oven, trattoria ambience, dark-wood booths and gleaming bar make **Pazzo Ristorante** a valuable member of the Portland restaurant scene. Dip a little of the fresh-baked bread in the special-press extra virgin olive oil, hoist a glass of the red and survey the Northern Italian menu. Wood oven–baked pizza, housemade pastas, line-caught fish, and organic, free-range Piedmontese beef are some of the popular entrées. ~ 627 Southwest Washington Street; 503-228-1515, fax 503-228-5935; www. pazzoristorante.com, e-mail pazzoristorante@pazzo.com. MODERATE TO DELUXE.

Pass the retsina and toast **Alexis Restaurant**. This family-style taverna brings the Aegean to the Columbia in the time-honored manner. Belly dancing on the weekend, wallhangings and long tables upstairs with checkered blue-and-white tablecloths add to the ambience. Lamb souvlaki, moussaka, charbroiled shrimp and vegetarian specialties are all on the menu. Be sure to try the dolmas and share an order of hummus and homemade pita. No lunch on Saturday. Closed Sunday. ~ 215 West Burnside Street; 503-224-8577, fax 503-224-9354; www.alexisfoods.com, e-mail restaurant@alexisfoods.com. MODERATE.

A memorable dining room is **Jake's Famous Crawfish**. This mahogany-paneled, late-19th-century landmark has a grand bar, big tables and a seafood menu that seems to stretch from here to Seattle. Inevitably packed, the restaurant offers tasty chowder, smoked and fresh salmon, halibut, oysters and a good bouillabaisse. For the non-seafood lover, they also offer pasta and steak dishes. ~ 401 Southwest 12th Avenue; 503-226-1419, 888-344-6861, fax 503-220-1856. MODERATE TO DELUXE.

With a vast menu of Northwest cuisine, the **Harborside Restaurant** is a kind of culinary United Nations. Window tables on the river and paneled booths on the upper levels provide great views of the harbor traffic. Excellent seafood salads, pasta dishes, stir frys, steaks, hamburgers and pizza are served. ~ 0309 Southwest Montgomery Street; 503-220-1865, 888-344-6861, fax 503-220-1855. MODERATE TO DELUXE.

The setting alone justifies a trip to **Old Town Pizza**. A landmark commercial building with stained glass, wicker furniture, enough antiques to furnish a store and old root beer advertising signs make this two-level establishment a genuine period piece. Over two dozen toppings from feta cheese to roasted garlic give you plenty of options. Focaccia, antipasti, lasagna and salads are also available. ~ 226 Northwest Davis Street; 503-222-9999; www.oldtownpizza.com, e-mail adam@oldtownpizza.com. BUDGET.

Obi is the place for sushi, *yaki soba*, shrimp tempura, salmon teriyaki and dozens of other Japanese specialties. The dark dining room has modest plastic tables and displays silk-screen art, watercolors and traditional costumes. No lunch Saturday. Closed Sunday. ~ 101 Northwest 2nd Avenue; 503-226-3826. MODERATE.

SHOPPING   The **Oregon Historical Society Museum Store** has an outstanding collection of local and regional history titles. From American Indian culture to walking tours of Portland, this admirable shop is definitely worth a look. Souvenir books, guides, children's literature, and historical toys as well as regional gifts are all found in abundance. ~ Corner of Southwest Broadway and Madison; 503-306-5230, fax 503-221-2035; www.ohs.org, e-mail museumstore@ohs.org.

Classic newsstands are rare these days. Fortunately, **Rich's Cigar Store**, dating to the late 1800s, continues this grand tradition. Browse for your favorite magazine or out-of-town newspaper in this beautiful wood-paneled shop. ~ 820 Southwest Alder Street; 503-228-1700, 800-669-1527; www.richscigar.com.

Whether you're on the lookout for hard-to-find vintage vinyl or the newest indie releases, look no farther than **2nd Avenue Records**. Punk music is well-represented here, as is metal, hip hop, electronica, ska, reggae and rock. The sheer volume of merchandise can be daunting, but the knowledgeable sales staff can

AUTHOR FAVORITE

Bigger than many libraries, **Powell's City of Books** is only one of Portland's many fine bookstores. What makes it unique is its size—it would be hard to dispute its claim of being the world's largest bookstore. With over a million new and used titles, this Goliath encourages customers to pick up a large map, indexed into hundreds of categories ranging from abortion to Zen. Somewhere in between you're likely to find the title you want. Powell's also hosts guest readings by well-known authors. Along the way, stop by the Coffee Room for a snack and a leisurely read. ~ 1005 West Burnside Street; 503-228-4651, 800-878-7323, fax 503-228-4631; www.powells.com. Powell's also has five other locations in the Portland area.

point you in the right direction. There's also a wide selection of T-shirts, buttons, patches and stickers. ~ 400 Southwest 2nd Avenue; 503-222-3783.

The **Attic Gallery** features paintings, sculpture, prints and ceramics by major Northwest artists. Closed Sunday. ~ 206 Southwest 1st Avenue; 503-228-7830; www.atticgallery.com.

Several major malls are in the downtown area. **Pioneer Place** boasts 80 stores spread across a three-block area. ~ 700 Southwest 5th Avenue; 503-228-5800; www.pioneerplace.com.

One of the region's best-known apparel makers offers its line at **The Portland Pendleton Shop**. Skirts, shirts, slacks, jackets and blankets are sold at this popular store. While its reputation was built on woolens, it also sells high-quality apparel in silk, rayon and other fabrics. ~ 905 Southwest 4th Avenue; 503-242-0037, 800-760-4844; www.pendleton-usa.com.

Elizabeth Leach Gallery presents an array of regional and national painters, sculptors, photographers and print makers. Closed Sunday and Monday. ~ 417 Northwest 9th Avenue; 503-224-0521; www.elizabethleach.com.

Nearly 300 artisans display handcrafted glass, jewelry, hats, clothing, furniture, rugs, music boxes and folk and fine art at the **Portland Saturday Market**. There's also live entertainment and food. Open Saturday and Sunday during the holiday season, open Tuesday through Thursday from mid-July to mid-August. Closed January and February. ~ Between Front and 1st streets underneath the Burnside Bridge; 503-222-6072, fax 503-222-0254; www.port landsaturdaymarket.com, e-mail info@saturdaymarket.org.

The city's cultural hub is the **Portland Center for the Performing Arts**. Included are the Arlene Schnitzer Concert Hall and the Newmark and Winningstad theaters. The center (which houses the world's largest electronic organ) is home to the **Oregon Symphony Orchestra** (503-228-1353, 800-228-7343; www.orsym phony.org), the **Keller Auditorium** and **Portland Center Stage** (128 Northwest 11th Avenue; 503-445-3700; www.pcs.org). ~ 1111 Southwest Broadway; 503-248-4335; www.pcpa.com.

NIGHTLIFE

Artists Repertory Theater is the place for off-Broadway productions with a focus on current contemporary playwrights and modern-day issues. ~ 1516 Southwest Alder Street; 503-241-1278 (box office); www.artistsrep.org.

Both the **Oregon Ballet Theatre** (503-222-7738; www.obt.org) and **Portland Opera** (503-241-1802; www.portlandopera.org) perform at the Keller Auditorium, located at 222 Southwest Clay Street.

At **The Heathman Lobby Lounge**, musicians like Johnny Martin play jazz on the Steinway. ~ 1001 Southwest Broadway at

Salmon Street; 503-241-4100, 800-551-0011; www.heathman hotel.com.

Enjoy a cocktail to the strains of live pop and jazz piano at **The Benson Hotel's Lobby Court Lounge**. This elegant setting includes plush sofas and wing chairs and walnut paneling. The lounge is a great place to impress your friends—or yourself. Live music Tuesday through Saturday nights. ~ 309 Southwest Broadway; 503-228-2000.

The **Portland Art Museum—After Hours** is the perfect way to spend a spring or fall Wednesday evening. Take a seat or explore the collection while the halls resonate to jazz or blues. Beer, wine and hors d'oeuvres are served. Admission. ~ 1219 Southwest Park Avenue; 503-226-2811.

With male strippers six nights a week, neon bar signs and a swinging dancefloor, **Silverado** has plenty of action. In addition, you'll encounter deejay music, a long bar and dining room. Cover Friday and Saturday. ~ 1217 Southwest Stark Street; 503-224-4493; www.silveradopdx.com.

The **Pilsner Room** is an upscale bar attached to a microbrewery, serving fish-and-chips, hamburgers and the like. ~ 0309 Southwest Montgomery Street; 503-220-1865.

Billiards, darts and beer on tap create a relaxed atmosphere at **Scandal's Restaurant and Lounge**, which has a loyal gay following. ~ 1038 Southwest Stark Street; 503-227-5887; www.scandalspdx.com.

Female impersonators perform Wednesday through Saturday nights at **Darcelle XV**, a small theater where dinner is available by reservation. Closed Sunday and Monday. Cover. ~ 208 Northwest 3rd Avenue; 503-222-5338; www.darcellexv.com.

Embers on the Avenue features drag shows Wednesday through Saturday. The rear of this brick building houses Portland's largest dancefloor, hosting a mixed crowd of gay and straight partygoers. With neon-lit walls, two bars and deejay music, this room is always jumping. Cover Friday and Saturday. ~ 110 Northwest Broadway; 503-222-3082; www.emberspdx.net.

Regarded as one of the top places in the world for jazz music, **Jimmy Mak's Bar & Grill** features soulful live acts almost every night. Intimate and often crowded, you can ensure a comfortable seat by arriving early for dinner. A basement lounge with two pool tables and a full bar provides a casual alternative to the main stage. Closed Sunday. ~ 221 Northwest 10th Avenue; 503-295-6542; www.jimmymaks.com.

▼▼▼▼▼▼▼▼▼▼
Portland East
Just across the Willamette from the frenzied downtown core are some of Portland's most inviting neighborhoods. The city planners have emphasized good public transportation throughout the entire metropolitan area, keeping the neigh-

borhoods east of the river unified with the downtown core. But only here can you glimpse Portland's lower-key charms: a shopping area devoted exclusively to antiques, a city park featuring an extinct volcano and a religious retreat doubling as a peaceful garden. Portland East is also home to a rare heirloom—a classic old-time amusement park.

This section of Portland also includes such suburbs as Oregon City and Milwaukie, the former of which once welcomed settlers who had made the arduous trek overland on the Oregon Trail. Today, Portland East is a network of streets and parks designed, like much of Portland, for maximum use by its residents.

Cross the Willamette via MAX Light Rail and disembark at the beautiful **Oregon Convention Center** plaza, landscaped with terraced planters. Stroll over for a look at the 18-acre campus of the center crowned by a matching pair of glass-and-steel spires soaring 250 feet above the hall. The center's interior contains art, dragon boats, a bronze pendulum and inspirational quotes about the state. Everywhere you go, even in the restrooms, you'll find talented artists and craftspeople have left their decorative touch. ~ 777 Northeast Martin Luther King Jr. Boulevard; 503-235-7575, 800-791-2250, fax 503-235-7417; www.oregoncc.org.

SIGHTS

A mile south of the convention center, the **Oregon Museum of Science and Industry** (OMSI) is a 220,000-square-foot science education center. Four exhibition halls offer displays on the physical, earth, life and information sciences, while another has traveling exhibits. In addition, you'll find an OMNIMAX theater and the Harry C. Kendall Planetarium presenting astronomy and laser

AUTHOR FAVORITE

sights No visit to the city's east side is complete without a stop at **The Grotto**. Near the Portland airport, this 62-acre Catholic sanctuary and garden is a peaceful refuge that seems to have as much in common with a Zen retreat as it does with the Vatican. Beautiful ponds and shrines, paths leading through flower gardens and expansive views of the mountains and the Columbia River make The Grotto a local favorite. In December, the grounds are illuminated by 200,000 lights during the Festival of Lights. Choral performances, a petting zoo and refreshments round out the experience. Admission for festival. ~ 8840 Northeast Skidmore Street (parking at Northeast 85th Avenue and Sandy Boulevard); 503-254-7371, fax 503-254-7948; www.thegrotto.org, e-mail gifts@thegrotto.org.

light shows (additional admission). Special exhibits focus on biotechnology, computers, engineering for kids, communications and chemistry. Closed Monday (unless it's a Portland public schools holiday). Admission. ~ 1945 Southeast Water Avenue; 503-797-6674, 800-955-6674; www.omsi.edu.

To the south are two popular Portland shopping districts. **Hawthorne Boulevard** from 30th to 40th avenues has become one of the city's more intriguing commercial districts. A great place to browse, shop and eat, this district is known for its used bookstores and offbeat boutiques. Another popular neighborhood is **Sellwood,** an antique center extending along 13th Avenue from Clatsop to Malden streets.

While cities across the land have scrapped these period pieces, Portland has held on to the **Oaks Amusement Park,** located just west of the Sellwood district. In addition to vintage thrill rides, you can enjoy roller skating to the strains of the last Wurlitzer organ playing at a rink in the United States. This pretty park is next to the **Oaks Bottom Wildlife Sanctuary,** a major Portland marsh habitat. Rides are closed mid-October to mid-March. ~ Oaks Park, east end of the Sellwood Bridge; 503-233-5777, fax 503-236-9143; www.oakspark.com.

One of the nation's most progressive liberal arts institutions, **Reed College** has a wooded, 98-acre campus cloaked in ivy. Reed's gothic buildings and old dorms are close to Crystal Springs Rhododendron Garden at 28th Avenue and Woodstock Boulevard (see "Parks" below for more information). Pick up a visitors guide in Eliot Hall or the Greywood Community Service Building. ~ 3203 Southeast Woodstock Boulevard; 503-771-1112, fax 503-777-7769; www.reed.edu.

LODGING

In northeast Portland's Irvington District, **The Lion and the Rose Victorian Bed and Breakfast** is a historical Queen Anne–style mansion with six guest rooms furnished in period antiques. The decor is warm with rich shades of plum and ivy green, and natural light makes the rooms bright and airy. Amenities range from jacuzzi and clawfoot tubs to wrought-iron and four-poster beds. Enjoy tea in the outdoor gazebo and English gardens. ~ 1810 Northeast 15th Avenue; 503-287-9245, 800-955-1647, fax 503-287-9247; www.lionrose.com, e-mail innkeeper@lionrose.com. MODERATE TO DELUXE.

HIDDEN ►

Hail to the Chief! **Portland's White House** strongly resembles the other White House in Washington, D.C. The stately Greek columns, circular driveway and crystal chandeliers would all make the First Family feel right at home. The difference here is that you don't have to stand in line for a tour, and there are no Secret Service agents to hustle you along. Originally built as a lumber baron's summer home, this White House features handpainted murals of garden scenes and oak-inlaid floors. Canopy and four-poster beds, clawfoot tubs and leaded glass adorn the eight rooms. Three additional rooms in an adjacent carriage house have feather beds and stained glass. The price of a room includes a full gourmet breakfast. ~ 1914 Northeast 22nd Avenue; 503-287-7131, 800-272-7131, fax 503-249-1641; www.portlandswhitehouse.com, e-mail pdxwhi@portlandswhitehouse.com. MODERATE TO DELUXE.

The 1908 **Sullivan's Gulch Bed & Breakfast** offers four guest accommodations with themed decor ranging from Bangkok to Scotland; the two with private baths also have sitting areas. There's

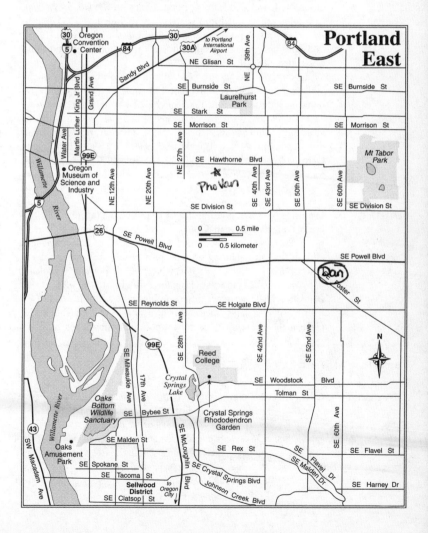

a garden with two decks and a stately dining room. A friendly resident dog helps provide furry companionship. Gay-friendly. ~ 1744 Northeast Clackamas Street; 503-331-1104, fax 815-327-1794; www.sullivansgulch.com, e-mail atlantisplace@yahoo.com. MODERATE TO DELUXE.

In the Hawthorne neighborhood, **Hostelling International— Portland Hawthorne** offers dorm accommodations for men and women, a family room and a couples room. This older home also has a self-serve kitchen and all-you-can-eat pancakes in the morning. Internet kiosks and free internet connections for laptops are available. Check-in begins at noon. Quiet time starts at 10 p.m. Complimentary bread and pastries are included. ~ 3031 Southeast Hawthorne Boulevard; 503-236-3380, 866-447-3031, fax 503-236-7940; www.portlandhostel.org, e-mail hip@portland hostel.org. BUDGET.

In Oregon City, south of Portland and on the banks of the Willamette, the **Rivershore Hotel** is pretty much the only remaining lodging option. Each of the 114 rooms has a balcony with a view and a queen- or king-size bed—clean and comfortable, but nothing to write home about. There is, however, an indoor spa and an outdoor heated pool. ~ 1900 Clackamette Drive, Oregon City; 503-655-7141, 800-443-7777, fax 503-655-1927; www.rivershorehotel.com, e-mail info@rivershore hotel.com. MODERATE.

DINING   Inventive Mexican food and an extensive cocktail menu distinguish **Dingo's Mexican Grill** from your run-of-the-mill burrito place. Entrées include lime chicken enchiladas, rock shrimp tacos and ahi burritos. Happy hour (4 p.m. to 6 p.m.) features $3-a-plate specials. Thursday is Girl's Night Out, popular with local lesbians. ~ 4612 Southeast Hawthorne Boulevard; 503-233-3996, fax 503-233-0778; www.dingosonline.com. BUDGET.

One of Portland's better breakfasts is found at **Tabor Hill Café** in the Hawthorne neighborhood. This small, red-brick es-

BRUNCH AND MORE

It's not easy to find a hearty Sunday brunch these days, but we did it at **Bread and Ink Café**. The coffee is strong, the lox is beautiful and the children are kept content with crayons and paper. In addition to bagels and cream cheese, challah and a variety of omelettes, you'll enjoy the family-style atmosphere. Set in an elegant commercial building adorned with terra cotta, this weekly happening is a Portland original. The restaurant is also famous for its burgers. Breakfast, lunch and dinner. ~ 3610 Southeast Hawthorne Boulevard; 503-239-4756. MODERATE.

######

tablishment with eclectic decor features modern art, gray carpet and red tables. The seasonal fruit pancake (that's singular, not plural) is large enough to blanket your entire plate. Other choices are chicken omelettes and a fresh fruit cup. Lunch specialties include avocado-and-bacon sandwich, burgers, marinated chicken breast and blackened-snapper salad. ~ 3766 Southeast Hawthorne Boulevard; 503-230-1231. BUDGET.

Located in the Sellwood district known for its antique stores, **Papa Haydn** is a yummy storefront café where fans twirl from the ceilings, watercolors grace the gray walls and wicker furniture accommodates guests who don't come to count calories. Weekend brunch features french toast brioche rolled in hazelnuts or an aged white cheddar omelette. Dinner entrées include wood-grilled steak with bleu cheese butter and organic chicken with bacon and bucatini pasta. An extensive wine list and espresso drinks are found here along with one of the longest dessert menus in the Pacific Northwest. ~ 5829 Southeast Milwaukie Avenue; 503-232-9440, fax 503-236-5815; www.papahaydn.com, e-mail east@papahaydn.com. MODERATE.

SHOPPING

Vestiges has two floors of funky and eclectic antique and new items, all artfully displayed. ~ 4743 Northeast Fremont Avenue; 503-331-3920.

Oregon Mountain Community is the ultimate shop for recreational equipment and supplies. In addition to a full line of outdoor wear, there's skiing, backpacking and climbing gear. ~ 2975 Northeast Sandy Boulevard; 503-227-1038, 800-538-3604; www.e-omc.com.

Along Hawthorne Boulevard are many small, independent shops with interesting selections. Stop by **Artichoke Music** for acoustic and folk instruments, guitar sheet music and lesson books. On a weekend you can catch live acoustic music or join the song circle; on the first Friday of every month check out the highly acclaimed variety revue. Closed Monday. ~ 3130 Southeast Hawthorne Boulevard; 503-232-8845, fax 503-232-3476; www.artichokemusic.com, e-mail folks@artichokemusic.com.

Death can be proud at **Murder by the Book**. Mystery addicts will get their fix here and also become acquainted with many well-known Northwest authors. In addition to new and used books, you can buy accessories, games and puzzles. ~ 3210 Southeast Hawthorne Boulevard; 503-232-9995, fax 503-232-2554; www.mbtb.com, e-mail books@mbtb.com.

NIGHTLIFE

The Moorish **Baghdad Theater and Pub** has a fairy-tale decor with painted walls and a fountain in the lobby. Every other row of theater seating has been removed to accommodate tables where patrons can order food and drinks and enjoy second-run films.

Customers under 21 years of age are welcome for the Saturday and Sunday matinees only when accompanied by a parent. ~ 3702 Southeast Hawthorne Boulevard; 503-236-9234, 503-249-7474 (movie line); www.mcmenamins.com, e-mail baghdad@mc menamins.com.

The **Echo Theater** is the home of **Do Jump! Extremely Physical Theater**. Shows include acrobatic and trapeze acts. Visiting dance troupes also use the theater's stage. ~ 1515 Southeast 37th Avenue; 503-231-1232, fax 503-231-2937; www.dojump.org, e-mail dojump@dojump.org.

One of the city's finest classical programs is **Chamber Music Northwest**. Nationally known groups perform year-round in the beautiful settings at Kaul Auditorium at Reed College, with a five-week festival in June and July. ~ 503-223-3202, fax 503-294-1690; for tickets, call 503-294-6400; www.cmnw.org, e-mail info@cmnw.org.

The 9000-square-foot **Egyptian Club**, located in a former milk plant, features three different rooms. There's a dancefloor in the Tomb and a retro bar room with pool tables and video games. A third bar, the Room, features open-mic night and karaoke. Every Monday and Wednesday nights there are poker tournaments in the Tomb. The crowd is primarily lesbian. Cover Friday and Saturday. ~ 3701 Southeast Division Street; 503-236-8689; www.eroompdx.com, e-mail egybobbi@aol.com.

For a listing of current shows and popular venues in the area, pick up a copy of *Willamette Week*, a free alternative newspaper available at groceries and newsstands. ~ www.wweek.com.

PARKS

HIDDEN ►

KELLEY POINT PARK 🏃 🛶 At the confluence of the Willamette and Columbia rivers, this forested site is popular for biking and hiking. The park, largely undeveloped, is busy during the summer months but wide open the rest of the year. There are picnic tables and restrooms. ~ Located in northernmost Portland at the intersection of Lomband Street and North Marine Drive; 503-823-7529, V/TDD 503-823-2223, fax 503-823-6007.

PENINSULA PARK 🏊 This 16-acre park features beautiful sunken rose gardens highlighted with fountains and a charming gazebo. Extensive recreational facilities, a formal rose garden and a small pond make Peninsula popular with families. Facilities include picnic tables, a basketball court, horseshoe pits, a pool, a soccer field, tennis courts and restrooms. ~ North Albina Street and Portland Boulevard; 503-823-7529, fax 503-823-6007.

POWELL BUTTE NATURE PARK 🏃 🚲 🐎 This rustic, 600-acre park centers around a 630-foot-high volcanic mound that offers great views of the city and the Cascades. If you can, circle this volcanic butte via a two-mile loop route at day's end and take advantage of the sunset. Facilities are limited to restrooms and picnic tables. ~ Northeast 162nd Avenue and Powell Boulevard; 503-823-2223, fax 503-823-6007.

LAURELHURST PARK Bordered by rhododendron, a pretty lake is the heart of this 27-acre park in a historic residential district. Along the way you're likely to spot geese, ducks, swans and turtles. Forested with fir and oak, the park also features glens, gardens and contemporary sculpture. You'll find restrooms, picnic tables, a playground, a soccer field and tennis, volleyball and basketball courts. ~ Southeast 39th Avenue and Stark Street; 503-823-2223, fax 503-823-6007.

MT. TABOR PARK 🏃 🚲 One of two extinct volcanoes within the limits of an American city, Mt. Tabor was discovered during excavations in 1912. While the cinder cone is the park's star attraction, it also offers an extensive network of trails for hiking and jogging. This forested setting affords smashing views of the city. There are picnic tables, restrooms, horseshoe pits, a playground, tennis courts, basketball courts, a volleyball court and an amphitheater. ~ Southeast Salmon Street and 60th Avenue; 503-823-2223, fax 503-823-6007.

When it comes to parks, Portland offers more than 80, covering 37,000 acres.

LEACH BOTANICAL GARDEN These 15 acres are home to over 2000 flowers and plants, including many native species. Johnson Creek meanders through the original Leach Property. You can explore the grounds of this one-time estate on your own or via a guided tour. You'll find a manor house, stone cabin and carriage house, a library, a gift shop and plant table, restrooms and self-guiding brochures. Closed Monday. ~ 6704 Southeast 122nd Avenue; 503-761-9503, fax 503-823-9504; www.leachgarden.org, e-mail info@leachgarden.org.

CRYSTAL SPRINGS RHODODENDRON GARDEN Boasting seven acres of flora and fauna, this park is at its best in April and May. The colorful panorama of more than 2000 rhododendron and azalea is enhanced by three waterfalls and two bridges spanning a creek that flows into Crystal Springs Lake. Ducks and other waterfowl are found year-round at this refuge near Reed College. Call ahead to arrange a guided tour. There are restrooms. Admission during the summer months. ~ 6015 Southeast 28th Avenue north of Woodstock Boulevard; 503-771-8386.

CLACKAMETTE PARK A haven for ducks and geese, Clackamette's 22 acres border the Willamette River in the Oregon City area. It's also a prime spot to see blue herons nesting on Goat Island. Restrooms are available. ~ Take Exit 9 from Route 205 toward Oregon City and Gladstone. Go west on Clackamette two-tenths of a mile; 503-657-8299, fax 503-656-7488.

▲ There are 38 RV hookup sites; $15 to $18 per night, ten-day maximum stay. No reservations taken.

Portland West

From vineyards to Japanese gardens, Portland's west side has many of the city's best parks, major museums and wildlife preserves. Charming Victorians line many streets and the city's fabled Pittock Mansion reminds visitors of Portland's glamorous past. Washington Park, the city's beloved green oasis, presides over Portland West in much the same way that Central Park does in New York. Most of the other worthwhile attractions here also involve the outdoors: just half an hour from downtown, you can enjoy wilderness areas or cycle along placid sloughs, in addition to other delights.

Heading south from downtown along the western side of the Willamette, you'll pass residential 'burbs like Tigard and Beaverton before encountering the vineyards that comprise Oregon's wine country. The original settlers believed the Willamette Valley to have some of the best soil in the world, and the area just beyond the city limits does maintain a rural flavor. But Portland's populace has also worked hard not to overdevelop all of its own land, and this section of the city definitely benefits as a result. Still, the area closest to downtown does maintain a cosmopolitan air.

SIGHTS

We begin our tour in one of the trendiest areas in Portland, **Nob Hill**. The district was given its name by a 19th-century San Franciscan who saw a similarity to his old neighborhood. At the **Portland Oregon Information Center** downtown (Pioneer Courthouse Square, 701 Southwest 6th Avenue; 503-275-8355), you can pick up the walking guide to this district focused around Northwest 23rd Avenue, north of Burnside Street. Home of many of the city's finest restaurants, bookstores and antique and art shops, Nob Hill also has noteworthy early-20th-century Victorian and Georgian homes, as well as churches and commercial buildings. Among them are the **Charles F. Adams House** (2363 Northwest Flanders Street) and the **Ayer-Shea House** (1809 Northwest Johnson Street).

This tree-lined district is also convenient to **Washington Park**, a 130-acre refuge created by the Olmsted brothers, from the family of landscape architects who gave the world Central Park in New York and Golden Gate Park in San Francisco. Home to several gardens and the zoo, this park is one of Portland's most worthy destinations. ~ Southwest Park Place, two blocks west of Vista Avenue; 503-823-7529, fax 503-823-6007.

Begin your visit at the **International Rose Test Garden**. Consisting of three terraces, this four-and-a-half-acre gem has over 8700 bushes, enough to make this park a true mecca for rose aficionados worldwide. In addition to the test area, visitors are welcome to see the Shakespearean Garden and Gold Medal Award Garden. ~ 400 Southwest Kingston Avenue; 503-823-3636 or 503-823-2555, fax 503-823-1667; www.rosegardenstore.org.

Directly west of the Rose Garden is the **Japanese Garden Society of Oregon**. Five traditional gardens spread across five and a half acres make this tranquil spot a great place for a quiet walk. The Flat Garden is a sea of raked sand. The Sand and Stone Garden is abstract and inspired by Zen Buddhism. The Tea Garden contains a Japanese teahouse, while the Natural Garden is filled with foliage growing in its natural state. Don't miss the Strolling Pond Garden with its Heavenly Falls, koi pools and beautiful moon bridge. There's also a pavilion overlooking Mt. Hood, Oregon's answer to Mt. Fuji. Admission. ~ 611 Southwest Kingston Avenue; 503-223-1321, fax 503-223-8303; www.japanesegarden.com.

Follow Kingston Avenue until you see signs leading to 64-acre **Oregon Zoo**. Also accessible by a steam train from the Japanese and International Rose Test gardens during the summer months, the zoo features an African rainforest as well as a savannah

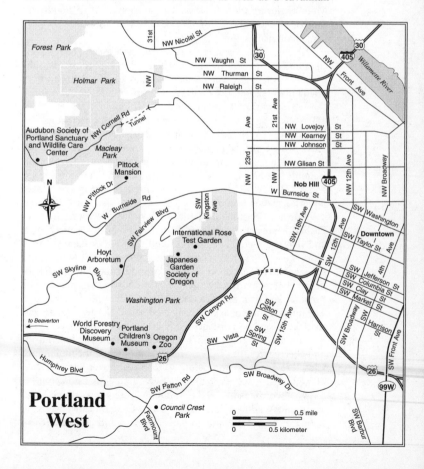

roamed by giraffes, zebras, rhinos and hippos. Stellar Cove is a marine environment with sea lions, sea otters, a kelp forest and a coastal tide pool display. Other points of interest are the zoo's Humboldt penguins, Arctic polar bears and orangutans. The staff is proud of the fact that it has one of the world's most successful Asian elephant–breeding programs. You'll also find an extensive collection of Pacific Northwest animals, including beavers and otters. Admission. ~ 4001 Southwest Canyon Road; 503-226-1561, fax 503-226-6836; www.oregonzoo.org.

> When the roses are in bloom (from late June to early September), it's hard to find a better vantage point for the city than the International Rose Test Garden.

Portland Children's Museum is a must for families with small children (infant through ten years of age). Fun-filled exhibits here include a pint-sized grocery complete with a bar-code scanner and a medical center where kids can "operate" on parents and friends. Closed Monday during the school year. Admission. ~ 4015 Southwest Canyon Road; 503-223-6500, fax 503-223-6600; www.port landchildrensmuseum.org.

Nearby is the **World Forestry Discovery Museum**. Here's your chance to learn about tree nomenclature, logging history and sub-terranean forest life. The center has a pro-logging slant but does offer a useful perspective on the state's lumber industry. Admission. ~ 4033 Southwest Canyon Road; 503-228-1367, fax 503-228-4608; www.worldforestry.org, e-mail mail@worldforestry.org.

One way to tell the trees from the forest is to visit the 185-acre **Hoyt Arboretum**. You'll have a chance to see over 1100 varieties of shrubs and trees, including one of the nation's largest collection of conifers. ~ 4000 Southwest Fairview Boulevard; 503-865-8733, fax 503-823-4213; www.hoytarboretum.org, e-mail info@hoytarboretum.org.

North of Washington Park is a favorite Oregon house tour, **Pittock Mansion**. Built by *Oregonian* publisher Henry Pittock and his wife Georgiana, this 16,000-square-foot, château-style residence features an Edwardian dining room, French Renaissance drawing room, Turkish smoking room and Jacobean library. Chandeliers, Italian marquetry, friezes on the doorways, a carved-stone fireplace and bronze grillwork make this 1914 home a treasure. The finest craftspeople of the day used native Northwest materials to make this house Portland's early-20th-century masterpiece. The 46-acre estate, landscaped with roses, azaleas, rhododendrons and cherry trees, has a great view of the city and the mountains. Closed in January. Admission. ~ 3229 Northwest Pittock Drive; 503-823-3623, fax 503-823-3619; www.pittockmansion.com.

Well worth visiting is the **Audubon Society of Portland Sanctuary and Wildlife Care Center**. The 143-acre facility helps rehabilitate over 3500 injured native animals and birds each year.

Visitors can watch the staff handle animals through an observation window and can also view up close a few of the center's permanent creatures: a red-tailed hawk, a peregrine falcon and a northern spotted owl. Naturalist guides often lead tours through the flora and fauna of the sanctuary, and miles of hiking trails here link up with Forest Park. ~ 5151 Northwest Cornell Road; 503-292-6855, fax 503-292-1021; www.audubonportland.org, e-mail general@audubonportland.org.

To experience one of the country's biggest wilderness parks fully, continue on Skyline Boulevard along the Tualatin Mountains. Overlooking the Willamette River, Forest Park extends west for eight miles. Turn right at Germantown Road and drive north through Forest Park's woodlands to Route 30. Continue west to the Sauvie Island Bridge. Cross the bridge and proceed one mile to **Howell Territorial Park**. ~ 13901 Northwest Howell Park Road; 503-797-1850; www.metro-region.org.

On the grounds of the James F. Bybee House is the **Agricultural Museum** displaying pioneer equipment, shops and hands-on exhibits. In addition you'll want to explore the **Pioneer Orchard**, containing over 120 varieties of apple trees, as well as pears and plums.

Washington County west of Portland has a number of excellent wineries. **Oak Knoll Winery,** known for pinot noirs and pinot gris, produces more than a dozen wines. This small vineyard has a white-tiled tasting room and a charming picnic area. ~ 29700 Southwest Burkhalter Road, Hillsboro; 503-648-8198, 800-625-5665, fax 503-648-3377; www.oakknollwinery.com, e-mail info@oakknollwinery.com.

Traveling south, the **Willamette Shore Trolley** offers a 105-minute, 14-mile roundtrip scenic tour along the Willamette River that takes you through two parks, stately mansions and a tunnel. Your trip aboard a vintage trolley runs along a section of the Jefferson Street Line built in the late 19th century. ~ 311 North State Street, Lake Oswego; 503-697-7436; www.trainweb.org.

The **Park Lane Suites** offers 44 contemporary rooms. Within walking distance of the popular shops and restaurants in the Nob Hill district, this five-story motel building is tucked into a residential neighborhood. Nondescript from the outside, the inn has attractive carpeted rooms with potted plants, desks, fully equipped kitchenettes and posturepedic beds. The upper-story rooms have great views of downtown Portland, Mount Hood and Mount St. Helens. ~ 809 Southwest King Avenue; 503-226-6288, 800-532-9543, fax 503-274-0038; www.parklanesuites.com, e-mail info@parklanesuites.com. MODERATE TO DELUXE.

LODGING

◄ HIDDEN

After a busy afternoon perusing Nob Hill's trendy boutiques, I doubly appreciate the quiet, secluded garden at **Heron Haus**. What's more, this beautifully renovated English Tudor provides pleasant views of the city, the Cascades, Mt. Hood and Mt. St. Helens. The blend of country casual and contemporary furniture, oak-parquet flooring, mahogany library, sun room and patio make the establishment a delight. Fireplaces, private baths and quilts add to the comfort of the six spacious rooms. Continental breakfast includes delicious pastries and fresh fruit. ~ 2545 Northwest Westover Road; 503-274-1846, fax 503-248-4055; www.heronhaus.com, e-mail julie@heronhaus.com. DELUXE TO ULTRA-DELUXE.

Just south of Portland in Beaverton, the **Shilo Inn Hotel** is a good choice for families and long-stay visitors. Each of the resort's 142 rooms features a queen- or king-sized bed, private bath and free high-speed internet access. Dad can smoke a cigar in the on-site sports bar while mom makes use of the 24-hour fitness center and junior splashes around in the seasonal outdoor pool. There's a picture-perfect gazebo and pond with geyser fountains in the courtyard. ~ 9900 Southwest Canyon Road, Beaverton; 503-297-2551, 800-222-2244, fax 503-297-7708; www.shiloinns.com, e-mail beaverton@shiloinns.com. MODERATE.

DINING

Inventive Continental/Mediterranean cuisine and a chic, postmodern setting draw a well-dressed crowd to **Bluehour**. Suspended draperies divide the converted warehouse space (with 20-foot floor-to-ceiling windows) into more intimate spaces. Savory starters may include salmon *tartare* and bacon-wrapped scallops; main dishes might feature Muscovy duck with chanterelle mushrooms or roasted suckling pig with polenta. Finish the meal off on a sweet note with chocolate truffle cake. Diners without reservations can

AUTHOR FAVORITE

For great views of the Willamette, head for **Ram Restaurant & Brewery**. The downstairs dining area, with its cherry-wood paneling, offers American fare in the form of steaks, chicken, pasta, burgers, salads and daily specials. The appetizers are especially popular. Alfresco seating is an option in the summer. Upstairs is a 21-and-over game room with pool tables, virtual-reality video games, a wall of TVs broadcasting sporting events and a dancefloor with occasional live music on Friday and Saturday nights in summer. ~ 320 Oswego Pointe Drive, Lake Oswego; 503-697-8818; www.theram.com. MODERATE TO DELUXE.

drop by the casual café/bar. Sunday brunch. ~ 250 Northwest 13th Avenue; 503-226-3394, fax 503-221-3005; www.bluehouron line.com, e-mail info@bluehouronline.com. ULTRA-DELUXE.

Wildwood Restaurant and Bar draws from local Northwest ingredients to create a distinctive Oregon flavor just as it displays regional artwork to enhance its decor. You'll find such dishes as beet, endive, pistachio and feta salad; pan-roasted confit of duck with lentils, bacon and raisins; and a risotto of walnuts and caramelized Brussels sprouts. The menu changes weekly to accommodate seasonal produce; a chalkboard details the day's specials. No lunch on Sunday. ~ 1221 Northwest 21st Street; 503-248-9663, fax 503-222-5153; www.wildwoodrestaurant.com. DELUXE.

Hurley's is an intimately elegant French restaurant furnished with oak furniture and white linen tablecloths. In the heart of Nob Hill, the restaurant presents entrées like duck with juniper-smoked sauce, ribeye bordelaise with pinot noir reduction and wild mushroom flan. There's an excellent wine list. Highly recommended. Dinner only. Closed Sunday and Monday. ~ 1987 Northwest Kearney Street; 503-295-6487; www.hurleys-restau rant.com, e-mail main@hurleys-restaurant.com. MODERATE TO DELUXE.

If sushi is what you crave, join the locals at **Mio Sushi**. You may have to huddle outside with the crowd that's arrived before you, but your tastebuds will thank you for your patience. The *maki* rolls are superb and include unique options like the Oregon roll, a succulent combo of avocado, fresh crab, asparagus and salmon. Non-fishy fare such as noodles and teriyaki is also available. Closed Sunday. ~ 2271 Northwest Johnson Street; 503-221-1469, fax 503-827-4932; www.miosushi.com, e-mail contact@ miosushi.com. BUDGET TO MODERATE.

Pulliam Deffenbaugh Gallery specializes in contemporary Northwest art but includes work from other regions. Closed Sunday and Monday. ~ 929 Northwest Flanders Street; 503-228-6665; www.pulliamdeffenbaugh.com.

SHOPPING

Another excellent place to look for fine local art is the **Laura Russo Gallery**. Paintings, original prints, drawings, watercolors and sculptures in a variety of media are all shown here. Closed Sunday and Monday. ~ 805 Northwest 21st Avenue; 503-226-2754; www.laurarusso.com.

We were impressed by the breadth of the offerings at **Contemporary Crafts Museum & Gallery**, a nonprofit organization showcasing everything from ceramic pins and medallions to metal sculpture. Highlighting crafts of the five disciplines (clay, glass, wood, fiber and metal), this eclectic gallery is a great place to shop

Text continued on page 344.

Oregon City—
The Trail's End

Wagons, ho! So you missed out on the 19th-century move west?
(Well, at least we weren't around then.) To get a sense of what it
must have been like, head to Oregon City. Just a half-hour south of
Portland, this community built along the 40-foot-high Willamette River
waterfalls is one of the best places in the Pacific Northwest to understand and appreciate manifest destiny. For this was the destination that
launched the migration of over 300,000 Americans to a blank slate
known as the promised land.

The center of human endeavor for more than 10,000 years, the
Willamette Falls was an important place long before the first white
immigrants arrived. But once they did show up, things moved quickly.
In 1818, just five years after the British took control of the Northwest
region from the Astorians, the Americans and British agreed to jointly
occupy Oregon Country. In 1829, Dr. John McLoughlin, the shrewd
operator of the Hudson's Bay Company base at Fort Vancouver, built
three homes at the Willamette Falls. Although the American Indians
responded by burning these buildings, McLoughlin forged ahead with
a new sawmill and flour mill.

American settlers began trickling in, and by 1841 the first wagon trains
started to arrive. Pouring in by boat and by land, the pioneers soon
spread across the Willamette Valley in search of farmsteads. Thankfully,
you don't have to retrace the entire trail to learn of this riveting history.
Just head to Oregon City's museums, homes, farms and cemeteries.

The place to begin your visit is the **End of the Oregon Trail Interpretive Center and Historic Site**. The center offers guided shows
featuring living history presentations, a multimedia presentation, a hands-
on area and exhibits displaying notable artifacts, photographs and maps.
You'll gain a well-rounded perspective on immigrant history. You can also
pick up helpful walking and driving tour guides to the community.
Admission. ~ 1726 Washington Street; 503-657-9336, fax 503-557-8590;
www.endoftheoregontrail.org.

Among the major Oregon City highlights are the **McLoughlin House**,
where the Hudson's Bay Company leader and "Father of Oregon" retired.

Although his employer was British, John McLoughlin generously aided the new settlers and helped lay the groundwork for Americanization. Regular 45-minute tours show off this 1846 home, which was a social hub in pioneer days. Highlights include a Chilkat Indian ceremonial robe, banjo-shaped clock, Hudson's Bay Company sideboard and lots of original McLoughlin family and Fort Vancouver furnishings. The home is closed on Monday and Tuesday and during the month of January. Incidentally, you can learn the rest of the McLoughlin story by visiting Fort Vancouver across the Columbia River from Portland. ~ 713 Center Street; 503-656-5146.

Step into the **Frances Ermatinger House**, a Federal-style residence showcasing antiques and memorabilia for another peak into this area's past. Admission. ~ 6th and John Adams streets. The **Stevens-Crawford Heritage House**, a historically preserved turn-of-the-20th-century site, has a small collection of American Indian artifacts. Closed Monday and Tuesday, and the month of January. Call ahead for hours. Admission. ~ 603 6th Street; 503-655-2866.

Well worth your time is the **Rose Farm Museum** (also known as the William Holmes House), one of the state's oldest residences. The first territorial governor was inaugurated at this home surrounded by rose plantings. A two-tiered piazza and second-story ballroom are highlights of this restored residence, now on the National Register of Historic Places. Open by appointment only. ~ 536 Holmes Lane, Oregon City; 503-656-5146.

The **Clackamas County Historical Society Museum of the Oregon Territory** explores the history of Clackamas County with exhibits covering geology, traders and trappers, immigration, government and religion. Closed Sunday and Monday. Admission. ~ 211 Tumwater Drive; 503-655-5574, fax 503-655-0035.

Also of special interest is the **Oregon City Municipal Elevator**. Founded in 1916, this ride was designed to make it easy for residents to journey from the riverfront to the upper part of town. One of only four municipal elevators in the world, the 90-foot ride is a great way to enjoy views of Willamette Falls, particularly at sunset. ~ 300 7th Street (at Main Street), Oregon City; 503-657-0891.

for a gift. Closed Monday. ~ 3934 Southwest Corbett Avenue; 503-223-2654, fax 503-223-0190; www.contemporarycrafts.org.

NIGHTLIFE Classical-music buffs will enjoy the **Portland Baroque Orchestra**. Make it a point to hear this group if they're performing during your visit (October through April). ~ First Baptist Church, 909 Southwest 11th Avenue; Kaul Auditorium at Reed College; 503-222-6000, fax 503-226-6635; www.pbo.org.

McMenamins Mission Theater is a historic movie theater that now doubles as a pub, with seating at tables and couches where you can dine and watch second-run films. There's also traditional theater seating on the balcony level. ~ 1624 Northwest Glisan Street; 503-223-4527, movie showtimes 503-249-7474 ext. 5, fax 503-294-0837.

PARKS **MACLEAY PARK** 🏃 This natural 104-acre park offers several excellent trails, a pond, creek and viewing windows overlooking a bird-feeding area. In addition, Pittock Mansion provides stunning views of the city and Mt. St. Helens. There's a good chance you'll spot deer and other wildlife on your walk. Hiking trails lead down to Lower Macleay Park, which is a gateway to 5000-acre Forest Park. The Portland Audubon Society's headquarters, bookstore and wildlife care center are adjacent to the park. Facilities include restrooms and a playground. ~ Take Lovejoy Street west to Northwest Cornell Road and continue to the park; 503-823-2223, fax 503-823-6007.

The trails that lead through orchards and gardens on Sauvie Island are ideal for leisurely exploration on foot.

COUNCIL CREST PARK 🏃 Atop a Tualatin Mountain peak, this forested 45-acre park is a great way to see the Cascades and the Coast Range. Make your way through stands of fir and maple via Marquam Hill Trail. There's also a sculptured fountain of a mother and child. Facilities include picnic tables. ~ Southwest Council Crest Drive near Fairmount Boulevard; 503-823-2223, fax 503-823-6007.

HIDDEN ► **SAUVIE ISLAND WILDLIFE AREA** 🏃 ⚓ ⛴ 🚤 ⛵ This 12,000-acre haven ten miles northwest of Portland is an ideal place to spot great blue heron, bald eagles, sandhill cranes (during March and April migration) and 230 other bird species. Featuring a sandy beach on the Columbia, the refuge is also home to 37 mammal species including black-tailed deer. Small craft explore the sloughs while oceangoing freighters cruise by on the Columbia. For fishing, try for catfish, perch and crappie from slough and pond banks. There are portable toilets and bird observation platforms. Some areas are open year-round; other areas are closed from October to mid-April. Day-use only; you must obtain a parking permit ($3.50 per day/$11 annually), available at the Cracker Barrel and the Redder Beach RV Park on the island or at any Fred Meyer department store or G.I. Joe's Sporting Goods throughout Portland. ~ Take Route 30 west from Portland toward Astoria. Four miles past St. John's Bridge, take the Sauvie Bridge turnoff to the Island; 503-621-3488, fax 503-621-3025.

ELK ROCK GARDEN Ever since 1957 this refuge, also known as   ◄ *HIDDEN*
the Garden of the Bishop's Close, has been a favorite of Portland's garden societies. And why not? A terraced 13-acre estate overlooking the Willamette River and Elk Rock Island, the garden is also home to the Episcopal Diocese of Oregon's main office. Formal gardens and native plants, including 77 magnolia varieties, make this a spot for Zen-like contemplation. Also here are lily ponds, a rock garden and a small spring. Self-guided tour information is available from the visitors center. ~ 11800 Southwest Military Lane; 503-636-5613, 800-452-2562, fax 503-636-5616; www.diocese-oregon.org/theclose.

TRYON CREEK STATE NATURAL AREA 🚶 🚲 🐎 Set in a shallow, steep-walled canyon, this 645-acre suburban park is a hot spot for hiking, biking and horseback riding. Tryon is forested with fir, alder and maple and also has a grassy meadow. Look for beaver and pileated woodpeckers. There's a trillium festival in the spring. Facilities here are restrooms, an observation area and a nature center. ~ Located six miles southwest of downtown Portland. Take the Terwilliger exit off Route 5 and follow signs to the park; 503-636-9886, 800-551-6949, fax 503-636-5318.

MARY S. YOUNG PARK 🚶 🚲 A popular day-use area forested in fir, maple, cottonwood and oak, the park sits on the Willamette River. With 133 acres, this leisurely spot is perfect for fishing from the riverbank, riding or walking. There are restrooms and picnic tables. ~ Located nine miles south of Portland on Route 43; 503-557-4700, fax 503-656-4106; www.ci.west-linn.or.us.

All visitors to Portland owe it to ▼▼▼▼▼▼▼▼▼▼▼▼▼▼▼▼▼▼
themselves to see the Columbia River **The Columbia River Gorge**
Gorge. The spectacular scenery includes one of the Northwest's most important historical sites, Fort Vancouver. Heaven for windsurfers, kayakers, waterfall lovers, hikers and history buffs, this is the ultimate Portland day trip. Of course, if you love it as much as we did, you'll probably want to spend the night.

Although it's only half an hour from downtown Portland and the   **SIGHTS**
logical starting point for touring the Columbia Gorge region, many visitors to the region miss **Fort Vancouver**. What a pity. Located across the Columbia River from Portland, on the Wash-

ington side, this National Historic Site is a cornerstone of Pacific Northwest history. Organized by the Hudson Bay Company in 1825, the fort was originally a British fur-trading post and focal point for the commercial development of an area extending from British Columbia to Oregon and from Montana west to the Hawaiian Islands.

Ten structures have been reconstructed on their original fort locations. Collectively known as **Fort Vancouver National Historic Reserve**, they give a feel for life during the arrival of the first white settlers. One of the best ways to start your tour is at the visitors center with the introductory video. On your tour you'll see the re-created **Chief Factor's House**, once home to Dr. John McLoughlin, the British agent who befriended American settlers and is remembered as the "Father of Oregon." The phenomenal ability of the British to instantly gentrify the wilderness is reflected in the fine china, copper kettles and elegant furniture of this white clapboard home wrapped with a spacious veranda. You may be surprised to learn that the male officers dined without their wives.

The **Fur Warehouse** interprets how furs were collected and prepared for shipment to England. Also worth a visit are the **Blacksmith Shop, Bake House, Kitchen, Wash House, Palisade, Bastion, Jail** and a **Carpenter Workshop**. At the **Indian Trade Shop and Dispensary**, you'll learn how American Indians skillfully bartered their collected furs for British-made goods. Because most of the items were imported, there was a two-year hiatus between ordering goods and receiving them. Fort Vancouver: Admission May 1 to September 30. ~ 612 East Reserve Street, Vancouver, WA; 360-816-6230, fax 360-816-6363; www.nps.gov/fova.

On nearby **Officer's Row**, you'll see 21 grand homes built for American Army leaders who served here during the latter half of the 19th and the early 20th centuries. These charming Victorians are the focus of a rehabilitation program combining interpretive and commercial use. Among the residences you can tour is the **Grant House**, which currently houses a restaurant serving classic Northwestern food. ~ 360-906-1101. The **George C. Marshall House**, an imposing Queen Anne structure, also offers tours every day. Call for weekend hours; tours are available Saturday and Sunday except during weddings or other event rentals. ~ 360-693-3103.

HIDDEN ▶   Next to Fort Vancouver is **Pearson Air Museum**. The field, opened in 1905, is the oldest operating airfield in the United States. Exhibits feature a display on the world's first nonstop transpolar flight (Moscow to Vancouver) in 1937—the Soviet aviators were greeted by General George Marshall, who hosted them at his residence—as well as the last remaining artifact from the *Hindenburg*. The airpark exhibit features flyable vintage aircraft, an avi-

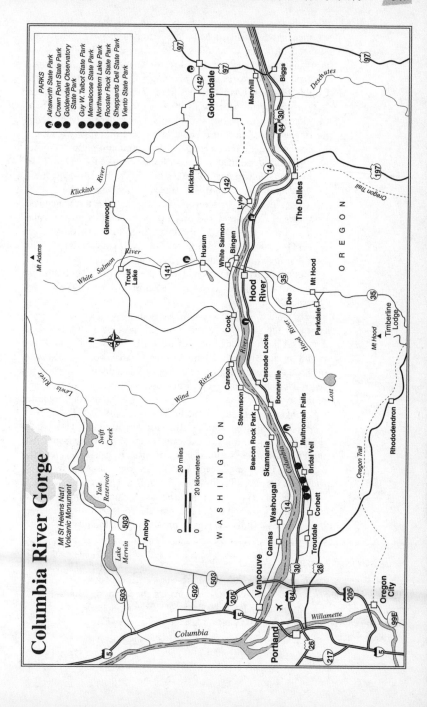

Columbia River Gorge

PARKS
- Ainsworth State Park
- Crown Point State Park
- Goldendale Observatory State Park
- Guy W. Talbot State Park
- Memaloose State Park
- Northwestern Lake Park
- Rooster Rock State Park
- Sheppards Dell State Park
- Viento State Park

20 miles

20 kilometers

ation theater, a hands-on activity room and the nation's oldest wooden hangar. Closed Monday. Admission. ~ 1115 East 5th Street, Vancouver, WA; 360-694-7026, fax 360-694-0824; www.pearsonairmuseum.org, e-mail director@pearsonairmuseum.org.

Originally constructed in 1909 as a Carnegie Library, **Clark County Historical Museum** has a better than good regional collection—from the American Indian artifacts and handicrafts to the historical doctor's office and general store. Not to be missed is the downstairs train room with a Pullman unit, railway telegram office, dining car china, a model train layout and photos of noteworthy local derailments. Closed Sunday and Monday. ~ 1511 Main Street, Vancouver, WA; 360-993-5679, fax 360-993-5683; www.cchmuseum.org, e-mail cchm@pacifier.com.

To see more of Vancouver stop by the **Greater Vancouver Chamber of Commerce** and pick up the handy downtown walking tour brochure. ~ 1101 Broadway, Suite 110, Vancouver, WA; 360-694-2588, fax 503-693-8279; www.vancouverusa.com, e-mail yourchamber@vancouverusa.com.

Returning to the Oregon side of the river take Route 84 east up the Gorge to the **Historic Columbia River Highway** (see "Scenic Drive").

The taming of the Columbia River to provide low-cost power is one of the most controversial issues associated with the river. You'll get the pro side of the picture at **Bonneville Lock and Dam**, including the **Bradford Island Visitors Center**. You can also witness salmon swimming up underwater fish ladders. Extensive interpretive displays and an informational film provide an overview of the dam's operation and history. ~ Route 84, Exit 40, three miles west of Cascade Locks, OR; 541-374-8820, fax 541-374-4516.

On the Washington side of the Gorge, you can also learn how the dam operates, enjoy underwater views of fish ladders and visit the **Fort Cascades National Historic Site**. To get there, cross the Columbia River at Cascade Locks, Oregon, using the **Bridge of the Gods** (named after an Indian legend) and head west two miles on Route 14. The 59-acre historic site includes a one-mile self-guided trail featuring the sites of the old Portage Railroad, a one-time Chinook Indian village, a pre–Civil War military fort and a

MUSEUMS GALORE

There are many different visitors centers and museums in Columbia River Gorge National Recreation Area because it is managed cooperatively by a board made up of representatives from the states of Washington and Oregon and each of the counties in which it falls, as well as the U.S. Forest Service.

nature preserve. A quiet nine-mile segment of the historic highway continues east of Hood River, between Mosier and The Dalles, winding onto the Rowena Plateau. Views include channeled scabland terraces, fruit orchards, and the **Tom McCall Preserve**, a beautiful and little-known nature reserve run by The Nature Conservancy that protects many of the hundreds of unique Columbia River Gorge wildflower species. ~ 541-427-4281, fax 541-374-4516.

Retrace your route across the Bridge of the Gods to the Oregon side and stop at the **Cascade Locks Museum** to see exhibits on American Indians, the first Columbia River locks, the portage road, logging and fishwheels. Water-powered, these rotating devices scooped so many salmon from the river that they were banned by the state in 1926. Closed November through April. ~ Marine Park, 1 Northwest Portage Road, Cascade Locks, OR; 541-374-8535.

The sternwheeler **Columbia Gorge** is docked in Cascade Locks year-round. The multidecked old paddlewheel steamboat leads daytime and weekend dinner cruises through the Gorge. ~ 503-224-3900, 800-224-3901, fax 503-231-9089; www.stern wheeler.com, e-mail sales@sternwheeler.com.

On the Washington side of the bridge in Stevenson is the spacious **Columbia Gorge Interpretive Center**, where the focus is on the cultural and natural history of the Gorge. Located on a ten-acre site overlooking the river, the center includes a 37-foot-high replica of a 19th-century fishwheel, a restored Corliss Steam Engine, a theater with a nine-projector slide show re-creating the cataclysmic formation of the Gorge and several exhibits drawn from the oral histories of local American Indians and pioneer settlers. The world's largest rosary collection is also housed here. Admission. ~ 990 Southwest Rock Creek Drive, Stevenson, WA; 509-427-8211, 800-991-2338, fax 509-427-7429; www.colum biagorge.org, e-mail info@columbiagorge.org.

Farther east on Route 14 is **Carson Hot Springs Resort**. On the Wind River, this resort is well-known by weary travelers for its mineral baths and massages, and can provide a restful stop for those who have been hiking all day on its beautiful hiking trails; there's also an 18-hole golf course. From here you can drive east along Route 14 to Route 141, which leads north along the White Salmon River Valley to Trout Lake, then return to Route 14 and the town of White Salmon. ~ 372 St. Martin's Spring Road, Carson, WA; 509-427-8292, 800-607-3678, fax 509-427-7242.

Just east of White Salmon in the small town of Bingen, Washington, is the **Gorge Heritage Museum**, where you can view historic photographs and American Indian artifacts, including tools, arrow points and beadwork. Closed Monday through Wednesday, and October through May. ~ 202 East Humboldt Street, Bingen, WA; 509-493-3228; e-mail ghm@gorge.net.

Historic Columbia River Highway

This magnificent scenic route parallels Route 84, skirting the foot of sheer cliffs of the Columbia River Gorge with its wonderland of waterfalls, side canyons and verdant forest. The road was built by concrete tycoon Sam Hill, creator of the Maryhill Museum of Art, in 1916 as an attempt to convince Oregon legislatures to let him extend a highway up the length of the Columbia River. It was the first rural paved road in the Pacific Northwest.

VISTA HOUSE   Turn off Route 84 at Troutdale (Exit 17) to reach the Historic Columbia River Highway. At the mouth of the gorge, a road turns off to the right and winds up to Vista House in Crown Point State Park. This octagonal structure, perched 733 feet above the river, has an information desk, a gift shop, an espresso bar and an awesome view.

WATERFALLS   Among the major waterfalls that plunge into the gorge alongside the highway are **Latourelle Falls** (249 feet) in Guy W. Talbot State Park, **Sheppards Dell Falls** (two tiers, 50 and 60 feet) in Sheppards

Your next stop should be on the Oregon side at **Hood River**, which has become a windsurfing capital thanks to the strong breezes here. Stop at the **Hood River County Visitors Center** for information on this scenic hub. Closed weekends from mid-October to mid-April. ~ 405 Portway Avenue, Hood River, OR; 541-386-2000, 800-336-3530, fax 541-386-2057; www.hood river.org, e-mail hrccc@hoodriver.org.

The **Hood River County Historical Museum** features exhibits on American Indian culture, the westward migration, pioneer farming, logging and the Columbia River. Also found here is a collection of period furniture and early-20th-century artifacts. Closed November through March. ~ 300 East Port Marina Park, Hood River, OR; phone/fax 541-386-6772.

If you're in town from mid-May to mid-October, visit the **Hood River Saturday Market**, which features local foods, crafts and artwork. ~ 5th Street and Cascade Avenue, across from the Full Sail Brewing Company; 541-387-8349.

HIDDEN ►   One of the prettiest drives in Oregon is the 20-mile trip from Hood River to **Lost Lake** (elevation 3140 feet). At the lake you'll have a stunning angle on Mt. Hood—have your camera ready— and can rent a canoe or paddleboat (motorized boats are banned on the lake). In addition to fishing for rainbow trout, visitors like to walk the three-mile Lakeshore Trail that circles the lake. To reach the idyllic retreat, take Route 281 south to Dee and then

Dell State Park, **Bridal Veil Falls** (two tiers, 100 and 60 feet) and **Wah-keena Falls** (242 feet), where a mile-long trail leads to **Fairy Falls**, a magical 30-foot fan-shaped fall.

MULTNOMAH FALLS   The most popular tourist attraction in Oregon, this cascade plunges 620 feet, making it the second-tallest waterfall in the United States. Walk up the paved trail to the observation bridge between the upper and lower falls, where you'll get a misty view of the entire falls. In 1995, a 400-ton rock the size of a Greyhound bus fell from the top of the falls to the upper pool as a result of the ongoing erosion that originally formed the gorge. It caused about 20 minor injuries from flying debris, reminding us that the amazing geology here is still transforming on a grand scale.

STILL MORE FALLS   Two and a half miles beyond Multnomah Falls is **Horsetail Falls** (176 feet). Nearby, a trail leads almost two miles through the lush greenery of Oneonta Gorge to **Triple Falls**, a 135-foot segmented fall. The historic highway rejoins the interstate at Ainsworth State Park—unbelievably a mere 18 miles from where it began.

follow the signs west to the lake. Do keep an eye out for logging trucks en route.

Although many visitors miss it, we strongly recommend a visit to **The Dalles**, on the Oregon side of the Gorge. The end of the Oregon Trail, where immigrants boarded vessels to float down the Columbia (the Barlow Trail later made it possible to complete the overland journey), this city has a superb old-town walking tour. Pick up a copy of the route map at **The Dalles Area Chamber of Commerce**. Closed weekends from Labor Day to Memorial Day. ~ 404 West 2nd Street, The Dalles, OR; 541-296-2231, 800-255-3385, fax 541-296-1688; www.thedalleschamber.com, e-mail td acc@gorge.net.

Highlights on this walk include the state's oldest bookstore, **Klindt's** (315 East 2nd Street), and the circa-1863 **Waldron Brothers Drugstore** nearby.

The **Fort Dalles Museum** is a favorite stop. Only two fort buildings, the Surgeon's Quarters and the Garden Cottage, remain today. But the museum does preserve an excellent collection of pioneer artifacts, rifles, quilts and historic photographs. Closed December through February. Call for hours otherwise. Admission. ~ 15th and Garrison streets, The Dalles, OR; phone/fax 541-296-4547.

Don't miss the attractive, new, 26,100-square-foot **Columbia Gorge Discovery Center and Whatcom County Historical Mu-**

seum in The Dalles. This is the official Columbia River Gorge National Recreation Area interpretive center and has exhibits on the natural and cultural history of the gorge, as well as artifacts from local collectors in its airy, barnlike structure. ~ 5000 Discovery Drive, The Dalles; 541-296-8600, fax 541-298-8660; www.gorgediscovery.org.

From here, take Route 30 east to Route 197 north. Cross the freeway to Bret Clodfelter Way and follow signs to **The Dalles Dam**. Perhaps the saddest part of this story focuses on the demise of the Gorge's best-known Indian fishing grounds. Wherever you go along this part of the Columbia River, in coffee shops and hotel lobbies, phone company offices and visitors centers, you're likely to see classic photographs of Indians dipping their nets into the river at heavenly Celilo Falls. To get the full picture, leaf through the scrapbook of Celilo Falls fishing pictures at the Fort Dalles Museum. One hopeful sign, though. If you look carefully below The Dalles Dam, you may see contemporary Indian dipnet subsistence fishermen fishing from platforms. Treaties have upheld the right of Indian fishers to half the annual take of fish along the river for subsistence and cultural use only.

If you continue on Route 84 east of The Dalles for 12 miles you'll come to a small **Celilo Falls Marker**, which indicates where these bounteous fishing waters prospered before being destroyed by the dam in the late 1950s.

HIDDEN ▶ A few miles farther east, on the Washington side, is one of the most isolated museums in America. **Maryhill Museum of Art** was designed in 1914 as the mansion residence of eccentric millionaire Sam Hill, and was supposed to oversee a Quaker agricultural town. But the plan for a new town flopped and the house on the hill eventually became a museum. This eclectic assemblage was dedicated in 1926 by Queen Marie of Rumania, which helps explain the presence of treasures from that nation's royal collection. Also here are Russian icons, a large collection of Rodin sculptures, Charles M. Russell's *Indian Buffalo Hunt*,

AUTHOR FAVORITE

sights You'll enjoy panoramic views of the Cascades from the restored coaches of the scenic **Mt. Hood Railroad**. This 44-mile roundtrip journey links the Gorge with Mt. Hood along a route pioneered in 1906. The trip climbs up the Hood River Valley through steep canyons, orchards and forests. Special fall foliage trips are well worth your while as are murder-mystery and four-course dinner rides. The railroad runs April through October, with selected holiday trips between Thanksgiving and Christmas. ~ 110 Railroad Avenue, Hood River, OR; 541-386-3556, 800-872-4661; www.mthoodrr.com, e-mail mthoodrr@gorge.net.

French decorative arts, a good display of American Indian hand-icrafts and artifacts, and contemporary Pacific Northwest art, as well as one of the world's great chess collections. The museum also includes the world's only collection of post–World War II fashion mannequins. Views of the Columbia Gorge are spectacular, as are the sunsets. Closed mid-November to mid-March. Admission. ~ 35 Maryhill Museum Drive, Goldendale, WA; 509-773-3733, fax 509-773-6138; www.maryhillmuseum.org, e-mail maryhill@maryhillmuseum.org.

Three miles east of Maryhill Museum of Art is **Stonehenge**, Sam Hill's memorial to local soldiers who died in World War I.

The **Cedarplace Inn Bed and Breakfast**, a yellow two-story home built in 1907, offers three large guest rooms and a two-bedroom suite, decorated with antique furnishings including canopy beds and soft featherbeds with down pillows and comforters. All these attributes may sound fairly typical of Victorian-style luxury B&Bs everywhere, but the location of this one, at the mouth of the Columbia River Gorge Scenic Area, makes it an extra special spot for a romantic getaway. ~ 2611 South Troutdale Road, Troutdale, OR; 503-491-1900, 877-491-1907, fax 503-465-1046; cedarplc inn.com, e-mail cedarplace@comcast.net. MODERATE TO DELUXE.

LODGING

Located just above the Columbia Gorge Interpretive Center in Stevenson, Washington, is the **Skamania Lodge**, a modern resort built in the tradition of the grand mountain lodges of the late-18th century. Guests can congregate in the wood-paneled Gorge Room with its deep sofas and three-story river-rock fireplace. Public areas and the 254 guest rooms are handsomely decorated with mission-style furniture, Pendleton fabrics, petroglyph rubbings and American Indian–inspired rugs. The grounds include an 18-hole golf course, fitness center, whirlpools, swimming pool, and more. ~ 1131 Skamania Lodge Way, Stevenson, WA; 509-427-7700, 800-221-7117, fax 509-427-2547; www.ska mania.com. ULTRA-DELUXE.

With rooms often in short supply during the summer windsurfing season, visitors who arrive in the Hood River area without reservations may want to call the **Hood River Bed and Breakfast Association** room-finder hotline for information on what is available at local inns. ~ 541-386-6767; www.hoodriver roomfinder.com.

In Cascade Locks, 20 miles west of Hood River, **Bridge of the Gods Motel** provides affordable rustic rooms. All 17 units have queen-size beds; 11 of them offer kitchens. ~ 630 WaNaPa Street, Cascade Locks, OR; 541-374-8628; e-mail bridgeofgodsmotel@ msn.com. BUDGET.

The **Columbia Gorge Hotel** is a 40-room landmark where strains of Bach waft through the halls, sculptured carpets highlight the public areas and the fireplace is always roaring. This Mediterranean-style hotel tucks guests into wicker, brass, canopy or hand-carved antique beds. The dining room, home of a popular five-course farm breakfast, offers splendid riverfront dining. Relax in the Valentino Lounge, take a walk through the manicured gardens or enjoy a mineral wrap at the in-house spa. ~ 4000 Westcliff Drive, Hood River, OR; 541-386-5566, 800-345-1921, fax 541-386-9141; www.columbiagorgehotel.com, e-mail cghotel@gorge.net. ULTRA-DELUXE.

The chandeliered **Hood River Hotel** is a restored brick landmark with 41 rooms and suites. Brightly painted rooms are appointed with oak furniture, four-poster beds, casablanca fans, wing chairs and antiques. Some offer views of the Columbia River. Comfortable sitting areas, a lobby offering jazz music and a cheery café are all part of the charm. Kitchenette suites are available. ~ 102 Oak Street, Hood River, OR; 541-386-1900, 800-386-1859, fax 541-386-6090; www.hoodriverhotel.com, e-mail hrhotel@gorge.net. DELUXE.

Situated in a restored 1909 historic downtown home, the charming **Oak Street Hotel** offers nine guest rooms (one of which is a suite). Queen-sized beds with intricate iron frames and handcrafted furnishings enliven the rooms, all of which have a private bath. There's a comfortable lounge downstairs with a fireplace. ~ 610 Oak Street, Hood River; 866-386-3845, fax 541-387-8696; www.oakstreethotel.com, e-mail reservations@oakstreethotel.com.

Beautifully located overlooking the Columbia, **Vagabond Lodge** offers 42 spacious, carpeted rooms—some opening right onto the riverfront. All feature contemporary furniture, doubles or queens, microwaves, refrigerators and a secluded garden setting. Some suites have fireplaces, whirlpools and full kitchens. For the price, it's hard to beat this motel west of town. ~ 4070

AUTHOR FAVORITE

One of the frustrating facts of life on the road is the Sunday brunch. If you crave broccoli quiche, Italian sausages, artichoke frittatas, baklava, date tarts, fresh fruit and a dozen other treats, Monday to Saturday just won't do. Fortunately, the **Inn of the White Salmon** has solved this problem in an imaginative way. This lovely bed and breakfast offers brunch seven days a week. All you need do is check in to one of the inn's 16 countrified rooms featuring brass beds and antiques, and this splendid feast is yours. Across the Columbia from Hood River, this inn also features a comfortable parlor. ~ 172 West Jewett Boulevard, White Salmon, WA; 509-493-2335, 800-972-5226; www.innofthewhitesalmon.com, e-mail innkeeper@innofthewhitesalmon.com. MODERATE TO DELUXE.

Westcliff Drive, Hood River, OR; 541-386-2992, 877-386-2992, fax 541-386-3317; www.vagabondlodge.com, e-mail info@vaga bondlodge.com. BUDGET TO MODERATE.

Located just five blocks from downtown Hood River is the 1908 Victorian **Inn at the Gorge Bed & Breakfast.** Three suites and two bedrooms have antique furnishings and private baths. Enjoy the surrounding gardens, nap in the hammock beneath the cedar tree or just laze the day away on the wraparound porch. Full breakfast included. ~ 1113 Eugene Street, Hood River, OR; phone/fax 541-386-4429; www.innatthegorge.com, e-mail stay@innatthegorge.com. MODERATE TO DELUXE.

The **Columbia Windrider Inn** is operated by an avid Columbia Gorge sailor and windsurfer who likes to play host to other sailboard afficionados. Situated on a quiet residential street, this historic 1921 home has maple wood floors and four large guest rooms, each with private bath, air conditioning, complimentary wi-fi internet and a queen- or king-size bed. Facilities include a swimming pool, a hot tub and a recreation room. ~ 200 West 4th Street, The Dalles, OR; 541-296-2607; www.windriderinn.com, e-mail chuck@windriderinn.com. BUDGET.

For contemporary motel accommodations try the **Cousins Country Inn.** The 93 fully carpeted rooms have oak tables and queen-size beds. Some have kitchenettes. Guests receive free use of the nearby health club. There's a pool on the premises, as well as Cousins, the only restaurant we know that has a John Deere tractor in the middle of the dining room. ~ 2114 West 6th Street, The Dalles, OR; 541-298-5161, 800-848-9378, fax 541-298-6411; www.cousinscountryinn.com, e-mail info@cousinscountry inn.com. MODERATE.

In Stevenson, Washington, the **Cascade Room** at Skamania Lodge has a grand dining room with massive wooden ceiling beams and superb views of the Gorge. The specialties are Northwest-inspired dishes prepared in a wood-burning oven, including wild salmon, meats and seafood, not to mention a Sunday champagne brunch. ~ 1131 Skamania Lodge Way, Stevenson, WA; 509-427-7700, 800-221-7117, fax 509-427-2547; www.skamania.com. DELUXE TO ULTRA-DELUXE.

DINING

About 20 minutes north of the Gorge, and well worth the trip, is one of the Gorge's most intriguing restaurants, **The Logs.** You'll be impressed by the roasted chicken, hickory-smoked ribs, giant fries and huckleberry pie served in this log-cabin setting. The battered and deep-fried chicken gizzards and cheese sticks are a big hit with the regular clientele, who include locals, rafters, skiers and devotees of the rich mud pie. In business for six decades, this is the place where city slickers will come face to face with their first jackalope, safely mounted on the wall. ~ 1258

◄ HIDDEN

Route 141, White Salmon, WA; 509-493-1402; e-mail logsres@ gorge.net. BUDGET.

HIDDEN ► Tucked away in the woods on the Oregon side is **Stonehedge Gardens**, an antique-filled home preparing Continental and Northwest dining at its finest. Set in a beautiful garden, this paneled restaurant has a tiny mahogany bar and a roaring fireplace. Among the dishes are scallop sauté, veal chanterelle, jumbo prawns and filet of salmon. Light entrées, such as a seafood platter, are also recommended. Dinner only. Closed Monday in winter. ~ 3405 Cascade Avenue, Hood River, OR; 541-386-3940; e-mail stone hedge@gorge.net. MODERATE TO DELUXE.

Cornerstone Cuisine has breezy indoor and sidewalk seating in the center of this resort town. The heart of the dining room is a handcrafted bar with an etched-glass mirror. Entrées include almond-crusted salmon, paella and braised lamb shank with gnocchi, dates and cinnamon butter. ~ In the Hood River Hotel, 102 Oak Street, Hood River, OR; 541-386-1900, 800-386-1859, fax 541-386-6090; www.hoodriverhotel.com, e-mail hrhotel@gorge. net. MODERATE TO DELUXE.

An elegant dining room overlooking the Gorge, **Columbia River Gorge Dining Room** is a romantic place to dine on roast pork tenderloin, fresh Oregon salmon, rack of lamb or Dungeness crab with lobster sauce and risotto. Done in an Early American design with oak furniture and candlelit tables, this establishment is well known for its lavish farm breakfast. ~ 4000 Westcliff Drive, Hood River, OR; 541-387-5428, fax 541-387-5414; www.colum biagorgehotel.com, e-mail cghotel@gorge.net. ULTRA-DELUXE.

Located in one of the most historic buildings in The Dalles, the **Baldwin Saloon** was built in 1876 and has an 18-foot-long mahogany back bar and turn-of-the-20th-century oil paintings on the brick walls. The restaurant is known for its seafood and oyster dishes (baked and on the half shell) and also serves thick sandwiches, burgers, soups and desserts. Breads and desserts are baked on the premises. Closed Sunday. ~ 1st and Court streets, The Dalles, OR; 541-296-5666. MODERATE TO DELUXE.

AUTHOR FAVORITE

After a visit to Multnomah Falls it makes sense to dine at **Multnomah Falls Lodge**. The smoked-salmon-and-cheese platter and generous salads are recommended. The European-style lodge building with a big stone fireplace, scenic paintings of the surroundings and lovely views will add to your enjoyment of the Gorge. Buffet champagne brunch on Sunday. ~ Off Route 84, Bridal Veil, WA; 503-695-2376, fax 503-695-2338; www.multnomahfallslodge.com, e-mail info@mult-nomahfallslodge.com. MODERATE TO DELUXE.

Fort Vancouver Gift Shop is the place to go for books, maps and
pamphlets on Pacific Northwest history. We recommend picking up a copy of *Outpost* by Dorothy Morris. ~ 1501 East
Evergreen Boulevard, Vancouver, WA; 360-816-6230.

Aviation buffs will want to stop by the gift shop at **Pearson
Air Museum**. The shop has an ace collection of memorabilia and
souvenirs for adults and juniors alike. Closed Sunday through
Tuesday. ~ 1115 East 5th Street, Vancouver, WA; 360-694-7026,
fax 360-694-0824; www.pearsonairmuseum.org.

Pendleton Woolen Mills and Outlet Store offers big savings on
irregulars. Tours of the mill, in operation since 1912, are available,
but call first for schedule information. ~ #2 17th Street, Washou-
gal, WA; 360-835-1118, fax 360-835-5451.

A good place to find books on the region is **Waucoma Bookstore**, which is also well stocked with fiction, children's books, cards,
magazines, children's toys and handcrafted pottery. Closed Sunday
in winter. ~ 212 Oak Street, Hood River, OR; 541-386-5353.

Columbia Art Gallery represents over 150 artists, primarily
from the Columbia Gorge region. Featured are the works of photographers, printmakers, potters, glassblowers, jewelers, weavers,
sculptors and painters. ~ 215 Cascade Avenue, Hood River, OR;
541-387-8877; www.columbiaartgallery.org.

Locally made jams, jellies, wine and other food products
make terrific presents for the folks back home. **The Gift House**
carries a variety of home-grown products, including wine and
jams. ~ 204 Oak Street, Hood River, OR; 541-386-9234. Pick
up a fine Oregon white or red at **The Wine Sellers**. ~ 514 State
Street, Hood River, OR; 541-386-4647. **Rasmussen Farms** sells
strawberries, Hood River apples, Comice pears and cherries.
Apples and pears can be shipped as gift packs. ~ 3020 Thomsen
Road off Route 35 south of Hood River, OR; 541-386-4622,
800-548-2243, fax 541-386-4702; www.rasmussenfarms.com,
e-mail info@rasmussenfarms.com.

On the Washington side of the Gorge, Stevenson's small, walkable downtown has some distinctive art galleries and gift shops.

The Dalles is home to Oregon's oldest bookstore, **Klindt's**,
which dates from 1870 and still has an old-time ambience with high
ceilings and glass-topped counters. Books on the Pacific Northwest,
both new and used, are a specialty, as are rare and out-of-print
books. ~ 315 East 2nd Street, The Dalles, OR; 541-296-3355.

A popular gay and lesbian nightspot in Vancouver, Washington,
is **North Bank Bar & Grill**, which has a dancefloor and outdoor
patio. Cover for drag shows. ~ 106 West 6th Street, Vancouver,
WA; 360-695-3862.

The **Power Station Pub and Theater** is located in the former
Multnomah County poor farm. The theater presents second-run

movies in the farm's former power plant. The pub serves a full menu in the converted laundry building. Also on the premises is the **Edgefield Brewery** and a working winery and distillery. ~ 2126 Southwest Halsey Street, Troutdale, OR; 503-669-8610, 800-669-8610; www.mcmenamins.com, e-mail power@mcmenamins.com.

The **Skamania Lodge** has occasional live music or speakers before a woodburning fireplace in summer. ~ 1131 Skamania Lodge Way, Stevenson, WA; 509-427-2527, fax 509-427-2547.

Bungalow Bar & Grill has televised sports, two pool tables and dart boards. ~ 812 Wind River Highway, Carson, WA; 509-427-4523.

Full Sail Brewing Company offers tastings of their very popular hand-crafted beers, as well as a pub-style menu and deck seating with fine views of the Columbia. ~ 506 Columbia Avenue, Hood River, OR; 541-386-2247, 888-244-2337; www.fullsail brewing.com.

PARKS

ROOSTER ROCK STATE PARK 🏃 🚲 🏊 ⛵ ⚓ 🚤 🎣 ⛴ Offering more than three miles of sandy Columbia River frontage, this 872-acre park is near the Gorge's west end. The rock, named for a towering promontory, is near a camping site chosen by Lewis and Clark in 1805. Well-known for swimming and beginner wind-surfing, Rooster Rock also has excellent hiking trails, a small lake and a forested bluff. Anglers can fish for salmon. There are picnic tables and restrooms. Day-use fee, $3, or $25 for an annual pass. ~ Located in Oregon 22 miles east of Portland on Route 84 at Exit 25; 503-695-2261, 800-551-6949, fax 503-695-2226.

VIENTO STATE PARK 🏃 🚲 🏊 ⛵ ⚓ 🎣 Originally a rest stop on the old Columbia River Highway, this 247-acre park includes a riverfront and Viento Creek forest section. Dramatic views of the Columbia River make this a popular camping and picnicking facility. It can get very windy, and be aware that trains pass through the gorge at night. Facilities include picnic tables, barbecue pits, showers and restrooms. Closed October through April. Day-use fee, $3. ~ Route 84 Exit 56, eight miles west of Hood River in Oregon; 541-374-8811, 800-551-6949.

▲ There are 18 tent sites ($10 to $14 per night) and 56 RV hookup sites ($12 to $16 per night).

AINSWORTH STATE PARK 🏃 Ranking high among the treasures of the Columbia River Scenic Highway is this 156-acre park. Near the bottom of St. Peter's Dome, the forested park has a gorgeous hiking trail that connects with a network extending throughout the region. A serene getaway, the only sound of civilization you're likely to hear is that of passing trains. There are picnic tables, showers and restrooms. Closed November through March. ~ Route 30, the Columbia River Scenic Highway, 37 miles east of Portland on the Oregon side; 503-695-2301, fax 503-695-2226.

▲ There are 45 RV hookup sites; $12 to $16 per night. There are also six walk-in sites; $10 to $14 per night.

MEMALOOSE STATE PARK The park is named for an offshore Columbia River island that was an American Indian burial ground. This 336-acre site spreads out along a two-mile stretch of riverfront and is forested with pine, oak and fir. Much of the park is steep and rocky. It can also be very windy. There are horseshoes, a playground, interpretive programs in summer, showers and restrooms. Closed November through March. ~ Off Route 84, 11 miles west of The Dalles in Oregon. Take the Memaloose Rest Stop exit, then make a right into the park. Westbound access only; 541-478-3008, fax 541-478-2369.

> "Memaloose," in case you were wondering, is a Chinook word linked to the sacred burial ritual.

▲ There are 66 tent sites ($12 to $16 per night) and 44 RV hookup sites ($16 to $20 per night). Reservations: 800-452-5687.

BEACON ROCK STATE PARK 🚶 🚴 🛶 Located next to Beacon Rock, a volcanic landmark on the Washington side of the river named by Lewis and Clark, this park has several lovely trails, including one that goes up 800-foot-high Beacon Rock itself. There is also fishing on the river and a 59-table picnic site. ~ Off Route 14; 509-427-8265.

▲ The attractive forested campground built in the 1930s by the Civilian Conservation Corps has 29 first-come, first-served private tent sites with restrooms and two showers; a group site at Hamilton Mountain Trailhead may be reserved (888-CAM-POUT) for groups of up to 100.

Skating may not be big-thrills adventure, but it sure is fun. In Portland, rollerskating even takes on an old-fashioned aura when you've got an amusement-park organ playing the music. Skaters are welcome to use any hard surface in the city's parks. ~ Portland Parks Department; 503-823-2223; www.portlandparks.org.

Outdoor Adventures

FISHING

PORTLAND EAST Rollerblade or rollerskate to the strains of the mighty Wurlitzer at the early-20th-century **Oaks Amusement Park** on the east bank of the Willamette. Skate rentals are available. ~ East end of the Sellwood Bridge; 503-233-5777; www.oakspark.com.

At **Skateworld,** you can rent skates, including inlines. Public skating sessions are held Tuesday through Sunday. ~ 4395 Southeast Witch Hazel Road, Hillsboro; 503-640-1333.

PORTLAND WEST City ordinance prohibits skaters (and skateboarders) from most city center streets. One happy exception is the esplanade in **Waterfront Park.** When the weather is particularly pleasant, the concrete pathway (it's about ten feet wide) can get congested with cyclists, runners, skaters, skateboarders and strollers. But the mood is always congenial. ~ Front Street, from Southwest Harrison Street to Northwest Glisan Street.

ICE SKATING

PORTLAND EAST At Lloyd Center Ice Rink, the music is recorded but the fun is genuine. Skate rentals are available here, too. Closed one week in May. ~ 953 Lloyd Center shopping mall, between Northeast Multnomah and Halsey streets and Northeast 9th and 15th avenues, Portland; 503-288-6073; www.lloyd centerice.com.

PORTLAND WEST The Valley Ice Arena hosts several public skating sessions a day. Skate rental is included in admission fee. Call for times. ~ 9250 Southwest Beaverton-Hillsdale Highway, Beaverton; 503-297-2521.

WINDSURFING

Between the high cliff walls of the Columbia Gorge, east of Portland, winds on the river can hit 60 knots, so it's no wonder this is one of the world's best windsurfing areas, with Hood River its capital. According to a local expert, "Once you learn the tricks and let the wind do the work for you, it's not as hard as it looks." And if you don't mind cool temperatures (50°F and lower) in winter, you can windsurf year-round.

COLUMBIA RIVER GORGE Big Winds offers rentals and instruction for children and adults, and a full-service retail shop. Kitesurfing equipment is also available. ~ 207 Front Street, Hood River, OR; 541-386-6086, 888-509-4210; www.bigwinds.com.

If you're experienced and want to rent equipment, contact **Doug's Sports**. ~ 101 Oak Street, Hood River, OR; 541-386-5787, 800-211-8207; www.dougsports.com. **Hood River WaterPlay** offers lessons and equipment, and has a beginner beach area in front of the Hood River Inn. ~ Port Marina Park, Hood River, OR; 541-386-9463, 800-963-7873; www.hoodriverwater play.com.

Swiss Swell also offers lessons in the Hood River area. Closed in winter. ~ 13 Oak Street, Hood River, OR; 541-490-7570; www. swiss-swell.com.

FISHING

Imagine catching a 350-pound sturgeon, even if you've never fished before. You can haul in these babies, which can come in at seven to ten feet and weigh upward of 300 pounds, year-round, right out of the Columbia. Walleye is another year-round favorite found in the Willamette; Tillamook Bay, about 65 miles west on the coast, is well known for trophy-size fall chinook salmon.

PORTLAND Page's Northwest Guide Service can set up a one-day Tillamook Bay fishing trip on a 25-foot, all-weather boat, or arrange an outing on the Willamette, Clackamas, Columbia or Sandy rivers. ~ Portland; 503-760-3373, 866-760-3370; www.fishingoregon.net.

PORTLAND EAST Don Schneider's Reel Adventures specializes in full-day fishing trips on the Columbia River but also provides trips on the Sandy and Willamette. Schneider can custom-tailor an outing in a drift boat. ~ 57206 East Marmot Road, Sandy; 503-622-5372, 877-544-7335; www.donsreeladventures.com.

COLUMBIA RIVER GORGE The art of flyfishing abounds on rivers in the Gorge region. The Gorge Fly Shop arranges fly-fishing excursions to such popular destinations as Deschutes. All levels of lessons are available. ~ 201 Oak Street, Hood River, OR; 541-386-6977; www.gorgeflyshop.com.

RIVER RUNNING

About 90 minutes from downtown Portland is a whitewater thrill ride—the White Salmon River, just north of the Columbia, in Washington. Designated a Wild and Scenic River, it moves "fast and furious" through the forest canyon. Southeast of Portland is the Clackamas, another popular whitewater river, with some Class III and IV rapids. It's about an hour away. Most whitewater-rafting trips are done in paddleboats (*you* paddle!), holding six to eight people, plus a guide. The passive adventurer who'd like to photograph the gorgeous mountain scenery instead of paddle should ask about oar-powered raft trips.

PORTLAND AREA About 35 miles southeast of Portland, the Clackamas River is the best bet for a one-day whitewater adventure. From March through October, the Clackamas River runs with some Class III and IV rapids (the water is too low the rest of the year). **River Drifters,** one of the only outfitters oper-ating in the spring on the Clackamas, can arrange a complete full-day trip on several rivers, including the Deschutes and White Salmon rivers. They also offer a whitewater and wine trip on the White Salmon, stopping for lunch or dinner at a local win-ery. ~ 405 Deschutes Avenue, Maupin; 800-972-0430.

AUTHOR FAVORITE

A little Washington gem on the White Salmon River north of the Columbia, **Northwestern Lake** is an ideal destination for a day trip where you can swim, fish, hike or just loaf. There are also summer cabins nearby for those who want to stay longer. ~ Head west from White Salmon on Route 14 to Route 141. Continue north five miles to the park.

GOLF

PORTLAND EAST   Eastmoreland Golf Course is an 18-hole regulation course rated by *Golf Digest* as one of the country's most affordable places to play. ~ 2425 Southeast Bybee Boulevard, Portland; 503-775-2900; www.eastmorelandgolfcourse.com. The two 18-hole courses at **Glendoveer Golf Course** are lined with fir trees. There's also a driving range. ~ 14015 Northeast Glisan Street, Portland; 503-253-7507. Across the state border you can tee off on the par-72, 18-hole **The Cedars on Salmon Creek**. ~ 15001 Northeast 181st Street, Brush Prairie, WA; 360-687-4233; www.thecedarsonsalmoncreek.com.

PORTLAND WEST   Just 30 minutes from downtown Portland, the four nine-hole greens at **Meriwether National Golf Club** are good walking courses. ~ 5200 Southwest Rood Bridge Road, Hillsboro; 503-648-4143; www.meriwethergolfclub.com. **King City Golf Club** is a challenging, nine-hole, semiprivate course that, says a local golf pro, is "harder than it looks." ~ 15355 Southwest Royalty Parkway, Tigard; 503-639-7986.

COLUMBIA RIVER GORGE   Hood River Golf and Country Club has 18 holes, full mountain views, pear orchards and a driving range. ~ 1850 Country Club Road, Hood River, OR; 541-386-3009; www.hoodrivergolf.com. **Indian Creek Golf Course**, with its gentle rolling hills, is a dry, year-round 18-hole course. ~ 3605 Brookside Drive, Hood River, OR; 541-386-7770, 866-386-7770; www.indiancreekgolf.com.

TENNIS

Among the numerous public clubs is **Portland Tennis Center**, which has four hardtop indoor (hourly per-person charge) and eight lighted outdoor courts (free). They also maintain a list of other public tennis courts throughout the city. ~ 324 Northeast 12th Street; 503-823-3189.

BIKING

To say that the Portland area is bicycle friendly is like saying New York has a lot of tall buildings—so what else is new? There are 260 miles of bike lanes in the metropolitan area (plus 83 miles of multi-use lanes), and city buses all have bike racks. *Bicycling* magazine has picked Portland as the country's top bicycle city. Morning, afternoon or entire-day bicycling in the area presents a variety of options, from a mountain-bike ride in a city park to a long-distance excursion along the Columbia River.

Visitors interested in bicycling in the Portland metropolitan area will find the going easier by first contacting one or more of these resources. The **Portland Bicycle Program** publishes a small map of the city's bikeway system; an accompanying brochure explains how to take your bike along on a bus. The map and brochure are free and available at the program's office and in some bike shops. ~ 1120 Southwest 5th Avenue, Room 800; 503-823-2925, fax 503-823-7576.

Multnomah County also puts out a map, but it just covers the east county area. ~ 1220 Southeast 190th Avenue; 503-248-5050.

The best resource is *Bike There*, a detailed bicycle map and safety guide for the metropolitan area. Bike and multi-use lanes are color coded to a use-suitability scale (off-street, low-traffic, etc.). *Bike There* is put out by Metro (an elected regional government). You can pick one up at Powell's Bookstore, most bike shops or at Metro headquarters at 600 Northeast Grand Street in Portland.

Just as the riders using them come in a variety of shapes and sizes, bike routes in the area are of varying lengths and distances. Beginners and intermediate riders would do well to contact **The Bike Gallery**, which sponsors weekend group rides that are open to the public. Two rides are usually offered: a road ride one day, a mountain ride the next. ~ 12345 Southwest Canyon Road, Beaverton; 503-641-2580; www.bikegallery.com.

City riders will find the northeast and southeast portions of the city more suitable. The terrain is relatively flat, and marked bike routes follow low- or medium-traffic streets.

PORTLAND EAST   The **Springwater Corridor** follows an old railroad route along the southern flank of the city. The 16-mile trail extends from Southeast McLoughlin Boulevard east through Powell Butte Nature Park and Gresham to the city of Boring in Clackamas County. Most of this multi-use trail is unpaved.

PORTLAND WEST   Mountain bikers will like **Forest Park**, which comprises 5000 acres west of downtown. The park has some rather hilly terrain, perfect for mountain biking, and one multi-use trail, Leif Erickson, is especially popular.

More experienced riders, of course, have the option of longer rides, perhaps west to the **vineyards** around Hillsboro. The Bike Gallery in Beaverton is a good source for information on suggested routes, distances and length of trips.

COLUMBIA RIVER GORGE   East of Portland, the Columbia River Gorge along Route 84 is prime cycling territory, particularly along any portion of the 62-mile route from Portland to Hood River. The old Columbia River Highway, which parallels Route 84, is less trafficked, calmer, scenic and a wonderful way

AUTHOR FAVORITE

An excellent cycling getaway in the area is **Sauvie Island**, located ten miles northwest of Portland. Light traffic makes it a pleasure to pedal through this wildlife sanctuary. You can drive or take a Tri-Met bus to the island.

to experience the Gorge. The Dalles Riverfront Trail, a paved bike trail, extends from the west part of The Dalles to Dalles Dam.

Bike Rentals **Discover Bicycles** rents and sells mountain and road bikes and can provide information about guided bike tours. ~ 116 Oak Street, Hood River, OR; 541-386-4820; www.disco verbicycles.com.

HIKING

A hiker's paradise, the Portland region has beautiful riverfront walks, urban trails and wilderness loops perfect for a brief interlude or an all-day excursion. Trail information is available from the Portland Oregon Information Center or the **Bureau of Parks and Recreation**. ~ 1120 Southwest 5th Avenue; 503-823-2223, fax 503-823-6007. All distances listed for hiking trails are one way unless otherwise noted.

CENTRAL PORTLAND Named for a former governor, **Tom McCall Waterfront Park** offers a 2-mile-long path along the Willamette River. This is an ideal way to get an overview of the downtown area.

PORTLAND EAST The **Springwater Corridor** (16.5 miles) begins at Tideman-Johnson Park and heads to Gresham and south to Boring, shadowing Johnson Creek. This multipurpose trail is a converted railway line that's part of the Rails to Trails project.

You don't have to go all the way to Mt. St. Helens to hike a volcano. Just take the **Mt. Tabor Perimeter Loop** (2.7 miles). Your hike on Southeast 60th Avenue, Southeast Yamhill Street, Southeast 71st Avenue and Southeast Harrison Drive (which becomes Southeast Lincoln Street) provides a pleasant overview of this landmark.

PORTLAND WEST Sauvie Island is ideal for short or long strolls. One of our favorite walks in the region is the hike from parking lot #5 in Crane Unit around **Willow Hole to Domeyer Lake** (1.5 miles). Another good bet is the hike from Walton Beach along the Columbia to **Warrior Rock Lighthouse** (3 miles).

With more than 5000 acres, Forest Park offers over 50 miles of connecting trails. Many of the routes are spurs off **Wildwood Trail** (27 miles), the primary route traversing this vast urban refuge. Depending on your time and mood, hike as much of this trail as you want, connecting easily to other convenient routes. Your starting point for Wildwood is Hoyt Arboretum's Vietnam Memorial. If you're feeling more ambitious, try **Marquam Nature Trail** (5 miles), leading from Hines Park to Washington Park via Terwilliger Boulevard and Council Crest Park.

Two mile-long walks will add to your enjoyment of Hoyt Arboretum. The **Conifer Tour** leads through a forest thick with spruce, fir and redwood. Also well worth your time is the **Oak Tour**.

COLUMBIA RIVER GORGE   Latourell Falls Trail (2.2 miles), on the Columbia River Highway three miles east of Crown Point, is a moderately difficult walk leading along a streambed to the base of the upper falls. To extend this walk another mile, take a loop trail beginning at the top of lower Latourell Falls and returning to the highway at Talbot Park.

Near the Bridal Veil exit off Route 84 is **#415 Angels Rest Trail** (4.5 miles), an easy hike leading to an overlook. This route can be extended another 15 miles to Bonneville Dam by taking the **#400 Gorge Trail**, an amazing path that passes many of the Gorge's stunning cascades, including Multnomah Falls, Triple Falls and Horsetail Falls.

A manmade tunnel passes behind the cascading water of Tunnel Falls.

Eagle Creek Campground at Exit 41 on Route 84 is the jumpoff point for the easy **#440 Eagle Creek Trail** to Punch Bowl Falls (2 miles) or Tunnel Falls (6 miles). You can continue to follow the wildflower-riddled path (part of the Pacific Crest Trail) through the Columbia Wilderness, up to Wahtum Lake (13 miles). Four campsites provide rest between Eagle Creek and the lake.

On the Washington side of the river west of Bonneville Dam is the one-mile trail leading to the top of **Beacon Rock**, an 800-foot monolith noted by Lewis and Clark. Ascended by a series of switchbacks guarded by railings, this trail offers numerous views of the Gorge.

East of Home Valley, Oregon, on Route 14 is the **Dog Mountain Trail** (6 miles), a difficult climb up 2900 feet for impressive views of Mt. Hood, Mt. St. Helens and Mt. Adams. During May and June, the surrounding hills are covered with wildflowers, making this an extraordinary time to hike the trail.

Transportation

Most visitors to Portland arrive on one of three primary highways. **Route 5** bisects the city and provides access from the north via Vancouver, Washington. This same highway also is the main line from points south like the Willamette Valley and California. From points east, **Route 84** along the Columbia River is the preferred way to enter Portland. From the west, **Route 26** is a major highway into town. Secondary routes include **Route 30** from the west and **Route 99** from the south. For road conditions, call 503-222-6721.

CAR

AIR

Portland International Airport is the major gateway. Located ten miles northeast of downtown, it is served by Air Canada Jazz, Alaska Airlines, American Airlines, Big Sky Airlines, Continental Airlines, Delta Air Lines, Frontier Airlines, Hawaiian Airlines, Horizon Air, JetBlue Airlines, Lufthansa, Mexicana, Northwest Airlines, Southwest Airlines, United Airlines and US Airways. ~ www.portlandairportpdx.com.

Limousines, vans and buses take visitors to downtown locations, including **Limousines Dot Com** (866-546-6726; www.limos.com).

BUS

Greyhound Bus Lines offers bus service to Portland from across the nation. The main downtown terminal is at 550 Northwest 6th Avenue. ~ 800-231-2222; www.greyhound.com.

Also consider the **Green Tortoise**, a New Age company with a fleet of funky buses. Each is equipped with sleeping platforms allowing travelers to rest as they cross the country. The buses stop at interesting sightseeing points en route. The Green Tortoise, an endangered species from the '60s, travels to and from the East Coast, Portland, Seattle, Los Angeles and elsewhere. It provides a mode of transportation as well as an experience in group living. ~ 494 Broadway, San Francisco, CA 94133; 415-956-7500, 800-867-8647; www.greentortoise.com.

TRAIN

Amtrak provides service from Washington and California via the "Coast Starlight." There is also a northerly connection to Spokane on the "Empire Builder." ~ 800 Northwest 6th Avenue; 800-872-7245; www.amtrak.com.

CAR RENTALS

At the Portland International Airport try **Avis Rent A Car** (503-249-4950), **Budget Rent A Car** (503-249-4556), **Dollar Rent A Car** (503-249-4793), **Enterprise Rent A Car** (503-252-1500), **Hertz Rent A Car** (503-249-8216).

PUBLIC TRANSIT

Tri-Met Buses/MAX Light Rail serve the Portland region. Buses blanket the city, while the MAX blue line extends east from downtown to the Gateway transit center and then on to Gresham. The red line provides direct service from downtown to the airport. There is free bus service downtown and in the Lloyd District in the "Fareless Square" region spanning 300 blocks. ~ 503-238-7433; www.tri-met.org.

TAXIS

Broadway Cab (503-227-1234), **Radio Cab** (503-227-1212) and **Yellow Cab** (503-253-2277) all provide convenient local service. In Hood River, call **Hood River Taxi and Transportation** (541-386-2255).

EIGHT

Oregon Coast

As you take in the wonders of the Oregon Coast, do it with respect, for in a very real sense you are stepping into a paradise borrowed. In 1805, when Lewis and Clark arrived at the mouth of the Columbia River, only about 10,000 American Indians in such coast tribes as the Tillamook and Yaquina called this home. With roughly three square miles per inhabitant, these tribes were undisputed masters of their realm. The American Indians traveled almost entirely by water, were intensely spiritual and had, for the most part, a modest and self-sufficient lifestyle. Working hard during the spring and summer months, they harvested enough from the sea and forests to relax during the winter.

But their world began to change, indeed it was doomed, when distant entrepreneurs set sights on the region's vast resources. These men believed that the Northwest did not belong to its native populace but was instead destined to be claimed by a new master race of settlers thousands of miles away. Among them was John Jacob Astor, the richest man in America. Eager to monopolize the lucrative fur trade in the uncharted Northwest, he dispatched the ship *Tonquin* from New York in the fall of 1810. Then, in the spring of 1811, just about the time the *Tonquin* was sailing across the Columbia River Bar, a second overland group sponsored by Astor left St. Louis. They began by following the river route pioneered by Lewis and Clark but then forged a new trail across the Rockies, eventually reaching the Snake River, where they were turned back by impenetrable rapids. By early 1812, when the party limped into Astoria, the little settlement created by men from the *Tonquin*, it was clear that their patron's great vision remained distant. For one thing, most of the *Tonquin* group had headed north to Vancouver Island, where dictatorial captain Jonathan Thorn spurned the American Indians, triggering a massacre that destroyed almost everyone aboard. In a final insane act of revenge, a surviving crew member lured the American Indians back on the ship, went below and lit the ship's magazine, killing everyone aboard.

In September 1812, not long after they received news of this tragedy, the Astorians left behind at the little Columbia River settlement were visited by a party from the rival North West Fur Company. These newcomers announced that a British warship was en route to seize Fort Astoria. To make matters worse, they declared that the British had just won the War of 1812. Cut off from the news that would have exposed this lie, the Astorians decided to sell off their pelts and the first American settlement west of the Mississippi for pennies on the dollar. Then they began the long journey home.

While the British took over the fur trade, Americans began heading west on the Oregon Trail, inspired by the dream of Manifest Destiny, which would unite the continent "from sea to shining sea." In 1846, the Oregon Country was returned to the Americans and new settlers gradually returned to the coast. Astoria and other settlements along the coast emerged as fishing, farming and logging centers. The arrival of the railroads spawned the development of resort towns like Newport and Seaside. Boardwalks, modeled after those found on the East Coast, soon sprang up to serve the growing clientele.

The coast may have been the magnet, but it didn't take the new arrivals long to discover that the lofty headlands, picturesque estuaries, rocky points, sand dunes and tidepools were only part of the attraction. Back behind the coastal rhododendron fields were rivers that offered legendary steelhead fishing. Sunny valleys forested with fir, spruce, hemlock and cedar were perfect for camping. Stands of weird carnivorous plants, plunging waterfalls, myrtle groves and pristine lakes were all part of the draw. And the Indians, decimated by white man's diseases, were subjugated by the new settlers and ultimately forced onto reservations.

Having pushed the natives conveniently out of the way, the pioneers soon began reaping nature's bounty from the coastal region. Coos Bay became a major wood-processing center, and commercial fishing dominated the economies of communities like Port Orford. In other towns, such as Tillamook, the dairy trade flourished. And, of course, farming also began to emerge in the sunnier valleys east of the coast.

Today, thanks in part to a comprehensive network of state parks, the coast is equally appealing to motorists, bikers and hikers. While it's hard to improve on this landscape, humans have done their best to complement nature's handiwork. From bed and breakfasts heavy on chintz and lace to bargain oceanfront motels furnished from garage sales, accommodations serve every taste. Everywhere you turn, another executive chef weary of big-city life seems to be opening a pasta joint or a pita stand. Theater, classical music, jazz, pottery and sculpture galleries have all found a home in towns ranging from North Bend to Cannon Beach. A major aquarium in Newport, a world-class maritime museum in Astoria, a printing museum in Coos Bay, an antiquarian curio shop in Florence—these are just a few of the special places that are likely to capture your attention.

If you must go down to the sea again, and you must, rest assured that this coast offers the space all of us need. True, some of the northern beaches draw a crowd on weekends and holidays. But traffic is lighter on the South Coast, where beachcombing can be a solitary experience. With vast national recreation areas, national forests and sloughs, it's easy to get lost in the region. Often foggy, the

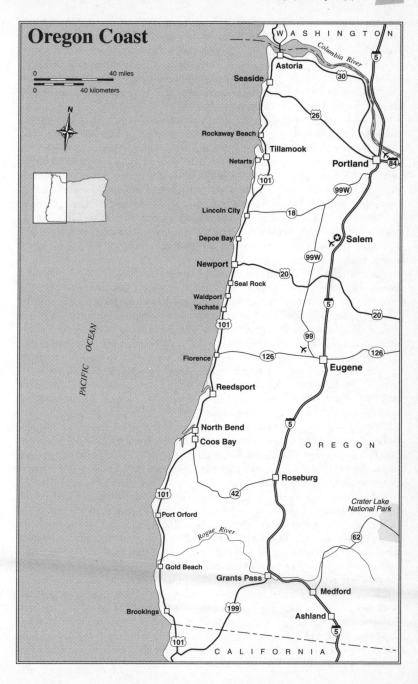

Oregon Coast

0 ————— 40 miles
0 ————— 40 kilometers

N

WASHINGTON

Columbia River

Astoria

Seaside

5

30

26

Rockaway Beach

Tillamook

Netarts

101

Portland

84

99W

Lincoln City

18

Depoe Bay

Salem

Newport

99W

Seal Rock

20

Waldport

Yachats

101

5

20

99

Florence

126

126

Eugene

Reedsport

North Bend

Coos Bay

5

OREGON

Roseburg

101

42

Crater Lake
National Park

Port Orford

Rogue River

62

Gold Beach

Grants Pass

Medford

Brookings

199

Ashland

101

5

CALIFORNIA

PACIFIC OCEAN

Oregon coast is hit by frequent storms in the winter months. But this rugged weather is offset by mild periods in the summer or early fall. Even when the coast itself is socked in, inland valleys just a few miles away can be warm and sunny. The contrast continues: temperatures along the coast seldom fall below freezing, but the adjacent coastal peaks are frequently snowbound in the winter months. And while the surf is bracing, lakes adjacent to the coast feature warmer waters ideal for swimming and waterskiing.

To fully experience the coast, you're well advised to see it border to border, from Astoria to Brookings. But many travelers prefer to focus on one or two areas. If you're history minded, Astoria is a must. For pure scenic grandeur and small-town charm, it's hard to beat the Tillamook–Three Capes area. Another winner in this category is the Otter Rock community north of Newport. Windy Port Orford is a very special place, scenic, uncrowded and ideal for steelheading.

Groups with diverse interests such as surf fishing, arcade games and shopping for folk art will want to consider well-rounded resort towns like Lincoln City, Seaside and Newport. They offer sporting life, cultural attractions and all the cotton candy you can eat. These towns are also convenient to rural gems when you're ready to make a great escape.

One of the most alluring communities on the coast is Florence. A delightful historic district, some of Oregon's finest dunes, a good restaurant scene and easy access to the Willamette Valley make this community a popular getaway. In the same category is Bandon, a charming port with a commercial district that will delight the shoppers in your group. Those who are eager to take a jet boat to the wilderness will doubtless find themselves in Gold Beach, a major fishing center. And Brookings is the gateway to one of our favorites, the Chetco River country.

The Bay Area, Coos Bay/North Bend/Charleston, is an ideal choice for clamming on the tidal flats. The parks, sloughs and country roads south of the area will keep you busy for days. And there is an impressive variety of museums, including one of the state's finest art institutions.

When it comes to a trendy resort atmosphere with tasteful shopping malls, sign ordinances, café au lait, classical music, French cuisine and gallery openings, Cannon Beach is the coast's class act. Every day the tourist tide from the east washes in patrons of the arts and Oregon varietals. This town may set the record for merchant-punsters operating shops with names like "Sometimes a Great Lotion."

There are many other destinations that don't appear on any map. In fact, the best of the Oregon Coast may not be its incorporated cities or parklands. Think instead of rocky points home only to sea lions. Eddies so beautiful you don't care if you catch anything. Offshore haystacks that don't even have names. Dunes that form the perfect backdrop for a day of kite flying. Points that seem to have been created solely for the purpose of sunset watching.

All these possibilities may seem overwhelming. But we believe the following pages will put your mind at ease. An embarrassment of riches, the Oregon Coast is more byway than highway. As you explore the capes and coves, visit the sea-lion caves and sea-cut caverns, you're likely to make numerous finds of your own.

Those hidden places we're always talking about will tempt you to linger for hours, maybe even days. And however long you stay, give pause to remember that another people once lived here.

Oregon's North Coast is one of the most heavily traveled tourist routes in the Pacific Northwest. From June to early October, you can expect to have plenty of company. While most travelers hug the shoreline, some of the best sightseeing is actually found a few miles inland. Less crowded and often sunnier, these hidden spots reward those willing to veer off Route 101.

North Coast

A special tip for those who prefer to drive during off-peak times: Around 5 p.m. most of the logging trucks are berthed and the RVs are bedded down for the night. In the summer consider allocating a good part of your day for sightseeing. Then, at 5 p.m., when many of the museums and attractions close, take a couple of daylight hours to proceed to your next destination. Not only is the traffic lighter, the sunsets are remarkable. Plus, you'll be able to dine fashionably late.

Why not follow the path of Lewis and Clark by taking Route 30 west from Portland along the Columbia River to **Astoria**, the first American settlement established west of the Rockies? Set on a hillside overlooking the Columbia River, Astoria is one of the Pacific Northwest's most historic cities. Grand Victorians, steep streets and skies that belong to the gulls and shorebirds make this river town a must. As you enter Astoria, stop at the **Uppertown Firefighters Museum**. The vintage collection, housed in a 1920s firehouse, includes a classic 1878 horse-drawn ladder wagon, antique motorized pumpers and fire-fighting memorabilia. Closed Sunday through Tuesday. ~ 30th Street and Marine Drive, Astoria; 503-325-2203, fax 503-325-7727; www.cumtux.org, e-mail cchs@cumtux.org.

SIGHTS

One of the most treacherous spots on the West Coast, the turbulent Columbia River Bar was a nautical graveyard claiming scores of ships.

Continue west to the **Columbia River Maritime Museum**. One of the nation's finest seafaring collections, this 40,000-square-foot building tells the story of the Northwest's mightiest river, discovered in 1792 by Captain Robert Gray and navigated by Lewis and Clark in 1805 on the final leg of their 4000-mile journey from St. Louis. Besides documenting shipwrecks, the museum offers exhibits on American Indian history, the Northwest fur trade, navigation and marine safety, fishing, canneries, whaling, sailing and steam and motor vessels. Interactive exhibits include a Coast Guard rescue mission, fishing on the Columbia River and taking the helm in a tugboat Wheelhouse. And that's not all. Docked outside is the *Columbia*, the last of numerous lightships that provided navigational aid along the Pacific Coast. Admission. ~ 1792 Marine Drive, Astoria; 503-325-2323, fax 503-325-2331; www.crmm.org.

Continue west along Marine Drive to Astoria, the city founded in 1812 by John Jacob Astor as a fur-trading post. Head to the

Astoria–Warrenton Area Chamber of Commerce to pick up a helpful map and background. ~ 111 West Marine Drive, Astoria; 503-325-6311, 800-875-6807, fax 503-325-9767; www.oldore gon.com, e-mail awacc@seasurf.com.

Among the many Astoria Victorians on the National Register of Historic Places is the **Flavel House**, a Queen Anne with Italianate columns and Eastlake-style woodwork around the doors and windows. Featuring six fireplaces, a library and a music parlor, this home is one of the most visited residences on the Oregon coast. Admission. ~ 441 8th Street, Astoria; 503-325-2203, fax 503-325-7727; www.cumtux.org, e-mail cchs@cumtux.org.

At the **Heritage Museum** exhibits feature the early pioneers, American Indians, immigrants and local industries of Clatsop County. A "vice and virtue" exhibit explores the county's colorful past. Admission. ~ 16th and Exchange streets, Astoria; 503-338-4849, fax 503-338-6265; www.cumtux.org, e-mail cchs@cumtux.org.

You'll also want to visit **Fort Astoria**. This small blockhouse replica was the home base for the Astorians when they settled here in the early 19th century. ~ 15th and Exchange streets, Astoria.

For a good overview, follow the signs up 16th Street to **Coxcomb Hill**. Pictorial friezes wrapping around the 125-foot-high Astoria column, built in 1926, cover the region's heritage from its American Indian past to modern times. Unless you're prone to vertigo, climb the circular stairway to the top for a panoramic view of Astoria.

About eight miles west of Astoria in the town of Hammond is **Fort Stevens Historic Area and Military Museum**. On June 21, 1942, the fort became the first American continental military installation shelled since the War of 1812. Nine shots fired by a Japanese submarine hit the fort. Fortunately none caused any damage. (The same pilot also dropped a few ineffective bombs near Brookings on the southern Oregon coast.) While visiting, you can tour the fort in a two-and-a-half-ton Army truck or take an underground tour of Battery Mishler (fee; May through September). Don't miss the wreck of the *Peter Iredale*, now a rusty skeleton easily reached by following signs inside the park. Parking fee. ~ Fort Stevens State Park, Hammond; 503-861-2000, fax 503-861-0879; www.visitfortstevens.com, e-mail foofs@teleport.com.

During the rainy winter of 1805–1806, the 33-member Lewis and Clark party built a fort and lived at what is today the **Lewis and Clark National Historical Park at Fort Clatsop** for three months before returning east. Named in honor of the Clatsop tribe, this reconstructed fort has introductory movie presentations and interpretive displays. In the summer, buckskin-clad rangers armed with flintlock rifles offer muzzle-loading demonstrations or show how Lewis and Clark's team made candles, did woodworking and

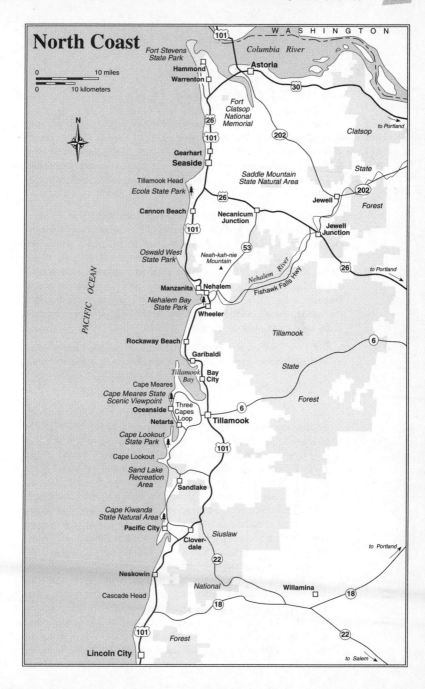

North Coast

0 ————— 10 miles
0 ————— 10 kilometers

N

WASHINGTON

Columbia River

101

Astoria

30

Fort Stevens
State Park

Hammond

Warrenton

Fort
Clatsop
National
Memorial

26

101

Clatsop

to Portland

202

State

Gearhart

Seaside

Saddle Mountain
State Natural Area

202

Jewell

Forest

Tillamook Head

Ecola State Park

Cannon Beach

26

Necanicum
Junction

Jewell
Junction

26

to Portland

101

53

Oswald West
State Park

Neah-kah-nie
Mountain

Nehalem River

Fishawk Falls Hwy

Manzanita Nehalem

Nehalem Bay
State Park

Wheeler

Tillamook

6

Rockaway Beach

Garibaldi

PACIFIC OCEAN

Tillamook
Bay

Bay
City

State

Cape Meares

Cape Meares State
Scenic Viewpoint

Oceanside

Netarts

Three
Capes
Loop

6

Forest

Tillamook

Cape Lookout
State Park

Cape Lookout

101

Sand Lake
Recreation
Area

Sandlake

Cape Kiwanda
State Natural Area

Pacific City

Clover-
dale

Siuslaw

to Portland

22

Neskowin

National

Willamina

18

Cascade Head

18

101

Forest

22

Lincoln City

to Salem

SCENIC DRIVE

Three Capes Loop

West of Tillamook is one of the most picturesque drives on the Oregon Coast, 35-mile **Three Capes Loop**. The three capes are Cape Meares, Cape Lookout and Cape Kiwanda, each of which contains a state park of the same name (see "Beaches & Parks" for more information). The route starts in central Tillamook. From Route 101, take Bay Ocean Road west, and when you reach the fork in the road, bear right along the coast.

BAY OCEAN PARK   As you follow Bay Ocean Road along the southern edge of Tillamook Bay, you'll come to one of the region's most fascinating ghost towns, Bay Ocean Park. Designed to become a pre-casino Atlantic City of the West, this 1912 subdivision eventually grew to 59 homes. But between 1932 and 1949 the sea cut a half-mile swath across the spit, turning it into an island. Over the next 20 years the ocean eroded the Bay Ocean landscape and one by one homes were swept into the sea. Finally, in 1959, the last five remaining houses were moved. Today only a sign marks the site.

CAPE MEARES   The Three Capes Loop continues past Cape Meares Lake, a haven for waterfowl and shorebirds, before continuing to Cape Meares

sewed hides. There are trails upon which visitors can wander. Admission. ~ Five miles south of Astoria off of Route 101; 503-861-2471, fax 503-861-2585; www.nps.gov/lewi.

Oregon's answer to Coney Island, the town of **Seaside** is the kind of place to go when you long for saltwater taffy and game arcades, boardwalks and volleyball. Just head down Broadway to find the carnival atmosphere. By the time you reach the beach you'll feel a restless urge to start building sandcastles. The oldest and one of the most popular resorts on the coast, it is easy to visit with a little help from the **Seaside Visitors Bureau**. ~ 7 North Roosevelt Drive, Seaside; 503-738-3097, 888-306-2326, fax 503-717-8299; www.seasideor.com, e-mail visit@seaside-oregon.com.

The two-mile boardwalk known as the **Prom** offers a historical look at Seaside. Along the way are Victorian-style homes, arts-and-crafts bungalows, Colonial revivals and English-style cottages. Another highlight is the Prom "Turnaround," marking the end of the Lewis and Clark Trail. At the south end is a reproduction of the cairn where the Lewis and Clark expedition boiled seawater

State Scenic Viewpoint. While here you'll want to visit the **Octopus Tree**, a legendary Sitka spruce with six trunks extending horizontally for up to 30 feet before making a skyward turn. With just two more limbs this could have been the world's largest Hanukkah menorah. You can also take the short trail to the century-old Cape Meares lighthouse, surrounded by wild roses in the warm months.

THREE ARCH ROCKS　　Continue south to Oceanside and Three Arch Rocks Wildlife Refuge, home of Oregon's largest seabird colony. Half a mile offshore, these islands harbor 200,000 common murres as well as tufted puffins, pigeon guillemots, storm petrels, cormorants and gulls. You might spot a noisy sea-lion colony perched on the rocks below.

CAPE LOOKOUT　　At Cape Lookout State Park, nature trails and coast walks delight visitors. With 2000 acres of forested headlands abutting sandy dunes, Cape Lookout has some of the best walking trails on the coast. Dune buffs will enjoy visiting the **Sand Lake Recreation Area** seven miles south of Cape Lookout State Park. These 1000 acres of dunes attract the ATV crowd, who zoom up and over the dunes ceaselessly. **Pacific City**, on Cape Kiwanda, is famous for its dory fleet launched into the surf from the Cape Kiwanda beach.

The Three Capes Loop returns to Route 101 two miles east of Pacific City, two miles south of Cloverdale, and eight miles north of Neskowin.

during the winter of 1806 to make salt. More than three and a half bushels were produced for the return trip.

Of special interest is the **Seaside Museum**. Inside are American Indian artifacts (some dating back 2000 years), turn-of-the-20th-century photos of boardwalk hotels and bathhouses, a linotype printing press, and antique fire-fighting equipment. Admission includes a tour of the historic Butterfield Cottage. ~ 570 Necanicum Drive, Seaside; 503-738-7065, fax 503-738-0761; www.seasidemuseum.org, e-mail office@seasidemuseum.org.

Also here in town is the **Seaside Aquarium**, where you can see marine mammals and feed local harbor seals. Kids love the hands-on interaction at the touch tank. Call for winter hours. Admission. ~ 200 North Promenade, Seaside; 503-738-6211, fax 503-717-0904; www.seasideaquarium.com, e-mail aquarium@seasideaquarium.com.

Eighteen miles east of Seaside on Route 26 is the **Camp 18 Logging Museum**. Steam donkeys, cranes, train cabooses and other vintage equipment are among the exhibits. (There's a restaurant on the premises.) ~ Milepost 18, Route 26; 503-755-1818, 800-874-1810, fax 503-755-2815.

Follow Route 26 east to Jewell Junction and continue north on Fishawk Falls Highway toward Jewell. Just north of town is the **Jewell Meadows Wildlife Area**. Run by the Oregon Department of Fish and Wildlife, the sanctuary is a good place to spot raptors, red-tailed hawks, songbirds and, in winter, bald eagles and Roosevelt elk. ~ Route 202; 503-755-2264, fax 503-755-0706.

HIDDEN ►

Located south of Seaside is **Tillamook Head Trail**, a seven-mile route that extends to Cannon Beach's northern edge. Most of the route is within Ecola State Park. A highlight of this park is the tidepools of rocky Indian Beach. From the head you'll enjoy excellent views of the coast and the **Tillamook Rock Lighthouse**.

Cannon Beach, one of the most popular villages on the North Coast, is an artists' colony and home of photogenic **Haystack Rock**. Rising 235 feet ("the third-largest coastal monolith in the world") and accessible at low tide, this geologic wonder is a marine and bird sanctuary, and a good place to explore tidepools and look for puffins. With its resorts and condos, boutiques and small malls, Cannon Beach (it's named for a cannon that drifted ashore after a shipwreck) can be a busy place, especially in summer when the population increases fourfold. Gallery shows, the Stormy Weather Festival (early November's artist showcase), sandcastle contests and concerts in the park add to the fun.

Twelve miles south of Cannon Beach, **Oswald West State Park** offers a series of beautiful viewpoints. Just south of the park is **Neah-kah-nie Mountain**, a 1631-foot promontory surrounded by a 200-year-old American Indian legend. Indian lore holds that a wrecked Spanish galleon carrying gold and beeswax washed up on the beach and the surviving crew members tucked the treasure into a hole dug at the base of the mountain. But treasure hunters, using everything from backhoes to bare hands, have failed to strike it rich here.

A lovely spot on the North Coast is **Nehalem Bay**, separated from the ocean by a sandspit. The Nehalem River, a waterway filled with Chinook salmon, empties into the bay, making it one of the best fishing spots in the Pacific Northwest. You'll see boats crowding the bay during the prime fall fishing months.

Along the bay are three small resort towns. The northernmost, **Manzanita**, sits amidst trees at the foot of Neah-kah-nie Mountain. Many residents of Portland and Seattle make Manzanita a weekend retreat. In fact, more than 60 percent of the homes here are owned by people who are not residents year-round. A five-block-long strip of gift shops, restaurants and motels make this the bay's center for provisions. The historic **Nehalem** waterfront, located right where the river meets the bay, was an American Indian community before being replaced by canneries, lumber mills and dairy farms. Today, despite disastrous flooding in 1966, Nehalem continues to thrive, sporting an increasing number of clothing, gift and specialty shops. Nearby **Wheeler** is an increasingly popular town situated on the southern side of Nehalem Bay on a hill sloping down to the Pacific. Boutiques are beginning to sprout up in Wheeler, which is also the site of the **Nehalem Bay Visitors Center**. You can pick up information about Wheeler, Manzanita and the entire Nehalem Bay area here. Closed weekdays from November through April. ~ 425 Nehalem Boulevard, Wheeler; 503-368-5100, 877-368-5100; www.nehalembaychamber.com, e-mail nehalem@nehalemtel.net.

Heading south, Route 101 follows the curving shoreline around Tillamook Bay. On your way into **Tillamook** you'll probably want to stop to sample the familiar orange cheddar at **Tillamook Cheese**. A self-guided tour makes it easy to see the Pacific Northwest's largest cheese factory, Tillamook County Creamery Association. An observation room offers a bird's-eye view of the packaging process. Free cheese samples. ~ 4175 North Route 101, Tillamook; 503-815-1300, 800-542-7290, fax 503-815-1305; www.tillamookcheese.com.

Next, stop by the **Tillamook Chamber of Commerce** to pick up helpful background information about this area. Closed weekends. ~ 3705 North Route 101, Tillamook; 503-842-7525, fax 503-842-7526; www.tillamookchamber.org, e-mail tillchamber@oregoncoast.com.

Among the musts is the **Tillamook County Pioneer Museum**. Unlike many museums that display only a small portion of their holdings, this one is packed with 35,000 antiques, artifacts, dioramas, mounted animals, gems and gemstones and other items connected with the coast's pioneer life and natural history. Highlights include Tillamook basketry, pioneer implements, antique-clock section and fire-lookout cabin. You'll also learn that the giant hangars south of town berthed blimps that patrolled the West Coast for the Navy during World War II. Closed Monday. Admission. ~ 2106 2nd Street, Tillamook; phone/fax 503-842-4553; www.tcpm.org, e-mail clb@tcpm.org.

❖❖

RADIO FREE ASTORIA

About 20 miles west of Portland you can tune in **KMUN** (91.9 or 89.5 FM), one of the finest public-broadcasting stations in the Northwest. A kind of Radio Free Astoria, this listener-sponsored station features local kids reading their favorite fiction, opera buffs airing Bellini, and river pilots doing classical and variety shows.

If you'd like to explore the world of dirigibles, head to the **Tillamook Air Museum**, housed in a former blimp hangar that dates from 1943. It's the largest wooden clear-span structure in the world. The museum's collection features photographs, artifacts and 30 vintage World War II and modern airplanes. Admission. ~ 6030 Hangar Road, Tillamook; 503-842-1130, fax 503-842-3054; www.tillamookair.com, e-mail info@tillamookair.com.

From Tillamook, Route 101 runs inland for 26 miles, much of it through **Siuslaw National Forest**, before returning to the seashore six miles north of Neskowin.

HIDDEN ► Seven miles south of town via Route 101, take the turnoff to 266-foot-high **Munson Creek Falls**, easily reached via a half-mile trail. This horsetail falls is the highest in the Coast Range, and is a popular spot for picnicking. The creek gorge is lovely.

South of Neskowin, Cascade Head Road leads to the **Cascade Head Scenic Research Area** and the **Cascade Head Experimental Forest**. These two areas, run as research facilities by the U.S. Forest Service, are full of colorful wildflowers and birds. The moderately difficult six-mile-long Cascade Head Trail follows the coast and provides plenty of opportunities to whale watch. Because these are special research areas, be sure to stay on the trails and not disturb any flora or fauna.

LODGING A neoclassical revival with fir wainscotting, leaded glass, traditional American furnishings and a formal dining room, the **Rosebriar Inn B&B** offers 12 rooms in a renovated former convent. The rooms have wing-back chairs and mahogany furniture; some have fireplaces. One unit is located in a separate carriage house with a kitchenette and jacuzzi. The Captain's Room has a great view of Astoria. A gourmet breakfast is included. ~ 636 14th Street, Astoria; 503-325-7427, 800-487-0224, fax 503-325-6937; www.rosebriar.net, e-mail rbinn@pacifier.com. MODERATE TO ULTRA-DELUXE.

East of town, the **Crest Motel** sits on a grassy hilltop overlooking the Columbia River. This trim and tidy establishment has 40 modernized units with watercolor prints and writing desks, a jacuzzi and laundry facilities. Try for one of the quieter rear rooms. ~ 5366 Leif Erickson Drive, Astoria; phone/fax 503-325-3141, 800-421-3141; www.crestmotelastoria.com. MODERATE.

Also on the Columbia River is **Best Western Lincoln Inn of Astoria**. The 75 motel units are spacious and comfortable, and most rooms have Columbia River or Young Bay views. The indoor pool, sauna and spa are open for guests' use; laundry facilities are a plus. Convenient to Astoria's historic district, this is an ideal spot to watch river traffic or fish. A full hot breakfast buf-

How old is your Tillamook cheese? Medium cheddar is aged for 60 days, sharp cheddar for 9 months and extra sharp for nearly a year and a half!

fet is included, and freshly baked cookies are offered nightly. Pet-friendly. ~ 555 Hamburg Avenue, Astoria; 503-325-2205, 800-621-0641, fax 503-325-5550; e-mail 38156@hotel.bestwestern.com. DELUXE TO ULTRA-DELUXE.

Hillcrest Inn offers 26 attractive, pine-shaded units in a quiet garden setting close to this resort town's beach, shops, restaurants and nightlife. Choose between studios and one- and two-bedroom units with kitchens. Eclectic furniture ranges from fold-out sofas to wicker living-room sets. Some units have fireplaces, decks and spas. Barbecue facilities and picnic tables are provided for guest use. Adjacent to the inn is an ultra-deluxe six-bedroom beachhouse that sleeps up to 16 people; it rents weekly in the summer and requires a two-night minimum in the off-season. Family groups will find this establishment a good value. Wi-fi internet available. ~ 118 North Columbia Street, Seaside; 503-738-6273, 800-270-7659, fax 503-717-0266; www.seasidehillcrest.com, e-mail hillcrest@email.com. MODERATE.

The **Ocean Front Motel** is an older, 35-unit motel with one- and two-room units on the beach. The carpeted rooms have wooden bedframes, refrigerators and picture windows ideal for sunset watching. Kitchenettes are also available. Number 13, a one-bedroom cottage, is a bargain for the budget-minded. ~ 50 1st Avenue, Seaside; 503-738-5661, fax 503-738-3084; www.oceanfrontor.com. MODERATE.

Located right on the beach, the three-story **Seashore Inn On the Beach** has 54 spacious guest rooms with comfortable furniture, vanities, an enclosed pool, sauna and whirlpool. Within walking distance of Seaside's most popular attractions, it overlooks volleyball courts and the surf. Continental breakfast and free wi-fi available ~ 60 North Promenade, Seaside; 503-738-6368, 888-738-6368, fax 503-738-8314; www.seashoreinnor.com, e-mail info@seashoreinnor.com. DELUXE TO ULTRA-DELUXE.

A mix of sleeping rooms and one-bedroom units, the completely non-smoking **McBee Motel Cottages** are conveniently located on the south side of town, only one block from the beach. Some of the ten units in this older, motel-style complex offer kitchenettes and fireplaces. Some rooms are pet-friendly. ~ 888 South Hemlock Street, Cannon Beach; 503-436-2569, 800-238-4107; www.mcbeecottages.com, e-mail cbhl@oregoncoastlodging.com. DELUXE.

Set on a hill with commanding views of Nehalem Bay, the motel rooms at **Wheeler Village Inn** are small, clean and brightly painted. All six rooms have carpets and kitchenettes. Pull up a chair and enjoy the sunsets or relax outside in the landscaped garden. All rentals are long term with a one-month minimum stay. ~ 2nd and Gregory streets, Wheeler; 503-368-5734; e-mail otoole@nehalemtel.net. BUDGET.

On Nehalem Bay, **Wheeler on the Bay Lodge and Marina** certainly is on the bay; it even has its own private docks. Ten motel-style units and suites, some with private decks, spas and kitchenettes, are furnished with fireplaces and VCRs. The lodge runs an on-site video store as well as kayak and canoe rentals and private bay cruises. Rooms range from Victorian style to art deco; all are carpeted. It's convenient to fishing, crabbing, sailboarding, hiking and birdwatching. ~ 580 Marine Drive, Wheeler; 503-368-5858, 800-469-3204, fax 503-368-4204; www.wheeleronthebay.com, e-mail wheelerlodge@nehalemtel.net. MODERATE.

Eclectic is surely the word for **Ocean Rogue Inn**, which features nine units overlooking Twin Rocks, a pair of giant rocks rising from the surf facing Rockaway Beach. Seven one-, two- and three-bedroom units have full kitchens and ocean views and two more-basic units offer beds, TVs, microwaves and refrigerators. Three units have gas fireplaces. Lawn furniture, a horseshoe pit, volleyball, barbecues, a fire pit, a play structure, and clam rakes and buckets make this family-oriented establishment appealing. ~ 19130 Alder Street, Rockaway Beach; 503-355-2093; www.oceanrogueinn.com, e-mail info@oceanrogueinn.com. MODERATE.

On the Three Capes Scenic Loop, **Terimore Motel** has 26 units ranging from sleeping rooms to cottages. Located on the beach, these clean, modernized units are comfortably furnished. Some have lofts, sitting areas, kitchens and fireplaces. A quiet retreat, it's ideal for fishing, crabbing, clamming, whale watching and agate collecting. ~ 5105 Crab Avenue, Netarts; 503-842-4623, 800-635-1821, fax 503-842-3743; www.oregoncoast.com/terimore, e-mail terimore@oregoncoast.com. MODERATE.

DINING

For fish-and-chips you'll have a hard time beating the **Ship Inn**. Huge portions of cod and halibut are served in the waterfront dining room along with chowder, generous salads and desserts. The full bar is one of the town's most crowded gathering places. Live music is featured Friday nights. Nautical decor gives diners the feeling they're out on the bounding main. ~ One 2nd Street, Astoria; 503-325-0033. MODERATE TO DELUXE.

Creekside Pizzeria overlooks a river that's home to gulls and ducks. Locals swarm this Italian eatery for its famous twice-baked Sicilian-crust pizza. Kids have a blast in the covered play area. Closed Monday. ~ 2490 North Route 101, Seaside; 503-738-7763. MODERATE.

The **Pig 'N Pancake** can seat over 200 patrons at booths and tables to feast upon Swedish pancakes, crêpes suzettes and strawberry waffles. Lunch and dinner entrées include patty melts, garden sandwiches, seafood and steaks. ~ 323 Broadway, Seaside; 503-738-7243, fax 503-738-7014; www.pignpancake.com. MODERATE.

Convenient to the city's popular attractions, **Dooger's Seafood and Grill** serves crab legs, prawns, fish and chips, pasta dishes, burgers and steaks. The carpeted dining room sports oak furniture. Dessert specialties include marionberry cobbler. ~ 505 Broadway, Seaside; 503-738-3773. MODERATE.

Start your day with an omelette or oatmeal waffles at the **Lazy Susan Café**, a cut above your average café. If you come during pear season (November to April), try the gingerbread waffles. Or try their seafood salad or seafood stew for lunch or dinner. The paneled dining room with bright-blue tablecloths and watercolor prints on the walls make the Lazy Susan a local favorite. Breakfast and lunch are served year-round, dinner only in the summer. Closed Tuesday. ~ 126 North Hemlock Street, Cannon Beach; 503-436-2816. BUDGET TO MODERATE.

With both take-out and in-house dining, **Pizza a fetta** is a good choice for a slice or an entire pie. In addition to regular toppings you can order sun-dried tomatoes, artichoke hearts, pancetta bacon or fruits. Cheeses include, Oregon blue, French feta, fontina and Montrachet chèvre. Closed Wednesday and Thursday during winter. ~ Village Center, 231 North Hemlock Street, Cannon Beach; 503-436-0333, fax 503-738-7104; www.pizza-a-fetta.com, e-mail jdf@pacifier.com. BUDGET TO MODERATE.

For elegant Continental dining try the **Bistro Restaurant and Bar**. Set in a small house, this intimate dining room serves specialties such as sautéed oysters in a lemon-butter sauce, a hearty seafood stew and fresh seafood dishes nightly. Dishes change seasonally. From November through April, call for weekday hours; open on weekends year-round. ~ 263 North Hemlock Street, Cannon Beach; 503-436-2661. MODERATE.

Many museums have cafés in the basement or out on the patio. But **Artspace** is a rare find, a fine restaurant in an elegant gallery setting. You'll walk past contemporary paintings, prints,   ◄ HIDDEN

AUTHOR FAVORITE

One of the most beautiful dining rooms on the coast is found at **Café Uniontown**. An elegant, paneled setting with a mirrored bar, white tablecloths and a river view make this restaurant the place to go to enjoy rib-eye steak with shiitake mushroom, almond baked halibut, cioppino, steaks and pasta dishes. Located under the bridge in the historic Uniontown district, this is also a relaxing spot for a drink after a hard day of sightseeing. Dinner only. ~ 218 West Marine Drive, Astoria; 503-325-8708, fax 503-338-0130; e-mail cafeuniontown@charterinter net.com. MODERATE TO ULTRA-DELUXE.

sculpture and jewelry by outstanding Northwest artists on the way to the dining area. Warm gold walls, a deep olive ceiling, and fun natural-paper tablecloths to draw on all add up to a cozy setting for homemade breads, soups and specialties like oysters Italia. Sunday brunch includes treats such as vegetarian eggs Benedict, eggs florentine and quiche. Open Friday, Saturday and Sunday. Call for winter hours. ~ 9120 5th Street, Bay City; 503-377-2782, fax 503-377-2010. MODERATE.

Thanks to an extensive trail network, Cape Lookout is an excellent place to observe sea lions and shorebirds.

If you're looking for good, honest deli fare with soup or salad on the side, head to the **Blue Heron French Cheese Company**. The deli counter in the midst of this jam-packed shop is stocked with goodies such as salami and provolone, smoked turkey and creamy brie or roast beef with cheddar cheese. ~ 2001 Blue Heron Drive, Tillamook; 503-842-8281, 800-275-0639, fax 503-842-8530; www.blueheronoregon.com, e-mail blue heron@oregoncoast.com. BUDGET.

Set in a shingled Craftsman house, **La Casa Medello** is the right place to go when you want south-of-the-border fare on the North Coast. The dark-wood interior featuring beautiful built-in cabinetry and casablanca fans is brightened by floral arrangements and plants. You can dine family-style at the big tables offering specialties like *chiles rellenos*, Spanish-rice salad, homemade tamales and generous burritos. If you're hungry try *la casa* fajita tostada with steak or chicken breast. ~ 1160 North Route 101, Tillamook; 503-842-5768. BUDGET TO MODERATE.

Nautical decor, pink walls and valances, ocean views and an oak counter make **Roseanna's Café** an inviting spot to enjoy Willapa Bay oysters, daily fish specials, vegetable penne, burgers, steaks and their famous gorgonzola-pear pasta. This board-and-batten building is packed on the weekend with a loyal clientele that likes to toast those delicious moments when the sun finally burns through the fog. ~ 1490 Pacific Street, Oceanside; 503-842-7351; www.roseannas.com. MODERATE TO DELUXE.

SHOPPING   **M and N Workwear** is where you can find flannel shirts, jeans, outerwear and casual menswear. Located beneath the bridge in the old Finnish Hall, this establishment is popular with fishermen, lumberjacks, farmers and tourists in the midst of shopping-mall deprogramming. Located in Astoria's historic Uniontown district, this is not a place for quiche eaters. ~ 248 West Marine Drive, Astoria; phone/fax 503-325-7610, 877-272-5100; www.mnwork wear.com, e-mail neilc@mnworkwear.com.

Caught in a downpour? Duck into **Let it Rain**, where you can find any imaginable accessory, from rain boots to water-proof purses, to keep you dry. Be sure to check out their gallery of fine art and unique umbrellas. ~ 1124 Commercial Street, Astoria; 800-998-0773; www.let-it-rain.com, e-mail sales@let-it-rain.com.

The **Wine Shack** offers a fine selection of rare, international and local wines. This funky little shack, with cozy wood-paneled walls and a stained glass chandelier, shimmies every Saturday afternoon during its wine tasting. ~ 124 Hemlock Street, Cannon Beach; 503-436-1100, 800-787-1765; www.beachwine.com, e-mail info@beachwine.com.

Our idea of a coastal gallery is **Artspace**. Contemporary Northwest sculpture and painting, jewelry and arts and crafts are all found in this intriguing showplace. WPA art from the '30s, '40s and '50s is also on display. There's a restaurant on the premises. ~ 9120 5th Street, Bay City; 503-377-2782, fax 503-377-2010.

◄ HIDDEN

Rainy Day Books focuses on new and used titles and has an excellent section on the Pacific Northwest as well as a large selection of greeting cards. This is also a good place to pick up inexpensive paperbacks that come in handy when you want to relax by the fireplace. Closed Sunday. ~ 2015 2nd Street, Tillamook; 503-842-7766; e-mail rdb@gorge.net.

Girtles presents rock bands every night except Monday and Tuesday, when locals show off with karaoke. Cover on Friday and Saturday. ~ 311 Broadway Street, Seaside; 503-738-8417; www.girtles.com.

NIGHTLIFE

In Cannon Beach, the **Bistro Restaurant and Bar** has a guitarist on the weekends. Take a seat at the bar or order drinks and dessert at one of the adjacent tables. This romantic setting is the ideal way to wind up the evening. Call for winter hours. ~ 263 North Hemlock Street, Cannon Beach; 503-436-2661.

For musicals and jazz piano, Broadway shows, murder mysteries, revivals, classical concerts, comedies and melodramas, check out the **Coaster Theatre Playhouse**. Closed in January. ~ 108 North Hemlock Street, Cannon Beach; 503-436-1242, fax 503-436-9653; www.coastertheatre.com, e-mail info@coaster theatre.com.

FORT STEVENS STATE PARK 🚶 🚲 ⚓ 🛶 ⛵ This 3762-acre state park embraces a Civil War–era fort that defended the coast during World War II. The site of a rare coastal attack by a Japanese submarine in 1942, the park includes shallow lakes, dunes, sand flats and a pine forest. The paved bike trails are also good for skating. Of special interest are the oceanfront remains of a wrecked British ship, the *Peter Iredale*. A museum and guided tours offer historical perspective on the region. Fish the surf for perch. The razor clamming is excellent. There are picnic tables, showers, restrooms and a gift shop. Day-use fee, $3. ~ Take Pacific Drive west from Hammond; 503-861-1671, fax 503-861-9890.

BEACHES & PARKS

▲ There are 42 tent sites ($13 to $18 per night), around 300 RV hookup sites ($18 to $22 per night) and 15 yurts ($30 per night). Hiker-biker sites ($4 per night) are available by request. Reservations: 800-452-5687.

ECOLA STATE PARK 🚶 🚲 🚣 🏄 🛶 Forested with Sitka spruce and western hemlock, this 1303-acre park includes Ecola Point and the steep shoreline leading to Tillamook Head. The name Ecola comes from the Chinook word for whale, which was hunted in the waters offshore. You may see deer and elk during your visit. You can fish for perch. At Indian Beach, you can take the Clatsop Loop Trail, an interpretive hike that lets you explore the same place as Lewis and Clark. You'll find barbecue pits, picnic tables, group picnic shelter (available by reservation at 800-551-6949) and restrooms. Day-use fee, $3. ~ Off Route 101, two miles north of Cannon Beach; 503-436-2844.

▲ There are 3 primitive Adirondack-style shelters located at the summit of the Clatsop Loop Trail; no fee.

SADDLE MOUNTAIN STATE NATURAL AREA 🚶 A 3283-foot twin peak is the heart of this natural heritage site that features unusual plants and flowers. Saddle Mountain was originally called Swallahoost for a chief who, after being murdered, was said to have returned to life as an eagle. From the mountaintop you can see both the Columbia River's mouth and the Pacific Coast. Douglas fir, spruce, hemlock and alder shade the 2911-acre park. There are picnic tables and restrooms. Closed in winter from November to March, or until the snow melts. ~ Off Route 26, eight miles northeast of Necanicum Junction; 503-368-5943, fax 503-368-5090.

▲ There are 10 primitive sites; $10 per night.

OSWALD WEST STATE PARK 🚶 🚣 🐟 🛶 With four miles of Pacific shoreline, this 2484-acre park provides great views of Nehalem Bay, as you walk only a half-mile from old growth forest to beach. Douglas fir, spruce and western red cedar dominate the rainforest in this park bounded on the south by legendary Neah-kah-nie Mountain. You'll want to visit the picturesque creeks, coves and scenic Arch Cape. Fishing is good at the beach for cod, perch and bass. You'll find picnic tables and restrooms. ~ Off Route 101, ten miles south of Cannon Beach; 503-368-3575, 800-551-6949.

▲ There are 30 primitive sites accessible by foot with wheelbarrows for walk-in campers; $10 to $14 per night. Closed November through February.

NEHALEM BAY STATE PARK 🚶 🚲 🐎 🚣 🛥 🛶 Encompassing a three-mile-long sandspit at Nehalem Bay's mouth, this 889-acre park is a popular recreational area. The open, wind-

Let There Be Light

No matter where you are on the Oregon Coast, a powerful beacon may be sweeping the high seas and shoreline. Nine of these classic sentinels built since 1857 still stand. Five continue to operate as unmanned Coast Guard stations, and three inactive lighthouses are restored and open to the public. Those not open to the public attract visitors who come to admire the architecture.

Tillamook Rock Lighthouse, opened in 1881 and the state's only lighthouse that is actually offshore, was built and then ferried to the construction site by tender.

One of the best, located at **Cape Meares**, five miles south of Tillamook Bay, is a dormant beam that was built in 1890. Open year-round for a self-guided look-see, the lighthouse is part of Cape Meares State Scenic Viewpoint. ~ Off Route 101, ten miles west of Tillamook; www.capemeareslighthouse.org.

Off Route 101, just north of Yaquina Bay Bridge, is **Yaquina Bay Lighthouse**, built in 1871. Authentically restored with 19th-century furniture, Yaquina Bay features an interpretive exhibit. Newport's **Yaquina Head Lighthouse** was constructed in 1873. This automated light flashes every 20 seconds and is supplemented by a powerful radio beacon. You can catch one of the self-guided tours (fee). ~ Four miles north of Yaquina Bay; www.yaquinalights.org.

One of the most photographed spots is **Heceta Head Lighthouse**, the brightest beacon on the coast. ~ Off Route 101, 13 miles north of Florence. Built in 1857, the **Umpqua Lighthouse** was the coast's first. Destroyed in an 1861 flood, it was replaced in 1894. The 65-foot tower emits a distinctive automated red-and-white flash and is adjacent to Umpqua Lighthouse State Park. Tours are offered Wednesday through Sunday from May through September. ~ Off Route 101, six miles south of Reedsport; 541-271-4631.

The 1866 **Cape Arago Lighthouse** is on a rocky island at the Coos Bay entrance. The unmanned Coast Guard beacon has been deactivated but the structure still stands. ~ Next to Sunset Bay State Park off Route 101.

The 1896 **Coquille River Lighthouse** was the last lighthouse built on the Oregon Coast. It serves as a public observatory with interpretive displays on the Coquille River region. ~ At the south end of Bullards Beach State Park, a mile north of Bandon.

In service since 1870, **Cape Blanco Lighthouse** is the westernmost navigational beacon in Oregon. It is also Oregon's oldest continuously operated light. This 300,000-candlepower light is near Cape Blanco State Park. Open Tuesday through Sunday from April to October for guided tours. ~ Nine miles north of Port Orford off Route 101.

swept landscape is ideal for kite flying. Nehalem Bay State Park is also a favorite for horseback riding, cycling and walking. There's good crabbing in the bay and, depending on the season, good fishing for steelhead, cutthroat trout, perch and chinook salmon. Facilities include picnic tables, restrooms, showers and an on-site airport. Day-use fee, $3. ~ Off Route 101, three miles south of Manzanita Junction; 503-368-5943, 800-551-6949.

▲ There are 267 RV hookup sites ($16 to $20 per night), 18 yurts ($27 per night), 17 horse camp sites ($12 to $14 per night) and hiker-biker sites ($4 per person per night). Reservations: 800-452-5687.

CAPE MEARES STATE SCENIC VIEWPOINT 🏃 Named for an 18th-century British naval officer and trader, this 94-acre park and adjacent wildlife refuge encompass a spruce-hemlock forest and memorable ocean headlands. While the historic lighthouse (closed November through March) no longer shines, the cape remains a landmark for tourists, who come to see the offshore national wildlife refuge and birds. It is a prime location for spotting migrating whales. There are picnic tables and restrooms. ~ Off Route 101, ten miles west of Tillamook; 503-842-3182, 800-551-6949; www.capemeareslighthouse.org.

If you stop at Cape Meares State Scenic Viewpoint, look for the Octopus Tree, an exotic Sitka spruce that was once a meeting point for Tillamook American Indian medicine men.

CAPE LOOKOUT STATE PARK 🏃 With two miles of forested headlands, a rainforest, beaches and sand dunes on Netarts Bay, it's hard to resist this 2000-acre gem. It is also one of the highlights of the Three Capes Loop. There's excellent crabbing in Netarts Bay. You'll find picnic tables, restrooms and showers. Day-use fee, $3. ~ Off Route 101, 11 miles southwest of Tillamook; 503-842-4981 or 503-842-3182.

▲ There are 173 tent sites ($12 to $16 per night), 39 RV hookup sites ($16 to $20 per night), 13 yurts ($27 per night), 3 deluxe log cabins ($45 to $66 per night) and a hiker-biker camp ($4 per person per night). Reservations: 800-452-5687.

CAPE KIWANDA STATE NATURAL AREA 🏃 This 185-acre headland area has a beautiful, sheltered beach. On the road between Pacific City and Sand Lake, it has wave-sculptured sandstone cliffs, tidepools and dunes. Shore fishing is good. There are picnic tables and restrooms. ~ Off Route 101, one mile north of Pacific City; 503-842-4981, 800-551-6949.

Central Coast Proceeding down the coast you'll appreciate an impressive state-park system protecting coastal beaches and bluffs, rivers and estuaries, wildlife refuges and forested promontories. With the Pacific to the west and the Siuslaw National Forest to the east, this section of the coast is sparsely populated but has more than its share of state parks and beaches. Anglers and hikers have plenty of options here, with many of the best spots only about 90 minutes away from Salem or Eugene.

One of the largest communities on the coast, **Lincoln City** stretches along the shore for roughly ten miles. While the coastal sprawl may turn some visitors off, this region offers many fine parks, lakes and restaurants, and seven miles of clean, sandy (not rocky) beaches. Stop by the **Lincoln City Visitors and Convention Bureau** for helpful details on beachcombing, shopping for crafts and recreational activities. ~ 801 Southwest Route 101, Suite 1, Lincoln City; 541-996-1274, 800-452-2151, fax 541-994-2408; www.oregon coast.org, e-mail info@oregoncoast.org.

SIGHTS

Many visitors flock to **Devil's Lake**, a popular water sports and fishing area. But few of them realize that **D River**, located at the lake's mouth, is reputedly the world's shortest river, just under 120 feet long at low tide. This is also a terrific place to fly a kite.

When it's foggy on the coast, it makes sense to head inland where the sun is often shining. One way to do this is to take Route 229 inland along the Siletz River. Six miles beyond the town of Kernville you'll come to **Medicine Rock**, a pioneer landmark. Indian legend held that presents left here would assure good fortune.

◄ *HIDDEN*

Proceed south to **Siletz**, named for one of the coast's better-known American Indian tribes. In 1856, at the end of the Rogue River Wars, the American Army created the Siletz Indian Agency, which became home for 2000 American Indians. Within a year, unspeakable conditions diminished their numbers to 600. The agency closed for good in 1925, and today the Siletz tribe gathers each August for its annual powwow featuring dancing and a salmon bake.

Continue on to visit the popular galleries and antique shops at **Toledo**. This small town operated one of the world's largest spruce mills during World War II.

From Toledo, follow Route 20 west to **Newport**. A harbor town with an array of tourist attractions, Newport is a busy place, especially during the summer. Like Seaside, Newport is filled with souvenir shops, saltwater-taffy stores and enough T-shirt shops to outfit the city of Portland. There are also fine museums, galleries and other sightseeing possibilities. Begin your visit to this popular vacation town with a stop at the **Greater Newport Chamber of Commerce**. Closed weekends from October through May. ~ 555 Southwest Coast Highway, Newport; 541-265-8801, 800-262-7844, fax 541-265-5589; www.newportchamber.org.

A short walk from the chamber are the Burrows House and Log Cabin Museum of the **Lincoln County Historical Society**. You'll see Siletz basketry, maritime memorabilia, farming, log-

ging and pioneer displays, Victorian-era household furnishings
and clothing, and many historic photographs. Closed Monday. ~
545 Southwest 9th Street, Newport; 541-265-7509, fax 541-
265-3992; www.oregoncoast.history.museum, e-mail coasthis
tory@newportnet.com.

The most popular tourist area in Newport is **Bay Boulevard**,
where canneries, restaurants, shops and attractions like **Undersea
Gardens** peacefully coexist. Located on Yaquina Bay, this waterfront extravaganza gives you a chance to view more than 5000
species including octopus, eel, salmon and starfish. Scuba divers
perform daily for the crowds in this bayfront setting. Closed
Tuesday and Wednesday from November to mid-February.
Admission. ~ 250 Southwest Bay Boulevard, Newport; 541-265-
2206, fax 541-265-8195; www.marinersquare.com.

The OSU **Mark O. Hatfield Marine Science Center** is the coast's
premier aquarium, featuring a quarter-mile-long, wheelchair-
accessible estuary nature trail. The center features hands-on displays, aquariums and exhibits interpreting the research being conducted at the center. Closed Tuesday and Wednesday from Labor
Day to Memorial Day. ~ 2030 Southeast Marine Science Drive,
Newport; 541-867-0100, fax 541-867-0138.

Next door is the **Oregon Coast Aquarium**, which has indoor
and outdoor exhibits showcasing seabirds, marine mammals, crustaceans and fish in a re-created natural environment. Children
love the interactive exhibits and the touch tank. A 200-foot underwater tunnel has you completely surrounded by sharks, halibut and other sea creatures. Admission. ~ 2820 Southeast Ferry
Slip Road, Newport; 541-867-3474, fax 541-867-6846; www.
aquarium.org, e-mail info@aquarium.org.

After crossing the bridge, follow the signs west to visit the
Yaquina Bay Lighthouse, the only wooden lighthouse still standing in Oregon, at Yaquina Bay State Park. Continue north on
Mark Street to **Nye Beach**. Newport's historic beach district is
more than a century old, but many of the early-day hotels, cabins
and beach houses survive.

In Nye Beach you'll find the **Cloe–Niemela–Clarke Gallery**,
where you can familiarize yourself with paintings, sculpture, pottery, handicrafts and photography by members of the Yaquina Art
Association. ~ 839 Northwest Beach Drive, Nye Beach; 541-265-
5133; www.yaquinaart.org.

Drive north on Route 101 to **Agate Beach**, a great spot for
rockhounds. Moonstones, jasper and tiger eyes are all found
here. Continue north on Route 101 to the Otter Crest Loop.
Begin by visiting **Devil's Punch Bowl State Natural Area**, near
Otter Rock, named after a collapsed cavern flushed by high tides.
There's a lovely beach here, and you can shop for a picnic or
mask art in the tiny oceanfront hamlet of Otter Rock. Continue

north past Cape Foulweather, named by Captain James Cook in 1778, to **Depoe Bay**, home to the smallest harbor in the world. This six-acre port is fun to explore on foot thanks to its seafood restaurants and shops.

While the harbor is the heart of this charming seaside village, you may also want to head across Route 101 to the coast, one of the best whale-watching spots in Oregon. A location for the movie *One Flew Over the Cuckoo's Nest*, Depoe Bay is also famous for

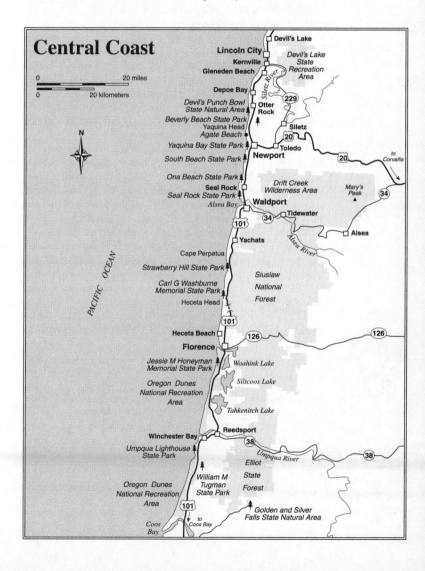

Central Coast

0   20 miles

0   20 kilometers

N

Devil's Lake

Lincoln City

Kernville

Gleneden Beach

Devil's Lake State Recreation Area

Siletz River

229

Depoe Bay

Devil's Punch Bowl State Natural Area

Otter Rock

Beverly Beach State Park

Yaquina Head

Agate Beach

Siletz

20

Yaquina Bay State Park

South Beach State Park

Toledo

Newport

20

to Corvallis

Ona Beach State Park

Seal Rock

Seal Rock State Park

Alsea Bay

Drift Creek Wilderness Area

Mary's Peak

34

Waldport

101

34

Tidewater

Alsea

Alsea River

Yachats

Cape Perpetua

Strawberry Hill State Park

Carl G Washburne Memorial State Park

Heceta Head

Siuslaw National Forest

101

Heceta Beach

126

126

Florence

Jessie M Honeyman Memorial State Park

Woahink Lake

Oregon Dunes National Recreation Area

Siltcoos Lake

Tahkenitch Lake

Reedsport

38

Winchester Bay

Umpqua Lighthouse State Park

Umpqua River

38

Elliot

William M Tugman State Park

State Forest

Oregon Dunes National Recreation Area

101

Golden and Silver Falls State Natural Area

Coos Bay

to Coos Bay

PACIFIC OCEAN

Spouting Horn, where the surf surges above the oceanfront cliffs in stormy weather.

Return to Newport on Route 101 and continue southward ten miles to **Seal Rock State Park**. This wayside park has some of the best tidepools in the area and is a great place to watch the barking pinnipeds and hunt for agates.

Continue south on Route 101 to **Waldport** and **Alsea Bay**, one of the best clamming spots on the coast and easily accessed from numerous parks. Walport is a relatively peaceful alternative to the coast's busy tourist hubs.

HIDDEN ►

Pick up Route 34 east along the Alsea River for nine miles to the **Kozy Kove Resort**. You can launch your boat here and explore this tributary bounded by the Siuslaw National Forest. You'll find a campground and a store that sells fishing and camping supplies. A great fishing spot, this section of the Alsea can be a sunny alternative to the foggy coast. ~ 9464 Alsea Highway, Tidewater; 541-528-3251, fax 541-528-3837; www.kozykove. com, e-mail kozykampmarina@yahoo.com.

HIDDEN ►

For a picturesque, albeit windy, drive, travel east 39 miles on Route 34 to the village of Alsea and follow the signs to **Alsea Falls**. The area around the 35-foot cascade makes a good spot for a picnic, and there's also three and a half miles of hiking trails through old-growth forest and Douglas firs. Along the way you may catch a glimpse of woodpeckers, beavers and white-tailed deer.

Return to Waldport and continue southward to **Yachats** (pronounced "Ya-HOTS"), a classy village with fine restaurants, inns and shops. This town is also home of the **Little Log Church**. Surrounded by a charming garden, this tiny house of worship has a handful of white pews for congregants warmed by a pioneer stove. ~ Located at 3rd and Pontiac streets, Yachats; 541-547-3976.

To the south is Cape Perpetua, discovered by Captain James Cook in 1778. The 2700-acre **Cape Perpetua Scenic Area** has

AUTHOR FAVORITE

sights   It's pinniped heaven at **Sea Lion Caves**, just south of Heceta Head Lighthouse. Ride the elevator down to the two-story-high cave to see the resident stellar sea lions enjoying a life of leisure. The outside ledges are a rookery where these marine mammals breed and give birth in the spring and early summer. The bulls vigilantly protect their harem's territory. An overlook adjacent to the entrance is a great whale-watching spot. Admission. ~ 91560 Route 101, 11 miles north of Florence; 541-547-3111, fax 541-547-3545; www.sealioncaves.com, e-mail info@sealioncaves.com.

miles of trails ideal for beachcombing and exploring old-growth forests and tidepools. The **Cape Perpetua Visitors Center** is a good place to learn about the region's original inhabitants, the Alsi. Known for their woodworking, canoes and decorative, watertight basketry, the Alsi hunted in the Coast Range hills. The visitors center is closed intermittently from November through April; call for seasonal hours. Admission. ~ Route 101, Cape Perpetua; 541-547-3289, fax 541-547-4616.

Two miles south of Cape Perpetua off Route 101 is **Strawberry Hill State Park**. The white blossoms of wild strawberries create a floral panorama in the spring months. This park is also a popular spot for seals that sunbathe on the shoreline's basalt rocks. A short path of steps will take you quite close to the seals. The tidepools shelter sea stars, anemones and bright-purple spin sea urchins. However, the pools are a protected reserve, so removal of anything is strictly forbidden. Down the road another two miles is the distinctive **Ziggurat**, a four-story pyramid-shaped bed and breakfast. ~ Ziggurat: 95330 Route 101, Yachats; 541-547-3925.

As you continue on toward Florence, about six miles north of the city is **Darlingtonia Botanical Wayside**, a short path that takes you to see the bog where Darlingtonia, serpent-shaped plants also known as cobra lilies, trap insects with a sticky substance and devour them. They are in full bloom from May to mid-June.

In Florence, the **Chamber of Commerce** will quickly orient you to this Siuslaw River community. Closed most Sundays. ~ 290 Route 101, Florence; 541-997-3128, fax 541-997-4101; www.florencechamber.com, e-mail florence@oregonfast.net. Then, with the help of a chamber walking-tour guide, explore Florence's old town. A small artists' colony with a gazebo park overlooking the Siuslaw waterfront, **Florence** has a popular historic district centered around Bay Street. Here you can browse or sip an espresso.

Florence is also the northern gateway to **Oregon Dunes National Recreation Area**. Forty miles of sandy beaches and forested bluffs laced by streams flowing down from the mountains make this region a favorite Oregon vacation spot. Woodlands and freshwater lakes provide a nice contrast to the windswept beaches. Numerous parks offer access to the dunes. Among them is **Oregon Dunes Overlook**, ten miles south of Florence. Fee. ~ 541-271-3611, fax 541-271-6019.

To gain perspective on the region's American Indian and pioneer history, visit the **Siuslaw Pioneer Museum**, a former Lutheran Church. Closed Monday and the month of January. Admission. ~ 278 Maple Street, Florence; 541-997-7884; e-mail museum@winfinity.com.

Near Reedsport on Route 38 about four miles east of Route 101 is **Dean Creek Elk Viewing Area**. The herd of Roosevelt elk make for an unusual photo opportunity.

LODGING

Located right on the beach, the **Inn at Spanish Head** has 125 rooms and suites, each with floor-to-ceiling windows and kitchens or kitchenettes. Many have balconies and each unit is uniquely decorated. A heated pool, spa, recreation room, lounge and restaurant add to the resort atmosphere. Wi-fi access is available. ~ 4009 Southwest Route 101, Lincoln City; 541-996-2161, 800-452-8127, fax 541-996-4089; www.spanishhead.com, e-mail info@spanishhead.com. ULTRA-DELUXE.

South of Reedsport is one of the most popular fishing ports in the dunes region, Salmon Harbor on Winchester Bay. The crabbing and rockfishing here are top-notch.

The **Salishan Spa & Golf Resort** offers 205 units. In a forested setting above Siletz Bay, this lodge accommodates guests in two- and three-story, hillside buildings. All units feature gas fireplaces and balconies. Golf, tennis, a fitness center, a library and an art gallery are just some of the amenities at this four-star resort. ~ 7760 North Route 101, Gleneden Beach; 541-764-2371, 800-452-2300, fax 541-764-3681; www.salishan.com, e-mail reservations@salishan. com. ULTRA-DELUXE.

One of the area's best deals is **Trollers Lodge**. Set on an oceanview bluff, this 12-unit establishment has clean rooms with eclectic furniture, picture windows, TV and VCR, and kitchenettes. Picnic tables and benches are the ideal spots for watching the residential whale pod and migrating whales in season. One- and two-bedroom suites with full kitchens are also available, as are three deluxe to ultra-deluxe-priced oceanfront homes. The location is good for deep-sea fishing trips. Wi-fi is available. Pets are welcome for an additional charge. ~ 355 Southwest Route 101, Depoe Bay; 541-765-2287, 800-472-9335; www.trollerslodge. com, e-mail trollers@newportnet.com. MODERATE.

Modeled after a 19th-century New England–style inn, **Seahag Inn** overlooks the nation's smallest harbor. While the inn's 13 rooms and suites have a standard motel appearance, all the suites have a balcony or patio overlooking this picturesque harbor; some have bathtubs with whirlpool jets and fireplaces. There is also a parlor with comfortable sofas, and a library with a fireplace. All ground-rooms are pet-friendly. Full breakfast is included. ~ 235 Southeast Bay View Avenue, Depoe Bay; 541-765-2322, 800-228-0448; www.seahaginn.com, e-mail stay@seahaginn.com. MODERATE TO DELUXE.

Don't be surprised if you find a couple sitting on an oceanview bench outside **Alpine Chalets**. They are probably coming back to remember a honeymoon spent at this oceanfront retreat adjacent to Devil's Punchbowl State Park. Blessed with its own private park and beach access, each two- and three-bedroom A-frame chalet here has a large, paneled sitting area furnished with contemporary foldout sofas. All 11 units are fully carpeted and come with kitchens and casablanca fans. Pet-friendly units are available. ~ Otter Crest Loop, Otter Rock; 541-765-2572, 800-825-5768, fax 541-765-3135; www.oregonalpinechalets.com, e-mail info@oregon alpinechalets.com. MODERATE.

The Inn at Otter Crest offers 100 rooms including one- and two-bedroom suites with fireplaces, fully equipped kitchens and decks. The semiprivate cove boasts great tidepools; you can look for seals and, in season, migrating gray whales. Set in a fir forest, with duck ponds and wild rhododendron, the inn also sports a playground, a workout room, a pool, a hot tub and a sauna. There's also a restaurant and lounge on the premises. ~ Otter Crest Loop off Route 101, Otter Rock; 541-765-2111, 800-452-2101, fax 541-765-2047; www.innatottercrest.com, e-mail havefun@ innatottercrest.com. DELUXE TO ULTRA-DELUXE.

The four-story Sylvia Beach Hotel, a honeymoon haven that had degenerated into a flophouse, was renovated and renamed for the proprietor of Shakespeare and Co. and first publisher of James Joyce's *Ulysses*. Her Paris bookstore and coffeehouse was a home away from home for writers like Joyce, Ernest Hemingway, T. S. Eliot and Samuel Beckett. Twenty rooms, each themed after an author, now accommodate guests. Our favorites are the ornate Oscar Wilde room featuring garish Victorian wallpaper (while dying in a Paris hotel room his last words were: "Either this wallpaper goes or I do"), the Dr. Seuss room (*The Cat in the Hat* is front and center), the Mark Twain room (fireplace, deck, clawfoot tub) and the Emily Dickinson room (marble dresser, green carpet, beautiful antique desk). While Henry Miller (*Tropic of Cancer*) didn't get his own quarters, this man of letters is appropriately commemorated in the basement restrooms. Incidentally, we'd love to see the owners add a James Joyce room in the years ahead. The hotel is completely nonsmoking and Aggie, the house cat, resides there. Breakfast is included. ~ 267 Northwest Cliff Street, Newport; 541-265-5428, 888-795-8422; www.sylviabeach hotel.com. MODERATE TO ULTRA-DELUXE.

The Summer Wind Budget Motel offers 33 fully carpeted rooms—seven with kitchenettes, all with woodframe beds, sofas, pine coffee tables and stall showers. One of many Route 101 strip motels serving the Newport crowd, it's set back from the highway, and the rear rooms are relatively quiet. ~ 728 North Coast Highway, Newport; 541-265-8076, fax 541-265-9475. BUDGET.

The Cliff House is a bed and breakfast on the ocean. It features a big fireplace in the living room and a gazebo in the front yard. Convenient to ten miles of walking beach, the inn also offers a jacuzzi and an on-call masseuse. Some of the four theme-decorated rooms have chandeliers and wall-to-wall carpeting. Full gourmet breakfast included. Reservations highly recommended. Gay-friendly. ~ 1450 Southwest Adahi Street, Waldport; 541-563-2506; www.cliffhouseoregon.com, e-mail innkeeper@cliffhouse oregon.com. DELUXE TO ULTRA-DELUXE.

Romantic, secluded accommodations on three-and-a-half forested acres above the ocean can be found at **The Oregon House**, an inn and retreat center. Cottages, guest rooms, suites and townhouse units housed within five buildings across the grounds, include kitchens, fireplaces and marble bathrooms. One of the most charming is Oak Cabin, which has red-and-white-checked curtains, a red fireplace, a hot tub and a brass-and-iron bed. The grounds include a private beach, trails and a creek. Gay-friendly. ~ 94288 Route 101, Yachats; 541-547-3329, fax 541-547-3754; www.oregonhouse.com, e-mail office@oregonhouse.com. MODERATE TO ULTRA-DELUXE.

The **Yachats Inn** has 35 pleasant motel accommodations, 16 of which are suites, some with a rustic knotty-pine look and superb ocean views. Especially nice are the upstairs units, which include a glassed-in sunporch, great for watching a winter storm roll in. There is an indoor swimming pool and a lounge with stone fireplace, books, games, puzzles and free coffee. Some suites feature decks or patios. Gay-friendly. ~ 331 South Coast Highway, Yachats; 541-547-3456, 888-270-3456, fax 541-547-4331; www.yachatsinn.com, e-mail geninfo@yachatsinn.com. DELUXE.

On a 40-foot cliff overlooking the Pacific six and a half miles south of Yachats, **See Vue** offers 11 units. Each is individually named and themed. All have plants and antiques, and some offer kitchens and fireplaces. Weekend reservations recommended well in advance. Pets are welcome. Closed weekdays in January. Gay-friendly. ~ 95590 Route 101, Yachats; 541-547-3227, 866-547-3237; www.seevue.com, e-mail seevue@seevue.com. MODERATE TO ULTRA-DELUXE.

AUTHOR FAVORITE

Turn up the Vivaldi and step right in to the circa-1914 **Edwin K Bed and Breakfast**, where the six rooms are named for six seasons (including Autumn and Indian Summer). Furnished with oak armoires, chandeliers and wool area carpets, this elegant home has a backyard waterfall and Siuslaw River views. A deluxe five-course meal is included for breakfast; tea, sherry and cookies are served each evening. Two vacation rentals are also available for families or couples seeking more space and privacy. ~ 1155 Bay Street, Florence; 541-997-8360, 800-833-9465, fax 541-997-1423; www.edwink.com, e-mail info@edwink.com. DELUXE TO ULTRA-DELUXE.

On the Siuslaw River, the 40-unit **River House Inn** is a one-block walk from this popular town's historic shopping district. Many of the units have decks overlooking the river traffic and drawbridge. Rooms feature oak furniture and queens and kings with floral-print bedspreads. Some rooms have jacuzzis and overlook the waterfront. ~ 1202 Bay Street, Florence; 541-997-3933, 888-824-2750, fax 541-902-2312; www.riverhouseflorence.com, e-mail riverhouse@harborside.com. MODERATE.

If you're interested in cetaceans, consider checking in to **Driftwood Shores Resort & Conference Center**. An estimated 21,000 whales migrate south past this inn each winter and return northward in the spring. Overlooking Heceta Beach, the 127-unit establishment has rooms and kitchenette suites featuring nautical prints, stone fireplaces, picture windows, decks and contemporary furniture. An indoor pool, hot tub and restaurant are located on the premises. ~ 88416 1st Avenue, Florence; 541-997-8263, 800-422-5091, fax 541-997-5857; www.driftwoodshores.com, e-mail reservations@driftwoodshores.com. MODERATE TO ULTRA-DELUXE.

DINING

Kernville Steak and Seafood has a reputation for reasonably priced, hearty meals. Feast in the dining room beneath a vaulted ceiling with A-framed views of the river. Known for its steaks, prime rib, steamers and french onion soup, the restaurant also has a few vegetarian selections. Enjoy music with your meal in the lounge every Saturday night. ~ 186 Siletz Highway, Lincoln City; 541-994-6200, fax 541-994-6208; www.kernvillesteakhouse.com. MODERATE.

The Salishan's casual **Sun Room** restaurant features views of the driving range and putting course. This lodge-style restaurant offers pasta dishes, pan-seared salmon, and a Dungeness crab melt, along with a variety of salads and sandwiches. Breakfast, lunch and dinner. ~ 7760 Route 101, Gleneden Beach; 541-764-2371, 800-452-2300, fax 541-764-3681; www.salishan.com, e-mail reservations@salishan.com. MODERATE TO DELUXE.

For a step above in price, try the **Dining Room**, Salishan's romantic, tri-level gourmet restaurant. Specialties include grilled breast of duckling with pecan-and-pear-bread pudding, ham-wrapped sturgeon chop and Chinook salmon. ~ 7760 Route 101, Gleneden Beach; 541-764-2371, fax 541-764-3681; www.salishan.com. ULTRA-DELUXE.

Popcorn shrimp with ale sauce, a pizza crust made with stout, bangers with beer mustard, oysters with ale sauce—do we detect a trend here? The **Rogue Ales Public House** serves these specialties with its golden ales, stouts, lagers, award-winning Old Crustacean barley wine and gold medal–winning Rogue Smoke in a wood-paneled lounge. Tiffany-style lamps illuminate the booths, and the walls are decorated with classic advertising signs and pieces of the pub's history. The game room in the rear is good for a round of pool, or try your hand at blackjack in the card room. Specialties include sandwiches, salads and fish-and-chips. ~ 748 Southwest Bay Boulevard, Newport; 541-265-3188, fax 541-265-7528; www.rogue.com. BUDGET TO MODERATE.

Gino's Seafood and Deli offers crab and deli sandwiches, chowder and fish-and-chips. You can dine alfresco on picnic tables. A good bet for picnic fare. No dinner. ~ 808 Southwest Bay Boulevard, Newport; 541-265-2424. BUDGET.

The Whale's Tale serves excellent breakfasts, vegetarian lasagna, cioppino, hamburgers, seafood poorboys and fish filets with mushrooms, lemon butter and wine. This dark-wood café has an open-beam ceiling, inlaid mahogany and oak tables and Tiffany-style lamps. A kayak frame, harpoon, whale's vertebrae and tail suspended from the ceiling complete the decor. Breakfast, lunch and dinner are served. Closed in January and on Wednesday from fall through spring. ~ 452 Southwest Bay Boulevard, Newport; 541-265-8660. MODERATE TO DELUXE.

Canyon Way Bookstore and Restaurant serves up a host of delectables in a contemporary setting. Choose between a main room with wood tables that has inlaid tiles, a garden room with view of the bayfront and, best of all, in the summer a handsome, enclosed brick patio with tables in a garden setting (lunch only). Dinner entrées change but may feature beef, seafood and chicken. Closed Sunday from Labor Day to July 4th. ~ 1216 Southwest Canyon Way, Newport; 541-265-8319. MODERATE TO DELUXE.

If you're looking for a sushi bar, try Yuzen Japanese Cuisine. Set in a former rathskeller with leaded glass windows and Tiffany-style lamps, the restaurant has been redecorated with red paper lanterns, paper screens and a wooden sushi bar. The menu includes tempura, sukiyaki, *katsu don*, bento dinners and sashimi. Closed Monday. ~ 10111 Northwest Route 101, Seal Rock; 541-563-4766; e-mail takaya@yuzen.com. MODERATE TO ULTRA-DELUXE.

While some restaurants may be advertising "fresh crab" just flown in from Anchorage, La Serre Restaurant Grill & Creperie insists on truth in labeling. Only fresh local fish and crab off the boat are served in the contemporary dining room decorated with oak tables and chairs, oil lamps, potted plants and polished-hardwood floors. A bistro with a fireplace and full bar also provides a relaxed setting for drinks or dinner. La Serre specializes in seafood like razor clams and bay oysters, vegetarian entrées, chicken pot pies, steaks and fresh pastries including crêpes made on an authentic French griddle. Dinner only. Closed Tuesday and the month of January. ~ 2nd and Beach streets, Yachats; 541-547-3420, fax 541-547-3042; www.laserreoregon.com. MODERATE TO DELUXE.

In Florence, the Traveler's Cove Gourmet Café and Import Shop provides a perfect lunch-and-shop stop. The open-air deck overlooks the Siuslaw River, and the kitchen turns out light seafood fare such as "crabby" caesar salad, Boston clam chowder and hot shrimp sandwiches. ~ 1362 Bay Street, Florence; 541-997-6845.

There are good beachwear and swimwear departments at the **SHOPPING** **Oregon Surf Shop**, which also sells and rents surfboards, boogie-boards, skimboards, wetsuits and kayaks for fun in and out of the water. ~ 4933 Southwest Route 101, Lincoln City; phone/fax 541-996-3957, 877-339-5672; www.oregonsurfshop.com.

Forget your kite? For stunt, quad-line, box, delta, cellular, dragon and diamond kites try **Catch The Wind**. A full line of accessories, repairs and free advice are also available from the resident experts. ~ 130 Southeast Route 101, Lincoln City; 541-994-9500, fax 541-994-4766; www.catchthewind.com.

The Wood Gallery shows the work of over 400 artists: beautiful wooden sculptures, myrtlewood bowls, cherry-wood cabinets and jewelry boxes. Also here are metal sculptures, jewelry, ceramics, pottery, photography and stained glass. Handmade children's toys, furniture and ceramic tables are all worth a look. ~ 818 Southwest Bay Boulevard, Newport; 541-265-6843, 800-359-1419, fax 541-265-7615; www.woodgalleryonline.com.

Oceanic Arts has innovative fountains as well as limited-edition prints, pottery, jewelry and decorative basketry. ~ 444 Southwest Bay Boulevard, Newport; 541-265-5963, fax 541-265-3946.

Check out the original chainsaw wood carvings by artist Timothy Robins at his shop **Mystic Woods Wildlife Designs**. He specializes in caricature statues and bear carvings, but you'll also find intricately carved benches and nautical pieces. ~ 05890 Mercer Creek Drive, Florence; 541-997-9262; www.mysticwoods.net.

To enjoy rock and jazz you can dance to, try the second-story **NIGHTLIFE** lounge at **Salishan Lodge** on Thursday, Friday and Saturday. When you're tired of the dancefloor, take a table by the fireplace or at the bar. There is also a deck that overlooks the golf course.

AUTHOR FAVORITE
The town of Toledo is home to one of the best galleries along the coast, **Michael Gibbons Gallery**. Located in the old vicarage of the city's Episcopal church, the gallery is both home and workspace for noted landscape painter Michael Gibbons. Closed Monday through Wednesday. ~ 140 Northeast Alder Street, Toledo; phone/fax 541-336-2797; www.michaelgibbons.net, e-mail gmg@newportnet.com.

Contemporary painting completes the decorating scheme. ~ 7760 Route 101, Gleneden Beach; 541-764-2371, fax 541-764-3681.

The **Newport Performing Arts Center** presents concerts, dance programs and theatrical events in the Alice Silverman Theater and the Studio Theater. Both local groups and touring companies perform. ~ 777 West Olive Street, Newport; 541-265-2787, 888-701-7123; www.coastarts.org, e-mail occa@coastarts.org.

At **Rookie's Sportsbar** in the Best Western Agate Beach Inn, large-screen televisions project every sporting event imaginable. There's a pool table, sports memorabilia, darts and a relaxing view. ~ 3019 North Coast Highway, Newport; 541-265-9411, fax 541-265-5342; www.agatebeachinn.com/restbar.html.

BEACHES & PARKS

DEVIL'S LAKE STATE RECREATION AREA Is there really a devil in the deep blue sea? That's what American Indian legend says right here in Lincoln City. Find out for yourself by visiting this 109-acre spot offering day-use and overnight facilities. The camping area is protected with a shore-pine windbreak. A day-use area is available at East Devil's Lake down the road. Fish for bass and trout. Facilities include picnic tables, restrooms, showers and a boat moorage. An interpreter conducts kayak nature tours. ~ The West Devil's Lake section is at 1450 Northeast 6th Drive off Route 101. The day-use section is located two miles east of Route 101 on East Devil's Lake Road; 541-994-2002, 800-452-5687.

▲ There are 54 tent sites ($13 to $17 per night), 33 RV hookup sites ($17 to $22 per night) in the Devil's Lake section, and 10 yurts ($29 per night). Hiker-biker sites ($4 per person per night) are available.

DEVIL'S PUNCH BOWL STATE NATURAL AREA Don't miss this one. The forested, eight-acre park is named for a sea-washed cavern where breakers crash against the rocks with great special effects. Besides the thundering plumes, the adjacent beach has impressive tidepools. There are picnic table and restrooms in the Marine Gardens area. ~ Off Route 101, eight miles north of Newport; 800-551-6949.

BEVERLY BEACH STATE PARK Numerous coastal creeks make ideal hiking and camping areas. Among them is Spencer Creek, part of this 130-acre refuge. The windswept beach is reached via a highway underpass. Some of Oregon's best surf fishing is found here. You'll find picnic tables, restrooms and showers. ~ Route 101, seven miles north of Newport; 541-265-9278.

▲ There are 128 tent sites ($13 to $17 per night), 128 RV hookup sites ($17 to $22 per night) and 21 yurts ($29 per night). Hiker-biker sites ($4 per person per night) are also available. Reservations: 800-452-5687.

SOUTH BEACH STATE PARK 🚶🚴🎣♨︎🛶🚤⛵️⚓️
South of Newport's Yaquina Bay Bridge, this 434-acre park includes a sandy beach and a forest with pine and spruce. Extremely
popular in the summer months, the park includes rolling terrain
and a portion of Yaquina Bay's south-jetty entrance. There is a
paved bicycle trail. For anglers, try for striped perch in the south
jetty area. Explore the Beaver Creek area on a guided kayak tour.
Boat ramps at the marina make it possible to boat in the bay. Facilities include picnic tables, restrooms and showers. ~ Route
101, two miles south of Newport; 541-867-4715.

▲ There are 228 RV hookup sites ($17 to $22 per night), 27
yurts ($29 per night), a hiker-biker camp ($4 per person per
night) and group tent sites ($44 to $65 per night). Reservations:
800-452-5687.

ONA BEACH STATE PARK ♨︎🛶🚤⛵️⚓️ Beaver Creek
winds through this forested, parklike setting to the ocean. Picturesque bridges, broad lawns and an idyllic shoreline are the draws
of this 220-acre gem. Good fishing can be found in the river for
perch or trout in season, and from the shore. There are picnic tables and restrooms. ~ Route 101, eight miles south of Newport;
800-551-6949.

CARL G. WASHBURNE MEMORIAL STATE PARK 🚶⚓️ Five miles
of sandy beach with forested, rolling terrain make this park yet
another coastal gem. Elk are often sighted at 1238-acre
Washburne Park. The south end of the park connects to Devil's
Elbow State Park's Cape Creek drainage. There are six miles of
hiking trails, including the spectacular Lighthouse Trail, which

AUTHOR FAVORITE

sights   Routes 42 and 33 between Coos Bay and Gold Beach are popu-
larly known as the **Inland River Route**. Following the Coquille River south
through the town of the same name, this route is the hidden Oregon of your
dreams. You'll see farms, pastureland, orchards, birdlife and towering stands
of fir. Twenty-three miles beyond the Route 101 turnoff is **Hoffman
Memorial Wayside**, the first of two protected groves of the distinctive
myrtlewood tree. Turning right onto Route 33 here, you'll come to the
other grove in a few miles at **Coquille Myrtle Grove State Park** and
soon enter **Siskiyou National Forest**. After traversing the east slope
of 4075-foot **Iron Mountain**, you'll follow the **Rogue River** from the
coastal mountains to the ocean, returning to Route 101 at Gold
Beach. Allow at least half a day to drive this winding 123-mile route.

leads along dramatic coastline to the Heceta Head Lighthouse. Nearby fishing is excellent: there's perch, tuna, bass and snapper in the sea, and several streams offer trout, salmon and steelhead. Clamming is also good. There are picnic tables, restrooms and showers. ~ Route 101, 14 miles north of Florence; 541-547-3416.

▲ There are 7 walk-in tent sites ($13 to $17 per night), 58 RV hookup sites ($17 to $22 per night), 2 yurts ($29 per night) and a hiker-biker camp ($4 per person per night).

SIUSLAW NATIONAL FOREST

With two sections on the coast, this 630,000-acre region has more seacoast, 54 miles, than any other national forest in the continental United States. The terrain includes the Coast Range, Mt. Hebo and Mary's Peak. Oceanfront areas include the Cascade Head Scenic Area, Oregon Dunes National Recreation Area, Sand Lake Recreation Area and the Cape Perpetua Interpretive Center. While hiking some of the forest's 125 miles of trails, you may see deer, elk, otter, beaver, fox and bobcat. Northeast of Waldport, several trails lead into the old-growth forests at Cape Perpetua Scenic Area. Furthermore, there's boating and horseback riding. Incidentally, Siuslaw is taken from a Yakona Indian word meaning "far away waters." More than 200 species of fish including salmon, perch and trout can be caught in local streams and along the coast. Facilities include picnic areas, restrooms, showers and horseback corrals. ~ Route 101 passes through the Siuslaw in Tillamook, Lincoln and Lane counties; 541-750-7000, fax 541-750-7234; www.fs.fed.us/r6/siuslaw.

> Several California gray whales have taken up summer residence along the Central Coast—one, at least, has returned to Depoe Bay since the 1970s and has been christened "Spot."

▲ There are 31 campgrounds, one with full hookups; $15 to $20 per night. Two of the best known are the Blackberry Campground between Corvallis and the coast on Route 34 (33 tent/RV sites at $15 per night; no hookups) and the Tillicum Beach site on the coast near Waldport (59 tent/RV sites at $20 per night; no hookups). The former is situated on the Alsea River near a boat landing and hiking trails; the latter is right beside a nice beach.

JESSIE M. HONEYMAN MEMORIAL STATE PARK

This park is richly endowed with 500-foot-high sand dunes, forested lakes, rhododendron and huckleberry. Bisected by Route 101, 505-acre Honeyman is ideal for water sports, dune walks and camping. As far as we know, it has the only bathhouse on the National Register of Historic Places. A stone-and-log structure at Cleawox Lake, the unit now serves as a store and boat rental. Anglers may find bass or crappie, but rainbow trout is the main catch at Cleawox and Woahink Lake.

Boating and waterskiing are allowed at Woahink. From October through April, off-road vehicles are allowed access to the dunes from the H-loop only. Picnic tables, restrooms, showers, a playground, a store (Memorial Day to Labor Day only) and boat rentals are available here. Day-use fee, $3. ~ Route 101, three miles south of Florence; 541-997-3641, 800-5851-6949.

▲ There are 187 tent sites ($13 to $17 per night), 168 RV hookup sites ($17 to $22 per night), 10 yurts ($29 per night), 6 group tent areas ($43 to $65 per night) and a hiker-biker camp ($4 per person per night). Reservations: 800-452-5687.

UMPQUA LIGHTHOUSE STATE PARK 🏃 🏊 🚣 🛶 ⛴ 🚤 South of Winchester Bay, this park offers beautiful sand dunes and a popular hiking trail. Forested with spruce, western hemlock and shore pine, the 320-acre park is at its peak when the rhododendron bloom. Lake Marie provides calm water for canoeing or fishing. Trout is the most common catch. Great views of the Umpqua River are available from the highway. The lighthouse (which belongs to neighboring Douglas County Park) was built to signal the river's entrance; catch a tour any day of the week during the summer. You'll find picnic tables, restrooms and showers. ~ Off Route 101, six miles south of Reedsport; 541-271-4118, 541-271-4631 (lighthouse).

▲ Camping options include 24 tent sites ($12 to $16 per night), 20 RV hookup sites ($16 to $20 per night), 8 yurts ($27 to $66 per night) and 2 cabins ($35 per night). Reservations: 800-452-5687.

WILLIAM M. TUGMAN STATE PARK 🏃 🚣 🎣 🛶 🚤 ⛴ 🚤 This 800-acre park includes Eel Lake, cleaned of logging debris and turned into a popular recreational area. An excellent day-use area, Tugman is ideal for swimming and boating. Fishing will get you either a largemouth bass or a variety of other fish, including crappie and rainbow trout. Restrooms and showers are available. ~ Route 101, eight miles south of Reedsport; 541-888-3778.

▲ There are 94 RV hookup sites ($12 to $16 per night), 16 yurts ($27 per night) and a hiker-biker camp ($4 per person per night).

GOLDEN AND SILVER FALLS STATE NATURAL AREA 🏃 🚤 A pair of 100-foot-high waterfalls, old-growth forest including myrtlewood trees, and beautiful trails make this 157-acre park an excellent choice for a picnic. Cutthroat trout is a common catch here, as are crawdads. There are picnic tables, fire pits and restrooms. Bring your own water. ~ Off Route 101, 24 miles northeast of Coos Bay; 800-551-6949.

South Coast

The quietest part of the Oregon coastline, Oregon's South Coast offers miles of uncrowded beaches, beautiful dunes and excellent lakes for fishing or waterskiing. The smaller towns make an excellent base for the traveler who appreciates fine restaurants, museums, festivals and shopping. The Rogue and Chetco rivers offer rugged detours from the coast, ideal for the angler or rafter.

SIGHTS

A real sleeper, the **Coos Bay/North Bend/Charleston Bay area** is the coast's largest metropolitan area, a college town, fishing center and former logging center. Historic residential and commercial buildings, a grand harbor and a wide variety of outdoor adventure options lend character to this area. The **Bay Area Chamber of Commerce** is the ideal place to orient yourself. Closed Saturday and Sunday. ~ 50 Central Avenue, Coos Bay; 541-269-0215, 800-824-8486, fax 541-269-2861; www.oregons bayareachamber.com, e-mail bacc@uci.net.

One of our favorite galleries in the Pacific Northwest is the **Coos Art Museum,** where 20th-century American graphic art and Northwest paintings, sculpture and prints form the heart of the collection. Special exhibits feature local and nationally known artists as well as occasional traveling international exhibitions. Closed Sunday and Monday. Admission. ~ 235 Anderson Avenue, Coos Bay; 541-267-3901, 866-526-4423, fax 541-267-4877; www. coosart.org, e-mail info@coosart.org.

The art museum is just one of 22 landmarks on the chamber of commerce's self-guided walking-tour brochure. This route includes Victorian homes, Greek Classic commercial buildings and the Myrtle Arms Apartments, a rare Oregon building done in the Mission/Pueblo style.

Worth a visit is the **Coos Historical Maritime Museum**, where the diverse history of this ocean-dependent region is examined. Pioneer logging and mining and maritime equipment, along with American Indian artifacts, are on display here. Closed Sunday and Monday. Admission. ~ 1220 Sherman Avenue, North Bend; 541-756-6320; www.cooshistory.org, e-mail cmuseum@verizon.net.

A popular recreational region, the Bay Area offers watersports and fishing at **Tenmile Lakes**. The **Charleston Boat Basin** is ideal for sportfishing, clamming, crabbing, birdwatching and boating.

From Charleston, continue south four miles to **Shore Acres State Park**. Although the mansion of lumberman Louis Simpson burned down years ago, the grand, seven-acre botanical garden, including a 100-foot lily pond, is preserved. Admission. ~ 89814 Cape Arago Highway, Coos Bay; 541-888-3732, fax 541-888-5650; www.shoreacres.net, e-mail shoreacres@state.or.us.

From here, head south to **Cape Arago State Park**, your best bet for local tidepools and seal watching. The road into the park is closed to vehicle traffic, but you can still walk in, feet willing. ~ End of Cape Arago Highway.

Return toward Charleston and head south on Seven Devil's Road to **South Slough National Estuarine Research Reserve**. An extension of the Coos Bay Estuary, this splendid nature reserve is a drowned river mouth where saltwater tides and freshwater streams create a rich estuarine environment. Even if you only have time to stop at the Interpretive Center, don't miss South Slough. Easily explored on foot, thanks to a network of trails and wooden walkways, the tideflats, salt marshes and open water of the estuary and forest communities are a living ecology textbook. A major resting spot for birds like the great blue heron, the slough can also be navigated by canoe. Open year-round, but the interpretive center is closed on Sunday from Labor Day to Memorial Day. ~ Charleston; 541-888-5558, fax 541-888-5559; www.southslough estuary.org.

Bandon is one of those popular resort towns that seems to have everything. From myrtlewood and cranberry bogs to salmon bakes, it's hard to be bored in Bandon. Swing by the **Bandon Chamber of Commerce** for brochures and information. ~ 300 Southeast 2nd Street, Bandon; 541-347-9616, fax 541-347-7006; www.bandon.com, e-mail bandoncc@mycomspan.com.

Bandon's **Old Town** is an engaging neighborhood where you can shop for cranberry treats and pottery or visit one of the local art galleries. Also here is the **Bandon Driftwood Museum**. Located in an old general store, the museum features driftwood sculptures well worth a look. ~ 1st and Baltimore streets, Bandon; 541-347-3719.

One of the town highlights used to be **Tupper Rock**, a site sacred to the Coquille tribe and returned to them in 1990. Unfortunately, most of this blue-colored rock was removed many years ago to build the town jetty, and what was left of it now lies buried underneath a new rest home operated by the Coquille. South of town, **Beach Loop Road** leads past Bandon's scenic trio—Table Rock, Elephant Rock and legendary Face Rock. One of Oregon's

COOS BAY'S LEGENDARY RUNNER

Of special interest in the Coos Art Museum is the **Prefontaine Memorial Room**, a collection honoring the life and times of Steve Prefontaine, the distance runner who died in a 1975 car accident at the age of 24. During his short life Prefontaine set 11 United States indoor and outdoor records including several that still stand. Every year, a running event commemorates the memory of this Coos Bay native.

most photographed spots, the offshore seastacks make an ideal backdrop at sunset.

West Coast Game Park Safari, located seven miles south of Bandon, gives visitors a chance to see more than 75 species including lions, tigers, snow leopards, bison, zebras and elk. On their walk through the park, children can pet cubs, pups and kits in the company of attendants. Many endangered species are found at this wooded, 23-acre site. In winter the park is only open weekends and holidays, weather permitting. Admission. ~ Route 101, seven miles south of Bandon; 541-347-3106; www.gameparksa fari.com, e-mail support@gameparksafari.com.

Port Orford, the first townsite on the Oregon Coast and westernmost town in the continental United States, is a major commercial and sportfishing center. Windsurfers flock to local Floras and Garrison lakes. The Sixes and Elk rivers are popular salmon and steelhead fishing spots.

Six miles south of Port Orford is **Humbug Mountain State Park,** where hiking trails offer majestic views of the South Coast. ~ 541-332-6774.

Continue another six miles to the **Prehistoric Gardens.** Filled with life-size replicas of dinosaurs and other prehistoric species, this touristy menagerie includes the parrot-beaked *Psittacosaurus*, an ancestral form of the horn-faced dinosaur. Open year-round, weather permitting; call for changing hours. Admission. ~ 36848 Route 101 between Port Orford and Gold Beach; 541-332-4463; www.theprehistoricgardens.com.

At **Gold Beach,** a settlement at the mouth of the Rogue River, you'll find yourself on the edge of one of the coast's great wilderness areas. Here you can arrange an ocean-fishing trip or a jet boat ride up the wild and scenic Rogue River. Along the way, you may see deer, bald eagle, bear or otter. Accessible only by water, some of the rustic Rogue lodges are perfect for an overnight getaway. It's also possible to drive along the Rogue to Agness. For more details, check with the **Gold Beach Visitor Center.** Closed Sunday and Monday in winter. ~ 94080 Shirley Lane, Gold Beach; 541-247-7526, 800-525-2334, fax 541-247-0187; www.gold beach.org, e-mail visit@goldbeach.org.

Fifteen miles south of Gold Beach is **Samuel H. Boardman State Scenic Corridor,** where you'll begin a 12-mile stretch that includes Arch Rock Point, Natural Bridges Cove, House Rock and Rainbow Rock. Many visitors and locals agree this is the prettiest stretch on the Oregon coastline.

Just when you thought it would never end, the Oregon Coast comes to a screeching halt. The end of the line is **Brookings,** the Chetco River port town that produces nearly 90 percent of the Easter lilies grown in America. They are complemented by exotic lilies and daffodils raised commercially in the area. **North Bank**

South Coast

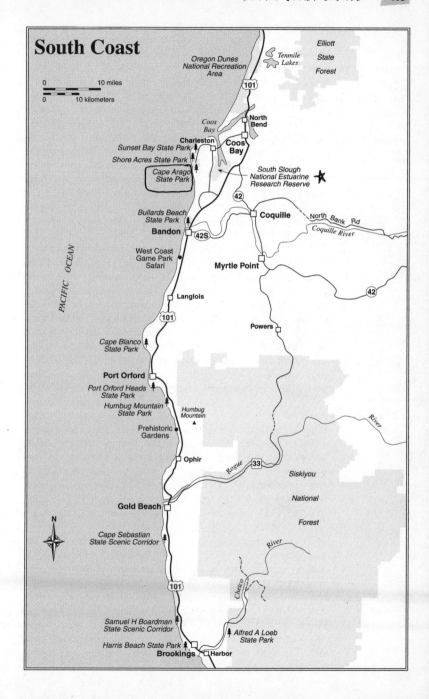

0   10 miles

0   10 kilometers

Oregon Dunes National Recreation Area

Tenmile Lakes

Elliott State Forest

101

Coos Bay

North Bend

Charleston

Coos Bay

Sunset Bay State Park

Shore Acres State Park

Cape Arago State Park

South Slough National Estuarine Research Reserve

42

Bullards Beach State Park

Coquille

North Bank Rd

Coquille River

Bandon

42S

West Coast Game Park Safari

Myrtle Point

Langlois

Powers

101

Cape Blanco State Park

42

Port Orford

Port Orford Heads State Park

Humbug Mountain State Park

Humbug Mountain

Prehistoric Gardens

PACIFIC OCEAN

Ophir

Rogue

33

River

Siskiyou

National

Gold Beach

Forest

Cape Sebastian State Scenic Corridor

River

101

Samuel H Boardman State Scenic Corridor

Alfred A Loeb State Park

Chetco

N

Harris Beach State Park

Brookings

Harbor

Chetco River Road provides easy access to the fishing holes upstream. One of the most popular destinations is **Alfred A. Loeb State Park** ten miles east of Brookings. Redwood and myrtlewood groves are your reward. You can loop back to Brookings on South Bank Road. En route consider turning off on **Forest Service Road 1205** (Bombsite Trail) and take the trail to one of only two continental United States locations bombed by a Japanese pilot during World War II. The other location, bombed by the same raider, is farther up the Oregon coast at Fort Stevens. The raider, who used a plane built aboard an offshore submarine, returned years later to give the city a samurai sword as a peace offering.

> Check out the world's largest Monterey cypress, found on the grounds of the Chetco Valley Historical Museum.

The **Brookings/Harbor Chamber of Commerce** can provide additional information on visiting this region. ~ 16330 Lower Harbor Road, Brookings; 541-469-3181, 800-535-9469, fax 541-469-4094; www.brookingsor.com, e-mail chamber@wave.net.

Shortly before reaching the California line, you'll see the Blake House, site of the **Chetco Valley Historical Society Museum** the oldest standing house in the region. Visitors can check out a turn-of-the-20th-century kitchen, antique sewing machines, Lincoln rocker, patchwork quilts dating back to 1844 and American Indian artifacts. Once a trading post and way station, the old home is filled with period furniture. A new attachment contains old logging equipment and details the area's settlement days. Closed weekdays in winter; closed Sunday through Tuesday the rest of the year. ~ 15461 Museum Road, Brookings; 541-469-6651.

LODGING   A 1912 Colonial-style house, **Coos Bay Manor** has five rooms (three with private baths) themed in Victorian, regal and country-style. Also here are a Colonial room with four-poster or twin beds and a garden room furnished with white wicker furniture. A rhododendron garden, redwoods and a delicious breakfast add to the fun. The ten-minute walk to downtown Coos Bay and the boardwalk is a bonus. ~ 955 South 5th Street, Coos Bay; 541-269-1224, 800-269-1224; www.coosbaymanor.com, e-mail cbmanor@charter.net. MODERATE.

If you're eager to crab or clam, consider unpretentious **Captain John's Motel**. On the small boat basin, this establishment is within walking distance of fishing and charter boats. Special facilities are available to cook and clean crabs. Forty-four newly renovated rooms and kitchenettes are fully carpeted and feature contemporary motel furniture. Other accommodations include a two-bedroom apartment. ~ 63360 Kingfisher Drive, Charleston; 541-888-4041, fax 541-888-6563; www.captainjohnsmotel.com, e-mail info@captainjohnsmotel.com. BUDGET TO DELUXE.

One block from Bandon's old-town district, **Sea Star Guest** ✱ **House** offers modern, carpeted units with brass or step-up beds, quilts and harbor views. These include rooms and suites with living rooms and lofts. There is also a two-bedroom penthouse. ~ 375 2nd Street, Bandon; 541-347-9632, 888-732-7871; www. seastarbandon.com, e-mail seastarban@earthlink.net. BUDGET TO DELUXE.

In the same complex is the **Sea Star Youth Hostel**. The two dorms are sex-segregated and feature ten bunk beds. There are also two family/couple rooms that should be reserved in advance. No curfew. ~ 375 2nd Street, Bandon; 541-347-9632; e-mail seastar oregon@earthlink.com. BUDGET.

You can hear the foghorn from the **Bandon Beach Motel** ✱ where many of the 28 units have balconies overlooking the ocean. Nautical decor, wood paneling and vanities make these rooms appealing. There's also a pool and spa. Small pets are welcome in some rooms. ~ 1110 11th Street, Bandon; 541-347-9451. MODERATE.

American Indian legend tells us that Ewauna, the willful daughter of Chief Siskiyou, wandered too far out into the surf and was snatched up by Seatka, the evil spirit of the sea. Today, Bandon visitors learn that images of all the protagonists in this tragedy have been frozen in stone at Face Rock. That may be one of the reasons proprietors of **Best Western Inn at Face Rock** caution guests to be wary of the local surf. Adjacent to a public golf course, this 74-unit resort—including 20 suites with fireplaces, kitchenettes and balconies—also has ocean views. Wallhangings and decks make the king- and queen-bedded rooms appealing. There's a restaurant on the premises. A pool, spa and exercise room are other amenities. ~ 3225 Beach Loop Road, Bandon; 541-347-9441, 800-638-3092, fax 541-347-2532; www.facerock. net, e-mail contact@facerock.net. DELUXE TO ULTRA-DELUXE.

Castaway-by-the-Sea Motel offers rooms and suites overlooking one of the South Coast's most picturesque, albeit windblown, beaches. Kitchenettes, glassed-in decks, contemporary upholstered furniture, wall-to-wall carpeting and easy access to fishing make this 13-unit motel a popular place. ~ 545 West 5th Street, Port Orford; 541-332-4502, fax 541-332-9303; www.castawaybythe sea.com, e-mail stay@castawaybythesea.com. MODERATE.

Breathtaking views of the coast are found at **Home by the** ◄ *HIDDEN* **Sea**. Ceramic tile floors, myrtlewood beds with quilted spreads, a leather loveseat, a rocking chair, oriental carpets and stained glass add to the charm of these units. The two rooms include private baths and mini-refrigerators; each room in this bed and breakfast comes with binoculars perfect for whale watching through the picture windows. Laundry and internet access are available. ~ 444 Jackson Street, Port Orford; 541-332-2855, 877-332-2855; www.homebythesea.com, e-mail reservations@home bythesea.com. MODERATE.

If you're an adventurer eager to deep-sea fish, raft the Rogue, boat, cycle or hike the coastal mountains, consider **Jot's Resort**. Jot's has 140 attractive, contemporary rooms, suites and condos with wall-to-wall carpet, oak furniture, vanities and decks featuring river views. Family units are available with two bedrooms, a kitchenette, and living and dining rooms. All deluxe rooms come with a microwave and refrigerator. Crabbing and clamming are great here. A full-service resort, there's a jacuzzi, sauna and two pools, an indoor and outdoor. ~ 94360 Wedderburn Loop, Wedderburn; 541-247-6676, 800-367-5687, fax 541-247-6716; www.jotsresort.com, e-mail information@jotsresort.com. MODERATE TO ULTRA-DELUXE.

On the Rogue River, **Tu Tu' Tun Lodge** can be a sunny alternative to the cloudy coast. Seven miles upriver from Gold Beach, this lodge offers 18 rooms with 12-foot-window walls, refrigerators, lounge chairs and decks or patios overlooking the water. Several have fireplaces and outdoor soaking tubs. There are also two houses for rent and two suites with kitchen facilities. Amenities here include hiking trails, horseshoes and, in the main lodge, a library and game tables. Outside you'll find a four-hole putt course and kayaks. ~ 96550 North Bank Rogue River Road, Gold Beach; 541-247-6664, 800-864-6357, fax 541-247-0672; www.tututun.com, e-mail tututunlodge@charter.net. ULTRA-DELUXE.

Located in a Craftsman-style home designed in 1917 by Bernard Maybeck, **South Coast Inn Bed & Breakfast** is an inn with four rooms in the main house and a separate private cottage. Especially choice is the Victorian Rose Room, which has a large picture window framing the Pacific, a high-rise four-poster bed, and an old-fashioned clawfoot tub in the bathroom. A fully furnished apartment with a deck and sleeper sofa is also available to rent. A full breakfast is included (continental breakfast only in the cottage). ~ 516 Redwood Street, Brookings; 541-469-5557, 800-525-9273, fax 541-469-6615; www.southcoastinn.com, e-mail innkeeper@southcoastinn.com. DELUXE.

At **Best Western Beachfront Inn**, 102 units, all with ocean views and some with kitchenettes, offer a quiet resting place. Furnished with contemporary oak dressers and tables, the king- and queen-bedded units come with microwaves, refrigerators, sofas and decks. Suites and some rooms have ocean-view jacuzzis. Inn amenities include a heated pool, an outdoor spa, sundeck and meeting rooms. ~ 16008 Boat Basin Road, Harbor; 541-469-7779, 800-468-4081, fax 541-469-0283; e-mail info@beachfrontinn.com. DELUXE TO ULTRA-DELUXE.

HIDDEN ▶   A one-lane road leads you to **Chetco River Inn Bed and Breakfast**, a get-away-from-it-all establishment on 40 wooded acres. An ideal retreat for fishing, swimming, hiking through myrtle groves or loafing on the riverbank, this contemporary solar-, propane- and battery-powered home is furnished with antiques and eclectic furniture. The inn has down comforters and large brass beds, casablanca fans and, by advance request, dinner. The cooking is innovative, and portions are generous. All five rooms have private baths. A private cottage is also available. Special discounts are offered for anglers who agree to catch and release their fish. ~ 21202 High Prairie Road, North Bank, 17.5 miles east of Brookings on the Chetco River; 541-251-0087, 800-327-2688; www. chetcoriverinn.com, e-mail chetcoriverinn@starband.net. DELUXE.

DINING

For *chiles rellenos*, *chilaquiles*, chicken *mole* and *carne asada*, try El Sol. Spanish carvings, sombreros and photographs of Mexico give this popular little restaurant a festive feel. ~ 63058 Route 101, Coos Bay; 541-266-8212. BUDGET TO MODERATE.

If you've been looking for Japanese or Chinese dishes, stop by **Kum-Yon's**. *Bulgoki*, sushi, yakitori, Mongolian beef, tempura *udon* and tofu dishes are just a few of the enticing specialties. Like the menu, the decor is pan-Asian with Japanese shell plaques, Korean wedding decorations and Chinese fans accenting the brick dining room. Closed Monday. ~ 835 South Broadway, Coos Bay; 541-269-2662. BUDGET TO DELUXE.

Wheelhouse Seafood Grill and Lounge serves fresh seafood, pasta and steak in an upstairs lounge that overlooks the water. A lighter lunch menu offers tasty burgers and sandwiches. ~ 1st and Chicago streets, Bandon; 541-347-9331. DELUXE.

Paula's Bistro, where the dimly lit bar and knotty pine–paneled dining room are decorated with local art for sale, provides an interesting mixture of artsy bohemian culture. You'll find pasta, steak, seafood and chowder on the menu; the kitchen accepts special requests from guests who want something not found on

AUTHOR FAVORITE

To get a big laugh at **Portside Restaurant and Lounge**, just ask if the fish is fresh. Grilled sole, deep-fried scallops, steamed clams, salmon and Coquille St. Jacques are among the specialties, as well as Maine lobster and Dungeness crab. I also recommend the cucumber boat, a salad with shrimp, crab and smoked salmon served with cucumber dressing and garlic toast. The contemporary dining room features photos of the fishing industry. ~ Charleston Bay Boat Basin, 63383 Kingfisher Road, Charleston; 541-888-5544, fax 541-888-9206; www.portsidebythebay. com. MODERATE TO DELUXE.

the menu. A piano is available for your use. Dinner only. Closed Sunday and Monday. ~ 236 Route 101, Port Orford; 541-332-9378, fax 541-751-1999. MODERATE TO DELUXE.

For waterfront dining, try the **Nor'wester Seafood Restaurant**. Cedar woodwork, local artwork on the walls and a large fireplace create an inviting and cozy atmosphere. Sample the fresh fish, steaks, pasta or chicken. Dinner only. Closed December and January. ~ 10 Harbor Way, Gold Beach; 541-247-2333. DELUXE TO ULTRA-DELUXE.

When the natives get restless for 4 a.m. breakfasts, fish and chips, burgers, clam chowder or shrimp cocktails, they head for the **Oceanside Diner**. This modest establishment seats customers at pine tables in the nautically themed dining room featuring fishing photos. ~ 16403 Lower Harbor Road, Brookings; phone/fax 541-469-7971. BUDGET.

A culinary time warp on the coast, **O'Holleran's Restaurant and Lounge** serves middle-of-the-road entrées in a modest dining room with wood tables and pictures on the wall. You'll find few bells or whistles on the traditional menu featuring steaks, prime rib and seafood. While you can't get blackberry catsup on the side, the food is well prepared. Dinner only. ~ 1210 Chetco Avenue, Brookings; 541-469-9907. DELUXE.

SHOPPING   Let's hear it for **Chris Merz, "The Bird Lady."** This folk artist, operating out of her home, produces outstanding wind-powered whirligigs perfect for your yard. You can choose between birds and other colorful Rube Goldberg–like contraptions. Closed during the winter months; call for hours. ~ 63347 Charleston Road, Charleston; 541-888-4425; www.whirligiglady.com.

For beaded earrings, silver and turquoise and other American Indian arts and crafts, visit **Klahowya!** The store also carries American Indian art originals, pottery, ceramics and gifts celebrating the natural world. ~ 175 2nd Street, in the Continuum Center Plaza, Bandon; 541-347-5099.

If you're looking for smoked salmon, smoked albacore, crab or shrimp, head for **Bandon Pacific Seafood**. Closed Monday. ~ 250 Southwest 1st Street, Bandon; 541-347-4454, fax 541-347-4313.

Zumwalt's Myrtlewood is the place to see the owner creating dinnerware, vases, sculptures, clocks and other popular souvenirs. ~ Route 101, six miles south of Bandon; 541-347-3654; www.zumwaltsmyrtlewood.com.

Jerry's Rogue River Museum and Gift Shop offers a broad selection of locally made arts and crafts. There is also an extensive collection of artifacts, photos and natural-history exhibits on the Rogue River area. ~ Port of Gold Beach; 541-247-4571, 800-451-3645; www.roguejets.com.

The Great American Smokehouse and Seafood Company produces gift packs with such delicacies as smoked salmon jerky, hand-packed tuna, sweet hot mustard and wild blackberry jam. ~ 15657 South Route 101, Brookings; 800-828-3474; www. smokehouse-salmon.com.

On Broadway Thespians presents contemporary drama, mysteries and musical theater in an intimate 90-seat auditorium. ~ 226 South Broadway, Coos Bay; 541-269-2501.

NIGHTLIFE

The bartenders at Timber Inn Lounge are cordial, and you can find some room out on the dancefloor. The ground-floor lounge features karaoke nightly. ~ 1001 North Bayshore Drive, Coos Bay; 541-267-4622; www.timberinnor.com.

For great sunsets, harbor views and music on the weekend, try the Portside Lounge. ~ 63383 Kingfisher Road, Charleston; 541-888-5544, fax 541-888-9206; www.portsidebythebay.com, e-mail dine@ portsidebythebay.com.

Lloyd's offers rock-and-roll bands on weekends year-round. There's a large dancefloor to let loose on. Occasional cover. ~ 119 2nd Street, Bandon; 541-347-4090.

Lord Bennett's offers jazz, country and pop in their antique-filled lounge on the third weekend of the month. Closed January. ~ 1695 Beach Loop Drive, Bandon; 541-347-3663, fax 541-347-3062; www.lordbennetts.com.

At Rascals Lounge, bands play occasionally to a dimly lit room with café seating and a full bar. If you don't want to dance, head on over to the low-stakes gaming tables and struggle against the odds. ~ Lower Harbor Road, Brookings; 541-469-5503, fax 541-469-7281.

> Harbor seals and sea lions breed on offshore rocks near Port Orford, an area known as the "Thousand Island Coast."

SUNSET BAY STATE PARK 🏃 ⛱ 🎣 🚤 ⛵ 🛶 A splendid park on dramatic headlands, Sunset is forested with spruce and hemlock. Highlights include Big Creek, a popular stream flowing into the bay. As the name implies, this is the place to be when the sun sets. Swimming, canoeing, boating, clamming and other crabbing are also popular activities in the surrounding area. Picnic tables, restrooms and showers are the facilities here. ~ Off Route 101, 12 miles southwest of Coos Bay; 541-888-4902, fax 541-888-5650.

BEACHES & PARKS

◄ HIDDEN

▲ There are 66 tent sites ($12 to $16 per night), 63 RV hookup sites ($16 to $20 per night), 8 yurts ($27 per night) and a hiker-biker camp ($4 per person per night). Reservations: 800-452-5687.

BULLARDS BEACH STATE PARK 🏃 🚲 🐎 ⛱ 🎣 🚤 ⛵ 🛶 All good things come to an end, even the Coquille River. Fortunately, this 1383-acre park makes it possible to enjoy the tail end of the stream as it flows into the estuary and the Pacific opposite the city of Bandon. The Coquille River lighthouse is located in the park (open May through October). A great recreation area, the park has fine dunes, beaches and forested lowlands. It's also ideal for crabbing and clamming. Fish for steelhead, silver and chinook salmon. Facilities include picnic tables, restrooms and showers. ~ Off Route 101, two miles north of Bandon; 541-347-2209, 800-551-6949.

▲ There are 185 RV hookup sites ($16 to $20 per night), 13 yurts ($27 per night), 8 primitive horse-camp sites ($12 to $16 per night) and a hiker-biker camp ($4 per person per night). Reservations: 800-452-5687.

CAPE BLANCO STATE PARK 🏃 🚲 🐎 ⚓ Settled by an Irish dairy farmer, these dramatic, pastured headlands include the westernmost lighthouse in Oregon. A windswept, 1856-acre retreat, Cape Blanco welcomes visitors to the Hughes House, built by a pioneer family in 1898. There's good surf fishing. You'll find picnic tables, restrooms and showers. ~ Off Route 101, nine miles north of Port Orford; 541-332-2973.

▲ There are 53 RV hookup sites ($12 to $16 per night), 4 log cabins ($35 per night), 6 primitive horse-camp sites ($10 to $14 per night) and a hiker-biker camp ($4 per person per night).

PORT ORFORD HEADS STATE PARK 🏃 ⚓ You'll love this windblown and unforgettable 126-acre wayside. It encompasses the ocean bluff as well as Nellies Cove. The park protects marine gardens and prehistoric archaeological landmarks. A former Coast Guard Station now houses a free museum that is open Thursday through Monday from April through October. There are picnic tables and restrooms. ~ Off Route 101, Port Orford; 800-551-6949.

HUMBUG MOUNTAIN STATE PARK 🏃 🐟 ⚓ A 1756-foot peak forested with fir, spruce, alder and cedar, Humbug is one of the coast's finest parks. Hiking trails, viewpoints, Brush Creek

AUTHOR FAVORITE

sights   Let's skip the superlatives and get to the point: Visit **Shore Acres State Park**. This 745-acre estate was once the site of a timber baron's mansion. Although the house burned down, the formal garden remains a showcase. Planted with azaleas, rhododendrons, irises, dahlias and roses, Shore Acres also offers trails on the forested bluffs. There are picnic tables, restrooms, an observation shelter and a gift shop. Between Thanksgiving and New Year's, check out the nightly Holiday Lights display. Dayuse fee, $3. ~ Off Route 101, 13 miles southwest of Coos Bay; 541-888-3732; www.shoreacres.net, e-mail shoreacres@state.or.us.

and ocean frontage make the 1765-acre sanctuary a great retreat. If you're feeling ambitious, why not take the three-mile hike up the wildflower-lined trail to the summit? You'll find picnic tables, restrooms and showers. ~ Off Route 101, six miles south of Port Orford; 541-332-6774.

▲ There are 62 tent sites ($10 to $14 per night), 32 RV hookup sites ($12 to $16 per night) and a hiker-biker camp ($4 per person per night).

CAPE SEBASTIAN STATE SCENIC CORRIDOR 🏃🔦 This narrow park includes several miles of exceptional coastline. The centerpiece of the 1224-acre place is the cape, carpeted with wildflowers and rhododendron in the spring. Views are magnificent and whale watching is excellent. A spectacular one-and-a-half-mile trail leads to the tip of the Cape. Old-growth Douglas fir and Sitka spruce form a handsome backdrop. There is no drinking water here. ~ Off Route 101, seven miles south of Gold Beach; 800-551-6949. Not recommended for long RVs or vehicles towing trailers.

HARRIS BEACH STATE PARK 🏃🚣🎣🏄🏊🚤🔦 Named for Scottish pioneer George Harris, this one-time sheep-and-cattle ranch is the southernmost state camping facility on the coast. The 172-acre park offers sandy beaches and great sunsets. The shoreline is punctuated with dramatic, surf-sculptured rocks, which make kayaking and surfing challenging. There's good fishing for salmon and perch. There are picnic tables, restrooms and showers. ~ 1655 North Route 101, Brookings; 541-469-2021.

▲ There are 63 tent sites ($13 to $16 per night), 86 RV hookup sites ($17 to $22 per night), 6 yurts ($29 per night) and a hiker-biker camp ($4 per person per night). Reservations: 800-452-5687.

ALFRED A. LOEB STATE PARK 🏃🚣🏊🔦 On the Chetco River, this park can be a warm place when the coast is not. A one-mile trail leads to Loeb's redwood grove. There's also a myrtle grove here. A popular fishing region, particularly during the steelhead season, the Chetco is one of Oregon's special havens. With 320 acres, the park provides easy access to a prime stretch of this river canyon. Picnic tables, firepits, restrooms and showers are some of the facilities. ~ Located ten miles northeast of Brookings along the Chetco River; 541-469-2021.

◄ HIDDEN

▲ There are 48 RV hookup sites ($12 to $16 per night) and 3 log cabins ($35 per night). Reservations: 800-452-5687.

From mid-May or June through September or mid-October, charter companies and outfitters up and down the coast regularly run ocean fishing trips: from a half day of bottomfishing to longer reef-fishing

▼▼▼▼▼▼▼▼▼▼▼▼
Outdoor Adventures
SPORT-
FISHING

outings. Tackle is usually provided, but a fishing license is required (you can purchase it through charter operators). And don't forget to bring lunch.

NORTH COAST   **Charlton Deep Sea** accommodates up to 15 people, May through September, on trips for tuna, salmon, sturgeon and halibut. ~ 470 Northeast Skipanon Drive, Warrenton; 503-338-0569. **Garibaldi/D&D Charters** runs an annual trip each May for halibut; it's so popular, however, it's booked a year in advance. They offer several other trips, so you should have no trouble getting a spot on the salmon, light-tackle or deep-reef bottomfish trips. ~ Route 101, Garibaldi; 503-322-0007, 800-900-4665; www.garibaldicharters.com.

> Well known for salmon, Oregon's coastal waters are also fished for ling cod, cabazon (a big, ugly bottom fish), sea bass, red snapper, albacore and halibut.

CENTRAL COAST   The oldest charter fishing company in the area, **Newport Tradewinds** has been running trips for halibut, salmon, tuna, bottomfish and crab since 1949. ~ 653 Southwest Bay Boulevard, Newport; 541-265-2101; www.newporttradewinds.com. **Depoe Bay Tradewinds** runs fishing trips year-round for tuna, halibut, salmon and clams, as well as bottomfish like sea bass and red snapper. ~ Depoe Bay; 541-765-2345, 800-445-8730; www.tradewindscharters.com. You can also arrange a guided fishing trip with **Dockside Charters**. ~ Depoe Bay; 541-765- 2545; www.docksidedepoebay.com.

SOUTH COAST   In Charleston, **Betty Kay Charters** has year-round half-day bottomfishing trips, as well as seasonal runs for tuna and halibut. ~ 7788 Albacore Street; 541-888-9021, 800-752-6303; www.bettykaycharters.com. Besides halibut fishing in May, **Bob's Sportfishing** offers several other trips, including a half-day bottomfishing excursion. ~ Charleston; 541-888-4241; www.bobssportfishing.com.

FISHING   You can rent a small boat and row out into a bay, such as Yaquina or Nehalem, for year-round recreational crabbing (always call first for tide information), as well as seasonal catches of perch, flounder, bass and salmon. Near Coos Bay, Ten Mile Lake is stocked with trout, crappie and catfish.

NORTH COAST   **Jetty Fisheries** rents 16-foot aluminum Klamath boats. August through November, a run of salmon moves through the bay to spawn in the Nehalem River. Crabbing is good year-round. Crab-cooking and fish-cleaning facilities are provided. ~ Route 101 at Nehalem Bay, Rockaway Beach; 503-368-5746; www.jettyfishery.com, e-mail jettyfishery@coastwipi.com.

CENTRAL COAST   The **Newport Marina Charter and Store** rents 14-foot aluminum fishing boats and equipment for fishing and crabbing year-round. ~ 2122 Southeast Marine Science Drive, South Beach; 541-867-4470; www.nmscharters.com. In Waldport try **McKinley's Marina**, which rents small boats that seat up to four. Boat rentals include bait. ~ Route 34; 541-563-4656. Near the Florence area try **Westlake Resort**, where you can rent 15-foot boats and try for perch, crappie and catfish. ~ Laurel Avenue, Westlake; 541-997-3722; www.westlakeresort.com.

The Oregon Coast provides a front-row seat to one of nature's magnificent shows: the annual migrations of the California gray whales. Although the southbound leg of the mammals' trip peaks in late December, it continues until February. Then, with calves in tow, the mammals begin the northbound journey in March. It continues through May. This is an excellent time to take a whale-watching tour: during this leg of the trip, the whales travel closer to shore and more slowly.

WHALE WATCHING

CENTRAL COAST Depoe Bay calls itself the whale-watching capital of the Oregon Coast. The mammals are probably attracted to the bay because of a unique environment that provides plenty for the whales to feed on. The **Oregon Parks and Recreation Department**'s whale-watching center has 200 volunteers who array themselves at 28 overlooks along the Oregon Coast and offer tips to whale watchers. Trained by researchers at Mark O. Hatfield Marine Science Center in Newport, the volunteers are mines of information about the gray whale's behavior and life cycle. Closed Labor Day through Memorial Day and May through October. ~ 119 Southwest Route 101, Depoe Bay; 541 765 3407; www.whalespoken.org.

Dockside Charters runs daily whale-watching tours. Once the boat reaches the migration route—usually about a mile or two offshore—it will stop and drift for a while so visitors can watch the whales feed. Owner Jim Tade will also take up to six people out in inflatable Zodiac boats for up-close looks at the mammals. ~ Depoe Bay; 541-765-2545; www.docksidedepoebay.com. **Depoe Bay Tradewinds** also operates daily one-hour whale-watching trips year-round. ~ Depoe Bay; 541-765-2345, 800-445-8730; www.tradewindscharters.com. **Newport Tradewinds** offers two-hour whale-watching trips all through the year. ~ 653 Southwest Bay Boulevard, Newport; 541-265-2101; www.new porttradewinds.com.

If you go surfing, keep in mind that you will be sharing the waves with cold water–loving great-white sharks so stick to common surfing areas. Surfing in Oregon hasn't reached the crescendo of activity that it has in California. Nevertheless, there are local contingents of surfers up and down the coast. Ecola State Park, Indian Beach and Oswald West State Park are recommended North Coast surfing spots, and good for all skill levels. Along the Central Coast, Otter Rock, south of Newport, is good place for

SURFING

beginners. But only a few shops rent surfboards, wetsuits and various other "board" sports equipment.

NORTH COAST   **Cleanline Surf Shop** in Seaside started out in 1980, renting wetsuits to diehard surfers ready to brave the cold winter waters. Now it rents just about everything, including wetsuits, surfboards and snowboards. ~ 725 1st Avenue, Seaside; 503-738-7888, fax 503-738-9793; www.cleanlinesurf.com.

CENTRAL COAST   **Safari Town Surf Shop** rents wetsuits, surfboards, bodyboards and skimboards. The shop is about a half-hour's drive north of Otter Rock. Closed Monday in the winter. ~ 3026 Northeast Route 101, Lincoln City; 541-996-6335. Surfboards, boogieboards, skimboards, kayaks and wet suits can be rented or purchased at the **Oregon Surf Shop**. ~ 4933 Southwest Route 101, Lincoln City; phone/fax 541-996-3957, 877-339-5672; www.oregonsurfshop.com.

WIND-SURFING & KAYAKING   Kayaking is popular on Coffenberry Lake at Fort Stevens State Park in Astoria. And in Langlois, on the South Coast, there's a windsurfing bed-and-breakfast inn, where you can take lessons after your continental breakfast.

NORTH COAST   For kayak rentals, contact **Pacific Wave Limited**. The shop also offers kayaking lessons and guided kayak tours of the area's rivers, bays and estuaries. ~ 2021 Route 101, Warrenton; 503-861-0866, fax 503-861-4319; www.pacwave.net.

SOUTH COAST   A sandspit separates the freshwater, spring-fed Floras Lake from the ocean. At the **Floras Lake House**, a bed and breakfast that sits just off the lake, the owners also operate a windsurfing school (equipment and wetsuit included for beginners). Mornings are best for lessons (steady northwest winds blow during the afternoon) on the lake, which is shallow and warm.

BEASTLY BEHAVIOR

Once you have spotted a whale, keep your eyes peeled for it to rise above the surface. Gray whales often "spyhop," thrusting their heads out of the water and balancing with their eyes exposed. Experts believe this is done to look around above the surface and possibly to orient themselves with reference to the shore or the sun. The most spectacular whale behavior, from a landlubber's viewpoint, is "breaching"—leaping completely out of the water, rolling sideways and falling slowly backward to land with an enormous splash. The reason for this is unknown. It could be to knock off barnacles or to signal other whales. It might be a courtship ritual, or then again, it might just be the giant beast's playful way of expressing the joy of life.

Closed November to mid-February; call for hours after Labor Day. ~ 92870 Boice Cope Road, Langlois; 541-348-2573; www. floraslake.com, e-mail floraslk@harborside.com.

Look no further than the Oregon Coast for impressive scenic backdrops to half-day guided rides through coastal mountain pine forest, open rides along beach dunes or mountain trail rides near the mouth of the Rogue River.

RIDING STABLES

NORTH COAST Based out of Nehalem Bay State Park, **Northwest Equine Outfitters** offers early-morning and sunset rides along the coast, as well as half- and full-day rides. Customized trips can be arranged. Open daily Memorial Day to Labor Day; by appointment only the rest of the year. ~ Nehalem Bay State Park; 503-801-7433; www.horserental.us.

CENTRAL COAST **C&M Stables** has guided rides through the dunes and along the beach or the mountains. Long (half-day) rides through the beaches and dunes can also be arranged. ~ 90241 Route 101, Florence; 541-997-7540; www.oregonhorsebackriding.com.

SOUTH COAST **Bandon Beach Riding Stables** specializes in open rides along the beach, and operates year-round. Maximum group of 16 people. Reservations recommended. ~ Beach Loop Drive, Bandon; 541-347-3423; www.bandonbeachridingstables.com.

When rainfall along the coast can measure 60, 70, even 80 inches a year, good drainage is important for a golf course. The courses listed here all report good drainage, making them playable year-round. You can rent clubs and carts at the courses listed below.

GOLF

NORTH COAST For a round of nine holes, try the public **Highlands Golf Course**, run by Discount Dan. It's a fun but challenging course, with ocean views from some holes. ~ 33377 Highland Lane, Gearhart; 503-738-5248; www.highlandsgolf course.com. At the 18-hole **Gearhart Golf Links**, ocean views are obscured by a condominium complex, but the terrain is relatively flat, making this public green quite walkable. ~ 1157 North Marion Street, Gearhart; 503-738-3538; www.gearheartgolf links.com.

CENTRAL COAST Public facilities also include **Chinook Winds Golf Resort**, which has a hilly, moderately challenging 18-hole course. ~ 3245 Northeast 50th Street, Lincoln City; 541-994-8442. In Gleneden Beach, try the 18-hole course at **Salishan Golf Links**. ~ Gleneden Beach; 541-764-3632; www.salishan.com. The scenic nine-hole, privately owned but publicly accessible **Agate Beach Golf Course** is fairly flat and walkable, with ocean views from some holes. This 3002-yard-long course has a driving range. ~ 4100 North Coast Highway

(Route 101), Newport; 541-265-7331; www.agatebeachgolf.net. In Florence, **Sand Pines Golf Links** has an 18-hole course built on sand dunes, which provide excellent drainage and spectacular scenery. ~ 1201 35th Street; 541-997-1940; www.sandpines. com. There's a "wee bit o' Scotland" in Florence at the 18-hole, public **Ocean Dunes Golf Links**, an older, well-known, "true" links course, with high slope and difficulty ratings. ~ 3345 Munsel Lake Road; 541-997-3232; www.oceandunesgolf.com. In Waldport, the nine-hole **Crestview Hills Golf Course** is flat and walkable, complete with a pro shop and a driving range. ~ 1680 Crestline Drive, Waldport; 541-563-3020, 888-538-4463; www. crestviewhillsgolf.com.

SOUTH COAST The John Zahler–designed **Sunset Bay Golf Course** is adjacent to Sunset Bay; it's public, nine holes, is walkable and is "about the only course in the area playable in the winter," according to a local pro. ~ 11001 Cape Arago Highway, Coos Bay; 541-888-9301; www.sunsetbaygolf.com. A little farther south is **Bandon Face Rock Golf Course**. Lessons are offered during the summer at this nine-hole executive course. ~ 3235 Beach Loop Road, Bandon; 541-347-3818; www.bandonby thesea.com/golf. About 12 miles north of Gold Beach, the nine-hole, public **Cedar Bend Golf Course** is set in a valley with a creek winding through it. Alder, hemlock and fir trees add to the scenic beauty. Cedar Bend is an 18-hole course. ~ 34391 Cedar Valley Road, Gold Beach; 541-247-6911.

TENNIS Time for tennis? A good possibility is the court at **Goodspeed Park**. ~ 3rd Street and Goodspeed Place, Tillamook; 503-842-7525. On the coast, try **Bandon High School**'s two courts. ~ 11th and Franklin streets, Bandon; 541-347-9616. In Port Orford, play at **Buffington Park**. ~ 14th and Arizona streets, Port Orford; 541-332-8055. Additional public courts are at 2nd and Spruce streets in **Cannon Beach** (these courts are lighted; 503-436-2623), Northeast 4th and Benton streets in Newport, and **Rolling Dunes Park** at Siano Loop and 35th Street in Florence (541-997-3436).

BIKING Route 101 is the state's most popular biking trail. Every year, thousands of travelers do the coast, taking advantage of many side roads, hiker-bike camps and facilities that cater to the cycling crowd. Even to nonbicyclists, the 370-mile **Oregon Coast Bike Route** is well known. There are numerous sections that take in scenic and quiet county and city streets that have low volume traffic and slow traffic speeds. There are also backcountry sites set up for cyclists.

NORTH COAST An eight-mile paved route through **Fort Stevens State Park** passes through the park's historic section, then leads into a wooded area before crossing to parallel the ocean and looping back into the park. In Seaside you can ride along the two-mile boardwalk or head back into the Lewis and Clark area for rides along paved roads and some old logging roads.

CENTRAL COAST   Newport's **Ocean View Drive** is an excellent, four-mile alternative to Route 101. This route leads past the Agate Beach area and takes you through the historic Nye Beach community, one of Newport's earliest resorts. You'll wind up at Yaquina Bay State Park, home of the community's signature lighthouse.

SOUTH COAST   Off Route 101 north of Bandon, **North Bank**   ◄ *HIDDEN*
Road winds for 16 miles along the Coquille River. This flat, scenic route is lightly trafficked (but watch out for logging trucks), lush and unforgettable. Then head south on Route 42 to Coquille and pick up South Route 42 back to Bandon. The roundtrip is 52 miles.

Bike Rentals   In Seaside, **Prom Bike and Hobby Shop** is just three blocks from the beach. The shop rents three-speed cruisers, mountain bikes, kids' bikes, tandems and beach tricycles. Or you might try a surrey, rollerskates or inline skates. Closed Tuesday and Wednesday. ~ 622 12th Avenue, Seaside; 503-738-8251. A few miles south, **Mike's Bike Shop** rents "fun-cycles"—big three-wheelers—for riding on the fairly level wide beach at low tide. Otherwise, you can rent mountain bikes to ride on nearby logging trails (they're private, however) or up to Ecola State Park, about a mile away. You may also rent beach cruisers. Closed Tuesday and Wednesday during the winter. ~ 248 North Spruce Street, Cannon Beach; 503-436-1266; 800-492-1266. In Newport, check out **The Bike Shop** for mountain, road and tandem bike rentals, as well as equipment and repairs. Closed Sunday. ~ 223 Northwest Nye Street, Newport; 541-265-2481,

BIKING THE OREGON COAST

If you're thinking about making the ride along the Oregon Coast Bike Route, get hold of the **Oregon Coast Bike Route Map**. It's free and published by the Oregon Department of Transportation. The department also publishes the **Oregon Bicycling Guide** that maps out bike routes throughout the state and provides information on various route conditions. It should be noted that Oregon Coast Bike Route is really for experienced cyclists. Besides the length of the trip (the journey takes about six or eight days), the route rises and falls 16,000 feet along the way. ~ Oregon Department of Transportation Bikeway Program: 355 Capitol Street Northeast, Room 210, Transportation Building, Salem, OR 97310; 503-986-3556, fax 503-986-3407; ww.oregon.gov/odot/hwy/bikeped.3.

800-446-9243. **Bicycles 101** in Florence rents mountain bikes and cruisers. Closed Sunday. ~ 1537 8th Street, Florence; phone/fax 541-997-5717.

HIKING   The Oregon Coast abounds with beautiful hiking opportunities within state parks and national forests. All distances listed for hiking trails are one way unless otherwise noted.

NORTH COAST   **Fort Stevens State Park** has several easy trails, including the two trail, 1.8-mile stroll from Battery Russell to the wreck of the *Peter Iredale.*

Saddle Mountain Trail (2.5 miles) ascends the highest mountain on the coastal range. A difficult climb offering great views. It's located off Route 26 near Necanicum.

Tillamook Head Trail (7 miles) begins south of the town of Seaside and ascends to 1200 feet on the route to Escola State Park's Indian Beach. This is believed to be the route followed by Lewis and Clark when they journeyed to Ecola Creek.

HIDDEN ►   Inland from Tillamook on Route 6 is the moderate-to-difficult **Kings Mountain Trail** (2.5 miles). This route takes you through the area of the famed Tillamook Burn, a series of 1933, 1939, 1945 and 1951 fires that took out enough lumber to build over one million homes. While the area, now the Tillamook State Forest, is covered with younger timber, some evidence of the old burn can still be seen.

Neah-kah-nie Mountain Trail (4 miles) is a challenging climb that begins 2.6 miles south of Oswald West State Park's Short Sands parking area. Great views of the coast.

CENTRAL COAST   In the Siuslaw National Forest east of Pacific City, the **Pioneer Indian Trail** (8 miles) is highly recommended. This moderately difficult trail runs from Itebo Lake to South Lake through a fir forest and a meadow that has a wide array of wildflowers in the summer.

HIDDEN ►

The **Estuary Trail** (.25 mile) at the Hatfield Marine Science Center is a great introduction to local marine life. This posted route is wheelchair accessible. ~ 2030 South Marine Science Drive, Newport; 541-867-0100.

Captain Cook's Trail (.6 mile) leads from the Cape Perpetua visitors center below Route 101 past American Indian shell middens to coastal tidepools. At high tide you'll see the spouting horn across Cook's Chasm. A bit more challenging is the **Cummins Creek Loop** (10 miles) up Cook's Ridge to Cummins Creek Trail and back down to the visitors center. Enjoy the old-growth forests and meadows.

At the southern end of the Oregon Dunes National Recreation Area, **Bluebill Trail** (1 mile roundtrip), two and a half miles off Route 101 near Horsefall Beach Road, offers an easy and beautiful loop hike around the marshy area once known as Bluebill Lake. It includes an extensive boardwalk system.

SOUTH COAST The **Estuary Study Trail** at South Slough National Estuarine Research Reserve south of Coos Bay (1.5 miles) is one of the finest hikes on the Oregon Coast. Leading down through a coastal forest, you'll see a pioneer log landing, use a boardwalk to cross a skunkcabbage bog and visit a salt marsh.

Shrader Old Growth Trail (1.5 miles) off Jerry's Flat Road, east of Gold Beach, is a pleasant loop where you'll see rhododendron, cedar, streams and riparian areas. The marked route identifies coastal species along the way.
◄ HIDDEN

To really get away from it all, hike the **Lower Rogue River Trail** (12.2 miles) south from Agness. You'll pass American Indian landmarks, see picturesque bridges and spot wildlife as you hike this wild and scenic canyon.
◄ HIDDEN

Bandon to Fourmile Creek (8.5 miles) is one of the coast's most scenic walks. Begin at Bandon Harbor and head south past the Bandon Needles, dunes, ponds and lakes to the creek. Of course you can abbreviate this hike at any point. One easy possibility is to head south on Beach Loop Drive to the point where it swings east toward Route 101. Park here and take the short .2-mile walk through the woods and up over the dune to Bradley Lake, a good swimming hole.

Redwood Trail (1 mile) north of Alfred A. Loeb State Park, ten miles east of Brookings, is a beautiful streamside walk leading past rhododendron, myrtlewood and towering redwoods.

▼▼▼▼▼▼▼▼▼▼

Transportation

From Northern California or Washington, the coast is easily reached via **Route 101**. Within Oregon, many roads link Portland and the Willamette Valley to resort destinations. **Routes 30** and **26** provide easy access to the North Coast communities of Astoria and Seaside, while **Route 6** connects with Tillamook. **Route 18** leads to Lincoln City, and **Routes 20** and **34** connect with the Central Coast region in the vicinity of Newport and Waldport. **Route 126** is the way to Florence. **Route 38** heads to Reedsport. To reach Bandon and the South Coast, take **Route 42**.

CAR

Horizon Air flies to **North Bend Municipal Airport** (www.coos baynorthbendairport.com). The **Portland International Airport** (503-460-4234, 877-739-4636) and **Eugene Airport** (541-682-5430), described in other chapters, also provide gateways to the coast.

AIR

Greyhound Bus Lines (800-231-2222; www.greyhound.com) serves many coast destinations. There is a stop in Florence, along with stops in Newport at 956 Southwest 10th Street, 541-265-2253.

BUS

CAR RENTALS   **Hertz Rent A Car** has a location at North Bend Municipal Airport, as well as one at 1492 Duane Street in Astoria. ~ 800-654-3131.

PUBLIC TRANSIT   In Otis, Lincoln City, Newport, Waldport, Yachats, Toledo and Siletz, local service is provided by **Lincoln County Transit**. The same company provides service from Siletz and Yachats to Newport, and from Newport to Lincoln City. ~ 541-265-4900; co.lincoln.or.us/transit. Connections can be made from Bend, Corvallis, Newport, Salem and Albany through **Valley Retriever Bus Lines**. ~ 541-265-2253.

TAXIS   For service in Seaside, try **Seaside Yellow Cab**. ~ 503-738-5252. On the South Coast, **Yellow Cab** operates in Coos Bay/North Bend. ~ 541-267-3111.

NINE

Oregon Cascades

Some questions are impossible to answer. Here's one that came to mind while we traveled the highways and byways of the Oregon Cascades, swimming in crystal-clear pools, basking at alpine resorts, fishing pristine streams, dining on fresh salmon and cooling off beneath the spray of yet another waterfall: Why isn't this heavenly space positively jammed with people who want to get away from it all?

Except for a handful of places, such as Mt. Hood on a Saturday afternoon, Route 97 in the vicinity of Bend or Crater Lake's Rim Drive, it's often hard to find a crowd in this seemingly inexhaustible resort area. Sure, there's a fair number of timber rigs out on major routes. And the No Vacancy sign does pop up a good deal at popular resorts during the summer and weekends. But who cares when you can head down the road half a mile and check into a glorious streamside campground where the tab is rock-bottom and there's no extra charge for the nocturnal view of the Milky Way? The fact is that mile for mile, the Oregon Cascades offer some of the best wilderness and recreational opportunities in the Pacific Northwest.

To really get a feel for the area, you need a week or longer. But even if you only have time to buzz up to Mt. Hood for an afternoon, this is the best place we know to gain perspective on the volcanic history of the Pacific Northwest. A chain of peaks topped by 11,235-foot Mt. Hood, the Cascades have an average elevation of about 5000 feet. Heavily forested, these mountains are also the headwaters for many important rivers such as the Rogue, the Umpqua and the McKenzie. Klamath Falls is the principal southern gateway to the region, and Bend and Redmond provide easy access from the east. Within the mountains are a number of charming towns and villages such as Sisters, McKenzie Bridge and Camp Sherman. While the summer months can be mild and sunny, winter snowfalls blanket the western slopes with 300 to 500 inches of snow.

For some perspective on the Cascades, take a look at the area's good-old days. Begin with the evolution of one of the Northwest's signature attractions, Crater

Lake. Looking at this placid sea, it's hard to imagine what this region looked like 60 million years ago during the late Cretaceous period. As Lowell Williams has written: "At that time the Coast Ranges of Oregon . . . were submerged and the waves of the Pacific lapped against the foothills of the Sierra Nevada and the Blue Mountains of Oregon. Where the Cascade peaks now rise in lofty grandeur, water teemed with shellfish . . . giant marine lizards swam in the seas, and winged reptiles sailed above in search of prey."

Later, in the Eocene and Oligocene periods, roughly 25 million to 60 million years ago, the Crater Lake region became a low plain. Throughout this period and the late Miocene, volcanoes erupted. Finally, about one million to two million years ago, in the last great Ice Age, the Cascades were formed. The largest of these peaks became 12,000-foot Mt. Mazama. About 7000 years ago, this promontory literally blew its top, leaving behind the caldera that is now Crater Lake.

The American Indians, who viewed this area as a sacred and treacherous place, went out of their way to avoid Crater Lake. It was only after the white man arrived in the 19th century that it became a tourist attraction and eventually a national park. Today the lake is considered a unique national treasure.

Because they provided a tremendous challenge to settlers heading toward the Pacific Ocean on the Oregon Trail, the Cascades also gained an important place in the history of the West. Landmarks surrounding Mt. Hood tell the dramatic story of pioneers who blazed time-saving new routes to the promised land across this precipitous terrain. Of course, their arrival permanently altered American Indian life. Inevitably, efforts to colonize the Indians and turn them into farmers and Christians met with resistance. American Indian leader Captain Jack led perhaps the most famous tribal rebellion against the miseries of reservation life in the 1872–73 Modoc War. This fighting raged in an area that is now part of the Lava Beds National Monument across the border in California. Captain Jack and his fellow renegades were ultimately hanged at Fort Klamath.

While logging became the Cascades' leading industry, tourism emerged in the late 19th century. Summer resorts, typically primitive cabins built at the water's edge, were popular with the fishing crowd. Later, the arrival of resort lodges like the Timberline on the slopes of Mt. Hood drew a significant winter trade. But even as Oregon's best-known mountain range evolved into a major resort area, it was able to retain carefully guarded secrets. Little-known fishing spots, obscure trails, waterfalls absent from the maps—this high country became Oregon's private treasure.

Today, Oregon, one of the nation's most environmentally conscious states, is trying to find peaceful coexistence between the logging industry and environmentalists. The continuing "spotted owl" controversy has led to logging restrictions in the past over the fight to save old-growth forests for future generations. But with political changes, the battle lives on.

In 2003 President George Bush signed the Healthy Forest Restoration Act, which allowed vast areas of forests to be logged as a fire prevention measure. The Act was in response to the massive 2002 Biscuit fire that devoured 500,000 acres of Oregon and California forests. Though by 2006 it was determined that the Act cost the federal government $2 million that had not yet been used to restore the logged trees or habitats, and despite appeals from environmentalist groups that

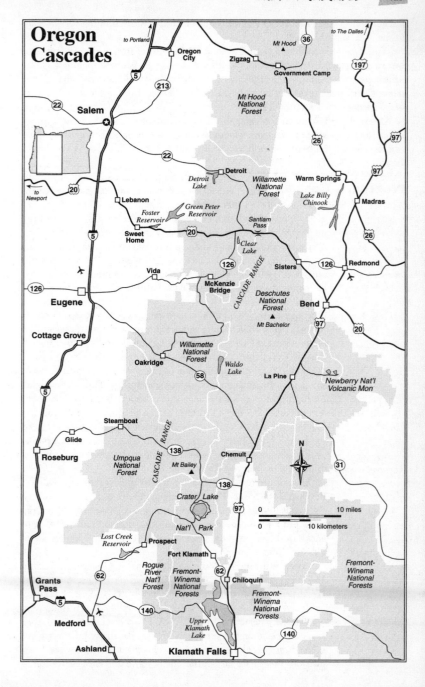

Oregon Cascades

to Portland

Oregon City

Zigzag

Mt Hood ▲ 36

to The Dalles

197

Government Camp

5

213

Mt Hood National Forest

26

97

22

Salem ✪

22

Detroit

Detroit Lake

Willamette National Forest

Warm Springs

Lake Billy Chinook

97

97

Madras

to Newport

20

Lebanon

Green Peter Reservoir

Foster Reservoir

Sweet Home

20

Santiam Pass

26

5

Clear Lake

Vida

126

Sisters

126

Redmond

CASCADE RANGE

McKenzie Bridge

Deschutes National Forest

126

Eugene

Mt Bachelor ▲

Bend

Cottage Grove

97

20

Willamette National Forest

Waldo Lake

Oakridge

58

La Pine

Newberry Nat'l Volcanic Mon

Steamboat

CASCADE RANGE

Glide

138

Chemult

Roseburg

Umpqua National Forest

Mt Bailey ▲

138

31

N

Crater Lake

97

0   10 miles

0   10 kilometers

Nat'l   Park

Lost Creek Reservoir

Prospect

Fort Klamath

Rogue River Nat'l Forest

Fremont-Winema National Forests

62

Chiloquin

Fremont-Winema National Forests

Grants Pass

62

Fremont-Winema National Forest

5

140

Medford

Upper Klamath Lake

140

Ashland

Klamath Falls

haven't let up since the Act's inception, Bush included more funding for the plan in the 2007 fiscal budget.

You'll be able to take a firsthand look at the subject in question on some of our recommended walks through old-growth preserves. Because logging has traditionally been such an important component of the local economy, many residents worry that further restrictions will threaten their livelihood.

Walking into the Cascades backcountry, you can easily spend hours on a road or trail with only yourself for company. This solitude is the area's greatest drawing card. Appreciate the fact that the only lines you'll have to bother with most of the time are the kind with a hook on the end.

Northern Cascades

Given their proximity to the state's major urban centers such as Portland and Eugene, the Northern Cascades are a popular destination, particularly on weekends and during the summer months. Most of the highlights, in fact, can be reached within a couple of hours. Pioneer history, American Indian culture and scenic wonders are just a few of the Cascades' treasures. And if you're looking for un-crowded, out-of-the-way places, relax. Those hidden spots are easily located, often just a mile or two off the most popular routes.

SIGHTS
Our visit to the **Mt. Hood** region begins on Route 26. Portions of this road parallel the time-saving trail first blazed in 1845 by pioneer Samuel Barlow. The following year he and a partner turned this discovery into a $5 toll road at the end of the Oregon Trail, the final tab for entry to the end of the rainbow. Today a series of small monuments commemorates the **Barlow Trail**. At Tollgate campground, a quarter-mile east of Rhododendron on the south side of Route 26, you'll want to visit a reproduction of the historic Barlow Tollgate. Continue five miles east of Rhododendron to the **Laurel Hill Chute** marker. You can take the short, steep hike to the infamous "chute" where wagon trains descended the perilous grade to Zigzag River Valley.

Two of the region's most popular fishing streams, the **Salmon River** and the **Sandy River** are convenient to old-growth forests, waterfalls and hiking trails. Continuing east, you'll reach Zigzag and **Lolo Pass Road**. This backcountry route on the west side of Mt. Hood leads to **Lost Lake**, a great escape (see Chapter Seven for more on the lake).

After returning to Route 26, drive east to Government Camp and head uphill to Mt. Hood's **Timberline Lodge**, one of the Northwest's most important arts and crafts–style architectural landmarks. Massive is the word for this skiing hub framed with giant timber beams and warmed by a two-level, octagon-shaped stone fireplace. In the summer you can hike the wildflower trails surrounding the lodge. Be sure to check out the lower-level display on the lodge's fascinating history and current restoration. ~

Timberline Ski Area; 503-622-7979, 800-547-1406, fax 503-622-0710; www.timberlinelodge.com, e-mail information@timberlinelodge.com.

Two miles east of Government Camp turn south on Route 26 to picturesque **Trillium Lake**, a popular fishing, swimming and non-motorized boating spot created by the damming of Mud Creek. This is an ideal place for a picnic lunch and wildlife viewing.

For more information on the area surrounding the great mountain, contact the **Mt. Hood Information Center**. ~ Located 15 miles east of Sandy on Route 26; 503-622-4822, 888-622-4822, fax 503-622-7625; www.mthood.info, e-mail infoctr@mthood.info.

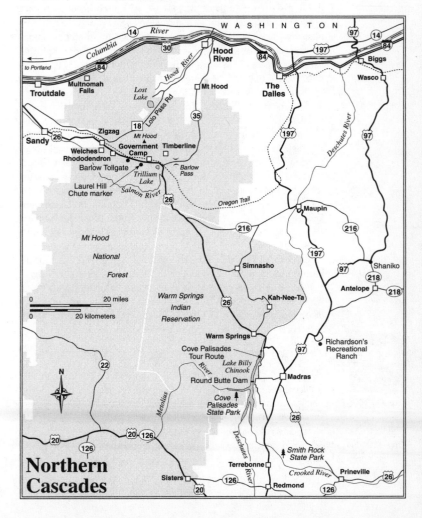

Northern Cascades

Returning to Route 26, pick up Route 35 over Barlow Pass. East of the junction of these two highways, you'll pass a stone cairn marking a **Pioneer Women's Grave**. It commemorates the heroism of all the women who bravely crossed the Oregon Trail. Continue another one and three quarters miles to Forest Road 3530 and the **Barlow Road Sign**. Hand-carved by the Civilian Conservation Corps, this marker is a short walk from the wagon ruts left behind by the pioneers.

Half a century after the pioneers arrived, tourism began to put down roots on this Cascades Peak. Overnight guests were accommodated at the turn-of-the-20th-century **Cloud Cap Inn**, the first structure built on Mt. Hood. Although it no longer accepts the public, the shingled inn is on the National Register of Historic Places. Today, it serves as a base for a mountain-climbing-and-rescue organization and provides views of Mt. Hood's north side. It is accessible in late summer and early fall via a washboard dirt road. ~ Located 10.5 miles north of Route 35, Mt. Hood.

Return south to Route 26 and continue southeast to Warm Springs, one of the Pacific Northwest's most intriguing American Indian reservations. Near the lodge entrance an interpretive display offers background on the Confederated Tribes of Warm Springs. American Indian dance performances and a traditional salmon bake are held at the lodge each Saturday in the summer months. Tribe members skewer Columbia River salmon on cedar sticks and cook it over alderwood coals. The hot springs pool is also highly recommended. **Kah-Nee-Ta High Desert Resort and Casino**, the tribe's arrow-shaped casino-hotel, is a great base for visiting the reservation. ~ Warm Springs; 541-553-1112, 800-554-4786, fax 541-553-1071; www.kahneeta.com.

Richardson's Rock Ranch could also be called the world's largest pick-and-pay thunder-egg farm. Formed as gas bubbles in rhyolite flows and filled with silica, these colorful stones range from the size of a seed to 1760 pounds. You can pick up, chisel or dig your thunder eggs out of 12 beds spread across this 4000-acre rock ranch. Make sure to arrive before 3 p.m. if you want

AUTHOR FAVORITE

An interesting side trip along Route 97 about 41 miles northeast of Madras is the ghost town of **Shaniko**, which was once the bustling terminus of the Columbia Southern Railroad and an important shipping center for cattle, sheep and gold at the turn of the 20th century. Tour the 1901 schoolhouse and the city hall, which once accommodated the jail and firehouse, and imagine the streets filled with boys in buckskin and girls in bonnets.

to dig. Closed mid-November to mid-April, depending on the weather. ~ Located 11 miles north of Madras on Route 97, at Milepost 81 turn right and continue southeast three miles; 541-475-2680, 800-433-2680, fax 541-475-4299; www.richardson rockranch.com, e-mail richardsonranch@bendnet.com.

The 31-mile **Cove Palisades Tour Route** off Route 97 is also a worthwhile excursion. Just southwest of Madras, the route circles Lake Billy Chinook, a popular place for recreational watersports. Three major rivers, the Deschutes, Crooked and Metolius, have cut canyons through this Oregon plain and merged at Lake Billy Chinook behind Round Butte Dam. Be sure to visit the observatory viewpoint on the lake's Metolius River arm. Adjoining the lake is **Cove Palisades State Park**, a mostly arid landscape interrupted by towering volcanic cones. Begin by picking up a brochure that details camping and hiking options for this excursion at the **Madras-Jefferson County Chamber of Commerce**. ~ 274 Southwest 4th Street, Madras; 541-475-2350, 800-967-3564, fax 541-475-4341; www.madraschamber.com, e-mail office@madraschamber.com.

After completing this tour, return to Route 97. Continue south 12 miles to Terrebonne. Then head east three miles to **Smith Rock State Park** (see "Central Cascades Parks" later in this chapter), a favorite of world-class rock climbers. Don't worry if you forgot to bring your spikes and pitons. You can still enjoy the Cascades scenery from your vantage point along the Crooked River Gorge. Day-use fee. ~ 800-551-6949.

LODGING

When it comes to architecture, history, location and ambience, few hotels in the Cascades match **Timberline Lodge**. A veritable museum of Northwest arts and crafts, the lodge was built in 1937 by the Works Progress Administration on the slopes of Mt. Hood. All of the 60 guest rooms and 10 chalet dorm rooms (with bunk beds) have handwoven draperies, bedspreads and rugs featuring a variety of themes; there are iron-and-oak beds, writing desks, WPA watercolors and views of the valley and mountain. While the rooms are small, there is nothing modest about the public areas, which feature a two-level, octagon-shaped stone fireplace and banisters. It's perfectly situated for skiing, hiking or climbing. In winter, sit inside and watch skiers glide by on snowbanks that reach halfway up the massive windows. ~ Timberline; 503-622-7979, 800-547-1406, fax 503-622-0710; www.timberline lodge.com, e-mail reservations@timberlinelodge.com. DELUXE TO ULTRA-DELUXE.

Huckleberry Inn offers 16 accommodations in varying price ranges. The units are spare and woodsy, and are popular with hikers scaling Mt. Hood. Standard rooms sleep small groups, while larger rooms with spiral staircases leading up to sleeping lofts accommodate more. Budget dorm rooms are sometimes available as well. The inn's 24-hour restaurant is also worth checking out for its wide selection of dishes using locally grown huckleberries. ~ Route 26 at Government Camp Business Loop, Government Camp; 503-272-3325, fax 503-272-3031; www.huckleberry-inn. com. MODERATE TO DELUXE.

In the mid-1960s the federal government built the Dalles Dam on the Columbia River, submerging the ancestral fishing grounds of local Indians. The Confederated Tribes of Warm Springs used their compensation to pay for **Kah-Nee-Ta High Desert Resort and Casino**. Located in the midst of the 600,000-acre reservation, this resort offers visitors a variety of lodging choices. There are 139 rooms at the lodge, 30 guest rooms at the village, an RV park, and tepees with cement floors. Set in a red-rock canyon about an hour southeast of Mt. Hood, this resort offers kayaking, golfing, horseback riding, swimming pools, tennis, a water slide, bike rentals and gambling in a casino. ~ Warm Springs; 541-553-1112, 800-554-4786, fax 541-553-1071; www.kahnee ta.com. MODERATE TO DELUXE.

HIDDEN ▶ A thriving bed-and-breakfast inn in the midst of a ghost town is the **Shaniko Hotel**, a fine, two-story brick establishment with a wooden balcony dating from 1900 that has been restored by its current owners. The hotel provides 18 rooms decorated with historic photos from the town's early days and antique reproductions including nightstands that resemble old-fashioned iceboxes. Some rooms are equipped with air conditioning and TVs. Closed in winter. ~ 4th and E streets, Shaniko; 541-489-3441, fax 541-489-3444; www.shanikohotel.com, e-mail cbrock@shanikohotel. com. MODERATE.

DINING Convenient to the Timberline area is **Mt. Hood Brewing Company and Brew Pub**. Located in a three-story, stone-and-wood building, this establishment features a flyfishing motif with knotty-pine paneling, a red-quarry tile floor and a 43-foot-long

AUTHOR FAVORITE

If you don't try the **Cascade Dining Room** in the Timberline Lodge, you'll be missing one of the best meals in the Pacific Northwest. Liveried waiters and waitresses preside over this arts-and-crafts establishment with a stone fireplace and views of the Cascade Mountains. On a frosty morning there's no better place to down fresh salmon hash or apple oat cakes. Dinner entrées include rack of lamb, wild salmon, roast duckling and vegetarian specialties. ~ Timberline; 503-272-3311, fax 503-272-3710. ULTRA-DELUXE.

copper bar. Through the large windows you can see the beer-brewing kettles. (Brewery tours are available on a limited basis.) The family-style menu offers gourmet pizza, pasta, steaks, salads and hamburgers. ~ Route 26 at East Government Camp Road, Government Camp; 503-622-0724, fax 503-622-0770; www.mthoodbrewing.com, e-mail pubinfo@mthoodbrewing.com. MODERATE.

At the Kah-Nee-Ta High Desert Resort, try the informal **Chinook Room** for a hearty buffet that may include anything from barbecued ribs to the lodge's famous Indian fry bread. The **Juniper Room** has specialties like venison steak, prawns, halibut, steamed clams blended in a seafood pot and birds in clay, a specialty that is cooked for three hours. ~ Warm Springs; 541-553-1112, fax 541-553-1071; www.kahneeta.com. MODERATE TO DELUXE.

The Oregon Candy Farm is the place to shop for homemade   **SHOPPING** hand-dipped chocolates. Even the nutmeats are roasted in-house. Part of the fun is watching the candy-making process (Monday through Friday) through big windows. Sugar-free chocolate is available. ~ 48620 Southeast Route 26, five and a half miles east of Sandy; 503-668-5066, fax 503-668-6830; e-mail theorecandy farm@aol.com.

When it comes to shopping for American Indian arts and crafts, why not go to the source? At **Kah-Nee-Ta High Desert Resort and Casino**, both the Lodge and Village have gift shops offering beautiful basketry, handicrafts, blankets and jewelry. Many are made right on the reservation. ~ Warm Springs; 541-553-1112, fax 541-553-1071; www.kahneeta.com.

For limited-edition prints, posters, books, cards and other high-country souvenirs, visit the **Wy'East Store** adjacent to Timberline Lodge. A cross between a gift shop and a mountain outfitter, this is also a good place to find sportswear that will make you even more stylish on your way down the slopes. ~ Timberline; 503-272-3311 ext. 763, fax 503-622-0709.

Richardson's Rock Ranch Gift Shop has a wide variety of polished spheres, as well as rocks from around the world. Choose from agates, jasper, marble, petrified wood, Moroccan fossils, novelty items and jewelry. ~ Located 11 miles north of Madras on Route 97, at Milepost 81 turn right and continue southeast three miles; 541-475-2680, fax 541-475-4299; www.richardson rockranch.com, e-mail richardsonranch@bendnet.com.

On Saturday, live bands play a variety of music at **Charlie's Moun-   NIGHTLIFE tain View**. This rustic mountain lodge offers booth, table and whiskey barrel seating. The walls and ceilings are appointed with old-time skis, boots, snowshoes, ski bibs and other high-country memorabilia. ~ Government Camp Loop off Route 26, Government Camp; 503-272-3333; www.charliesmountainview.com, e-mail englesby25@oregontrail.net.

At the **Appaloosa Lounge** at Kah-Nee-Ta High Desert Resort, you can dance to live bands in a disco setting through the summer months. It's also fun to enjoy the music outside on the adjacent deck. When the stars are out this is a particularly romantic setting. ~ Warm Springs; 541-553-1112, 800-831-0100, fax 541-553-1071; www.kahneeta.com.

PARKS

MT. HOOD NATIONAL FOREST This one-million-acre national forest is named for the 11,235-foot Cascades peak that dazzles newcomers and natives alike. Extending from the Columbia River Gorge south to the Willamette National Forest boundary, the resort region includes four major wilderness and roadless areas. Popular destinations include the Olallie scenic area, known for its beautiful lakes and wildflowers, and the Mt. Hood Loop, a 150-mile scenic drive circling Oregon's highest peak. Along the way, you'll see mountain meadows, waterfalls, scenic streams, major ski areas and the magical Columbia River Gorge. More than 4500 miles of rivers and streams and more than 160 lakes and reservoirs will delight anglers seeking trout, salmon or steelhead. Some trails are wheelchair accessible. Restrooms are available. The forest headquarters is located outside the forest in Sandy and there are ranger stations scattered throughout the park. Trailhead fee, $5 per vehicle for some trails, available at the visitors center. ~ Access is via Routes 84, 30, 35, 224 and 26; 503-668-1700, fax 503-668-1794; www.fs.fed.us/r6/mthood.

▲ Permitted in 106 campgrounds; $16 to $18 per night; RV sites without hookups are available. Three of the best sites for tent/RV camping are on Timothy Lake: the Gone Creek, Hood View and Oak Fork sites. Or try Trillium Lake, with 57 tent/RV sites close to boating and fishing. No hookups are available at any of the sites. Reservations: 877-444-6777 ($9 reservation fee).

COVE PALISADES STATE PARK Located at the junction of the Crooked, Deschutes and Metolius rivers, this 4129-acre park encompasses two arms of Lake Billy Chinook. The cove is set beneath towering palisades and located on benchland punctuated by volcanic cones. Rich in petroglyphs and American Indian history, this region is a geological showcase. Fishing is excellent for smallmouth bass, trout and kokanee. Ten miles of hiking trails offer excellent panoramic views and opportunities to see wildlife. There is also a picnic area, restrooms, a marina, a playground, nature trails and concessions. Day-use fee, $3. ~ Off Route 97, 15 miles southwest of Madras; 541-546-3412, fax 541-546-2220.

▲ There are 94 tent sites ($13 to $17 per night), 174 RV hookup sites ($17 to $21 per night) and 3 cabins ($48 to $69 per night). Reservations: 800-452-5687.

▼▼▼▼▼▼▼▼▼▼▼▼
Central Cascades

One of Oregon's top recreational areas, the Central Cascades include some of the state's finest museums and interpretive centers. A year-round getaway for hiking, fishing, climbing and skiing, this area is also famous for its volcanic scenery, mountain lakes and rafting. Within the national forests are some of the West's leading wilderness areas and great opportunities for wildlife viewing. The region is an ideal family resort and also boasts one of the best scenic drives in the Northwest, the Cascades Loop Highway.

Although none of the peaks have the name recognition of Mt. Hood, the Central Cascades are by no means inferior mountains. A trio known collectively as the Three Sisters rises above 10,000 feet, while relatively diminutive Mt. Bachelor (a mere 9065 feet) provides some of the Northwest's best alpine skiing. The topography is so daunting, in fact, that not many roads cross the Central Cascades, although a few open up in the summer to provide access to the area's voluminous mountain lakes and rivers. Still, plenty of destinations can be reached year-round, and there are enough outdoor activities to keep you busy for weeks.

Thanks to dependable snowpack throughout the summer months, it is possible to spend the morning skiing on Mt. Hood and devote the afternoon to swimming in the warm waters of nearby Cascade Lake.

SIGHTS

A good way to begin your visit is by heading west from Redmond 20 miles on Route 126 to **Sisters**. Gateway to some of the Cascades' most memorable scenery, this small town has a Wild West–style main street that delights tourists driving between the Willamette Valley and the Bend area.

After pausing to shop, dine or provision, head west nine miles on Route 20 and then turn north to the Metolius River Recreation Area. Here you can enjoy flyfishing and, in the winter, cross-country skiing. Stop by the **Sisters Area Chamber of Commerce** to find out more information. ~ 541-549-0251, fax 541-549-4253; www.sisterschamber.com, e-mail info@sisterschamber.com.

Nearby **Black Butte Ranch** is a resort area (see "Lodging" below) named for a towering volcanic cone. ~ Route 20, eight miles west of Sisters; 541-595-6211, fax 541-595-2077; www.black butteranch.com, e-mail info@blackbutteranch.com. To the west off Route 20, **Blue Lake** is a resort destination as well, with easy access to the scenic treasures of the Mt. Washington Wilderness to the south. Continue west on Route 20 to Route 22 and **Detroit Lake**, a recreational area ideal for waterskiing.

HIDDEN ▶   This area is also home of the **Shady Cove Bridge**, an unusual, three-span, wooden-truss structure. The bridge, handcut and hand-assembled using hundreds of small interlocking pieces, links French Creek Road with Little North Santiam drainage.

From Detroit Lake, take Forest Road 46 northeast ten miles to **Breitenbush Hot Springs Retreat and Conference Center**, a New Age wilderness resort. Before the arrival of the white man, American Indians conducted rituals and ceremonies here. Now, yoga, guided forest hikes, meditation, hot-springs pools, steam saunas and massage therapy are all part of the fun. The artesian hot springs boast 30 minerals said to have curative powers. ~ Forest Road 46, Milepost 10, Detroit; 503-854-3314, fax 503-854-3819; www.breitenbush.com, e-mail office@breitenbush.com.

Return to Route 22 and head southeast. Along this route is a major volcanic landmark, **Clear Lake**, the source of the McKenzie River. Created when lava blocked a canyon, this lake lives up to its name in every respect.

Continue south on Route 126 to **Sahalie Falls**, a wheelchair-accessible spot where the McKenzie River cascades 100 feet over lava cliffs. A short drive south is **Koosah Falls**, which plunges more than 80 feet. In the fall this waterfall divides into several sections. Southeast on Route 126 another 17.6 miles is the hamlet of **McKenzie Bridge**, gateway to many scenic highlights of the Central Cascades. The town proper consists of little more than the Log Cabin Inn and a small market.

Head east to the **McKenzie River Ranger District and Cascade Center** (541-822-3381) and pick up the **Aufderheide National Scenic Byway** audio tape. Following old logging roads, the byway winds through the Three Sisters Wilderness, passing mid-size peaks like Olallie Mountain (5708 feet) and Grasshopper Mountain (5651 feet). The byway parallels the south fork of the McKenzie River for much of the way. You can also begin this 60-mile tour from the south end at the **Westfir Lodge Bed and Breakfast Inn**. The same tape is available here. ~ Route 58, Westfir; 541-782-3103; www.westfirlodge.com.

Before returning north to the McKenzie Bridge area, take a look around the Oakridge area. We liked the **Oakridge Pioneer Museum**, located south of Westfir on Route 58. Even if you're not into chainsaws—one of the Northwest's best collections is found here—you'll enjoy seeing the antique logging implements, grocery displays, American Indian artifacts and vintage crockery. Parked just down the street are an antique logging truck, fire truck and caboose. The museum is open Saturday from 1 to 4 p.m., Tuesday and Thursday from 10 a.m. to noon, and with advance notice. ~ 76433 Pine Street, Oakridge; 541-782-2402; e-mail del.spencer@yahoo.com.

Twenty miles east of Oakridge is pristine **Waldo Lake**. Clean ◀ *HIDDEN* enough to qualify as distilled water, the six-mile-long lake has astonishing visibility. Out on the water you can see down 100 feet to the bottom. While there are facilities, the lake, one of Oregon's largest, also has wilderness on the west and north shores. ~ Route 58.

Heading north to the McKenzie Bridge area again, pick up Route 126 east to Route 242 (a narrow route not recommended for long motor homes) up McKenzie Pass to the **Dee Wright Observatory**, where a half-mile paved trail leads through one of the Cascades' largest lava fields. From the observatory you can see 11

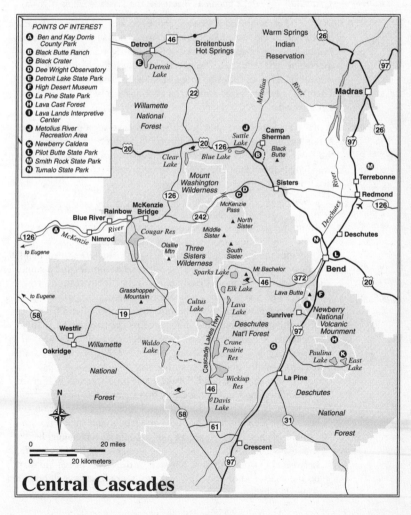

POINTS OF INTEREST

- Ⓐ Ben and Kay Dorris County Park
- Ⓑ Black Butte Ranch
- Ⓒ Black Crater
- Ⓓ Dee Wright Observatory
- Ⓔ Detroit Lake State Park
- Ⓕ High Desert Museum
- Ⓖ La Pine State Park
- Ⓗ Lava Cast Forest
- Ⓘ Lava Lands Interpretive Center
- Ⓙ Metolius River Recreation Area
- Ⓚ Newberry Caldera
- Ⓛ Pilot Butte State Park
- Ⓜ Smith Rock State Park
- Ⓝ Tumalo State Park

Central Cascades

Cascade Lakes Highway

This 87-mile mountain highway takes motorists close to Mount Bachelor and the Three Sisters Peaks on the Pacific Crest. Along the way are dozens of alpine lakes—large and small, natural and manmade—offering great fishing, camping, boating (mostly nonmotorized) and chilly swimming. From Bend, take Century Drive west. As it leaves town, it becomes Route 46, the Cascade Lakes Highway.

TODD LAKE Following Route 46 west from Bend, after 23 miles you'll pass the turnoff to the Mount Bachelor Ski Area. Another two miles brings you to an unpaved road that turns off to the right and leads about a quarter-mile to Todd Lake. Though close to the highway, this lake has a wonderful sense of seclusion in a glacial valley filled with wildflowers. There's a fishermen's trail around the 60-foot-deep lake and a primitive campground.

SPARKS LAKE About two miles past the Todd Lake turnoff, Sparks Lake has one of the prettiest views on this route, reflecting the snowcaps of the Three Sisters in its placid water. Although motorboats are allowed, the 10-mph speed limit and shallow water areas discourage them. The lake is ideal for canoeing and flyfishing.

mountain peaks. Also worth a visit nearby is **Black Crater,** a volcanic summit close to North Sister Mountain.

Continue east to Sisters and pick up Route 20 east to **Bend.** One of Oregon's fastest-growing resort communities and a sunny alternative to the more drizzly parts of the Northwest, this town has become a year-round recreational center.

As you drive into town, be sure to stop at the **Bend Chamber of Commerce.** This is the best place to orient yourself. Closed weekends. ~ 777 Northwest Wall Street, Suite 200, Bend; 541-382-3221, 800-905-2363, fax 541-385-9929; www.bendchamber.org, e-mail info@bendchamber.org.

In the center of Bend, **Drake Park** on Riverside Boulevard shouldn't be missed. On the Des Chutes River, this urban sanctuary features picturesque **Mirror Pond.** Put out a blanket on the lawn, have a picnic, feed the ducks and study your own reflection.

Although strip development along Route 97 is changing Bend's small-town character, the past is well preserved at the **Des Chutes Historical Center Museum.** Located in the Reid School building on the south end of downtown, the museum features exhibits on American Indian history, early-day trappers and explorers, pio-

DEVILS LAKE   Four miles farther on, glacier-fed Devils Lake is one of the few lakes that can be seen from the highway and one of the high points of this drive. The crystalline turquoise water and 10-foot-deep white pumice bottom make it easy to see the trout that swim below, though catching them may be a challenge. There's a small campground, a hiking trail, and a trailhead for longer trails into the Three Sisters Wilderness.

HOSMER LAKE   Five miles beyond Devils Lake is the turnoff to Hosmer Lake, a popular catch-and-release fishing lake that supports a landlocked salmon population. The tiny islands in the north part of the lake are home to otters and minks. Reeds and marshes make it hard to walk close to the water's edge, but hikers in the surrounding wildflower meadows and conifer forests may spot elk, deer and porcupines.

CRANE PRAIRIE RESERVOIR   About 20 miles beyond the Hosmer Lake turnoff, manmade Crane Prairie Reservoir is one of the most popular destinations on the east slope of the Cascades for recreational motorboating. It's also a major habitat for ospreys, and visitors can watch as these big "fish eagles" dive at high speed to snag fish with their talons.

The Cascade Lakes Highway passes two other large manmade lakes, Wickiup Reservoir and Davis Lake, before returning to Route 97 at Crescent, midway between Bend (46 miles) and Crater Lake (51 miles). If you're planning to return to Bend, shortcut roads return due east to Route 97 from both Crane Prairie and Wickiup reservoirs.

neer trails and the lumber industry. Closed Sunday and Monday. Admission. ~ 129 Northwest Idaho Avenue, Bend; 541-389-1813, fax 541-317-9345; www.deschuteshistory.org, e-mail info@des chuteshistory.org.

Three miles south of Bend is the **High Desert Museum.** One of the finest collections in the Pacific Northwest, the indoor galleries are complemented by 20 acres of nature trails and outdoor exhibits. Permanent exhibits share the contemporary reservation experience of the Columbia Plateau Indians, as well as the natural history and settlement. A nice display here is a dawn-to-dusk "walk through time" that showcases the past. The Brook and Collins galleries feature regional art, culture and history exhibits. Visitors head outdoors to view the river-otter pool and a birds-of-prey show. Admission. ~ 59800 South Route 97; 541-382-4754, fax 541-382-5256; www.highdesertmuseum.org, e-mail info@highde sertmuseum.org.

Continue south on Route 97 to **Newberry National Volcanic Monument,** one of Oregon's geologic showcases and the product of more than 500,000 years of volcanic eruptions. Part of the Deschutes National Forest, the monument encompasses numerous volcanic landmarks. At the **Lava Lands Interpretive Center**, you'll find exhibits, dioramas, videos and interpretive staff who can suggest a variety of nature trails that lead through the lava flow. Remodeling begins in 2007; call for hours. Admission. ~ 58201 South Route 97; 541-593-2421, 541-383-4771 (winter), fax 541-383-4700; www.fs.fed.us/r6.

One piece of Devils Hill Flow volcanic rock was flown to the moon by Apollo astronaut James Irwin, who as an astronaut candidate trained in the area. The flow is located on Cascade Lakes Highway, between Devils and Sparks lakes.

Within this ten-square-mile lava flow are highlights like 6650-year-old **Lava Butte**, which changed the course of the Deschutes River. Reached by a paved road from the interpretive center, the butte offers a 360-degree view of the Cascades, the Lava Lands and the high desert to the east. You'll have to hike the final 100 yards to the summit. After enjoying the vista, you can continue west four miles from the interpretive center (follow the signs saying "Deschutes River Views") to reach **Benham Falls**, a popular picnic spot next to the Deschutes. To reach the falls, continue on the trail another quarter of a mile.

Much of the best sightseeing in the monument is found on the east side of Route 97. Two worthy spots in this fascinating region are **Lava River Cave** and **Lava Cast Forest**. The former, a lava tube, is great for spelunkers (fee). Flashlight in hand, you can walk a mile down this eerie tunnel (Oregon's longest uncollapsed lava tube), but bring warm clothing since it stays around 40° in the tube; it's closed in winter because of hibernating bats. The latter, explored via a mile-long, self-guided trail, is a unique piece of Oregon scenery. This unusual landscape was shaped when lava swept across a stand of pine 6000 years ago, creating molds of each tree.

The region's largest geologic feature is 500-square-mile **Newberry Volcano**, created by eruption from thousands of volcanos over the past half-million years in the area just south of Bend. **Paulina and East lakes**, two popular resort areas for anglers, are found in the 20-square-mile **Newberry Caldera**. Also worth a visit is the crater's shiny, black obsidian flow.

West of Bend is **Mt. Bachelor**, central Oregon's premier ski area (see "Outdoor Adventures" below). Continue up the **Cascade Lakes Highway** to tour one of the region's most idyllic resort regions. Todd, Sparks, Devils, Elk, Hosmer, Lava, Cultus and Davis lakes are a few of the popular spots for fishing, boating, swimming and camping. For those eager to head for the outback, there's easy access to high-country lakes, streams and creeks in the Three Sisters Wilderness.

HIDDEN ►

Scenic highlights in this region include spots like **Devils Garden**, a beautiful meadow where you can spot pictographs left behind by Warm Springs Indians.

Sisters Motor Lodge offers comfortable bed-and-breakfast-style accommodations with funky, antique-decorated rooms. Four of the 11 rooms have kitchenettes; two-bedroom units are available. A patio area with a firepit is available for a backyard barbecue. ~ 511 West Cascade Street, Sisters; 541-549-2551, fax 541-549-9399; www.sistersmotorlodge.com, e-mail info@sisters motorlodge.com. MODERATE TO ULTRA-DELUXE.

LODGING

When it comes to lodging, you really can get just about anything you want at **Black Butte Ranch**. This 1830-acre resort offers more than 100 condos, cabins and private homes. Chalet-style accommodations nestled in the pines have paneled walls and ceilings, decks, fireplaces and, in some condos, fully equipped kitchens. Choose between two golf courses, four swimming pools, 18 miles of bike and jogging trails and 23 tennis courts. There's canoeing in a spring-fed lake, as well as skiing, hiking, fishing, boating and horseback riding. ~ Route 20, eight miles west of Sisters; 541-595-6211, 800-452-7455, fax 541-595-2077; www.blackbutteranch.com, e-mail info@blackbutteranch.com. MODERATE TO ULTRA-DELUXE.

The **Metolius River Lodges** in Camp Sherman include 13 cabins with one, two or three bedrooms. Located about 15.5 miles northwest of Sisters, this wooded retreat is in an area ideal for mountain biking, cross-country skiing, flyfishing and water sports. The wood-paneled units have carpeting, fireplaces, kitchens, barbecues and rustic cabin furniture. ~ Five and a half miles north of Route 20, Camp Sherman; 541-595-6290, 800-595-6290; www. metoliusriverlodges.com, e-mail cabins@metoliusriverlodges.com. DELUXE TO ULTRA-DELUXE.

A small lake created by a dammed stream is just one of the attractions at Camp Sherman's **Lake Creek Lodge**. Eighteen two- or three-bedroom knotty pine–paneled cabins feature early American furniture, full kitchens; some have fireplaces. Near the Metolius River, this 60-acre resort has tennis courts, a swimming pool, bike and hiking trails. In the summer they serve meals family style and offer special activities for children. ~ Forest Service Road, four miles north of Route 20, Camp Sherman; 541-595-6331, 800-797-6331, fax 541-595-1016; www.lakecreeklodge. com, e-mail stay@lakecreeklodge.com. DELUXE TO ULTRA-DELUXE.

Providing an extensive variety of children's programs during the summer, **Rock Springs Guest Ranch** is a family-oriented resort with comfortable, contemporary cabins in a forested setting. The pine-paneled cabins feature vaulted ceilings, light-pine furnishings, fireplaces, wet bars and sitting areas. On the grounds are horse stables, tennis courts, a pool, trout pond, a volleyball area and a hot tub. Rates include three meals daily. Three-day to one-week minimum. Groups only. ~ 64201 Tyler Road, Bend; 541-382-1957, 800-225-3833, fax 541-382-7774; www.rock springs.com, e-mail info@rocksprings.com. ULTRA-DELUXE.

McKenzie Riverside Cottages has roomy units complete with fireplaces, decks and kitchenettes. The cottages make an ideal fishing retreat—you can cast for trout from your porch! For larger gatherings, there is a suite complete with kitchen and deck that can easily sleep 16 people. ~ 54466 McKenzie River Drive, Blue River; 541-822-3715, 800-823-3715, fax 541-822-0346; www.mckenzieriversidecottages.com, e-mail mckenzierivercottages@aol.com. ULTRA-DELUXE.

Just a few miles northeast of Oakridge, the Westfir Lodge Bed and Breakfast Inn is right across the street from Oregon's longest covered bridge. This hostelry offers eight rooms decorated in English country antiques with private baths. Evening dessert and a full breakfast are provided. ~ Across from the covered bridge, off Route 58, Westfir; phone/fax 541-782-3103; www.westfir lodge.com. MODERATE.

The Riverhouse in Bend is one of over a dozen motels on the city's main drag. There are 220 rooms featuring contemporary furniture, floral-print bedspreads and sitting areas. In the evening you can relax in front of the fireplace or have a drink on your deck overlooking the Deschutes River. Deluxe-priced suites are available with kitchen facilities. An 18-hole golf course, jogging trail, two pools, two saunas and three whirlpools make this a good place to relax. ~ 3075 North Route 97, Bend; 541-389-3111, 800-547-3928, fax 541-389-0870; www.riverhouse.com, e-mail reserva tions@riverhouse.com. DELUXE TO ULTRA-DELUXE.

In the same part of Bend is the Econo Lodge, located directly beside the Bend Welcome Center and featuring 36 uniform motel rooms, a swimming pool and a hot tub. Continental breakfast served. ~ 3705 North Route 97, Bend; phone/fax 541-382-2211, 800-507-2211; www.econolodge.com. BUDGET.

RUSTIC RELAXATION

As far as luxurious New Age facilities go, secluded **Breitenbush Hot Springs Retreat and Conference Center** has it all. Located in the western Cascades, this retreat provides everything from massage therapy to yoga to a spiritual/self-help workshop. Guests bring their own bedding and are housed in spartan, cedar-shake cabins paneled with fir; platform tents and campsites are available in summer. Geothermal heat and electricity from hydropower provide energy self-sufficiency. Guests can choose between hot tubs, *au naturel* hot springs overlooking the river and mountains and a hot natural-steam sauna complete with a cold-water tub. Vegetarian meals are included. Reservations required. ~ Forest Road 46, Milepost 10, Detroit; 503-854-3314, 503-854-3320 (day-of reservations), fax 503-854-3819; www.breitenbush.com, e-mail office@breitenbush.com. MODERATE.

The **Dunes Motel,** with 30 rooms, is close to downtown Bend. ~ 1515 Northeast 3rd Street, Bend; 541-382-6811, fax 541-389-7504. MODERATE.

Located across from Drake Park, **Lara House Bed and Breakfast** hosts guests in six rooms, all with private baths. You can take your full breakfast on the sun porch. Wine and hors d'oeuvres are served in the afternoon. This 1910 Craftsman also has a comfortable living room and a candlelit front porch. ~ 640 Northwest Congress Street, Bend; phone/fax 541-388-4064, 800-766-4064; www.larahouse.com, e-mail larahousebandb@bendbroadband. com. ULTRA-DELUXE.

The **Bend Riverside Motel** offers 100 rooms, studios and suites with river views. The studios and suites have fireplaces, kitchen facilities, saunas, hot tubs and tennis facilities. Convenient to downtown in a secluded setting. ~ 1565 Northwest Wall Street, Bend; 541-389-2363, 800-284-2363, fax 541-312-3900; www.bendriversidemotel.com, e-mail bendrivers@aol.com. MODERATE TO DELUXE.

At the 3300-acre **Sunriver Resort,** you can choose between 300 rooms and suites featuring pine furniture, fireplaces, wall-to-wall carpets and decks with views of the Cascades. About 400 condos and homes are also available. All guests can take advantage of the pools, tennis courts, bicycles, canoes, skiing, golf, horseback riding and spa and fitness facilities. ~ Route 97, 15 miles south of Bend, in Sunriver; 541-593-1221, 800-547-3922, fax 541-593-5458; www.sunriver-resort.com, e-mail info@sunriver-resort. com. ULTRA-DELUXE.

In the wooded Cascades foothills, **The Seventh Mountain Resort** may be the only resort in Oregon with its own skating rink and outdoor pool open in the winter. The 327 rooms, suites and apartments have kings, queens and Murphy beds, knotty-pine paneling, fireplaces and contemporary prints. Convenient to Mt. Bachelor, the inn is ideally located for horseback riding, whitewater rafting and mountain biking. ~ 18575 Southwest Century Drive, five miles west of Bend; 541-382-8711, 800-452-6810, fax 541-382-3517; www.seventhmountain.com, e-mail info@seventhmountain.com. MODERATE TO ULTRA-DELUXE.

Built around a circa-1923 lodge, ten-unit **Elk Lake Resort** is a forested retreat ideal for fishing, canoeing, kayaking and loafing. The knotty-pine cabins, with two or three bedrooms, kitchens and small decks, are near wilderness hiking and Nordic skiing. For the adventurous, the resort is accessible only by cross-country skiing, snowcat and snowmobile in the winter months. ~ Cascade Lakes Highway, 30 miles west of Bend; 541-480-7378, fax 541-410-4917; www.elklakeresort.net, e-mail elkinfo@elklakeresort. net. DELUXE TO ULTRA-DELUXE.

◄ HIDDEN

DINING

In Sisters, **Ali's** provides a convenient solution for those who can't decide between a sandwich or a salad. Generous sandwiches served on an open-faced bagel or wrapped pita bread include curry chicken, dilly tuna, and lemon-ginger chicken. A wide variety of vegetarian sandwiches and smoked-turkey sandwiches are offered, as well as soups, pasta salads, bagels and ice cream. Lunch only. ~ Town Square, Sisters; 541-549-2547. BUDGET.

One of the most popular pizza parlors in these parts is **Papandrea's**. The modest board-and-batten establishment has indoor seating and patio service on picnic tables covered with green tablecloths. Antique farm implements decorate the dining room. All dough and sauces are homemade, and the tomatoes are fresh. ~ 442 East Hood Street, Sisters; 541-549-6081, fax 541-549-7407. MODERATE.

For dining in a contemporary setting, consider the **Restaurant at Black Butte Ranch**. This split-level establishment has cathedral ceilings, picture windows and early American furniture. While enjoying the panoramic Cascades view, you can order prime rib, roast duck, oysters, halibut filet, pasta primavera with chicken or vegetables. Closed Monday through Wednesday in winter. ~ Route 20, eight miles west of Sisters; 541-595-1260, fax 541-595-1212; www.blackbutteranch.com, e-mail info@black butteranch.com. DELUXE.

HIDDEN ►

Located in a shingled lodge-style building adjacent to the Metolius River, **Kokanee Café** is recommended for Pacific Northwest cuisine, including fresh wild-caught seafood dishes and organic meats and produce. The desserts are exceptional. Worth a special trip. Dinner only. Closed January to April. Call for hours and reservations. ~ Camp Sherman; 541-595-6420; www.kokaneecafe.com. DELUXE TO ULTRA-DELUXE.

In a café-style dining room set in an old church, the family-run **Ernesto's Italian Restaurant** serves up rich, homemade lasagna, veal

AUTHOR FAVORITE

A Bend tradition since 1936 and one of my state-wide top spots, **Pine Tavern** has an enviable location overlooking Mirror Pond. Built around late-18th-century ponderosa pines, the restaurant prides itself on home-cooked dishes like Marsala chicken, fresh salmon and their specialty, Oregon County prime rib using grain-fed beef. Don't miss the sourdough scones with honey butter. Seafood specials are offered each evening; there's also a children's menu. No lunch on Sunday. ~ Foot of Northwest Oregon Street, Bend; 541-382-5581, fax 541-382-5583; www.pine tavern.com, e-mail pinetavern@pinetavern.com. MODERATE TO DELUXE.

parmigiana and calzone. ~ 1203 Northeast 3rd Street, Bend; 541-389-7274, fax 541-389-1686. MODERATE.

For some different fare, head for **Deschutes Brewery and Public House**. This microbrewery, known for its Cascade Golden Ale and Black Butte Porter, homemade root beer and ginger ale, serves upscale pub fare like a pastrami Reuben, buffalo wings and vegetarian chili. ~ 1044 Northwest Bond Street, Bend; 541-382-9242, fax 541-385-8095; www.deschutesbrewery.com, e-mail info@deschutesbrewery.com. MODERATE TO DELUXE.

Located in a chalet-style building, **Marcello's Cucina Italiana**   ◄ HIDDEN
packs locals into its carpeted brick dining room nightly. Their reward is pasta, veal and chicken specialties, as well as calzones, seafood and, of course, a dozen varieties of pizza. Dinner only. ~ Beaver Drive and North Ponderosa Road, Sunriver; 541-593-8300, fax 541-593-5965. MODERATE TO DELUXE.

For dining with a view of the Cascades, a good choice is **The Meadows**. The restaurant serves fresh seafood and Northwestern cuisine. In summer you can dine on the outdoor deck with its panoramic view. ~ Sunriver Resort, Sunriver; 541-593-3740 or 541-593-1221, fax 541-593-4678; www.sunriver-resort.com, e-mail info@sunriver-resort.com. DELUXE TO ULTRA-DELUXE.

Also at Sunriver Resort is the more casual **Merchant Trader Café**, with outdoor patio seating. The breakfast menu includes homemade scones and granola. Baby back ribs, sandwiches, wraps and gourmet salads are offered for lunch and dinner. ~ Sunriver Resort, Sunriver; 541-593-3790, fax 541-593-4678; www.sunriver-resort.com, e-mail info@sunriver-resort.com. BUDGET TO MODERATE.

If you're looking for a hearty breakfast or coffee-shop lunch fare, try the counter at the rustic **Elk Lake Resort**. The dining area   ◄ HIDDEN
is a great place for bacon and eggs, pancakes or french toast. Burgers, salads and sandwiches fill the lunch menu. Although table service is available, we recommend taking a stool for the maximum waterfront view. Dinner specials served nightly. Closed Tuesday. Call for spring and fall hours. ~ Cascade Lakes Highway, 30 miles west of Bend; 541-480-7378, fax 541-410-4917; www.elklakeresort.net, e-mail info@elklakeresort.net. MODERATE TO DELUXE.

If you're in the market for jewelry, wood sculpture, pottery or   **SHOPPING**
basketry, try the **Folk Arts Gallery**. More than 120 Pacific Northwest artists are represented. Call for winter hours. ~ 222 West Hood Street, Sisters; phone/fax 541-549-9556.

Stop by the **Blue Spruce Gallery & Pottery Studio**, which car-   ◄ HIDDEN
ries a beautiful collection of pottery, ceramic vases, custom-made lamps and dinnerware, paintings and decorative art. Closed Sunday. ~ 550 Southwest Industrial Way #45, Bend; 541-389-7745; www.thebluesprucegallery.com, e-mail sant@ipris.com.

Deschutes Gallery displays Northwest American Indian and Inuit art pieces, including masks, boxes, bowls, blankets, jewelry and dolls, as well as prints and paintings. ~ 521 Northwest Colorado Avenue, Bend; 888-981-8200; www.deschutesgallery.com.

NIGHTLIFE For live Top-40 and classic-rock music nightly, head to the **Riverhouse**. This contemporary lounge has a roomy dancefloor, full bar and spacious deck overlooking the Deschutes. In warm weather you can enjoy dining and drinks on the deck. ~ 3075 North Business 97, Bend; 541-389-8810, fax 541-389-0870; www.riverhouse.com.

The **Cascades Theatrical Company** has presented musicals, dramas, comedies and Broadway hits since 1978. This theater produces six shows from early September to late June. ~ 148 Northwest Greenwood, Bend; 541-389-0803; www.cascadestheatri cal.org.

The **Obsidian Opera Company** performs a mix of classics and new productions November through June. ~ P.O. Box 182, Bend, OR 97709; 541-385-7055; www.obsidianopera.org.

PARKS **DETROIT LAKE STATE PARK** 🛶 🚤 🚤 ↵ This 104-acre park is a popular day-use and overnight facility on the shore of one of the busier Cascade Lakes. A forested spot on the north shore of Detroit Reservoir, the park is divided into two units. The smaller Mongold is for day-use picnicking, boat launching and swimming. To the east is the Detroit Lake State Park campground, with a boat launch and boat slips. You can fish for trout and kokanee salmon. There are restrooms, showers, a visitors center and picnic areas. Closed December through February. Day-use fee, $3. ~ Route 22, two miles west of Detroit; 503-854-3406.

▲ There are 133 tent sites ($12 to $16 per night), 178 RV hookup sites ($16 to $20 per night). Reservations: 800-452-5687.

WILLAMETTE NATIONAL FOREST 🚶 🚲 🚣 🏕 🥾 🚤 🚤 ↵ This 1.6-million-acre region (larger than the state of Connecticut!) covers from 10,495-foot Mt. Jefferson to the Calapooya Mountains northeast of Roseburg. Diverse terrain ranges from volcanic moonscapes to wooded slopes and cascading rivers. The National Forest recently annexed Opal Creek Wilderness; more than 400,000 acres of wilderness encompass seven major Cascade peaks. Home to more than 300 animal species, including deer, cougar, grouse and Roosevelt elk, this forest also boasts more than 600 varieties of rhododendron. There are over 1600 miles of hiking trails here, and mountain bikers cluster near the town of Oakridge to ride the foothills. In the winter months, heavy snowfall blankets the popular Nordic and alpine skiing areas at Willamette Pass and Hoodoo Ski Bowl. More than 1500 miles of rivers and streams, as well as 375 lakes, offer countless opportunities for fishing. You'll find picnic tables, interpretive centers and restrooms. Trailhead parking fee, $5. ~ Access via Routes 22, 20, 126, 242 and 58; 541-225-6300, fax 541-225-6337; www.fs.fed.us/r6/willamette.

▲ Permitted at over 60 campgrounds; free to $18 per night; RV sites available at most campgrounds. Some of the most popular sites are the Hoover Campground at Detroit Reservoir, and the Paradise and McKenzie Bridge campgrounds near the town of McKenzie Bridge along Route 126. One of the more secluded sites (Homestead Campground) can be accessed by Forest Service Road 19 near Blue River. For details, access the National Forest website (above). Reservations: 877-444-6777; www.reserve usa.com.

BEN AND KAY DORRIS COUNTY PARK 🏃 ⛴ 🎣 ⛵ A picturesque, 92-acre park at the head of Martin Rapids blending river frontage with an old orchard, this park is shaded by Douglas fir and big-leaf maple that add color to the region in the fall months. While a mile of river frontage is the park's leading attraction, the "Rock House," an outcropping that provided shelter for pioneers traveling the historic wagon road, is also worth a visit. This is one of Oregon's better places to catch trout. Facilities include picnic areas and restrooms. ~ Route 126, 31 miles east of Springfield; 541-682-2000, fax 541-682-2009; www.lanecounty.org/parks, e-mail laneparks@co.lane.or.us.

SMITH ROCK STATE PARK 🏃 ⛵ Along steep Crooked River Canyon, this day-use park is popular with climbers. They enjoy scaling striated Smith Rock, a formation rising several hundred feet above the tributary's north bank. Named for John Smith, a 19th-century pioneer, the park features decent fishing for rainbows and smallmouth bass. There are picnic areas and restrooms. The forest on the south bank suffered a fire in 1996, but the area has been replanted and is recovering. Day-use fee, $3. ~ Northeast Crooked River Drive, east of Route 97, nine miles northeast of Redmond; 800-551-6949.

Text continued on page 448.

Gorges in the Mist

The land of falling waters, the Pacific Northwest is the place to go for plunging rivers. Thousands of waterfalls are found here, often convenient to major highways or trails. Reached via fern canyons, paths through old-growth forests and along pristine streams, waterfall hunting is great sport, even on a rainy day. And part of the fun is getting misted or sprayed by the raging waters.

In the Cascades, these falls are at their peak in late spring or early summer. But even if you come later in the summer or fall, there will still be plenty to see: deep, plunging streams, tiered falls that split into roaring ribbons before converging in swirling pools, horsetails that drop at a 90-degree angle while retaining contact with bedrock. And, of course, you can count on frequently spotting the distinctive waterfall that gives this region its name—the Cascades that drop down in a series of steps.

The Mt. Hood area offers some of the loveliest falls. Head east to Route 35 to the entrance of the Mt. Hood Meadows ski area. You'll see a sign marking the .2-mile trail to **Umbrella Falls**. Although these falls drop only about 60 feet, the verdant setting and fields of wildflowers make this an excellent choice, especially for families with small children. In early summer, the falls trail is reached via a hike through fields of wildflowers. Return to Route 35 and continue 1.4 miles east to **Switchback Falls**. At its peak, in the late spring, North Fork Iron Creeks drops 200 feet.

To the south, the McKenzie River has two highly recommended falls accessible via Route 126. Located 5 miles south of the Route 20 junction, the river drops more than 100 feet at **Sahalie Falls**. Continue south another .4 mile to **Koosah Falls**. A trail takes you down the river canyon to enjoy the view from a series of overlooks. Continue another 5.2 miles south to a road that heads to the McKenzie River Trailhead. After hiking upriver for 2 miles you'll discover that **Tamolitch Falls** have now run dry. Although the river has been diverted to a reservoir at this point, it remains a scenic spot. Thanks to local springs, the river begins anew at this location.

The Bend area is an excellent choice for waterfall lovers. **Tumalo Falls**, ten miles west of town, is reached via Galveston Avenue and Route 1828. The falls drop nearly 100 feet in an area badly damaged by a fire in 1979. South of town, off Route 97, is **Paulina Creek Falls**. Located in

Newberry Crater, this 100-foot drop is an easy walk from Paulina Creek Falls picnic ground. Accessible only in summer.

Century Drive, the beginning of the Cascade Lakes Highway west of Bend, provides easy access to **Lava Island Falls** on the Deschutes River. Take this road to Route 41 and drive south for .4 mile. Go left on Route 620 for .8 mile to reach the falls. If you take Route 41 south from Century Drive 3 miles and pick up Route 100 for .9 mile you'll reach Dillon Falls. Take Route 620 south about 3 miles from the intersection of Route 100 to see a 50-foot cataract called **Benham Falls**.

In the Umpqua River Valley, Route 138, nicknamed "The Highway of Waterfalls," provides access to 11 falls within a 50-mile stretch. Among them is **Susan Creek Falls**, located via a trail 7.5 miles east of Idleyld Park. You'll hike 1 mile north of the highway to reach the falls. Drive Steamboat Road northeast from Steamboat 4.2 miles to reach **Steamboat Falls**. Located at a forest-service campground, this small waterfall is circumvented by fish that use an adjacent ladder. Near mile marker 42 about 3 miles southeast of Steamboat are **Jack Creek** and tiered **Jack Falls**. These three falls are particularly rewarding for photo buffs.

Also popular are **Toketee Falls**. To see this 90-foot drop, take Route 138 to the Toketee Lake turnoff. Continue north .3 mile to the trail leading west .6 mile to the falls. East of Toketee Lake is Lemolo Lake, a popular resort destination. From here, Thorn Prairie Road leads to Lemolo Falls Road. Hike the Lemolo Falls Trail 1 mile west to this cataract.

Off Route 62, the main highway from Medford to Crater Lake, is one of the Cascades' grander waterfalls, 175-foot **Mill Creek Falls**. Accessible by Mill Creek Road, this scenic spot is an easy .3-mile hike from the Mill Creek Falls Scenic Area trailhead on the south side of Prospect. Also accessible on this hike are **Barr Creek Falls**, **Prospect Falls**, **Pearsoney Falls** and **Lower Red Blanket Falls**.

Within Crater Lake National Park, **Annie Falls** is off Route 62, 4.7 miles north of the park's southern entrance. Because this falls is located in an unstable canyon-rim area, visitors should approach it with extreme caution. Also in the park, close to Applegate Peak, is **Vidae Falls**.

To get a complete rundown on these watery delights, check with local park or ranger offices. Or pick up a copy of the definitive guide to this subject, *A Waterfall Lover's Guide to the Pacific Northwest* by Gregory A. Plumb (The Mountaineers).

▲ Permitted in the Bivouac Area for primitive hike-in camping. Space limited by parking; $4 per person per night.

TUMALO STATE PARK 🏃 🏊 ⤵ Convenient to the Bend area in Deschutes River Canyon, it is forested with juniper, ponderosa pine, willow and poplar. This 333-acre park has handsome basalt bluffs above the canyon. There's fair trout fishing, too. Facilities include a picnic area, restrooms, showers and nature trails. Day-use fee, $3. ~ Located five miles northwest of Bend on O. B. Riley Road off Route 20; 541-382-3586, 800-551-6949, fax 541-388-6405.

▲ There are 58 tent sites ($13 to $17 per night), 23 RV hookup sites ($17 to $22 per night) and 7 yurts ($29 per night). Reservations: 800-452-5687.

DRAKE PARK 🏃 This verdant, 13-acre park is along the Deschutes River and includes a riverfront strollway and footbridge across the river. Beloved by the local populace, the park is home to most of Bend's community events. Stroll alongside the river and be serenaded by geese and ducks. Adjacent to downtown Bend, it includes picturesque Mirror Pond, actually just a part of the river that was widened and made into a peaceful place to sit beside. You'll find picnic areas and a playground (across the bridge at Harmon Park). ~ Take Franklin Avenue west from Route 97 into downtown Bend where it becomes Riverside Boulevard. Continue west to the park; 541-388-5435, fax 541-388-5429; www.bendparksandrec.org.

One of the world's purest bodies of water, Waldo Lake, is found in Willamette National Forest.

PILOT BUTTE STATE PARK 🏃 🚴 A cinder cone that served as a landmark for Oregon pioneers is the heart of this 100-acre urban park. The 511-foot-high volcanic dome is located on the east side of Bend and is a very popular climb (it takes only about 15 minutes to scale). Ascend the spiral road to the top of this pine-covered butte to enjoy great views of the Cascades from Mt. St. Helens to the Three Sisters. In the winter, car access is not available. Bring your own water. ~ Greenwood Avenue (Route 20), Bend; 800-551-6949.

LA PINE STATE PARK 🏊 🏄 ⤵ 🚣 This rolling Deschutes River Valley park is shaded by pine and old-growth forest. Expect to spot mule deer as you explore this uncrowded 2333-acre getaway. It's ideal for kayaking or canoeing, and a good base for visiting the surrounding volcanic landmarks including Newberry Crater. Small motorized boats can launch from here but can only go downstream. Anglers can fly cast for rainbow and brown trout. There are restrooms, showers and picnic areas. ~ Located west of Route 97 on State Rec Road, 27 miles southwest of Bend; 541-536-2071, 800-551-6949, fax 541-536-2143.

▲ There are 137 RV hookup sites ($13 to $17 per night), rustic cabins ($39 per night) and 5 deluxe cabins ($49 to $70 per night). Reservations: 800-452-5687.

DESCHUTES NATIONAL FOREST 🏃 🎿 🏊 🚣 ⛵ ⛴ Named for the popular river that descends the east slope of the Cascades, this 1.6-million-acre forest embraces Mt. Bachelor, the Three Sisters Wilderness, the Cascade Lakes region and Newberry National Volcanic Monument. Many popular resorts and five wilderness areas are found in the Deschutes forests, meadows and high country. Climbing from 3000 to 10,358 feet, the forest is dominated by ponderosa pine. You can explore the Three Sisters Wilderness via the South Sisters Climbing Trail from the Cascade Lakes Highway at Devils Lake Campground. The forest is known for its raftable rivers, spelunking and skiing. There are innumerable places to ski cross-country, including Dutchman Flat, Edison Butte and the Skyliner/Meissner area. Bend is the most convenient jump-off point. More than 240 miles of streams and 158 lakes and reservoirs make for ideal fishing. There are picnic tables, interpretive centers, marinas and restrooms. ~ Access via Routes 126, 242, 58, 97, 31, 20 and 46; 541-383-5300, fax 541-383-5531; www.fs.fed.us/r6/centraloregon.

▲ There are over 100 campgrounds for tents and RVs throughout the national forest; $5 to $17 per night; call for details. The best camping is found off the Cascade Lake Highway near one of the many lakes in the area. Paulina Lake in the Newberry National Volcanic Monument has 69 tent/RV sites ($10 to $12; no hookups). South of Elk Lake, the Hosmer campground has two campgrounds with lots of room for tent camping ($5; no hookups).

Southern Cascades

Blessed with several major wilderness areas that are great for viewing wildlife or birdwatching, the Southern Cascades are also the home of Oregon's only national park, Crater Lake. In addition to being drop-dead gorgeous—its chilly waters are an extraordinarily piercing shade of blue—the lake offers many recreational possibilities, from Nordic skiing to snowshoeing to hiking. The Southern Cascades also include a real sleeper, the Klamath Lake area.

SIGHTS

CRATER LAKE   One of the world's most famous mountain lakes, tucked inside the caldera of a collapsed volcano, Crater Lake is known for its shimmering vistas and dark, cold depths. The best way to see this geologic wonder is to take **Rim Drive,** the 33-mile road circling Crater Lake. With more than 20 turnouts, it provides a thorough overview of this mountain-rimmed, deep-blue lake. Vertical lava flow patterns add to the majesty of the volcanic scenery. The drive is seasonal; contact the visitors center (541-594-3000; www.nps.gov/crla) to be sure the road is open.

While the crystal-clear waters are the prime attraction, the 1000- to 2000-foot-high rim walls create an excellent cutaway view of the remains of Mt. Mazama. Allow at least two hours for this trip around the 20-square-mile, 1194-foot-deep lake (the road itself is about 33 miles around). You'll want to begin your tour at the **Rim Village Visitor Center** (open June through September). A short walk below the visitors center is **Sinnott Memorial Overlook**. There's a small museum on this rock ledge where rangers present interpretative geology talks during the summer months. Drive clockwise around the lake to **Discovery Point**, where in 1853 explorer John Wesley Hillman became the first white man to spot this treasure. ~ Visitors Center: 541-594-3100; www.nps.gov/crla.

From here you'll want to go to major viewpoints. About three miles past Discovery Point is a turnout ideal for seeing one of the park's major volcanoes, **Union Peak**. Continue another seven-tenths of a mile to **Wizard Island Overlook**. It's named for the small Crater Lake island that is actually the top of a small volcano. Rim Drive's highest viewpoint is **Cloudcap**. This is a great spot to see how part of Mt. Mazama was sliced away by the caldera's collapse. Also of special interest is **Pumice Castle**, an orange and pink landmark sculpted by the elements into a fortress-like formation.

The only access to the lakeshore is found at **Cleetwood Cove Trail**. This steep route takes you down to Cleetwood Boat Landing, where you can tour the lake by boat (admission). On this two-hour tour you'll be able to explore **Wizard Island**, a 700-foot-high cinder cone and see remnants of an older volcano called the **Phantom Ship**. ~ Boat tours: 541-594-2255.

Although America's deepest (1943 feet) lake is the centerpiece of this national park, other attractions are well worth your time. Southeast of Rim Village you'll find the **Steel Information Center** (open year-round), where you can see an 18-minute video on the lake, as well as interpretive exhibits. ~ 541-594-3100.

We also recommend visiting **The Pinnacles** area on the park's east side. Pumice and ash left behind by the Mt. Mazama collapse were gradually eroded by rain and snow. These formations evolved into rock pinnacles, further eroded by the elements into weird, hoodoo shapes.

Sixteen miles west of Crater Lake National Park in the vicinity of Union Creek is **Rogue River Gorge**. Here this mighty river is channeled into a beautiful little canyon easily accessed on foot. In the same area, a mile west of Union Creek, is **Natural Bridge** where the Rogue flows into a lava tube for a short distance before reappearing. The bridge is well worth a visit and an easy walk.

KLAMATH LAKE REGION   Although not in the mountains, its proximity to the high country makes the area around Upper Klamath Lake a favorite of travelers coming or going to them.

One of the best ways to explore the Klamath Lake area is via the **Upper Klamath Lake Tour Route.** Several state parks, botanical areas, nature sites, canoe trails and waterfowl observation points make this tour a winner. Take Route 97 south to Chiloquin and then turn north on Route 62 to Fort Klamath. (If you're coming direct from Crater Lake simply take Route 62 south.)

The centerpiece of your tour is **Upper Klamath Lake.** At nearly 64,000 acres, this is one of the state's largest lakes, extending south more than 25 miles to the town of Klamath Falls. The shallow waters here are prime fishing territory and a major wildlife refuge. One of the best birdwatching areas in the Pacific Northwest, these wetlands and marsh are also home to otter, beaver and muskrat.

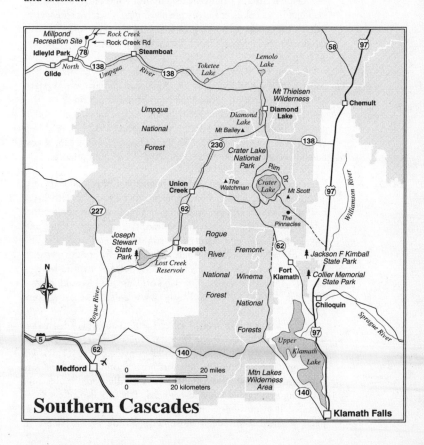

Southern Cascades

For a different view of Klamath Lake, take a ride on a guided tour boat. The **Klamath Belle Paddlewheel** offers lunch and dinner tours and ice cream socials April through November. Dockside dining is also available. ~ Phone/fax 541-883-4622; www. klamathbelle.com, e-mail reservations@klamathbelle.com. Or climb aboard **Klamath Excursions** for a one-, two- or four-hour tour. Longer tours stop at the islands for a chance to explore on foot. ~ 541-850- 6391.

In Klamath Falls, the **Senator Baldwin Hotel Museum** has been restored to its early-20th-century heyday. A guided tour shows off the four-story building's architectural gems and historic memorabilia. The building is not wheelchair accessible. Closed Monday and from October through May. Special tours can be made in the winter by request. Admission. ~ 31 Main Street, Klamath Falls; 541-883-4207, in the winter 541-883-4208.

At the **Klamath County Museum**, flora and fauna and American Indian and pioneer history are on display. There's also a special exhibit on geothermal energy. Closed Sunday and Monday. Admission. ~ 1451 Main Street, Klamath Falls; 541-883-4208, fax 541-883-5170.

Also in the Klamath Falls area is the **Favell Museum**. The contemporary building features American Indian and Western art and artifacts and a vast collection of miniature firearms. You won't have trouble finding arrowheads because more than 60,000 are on display. Closed Sunday. Admission. ~ 125 West Main Street, Klamath Falls; 541-882-9996, fax 541-850-0125; www. favellmuseum.org, e-mail favellmuseum@favellmuseum.org.

LODGING   For cabins in a wooded setting, head for **Cultus Lake Resort**. Twenty-three spacious, pine-paneled units equipped with brick fireplaces, alcove kitchens and drop-beam ceilings are set in a forest glen. The lake is great for sailing, fishing, waterskiing and kayaking. There's also a beach for sunbathing and swimming. Be advised: some readers have had rude service from management. Units are rented by the week. Closed October to mid-May. ~ Located 45 miles southwest of Bend off Cascade Lakes Highway; 541-408-1560, 800-616-3230; www.cultuslakeresort.com. DELUXE.

Twenty-five miles from Crater Lake in the small highwayside town of Chemult is the **Dawson House Lodge**, a 1929 train station boarding house that has been converted into a rustic yet cozy inn. Choose from five upstairs hotel rooms (all with private bathrooms) furnished with antiques, including one double unit featuring log-framed four-poster beds. The inn also offers three motel-style rooms. A continental breakfast awaits in the fireplace-warmed lobby each morning. ~ Route 97 at 1st Street,

Chemult; 541-365-2232, 888-281-8375, fax 541-365-4451; www. dawsonhouse.net, e-mail dawsonhouse@hotmail.com. MODERATE.

Zane Grey loved the north Umpqua River, and today a 31-mile stretch has been limited to "flyfishing only." In the heart of the river region 18 miles east of Idleyld Park is **Steamboat Inn**. An eclectic mix of streamside cabins, hideaway cottages, river suites and ranch-style homes, the inn serves meals family-style in the main lodge. Some of the 20 units are pine paneled; others offer river views, mini-kitchens, fireplaces, soaking tubs, quilted comforters and paintings by leading Northwest artists. A massage center is open from June to mid-October. Closed in January and February. ~ Route 138, Steamboat; 541-498-2230, 800-840-8825, fax 541-498-2411; www.thesteamboatinn.com, e-mail steamboat inn@hughes.net. ULTRA-DELUXE.

Crater Lake Lodge is a magnificent wood and stone structure built between 1909 and 1924 on the rim overlooking Crater Lake. The lodge has 71 rooms including a few lofts, all with natural-wood furnishings and many with views of the lake. Other superb views can be enjoyed from the lodge's Great Hall, which features a massive stone fireplace, historic photographs and floor-to-ceil-

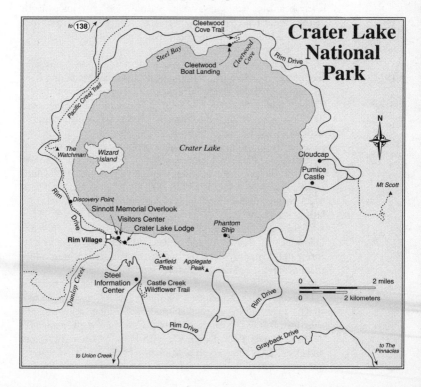

ing windows framed in rustic wood bark. Closed mid-October to mid-May. ~ Crater Lake National Park; 541-830-8700, fax 541-830-8514; www.craterlakelodges.com. DELUXE TO ULTRA-DELUXE.

Additional lodging in the national park can be found at **The Cabins at Mazama Village.** Forty modern units are available from June to October. Board-and-batten exteriors, paneled interiors and wall-to-wall carpeting make these gray-toned accommodations rather appealing. ~ Crater Lake National Park, Route 62; 541-830-8700, fax 541-830-8514; www.craterlakelodges.com. DELUXE.

Teddy Roosevelt and Zane Grey once stayed at Prospect Historical Hotel and Motel, a former stagecoach inn.

With 92 units, **Diamond Lake Resort** is the largest hostelry in the Crater Lake region. This complex includes 38 motel rooms, 10 studios and 42 cabins, all a short walk from the busy waterfront. Expect paneled, carpeted rooms with fireplaces, Franklin stoves and marine views. The studios and cabins come with kitchen facilities and, in some cases, private decks. An 11.5-mile biking trail circles the lake, and there are boat and bike rentals and hiking trails as well. The resort also has a café and a restaurant. While some find Diamond Lake too crowded for their tastes, it is convenient to many beautiful wilderness areas. ~ Route 138, five miles north of the Crater Lake entrance; 541-793-3333, 800-733-7593, fax 541-793-3309; www.diamondlake.net, e-mail info@diamondlake.net. MODERATE TO ULTRA-DELUXE.

HIDDEN ►

If you like the ambience of a historic inn but prefer the comfort of motel-style units, the **Prospect Historical Hotel and Motel** may be just the place. Located just a quarter mile off Route 62 and 28 miles from the south entrance to Crater Lake National Park, the white frame 1890 hotel has ten cozy rooms decorated with antiques, historical photos, quilts, vanities and access to a pleasant front porch. Once a stagecoach inn, it's now a National Historic Site. Famous former guests include Jack London and Teddy Roosevelt. There are also 14 motel rooms. ~ 391 Mill Creek Drive, Prospect; 541-560-3664, 800-944-6490, fax 541-560-3825; www.prospecthotel.com, e-mail info@prospecthotel.com. MODERATE TO DELUXE.

Motel-style units and cabins convenient to Upper Klamath Lake's Pelican Bay are found at **Rocky Point Resort.** Set in a fir forest frequented by deer, this waterfront resort is a good place to photograph bald eagles, osprey and white pelican colonies. The five paneled rooms are clean and comfortable, and the four cabins offer kitchen facilities. Camping (33 RV hookups, 5 tent sites), canoe and kayak rentals, moorage, fishing tackle and gift shop are all available on the premises. Closed November to April. ~ 28121 Rocky Point Road, Klamath Falls; 541-356-2287, fax 541-356-2222; www.rockypointoregon.com, e-mail rvoregon@aol.com. MODERATE TO DELUXE.

For inexpensive lodging try the **Maverick Motel**. Forty-nine carpeted guest rooms are brightly painted and furnished with dark-wood furniture. There's an outdoor pool here. ~ 1220 Main Street, Klamath Falls; 541-882-6688, 800-404-6690, fax 541-885-4095. BUDGET.

DINING

With American Indian and pioneer decor, a menu featuring specialties like the buckaroo breakfast, and a parking lot filled with diesel rigs, station wagons and motorcycles, it's obvious that the **Wheel Cafe** cultivates an eclectic clientele. Take a seat at the counter and order turkey, swiss cheese, bacon and tomato on a sourdough roll or a chef's salad. ~ Route 97, Chemult; 541-365-2284, fax 541-365-2202; e-mail wagonwheel@presys.com. BUDGET TO MODERATE.

You'll have a hard time beating the **Steamboat Inn**. This establishment is famous for its fisherman's dinner. After enjoying hors d'oeuvres, wine and champagne in the library, guests head inside to the lodge where dinner is served family-style on gleaming wood tables illuminated by the glow of the fireplace. Appetizers are followed by an entrée, side dishes, homemade bread and dessert. One set dinner menu is served nightly. Entrées may include beef, fish, lamb or pork. Breakfasts here are also memorable. Don't miss the fruit rollups, an inn tradition. Dinner by reservation only. Closed January and February. ~ Route 138, Steamboat; 541-498-2230, 800-840-8825, fax 541-498-2411; www.thesteamboatinn.com, e-mail steamboatinn@hughes.net. ULTRA-DELUXE.

For Mexican food, hamburgers, sandwiches and homemade soups, try **Munchies**. This full-service restaurant also serves fresh-baked pie. ~ 20142 Route 138, Glide; 541-496-3112. BUDGET.

An early American setting makes the carpeted **Prospect Historical Hotel and Motel Restaurant** a comfortable dining spot. A fixed-price dinner includes salad, antipasto, bread, choice of an entrée (including prime rib or lemon-dill roasted salmon) and dessert. There's also a selection of Northwest wines to complement your meal. The ambience is elegant. Dinner only. Closed October through April. ~ 391 Mill Creek Drive, Prospect; 541-560-3664, 800-944-6490, fax 541-560-3825; www.prospecthotel.com, e-mail info@prospecthotel.com. DELUXE.

◄ HIDDEN

With its beautiful setting overlooking Klamath Lake, rustic **Rocky Point Resort** is best known for its steaks and seafood. Closed Monday and Tuesday, and from Labor Day to Memorial Day; call for spring and fall hours. ~ 28121 Rocky Point Road, Klamath Falls; 541-356-2287, fax 541-356-2222; www.rockypointoregon.com, e-mail rvoregon@aol.com. MODERATE TO DELUXE.

SHOPPING An excellent collection of limited-edition prints, American Indian and Western art, American Indian jewelry and arrowheads is found at the **Favell Museum Gift Shop**. Exhibited in an attractive, two-story shop, this store features many one-of-a-kind pieces on consignment from local and well-known artists, as well as a multitude of "made in Oregon" products like jams, syrups and candies. ~ 125 West Main Street, Klamath Falls; 541-882-9996, fax 541-850-0125; www.favellmuseum.org, e-mail favellmuseum@favellmuseum.org.

Over 150 artists and antique dealers at the Crafters Market sell wares including wood products, dolls, clocks, jewelry, quilts and toys. Only open in summer. ~ 3040 Washburn Way, Klamath Falls.

For knives, cutlery, beads and beading supplies, American Indian earrings, mocassins, buckskins and leather goods, visit **Oregon Trail Outfitters**. This board-and-batten building is extremely popular with visitors searching for a piece of the Old West. Closed Sunday. ~ 5728 South 6th Street, Klamath Falls; 541-883-1369, 800-511-1369, fax 541-883-8881; www.oregontrailoutfitter.com, e-mail info@ oregontrailoutfitter.com.

NIGHTLIFE **Ross Ragland Theater** hosts touring theater companies, country-and-western bands, jazz and blues and classical performers. The year-round calendar also includes special children's shows and, in the summer, locally produced musicals. ~ 218 North 7th Street, Klamath Falls; 541-884-5483, fax 541-884-8574; www.rrthea ter.org, e-mail rrt@rrtheater.org.

The Linkville Playhouse offers a variety of plays and musicals from August through June. The local productions feature classics such as *A Funny Thing Happened on the Way to the Forum*.~ 201 Main Street, Klamath Falls; 541-884-6782, 541-882-2586 (tickets).

PARKS

HIDDEN ►

UMPQUA NATIONAL FOREST 🚶 🚲 🎣 🏕 ⛷ 🛷 Named for the Umpqua Indians, this forest spans almost a million acres and embraces three wilderness areas, numerous waterfalls and high-country trails. Among the Umpqua landmarks are the world's tallest sugar pine, bedrock gorges and volcanic-rock formations. Within the Umpqua are volcanic ridges, pine benches, alpine forests and meadows laced by snow-fed streams. Major destinations include the scenic Umpqua River and Diamond, Lemolo and Toketee lakes. Most lakes allow swimming; only Lemolo Lake allows waterskiing. The forest is also convenient to Crater Lake. Kayaking and rafting are popular on the North Umpqua River. Mt. Bailey near Diamond Lake has downhill skiing, while the areas around Diamond and Lemolo lakes offer good cross-country trails. Hundreds of miles of streams and numerous lakes make this a great spot for angling, especially in the North Umpqua River. There are picnic tables, history programs, pack stations and restrooms. Trailhead parking fee, $5. ~ Access via Routes 138, 1, 62 and 230; 541-672-6601, fax 541-957-3495; www.fs.fed.us/r6/umpqua.

▲ There are numerous campgrounds in the forest; $5 to $12 per night; RV sites without hookups are available. The Diamond Lake area is probably the most developed for camping, with three campgrounds around the lakeshore. Even better for those who want to be away from drive-in sites is the Twin Lakes campground (43 miles east of Glide), a walk-in (or bike-in) campground 10 miles from Route 138. You'll be camping in a primitive site under the stars amidst cold, clear high mountain lakes.

MILLPOND RECREATION SITE 🏊 With half a mile of frontage ◄ *HIDDEN*
on Rock Creek, this serene campground is a beautiful getaway near the community of Idleyld Park. It has a picturesque swimming hole and towering, moss-covered trees, and is the small Oregon park at its finest. You'll find picnic areas, a pavilion, a group campground, a softball field and restrooms. Closed mid-October to early May. ~ From the town of Idleyld Park take Route 138 east to Route 78 (Rock Creek Road) and head north five miles; 541-440-4930, fax 541-440-4948.

▲ There are 12 tent/RV sites (no hookups); $8 per night. The group campground includes 10 sites for $125 per night.

CRATER LAKE NATIONAL PARK 🚶🚴🏕️⛷️ One of the unique geologic features of the Pacific Northwest, Crater Lake is irresistible. The 183,224-acre park offers 100 miles of hiking and cross-country skiing trails, a fascinating boat tour of this volcanic lake and opportunities for biking, fishing and backpacking. For anglers there's nothing to get excited about though there are rainbow trout and kokanee salmon off Wizard Island. There are picnic areas, restaurants, lodging, exhibits and a ranger-guided boat tour. Entrance fee (good for seven days), $10 per vehicle, $5 walk-in. ~ Route 62, 54 miles northwest of Klamath Falls; 541-539-3000, fax 541-539-3010; www.nps.gov/crla.

▲ There are 213 tent/RV sites at Mazama Campground; $18 to $20 per night (without electrical hookups) or $23 per night (with electrical hookups). There are 16 tent sites at Lost Creek; $10 per night, no hookups. Backcountry camping by permit only. Campgrounds and lodging are closed in winter.

FREMONT-WINEMA NATIONAL FOREST 🚶🏕️⛵🚤⛷️
The Fremont-Winema National Forests lie on the eastern slopes of the Cascade Mountain Range in south central Oregon and expand east to "Oregon's Outback" and the Warner Mountains. The 203-million-acre forests are famous for their fishing and waterfowl habitat, expansive views, dramatic cliffs and solitude. Although the forest elevation ranges from roughly 4100 to 9200

feet, much of the eastern portion of this semiarid region is high-plateau country. The Fremont-Winema are forested with pine and fir and have four designated wilderness areas, including the Mountain Lakes Wilderness Area. More than 200 bird species have been identified on this Pacific Flyway. In addition, antelope, elk, deer, bear, coyote, bobcat, beaver, otters and many other species live here. Dozens of lakes and rivers like the Sycan, Sprague and Williamson offer good opportunities to catch trout and mullet. Rock hounds can be happy here. You'll find picnic tables and restrooms. ~ Routes 97, 395, 31 and 140 all provide easy access; 541-883-6715, fax 541-883-6709; www.fs.fed.us/r6/frewin.

> Crater Lake National Park rangers lead free snow-shoe ecology walks on Saturday and Sunday (they provide the snowshoes).

▲ Camping is permitted anywhere in the forest and there are 11 developed campgrounds with tent/RV sites; free to $13 per night.

HIDDEN ▶ **JACKSON F. KIMBALL STATE PARK** ⌐ This 19-acre Oregon state park is a scenic, forested spot on the headwaters of the Wood River. It's ideal for those seeking a quiet getaway. There's good fly-fishing for rainbow and brown trout. There is a picnic area. Closed November through March. ~ Route 232, three miles north of Fort Klamath; 541-783-2471, fax 541-783-2707.

▲ There are ten primitive sites; $5 to $9 per night.

COLLIER MEMORIAL STATE PARK 🚶 ⌐ Set in a ponderosa-pine forest at the junction of Spring Creek and Williamson River, this 655-acre park is a perfect place to spend the day or the night. The park is also a logging heritage site, filled with important memen-tos and lumberjack equipment. There's good trout fishing in the streams. You'll find picnic tables, showers, restrooms, a laundry fa-cility, a playground and a museum. ~ Route 97, 35 miles north of Klamath Falls; 541-783-2471, fax 541-783-2707.

▲ There are 18 tent sites ($15 per night) and 50 RV hookup sites ($17 per night). Closed November through March. Reserva-tions: 800-452-5687.

HIDDEN ▶ **JOSEPH STEWART STATE PARK** 🚶 🚲 ⚓ ⌐ 🏊 🚤 ⌐ A lush lawn leads down to Lost Creek Reservoir, making this park on the road to Crater Lake particularly inviting on a warm day. With 910 acres, there's room to spare for day and overnight use. Take a seat on a blanket beneath one of the pine groves and watch the waterskiers. Or toss in a line and wait for the big ones to nibble. With more than a mile of waterfront, this Rogue River Canyon park is a great place to take the kids. There's excellent fishing for bass, rainbow, brook or brown trout. Facilities include a picnic area, restrooms, showers and a marina. ~ Route 62, 35 miles northeast of Medford; 541-560-3334, fax 541-560-3855.

▲ There are 50 tent sites ($10 to $14 per night) and 151 RV hookup sites ($12 to $16 per night). Closed November through February.

The Cascades are famous for rivers and lakes
brimming with trout, salmon, bass and steelhead. Now that more and more people are try-
ing to fish these waters, "We've got a shrinking resource," as one
guide says; that's why you'll find him and others encouraging a
catch-and-release policy for all fish caught. The point is that you
can still wade out into the Deschutes to flyfish for wild trout or pull
steelhead out of the Umpqua from aboard a drift boat and have
the kind of experience immortalized in the fiction of Zane Grey.

Outdoor Adventures

FISHING

NORTHERN CASCADES   Whether you're an experienced fisher
or a beginner, **Wy'East Expeditions** can arrange a day-long Deschutes River flyfishing trip for fall steelhead or, in the spring, wild
rainbow trout. Overnight trips let you get out into areas that are
a bit more remote. ~ 6700 Cooper Spur Road, Mt. Hood; 541-352-
6457; e-mail info@wyeastexpeditions.com.

If you need gear, contact **Gorge Fly Shop** in Hood River.
Besides renting gear and obtaining information, you can set up a
guided trip on the Deschutes River, the John Day River, and other
prime fishing spots in the area. ~ 201 Oak Street; 541-386-6977;
www.gorgeflyshop.com. In Maupin, **Michael McLucas** has been a
fishing guide for over 25 years. He or his partner Mike Malefyt can
take you out on the Deschutes for trout or steelhead fishing trips.
~ Oasis Resort; 541-395-2611; www.deschutesriveroasis.com.

CENTRAL CASCADES   Although there's no commercial use permitted on the Metolius River (that is, no guided trips), it's a very
popular flyfishing spot. **Fly Fisher's Place** can rent or sell you gear
or arrange a guided trip on the McKenzie, the Deschutes or, near
Prineville, on the Crooked River, where you can catch wild trout.
~ 151 West Main Street, Sisters; 541-549-3474; www.theflyfishers
place.com. **High Desert Drifters, Guides, & Outfitters** specializes
in flyfishing float trips for rainbow trout and steelhead on the
Deschutes for either one day or several days. ~ 1710 Northeast
Hollow Tree Lane, Bend; 541-389-0607, 800-685-3474; www.
theflyfishersplace.com. **Sunriver Fly Shop**, also a guide service,
offers fishing classes if you want to learn more. Some of its popular trips are to the Davis, Hosmer and Crane Prairie lakes, where
you will catch a variety of trout between April and November. ~
56805 Venture Lane, Sunriver; 541-593-8814; www.sunriverfly-
shop.com. Guided expeditions are also available through **Helfrich River Outfitters**, who specialize in fly-fishing trips on the
McKenzie and Rogue rivers. Trips are led by a third-generation
guide. ~ 42091 McKenzie Highway, Springfield; 541-896-3017,
800-507-9889; www.helfrichoutfitter.com.

SOUTHERN CASCADES   Bill Conner of **North River Guide Service** primarily fishes the Umpqua, specializing in drift boat trips
for two people per boat. Up to four couples may go at a time.

Conner also leads flyfishing trips. ~ P.O. Box 575, Glide, OR 97443; phone/fax (main) 541-496-0309, (direct) 541-784-6714.

RIDING STABLES

The fun and excitement of a day of whitewater rafting is hard to beat, even with a crowd. Guided full-day trips usually include a riverside lunch stop along the way.

CENTRAL CASCADES   A. Helfrich Outfitters (not to be confused with their cousins who run the fly-fishing trips) leads full- and half-day rafting on the McKenzie River. ~ 2605 Harvest Street, Springfield; 541-726-5039, 800-328-7688; www.mckenzieraft ing.com. For a 17-mile run through Class III and IV rapids on the Deschutes, **Rapid River Rafters** puts in at Maupin, about 89 miles north. There are also whitewater trips down the McKenzie River (Class III). ~ 500 Southwest Bond Street, Bend; 541-382-1514, 800-962-3327; www.rapidriverrafters.com. **Sun Country Tours** rafts only on the Class III rapids; they run the Upper and Lower Deschutes, Upper McKenzie and North Umpqua from May through September. ~ 531 Southwest 13th Street, Bend; 541-382-6277, 800-770-2161; www.suncountrytours.com.

GOLF

In the Cascades, where resort courses comprise most of the golf options, forested mountain sides, emerald meadows, rivers coursing through fairways, elk lingering on the perimeters and wild geese flying overhead add a unique dimension to the experience.

NORTHERN CASCADES   Resort at the Mountain has three nine-hole courses that are open to the public. The mountain setting makes all three scenic; the first nine is the longest, but fair and forgiving; the third nine, Fox Glove, is fairly narrow and the most challenging. ~ 68010 East Fairway Avenue, Welches; 503-622-3101; www.theresort.com. Located on an American Indian reservation, the championship 18-hole **Kah-Nee-Ta Golf Course** is a fairly flat course, set in a valley. This location is often sunny, so the course is open year-round. ~ Off Route 26, Warm Springs; 541-553-1112; www.kahneeta.com.

CENTRAL CASCADES   The resort of **Black Butte Ranch has two award-winning 18-hole courses: Big Meadow (flat and open) and Glaze Meadow (hilly and narrow). Big Meadow is closed from late October to mid-March, while Glaze Meadow stays open until the snow flies. ~ Route 20, eight miles west of Sisters; 800-399-2322 for tee times, 541-595-1500 for pro shop. At the semiprivate **Widgi Creek Golf Club**, an 18-hole championship course meanders beneath huge pine trees along the rim of the Deschutes River canyon. Closed November through March. ~ Century Drive, five miles south of Bend; 541-382-4449; www.widgi.com. Probably the most famous course in the Cascades and certainly one of the most picturesque in the Northwest, **Tokatee Golf Club** is set majestically in the McKenzie River Valley. "It's a walk with

nature," says the pro. Tokatee, which is considered among the
nation's top public courses, is closed December and January.
Walk-ins are welcome. ~ 54947 McKenzie Highway, Blue River;
541-822-3220, 800-452-6376.

SOUTHERN CASCADES The **Circle Bar Golf Club** has a challenging public nine-hole course. ~ 48447 West Oak Road, Oakridge; 541-782-3541. The 18-hole public **Harbor Links Golf
Course** isn't near a harbor, but it is near a lake. It's a short course,
fairly flat and narrow, and has lots of water. This course is set in
a more developed region. ~ 601 Harbor Isles Boulevard, Klamath Falls; 541-882-0609; www.harborlinksgolf.org.

Many resorts in the Cascades have tennis courts available to guests;
the public is permitted access sometimes as well.

TENNIS

CENTRAL CASCADES The Bend Metro Park and Recreation
District maintains a number of tennis courts in the city. None of
them are nightlighted, but they're free and
available on a first-come, first-served basis
(access to the courts at schools, however, may
be restricted due to school-related activities).
There are four courts at **Juniper Park** (Franklin
Avenue and Northwest 8th Street); two courts at
Sylvan Park (Three Sisters Drive at Fairwell Drive,
on the north side of Aubrey Butte); two courts at
Summit Park (Summit and Promontory drives); and
four courts at **Bend High School** (230 Northeast 6th
Street), **Mountain View High School** (2755 Northeast
27th Street), **Summit High School** (2855 Clearwater Drive) and
Central Oregon Community College (2600 Northwest College
Way). ~ Call 541-389-7275 for more information.

The increasing popularity of whitewater rafting in the Northwest
means that a river like the Deschutes, where access is less
restricted than on the
North Umpqua and other
rivers, can get pretty
crowded—especially
in the summer.

SOUTHERN CASCADES In Klamath Falls, courts are available
at **Moore Park**. ~ Lakeshore Drive; 541-883-5351. There are
four indoor courts at **Harbor Isles Club**. ~ 541-884-3299. You
can also play on one of the four courts at **Crest Park**. ~ Hilyard
Avenue and Crest Street; 541-884-5351. If you time it right you
may get on one of the four lighted courts at **Wiard Park**. ~ Wiard
Street; 541-884-5351.

Skiing in July? It's possible in Oregon's endless winter and the
Cascades offer a ton of alpine and Nordic opportunities.

SKIING

NORTHERN CASCADES In the Northern Cascades, the best-
known resorts are found on the slopes of Mt. Hood. They include
the venerable **Timberline Lodge and Ski Area**, the only year-
round ski resort in North America with six chairlifts serving an
above-timberline snowfield and tree-lined runs. Three lifts operate on Friday and Saturday nights. From June to September, the

resort offers a summer season at the 8500-foot level. ~ Timber-line; 503-272-3311; www.timberlinelodge.com, e-mail info@tim berlinelodge.com.

Another resort serving the same area is **Mt. Hood Skibowl**, with nearly 65 trails, 34 of which are lit for night skiing. ~ 503-272-3206, 503-222-2695 (snowphone); www.skibowl.com. **Mt. Hood Meadows** offers 11 chairlifts serving 87 trails, rated 15 percent beginner, 50 percent intermediate and 35 percent expert. This resort offers runs for the physically challenged in conjunction with area organizations. ~ 503-337-2222, 503-287-5438, 800-754-4663; www.skihood.com.

CENTRAL CASCADES   On Route 20's Santiam Pass west of Sisters, **Hoodoo Ski Area** is a good bet for families looking for alpine or Nordic skiing. ~ 541-822-3799, 541-822-3337; www. hoodoo.com. **Mt. Bachelor** west of Bend is Oregon's largest ski area, offering dry powder and a season extending to mid-May. Ten chairs serve 3683 skiable acres, with 1600 acres groomed daily. ~ 800-829-2442; www.mtbachelor.com, e-mail info@mt bachelor.com. For full-service rental and repair of downhill skis and snowboards, try **Skjersaa's Sports Shop**. ~ 130 Southwest Century Drive, Bend; 541-382-2154. A full selection of skis, snowboards and snowshoes can be rented at **Eurosports**. ~ 182 East Hood Avenue, Sisters; 541-549-2471.

SOUTHERN CASCADES   Crater Lake National Park has extensive Nordic trails with views of the blue water beneath the snow-capped rim. ~ 541-594-3100. Diamond Lake Resort also has Nordic trails, as well as snowcat skiing on **Mt. Bailey**. The latter, limited to just 14 people per run (approximately 5 to 7 runs), transports skiers uphill to enjoy 6000 acres of deep-powder terrain. ~ 800-733-7593 ext. 754; www.catskimtbailey.com.

RIDING STABLES

NORTHERN CASCADES   From March to the end of September, guided hour-long rides wind through the hills or scenic red-rock country at **Kah-Nee-Ta High Desert Resort**. ~ Warm Springs; 541-553-1112; www.kahneeta.com.

CENTRAL CASCADES   In the Sisters area, guided half-hour to all-day trail rides and overnight pack trips into the Cascades are operated by **Equine Management**, which operates stables at Black Butte Ranch. ~ Route 20, eight miles west of Sisters; 541-480-4394, 541-280-4892; www.oregoncowboy.com. **Sunriver Stables** offers rides anywhere in length from half an hour to a full eight-hour trip. Hay rides and sleigh rides in the winter are also available. ~ Sunriver Resort; 541-593-6995.

SOUTHERN CASCADES   Near Crater Lake, **Diamond Lake Corrals** is the place to go for one-hour, three-hour and all-day rides; there are also pack trips and chuckwagon rides. ~ 541-793-3337; www.diamondlakecorrals.com.

Llamaland

One of the most singular sights you're likely to see while exploring the dry side of the Cascades is pastures full of llamas (pronounced "YA-mas"), those wooly long-necked South American cousins of camels. Llama ranching in the United States first appeared in central Oregon in the mid-1970s. The state now boasts about 170 llama ranches, of which more than half are located around Bend and the nearby towns of Sisters, Redmond and Prineville.

Llamas have been domesticated by the Inca people of the South American Andes for at least two thousand years. They have traditionally been raised there for wool and meat. Since they were imported to the United States, their main use has been as beasts of burden and companions, accompanying trekkers into mountain wilderness. Although a llama is not strong enough to carry a human rider, it can carry at least 40 pounds of backpacking and camping gear. Some outfitters rent llamas for independent hiking expeditions, while others organize guided trips. A growing number of outfitters use llamas to carry gear into the mountains in advance and await hikers with a fully set-up campsite.

Llamas also provide specialty wool, which is gathered by either frequent brushing or shearing. Llama wool has a higher warmth-to-weight ratio than sheep wool and comes in 22 natural shades of white, cream, beige, tan, brown, rust, gray and black. Although there is no organized commercial market for llama fiber, it is widely used by weavers and other craftspeople to make everything from scarves, ponchos, blankets and rugs to fishing flies. You'll find these products at galleries and arts-and-crafts shows throughout Oregon.

Perhaps the most unusual use of llamas is to guard livestock. Over the centuries they have developed instinctive behaviors for fighting off cougars and coyote-like Andean wild dogs. These behaviors, along with the Llama's larger size and almost impenetrable wool coat, make llamas more effective than dogs for protecting sheep flocks. They are also used to guard deer, cattle, and ducks and geese.

The economics of llama ranching is similar to horse ranching. Untrained llamas suitable as pets or guards sell for $250 to $1800. Llamas trained for trekking sell for up to $2000. Breeding males bring $2000 to $10,000 each, and breeding females $2000 to $12,000. For more information and to find out about llama ranch tours, contact the **Central Oregon Llama Association**. ~ P.O. Box 5334, Bend, OR 97701; 541-389-6855; www.centraloregonllamas.com, e-mail info@centraloregonllamas.org.

BIKING

From easy town rides to mountain biking on rugged backcountry trails, the Oregon Cascades offer thousands of miles of scenic cycling.

CENTRAL CASCADES In the Bend area, take **West Newport Avenue** for a six-mile trip to Shevlin Park or follow **O. B. Riley Road** five miles to Tumalo State Park. Another possibility is to take the road south 23 miles from Route 97 to **Newberry Volcano**.

At Black Butte Ranch, 18 miles of bike paths include the **Lodge Loop** (5 miles), the scenic **Glaze Meadow Loop** (4 miles) and the **Aspen Loop** (1.6 miles).

About ten miles from Sisters, **Suttle Lake**, with its "upsy-daisy" loop of about 13 miles, is a pleasant outing of moderate exertion for most people.

A popular **Cascades Loop** trail begins in Bend, heads west on Century Drive to Mt. Bachelor and then continues on Cascades Lakes Highway to Route 58. Allow several days to enjoy these demanding 74 miles.

SOUTHERN CASCADES One of the most popular biking trails in the Southern Cascades is the 11.5-mile **Diamond Lake Bike Path**. This level route is ideal for the whole family. The route takes cyclists from Thielsen View Campground to Silent Creek. Complete the loop on the highway returning to Thielsen View. A two-mile section of this route is wheelchair accessible.

The ultimate biking experience at Crater Lake is **Rim Drive**, offering the complete 33-mile overview of this volcanic landmark. Another excellent possibility is **Grayback Drive**, a scenic, unpaved route ideal for mountain bikes. In Klamath Falls, **Nevada Avenue** and **Lakeshore Drive** provide convenient bike-touring access to Upper Klamath Lake. This route continues west to Route 140 along the lake's west shore. **Kit Carson Way** also has a separated bike path.

Bike Rentals In Sisters, **Eurosports** rents mountain bikes in addition to children's bikes. The shop also has bike route maps as well as suggestions for rides in the area. Bikes are available in spring and summer. ~ 182 East Hood Avenue, Sisters; 541-549-2471. For mountain bike rentals or other sporting goods in Bend, stop by **Pine Mountain Sports**. No rentals in the winter. ~ 255 Southwest Century Drive, Bend; 541-385-8080.

AUTHOR FAVORITE

I can't resist the mountain-bike trails in the **Zigzag Ranger District**, with their scenic views of the Mt. Hood region. Among the best is the 12-mile Still Creek Road. This rarely traveled route connects Trillium Lake with the town of Rhododendron. You might also try the ten-mile Sherar Burn Road/Veda Lake trail which leads up to outstanding viewpoints.

In the Bend area, **Paulina Plunge**, as it's known, is a six-mile downhill waterfall mountain-bike tour that descends 3000 feet on groomed trails, with two stops along the way at several waterfalls and two waterslides in the Newberry Crater region. **Paulina Plunge Inc.** operates this activity from May to late September. Call ahead for availability. ~ P.O. Box 8782, Bend, OR 97708; 541-389-0562, 800-296-0562; www.paulinaplunge.com.

With hundreds of miles of trails, including many in wilderness areas, the Cascades are ideal for relaxed rambles or ambitious journeys. All distances listed for hiking trails are one way unless otherwise noted.

HIKING

NORTHERN CASCADES Many of Mt. Hood National Forest's trailheads are rather tricky to find. Stop by Clackamas' County Regional Visitors Center on Route 26, just before the 39-mile marker (before Welches), or at the Mt. Hood information center, 3 miles east of the Clackamas Center, on the right.

Zigzag Trail (2 miles) takes you across the Hood River's east fork via a drawbridge (closed in winter). You'll continue up the canyon to Dog River Trail, which leads to a viewpoint overlooking Mt. Hood and the Upper Hood River Valley.

Tamanawas Falls Loop (5.5 miles) leads along the north bank of Mt. Hood National Forest's Cold Spring Creek. After hiking to scenic Tamanawas Falls, you'll return to the trailhead via Elk Meadows Trail.

Also in Mt. Hood National Forest is **Castle Canyon Trail** (.9 mile) climbing out of the rhododendron area to rocky pinnacles. Views of the scenic Zigzag Valley are your reward.

Another relatively easy possibility is **Bonney Meadow Trail**, reached by taking Route 35 to Bennett Pass and then following Routes 3550 and 4891 to Bonney Meadows Campground. Take trail #473 (3.5 miles) east along the ridge to enjoy the views of Boulder and Little Boulder lakes. Return to the campground by turning right on trail #472.

CENTRAL CASCADES Located 33.4 miles west of Sisters off Route 20 is the **Black Butte Trail** (2 miles), a steady, moderate climb to the top of a volcanic cone.

In the Detroit Lake area, you might want to try **Tumble Ridge Trail** (5.3 miles), which begins on Route 22. This demanding trek heads up through second-growth forest, past Dome and Needle rocks to Tumble Lake.

Built along the Little North Santiam River, the (H)**Little North Santiam Trail** (4.5 miles) crosses eight tributaries with stringer bridges. Fishing and swimming holes are easily reached from this trail leading through some old-growth forests.

Return east on Route 20 and turn south on Route 126. Continue for eight miles to Forest Service Road 2664 and go east 4.4

miles to **Robinson Lake Trail** (.3 mile). It's an easy family hike leading to a pleasant hideaway.

In the McKenzie Bridge area, the **Olallie Trail** (9.7 miles) is an all-day hike with memorable views of the Three Sisters, Mt. Washington, Mt. Jefferson and Bachelor Butte. Take this trail in summer and fall. The trailhead is three miles from Horse Creek Road.

For an easier hike off McKenzie Pass Highway (Route 242), take the **Lava River Trail** (.5 mile). This interpretive trail beginning near the Dee Wright Observatory leads through lava flows. Signs add to your understanding of this moonscape's volcanic past. Wheelchair accessible.

To the south, the Willamette National Forest's Middle Fork Ranger District offers many fine hikes including **Fisher Creek Trail** (6.5 miles). A great way to see a primitive-forest region, you'll get a closeup view of old-growth trees. The silence is deafening. The **Waldo Lake Trail** (21.8 miles) is a challenging route around this incredibly pure lake.

The **Lava River Cave Trail** (1.2 miles) is an easy, rather chilly trail through the state's largest lava tube. It's south of Bend off Route 97, one mile south of Lava Lands Interpretive Center, which is an excellent place to stop for some information on the area. Lanterns are available (seasonally) close to the parking lot.

Fourteen miles south of Bend off Route 97, **Lava Cast Forest Nature Trail** (.9 mile) takes you through one of the Pacific Northwest's weirdest landscape. You'll see tree molds created when molten lava destroyed a forest thousands of years ago.

SOUTHERN CASCADES Off Route 62, the road from Medford to Crater Lake, the **Upper Rogue River Trail** (6.5 miles) is an easy ramble. Begin at the Prospect Ranger Station in Rogue River National Forest and make your way through sugar pines, pausing along the way to cool off in the stream.

Toketee Lake Trail (.4 mile) runs parallel to this spot. Short spurs lead to the waterfront where you'll find otter, beaver, osprey and ducks complementing the scenery.

The **North Umpqua Trail** (79 miles) offers a wide variety of hiking opportunities. Skirting both the Boulder Creek and Mt. Thielsen wilderness areas, this route ranges from easy to difficult. The last nine miles are in the Oregon Cascades Recreation Area and Mt. Thielsen Wilderness Area. Spur trails lead to waterfalls, fishing spots and campgrounds. Among the North Umpqua's most popular segments are **Panther Trail** (5 miles), beginning at Steamboat, and **Lemolo Trail** (6.3 miles), starting at Lemolo Lake.

Mt. Bailey Trail (5 miles) is a steep route located west of Diamond Lake. Your reward for climbing 3000 feet is a panoramic view of Diamond Lake, Mt. Thielsen and the Southern Cascades.

Running 2570 miles from Canada to Mexico, the **Pacific Crest Scenic Trail** is western America's back door to the wilderness, the kind of place John Muir lived for. Scenic, un-crowded, larger than life, it's worth a special trip. You can pick up a 30-mile segment at the North Crater Trailhead, a mile east of the Crater Lake Na-tional Park Trailhead on Route 138. Hike as much of this section as you care to. You can exit via the Tipsoo, Howlock Mountain, North Umpqua or Mt. Thielsen trails.

> All hiking trails in the Cascades are best tack-led in the warmer sea-sons and not recom-mended to try in the winter months.

CRATER LAKE NATIONAL PARK Watchman Peak Trail (.7 mile) is a steep route up Watchman Peak. From the top you'll have a great view of Wizard Island.

It's ironic that most visitors to Crater Lake never actually reach the shore. Doing so requires a steep descent on **Cleetwood Cove Trail** (1.1 miles). This is the route that leads to boat tours of Crater Lake. Bring water and good shoes.

For a good workout, try the **Mount Scott Trail** (2.5 miles). ◀ *HIDDEN* Along the way you'll spot many small animals and birds. The gnarled whitebark pines make a good photographic backdrop. On top you'll have a 360-degree view of the park.

To see some of the national park's impressive pinnacles, take **Godfrey Glen Trail** (1-mile loop). This route leads through a hem- ◀ *HIDDEN* lock and red-fir forest to a view of Sand Creek Canyon.

Located east of Crater Lake Lodge, **Garfield Peak Trail** (1.7 miles) is a fairly steep route offering views of the lake. Look for eagles and hawks along the way.

A short walk in the park is **Castle Crest Wildflower Trail** (.4-mile loop). This easy loop is the best way to sample Oregon wild-flowers in mid-summer. An eden-like setting with small streams trickling down the hillside, the trail is one of Oregon's best-kept secrets.

Sevenmile Trail/Pacific Crest Trail (15 miles) west of Fort Klam-ath off Route 3334 West leads through the Sky Lakes Wilderness south of Crater Lake National Park. Sevenmile Trail hooks up with the Pacific Crest Trail for a 2.5-mile stretch and then cuts off to Seven Lakes Basin. You can also follow the Pacific Crest Trail to Devil's Pass and the steep ascent of Devil's Peak.

The Cascades are a 50-to-100-mile-wide band extend-ing almost the entire length of the state. They begin on the eastern edge of the Willamette Valley and Ashland-Rogue River area and extend to the high-desert region of central Oregon.

Transportation

CAR

Route 26 travels east from Portland to the Mt. Hood area. You can also reach Mt. Hood by taking **Route 35** south from the Hood River area.

From Salem, take **Route 22** east to the Detroit Lakes and Santiam Pass area. **Route 20** east of Albany leads to the same destination, while **Route 126** is Eugene's mainline east to the McKenzie Bridge and McKenzie Pass area. **Route 58** southeast of Eugene is convenient to the Deschutes National Forest, and **Route 138** takes you from Roseburg to the Umpqua River Canyon.

From Medford, take **Route 62** northeast to Crater Lake. An alternate route to Crater Lake is **Route 97** north of Klamath Falls. This same highway also provides access to the Bend area and the Central Cascades. If you're coming from the east, Routes 20 and 26 are the most convenient ways to reach the mountains.

AIR

Redmond Airport, 16 miles north of Bend, is served by Delta Airlines, Horizon Airlines and United Express. **Klamath Falls Airport** is served by Horizon Airlines. The **Portland International Airport, Eugene Airport** and **Rogue Valley International–Medford Airport** are also convenient to the Cascades.

Redmond Airport Shuttle provides service from the Redmond Airport to Bend and Cascades destinations like Sunriver, Mt. Bachelor, Sisters and Black Butte Ranch. ~ 541-382-1687.

Luxury Accommodations offers limousine van service from the Portland airport to popular Northern Cascades recreation areas. ~ 503-668-7433.

BUS

Greyhound Bus Lines services Bend. ~ 120545 Builders Street; 541-382-2151, 800-231-2222; www.greyhound.com.

TRAIN

Amtrak's "Coast Starlight" is a scenic and comfortable way to reach the Cascades. It serves stations in Klamath Falls, Chemult, Eugene, Salem, Albany and Portland, all convenient starting points for the mountain resorts. ~ 800-872-7245; www.amtrak.com.

CAR RENTALS

Arriving passengers at the Redmond Airport are served by **Budget Rent A Car** (800-527-0700), **Hertz Rent A Car** (800-654-3131), **Avis Rent A Car** (800-831-2847) and **Enterprise** (800-736-8222).

Car-rental agencies at the Klamath Falls Airport are **Enterprise** (800-736-8222), **Budget Rent A Car** (800-527-0700), and **Hertz Rent A Car** (800-654-3131).

In Bend, you can rent from **Hertz Rent A Car** (800-654-3131).

PUBLIC TRANSIT

Lane Transit District (541-687-5555) serves McKenzie Bridge. **Basin Transit Service** (541-883-2877) operates in the Klamath Falls area.

TAXIS

For taxi service, contact **Redmond Taxi** (541-548-1182) in Redmond. In Klamath Falls, call **Classic Taxi** (541-885-8294).

TEN

The Heart of Oregon

Drivers in a hurry barrel down Oregon's 280-mile Route 5 corridor in about five hours. Incredibly, that's the way many people see the region that lies at the end of the fabled Oregon Trail. Tempted by free land or the prospect of finding gold, the pioneers risked everything to get here. Today a new generation, rushing to reach Crater Lake, Mt. Hood or the Oregon Coast, speeds through, never knowing what they've missed.

That's progress. Fortunately, all it takes is a trip down a Route 5 offramp to get hooked on the Heart of Oregon, the 60-mile-wide region that extends from Salem to the California border. With the freeway left behind in the rearview mirror, you may understand why residents say God spent six days creating the Earth and on the seventh He went to Oregon.

Framed by the Klamath and Coast ranges on the west and the Cascades on the east, this is the place to find peaceful covered bridges and exciting rafting runs, the nation's oldest Shakespeare festival and a legislature that has made Oregon America's most environmentally conscious state. Home to two major universities, the center of Oregon agriculture and some of its most historic towns, the Heart of Oregon is where you'll find many of the state's best-known writers, poets, artists and artisans.

Just an hour from the state's famous mountain and seaside resorts, the Willamette Valley and the Ashland–Rogue River areas are the primary destinations in the Heart of Oregon. Fields of wildflowers, small towns with falsefront stores and gabled homes, businesses with names like "Wild and Scenic Trailer Park," pies made with fresh-picked marionberries—this is the Oregon found in the postcard rack. Soda fountains with mirrored backbars, jazz preservation societies, old river ferries, museums built out of railroad cars, music festivals and folk-art shrines—you'll find them all and even more here.

In many ways this area's heritage, touted by writers ranging from Washington Irving to Zane Grey, sums up the evolution of the West: American Indians followed by British fur traders, American explorers, missionaries, pioneer settlers, gold miners and the merchants who served them. The 19th-century nouveau riche tapped the hardwood forests to create Victorian mansions. As the mines were played out, lumber and agriculture became king. Strategically located on the main stage and rail lines to California and Washington, this corridor also became the principal gateway to most of Oregon's cities, as well as its emerging mountain retreats and coastal beaches.

But the Heart of Oregon story also has a special dimension, one told at local museums and historic sites. The fatal impact of American expansion on the American Indian culture began with the arrival of missionaries, who preached Christianity but left behind diseases that decimated their converts. In 1843 the promise of free land triggered a stampede as "Oregon or bust" pioneers sped west. Many became farmers who prospered in the California trade after gold was discovered in 1848 at Sutter's Mill. Three years later, after gold was found closer to home near Jacksonville, many settlers put down their plows and made a beeline for the mines. A new boom brought instant prosperity to this sleepy town as millions in gold dust poured through banks on California Street and miners dazzled their brides with mansions shipped in piecemeal from Tennessee.

Not sharing in this windfall were American Indians pushed from their ancestral lands by the settlers and miners. The Indians fought back in the Rogue River Wars between 1851 and 1856. But they were ultimately forced onto reservations, easing the path to statehood in 1859. Settled by Methodist missionaries in 1840, Salem was one of several towns that emerged as a regional supply center. Others included Eugene and Corvallis.

As the railroad improved access, businessmen discovered there was more to sell in Oregon than gold, lumber, dairy products and bountiful crops. Visitors began to explore the fishing streams, caves and forests. Chautauqua tents brought intellectuals and entertainers to Ashland, as Jacksonville offered a different kind of nightlife that gave preachers something to denounce on their pulpits. When Zane Grey showed up to fish the Rogue and the Umpqua rivers, the entire country read about it in his articles. As the good word spread, more visitors began arriving to raft these and other rivers, to see the waterfalls and photograph the vernacular architecture.

Although it was a long way from Middle America, tourists loved the Main Street look and unspoiled countryside of the Heart of Oregon. Culturally it became a hub for social experiments and alternative lifestyles, happily exported by local celebrities like Ken Kesey, who took his famous traffic-stopping bus on a national tour with the "Merry Pranksters" in the 1960s.

Although the Heart of Oregon can be overcast and wet during the winter months, summers tend to be sunny and hot, particularly in the Ashland–Rogue River area. While Route 5 is the mainline, Route 99 is a pleasant alternative. Because the Willamette Valley is flat, it's ideal terrain for cyclists. South of Eugene, the Klamath mountains frame picturesque valleys and towns such as Medford, Ashland and Jacksonville. At the bottom of the state the Siskiyous form the backdrop to the California border.

Because this is the state's primary transportation corridor, it's convenient to scores of popular attractions. Since you're only an hour from the beach or the Cascades, you can easily spend your days waterskiing or spelunking and your

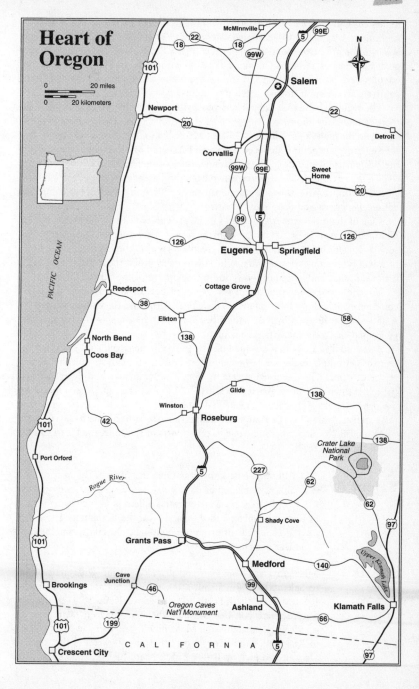

Heart of Oregon

0 ——— 20 miles
0 ——— 20 kilometers

nights enjoying *King Lear*. Blessed with some of the state's finest resorts and restaurants, the Heart of Oregon also offers plenty of birdwatching thanks to several wildlife preserves found along the Willamette River. Here you're likely to spot great blue herons, red-tailed hawks, quails and woodpeckers. Deer, fox, opossums, coyotes and raccoons abound in the valley, while elk, bobcats, bear and flying squirrels are found in the southern mountains.

The region's highlands are pocketed by pristine lakes, hundreds of miles of remote hiking trails and resort lodges paneled in knotty pine. There's even downhill skiing on the highest peak here, 7533-foot Mt. Ashland. But there's little doubt that the signature attractions between Salem and Ashland are the river valleys. From the Willamette wetlands to the swimming holes of the Applegate River, it's hard to beat the streamside life. Rushing down from the Cascades, roaring through Hellgate Canyon, flowing through restaurants at the Oregon Caves, these tributaries define every area and delight every visitor.

One of the most attractive features is the proximity to the wilderness. You are seldom more than 15 or 20 minutes from the countryside, and even the bigger towns, such as Eugene and Salem, have major greenbelts within the city limits. Just north of Salem is Oregon's wine country. While the state capitol is the biggest draw, many historic homes and neighborhoods add to the charm of the central city.

Eugene's college-town status gives it the amenities you would expect in a larger community. Its central location makes the city an ideal base for visiting most of the state's popular destinations. And the city's Ecotopian fervor shows what can happen when environmentalists take control.

Jacksonville, a city that boomed during the rollicking gold rush days, is a delightful period piece, the kind of town where bed and breakfasts outnumber motels ten to one. The tree-lined streets, red-brick office blocks and dusty old bars make the town a favorite. Artists flock here and to Ashland, an Oregon mecca for the dramatic arts. Thoroughly gentrified, heavily booked and loaded with great restaurants, Ashland is the state's last temptation and a hard one to leave on the route south. No mere stepping stone to other parts of the state, the Heart of Oregon is an end in itself.

Salem Area

Although best known as Oregon's capital, Salem is a desirable place to spend a day for many other reasons. A short drive from Oregon's wine country, Salem is also close to several historic Willamette Valley ferries. Near the Willamette, the downtown area is rich with restored buildings, museums, churches and a pioneer cemetery.

SIGHTS　　Most travelers from Portland drive down the Willamette Valley to Salem via Route 5. But a far more scenic approach is to exit Route 5 in southern Portland and pick up **Route 99 West** through Tigard. Here you can continue through Oregon's wine country on 99 West, head through McMinnville and then cut east to Salem at Rickreall. Even better, turn off Route 99 West at the town of Dayton and pick up **Route 221**, a beautiful backroad paralleling the Willamette River. Near Hopewell it's fun to cross the river on the Wheatland Ferry.

In Salem, you'll find **Mission Mill Museum**, a historic restoration that turns back the clock to Oregon's pioneer days. Built in the 19th century is the Thomas Kay Woolen Mill, a factory-turned-museum. Adjacent are the Jason Lee House, the oldest residence standing in the Pacific Northwest, and the John Boon House, where you'll learn what family life was like in the mid-19th century. The 1841 Methodist Parsonage is open for tours. Enjoy a picnic here by the millstream. The **Salem Convention and Visitors Association** (503-581-4325, fax 503-581-4540; www. travelsalem.com, e-mail information@travelsalem.com) has an office in the complex. Closed Sunday. ~ 1313 Mill Street Southeast, Salem; 503-585-7012, fax 503-588-9902; www.missionmill.org, e-mail info@missionmill.org.

Situated in formal gardens is the **Deepwood Estate**. With its stained-glass windows, oak woodwork and solarium, this Queen Anne is a monument to turn-of-the-20th-century craftsmanship. A nature trail leads through the adjacent Bush's Pasture Park. Closed Sunday in summer; closed Sunday, Tuesday, Thursday and Friday in winter. Admission. ~ 1116 Mission Street Southeast, Salem; 503-363-1825; www.historicdeepwoodestate.org, e-mail historicdeepwoodestate@yahoo.com.

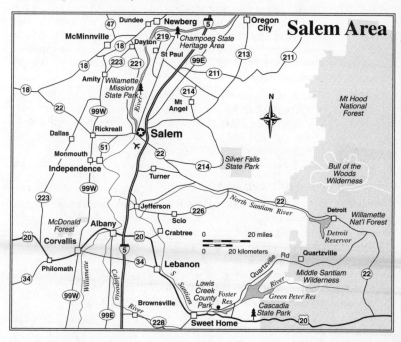

Court-Chemeketa Residential Historic District showcases 117 historic Queen Anne, Italianate, gothic, Craftsman and salt-box homes. On this mile-long walk you'll see many of the fine homes built by the city's founders. ~ Court and Chemeketa streets, Salem; 503-581-4325, 800-874-7012, fax 503-581-4540; www.travelsalem.com.

The **Oregon State Capitol** is a four-story Greek-style structure boasting half a dozen bronze sculptures over the entrances. Built from Vermont marble, the state building is crowned by the 23-foot-high gilded statue *The Oregon Pioneer*. The tower and rotunda have reopened after repairs were made to fix damage caused by an 1993 earthquake (the quake measured 5.5 on the Richter scale). Tours up the 121 stairs of the tower run every hour in summer. The surrounding Wilson Park has a pretty fountain and gazebo. ~ 900 Court Street, Salem; 503-986-1387, fax 503-986-1131; www.leg.state.or.us.

Across from the capitol, **Willamette University** is the state's oldest institution of higher learning and the first university in the West (founded in 1842). On this shady campus you'll want to see the exhibit on the history of the school (which in many ways mirrors the history of Salem) at venerable **Waller Hall**. Cone Chapel (also in Waller Hall) is the place of worship for this one-time Methodist school. The campus is also home to an unusual formation of five giant sequoias known as the **Star Trees**; if you stand in the middle of them and look upward, you'll see the shape of a star. The trees are near the **Sesquicentennial Rose Garden**, a blooming place for a walk across State Street from the capitol. ~ Willamette University: 900 State Street, Salem; 503-370-6300; www.willamette.edu.

NORTH OF SALEM   The byways and secondary highways of the Willamette Valley north of Salem offer great possibilities for a day of sightseeing. Many of Oregon's best wineries are along Route 99 West—a rural and scenic alternative to Route 5. (See "Oregon's Wine Country" Scenic Drive.)

AUTHOR FAVORITE

In the spring, don't miss **Schreiner's Gardens**, located five miles north of Salem. Although there are over 200 acres here, only 10 of them are open to the public, and that is only during the May-to-June blooming season. Still, a visit to this photographer's dream is a must during those months; the rest of the year, the gardens are closed while Schreiner's ships irises all over the world through its catalog business. ~ 3625 Quinaby Road Northeast; 503-393-3232, 800-525-2367, fax 503-393-5590; www.schreinersgardens.com, e-mail iris@schreinersgardens.com.

Mt. Angel Abbey is a 19th-century Benedictine monastic community 18 miles northeast of Salem. Visitors are welcome to take a walking tour of the Abbey, including the Romanesque church and retreat houses. A small museum focuses on the Russian Old Believer community, while another building emphasizes the natural history of the region. The beautiful library, designed by Alvar Aalto, features a display of rare books. Near the top of a 300-foot butte is the grotto of Our Lady of Lourdes. In July, the retreat hosts the Abbey Bach Festival. ~ 1 Abbey Drive, St. Benedict; 503-845-3030, fax 503-845-3027; www.mt angel.edu.

SOUTH OF SALEM   Heading south from Salem, you may want to skip Route 5 altogether. A fun loop drive, beginning in Albany (about 25 miles south of Salem), leads through Corvallis, home to one of Oregon's biggest universities, as well as through some accommodating rural towns and sights.

Take the kids to **Enchanted Forest**, located in a park setting seven miles south of Salem on Route 5. The dream of creator Roger Tofte, this family fun spot has fairytale attractions like a crooked house, Seven Dwarfs' cottage, an Alice in Wonderland rabbit hole, old-lady's-shoe slide, haunted house and the Big Timber log ride. Plays are performed in an outdoor theater. Closed October to mid-March, and weekdays in September and April. Admission. ~ 8462 Enchanted Way Southeast, Turner; 503-363-3060; www.enchantedforest.com.

Heading southeast from Salem on Route 51, continue past the town of Independence and follow the signs seven miles south to the historic **Buena Vista Ferry**, which carries a handful of cars and cyclists across the Willamette in the time-honored manner. No trip to Oregon is complete without a ride on one of these old-timers. Closed Monday and Tuesday, and from November through April. ~ 503-588-7979.

Proceed south to Albany, where you can begin a circular drive of the area north of Eugene. South of Albany, Route 34 leads east to the town of Lebanon. Continue east to Sweet Home and one of the Northwest's better pioneer museums. In a 1905 woodframe church, the **East Linn Museum** collection is big on logging equipment, antique dolls, quilts, butter churns, linotypes and saddles. There's also a full blacksmith shop here. Closed December through January; closed Monday from June through September, and Monday through Wednesday from September through April. ~ 746 Long Street, Sweet Home; 541-367-4580.

The **Sweet Home Chamber of Commerce** provides information on this Cascades gateway. Closed Saturday and Sunday. ~ 1575 Main Street, Sweet Home; 541-367-6186, fax 541-367-6150; www.sweethomechamber.org.

Oregon's Wine Country

Oregon's leading wine region, Yamhill County is an easy drive north from Salem or southwest from Portland. This area has more than 40 wineries and 100 vineyards, and is known for its exceptional pinot noir. Many wineries here also produce pinot gris, pinot blanc, chardonnay, riesling and champagne-process sparkling wines. Most wineries lie along pastoral Route 99W. The establishments listed here offer tours; call ahead to confirm visiting hours, which vary seasonally.

AMITY & MCMINNVILLE   From Salem, follow Edgewater Street westbound. It becomes Route 22 as it takes you ten miles to the intersection with Route 99W. Turn north (right) and follow 99W for 20 miles to McMinnville, the Yamhill county seat. **Yamhill Valley Vineyards** is on a 150-acre estate. Try their pinot noir, pinot blanc and pinot gris wines in the elegant tasting room set in an oak grove. The cathedral ceiling and balcony overlooking the vineyard add to the charm. Closed Monday through Wednesday from mid-March to Memorial Day. ~ 16250 Southwest Oldsville Road (off Route 18), McMinnville; 503-843-3100; www.yamhill.com, e-mail info@yamhill.com.

CARLTON   From McMinnville, take Route 47 north to Carlton, a distance of seven miles. In the center of this historic town, **The Tasting Room** presents a selection of fine wines from around Oregon, with tastings each afternoon. Closed January through March. ~ Main and Pine streets, Carlton; 503-852-6733; www.pinot-noir.com, e-mail info@pinot-noir.com. Nearby, **Carlo & Julian** is known for innovative viticulture techniques including the use of frost for crop control and trained cats for gopher eradication. Producing fewer than 1000 cases of handcrafted pinot noir, tempranillo and nebbiolo annually, the winery is open for tastings and sales over Memorial Day and Thanksgiving weekends and by appointment. ~ 1000 East Main Street, Carlton; 503-852-7432; e-mail carlojulwine@yahoo.com. Half a mile farther down Route 47 is **Cuneo Cellars**. Taste their range of handcrafted varietals. ~ 750 Lincoln Street,

Perched in the foothills ten miles east of the town of Sweet Home are **Foster Reservoir** and the adjacent **Green Peter Reservoir** on Quartzville Road. Green Peter Reservoir offers the kind of views you'd expect to find in Switzerland.

Brownsville, west of Sweet Home on Route 228, is one of the valley's most charming small towns. You can pick up a walking-tour brochure that guides you to local museums, including the century-old **Moyer House**. Built from lumber milled in John

Carlton; 503-852-0002; www.cuneocellars.com. Continue east on Main Street as it becomes Northeast Hendricks Road, then left on Northeast Kuehne Road to visit **Laurel Ridge Winery** and sample their pinot noir, riesling and gewürztraminer. Closed January. ~ 13301 Northeast Kuehne Road, Carlton; 503-852-7050.

NEWBERG   Continue four miles farther north to Yamhill, then turn east (right) on Route 240. A drive of 12 rural miles brings you to Newberg, where **Rex Hill Vineyards** is a beautifully landscaped 25-acre winery with an inviting terraced picnic area. Furnished with antiques, the tasting room has a fireplace. ~ 30835 North Route 99W, Newberg; 503-538-0666, 800-739-4455; www.rexhill.com, e-mail info@rexhill.com.

DUNDEE & DAYTON   At Newberg, turn southeast (right) and you'll find yourself back on Route 99W. Driving two miles south will bring you to Dundee, where **Sokol Blosser Winery**, established in 1971, was one of Oregon's first wineries. Here you'll enjoy great views of the Willamette Valley, along with a pleasant picnic area and contemporary tasting room offering not only the winery's fine pinot noir and pinot gris but also fruit preserves, gourmet mustards, salad dressings and candies. ~ 5000 Sokol Blosser Lane, Northeast Dayton; 503-864-2282, 800-582-6668; www.solkolblosser.com, e-mail info@solkolblosser.com. Established in 1987 by an Australian vintner in a one-time hazelnut processing plant, **Argyle** specializes in champagne-like sparkling wines and pinot noirs. The inviting tasting room is in a restored Victorian farmhouse. ~ 691 North Route 99W, Dundee; 503-538-8520, 888-427-4953; www.argylewinery.com. **Erath Winery** is set high above the Willamette Valley in the lovely Dundee Hills. You can sample the winery's wares in a rustic, wood-paneled tasting room. ~ 9409 Northeast Worden Hill Road, Dundee; 503-538-3318, 800-539-9463, fax 503-538-1074; www.erath.com, e-mail info@erath.com. Four miles south of Dundee, **Wine Country Farm Cellars** makes rare varietals such as Muller-Thurgau in addition to pinot noir and riesling. You'll find a picnic area and a B&B, and visitors can get acquainted with the resident Arabian horses. ~ 6855 Breyman Orchards Road, Dayton; 503-864-3466, 800-261-3446, fax 503-864-3109; www.winecountryfarm.com, e-mail jld@winecountryfarm.com. From here, it's a 20-mile drive back to Salem via Route 221.

Moyer's own sash and door factory, this Italianate home features 12-foot ceilings. Landscapes are painted on the walls and window transoms. ~ 204 Main Street at Kirk Avenue, Brownsville.

Howard Taylor and his wife, Faye, devoted 20 years to the creation of the folk-art capital of central Oregon, the **Living Rock Studios**. Howard created this memorial to his pioneer ancestors with 800 tons of rock. The circular stone building is inlaid with pioneer wagon-wheel rims, an American Indian mortar and pes-

◄ *HIDDEN*

tle, fool's gold, obsidian and coffee jars filled with crystals. A series of illuminated biblical pictures is displayed downstairs, while a circular staircase leads upstairs to a display of Taylor's carvings. Antiques and unique gifts are on display in the shop. Self-guided tours are available. Closed Sunday and Monday. ~ Route 228, west of Brownsville; 541-466-5814; www.pioneer.net/~mackey, e-mail mackey@pioneer.net.

A popular Oregon college town located on the west side of the valley at the edge of the coast range, **Corvallis** is also the seat of Benton County. A prominent landmark here is the **Benton County Courthouse**. The building, dating to 1887 and still in use, has an impressive clock tower. Closed weekends. ~ 120 Northwest 4th Street, Corvallis.

On the 500-acre **Oregon State University** campus in Corvallis, you'll find the OSU art department's **Fairbanks Gallery** in Fairbanks Hall (closed weekends; 541-737-4745) and **Giustina Gallery** at 26th and Western streets (541-737-2402), two small gallery spaces that usually feature rotating exhibits, often by the university's students. ~ OSU: Campus Way, Corvallis; 541-737-0123, fax 541-737-0625; www.oregonstate.edu/dept/arts.

For information on other local attractions, contact **Corvallis Tourism**. Closed weekends in fall and winter. ~ 553 Northwest Harrison Boulevard, Corvallis; 541-757-1544, 800-334-8118; fax 541-753-2664; www.visitcorvallis.com, e-mail info@visitcor vallis.com.

East of Corvallis on Route 20 is **Albany**, where you'll find nearly 500 Victorian homes. One of the best is the **Monteith House**, which is a frame residence with period 19th-century furnishings. Dressed in Victorian costumes, docents lead intriguing tours. Closed Monday and Tuesday, and from mid-September to mid-June, except by appointment. ~ 518 Southwest 2nd Avenue, Albany; 541-967-8699, 800-526-2256. At the **Albany Regional Museum** are an old-time general store, a shoe-shine shop and an exhibit on Camp Adair, a World War II Army training site. Closed Sunday. ~ 136 Lyon Street South, Albany; 541-967-7122.

To arrange tours of either location contact the **Albany Visitors Association**, where you can pick up a helpful walking-tour map. ~ 250 Broadalbin Street Southwest, Suite 110, Albany; 541-928-0911, 800-526-2256, fax 541-926-1500; www.albany visitors.com, e-mail info@albanyvisitors.com.

LODGING Convenient to Route 5, the **Best Western Mill Creek Inn** has 109 units including junior suites with microwaves, refrigerators and wet bars. The large rooms have contemporary furniture and ample closet space. ~ 3125 Ryan Drive Southeast, Salem; 503-585-3332, 800-346-9659, fax 503-375-9618; www.bestwestern.com/millcreekinn, e-mail bwmci@msn.com. MODERATE TO DELUXE.

George Washington never slept at **A Creekside Garden Inn**, but it looks as if he might have. Located just six blocks from the state capitol, this Mount Vernon colonial–style home has two-story columns and a veranda overlooking parklike grounds along Mill Creek. Each of the five antique-furnished rooms is decorated with a garden theme; three have private baths. Classic films are shown nightly with a "bottomless" popcorn bowl. A hearty full breakfast in the dining room or on the veranda is included in the room rate. ~ 333 Wyatt Court Northeast, Salem; 503-391-0837, fax 503-391-1713; www.salembandb.com, e-mail rickiemh@open.org. MODERATE.

Econolodge offers lodging just 50 yards from the Willamette River. Clean, air-conditioned rooms are furnished in modern decor. The price is right for this 61-room motel convenient to downtown. ~ 345 Northwest 2nd Street, Corvallis; 541-752-9601. BUDGET.

clean & cheap!

The **Sweet Home Inn Motel** has clean rooms with white and pink brick walls and contemporary furniture. A small garden is located at the inn, which is a block away from the museums and shops of this gateway to some of the valley's best boating and fishing. ~ 805 Long Street, Sweet Home; 541-367-5137, fax 541-367-8859. MODERATE.

There's no MSG at **Kwan's**, a Chinese establishment with seating for more than 400 at comfortable booths and large tables ideal for the whole family. Specialties like imperial fried rice, curry lamb, Mongolian emu and mango chicken have won a loyal following. They offer six varieties of whole-grain rice as well as an assortment of fresh produce and meats. Entering this pagoda-style building, you'll find a 15-foot-tall redwood Buddha in the lobby. ~ 835 Commercial Street, Salem; 503-362-7711, fax 503-373-5818; www.kwanscuisine.com. MODERATE.

DINING

AUTHOR FAVORITE

Just when you're about ready to give up on McMinnville as another franchise landscape, the chain stores of Route 99 give way to the town's well-preserved downtown. Tucked away in a storefront is **Nick's Italian Café**, where the kitchen prepares memorable dishes such as smoked salmon with pinenuts, veal parmesan and homemade lasagna with pesto, mushrooms and Oregon filberts. The prix-fixe menu is standard, but all items can be ordered à la carte. Don't despair if you can't get a reservation because there's nearly always seating available at the counter. Dinner only. Closed Monday. ~ 521 Northeast 3rd Street, McMinnville; 503-434-4471, 888-456-2511; www.nicksitaliancafe.com, e-mail nickscafe@onlinemac.com. MODERATE TO ULTRA-DELUXE.

Excellent— but a bit pricy

Michael's Landing serves prime rib and seafood salad in the restored Southern Pacific Station. One of the city's most popular restaurants, it has a great view of the Willamette. ~ 603 Northwest 2nd Street, Corvallis; 541-754-6141, fax 541-754-9578. MODERATE TO DELUXE.

For steaks, prime rib and fresh seafood, try **The Gables**. Portions are generous, and there's an extensive wine cellar. Dinner only. ~ 1121 Northwest 9th Street, Corvallis; 541-752-3364. MODERATE TO DELUXE.

HIDDEN ►

Located in a strip shopping center, **Amador's Alley** is one of the most popular Mexican restaurants in the area. Huge portions of *huevos con chorizo*, chile colorado and enchiladas rancheros are served up steaming. Diners are seated at plastic tables and chairs. Arrive early or be prepared to wait. Closed Sunday. ~ 870 North Main Street, Independence; 503-838-0170, fax 503-838-1710. BUDGET TO MODERATE.

Take one of the window booths at **The Point Restaurant** and enjoy a perfect waterfront view. Fresh fish, steak, prawns, lobster and generous salads are a few of the specialties. A fresh-baked loaf of bread comes with dinner. Breakfast also available. ~ 6305 Route 20, Sweet Home; 541-367-1560. MODERATE TO DELUXE.

SHOPPING

The **Reed Opera House Mall** at Court and Liberty streets in Salem is a restored landmark that once presented old-time minstrel shows. Now the building is a prime shopping area. ~ 189 Northeast Liberty Street, Salem; 503-391-4481; www.reedoperahouse.com.

The Mission Mill Museum's **Mission Mill Store** sells the usual assortment of postcards, gifts and collectibles as well as blankets, clothes and hats. Closed Sunday. ~ 1313 Mill Street Southeast, Salem; 503-585-7012; www.missionmill.org.

An excellent place for regional arts and crafts—pottery, sculpture, paintings, prints and jewelry, for example—is the **Bush Barn Art Center**. Closed Monday. ~ 600 Mission Street Southeast, Salem; 503-581-2228, fax 503-371-3342; www.salemart.org.

NIGHTLIFE

The **Oregon Symphony Association** offers classical concerts as well as a pops series. ~ 707 13th Street Southeast, Salem; 503-364-0149, 800-992-8499 (tickets).

Pentacle Theatre is a well-established community theater with eight plays each season. ~ 324 52nd Avenue Northwest, Salem; 503-364-7121, 503-485-4300 (tickets); www.pentacletheatre.org.

For belly dancing, big band music, folk, reggae, rock or bluegrass, check out **McMenamin's Boon's Treasury**. This circa-1860 two-story brick building has live music Wednesday through Saturday nights. Artworks are frequently exhibited. ~ 888 Liberty Street Northeast, Salem; 503-399-9062, fax 503-399-0074.

For live bluegrass, try **Lenora's Ghost** every other Thursday. On Saturday night, a deejay will play CDs you bring in. Friday nights, there's karaoke. Occasional cover. ~ 114 Main Street, Independence; 503-838-2937.

BUSH'S PASTURE PARK   The Bush Collection of old garden roses is one of the highlights in this 89-acre park south of the capital. They were originally collected from pioneer homesteads to represent roses brought west on the Oregon Trail. Also here are natural wildflower gardens, a collection of flowering trees, the **Bush Barn Art Center**, featuring Northwestern artists, and the **Bush Conservatory**, the West's second-oldest greenhouse. Amenities include a picnic area, restrooms and tours of the **Bush House Museum** (fee), a playground and gardens. ~ 600 Mission Street, entry off High Street Southeast, Salem; 503-588-2410.

PARKS

WILLAMETTE MISSION STATE PARK   Set in orchards and hop fields south of Wheatland's landing, this 1680-acre Willamette River park is the site of an 1830s Methodist Mission. A monument commemorates these early settlers. In the midst of the park are the historic Wheatland Ferry landings. This shady spot is a delightful retreat on a warm day. Fishing for bass and bluegill is popular with anglers. There are picnic tables, kitchen shelter areas, electricity, fire rings, restrooms, and bike and equestrian trails. Parking fee, $3. ~ Wheatland Road, 12 miles north of Salem; 503-393-1172, fax 503-393-8863; http://egov.oregon.gov/OPRD/index.

Silver Falls State Park's South Falls Lodge, home to the visitors center, was built by the CCC, which used native stone and logs in its construction.

SILVER FALLS STATE PARK   If you're addicted to waterfalls, look no further. Located in twin lava-rock gorges created by Silver Creek's north and south forks, the 8700-acre park has ten waterfalls. Also here are hiking, biking and equestrian trails leading through an old-growth fir forest with towering maples and quaking aspen ideal for fall-color buffs. South Falls, a seven-mile roundtrip hike from the highway, has the biggest drop, 177 feet, or 25 feet more than Niagara Falls. You'll find picnic tables, a snack bar, a playground, a swimming area, restrooms, rustic group lodging, a nature lodge, a jogging trail, bike trails and a horse camp. Parking fee, $3. ~ Route 214, 26 miles east of Salem; 503-873-8681, fax 503-873-8925.

▲ There are 46 tent sites ($12 to $16 per night), 47 RV hookup sites ($16 to $20 per night), 6 horse-camp sites ($16 to $48 per night) and 14 cabins ($35 per night). Reservations: 800-452-5687.

McDOWELL CREEK FALLS COUNTY PARK   This forested glen is a perfect refuge. An easy hike across the creek and up through   ◀ HIDDEN a fir forest takes you to a pair of scenic falls. On a weekday you may have this park to yourself. There are picnic tables and vault toilets. ~ Located 12 miles southeast of Lebanon via Fairview Road and McDowell Creek Drive; 541-967-3917, fax 541-924-6915; www.co.linn.or.us/parks, e-mail parks@co.linn.or.us.

LEWIS CREEK COUNTY PARK On the north shore of Foster Reservoir, Lewis Creek Park is a good spot to swim and enjoy other water sports. Troll for bass and trout in the lake. This day-use park includes 20 acres of open space and 20 acres of brush and forest, as well as plenty of fine views of the Cascades. Picnic tables and a boat dock are the facilities here. Closed October through April. Parking fee, $3. ~ Four miles northeast of Sweet Home. Take Route 20 east to Foster Dam and turn left at Quartzville Road. At North River Road turn left to the park; 541-967-3917, fax 541-924-6915; www.co.linn.or.us/parks, e-mail parks@co.linn.or.us.

CASCADIA STATE PARK On the South Santiam River Canyon, this 253-acre park has a beautiful one-mile trail leading to a waterfall. Largely forested with Douglas fir, the park also has an open meadow on the north river bank. You can fish for trout in the river. Facilities include restrooms and picnic tables. ~ Route 20, 14 miles east of Sweet Home; 541-367-6021, fax 541-367-3757.

▲ There are 25 primitive sites ($14 per night).

HIDDEN ► **WHITCOMB CREEK COUNTY PARK** With its stunning rainforest terrain on the shores of ten-mile-long Green Peter Reservoir, this 328-acre park in the foothills east of Sweet Home is a winner. It offers spectacular views of the Cascades and good trout fishing. The park is forested with fir and deciduous trees. You'll find picnic tables and restrooms. Boat ramps into the reservoir are located about a mile away. Closed October through April. ~ From Sweet Home take Route 20 east to Foster Dam and turn left at Quartzville Road. Continue north 15 miles to the park; 541-967-3917, fax 541-924-6915.

▲ There are 39 tent sites ($11 per night).

Eugene Area

College towns are often inviting and Eugene is no exception. Climb one of the town buttes and you'll find the city surrounded by rich farmland and beckoning lakes and streams. With the Cascades and the McKenzie River Valley to the east and the Coast Mountains to the west, Eugene has an ideal location. Eugene is at its best in the fall when maples, black walnuts, chestnuts and cottonwood brighten the landscape. The city, used for the filming of the movie *Animal House*, offers sidewalk cafés, malled streets and upscale shops.

SIGHTS

Pick up touring ideas at the **Convention and Visitors' Association of Lane County Oregon**. Closed Sunday in winter. ~ 754 Olive Street, Eugene; 541-484-5307, 800-547-5445, fax 541-343-6335; www.travellanecounty.com, e-mail info@cvalco.org.

Stop by the **University of Oregon**'s 250-acre campus. You'll find an arboretum with over 2000 varieties of trees; weekday tours for prospective students are offered from Oregon Hall at 13th and Agate streets. ~ 541-346-3111, 800-232-3825; www.uoregon.edu.

Among the campus highlights is the **Museum of Natural and Cultural History**. This collection is a good way to orient yourself to the state's geology, flora, fauna and anthropology. Permanent exhibits cover Oregon's fossil history and archaeology. Closed Monday, Tuesday and during university holidays. Admission. ~ 1680 East 15th Avenue, Eugene; 541-346-3024, fax 541-346-5334; natural-history.uoregon.edu, e-mail mnh@uoregon.edu.

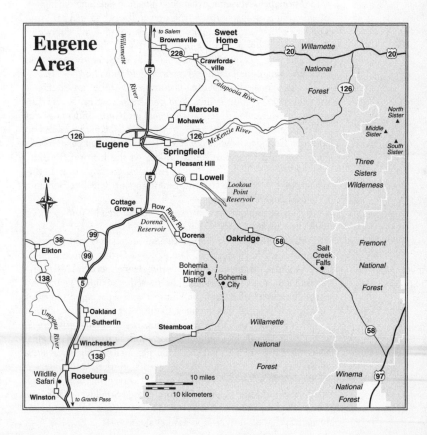

Also recommended is the **Jordan Schnitzer Museum of Art** at the University of Oregon. The colonnaded sculpture court with pool adjacent to the entrance is one of the campus's architectural highlights. The collection, one of the best in the state, displays American, European and a wide range of Asian artworks. Call for hours. ~ Just east of 14th and Kincaid streets, Eugene; 541-346-3027, fax 541-346-0976; jsma.uoregon.edu.

> The mountainous Bohemia Mining District was the scene of a mid-19th-century gold rush that unfortunately proved to be a bust.

Eugene is big on adaptive reuse of commercial buildings like the **5th Street Public Market,** home to a distinctive collection of over 100 percent Oregon-owned retail shops, restaurants, international cafés and offices. It is located in the heart of Eugene's historic market district. ~ 296 East 5th Avenue, Suite 300, Eugene; 541-484-0383, fax 541-686-1220; www.5thstreetmarket.com.

The prime attraction in the neighboring town of Springfield is the **Springfield Museum,** which has a section detailing the history of this timber-industry town (the first mill opened in 1853) and a gallery with changing exhibits of artwork, antique collections and Americana. Closed Sunday and Monday. ~ 590 Main Street, Springfield; 541-726-2300, fax 541-726-3688; www.springfield museum.com, e-mail dstaton@ci.springfield.or.us.

No trip to the Eugene area is complete without an excursion into the nearby countryside. You can head east on **Route 126** along the McKenzie River or southeast on **Route 58** to Lookout Point Reservoir, Oakridge and Salt Creek Falls. **Route 5** takes you south to Cottage Grove. Row River Road leads east past Dorena Reservoir and several covered bridges to the historic **Bohemia Mining District**. Today, tourists roam the district by car and four-wheel-drive vehicles to see lost mines, ghost towns like Bohemia City and covered bridges.

Before setting out for this national forest area be sure to check with the **Cottage Grove Ranger Station** (541-767-5000, fax 541-767-5075). Because there are active mining claims in the area, it is important not to trespass. The **Cottage Grove Museum** has a major exhibit on the Bohemia District, as well as displays on the *Titanic* and a covered bridge. The museum is open Wednesday through Sunday afternoons in summer and weekend afternoons in winter. ~ Birch and H avenues, Cottage Grove; 541-942-3963.

The **Willamette Valley Scenic Loop** is a 195-mile adventure. It begins and ends in Cottage Grove, looping through Corvallis, Salem and Albany. This backroad journey includes historical sites, museums, covered bridges, ferries, parks, gardens and wineries. A detailed brochure is available at the **Convention and Visitors' Association of Lane County Oregon**. Closed Sunday. ~ 754 Olive Street, Eugene; 541-484-5307, 800-547-5445, fax 541-343-6335; www.travellanecounty.com, e-mail cvalco@cvalco.org.

The **Roseburg Visitors Center and Chamber of Commerce** offers a handy city tour guide. Closed Sunday in winter. ~ 410 South east Spruce Street, Roseburg; 541-672-9731, 800-444-9584, fax 541-673-7868; www.visitroseburg.com, e-mail info@visitroseburg.com. Highlights include the **Roseburg Historic District** in the Mill Street/Pine Street neighborhood. You'll find many modest cottages built in the late 19th century. The **Floed-Lane House** is a Classic revival featuring a full-length, two-tier veranda with half a dozen square columns supporting each level. It's open for tours on Sunday or by appointment. ~ 544 Southeast Douglas Street, Roseburg.

The **Douglas County Museum of History and Natural History** features American Indian and pioneer artifacts, a 19th-century railroad depot and natural history wildlife dioramas. Admission. ~ 123 Museum Drive, Roseburg; 541-957-7007, fax 541-957-7017; www.co.douglas.or.us/museum, e-mail museum@co.douglas.or.us.

Wildlife Safari is Oregon's drive-through adventure, a 600-acre park where over 500 animals and birds roam freely. Visitors motor past Bactrian camels, hippopotamuses, lions, and scores of other species. In addition to the self-paced driving tour, the Safari Village has a petting zoo. Elephant and camel rides are also available in the summer. Admission. ~ 1790 Safari Road, Winston; 541-679-6761, fax 541-679-9210; www.wildlifesafari.org.

LODGING

Valley River Inn enjoys an enviable view of the Willamette River. Adjacent to the 140-store Valley River Center, this 257-room hotel features Indian quilts hanging over the big lobby fireplace that faces a conversation pit. Large rooms, decorated with either wicker furniture and impressionist prints or Laura Ashley designs, open onto small patios. Bicycling and jogging paths are adjacent to the inn, which rents bikes and has its own workout room. You'll also find a pool, sauna and jacuzzi as well as a full-service restaurant and lounge. All rooms are nonsmoking. ~ 1000 Valley River Way, Eugene; 541-687-0123, 800-543-8266, fax 541-687-0289; www.valleyriverinn.com, contact@valleyriverinn.com. DELUXE TO ULTRA-DELUXE.

The 65-unit **Best Western Greentree Inn** offers attractive, contemporary rooms with sitting areas and balconies, some with creek views. All units have refrigerators. Adjacent to the University of Oregon campus, this establishment has a pool, jacuzzi, exercise center, restaurant and sports bar. Continental breakfast is included. ~ 1759 Franklin Boulevard, Eugene; 541-485-2727, 800-528-1234, fax 541-686-2094; e-mail greentreeinn@aol.com. MODERATE.

Tucked away in a quiet university neighborhood, the **Secret Garden Bed & Breakfast** features ten unique rooms, each with a different garden theme. The Scented Garden room is furnished in sumptuous colors and Indian and Tibetan antiques, while the Apiary is decorated in French country style. A striking mural in the upstairs sitting room depicts the mythical Daphne in the middle of her metamorphosis into a tree. Naturally, the landscaped grounds are meticulous and lovely. Full breakfast included. ~ 1910 University Street, Eugene; 541-484-6755, 888-484-6755, fax 541-431-1699; www.secretgardenbbinn.com, e-mail innkeeper@ secretgardenbbinn.com. DELUXE TO ULTRA-DELUXE.

Pick your favorite musician at the **Excelsior Inn**, where classical composers such as Beethoven, Strauss and Verdi lend their names to guest accommodations. Each of the 14 musical rooms is distinctly decorated in dark cherry furniture, with elegant touches like writing desks, armoires, sleigh beds, arched windows and vaulted ceilings. Full breakfast from the inn's fine restaurant included. ~ 754 East 13th Street, Eugene; 541-342-6963, 800-321-6963; www.excelsiorinn.com, e-mail info@excelsiorinn.com. DELUXE TO ULTRA-DELUXE.

Overlooking Eugene, **The Campbell House** offers peaceful and elegant accommodations within walking distance to both city center and outdoor pursuits. The 18 rooms are individually decorated; all have a Victorian flavor with modern amenities. Some have fireplaces and jacuzzis. You'll also find a comfortable parlor and library. Full breakfast is served. ~ 252 Pearl Street, Eugene; 541-343-1119, 800-264-2519, fax 541-343-2258; www. campbellhouse.com, e-mail campbellhouse@campbellhouse.com. MODERATE TO ULTRA-DELUXE.

DINING

The emphasis at **Sweetwaters** is on Oregon cuisine featuring locally grown veal, lamb, lettuce, herbs, mushrooms and fruits. Seafood entrées include grilled salmon, Dungeness crab chowder and fresh swordfish. This contemporary dining room overlooking the Willamette River is complemented by a deck ideal for drinks before or after dinner. ~ Valley River Inn, 1000 Valley River Way, Eugene; 541-341-3462, fax 541-683-5121; www.val leyriverinn.com. DELUXE TO ULTRA-DELUXE.

AUTHOR FAVORITE

For a lively night on the town, I head to the **Oregon Electric Station Restaurant and Lounge**, a historic building magnificently reborn as a club-like dining and entertainment venue with oak paneling, high-backed tapestry chairs and antique train cars serving as dining areas. On weekends, jazz and blues bands elevate the mood. Fresh grilled seafood and prime rib highlight the menu. No lunch on weekends. ~ 27 East 5th Avenue, Eugene; 541-485-4444, fax 541-484-6149; www.oesrestaurant. com. DELUXE TO ULTRA-DELUXE.

Ambrosia prepares Italian specialties in a red-brick building distinguished by leaded glass, a mirrored oak and mahogany backbar, Tiffany-style lamps and a tintype ceiling. You'll find pizzas and calzones made with a plum tomato sauce, pasta and entrées like grilled fresh lamb and fresh seafood. There are 325 vintages on the wine list, including 30 ports. Outdoor dining is available. No lunch on Saturday and Sunday. ~ 174 East Broadway, Eugene; 541-342-4141, fax 541-345-6965. MODERATE TO DELUXE.

For pasta dishes, fresh salmon, lamb, steaks and generous salads, the Excelsior Inn and Ristorante Italiano is a good choice. Located in a Victorian near the university, this pleasing restaurant also has an excellent Oregon and Italian wine list and a generous brunch on Sunday. Ask for a table on the terrace. Open for breakfast, lunch and dinner; but no lunch on Saturday. ~ 754 East 13th Avenue, Eugene; 541-342-6963, 800-321-6963, fax 541-342-1417; www.excelsiorinn.com, e-mail info@excelsiorinn.com. MODERATE TO DELUXE.

Café Zenon, an elegant, yuppified establishment with slate   ◄ HIDDEN
floor, marble tables, white tile and outdoor seating, has an eclectic menu that changes daily. Some of the more popular items are oysters Bienville, fettuccine rustica and Tuscan roast rabbit. There are an extensive wine list and excellent desserts. Open for breakfast, lunch and dinner. ~ 898 Pearl Street, Eugene; 541-343-3005. DELUXE.

Mekala's Thai Cuisine serves authentic Thai recipes and boasts nearly 100 items, including traditional curries, noodle dishes, stir frys, soups and seafood. There is heated outdoor seating in summer only, and a full bar downstairs. ~ 1769 Franklin Avenue, Eugene; 541-342-4872. MODERATE.

Tolly's Soda Fountain is one of the most inviting lunch counters in Oregon. Located in a brick building, Tolly's is an architectural landmark with a mirrored backbar, varnished mahogany counters and stools, brass footrests and Tiffany lamps. Enjoy a soda, milkshake or banana split. Also available are breakfast potatoes and eggs, as well as Reuben sandwiches, croissants, lasagna and fresh strawberry pie. The budget-priced breakfasts and lunches are bargains; dinner brings a higher price tag. No dinner on Monday and Tuesday. ~ 115 Locust Street, Oakland; 541-459-3796, fax 541-459-1833. MODERATE TO DELUXE.

The 5th Street Public Market has an impressive collection of   **SHOPPING**
shops and galleries. ~ 296 East 5th Street, Eugene; 541-484-0383; www.5stmarket.com.

Dozens of other arts-and-crafts galleries are found in the Eugene area. Ruby Chasm sells necklaces, books, ceramics and tribal art. ~ 152 West 5th Avenue, Eugene; 541-344-4074; www.ruby chasm.com.

Eugene's **Saturday Market** is an open-air marketplace held weekly from April through November, with more than 200 vendors selling handcrafted items, from clothing and jewelry to pottery and more. There are also a farmer's market, an international food court and live music. Holiday Market is held at the Lane County Fairgrounds weekends from mid-November to Christmas Eve. ~ 8th and Oak streets, Eugene; 541-686-8885, fax 541-338-4248; www.eugenesaturdaymarket.org, e-mail info@eugene saturdaymarket.org.

If you're searching for rocks and minerals, American Indian art or books on Northwest natural history, head for the **University of Oregon Museum Store**. Open Wednesday through Sunday afternoons. ~ 1680 East 15th Avenue, Eugene; 541-346-3024.

One of the most comprehensive feminist women's bookstores in the Northwest is **Mother Kali's Books**. ~ 1849 Wilamette, Eugene; 541-762-1077; www.motherkalis.com.

NIGHTLIFE The **Hult Center for the Performing Arts** is the home of the summer Oregon Bach Festival, Oregon Mozart Players, Eugene Concert Choir, Eugene's symphony, opera and ballet, as well as visiting artists from around the world. Performances take place in Silva Hall or the smaller Soreng Theater. ~ Between 6th and 7th avenues and Willamette and Olive streets, Eugene; 541-682-5000, fax 541-682-2700; www.hultcenter.org.

Three theater companies make their home in Eugene. The **University Theater** stages full-scale productions in the Robinson Theater and smaller plays in the Arena Theater. ~ Villard Hall; 541-346-4191, fax 541-346-1978; theatre.uoregon.edu. The **Very Little Theater,** which stages five productions a year, is considered one of the best community theaters in the Eugene area. ~ 350 Hilyard Street; 541-344-7751; www.thevlt.com. The **Actors Cabaret/Mainstage Theater** presents Broadway and off-Broadway comedies, dramas and musicals. ~ 996 Willamette Street; 541-683-4368; www.actorscabaret.org.

An old standby for live reggae, rock, and folk shows is **W.O.W. Hall**, a 400-person venue and beer garden. Shows here are sponsored by the Community Center for the Performing Arts. ~ 291 West 8th Avenue, Eugene; 541-687-2746; www.wowhall.org.

Allann Brothers Coffee House hosts an array of live performances including zydeco, blues, salsa, jazz, folk and classical trios on some Friday and Saturday nights. ~ 152 West 5th Street, Eugene; 541-342-3378, 800-926-6886, fax 541-342-4255.

One of Eugene's premier brewpubs is **Steelhead Brewery & Café**, which has a handsome brick interior filled with large palms and ficus trees, marble tables and a mahogany bar. The pub offers cable sports stations, beers from the adjoining microbrewery and a casual menu. ~ 199 East 5th Avenue, Eugene; 541-686-2739, fax 541-342-5338.

Bridging the Past

Oregon takes pride in the fact that it has more covered bridges (53) than any other state west of the Mississippi. Most of these wooden spans are found in the Willamette Valley, although a handful are scattered along the coast, in the Cascades, the Ashland–Rogue River area and around Bend. Although some have been retired and now serve only pedestrians and cyclists, all these bridges are worth a special trip.

Originally the idea of covering a bridge was to protect its plank deck and trusses from the elements. But aesthetics eventually proved as important as engineering, and Oregon's beautiful hooded spans became one of the state's signature attractions.

Highly recommended is the Calapooia River's **Crawfordsville Bridge** (Route 228) east of Brownsville. Clustered around the nearby agricultural communities of Crabtree and Scio are many other "kissing bridges" such as **Shimanek**, **Larwood** and **Hannah**. To the south, Lane County is home to 18 covered bridges, all listed on the National Register of Historic Places. The Lowell area, on Route 58 southeast of Eugene, has four spans, including the **Lowell Bridge**, which crosses a river later flooded to create a lake. Other bridges are at **Pengra**, **Unity** and **Parvin**. A highlight in the Cottage Grove area is **Chambers Bridge**, the only "roofed" railroad bridge on the West Coast. In the same region, south of Dorena Reservoir, is **Dorena Bridge**. Other covered bridges in the same area are found at **Mosby Creek** and **Currin**.

Douglas County has a number of fine spans. One is **Mott Bridge**, 22 miles east of Glide. Constructed in the 1930s, this on-deck wood-truss arch bridge may be the only bridge of its type in the country. The **Rochester Bridge** (County Road 10A) west of Sutherlin is also historic. After county highway workers burned down a bridge in the late 1950s, residents feared the beloved Rochester nearby was destined for the same fate. Armed with shotguns, they kept an all-night vigil and saved the span.

Take the time to visit **Weddle Bridge** in Sweet Home. In 1987, after 43 years of service, it was damaged but, thanks to strong protests, the county wisely decided to take the bridge apart piece by piece and put it in storage. Donations and promotions raised $190,000 to reassemble the bridge, originally built in 1937 for $8500.

Great guides include *Roofs over Rivers* (Oregon Sentinel Publishing) by Bill and Nick Cockrell and *Oregon Covered Bridges: An Oregon Documentary in Pictures* (Pacific Northwest Book Company) by Bert and Margie Webber. Or contact the **Covered Bridge Society of Oregon**. ~ 503-399-0436.

For jazz, try **Jo Federigo's Café & Jazz Bar**. An intimate cellar setting with hanging plants, fans and modern art provides the background for some of the region's finest musicians. Cover Friday and Saturday. ~ 259 East 5th Avenue, Eugene; 541-343-8488; www.jofederigos.com.

The Valley River Inn's **Sweetwaters** presents live entertainment in a fireplace lounge setting on Friday and Saturday nights. On warm nights the strains of rhythm-and-blues, rock and standards drift out to the big deck overlooking the Willamette. ~ 1000 Valley River Way, Eugene; 541-341-3462, fax 541-683-5121; www.valleyriverinn.com.

PARKS   **BROWNSVILLE PIONEER PARK** 🏃 ⛵ 🛶 ⛵ The forested, 25-acre city park along the banks of the Calapooia River is a short walk from the center of a historic Willamette Valley community. There are big playfields, shady glens and a spacious picnic area with picnic tables and restrooms. ~ Take Route 5 north from Eugene 22 miles to Route 228 and continue east four miles. An alternative scenic loop heads north from Springfield via Mohawk, Marcola and Crawfordsville; 541-466-5666, fax 541-466-5118; www.ci.brownsville.or.us.

During the 1850s, when U.S. currency was scarce in the Northwest, Oregon Territory minted its own "beaver money" —$5 and $10 gold coins stamped with a beaver image.

▲ Permitted, though there are no formal sites; $10 per night for tents, $15 per night for RVs. Campgrounds are closed mid-October to mid-April.

HENDRICKS PARK AND RHODODENDRON GARDEN 🏃 🚲 A glorious springtime spot when over 3500 rhododendrons and azaleas brighten the landscape. An expansive native plant garden is also on view. The 78-acre park is shaded by Oregon white oaks and Douglas fir. There are picnic tables, restrooms, trails and occasional Sunday tours year-round (call ahead). ~ Located at the east end of Summit Avenue, Eugene; 541-682-5324, fax 541-682-6834.

▼▼▼▼▼▼▼▼▼▼
Ashland–Rogue River Area

If your vision of a good vacation is river rafting by day and Shakespeare by night, look no further. With the Klamath-Siskiyou mountains providing a rugged backdrop, this section of southern Oregon supports an array of fun activities: river rafting, downhill skiing, and, yes, the West Coast's best Shakespeare festival. Home of the largest concentration of bed and breakfasts in Oregon, Ashland is also your gateway to backcountry famous for its hidden gems.

The wild and scenic Rogue River is one of Oregon's signature attractions. It is also convenient to wilderness areas, mountain lakes, thundering waterfalls, marble caves and popular resort communities.

A good place to orient yourself is the **Grants Pass Visitors Center.** **SIGHTS**
Closed weekends from September through May. ~ 1995 Northwest
Vine Street at 6th Street, Grants Pass; 541-476-5510, fax 541-476-
9574; www.visitgrantspass.org, e-mail vcb@visitgrantspass.org.

Wildlife Images is a fascinating animal rehabilitation center. *HIDDEN*
Each year more than 1500 injured animals are nursed back to
health by veterinary staff and volunteers. Among the creatures you
can see being treated are owls, eagles, black bears and cougars.
Highly recommended. Daily tours are offered by appointment. ~
11845 Lower River Road, Grants Pass; 541-476-0222, fax 541-
476-2444; www.wildlifeimages.org, e-mail officemanager@wild
lifeimages.org.

Pottsville Powerland has a vintage collection of tractors, farm *HIDDEN*
and logging equipment, antique cars and fire trucks. A fair on
Father's Day weekend features music, food, arts and crafts. It's
five miles north of Grants Pass. ~ Pleasant Valley Road west of
Monument Drive, Pleasant Valley; 541-479-2981.

Although it's far from the core of Oregon's wine country,
Bridgeview Vineyards is attracting a loyal following. Situated on
74 acres in the Illinois Valley, this European-style winery offers tastings. Try the gewürztraminer, chardonnay, merlot, pinot gris, pinot
noir or riesling. ~ 4210 Holland Loop Road, Cave Junction; 541-
592-4688, 877-273-4843, fax 541-592-2127; www.bridgeview
wine.com, e-mail bvw@bridgeviewwine.com.

The **Oregon Caves National Monument** is the Pacific Northwest's grandest spelunking adventure. Fifty miles southwest of
Grants Pass, it's reached by taking Route 199 to Cave Junction
and then turning south on Route 46. Hourly guided tours are led
through the cave, which has over three miles of damp and drip-
ping passageways lined with stalagmites, flowstone, translucent
draperies and cave coral. Wear sturdy walking shoes that you
don't mind getting muddy and a jacket—the caves are a constant
43°F. The tour is not recommended for those with respiratory or
heart problems. To avoid the summer crowds at Oregon Caves
National Monument, arrive when the park opens at 9 a.m. If you
can't make it before 11 a.m., your best bet is to visit after 4 p.m.
for a late afternoon tour. Closed December through March. Admission. ~ 19000 Caves Highway, Cave Junction; 541-592-
2100; www.nps.gov/orca.

Southeast of Grants Pass is **Jacksonville,** a 19th-century mining
town that has clung to its legendary frontier tradition. The entire
town has been designated a National Historic Landmark with over
100 homes, stores and public buildings. Stop at the **Jacksonville
Visitor's Center and Chamber of Commerce** to pick up a walking-
tour map of the town's tree-lined streets. Closed Sunday in winter.
~ 185 North Oregon Street, Jacksonville; 541-899-8118, 800-
727-7570, fax 541-899-4462; www.jacksonvilleoregon.org, e-
mail chamber@jacksonvilleoregon.org.

Along the way you'll want to stop at the **Jacksonville Museum of Southern Oregon History**. Among the exhibits are gold-mining artifacts and a large-scale exhibit about the life of Peter Britt, pioneer photographer and Renaissance man of Jacksonville. In the same complex is the **Children's Museum**. Kids, take your parents to this former jail filled with "please touch" exhibits including a miniature kitchen and 1890s general store. Closed Monday and Tuesday, and during the month of January. ~ 206 North 5th Street, Jacksonville; 541-773-6536, fax 541-776-7994; www.sohs. org, e-mail publicrelations@sohs.org.

California Street, the heart of Jacksonville, is a step back in time. The graceful balustraded brick buildings have been lovingly restored. Worth a visit is the gothic **C. C. Beekman House**. The living history tour re-creates the lifestyle of the rich and famous, circa 1876. Along the way you see banker Beekman's carved oak bedframe, overstuffed furniture, lap desk and summer kitchen. Nearby at California and 3rd streets, visit the **Beekman Bank,** one of the first buildings in Jacksonville to be restored. Open the first weekends of the month from June to September. Admission. ~ Laurelwood and California Streets east of Beekman Square, Jacksonville; 541-773-6536, fax 541-776-7994; www. sohs.org, e-mail info@sohs.org.

Route 238 southwest of Jacksonville leads to the picturesque **Applegate Valley**, a two-mile-wide, fifty-mile-long canyon with memorable views and few tourists. After reaching the town of Applegate you can continue south on Applegate Road to the foot of the Siskiyous. Alternatively, Little Applegate and Anderson Creek roads loop back to Route 99.

Located about ten miles east of Jacksonville via Route 238, **Medford** is by far the largest city in the vicinity of Ashland and the Rogue River. A much-frequented stop in the area is **Harry and David's Original Country Village**, famous for the gift packs it ships nationwide. The store has a fruit stand, gourmet pantry and gift shop. Weekday tours of the packinghouse depart from the gift store. ~ 1314 Center Drive, Medford; 541-864-2277, 877-322-8000.

The **Medford Visitors & Convention Bureau** is an excellent source of information on southern Oregon. ~ 101 East 8th Street, Medford; 541-779-4847, fax 541-776-4808; www.visit medford.org.

The nearby **Southern Oregon Historical Society's History Center** has an extensive collection of Jackson County artifacts as well as a large photography exhibit and research library. Nonmember admission. ~ 106 North Central Avenue, Medford; 541-773-6536, fax 541-776-7994; www.sohs.org, e-mail info@sohs.org.

HIDDEN ►

Ten miles north of Medford off Route 62, **Butte Creek Mill** has been producing stone-ground products since 1872. Occasionally you may see the miller grinding wheat, rye and corn on giant white stones quarried in France, assembled in Illinois, shipped around the Horn to California and finally brought over the Siskiyous by wagon. ~ 402 Royal Avenue North, Eagle Point; 541-826-3531.

While **Ashland** is best known for the Oregon Shakespeare Festival, the play is not the only thing here. From shopping to restaurants to biking, this city offers plenty of diversions. Home to more bed and breakfasts than any other city in the state, Ashland has strict zoning controls that protect the architectural landscape.

To explore the possibilities, stop by the **Ashland Chamber of Commerce**. ~ 110 East Main Street, Ashland; 541-482-3486, fax 541-482-2350; www.ashlandchamber.com, e-mail dana@ashland chamber.com. A good place to begin your visit is the downtown plaza and verdant Lithia Park (see "Parks" below).

Across the street is the **Oregon Shakespeare Festival** and the fascinating **Backstage Theatre Tour**. This excellent behind-the-scenes program is a helpful introduction to stagecraft and the history of the OSF. Members of the theater company guide you through this 90-minute look at the dramatic arts. Closed November to mid-February. Admission. ~ 15 South Pioneer Street, Ashland; 541-482-4331, fax 541-482-8045; www.osfashland.org.

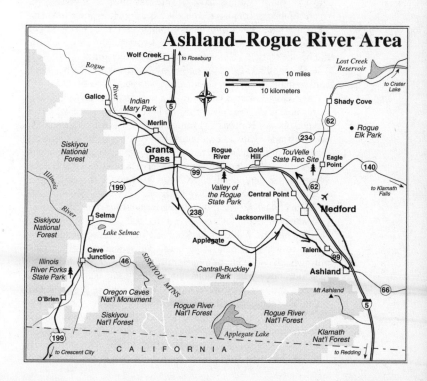

Ashland–Rogue River Area

Most people come to Ashland for the plays, but the mountain lakes east of town are a tempting day trip. Take Route 5 north and pick up Route 140 east to Dead Indian Road. Turn south to the first and most picturesque of these retreats, **Lake of the Woods**, an ideal place for a picnic, swimming or sunbathing. Continue southeast to **Howard Prairie Reservoir** and **Hyatt Reservoir**, both popular for water sports and fishing. Return to Dead Indian Road for the cliffhanging descent back into Ashland, an entrance that rivals anything you're likely to see on the Elizabethan stage.

LODGING

An 1880s stage stop, **Wolf Creek Inn** now operates as a state historic property. The handsomely restored inn offers nine guest rooms with private baths. You'll find antiques, old photographs and brass beds in the medium-sized rooms. There's an on-site restaurant, and full breakfast is included in your stay. You can also see the room where Jack London stayed on his visit here. Closed Monday and Tuesday from October to May. ~ 100 Front Street, Wolf Creek; 541-866-2474, fax 541-866-2692; www.thewolf creekinn.com, e-mail wolfcreek.info@state.or.us. MODERATE.

The **Riverside Inn** is the largest motel in town with an enviable location on the Rogue River across from Riverside Park. Most of the 63 rooms have private balconies overlooking the river; some have fireplaces. There is a beauty salon and a full-service conference center, plus a swimming pool and spa. A Rogue jet-boat dock is next door, and there is some highway noise from the bridge traffic. ~ 986 Southwest 6th Street, Grants Pass; 541-476-6873, 800-334-4567, fax 541-474-9848; www.riverside-inn. com, e-mail info@riverside-inn.com. MODERATE TO DELUXE.

The **Oregon Caves Chateau**, in a wooded glen surrounded by waterfalls, is an ideal place to spend the night after a visit to the Oregon Caves National Monument. Faced with cedar shakes, this National Historic Landmark has two big marble fireplaces framed with fir timbers in the lobby. Moderate-sized rooms with 1930s furnishings and Pendleton bedspreads offer forest and pond views in this serene setting. Closed November through April. ~ 20000 Caves Highway, Cave Junction; 541-592-3400, 877-245-9022, fax 541-592-5021; www.oregoncavesoutfitters.com, e-mail caves@cavenet.com. MODERATE TO DELUXE.

The historic red-brick **Jacksonville Inn** offers eight nicely restored rooms with oak-frame beds, quilts, wall-to-wall carpets, antiques, gas-style lamps and floral-print wallpaper. The inn also has four honeymoon cottages, featuring king beds, fireplaces, jacuzzis and steam showers, located on a separate property. Full breakfast included. ~ 175 East California Street, Jacksonville; 541-899-1900, 800-321-9344, fax 541-899-1373; www.jackson villeinn.com, e-mail jvinn@mind.net. DELUXE TO ULTRA-DELUXE.

Convenient to downtown Jacksonville, the **McCully House Inn** is a charming 19th-century home where a grandfather clock sounds the hour and guests sip wine around the fireplace. This immaculate white house has hardwood floors, painted friezes on the walls and three rooms big on lace, walnut furniture and clawfoot tubs. The adjacent restaurant serves breakfast to all guests. ~ 240 East California Street, Jacksonville; 541-899-1942, 800-367-1942, fax 541-899-1560; www.jacksonvillecountryhouseinns.com, e-mail ryan@countryhouseinns.com. DELUXE.

Take an 1862 country estate, complete with a three-story barn, add a redwood deck, an English garden with 140 rose bushes and an orchard with hammocks and what do you get? **Under the Greenwood Tree Bed and Breakfast Inn.** Overfurnished with Persian rugs, Chippendale and chintz, this is the place for travelers who want to wind down with a full afternoon tea and pluck a truffle off their freshly ironed pillow before climbing into bed. Five rooms have queen beds and private baths. A regional three-course, farm-fresh breakfast prepared by a Cordon Bleu chef is included. ~ 3045 Bellinger Lane, Medford; 541-776-0000; www.greenwoodtree.com, e-mail utgtree@quest.net. DELUXE.

◀ HIDDEN

Tour the world at the **Ashland Creek Inn**, where you can "visit" New Mexico, Marrakesh or Japan, depending on which internationally themed suite you choose. All nine suites include private entrances, baths, kitchenettes and decks. Full breakfast included. ~ 70 Water Street, Ashland; 541-482-3315; www.ashlandcreekinn.com, e-mail reservations@ashlandcreekinn.com. ULTRA-DELUXE.

Reached via a redwood staircase, the **Columbia Hotel** is a comfortable European-style inn. Rooms are furnished with brass beds, floral-print drapes, fans and wall-to-wall carpet. Some provide views of downtown and the surrounding mountains. Guests share a bathroom; suites with private baths are available ~ 262½ East Main Street, Ashland; 541-482-3726, 800-718-2530; www.columbiahotel.com. MODERATE.

AUTHOR FAVORITE

Choose one of the Bard's works from the library and wander out to the lush gardens that surround the **Arden Forest Inn**. Nestle into a secluded spot and catch up on the play you're about to see at the Shakespeare Festival. The inn also has fine views of Mt. Ashland and Grizzly Peak. Two rooms in the main house and three in the carriage house feature tasteful, comfortable furnishings; some have mountain or garden views, others have private patios. The two-course gourmet breakfast is a delight. Gay-owned and gay-friendly. ~ 261 West Hersey Street, Ashland; 541-488-1496, 800-460-3912, fax 541-488-4071; www.afinn.com, e-mail aforest@afinn.com. DELUXE TO ULTRA-DELUXE.

The **Windmill Inn of Ashland** has 230 affordable and charming rooms with the amenities of a city hotel. Tennis courts, a heated outdoor pool and spa, and a fitness room on 14 acres add to the comfort of this country inn. ~ 2525 Ashland Street, Ashland; 541-482-8310, 800-547-4747, fax 541-488-1783; www.windmillinns. com. DELUXE.

Cedarwood Inn of Ashland is one of several modern motels found south of downtown. Choose between rooms with queens and courtyard family units with kitchens and decks. All 64 rooms have contemporary oak furniture. Pools, saunas and barbecue facilities are available. ~ 1801 Siskiyou Boulevard, Ashland; 541-488-2000, 800-547-4141, fax 541-482-2000; www.brodeur-inns. com/cedarwood. MODERATE TO DELUXE.

For information on Ashland bed and breakfasts, and other inns across Oregon, check out **The Oregon Bed and Breakfast Guild**. ~ www.obbg.org. You may also contact **Ashland's Bed and Breakfast Network**. ~ 800-944-0329; www.abbnet.com.

DINING

Clam chowder is the staple at **The Laughing Clam**. Stop by for lunch or dinner and choose from sandwiches, large salads, fresh seafood and pasta (including the Seafood Mama—shrimp, scallops and clams in a cream sauce over lemon linguine), and steak. ~ 121 Southwest G Street, Grants Pass; 541-479-1110. MODERATE TO DELUXE.

Traversing a stream, the **Oregon Caves Chateau Restaurant** offers steaks, seafood, chicken and pasta dishes for dinner in the deluxe-priced formal dining room. There's also a 1930s-style budget-priced soda fountain. Scores of patrons seated on red stools enjoy sundaes, omelettes, french toast, salads, deli sandwiches and hamburgers. Don't miss this knotty-pine-paneled classic. Closed November through April. ~ 20000 Caves Highway, Cave Junction; 541-592-3400; www.oregoncavesoutfitters.com, e-mail caves@cavenet.com. MODERATE TO ULTRA-DELUXE.

AUTHOR FAVORITE

On a warm evening, the garden patio at the **Winchester Country Inn** is an ideal place to enjoy a rich, leisurely meal. Temptations here include Teng Dah beef, duck medallions, seafood cioppino, seasonal fish and lamb *du jour*. For dessert, try the award-winning bread pudding. This opulent Victorian, surrounded by a colorful garden, also has gazebo seating and a dining room decorated in burgundy tones with accents of blue. Dinner and Sunday brunch. ~ 35 South 2nd Street, Ashland; 541-488-1113, 800-972-4991; www.winchesterinn.com, e-mail ashlandinn@ aol.com. DELUXE.

The **Jacksonville Inn** serves breakfast, lunch, dinner and Sunday brunch in the restored 19th-century Ryan and Morgan general-store building. The dimly lit, brick-walled dining room with red carpets and tablecloths creates a great setting for vast, seven-course dinners or à la carte dishes. A large menu features Oregon cuisine, including razor clams, scallops, prime rib and vegetarian dishes. The wine list is endless. Open for Sunday brunch. No lunch on Monday. ~ 175 East California Street, Jacksonville; 541-899-1900; www.jacksonvilleinn.com, e-mail jvinn@mind. net. DELUXE TO ULTRA-DELUXE.

For patio dining, it's hard to beat the **McCully House Inn**. Entrées served outside or in one of the lovely dining rooms include mango-glazed salmon, tequila lime prawns and whiskey-peppered New York steak. You'll find Oregon wildflowers on every table. ~ 240 East California Street, Jacksonville; 541-899-1942, fax 541-899-1560; www.jacksonvillecountryhouseinns.com, e-mail ryan@ countryhouseinns.com. MODERATE TO ULTRA-DELUXE.

Phoenix-like, the **Bella Union** has risen from the ashes of one of Jacksonville's best-loved 19th-century saloons. Like its predecessor, this establishment is an important social center. On the menu you'll find pizza, seafood, pasta and sandwiches. You have your choice of several noisy dining rooms or the more serene heated patio out back. Open for Sunday brunch. ~ 170 West California Street, Jacksonville; 541-899-1770, fax 541-899-3919; www.bellau.com, e-mail greatfood@bellau.com. MODERATE TO DELUXE.

Whether you choose a seat at the counter or one of the glass-paneled booths, you'll find the country-casual **Geppetto's** a comfortable place to enjoy Italian and Ashland cuisine like linguine, five-spice chicken, steak, prawns and snapper. Try the fresh fruit pies. Breakfast, lunch and dinner. ~ 345 East Main Street, Ashland; 541-482-1138; www.geppettosrestaurant.com, e-mail dan@ ashlanddirectory.net. MODERATE TO DELUXE.

Looking for Asian cuisine served at a creekside setting? Consider **Thai Pepper**. Step into the romantic gray-walled dining room, take a seat on the wicker furniture and order such dishes as green chicken curry, yellow shrimp curry and crispy fish served with cold Singha beer. But your best bet, especially on a warm evening, is a seat on the shady patio next to the creek. Dinner only in winter. ~ 84 North Main Street, Ashland; 541-482-8058. BUDGET TO MODERATE.

A French bistro with stained-glass windows and dark wood-booths illuminated by Tiffany-style lamps, **Chatêaulin Restaurant** prepares such dishes as *crêpe Mediterranées*, pan-roasted duck breast and filet mignon *au poivre verte*. Dinner only. Closed Monday from October through June. ~ 50 East Main Street, Ashland;

541-482-2264; www.chateaulin.com, e-mail doss@chateaulin.com. DELUXE TO ULTRA-DELUXE.

Alex's Plaza Restaurant has a good house pizza with your choice of two toppings. Also on the menu are a vegetarian pasta with portobello mushrooms, seafood stew, New York steak and rack of lamb. Located in the first brick building built following the disastrous 1879 downtown fire, this second-story dining room still has its original fir floors. It's flanked by patios. No lunch on Monday. ~ 35 North Main Street, Ashland; 541-482-8818; www.alexsrestaurant.net, e-mail alexs@mind.net. MODERATE TO DELUXE.

Mediterranean, Italian and vegetarian fare served in a creekside setting make the **Greenleaf Restaurant** worth a visit. Specialties may include breakfast dishes like mushroom frittatas and tofu scrambles. For lunch or dinner, try pasta primavera, fruit salad or red snapper. An excellent choice for to-go fare, they will also prepare picnic baskets. Closed the month of January. ~ 49 North Main Street, Ashland; 541-482-2808; www.greenleaf restaurant.com, e-mail daniel@greenleafrestaurant.com. BUDGET TO MODERATE.

Brother's Restaurant and Delicatessen has an eclectic menu including shrimp omelettes, *huevos rancheros*, bagels and lox, and caesar and Greek salads. There's also a variety of vegetarian options. The carpeted, wood-paneled dining room with indoor balcony seating puts Brother's a cut above your average deli. Breakfast and lunch only. ~ 95 North Main Street, Ashland; 541-482-9671. BUDGET TO MODERATE.

SHOPPING

HIDDEN ►

Fifteen miles northwest of Grants Pass is **Windy River Farms**, which has organic teas and culinary and medicinal herbs. ~ 348 Hussey Lane, Grants Pass; 541-476-8979.

Thread Hysteria stocks new name-brand clothing and accessories at discount prices. ~ 19 North Main Street, Ashland; 541-488-3982.

As befits a town dedicated to Shakespeare, Ashland's Main Street is lined with bookstores, including **Bloomsbury Books**, which is a good source for regional books and newspapers. Coffee and espresso drinks are served in an upstairs café. ~ 290 East Main Street, Ashland; 541-488-0029, fax 541-488-2942.

Tudor Guild Gift Shop, adjacent to the Elizabethan Theatre, sells all the Bard's works, as well as Oregon Shakespeare Festival merchandise, gifts, educational books, jewelry and toys with a dramatic flair. Closed Sunday from November through March. ~ 15 South Pioneer Street, Ashland; 541-482-0940, fax 541-488-4708; www.tudorguild.org, e-mail tudorguild@tudorguild.org.

The Northwest Nature Shop is a wonderful place to shop for birdhouses, minerals, wind chimes, hiking maps and nature and travel books. In a Craftsman-style house near downtown, this shop has a good selection of nature-oriented children's games. ~ 154 Oak Street, Ashland; 541-482-3241.

Britt Festivals offers classical, jazz, folk, dance, blues, bluegrass, world, pop and country music performances from mid-June to mid-September. Headliners such as Jewel, Brad Paisley and B.B. King make this event a worthy companion to the nearby Oregon Shakespeare Festival. At this outdoor theater, you can choose between lawn and reserved seating in the natural setting of the historic Britt estate. ~ Britt Pavilion, Jacksonville; 541-773-6077, 800-882-7488; www.brittfest.org, e-mail info@brittfest.org.

NIGHTLIFE

Ashland is heavily booked during the Shakespeare season (mid-February to late October) when street vendors are out in force selling espresso.

The Oregon Shakespeare Festival is the nation's oldest and largest regional repertory theater, attracting more than 120,000 people each season. The most popular venue is the **Elizabethan Theatre**, which stages plays from June through October. The indoor **Angus Bowmer Theatre** also presents Shakespearian performances, as well as classics by Shaw and Wilder and contemporary playwrights. Both new and classic works are presented at the **New Theatre**. The season runs from mid-February to late October. Advance reservations are strongly recommended in peak season. ~ 15 South Pioneer Street, Ashland; 541-482-4331, 800-219-8161, fax 541-482-8045; www.osfashland.org.

The **Oregon Cabaret Theatre** holds professional productions including musicals, revues and comedies in a renovated church with table seating on the tiered main floor and in the balcony. Dinner theater also available. ~ 1st and Hargadine streets, Ashland; 541-488-2902, fax 541-488-8795; www.oregoncabaret.com.

Jefferson State Pub features a deck overlooking Lithia Creek, 15 brews on tap and live entertainment. Bands of all kinds play on various nights. Occasional cover. ~ 31-B Water Street, Ashland; 541-482-7718.

VALLEY OF THE ROGUE STATE PARK 🏃 🚵 ⚓ 🚤 🛥 🛶

PARKS

This 316-acre park on the Rogue River is convenient to the Grants Pass Area. Near the interstate, it's central to many rafting operators. Trout, steelhead and chinook salmon are caught in the Rogue River. The grassy, mile-long riverfront park is shaded by madrone, black locust and oak. Facilities include picnic areas and restrooms. ~ Off Route 5, 12 miles east of Grants Pass; 541-582-1118, fax 541-582-1312.

▲ There are 21 tent sites ($16 per night), 147 RV hookup sites ($16 to $20 per night) and 6 yurts ($27 per night). Showers are available. Reservations: 800-452-5687.

BEN HUR LAMPMAN WAYSIDE On the south bank of the Rogue River opposite Gold Hill, the 23-acre wayside park is named for the late Ben Hur Lampman, a popular Oregon newspaper editor, fisherman and poet laureate. Emulate his fishing prowess by angling for trout and steelhead in the Rogue. Day-use only. ~ Off Route 5, 16 miles east of Grants Pass; 541-582-1118, fax 541-582-1312.

INDIAN MARY PARK This half-mile-long park on the Rogue River west of Merlin is another ideal retreat for the entire family. Kids can play on the sandy beach or enjoy themselves at the playground. If you're towing a boat or raft, you can launch it here. You can also fish from the beach. You'll find picnic areas, restrooms, playgrounds and a sand volleyball court. ~ From Grants Pass take Route 5 north to the Merlin exit. Continue west ten miles on Merlin-Galice Road; 541-474-5285, fax 541-474-5280.

▲ There are 36 tent sites ($17 per night), 56 RV hookup sites ($20 per night) and 2 yurts ($28 per night). Reservations: 800-452-5687; www.reserveamerica.com.

Prior to evening shows at the Elizabethan, the Green Show Renaissance Musicians and Dancers offer free half-hour performances in the Oregon Shakespeare courtyard.

LAKE SELMAC A large Illinois Valley lake convenient to the Grants Pass area, this is a popular summer resort. The 160-acre lake near Selma is a good choice for fishing (trout, bass and crappie), canoeing and sailing. The waters here tend to be warmer than the nearby rivers. Facilities include a playground, picnic area, day-use park, disc golf course and horse corrals. ~ Located 2.3 miles east of Selma via Upper Deer Creek Road; 541-474-5285, fax 541-474-5280.

▲ There are 53 tent sites ($17 per night), 35 RV hookup sites ($20 per night) and 1 yurt ($28 per night). Reservations: 800-452-5687; www.reserveamerica.com.

ILLINOIS RIVER FORKS STATE PARK The largely undeveloped 511-acre day-use park at the junction of the east and west forks of the Illinois River is a secluded spot perfect for trout and steelhead fishing and birdlife and wildlife viewing. You'll find picnic tables and restrooms. ~ Route 199, one mile south of Cave Junction; 541-582-1118, 800-551-6949, fax 541-582-1312.

▲ Permitted in nearby U.S. Forest Service campgrounds in the Illinois Valley. Among them are Grayback and Cave Creek campgrounds (541-592-4440), respectively 12 and 16 miles east of Cave Junction on Oregon Caves Highway. Grayback has 39 tent sites ($10 per night); Cave Creek has 18 tent sites ($10 per night).

TOUVELLE STATE RECREATION SITE The 54-acre day-use facility is adjacent to Table Rock, an 1890-acre biologic, geologic and historic preserve forested with Pacific madrone, white oak and ponderosa pine. In the park you can swim or fish for salmon and trout. Facilities include picnic tables, restrooms and wildlife viewing platforms. Parking fee, $3. ~ Take Route 62 nine miles north of Medford to Table Rock Road; 541-582-1118, 800-551-6949, fax 541-582-1312.

CANTRALL-BUCKLEY PARK 🏃 ⛵ ⛴ Just eight miles southwest of Jacksonville on a wooded hillside above the Applegate Valley, Cantrall-Buckley extends half a mile along the inviting Applegate River and offers beautiful views of this farming region. Swimmers head to the small cove, while anglers try for trout in the river. There are picnic areas, barbecue pits, showers and restrooms. Parking fee, $3. ~ Take Route 238 eight miles southwest from Jacksonville and turn left on Hamilton Road; 541-774-8183, fax 541-774-6320.

▲ There are 30 primitive sites ($10 per night).

ROGUE ELK PARK ⛵ ⛴ 🚣 ⛴ The nearly mile-long park on the Rogue includes a warm creek ideal for swimming, and the kids can swing out into the river Tarzan-style on a rope hanging from an oak limb. There's good rafting and fishing (steelhead and trout) in the Rogue. Shade trees make this park a good choice on warm days, and an ideal stopover en route to Crater Lake. You'll find picnic tables, restrooms and showers. Day-use fee, $3. ~ Route 62, eight miles north of Shady Cove; 541-776-7001, fax 541-774-6320; e-mail parksinfo@jacksoncounty.org.

▲ There are 22 tent sites ($16 per night) and 15 RV hookup sites ($18 per night). Closed mid-October to mid-April.

LITHIA PARK 🏃 ⛵ A beautiful place to walk or jog, Lithia Park was originally designed by John McLaren, the creator of Golden Gate Park in San Francisco. This 93-acre urban forest is filled with towering maples, black oaks, sycamore, sequoia, bamboo, European beech and flowering catalpa. Also here are a Japanese garden, rose garden and two duck ponds. Facilities include picnic tables, fire pits, a playground, a tennis court, a swimming hole, a band shell, a fountain and restrooms. ~ On the south side of the Ashland Plaza in Ashland; 541-488-5340, 800-735-2900, fax 541-488-5314; www.ashland.or.us.

Outdoor Adventures

FISHING

In a Northwest wonderland of sparkling lakes, rivers and mountain streams, it's no surprise that fishing is such a part of the scene. Even novice anglers should try casting a line; they're bound to catch something: fall salmon from coastal rivers and streams in October and November; winter steelhead, from December through March. Spring and summer bring trout (try Detroit Lake, or the McKenzie River for huge rainbow trout) and summer steelhead (the North and South Santiam rivers are the best spots).

SALEM AREA   Bill Kremers arranges daily fishing trips on the west side of the Cascades, longer excursions on the Deschutes River. ~ 29606 Northeast Pheasant Street, Corvallis; 541-754-6411; www.oregonrivertrails.com. White Water Warehouse runs camping and rafting trips on the Rogue River from May to September; all levels of expertise are welcome. ~ 625 Northwest Starker Avenue, Corvallis; 541-758-3150, 800-214-0579; www. whitewaterwarehouse.com, e-mail fun@whitewaterwarehouse.com.

EUGENE RIVER AREA   Wilderness River Outfitters runs one-day and overnight fishing trips locally on the Willamette, Umpqua and McKenzie rivers and throughout Oregon. They also have a fly-fishing school, offering a four-day course on the river. ~ 1567 Main Street, Springfield; 541-726-9471, fax 541-726-6474.

ASHLAND–ROGUE RIVER AREA   For salmon and steelhead fishing, contact Rogue Wilderness Adventures, which has specialized in drift-boat fishing since 1975. Trips of one to four days can be arranged. ~ 325 Galice Road, Merlin; 541-479-9554, 800-336-1647; www.wildrogue.com. For a day trip to fish for salmon and steelhead on the Chetco near Brookings, or in the Rogue estuary at Gold Beach, contact Briggs Guide Service. ~ 1815 Southwest Bridge Street, Grants Pass; 800-845-5091.

RIVER RUNNING   A rafting or kayaking adventure can take you from the wild and scenic whitewater ruggedness of the Rogue River (where some of the rapids are Class III and IV) to an outing on the more gentle Willamette River or one of the local lakes. With dozens of rivers in the foothills surrounding Salem, Eugene and Ashland, you're never far from an enjoyable stretch of river. The North Santiam River near Salem is popular for both its rapids and views of the surrounding woods, while the McKenzie and Willamette near Salem lean more toward the serene than the adventurous. But by far the most popular area is around Ashland. Here the Rogue River offers everything from casual floats to spectacular rapids, like those in Hellgate Canyon.

One of the best regional resources for outdoor adventurers interested in fishing, hunting and rafting is the Oregon Guides & Packers Association in Eugene. The group publishes an extensive directory of guides and outfitters throughout the state. ~ 800-747-9552; www.ogpa.org.

SALEM AREA   White Water Warehouse can set you up with hardshell kayaks, sea kayaks, canoes and rafts. Instruction in whitewater kayaking is also available. The company also runs overnight camp and float trips locally on the Rogue River from May to September. ~ 625 Northwest Starker Avenue, Corvallis; 541-758-3150, 800-214-0579; www.whitewaterwarehouse.com.

EUGENE AREA Wilderness **River Outfitters** runs a moonlit evening float along serene stretches of the Willamette. ~ 1567 Main Street, Springfield; 541-726-9471.

ASHLAND–ROGUE RIVER AREA Whether you paddle your own kayak or float with a guide, rafting is the ideal way to see the Rogue's wild and scenic sections. Choose between one-day trips and overnight trips. **Orange Torpedo Trips Inc./**

Grants Pass Float Co. specializes in inflatable kayaking, with one-day and multiday whitewater trips on the Rogue, Klamath, Salmon and North Umpqua rivers. ~ 209 Merlin Road, Merlin; 541-479-5061; www.orangetorpedo.com. **Rogue Wilderness Adventures** can set you up for a one-day, 13-mile scenic adventure in an inflatable kayak or an oar or paddle raft, and also arrange longer wilderness trips on the Rogue. ~ 325 Galice Road, Merlin; 541-479-9554, 800-336-1647; www.wildrogue.com. For a full- or half-day whitewater adventure led by a naturalist along the middle Rogue (water ratings range from Class I to IV) or the upper Klamath in a six-person paddleboat, contact **The Adventure Center**. Multiday rafting and camping trips are also available on seven rivers. Food, lodging and gear are included. ~ 40 North Main Street, Ashland; 541-488-2819; www.raftingtours.com.

> Kayakers should look for a copy of the book *Soggy Sneakers*, a regional guide to kayaking published by the Willamette Kayak and Canoe Club.

Hellgate Jetboat Excursions will take you through the Rogue River's rugged Hellgate Canyon wilderness on one of several jetboat tours it operates. They also offer dinner and brunch trips. Closed Sunday. ~ 966 Southwest 6th Street, Grants Pass; 541-479-7204, 800-648-4874; www.hellgate.com, e-mail info@hellgate.com.

ASHLAND–ROGUE RIVER AREA Although most of the Heart of Oregon lies in a valley between the Cascades and the Coast Range, the southern section of the Route 5 corridor passes through the Klamath-Siskiyou Mountains. Skiers in that area head for **Mt. Ashland**. At 7500 feet, it's the highest peak in the range and just 18 miles south of Ashland off Route 5. Facilities include a day lodge, rental shop, four lifts and 23 runs. You'll also find ungroomed cross-country trails here. ~ Route 5, Exit 6; 541-482-2897; www.mtashland.com.

SKIING

SALEM AREA The quiet exhilaration of floating above it all—wine country, the river, rolling farmland—explains why ballooning is popular in the Salem area. From April to November, **Vista Balloon Adventures** operates one-hour flights over the wine country of Newburg (about 25 minutes north of Salem), followed by a catered breakfast. The company has seven balloons and can fly

BALLOON RIDES

six to ten passengers in each. If you're the participatory type, you can put on some gloves and help inflate the balloon. Closed Tuesday. ~ Sherwood; 503-625-7385, 800-622-2309; www.vista balloon.com, e-mail roger@vistaballoon.com.

RIDING STABLES

Along the western slopes of the Cascades, within a 30-mile drive of the Willamette Valley, lie some of the most pristine wilderness areas in the state, much of them U.S. Forest Service land. One of the best ways to explore these alpine meadows, old-growth forests and scenic mountain peaks is on a guided day-long or multiday trail ride from a local outfitter. Even if you only have a couple of hours, Mt. Pisgah just outside Eugene provides a good opportunity for a casual ride.

The Rogue River's Hellgate Canyon—where sheer rock walls rise 250 feet—was the setting for the Meryl Streep film *The River Wild*.

EUGENE AREA Three Sisters Wilderness, just east of Eugene in Willamette National Forest, takes its name from the North, Middle and South Sisters, three 10,000-foot-plus peaks that define the area. **Smart Ass Ranch** offers year-round trail rides in this wilderness area. Hunting, fishing and pack trips are also available. ~ Redmond; 541-280-9356; www.smartassranch.com.

GOLF

Public courses in the area offer a variety of landscapes, course lengths, and difficulty ratings.

SALEM AREA Built in 1928, **Salem Golf Club** is a lush, old-style Northwest course: 18 holes with meandering greens and big old fir trees. ~ 2025 Golf Course Road South, Salem; 503-363-6652. Near Stayton, the 18-hole **Santiam Golf Course** has lots of water and trees and is fairly flat. ~ 8724 Golf Club Road, Aumsville; 503-769-3485.

EUGENE AREA The relatively flat 18-hole **Fiddler's Green** is famous for its pro shop. ~ 91292 Route 99 North, Eugene; 541-689-8464; www.fiddlersgreen.com. The circa-1920 nine-hole **Hidden Valley Golf Course** is tucked away in a picturesque little valley and lined with mature fir and oak trees. ~ 775 North River Road, Cottage Grove; 541-942-3046.

ASHLAND–ROGUE RIVER AREA Oak Knoll Golf Course's nine holes are regulation length and set on gently rolling greens. ~ 3070 Route 66, Ashland; 541-482-4311. The 18-hole, par-70 **Cedar Links Golf Course** is 6000 yards but an easy walk for the most part. ~ 3155 Cedar Links Drive, Medford; 541-773-4373.

TENNIS

SALEM AREA The Salem Parks and Recreation Department operates free courts in the capital. At **Bush's Pasture Park** (Mission and High streets) there are four lighted courts; **Highland School Park** (Broadway and Highland Avenue Northeast) has two lighted courts; and there are four lighted courts at **Orchard Heights** (Orchard Heights Street and Parkway Drive). Courts are also available at **Hoover School/Park** (1104 Savage Road Northeast) and **Woodmansee Park** (4629 Sunnyside Road Southeast). ~ 503-588-6261, fax 503-588-6305; www.cityofsalem.net/~parks.

EUGENE AREA Eugene Parks and Recreation operates two lighted courts at **Washington Park** (2025 Washington Street) and four lighted courts at each of the following locations: **Churchill Courts** (1850 Bailey Hill Road), **Amazon Courts** (Amazon Parkway and 24th Avenue), **Sheldon Courts** (2445 Willakenzie Road), **Echo Hollow Courts** (501 Echo Hollow Road) and **West Mooreland Courts** (20th and Polk streets). ~ 541-682-4800.

For $20 per court (one hour), indoor courts are available to nonmembers at **Willow Creek Racquet Club.** ~ 4201 West 13th Avenue, Eugene; 541-484-7451.

ASHLAND–ROGUE RIVER AREA The Medford Parks Department operates four unlighted courts at **Fichtner Mainwaring Park** (Stewart Avenue and Holly Street), four lighted courts at **Bear Creek Park** (Siskiyou Boulevard and Highland Drive), ten courts (five lighted) at **North Medford High School** (Keene Way Drive and Crater Lake Road), and two unlighted courts at **Holmes Park** (185 South Modoc Avenue). ~ 541-774-2400.

BIKING

For recreational bicyclers, there are hundreds of miles of relatively flat, scenic bike trails that parallel beautiful rivers, parks and lakes throughout the valley. Experienced, active riders will enjoy the more challenging mountain trails or some of the longer loops in and around the region.

SALEM AREA The **Oregon Trans-America Trail** from the Dallas area near Salem heads south through the scenic wine country to Corvallis. Four miles of bike trails traverse **Willamette Mission State Park** (503-393-1172), which is surrounded by orchards and farm fields. **Silver Falls State Park** (503-873-8681), with its waterfalls and gorges carved out of lava, has a popular four-mile paved bike trail. There is also a 27-mile perimeter trail. East of the city, there are trails "all over **Lyons and Detroit lakes**," according to one local enthusiast.

Near Corvallis, Oregon State University has its own gated research forest called **McDonald Forest** (541-737-4434). It's a hilly tract, but not steep, and its 12-mile trail system is very popular. From the top of Dimple Hill, which gains 800 feet in about four miles, you'll get a good view of the surrounding area. The university maintains several trails and outlines them in a map available at bike shops.

Bike trails can be found in state parks throughout the area, including **Holman** (four miles west of Salem).

The **Salem Bicycle Club** publishes a monthly newsletter that includes a two- or three-page "Ride Sheet," which lists club-sponsored rides and is usually posted in bike shops around town. Club rides vary from beginner (15 to 20 miles) to expert (100-mile loops to the coast). Weekend rides are held year-round; in the summer, evening and overnight rides are held during the week. ~ P.O. Box 2224, Salem, OR 97308; www.salembicycleclub.org.

EUGENE AREA Eugene is one of the nation's top biking cities: more than 8500 people commute to school and work on bikes, and there are 200 miles of bike paths. All this in a city with a population of only 120,000.

Eugene's **Willamette River Recreation Corridor** offers five bridges that connect the north and south bank bike trails. The flat 15-mile loop from Knickerbocker Bridge to Owosso Bridge takes you through or past parks and rose gardens, shops and restaurants in downtown Eugene, and the University of Oregon campus.

Eight miles south of Eugene, the **Fox Swale Area** has eight miles of off-road trails ideal for mountain biking. Ride the Fox Hollow Road nine and a half miles over the summit and down into the valley to BLM Road 19-4-4. *Note:* The area gets muddy during the rainy season. Be sure to stay off private property in this area.

ASHLAND–ROGUE RIVER AREA From the town of Rogue River, east of Grants Pass on Route 5, head north eight miles along Evans Creek to Wimer and the glorious **Evans Valley**. It's a scenic, relatively easy four-mile ride out Pleasant Creek Road to the covered bridge. Look for elk in the meadows alongside the road.

If you'd like to join an escorted downhill bike tour on Mt. Ashland, contact **The Adventure Center**. Beside bike rentals (and insider tips about the more pleasant route past small rural farms and ranches for a two-hour loop to Emigrant Lake), this outfitter offers several different off-road bike tours, all guided, with extras like picnic brunch. ~ 40 North Main Street, Ashland; 541-488-2819, 800-444-2899, fax 541-482-5139; www.rafting tours.com.

AUTHOR FAVORITE

The best part about ascending **Mary's Peak**, about 15 miles south of Corvallis, is that you can cheat. The summit rises over 4000 feet—it's the highest in the Coast Range—but you can drive to a parking lot about three miles from the top. From there you can bike along the pavement to the summit, from which you'll get great views of the ocean and mountains to the east. When you're ready to descend, you can can follow one of several trails down.

Bike Rentals Bike rentals in Salem are hard to come by. Try **South Salem Cycleworks** for tandem, hybrid and road bikes. ~ 4071 Liberty Road South, Salem; 503-399-9848.

Pick up mountain and cruise bikes at **Peak Sports**, the only rental shop in the city. The shop also still has a few three-speeds, which are perfect for an easy afternoon ride around town. ~ 129 Northwest 2nd Street, Corvallis; 541-754-6444.

Eugene Mountain Bicycle Resources Group publishes *Mountain Bike Ride Guide*, available at bike shops in the Eugene area. Of the more than 14 bike shops in Eugene, there are only two places to rent. **Hutch's** rents out city bikes and is attached to the Rack and Roll sales/repair shop. ~ 960 Charnelton Street, Eugene; 541-345-7521. **Blue Heron Bicycles** rents mountain and hybrid bikes in the spring and summer. ~ 877 East 13th Avenue, Eugene; 541-343-2488.

Hiking does not necessarily mean huffing and puffing up steep mountain slopes. Several of the hikes mentioned here may be more aptly described as "walks." In any event, a hike or a walk along the river or through a park is a great way to get some exercise and to get to know the area. All distances listed for hiking trails are one way unless otherwise noted.

HIKING

SALEM AREA Riverfront Loop Trail (4 miles) in Willamette Mission State Park offers a secluded stretch of river.

The Ten Falls Loop Trail (7 miles) at Silver Falls State Park reaches all ten waterfalls along Silver Creek Canyon. Shorter hikes (less than 2.5 miles) can also be taken from roadside trailheads to the individual falls.

Salem's **Rita Steiner Fry Nature Trail** (.3 mile) offers a pleasant stroll through Deepwood Park, adjacent to the historic Deepwood Estate.

On River Road South, a mile south of downtown, **Minto-Brown Island Park** has around 15 miles of trails and paths.

EUGENE AREA Convenient to Eugene, the **Fall Creek National Recreation Trail** (13.7 miles) is ideal for day hikes and overnight trips in the hardwood and conifer Willamette National Forest. Pristine Fall Creek is visible from most of the trail, which begins south of the Dolly Varden Campground.

◄ *HIDDEN*

Eugene's **Mount Pisgah Arboretum** has more than seven miles of hiking trails. You can enjoy a lovely walk through oak savanna, a Douglas fir forest or along a seasonal marsh.

Pre's Trail is a Eugene memorial to legendary Oregon runner Steve Prefontaine. This all-weather trail through the woods and fields of Alton Baker Park offers parcourse-style routes ranging from .5 to 1.5 miles.

The **Kentucky Falls Recreation Trail** (8.5 miles) runs along Kentucky Creek through a forest of Douglas fir and western hem-

◄ *HIDDEN*

lock. Located 41 miles southwest of Eugene, it leads down 760
feet to the twin falls viewpoint.

ASHLAND–ROGUE RIVER AREA More than 30 trail systems, including 200 trails, are found in the **Illinois Valley Ranger District**
surrounding the Cave Junction/Oregon Caves
area. Trails run from half a mile to almost 50 miles.
Possibilities include **Tin Cup Mine**, the **Kalmiopsis
Rim**, **Black Butte** and **Babyfoot Lake**.

A good time to visit
the Fall Creek National
Recreation Trail is
spring when wild-
flowers abound.

Try Medford's **Bear Creek Greenway Trail** (5.5
miles), beginning at Bear Creek Park and running north
through Medford to Pine Street in Central Point. The
trail has two segments. One is near the Route 5 south in-
terchange off Table Rock Road. A series of 18 interpretive
stations points out more than 20 kinds of trees and berries as
well as landmarks along the creek. The other trail segment (3.5
miles) is in the Talent area with the trailhead in Lynn Newbry
Park. The trail runs south toward Ashland, passing wetland
habitats and historical sites, with an interpretive guide available.
~ 541-774-6231.

Transportation

CAR

From Northern California, **Route 5** runs north over the
border to Ashland and the Rogue River Valley. Route 5
also takes you southbound from Washington across the
Columbia River into Portland. If you're arriving from the Northern
California coast, pick up **Route 199**, which heads northeast
through the Siskiyous into Southern Oregon and Grants Pass.
Many other highways link the Willamette Valley with the Oregon Coast and central Oregon, including **Routes 126, 20 and 22**.

AIR

Two airports bring visitors to the Heart of Oregon: Eugene and
Medford. In addition, the big **Portland International Airport** an
hour north of Salem has convenient connections to all major cities
and is serviced by Air Canada, Alaska Airlines, America West,
American Airlines, Big Sky Airlines, Continental Airlines, Delta
Air Lines, Frontier, Hawaiian Airlines, Horizon Air, JetBlue,
Lufthansa, Mexicana Airlines, Northwest Airlines, Southwest
Airlines, United Airlines and United Express. ~ 877-739-4636;
www.fly.pdx.com.

Eugene Airport is served by America West Express, Delta
Connection, Horizon Air, United Airlines, United Express and
US Airways.

In Medford, **Rogue Valley International–Medford Airport** is
served by Horizon Airlines, United Airlines and United Express.

For ground transportation to and from the Eugene Airport
call **Airport City Taxi & Limo**. ~ 541-484-4142.

In Medford, **Yellow Cab** serves the airport and links the
Shakespeare capital with the Medford Airport. ~ 541-772-6288.

Greyhound Bus Lines (800-231-2222; www.greyhound.com) serves the Willamette Valley and Ashland–Rogue River area, with stations in Salem, Corvallis, Eugene, Grants Pass and Medford. ~ Salem: 450 Church Street Northeast; 503-362-2428. Corvallis: 153 Northwest 4th Avenue; 541-757-1797. Eugene: 987 Pearl Street; 541-344-6265. Grants Pass: 460 Northeast Agness Avenue; 541-476-4513. Medford: 212 North Bartlett Street; 541-779-2103.

BUS

Amtrak's "Coast Starlight" has daily service to the Willamette Valley, with stations in Eugene (433 Willamette Street), Albany (110 10th Avenue Southwest) and Salem (500 13th Street Southeast). ~ 800-872-7245; www.amtrak.com.

TRAIN

You'll find many of the major agencies at the airports in Eugene and Medford. In Eugene, there are **Avis Rent A Car** (800-331-1212), **Budget Rent A Car** (800-527-0700) and **Hertz Rent A Car** (800-654-3131). In Medford, try **Avis Rent A Car** (800-331-1212), **Budget Rent A Car** (800-527-0700), **Hertz Rent A Car** (800-654-3131) and **National Car Rental** (800-328-4567).

CAR RENTALS

All the major Willamette Valley and Ashland–Rogue River cities have local public transit systems. While there are bus connections to many of the smaller towns, you'll need to rent a car to see many of the rural highlights.

The Salem area is served by **Cherriots** (503-588-2877). Contact the **Corvallis Transit System** (541-757-6998) in Corvallis. In Eugene, the **Lane Transit District** (541-687-5555) blankets the city. Medford, Jacksonville and Ashland are served by the **Rogue Valley Transportation District** (541-779-2877).

PUBLIC TRANSIT

In Eugene, **Airport City Taxi** (541-484-4142) can take you downtown. In Medford, call **Yellow Cab** (541-772-6288).

TAXIS

ELEVEN

Vancouver and
the Sunshine Coast

Mother Nature went all out in British Columbia, a Canadian province larger than California, Oregon and Washington combined. Stretched along the upper west coast of North America, the coastline is dotted by thousands of islands, only a few inhabited. Inland are thick forests, rugged mountain ranges and high deserts. The more remote northern regions contain vast, pristine wildernesses.

Bordered by the Pacific to the west, the United States to the south and the Coastal Range to the east, the southwestern corner of the province, including Vancouver, Whistler and the Sunshine Coast, contains unrivaled scenic splendors. The waters of the region, fed by heavy rains (45 inches annually in Vancouver, more at higher elevations), shape this land: the ocean, high lakes, mountain streams, broad rivers, inlets and fjords carve through alpine meadows and mold shorelines.

Nature has long provided for human needs here. Myriad indigenous tribes, living in peaceful coexistence with the earth, thrived in the mild climate of the region for centuries, hunting and camping in verdant forests, fishing salmon-filled waters and traversing the many streams and rivers. Europeans made an appearance in the 1770s, when Captain James Cook sailed through searching for the Northwest Passage and stopped to trade with the native inhabitants. Britain didn't lay claim to the area until Captain George Vancouver's visit in 1792.

Stories of the incredible abundance of wildlife brought in trappers and traders; a string of posts established by Hudson's Bay Company soon followed, with a steady flow of settlers not far behind. Friction arose when American settlers moved in and sought United States government authority. Eventually, the boundary between the United States and British Columbia was settled in 1846 by the Oregon Treaty.

As the fur trade began to wane, the Fraser Gold Rush of 1858 was just gaining speed, so the stream of settlers continued. Logging took off not long after the gold petered out. Gastown, the first settlement in what is now Vancouver, grew around an early saw mill. The city's future was ensured with the arrival of the transcontinental railroad in 1887 and, with its natural harbor, its importance as a shipping center soon became evident.

Industry in British Columbia is still largely based on what the land provides—logging, fishing and mining—with Vancouver the processing and shipping center. Since the Vancouver World's Fair in 1986 focused worldwide attention on all the region had to offer, tourism has grown to become the second major industry in the province, after logging. Add to this mix Swiss-style banking regulations that attract investment from around the world and you have a truly dynamic city.

Canada's Pacific gateway in fact as well as image, Vancouver is one of the economic centers of the Pacific Rim, and a major North American shipping center. It's also a bustling cruise-ship departure port. The city has long attracted immigrants from Asia, most recently from Hong Kong, although that tide has slowed now that control of the colony has reverted to China. Even so, Vancouver's Chinatown is second largest in North America, behind San Francisco. The city also has strong Italian, Greek, French, Indian, Japanese and Russian communities, and is a popular destination for European travelers. The West End (adjoining Stanley Park) is the most densely populated urban district in North America, much resembling a European city neighborhood with its residential towers, streetside shops and cafés. The Vancouver visitor can hear more than a dozen languages in a day's journey through the city, a reflection of its vital, cosmopolitan nature.

The combination of exceptional scenery, heady cultural life, economical production costs and attractive exchange rates has made Vancouver the third-largest film and television production center in North America, after Los Angeles and New York, with more than 200 movies filmed in B.C. in 2005 alone. "The X-Files" was taped here, along with a half-dozen other American TV shows and, sometimes, literally dozens of films a year. Aside from the cachet this brings the city, it's an economic boon—more than US$1.2 billion a year.

Whistler, 75 miles northeast of Vancouver, is close enough for a day trip from the city (though there's too much to see and do in just one day). With island-dotted Howe Sound to the west and the verdant Coastal Range to the east, there are enough sights along the picturesque Sea to Coast Highway to make driving the narrow, winding road slow but enjoyable. Parks and scenic pullouts along the way are perfect for a picnic or stretch.

The first settlers to arrive in Whistler in the early 1900s realized right away the potential in the area's beauty, so it comes as no surprise that some of the first structures were built as vacation retreats, most geared toward fishing and hunting. Skiing began in earnest in 1966 with the opening of the Garibaldi Lift Company in Whistler. A stylized European village resort was constructed 12 years and $550 million later at the convergence of the Blackcomb and Whistler mountains. In its short time, this ski destination has gained a strong international reputation and is now among the top attractions in North America. The resort is consistently rated number one in North America by *Ski Magazine*—ahead of such better-known destinations as Aspen, Vail and Sun Valley.

Although summer used to be the slow season at Whistler, an explosion of golf development is attracting a rapidly growing crowd of warm-weather visitors. Hiking, tennis, sailing, fishing, biking and horseback riding are among the other activities that occupy visitors; lodging and dining rates are still somewhat lower than in winter. Boutiques and eateries line the cobbled walkways of Whistler Village, which are often alive with street entertainers, from jugglers and clowns to dancers and musicians. The warmer months (June–September) are a favorite time to visit since crowds are minimal, prices for accommodation are drastically lower and there are so many outdoor activities to enjoy in the area's quiet alpine meadows, dense green forests and cool mountain lakes. However, even during ski season (November–May), you'll find no shortage of parking—a big problem at many resorts—because the main village of this carefully planned resort is built atop a massive underground garage.

With approximately 2400 hours of sunshine each year, the Sunshine Coast lives up to its well-deserved name. It is made up of small, quiet fishing and logging communities strung along a 90-mile coastline. These pleasant sights lie between Langdale, a short ferry ride from Horseshoe Bay in West Vancouver, and Lund, the gateway to Desolation Sound Marine Park. Another short ferry ride between Earls Cove and Saltery Bay connects the northern and southern sections of the coast. The ferry trips give visitors the sense that they are touring a series of islands even though the Sunshine Coast is firmly attached to the mainland.

The region is a gem for anyone who loves the great outdoors, with mild weather and enough hiking, camping and water activities—fishing, diving, canoeing, kayaking, sailing or simply lounging on one of many beaches—to please one and all. The locals, mainly loggers, anglers and artists, are friendly and upbeat, willing to share recommendations for what to see and do in their neck of the woods. Except for warm summer weekends, the Sunshine Coast is not yet inundated by tourists and retains a rustic, provincial air.

Southwestern British Columbia offers something for everyone tucked into a neat package: the urbane and worldly pleasures of Vancouver, the bustle and excitement of resort life at Whistler and the undeveloped, uncrowded scenic beauty of the Sunshine Coast. Simply put, it is a vacationer's paradise in the Pacific Northwest.

▼▼▼▼▼▼▼▼▼▼▼
West Side– Granville Island

If museums are your passion, this is a good place to start your visit to Vancouver. A number of the city's leading facilities are found here. Marvelous Granville Island offers some cultural attractions as well.

SIGHTS

Begin your visit with a pleasant stroll through several of the city's leading museums. One of the finest is the University of British Columbia's **Museum of Anthropology**, with sunlit galleries of Northwest Coastal First Nation totems, chests, canoes, jewelry, ceremonial masks, clothing and contemporary native artwork. There's no charge to visit the true-to-life Haida longhouse and totems behind the museum; occasionally you may even find a carver at work on a totem there. Closed Monday from September through May. Admission. ~ 6393 Northwest Marine Drive; 604-822-3825; www.moa.ubc.ca.

Further samples of First Nation artifacts along with intriguing collections of European costumes, tools, furniture and relics portraying the rapid colonization of the area are at the **Vancouver Museum**, located on a small green peninsula in English Bay known as Vanier Park. The **H. R. MacMillan Space Centre** upstairs stages regular astronomy programs and musical laser light shows, as well as live science presentations and hands-on exhibits. Closed Monday in winter. ~ 1100 Chestnut Street; 604-738-7827; www.spacecentre.com, e-mail info@hrmacmillanspacecentre.com.

Nearby is the **Vancouver Maritime Museum**, documenting the maritime history of British Columbia including the glory of international steamship travel. Housed in the connected A-frame is the Royal Canadian Mounted Police supply ship, the **St. Roch**, now a National Historic Site since it was the first ship to pass successfully through the Northwest Passage in both directions. Closed Monday from September to mid-May. Admission. ~ 1905 Ogden Avenue; 604-257-8300, fax 604-737-2621; www. vmm.bc.ca, e-mail genvmm@vmm.bc.ca.

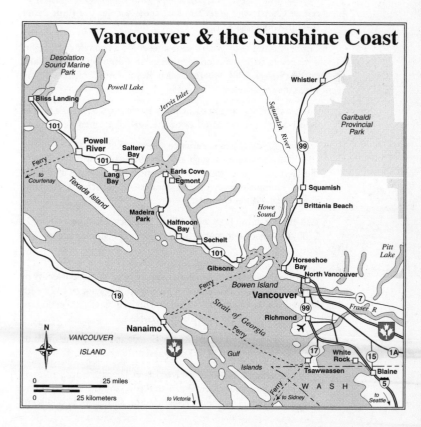

Vancouver & the Sunshine Coast

Text continued on page 516.

Three-day Weekend

Vancouver and Victoria

Day 1
- Cross into Canada. If you're coming from Seattle, it's a two-hour drive via Route 5 to the border, where the same highway becomes Route 99. Expect to spend another hour waiting in line, answering a few formal questions, and driving the 30 miles or so into Vancouver. After crossing the Oak Street Bridge, stay alert: Route 99 makes a couple of tricky turns before becoming Granville Street, the city's main north–south thoroughfare. Cross the Granville Street Bridge and keep going until you reach the harbor at Canada Place.

- Spend a pleasant day in downtown Vancouver. Take our suggested walking tour (pages 524–25), stopping for lunch along the way in one of Chinatown's great dim sum spots such as the **Pink Pearl Restaurant** (page 531).

- Check into the hotel where you've reserved a room for one night. If money is no object, consider the posh **Fairmont Hotel Vancouver** (page 528), where British Royal Family members stay when they're in town.

- Later in the day, head out to **Stanley Park** (page 525) for a peaceful drive and a sunset stroll along the seawall promenade.

- For dinner, you might experience the gourmet fare at one of the city's finest restaurants, such as **The William Tell** (page 532) in the Georgia Court Hotel. Or seek out fun, deliciously affordable dining—complete with dancing monks—at **Brother's Restaurant** (page 498) in Gastown.

- Call the **Coastal Jazz and Blues Society Hotline** (604-872-5200) for what's hot on the lively Vancouver nightclub scene.

Day 2
- Before leaving Vancouver, make a morning visit to the University of British Columbia's **Museum of Anthropology** (page 512), with its impressive totem pole garden and the finest collection of Northwest Coast Indian artifacts anywhere.

- Take Route 99 south to the Route 17 exit and drive nine miles to the B.C. Ferries terminal at Tsawwassen.

- Ride the ferry across to Vancouver Island. There are departures at least every two hours from 7 a.m. to 9 p.m., and the trip takes one and a half hours. The *Spirit* ferries, used on all sailings at odd-numbered hours, carry 2000 passengers and 470 vehicles per sailing, reducing the long ferry waits (sometimes six hours) that plagued Victorians until recently.

- Debarking at Swartz Bay, drive 19 miles into Victoria. Check into your downtown hotel: the **James Bay Inn** (page 570) is affordable and within walking distance of everything; the elegance of the **Fairmont Empress** (page 570) is astounding, with room rates to match.

- Spend the afternoon strolling Victoria's compact urban center, where you'll see architecture worthy of Buckingham Palace—plus totem poles. Start with a horse-drawn carriage tour, followed by a guided tour of the **Parliament Buildings** (page 567).

- Enjoy afternoon tea in the British manner at the **James Bay Tea Room and Restaurant** (page 573).

- Visit the **Royal British Columbia Museum** (page 566), then check out the Empress hotel's **Miniature World** (page 566).

- For dinner, might we suggest **Camille's Restaurant** (page 573).

- Take in a theater presentation at the delightfully old-fashioned **McPherson Playhouse** (page 576).

- Stop in for a drink at the Empress hotel's **Bengal Lounge** (page 575). A little pricey, but the setting is worth it.

Day 3
- No visit to Vancouver Island is complete without seeing **Butchart Gardens** (page 582), one of the largest and most beautiful formal gardens in the Pacific Northwest. Stay for lunch, then head for the ferry.

- The ferry schedule to the mainland is virtually identical to the one from the mainland: sailings at least every two hours from 7 a.m. to 9 p.m. Leaving on the 3 p.m. boat, you can be back in Seattle by 8 or 9 this evening. Bear in mind that the southbound border crossing can take longer, since U.S. Customs has been keeping a sharper-than-usual eye out for drug smugglers and terrorists recently. (You and I don't look suspicious, of course, but the folks in the vehicle ahead of us just might.)

Across a short bridge from downtown Vancouver lies **Granville Island**. Refurbished by the federal government, Granville contains everything from parkland to craft studios to a cement factory. Once an industrial area, today it is a classic example of native funk gone chic. Corrugated-metal warehouses have been transformed into sleek shops, while rusting cranes and dilapidated steam turbines have become decorative pieces. There are several **working studios** to view. The focal point is the **Granville Public Market**, a 50,000-square-foot collection of stalls selling fresh fish, fruits, vegetables and other goodies.

In July 2005, the Equal Marriage Act was signed into law, allowing same-sex couples to tie the knot legally throughout Canada.

A quick stop at the **Info Centre** to pick up a map helps you focus on what you want to see and do. ~ 1398 Cartwright Street; 604-666-5784; www.granvilleisland.com, e-mail info@granville island.bc.ca.

Leave time for an informal, one-hour tour of the **Granville Island Brewing Company**, the first microbrewery in Canada and home of the popular Island Lager. Tastings are offered at the end of the tour. Admission. ~ 1441 Cartwright Street; 604-687-2739; www.gib.ca, e-mail info@gib.ca.

Of course, getting to the market is half the adventure: you can walk, drive or catch the **False Creek Ferry** from behind the Vancouver Aquatic Centre (under the Burrard Street Bridge). ~ 604-684-7781; www.granvilleislandferries.bc.ca. The **Aquabus**, a competing enterprise, also offers passage across and along False Creek in small jitneys from various docks. ~ 604-689-5858; www.aquabus.bc.ca, e-mail mail@theaquabus.com.

LODGING

The **Hostelling International—Vancouver Jericho Beach**, the second-largest youth hostel in North America, enjoys a prime setting on English Bay. Housed in what was once military barracks, there is space here for over 250 hostelers in the many dorm-style rooms with shared baths; the few couple/family rooms go quickly. With fully equipped communal kitchens, laundry facilities, cafeteria and lounge with big-screen television, this is easily one of the fanciest hostels you could hope to visit. The hostel is open May through September. ~ 1515 Discovery Street; 604-224-3208, 888-203-4303, fax 604-224-4852; www.hihostels.ca. BUDGET.

The welcoming glass lobby full of greenery bustles with businesspeople, the majority of the clientele at the **Executive Airport Plaza**. This quiet, friendly hotel near the airport has 235 standard guest rooms and 115 suites in pastel tones with full kitchens and modern furnishings in separate seating and sleeping areas. Rooms with jacuzzis or kitchenettes are also available. ~ 7311 Westminster Highway, Richmond; 604-278-5555, 800-663-2878, fax 604-278-0255; www.executivehotels.net, e-mail reservationsr@executivehotels.net. ULTRA-DELUXE.

Although it's on a back street in a quiet neighborhood, near-by public transportation makes **Beautiful Bed & Breakfast** accessible to Vancouver's main attractions, including downtown and the UBC, both of which are just minutes away by bus. Housed in a spacious, attractive colonial-style home, the inn's four rooms include a honeymoon suite with marble fireplace and a balcony. Breakfast is served in a formal dining room with silver service. No children under 14 allowed. ~ 428 West 40th Avenue; 604-327-1102, fax 604-327-2299; www.beautifulbandb.bc.ca, e-mail sandbbb@portal.ca. MODERATE TO ULTRA-DELUXE.

◄ HIDDEN

The Kitsilano neighborhood, a long, narrow district that runs from around Burrard Street to Alma Street and features commer-

DINING

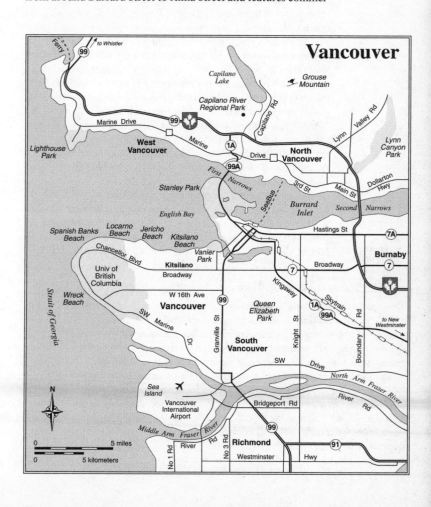

cial corridors along 4th Avenue and Broadway, boasts many excellent, small restaurants.

HIDDEN ►   The last time we stopped by **Sophie's Cosmic Café** on a weekend, diners were lined up outside the door. Inside, people were piling into Naugahyde booths and gazing at the pennants, pictures and antique toys that line this quirky café. There are omelettes and high-fiber Belgian waffles for breakfast, and falafel and veggie burgers later in the day. Dinner gets downright sophisticated as Sophie cooks up quesadillas, vegetarian pastas, salmon dishes, oysters and nightly specials. There's a heated outdoor patio. ~ 2095 West 4th Avenue; 604-732-6810, fax 604-732-9417; www.sophiescosmiccafe.com. BUDGET TO MODERATE.

Shijo Japanese Restaurant, atmospherically appointed with tatami, bronze lamps and black wood accents, is popular with the downtown crowd. Sushi, vegetarian dishes and traditional Japanese fare are prepared with an innovative twist. Barbecued shiitake mushrooms is one of the standout dishes. ~ 1926 West 4th Avenue; 604-732-4676, fax 604-731-4589. MODERATE.

Set near the conservatory at the peak of Queen Elizabeth Park, the elegant **Seasons in the Park Restaurant** enjoys sweeping views of the Vancouver skyline and the mountains towering above the North Shore. The seafood and West Coast cuisine dishes are seasonal, and specials from the daily menu are always on a par with the outstanding view. Weekend brunch. ~ Cambie Street at 33rd Avenue; 604-874-8008, fax 604-874-7101; www.vancouverdine.com, e-mail info@vancouverdine.com. MODERATE TO DELUXE.

Spicy northern Chinese cuisine is showcased brilliantly at **Kirin Mandarin**, a large, stylish restaurant handsomely adorned with creamy gold walls decorated with prints. An emphasis on fresh local seafood is evidenced by well-stocked fish tanks at the rear of the dining area. Shellfish dishes are especially notewor-

AUTHOR FAVORITE

Throughout the year there are affordable rooms available at the **Conferences and Accommodation at UBC**, a budget alternative to Vancouver's pricey downtown hotels. Staying here makes me feel like a student again—without the inconvenience of attending class. Single and twin rooms in the dorm buildings are generally full of students during the school term but are available in the summer. "West Coast suites" (one-bedroom apartments with kitchenette and private bath) are closed for renovations until May 2007. Guests can get an inexpensive meal in the Student Union Building cafeteria. ~ 5961 Student Union Boulevard; 604-822-1000, 888-822-1030, fax 604-822-1001; www.ubcconferences.com, e-mail reservations@housing.ubc.ca. MODERATE TO DELUXE.

thy, including lobster and crab prepared with ginger sauce or chili-spiked sea scallops. Stop by for daily dim sum. ~ 1166 Alberni Street; 604-682-8833, fax 604-688-2812; www.kirin restaurant.com. DELUXE TO ULTRA-DELUXE.

Gourmands literally come from around North America to line up at **Vij's**, the namesake high-style Indian bistro of Vikram Vij's path-breaking cuisine. The culinary inventions are simply astounding—just imagine cinnamon and red wine curry or lamb popsicles! The line heads out the door as Vij's does not take reservations, so get there early. ~ 480 West 11th Avenue; 604-736-6664; www.vijs.com. DELUXE TO ULTRA-DELUXE.

Another spot for a fine view of the city lights, this time from water level on the Granville Island Wharf, is **Bridges**. The restaurant is one of the current hot spots of the dining elite who have the choice of the refined elegance of the dining room, the relaxed bistro, the fresh air on the deck or the convivial pub. The fare here ranges from standard and nouvelle preparations of seafood and meats to basic pasta and finger foods. Be forewarned: Some readers claim it's too touristy. ~ 1696 Duranleau Street; 604-687-4400; www.bridgesrestaurant.com. ULTRA-DELUXE.

Inevitably you are going to end up on Granville Island. Should hunger strike while you're touring the shops and artist studios, check out the food stalls at the **Granville Public Market**. Here you'll find a fish-and-chips shop, a souvlaki stand, a juice and salad bar, a deli and even a fresh soup outlet. BUDGET.

A strip of intriguing shops lies along **4th Avenue** between Burrard and Alma streets. Situated between Granville Island and the University of British Columbia campus, this is the Kitsilano neighborhood. Back in the 1960s and 1970s, it was a center for Vancouver's counterculture. Since then, time and gentrification have transformed the area into a spiffy district of smart shops and comfortable homes.

SHOPPING

In the same neighborhood, along Broadway, is **T**, one of the district's more intriguing shops, which also doubles as a tearoom. Devoted entirely to teas, T has over 250 varieties, ranging from common types such as Earl Grey to rarities such as a robust Tanzanian leaf. Fruit and herbal teas and pastries round out the offerings. ~ 1568 West Broadway; 604-730-8390; www.tealeaves. com, e-mail tearoom@tealeaves.com.

◄ *HIDDEN*

The main draw on Granville Island is the **Public Market** (www.granvilleisland.com), with rows of vendors selling fresh produce, flowers, pastas, wines, baked goods, seafood and meats, along with the section brimming with fast-food outlets proffering an international array of delectables. The **Kids Market** within the market is a mall full of toy stores, children's clothing shops and a tykes' beauty salon. ~ 1496 Cartwright Street; 604-689-8447; www.kidsmarket.ca.

NIGHTLIFE   There is plenty of innovative theater to choose from on Granville Island. The **Carousel Theatre Company** offers family-oriented classical and contemporary productions at the **Waterfront Theatre.** ~ 1410 Cartwright Street; 604-685-6217 (box office), 604-669-3410, fax 604-669-3817; www.carouseltheatre.ca. The **Playwrights Theatre Center** hosts the Annual Vancouver New Play Festival, showcasing the works of Canadian playwrights. ~ 1398 Cartwright Street; 604-685-6228; www.playwrightstheatre.com. The second largest nonprofit theater in Canada is the **Arts Club Theatre.** ~ 1585 Johnston Street; 604-687-1644; www.artsclub.com.

Bridges, a subdued but trendy bistro on Granville Island, is fairly quiet and a good place to savor a glass of wine and the lights of the city dancing on the water of False Creek. ~ 1696 Duranleau Street; 604-687-4400.

BEACHES & PARKS   **QUEEN ELIZABETH PARK** 🏃 Taking the place of two stone quarries that once supplied building materials for the city, this 130-acre park now features various ornamental gardens showcasing the indigenous plants of the coast along with two rock gardens that reflect the land's past. At 505 feet above sea level, the park affords some of the best views of downtown Vancouver, crowned by the mountains of the North Shore. Bloedel Floral Conservatory rests at its peak. You'll find a restaurant, restrooms, picnic facilities, 18 tennis courts, lawn bowling lanes, frisbee golf and a pitch-and-putt golf course. ~ Located at Cambie Street and 33rd Avenue; 604-257-8400, fax 604-257-8427.

HIDDEN ►   **WRECK BEACH** 🏖 Of the many beaches in and around Vancouver, this highly undeveloped (and unspoiled) sandy stretch across from the University of British Columbia on the tip of Point Grey Peninsula is the only *au naturel* spot in town. Students make up the majority of the sun worshippers here. Located within Pacific Spirit Regional Park, there are outhouses, seasonal concession services and a telephone at the top of the trail. ~ Located south of Nitobe Garden and the Museum of Anthropology off Northwest Marine Drive; a steep, twisting trail opposite the university residences leads from the road to the beach; 604-224-5739.

ENGLISH BAY BEACHES (SOUTHERN SHORE) 🏖 Stretched around the north face of Point Grey Peninsula on the opposite side of the bay, Kitsilano Beach, Jericho, Lacarno and Spanish Banks beaches attract hordes of windsurfers, sunbathers, picnickers and swimmers, but are spacious enough not to feel overcrowded. There is a heated outdoor saltwater pool (open during the summer; fee) at Kitsilano Beach in case the sea is too nippy. You'll find restrooms, lifeguards (in summer), changing rooms and intermittent food stalls. ~ Kitsilano Beach is at Cornwall Avenue and Arbutus Street; Jericho, Lacarno and Spanish beaches are accessible off of Northwest Marine Drive; 604-665-3424.

If your vision of downtown is an office world that rolls up the sidewalk at 6 p.m., get ready for a pleasant surprise. A beautiful harbor setting, intriguing historic districts, galleries and gardens set downtown Vancouver apart from most cities.

Downtown Vancouver

SIGHTS

Vancouver Tourist Info Centre offers detailed information to visitors. ~ Plaza Level, Waterfront Centre, 200 Burrard Street; 604-683-2000, fax 604-682-6839; www.tourismvancouver.com. The best guide to Vancouver dining, theater, music and other events is the *Georgia Straight*, a free weekly with comprehensive coverage of the city's cultural life. It's available at most coffee shops, bookstores, hotels, restaurants and newsstands ~ www.straight.com.

The shining geodesic dome so prominent on the Vancouver skyline as you approach the city from the south was Expo Centre during the 1986 Exposition and is now home to **Science World British Columbia**. Fascinating hands-on exhibits let you blow square bubbles, light up a plasma ball, dance on a giant synthesizer keyboard and more. The OMNIMAX **Theatre** (604-443-7443) upstairs features a variety of exciting films shown on one of the largest screens in the world. Separate admission to museum and theater. ~ 1455 Quebec Street; 604-443-7440, fax 604-443-7430; www.scienceworld.bc.ca, e-mail info@scienceworld.ca.

Dedicated in 1995, **Library Square** is a stunning architectural highlight of Vancouver's decade-long building boom. Vancouver Public Library's Central Branch is the centerpiece: a fascinating oval building cast in reddish concrete, designed by famed Canadian architect Moshe Safdie to hint at the Roman Coliseum. Its many windows and unusual angles capture and reflect light like a prism. With nine floors of books and reference materials, the library is one of the largest in North America. ~ 350 West Georgia Street; 604-331-3600; www.vpl.vancouver.bc.ca.

LET THE GAMES BEGIN

Vancouver will host the Winter Olympic and Paralympic Games in 2010. The Richmond Oval, home of 12 speed-skating events during the games, along with an adjoining waterfront plaza and park, will be the centerpiece of a major new City Centre community to be developed on 32 acres along the banks of the Fraser River. ~ 877-408-2010; www.vancouver 2010.com, e-mail info@vancouver2010.com.

There are numerous photo-worthy spots in **Chinatown**, which stretches along Pender Street between Carrall and Gore streets. North America's third-largest Chinese community, this crowded neighborhood is particularly festive during holiday periods. Among the most remarkable sites is the extremely narrow **Sam Kee Building** (Pender and Carrall streets) listed in *Ripley's Believe It or Not!* as the skinniest building in the world at just six feet wide. Along the way you'll also see brightly colored, elaborately carved facades of buildings housing herbalists, bakeries, dim sum parlors, silk or souvenir shops and open-front produce stands. Also be sure to stop by the **Dr. Sun Yat Sen Classical Chinese Garden** (see "Vancouver in Bloom" below), a unique garden that seems to have been magically transported to Vancouver from China.

A bit farther on Pender Street is the 1912 **Sun Tower Building**, which, at 272 feet, was once the tallest building in the British Empire and site of a daring escape stunt pulled off by Harry Houdini during the height of his career. Builder Louis Taylor, a newspaper publisher, deliberately intended the half-clad caryatids (maidens) atop the tower to offend Edwardian sensibilities. ~ 100 West Pender Street; 604-683-2000.

Colorful **Gastown**, named after saloon keeper "Gassy" Jack Deighton whose statue stands in Maple Tree Square (Alexander and Carrall streets), is where the original townsite began in 1867. This touristy heritage area of cobbled streets, Victorian street lamps and storefronts, charming courtyards and mews is chock-full of antique and souvenir shops and international eateries. On the corner of Cambie and Water streets is the **Gastown Steam Clock**, the world's first, wheezing out musical chimes on the quarter hour. ~ 604-669-3525.

A few steps farther on Carrall there's a great view of the harbor from **Canada Place**, Vancouver's trade-convention center and cruise-ship terminal, complete with hotel and IMAX theater. From the bow of this landlocked behemoth you can scan the waterfront, taking in the broad sweep of North Vancouver and the spectacular mountains behind it. Bridges arch to port and starboard, ships lie at anchor in the harbor and an occasional ferry plies the narrow waterway. ~ At the foot of Howe Street.

Just a few blocks away, a glass elevator zips you up to the aptly named **Lookout!** circular viewing deck high atop Harbour Centre. With a tremendous 360-degree view of Vancouver and environs, plaques pointing out all the major sights, guides present to answer all questions and a brief multimedia presentation on the highlights of the city, this is one of the best places to get your bearings. It's over-priced, though, and if you want the best view, try Grouse Mountain or Queen Elizabeth Park. Admission. ~ 555

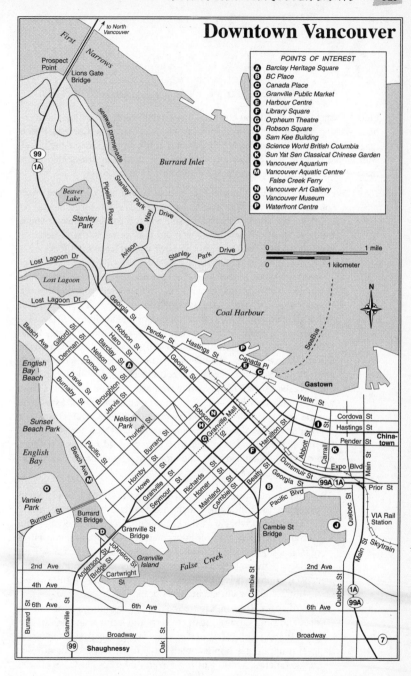

Downtown Vancouver

POINTS OF INTEREST

- Ⓐ Barclay Heritage Square
- Ⓑ BC Place
- Ⓒ Canada Place
- Ⓓ Granville Public Market
- Ⓔ Harbour Centre
- Ⓕ Library Square
- Ⓖ Orpheum Theatre
- Ⓗ Robson Square
- Ⓘ Sam Kee Building
- Ⓙ Science World British Columbia
- Ⓚ Sun Yat Sen Classical Chinese Garden
- Ⓛ Vancouver Aquarium
- Ⓜ Vancouver Aquatic Centre/
  False Creek Ferry
- Ⓝ Vancouver Art Gallery
- Ⓞ Vancouver Museum
- Ⓟ Waterfront Centre

WALKING TOUR
Downtown Vancouver

Much of Vancouver's distinctive character can be discovered on a three- to four-hour walking tour of the downtown area. Start your stroll at **Canada Place** (page 522), situated where Burrard Street ends at the harbor. One of the places with ample parking, this combination convention center and cruise ship pier's massive, distinctive architecture makes it an easy-to-find landmark.

GASTOWN   From the Canada Place pier, walk one block inland and turn southeast (left) on Cordova Street. Continuing for three blocks on Cordova, you'll pass Granville Square and the Seabus Terminal, where the ferry runs to North Vancouver, and then come to the skyscraping Harbour Centre, where a glass elevator named **Lookout!** (page 522) takes you up to an observation deck from which you can see all of Vancouver laid out at your feet. After this not-so-cheap thrill, angle east (left) onto Water Street, the main street of **Gastown** (page 522), where Vancouver got its start as a saloon-lined lumber mill port in 1870. Although the townsite was officially incorporated as Granville, it was locally known as Gastown for its colorful founder, barkeep "Gassy Jack" Deighton. One block east at Water and Cambie stands the **Gastown Steam Clock**; built by the owner of a nearby shop, this fun-to-watch two-ton timepiece has become Vancouver's trademark and most often photographed sight. Walking two more historic blocks of Water Street with its endless T-shirt and curio shops, you'll find the **Gassy Jack Statue** near the oddly angled intersection of Water, Carrall, Powell and Alexander streets. Since no one knows what Deighton actually looked like, the statue was made in 1986 from a century-old, randomly selected photo of an unidentified man who looked as if he could be Gassy Jack.

West Hastings Street; 604-689-0421, fax 604-689-5447; www. vancouverlookout.com, e-mail info@vancouverlookout.com.

Housed in what was once the central courthouse, the **Vancouver Art Gallery** has four floors of galleries showcasing the works of international and Canadian contemporary artists; the Emily Carr Gallery, featuring many of her drawings and paintings of the coastal rainforests is a must-see. Admission. ~ 750 Hornby Street; 604-662-4700; www.vanartgallery.bc.ca.

Adjacent **Robson Square**, below the current government offices and courts, is the site of concerts and lectures and has an outdoor skating rink. The various steps and plazas beside the multilevel fountain are popular with downtown workers for alfresco picnic lunches. ~ 800 Robson Street; 604-822-3333.

CHINATOWN   Turn south (right) on Carrall Street. Three blocks up is the intersection with Pender Street, where the six-foot-wide **Sam Kee Building**—the world's skinniest building, it's said—marks the entrance to **Chinatown** (page 522). Across the street, the **Chinese Cultural Centre** offers slide show presentations on the history of Chinatown as well as guided tours of the neighborhood. Take time to appreciate the urban serenity of the adjacent **Dr. Sun Yat Sen Classical Chinese Garden** (page 522), secluded behind high white walls and designed to blend water, rock, plants and architecture in Taoist harmony. Every detail of the garden has a symbolic meaning. Pause to write a poem or simply meditate. Then plunge back out onto teeming Pender Street, Chinatown's main street, where a three-block walk east to Gore Street will take you past exotic shops, apothecaries and restaurants. Then turn around and walk back up the other side of the street to Pender and Carrall. Be sure to check out **Market Alley** (aka Columbia Street), where street vendors sell exotic fruits, ginseng, seafood, baked goods, and assorted treasures and curiosities.

GRANVILLE MALL   Continuing west on Pender for eight blocks as it angles to the northwest will bring you to the **Granville Mall**, the modern urban heart of Vancouver. From here, it's an easy five-block walk northeast (right) back to Canada Place, where you started. But if you have more energy, head southwest (left) on Granville for three blocks, then northwest (right) on Robson for one block to **Robson Square** (page 524) and the **Vancouver Art Gallery** (page 524). Continuing north on Robson, you'll find yourself on **Robsonstrasse** (page 536), the city's chic shopping zone. Tired yet? from any place along this route you can walk about seven blocks back to Canada Place.

STANLEY PARK   Easily ranked as one of the most outstanding city parks in the world, 1000-acre Stanley Park offers more recreational and entertainment options than you can imagine. Only the outer 20 percent of this green grove poking out into Burrard Inlet at the head of the downtown peninsula is developed for recreational use. On December 15, 2006, hurricane-force winds decimated Stanley Park's famous old-growth forests, blowing down some 3000 mature conifers and causing an estimated $9 million worth of damage. The park is now open again, but clearing, replanting and repairs to the damaged six-mile seawall will continue for the foreseeable future. ~ 604-257-8400.

Within the park you'll find the **Vancouver Aquarium**, where you can view dolphins and whales, as well as nearly 700 species of marine life in the museum's numerous exhibits. Then stroll through the tropical rainforest room and listen to the birds chitter while peering at crocs or piranhas. An outdoor viewing deck on the west side of the compound allows free looks at the seal and beluga whale pools. Check out the brand new Cannaccord Capital Exploration Gallery, with an expanded children's area and new gallery space. Admission. ~ 604-659-3474; www.vanaqua.org.

You can enter the nearby **Children's Farm Yard** to frolic with the llamas, goats and other little critters. You can also ride the miniature railway, a scaled-down version of the first train to cross Canada. Call for winter hours. Admission. ~ 604-257-8531.

The best way to take in all the sights is to bike or hike along the divided six-mile **seawall promenade** (see "Outdoor Adventures" for more information). If you're pressed for time or just not up for the several-hour jaunt around the perimeter path, hop in the car and follow the one-way **scenic drive** signs from the park's main entrance off Georgia Street to hit most of the highlights.

Making your way around the promenade, you'll pass a statue of Lord Stanley, the rose gardens, the Royal Vancouver Yacht Club, Deadman's Island, the Nine O'Clock Gun, and the "girl in a wetsuit" statue next to the historic figurehead from the S.S. *Empress of Japan*. You will also pass the newly built **Brockton Visitor Centre**, located near the park's collection of Kwakiutl and Haida totem poles. Composed of two pavilions covered by a floating roof, the center now provides easily accessible restrooms and concessions since the totem poles are one of the park's biggest draws.

Continue along the promenade to **Prospect Point Lookout**, at the far northern tip of the park, which boasts a great view of the **Lions Gate Bridge**. One of the longest suspension bridges in the world, it stretches over Burrard Inlet to the slopes of West Vancouver. Siwash Rock, the hollow tree and Second, Third and English beaches, extremely popular among sunbathers and water enthusiasts, finish out the seawall route. Second Beach has a heated outdoor pool.

To get to know the wild interior of the park, visit the **Nature House**, an interpretive center at the northeast edge of Lost Lagoon where visitors learn about the flora and fauna in the park. Hikers will enjoy the miles of trails through thick coniferous forest while birdwatchers will probably prefer to perch quietly at the edge of **Beaver Lake** or **Lost Lagoon** to peer at Canadian geese, rare trumpeter swans and other waterfowl. For children, there's the **Variety Kid's Water Park** (a wonderful, watery play area complete with slides, water cannons and a pint-size, full-body blow drier), a miniature steam locomotive, pony rides, Kids Traffic School and a fire-engine playground. Admission.

Vancouver in Bloom

Rain is a common sight in this neck of the woods during the winter months, but the payoff bursts forth in the spring. Vancouver is a green, green city overflowing with international parks and gardens that are a flourishing testament to the forethought of the city's founders.

Rose aficionados will want to stroll through Stanley Park's lovely **Rose Garden**, crowning glory of the city's parks. The fragrant collection in this mid-size formal garden is sure to contain one or two specimens you'd like to have in your own yard. Late summer is the best time to visit. ~ Located near the park's entrance just off Georgia Street; 604-257-8400.

There's also a wonderful rose garden in Queen Elizabeth Park, but it is often overshadowed entirely by the star of the show here, the **Bloedel Conservatory**. Set at the crown of Little Mountain, the conservatory houses over 500 tropical plant species under a 70-foot-high triodetic geodesic dome. Admission for the conservatory only. ~ 604-257-8570.

With over 16,000 species, the award for variety goes to the **University of British Columbia Botanical Garden**. This 70-acre research facility is filled with exotic and familiar specimens separated into alpine, Asian, British Columbian natives and food gardens. Summer admission. ~ 6804 Southwest Marine Drive; 604-822-9666; www.ubcbotanicalgarden.org.

VanDusen Botanical Garden has over 6500 species of plants from six continents divided into theme areas. It takes a full day to make it through the 55-acre complex, but you can hit the major sites—the Elizabethan hedge maze, the hanging basket display, rock and stone gardens, Canadian Heritage garden, fragrance garden and herb garden—in two to three hours. Admission. ~ 5251 Oak Street; 604-878-9274.

Nitobe Memorial Garden is an authentic Japanese strolling garden with teahouse. Narrow paths wind through two and a half acres of serene traditional Japanese plantings. Folks come here for the cherry blossoms in April, irises in June and flaming red Japanese maples in October. Closed weekends in winter. Summer admission. ~ University of British Columbia campus, 1903 Lower Mall; 604-822-6038; www.nitobe.org.

The jewel of Chinatown is the **Dr. Sun Yat Sen Classical Chinese Garden**. Designed and constructed by craftsmen brought in from China, this Ming Dynasty–style garden is the first such garden to be built outside China. Many of the elements, including the architectural and artistic components, rocks and pebbles (but not the plants) were shipped in from China. Closed Sunday in winter. Admission. ~ 578 Carrall Street; 604-662-3207.

LODGING Hello BC operates a free reservation hotline to assist visitors in arranging for accommodations in all price categories. It's expensive to stay in the city, especially in the downtown core, and especially in high season (June through August). If you bring your car, expect to pay an additional $10–$25 per day to park at most downtown hotels. You will also pay the Goods and Services Tax (16 percent) on all hotel accommodations; if 7 percent of this tax amounts to over C$7, you can claim a rebate for this percentage by filling out a form (available from your hotel) and mailing it to Revenue Canada. ~ 800-663-6000; www.hellobc.com.

Located in the heart of the business and entertainment district of cosmopolitan Vancouver, the luxurious **Sutton Place Hotel** offers five-star accommodations at prices comparable to (and in some cases lower than) other top hotels in town, while assuring guests more for their money in terms of space and personal attention. The hotel was refurbished in 2005, and rooms are elegant, with classical decor punctuated by a blend of antique reproductions and fine botanical prints; the suites have enormous marbled bathrooms with deep European-style tubs and separate showers. Personal service is the signature here. ~ 845 Burrard Street; 604-682-5511, 866-378-8866, fax 604-682-5513; www.suttonplace.com. ULTRA-DELUXE.

Home away from home for the British royal family since it opened in 1939, the **Fairmont Hotel Vancouver**, peaked by a château-style oxidized copper roof, is a landmark. The calling card of this posh property is Old World elegance. Rooms are spacious and well appointed with polished antiques, plump chairs, large writing desks and tall windows that open to the surrounding scenery. Bathrooms are a bit small (typical of the period in which they were built) but elegant nonetheless. ~ 900 West Georgia Street; 604-684-3131, 800-257-7544, fax 604-662-1929; www.fairmont.com, e-mail concierge@fairmont.com. ULTRA-DELUXE.

TIMING IS EVERYTHING

July, August and early September are the peak tourist times in the lower mainland of southwestern B.C., and that is indeed when the weather is most reliable. However, visitors would do well to consider off-season travel—that's when local hotels offer special packages that can be incredible bargains. Luxury accommodations are sometimes half-price—which, when you take into account the favorable exchange rate, can mean that a super-deluxe room can be had for less than US$100. For more information call Tourism Vancouver (604-682-2222; www.tourismvancouver.com) or Super, Natural British Columbia (800-663-6000; www.hellobc.com).

There's a reason **Four Seasons Hotel Vancouver** consistently shows up in top-ten rankings for North America. The service here is incomparable, composed of dozens of tiny details that escape the average hotel. Head out the door to go jogging, for instance, and the doorman will greet your return with a dry towel. The location is superb and the 376 spacious rooms are well equipped for business travelers. The extensive fourth-floor fitness center opens onto a remarkable waterfall garden, perfect for contemplation. ~ 791 West Georgia Street; 604-689-9333, 800-268-6282, fax 604-689-3466; www.fourseasons.com/vancouver, e-mail res.vancouver@fourseasons.com. ULTRA-DELUXE.

The view from **The Fairmont Waterfront** captures the essence of Vancouver: In the foreground is the commercial hub of Canada Place; beyond that is Burrard Inlet, with sailboats and container ships; beyond that, the Lion's Gate Bridge and Grouse Mountain. More than half the 489 rooms in this deluxe business-class hotel are positioned to look out on this vista; be sure to ask for one. There's also an extensive herb garden on the patio adjoining the swimming pool. ~ 900 Canada Place Way; 604-691-1991, 800-441-1414, fax 604-691-1999; www.fairmont.com/waterfront, e-mail thewaterfronthotel@fairmont.com. ULTRA-DELUXE.

The **Coast Plaza Hotel & Suites at Stanley Park** is by far the best lodging near Stanley Park, just steps away from local beaches. With 269 airy, large rooms and suites looking out over the park and English Bay, its location is unsurpassed for West End visitors. ~ 1763 Comox Street; 604-688-7711, 800-663-1144, fax 604-688-5934; www.coasthotels.com, plazasuiteinfo@coasthotels.com. ULTRA-DELUXE.

With a prime downtown location and lots of space, **Pacific Palisades** is conveniently located near shops, restaurants, English Bay beaches and Stanley Park. The well-furnished studios and suites are roomy with modern, bright decor; all are equipped with kitchenettes, and many have breezy patios with grand views of the harbor or mountains. An evening wine reception is just part of the pampering service that includes pluses like thick robes, French milled soaps and other extras. Check for off-season promotions. ~ 1277 Robson Street; 604-688-0461, 800-663-1815, fax 604-688-4374; www.pacificpalisadeshotel.com, e-mail reservations@pacificpalisadeshotel.com. ULTRA-DELUXE.

The West End Guest House, a pink Victorian a block off bustling Robson Street, offers a more personable alternative to the area's hotels and motels. Each of the eight guest rooms (one of which is hypoallergenic) filled with a mixture of antiques has a personality of its own. All have private baths and plush feather mattresses, duvets and luxurious linens. Meals here, from the afternoon sherry with nuts and summertime iced tea on the sun deck to the multicourse morning repast, are a gourmand's delight. Free bike use. Gay-friendly. ~ 1362 Haro Street; 604-681-2889, 800-546-3327, fax 604-688-8812; www.westendguesthouse.com, e-mail info@westendguesthousecom. DELUXE TO ULTRA-DELUXE.

It's not hard to tell from its layout that the three-story **Barclay Hotel** was at one time an apartment building, though renovations have really spruced up the public areas. Rooms are a bit tight, with mix-and-match furniture, minuscule bathrooms and air conditioning. The suites provide an affordable (though not cheap) alternative for families. Facing on Robsonstrasse near all the restaurants and boutiques, the location is its best attribute. ~ 1348 Robson Street; 604-688-8850, fax 604-688-2534; www.barclay hotel.com, e-mail infos@barclayhotel.com. MODERATE TO DELUXE.

The **Burrard Inn** has standard, motel-style accommodations in a good central location. A crotchety old elevator takes guests to upper-level, medium-size rooms arranged in a quadrangle around the carport hidden under a rooftop garden. Furnishings are run of the mill. There are a few kitchenette units available. There are a 7-Eleven and a coffee shop on the premises. ~ 1100 Burrard Street; 604-681-2331, 800-633-0366, fax 604-681-9753; www.burrardinn.com, e-mail burrardinn@burrardinn. com. MODERATE.

Offering six guest rooms, **Nelson House** is a three-story Edwardian located near Barclay Heritage Square. Each room is individually decorated. Lounge by the cozy fireplace in the living room. Enjoy the full breakfast. Nonsmoking; children allowed by prior arrangement only. Gay-friendly. ~ 977 Broughton Street; 604-684-9793, 866-684-9793, fax 604-689-5100; www.down townbedandbreakfast.com, e-mail info@downtownbedand breakfast.com. MODERATE TO ULTRA-DELUXE.

The **Kingston Hotel Bed and Breakfast** is an unusual find in downtown Vancouver. This 1910 woodframe with the large green awning and red neon sign was recently renovated inside and out to look more like a European bed and breakfast. The tiny rooms are clean and offer the bare necessities—vanity sink, dresser, bed, small closet—and a shared bath down the hall; eight rooms with private bath and television are larger. The hotel has a restaurant with a sports lounge, and also a sauna. ~ 757 Richards Street; 604-684-9024, 888-713-3304, fax 604-684-9917; www.kingston hotelvancouver.com. DELUXE.

Hostelling International—Vancouver Downtown is perfectly located—10 to 15 minutes' walk from Stanley Park, Granville Island, Gastown and the business district. With space for more than 200 hostelers, its rooms are clean and functional. Laundry, recreation, cooking, meeting and studying facilities are available. Dozens of organized activities are offered every day, but wanderers will find almost limitless opportunities within easy reach. A free continental breakfast is included. ~ 1114 Burnaby Street;

604-684-4565, 888-203-4302, fax 604-684-4540; www.hihostels.
ca, e-mail info@hihotels.ca. BUDGET.

Located several blocks east on bustling Granville Street is **Hostelling International—Vancouver Central**, which offers private rooms with private baths in addition to four-bed dorm rooms. There's also a lively bar on-site. ~ 1025 Granville Street; 604-685-5335, 888-203-8333, fax 604-685-5351; e-mail vancouver.cen tral@hihostels.ca. BUDGET.

Housed in a huge, exquisitely renovated 1897 Victorian home, **O Canada House**'s six elegant, comfortable guest rooms all feature private bath and are furnished with period antiques. Guests are served a gourmet three-course breakfast in the morning and complimentary sherry in the afternoon. There's a pantry stocked with baked goods, teas and sodas. It's just a ten-minute walk to Granville Island, and 15 minutes to Stanley Park. Free parking. Gay-friendly. ~ 1114 Barclay Street; 604-688-0555, 877-688-1114, fax 604-488-0556; www.ocanadahouse.com, e-mail info@ ocanadahouse.com. ULTRA-DELUXE.

Dining in Chinatown is spelled dim sum. And the **Pink Pearl Restaurant** is a dim sum emporium, a cavernous dining room where black-clad waiters and waitresses roll out dozens of steam-tray delectables on trundle carts. Dine on this finger food while enjoying the Chinese artwork adorning the walls. ~ 1132 East Hastings Street; 604-253-4316, fax 604-253-8525; www.pinkpearl. com. MODERATE.

DINING

The decor at **C**, the snazzy seafood restaurant overlooking False Creek, is flashy—lots of wood, metal and glass, exposed pipes and modern furniture, along with kitschy touches such as fishing lures on the restroom doors. The food is equally inventive, including entrées such as foie gras with persimmon jam. Fish

AUTHOR FAVORITE

Don't miss **Liliget Feast House**, a "First American" (Canadian for American Indian) "longhouse" serving the native cuisine of the Pacific Northwest. You'll feast your eyes on Vancouver's most unique menu, then fill your belly with smoked salmon chowder, toasted seaweed and steamed rice, and alder-barbecued venison. On the side are steamed fern shoots and wild rice. For dessert, how about cold raspberry soup or whipped soapallalie (Indian ice cream), washed down with a cup of juniper tea? Call for winter hours. Reservations recommended. ~ 1724 Davie Street; 604-681-7044, fax 604-681-7074; www.liliget.com, e-mail info@liliget.com. DELUXE.

dishes are cooked to perfection, with only the freshest of seafood used, and you can round off dinner with one of C's 15 types of tea. Seasonal lunch. ~ 1600 Howe Street (on the False Creek Pier); 604-681-1164, fax 604-605-8263; www.crestaurant.com, e-mail info@crestaurant.com. ULTRA-DELUXE.

I find that seafood is rarely executed as expertly as at **Blue Water,** the sensational centerpoint of Yaletown dining. The signature appetizer tower features a dozen delights, ranging from crab cakes to sushi; the entrées take peerless ingredients such as salmon and cod, fancy them up a bit (pumpkin-seed crust) and leave the flavor intact. Desserts include handmade sorbets and a sensational lemon tart. Lots of glitz and glamour here, with black-clad young professionals hugging the sushi bar. The wood-decor and open ceiling are a delight, and the service is matchless. ~ 1095 Hamilton Street; 604-688-8078; www.bluewatercafe.net. DELUXE.

When the wallet is plump and it's time to indulge the taste buds, head for longtime favorite **The William Tell,** poshly appointed with fine European art and a few antique crossbows in keeping with its name. Your gastronomic experience might start with smoked B.C. salmon tartar or escargot, followed by seared veal with morel mushrooms or Fraser Valley duck breast with cherry compote in a terragon *jus.* Try the extraordinary set meals presented in conjunction with shows at the Queen Elizabeth Theatre or other local playhouses. Reservations recommended. No dinner on Monday. ~ Georgian Court Hotel, 765 Beatty Street; 604-688-3504, fax 604-683-8810; www.thewmtell.com. ULTRA-DELUXE.

If you're in the mood for Italian food, you can't go wrong by heading to one of the region's five restaurants in the Umberto dynasty. The service and decor are impeccable and the food always tasty: Caprese salad, antipasti and pasta are reliable choices. Specials included rack of lamb, venison and Chilean sea bass. For alfresco dining on sunny days, we recommend the villa-style, terra-cotta courtyard of **Il Giardino.** Check their website or the phone book for addresses and phone numbers of other Umberto locations. No lunch on Saturday. Closed Sunday. ~ 1382 Hornby Street; 604-669-2422; www.umberto.com, e-mail ilgiardino@umberto.com. DELUXE TO ULTRA-DELUXE.

HIDDEN ▶

Presto Panini is inconspicuous, but not hard to find—right in the heart of downtown—no doubt the reason it's hard to get a table here at lunch. The menu is simple—Italian soups, salads, pastas and panini sandwiches. The list of sandwiches is extensive—with two dozen concoctions scooped onto toasted focaccia—and excellent. Service is efficient, portions filling. Closed Sunday. ~ 859 Hornby Street; 604-684-4445. BUDGET TO MODERATE.

HIDDEN ▶

Fleuri Restaurant, well-known for outstanding Continental cuisine, also serves an incredible Chocoholic Bar from 6 to 10 p.m. each Thursday, Friday and Saturday night that attracts hordes of sweet-toothed locals. There are 12 to 16 different chocolate items on the buffet (crêpes, fondues, cakes, covered fruits) that change daily. They also feature a Sunday jazz brunch (be sure to try the croissant bread pudding), monthly winemakers dinners and afternoon tea daily. Reservations highly recommended. ~ Sutton Place Hotel, 845 Burrard Street; 604-642-2900, fax 604-682-5513; www.suttonplace.com, e-mail fleuri@suttonplace.com. MODERATE TO DELUXE.

Success can be a dangerous thing. Long cited as the premier French restaurant in Vancouver, **Le Crocodile** shows the signs of complacency: Service is a bit snotty, the bread can be stale, portions are shrinking. Champagne glasses are not much larger than thimbles, but the prices aren't equally minuscule! However, the Alsatian main dishes, such as venison with spätzl or roasted lamb in a mustard sabayon, remain hearty and rich. The nightly specials are inviting, and the crowded buzz of the place creates an energizing, cosmopolitan air. No lunch on Saturday. Closed Sunday. ~ 909 Burrard Street; 604-669-4298, fax 604-669-4207; www.lecrocodilerestaurant.com. ULTRA-DELUXE.

At **Villa del Lupo**, chef Julio Gonzalez-Perini practices food as art. Each dish is not only exquisitely flavorful, it's visually striking—swirls of sauce, artfully layered dashes and splashes of ingredients. The pastas, all handmade, are especially fine. The basement wine cellar (which guests can sometimes use for very intimate private parties) is extensive. Dinner only. ~ 869 Hamilton Street; 604-688-7436, fax 604-688-3058; www.villadellupo.com, e-mail info@villadellupo.com. DELUXE TO ULTRA-DELUXE.

Vancouver's explosion of coffee shops has become, if anything, greater than Seattle's. There are many fine local purveyors; the best downtown is **Trees**, a small enclave in the financial district just a couple of blocks from Canada Place. They roast their own ◄ HIDDEN

VANCOUVER'S HOLLYWOOD

Yaletown, on downtown's south side roughly bounded by Richards and Smithe streets and Pacific Boulevard, was an industrial warehouse district as recently as the early 1990s. Today it is a neighborhood of sophisticated cafés, restaurants and exclusive galleries and boutiques. The change was brought about by Vancouver's fast-growing motion picture and TV industry, which made the low-rent district its headquarters during the rise of the independent film movement, when Canada offered tax incentives and a chance to avoid big-studio guild restrictions. Its reputation having been enhanced by the success of high-profile Vancouver-based productions such as *Smallville* and *Battlestar Galactica*, British Columbia has emerged as the third-largest film production community in North America, after Los Angeles and New York.

all-organic coffees; even better, the very best cheesecake muffins in town are baked in the kitchen out back. ~ 450 Granville Street; 604-684-5060, fax 604-684-5026; www.treescoffee.com. BUDGET TO MODERATE.

Of the dozens of cafés and small eateries along Denman, near Stanley Park, **Bojangles** is a bit snazzier than most, but still offers an economical lunch for visitors who've spent the morning in the park. The deluxe sandwiches are exceptionally good; soups and salads are dependable. A small outdoor seating area faces south, into the sun, along a side street. ~ 785 Denman Street; 604-687-3622, fax 604-687-3613; www.bojanglescafe.com, e-mail denman@bojanglescafe.com. BUDGET TO MODERATE.

If a customer fails to finish the food ordered at the Elbow Room Cafe, he or she is required to give a donation to a local charity. How much? Past donations have ranged from 50 cents to $50.

Its entrance is right on Robson, but **Cin Cin** would be easy to miss if you weren't looking. The restaurant itself is upstairs, a surprisingly large and spacious dining room whose Mediterranean decor and cuisine have long been among the city's most popular. The fresh-baked bread, rich soups and grilled meats and seafoods here are all highly flavored and imaginatively conceived. No lunch on Saturday and Sunday. ~ 1154 Robson Street; 604-688-7338, fax 604-688-7339; www.cincin.net, e-mail info@cincin.net. DELUXE TO ULTRA-DELUXE.

Tropika offers a fine introduction to Malaysian cuisine. If you really don't know what you're getting into, order satay (marinated meat skewered and grilled over charcoal); if you've had some exposure, you'll appreciate the spicier starred selections. They specialize in curries. ~ 1128 Robson Street; 604-737-6002, fax 604-737-1433; www.tropika-canada.com. MODERATE.

A just-for-fun diner is **Fogg 'n' Suds**, a fancified hamburger joint with relaxed atmosphere and a friendly crowd. Their menu includes Thai noodle salad, steaks and a variety of pastas. You probably won't have time to try each of the 150 beers from around the globe, but regulars get a chance to fill out a stylized passport of brews. ~ 1323 Robson Street; 604-683-2337, fax 604-669-9297; www.foggnsuds.com. BUDGET TO MODERATE.

Unlike most tapas cafés, the menu at **Tapastree** is not so long you need a lengthy perusal to satisfy your curiosity. The two dozen plates here vary from Asian to comfort food—Oriental seafood salad with sesame lime dressing, prawn won tons and buttermilk fried chicken. It's just two blocks from Stanley Park, perfect after a trek around the seawall. ~ 1829 Robson Street; 604-606-4680, fax 604-682-6509; www.tapastree.ca, e-mail tapastree@gmail.com. MODERATE.

Generous breakfasts and lunches attract a mixed clientele to the **Elbow Room Cafe**, which is decorated with autographed photos of movie stars. Start your day with the lumberjack or English breakfast, eggs Benedict, pancakes or an omelette. For lunch try a Monte Cristo, clubhouse or shrimp and crab sandwich. Hamburgers are big and popular. The owners say you have to have personality to fit in. Weekend breakfasts are popular. ~ 560 Davie Street; 604-685-3628, fax 604-685-4338; www.theel bowroomcafe.com. BUDGET.

Local office workers line up on the sidewalk at lunchtime to get a table at **Stepho's**, a fairly traditional Greek taverna that serves up souvlakis as well as heaping platters of excellent roast lamb. One platter is a huge meal at a most reasonable price—about US$9. ~ 1124 Davie Street; 604-683-2555. BUDGET.

With its bordello decor and prime Northwest haute cuisine, funky **Delilah's** in the West End is one locals usually prefer not to share. As you arrive, you'll be handed a seasonal menu—perhaps grilled venison, pan-roasted duck, tagliatelle pasta tossed with roasted potatoes and seared artic char with a sweet paper oil. Next, sidle up to the bar for one of their famous martinis to keep you happy during the wait to be seated and served. Dinner only. Closed Monday. ~ 1789 Comox Street; 604-687-3424; www. delilahs.ca, e-mail info@delilahs.ca. DELUXE TO ULTRA-DELUXE.

There are enough shops in Vancouver to overwhelm even the most serious of the "I'd-rather-be-shopping" crowd. Here are a few in the most popular shopping districts.

SHOPPING

In Chinatown, the **Beijing Trading Company** carries an intriguing selection of herbs, teas and food products. ~ 89 East Pender Street; 604-684-3563.

Nearby, Gastown teems with souvenir shops full of T-shirts, totems, maple sugar, smoked salmon and other regional items. The **Inuit Gallery** has high-dollar Northwest Coast First Nation and Inuit art. ~ 206 Cambie Street; 604-688-7323, fax 604-688-5404; www.inuit.com.

Located on the edge of Gastown, **Sikora** is a modern oddity, a store with just one type of merchandise—classical music. But what a selection! With close to 25,000 CDs, classical music lovers will find artists and versions of standards that you'll never see in mainstream American music stores, no matter how large. ~ 432 West Hastings Street; 604-685-0625; www.sikorasclassical.com.

◄ HIDDEN

It seems like there are a zillion antique and curio shops in the Gastown area; one of the best is **Salmagundi West**, an engaging collection of clothes, jewelry and greeting cards. The owner has a fetish for horns, so if you need an antique trumpet or other heraldic instrument, this is the place. ~ 321 West Cordova Street; 604-681-4648.

Lush is exactly what its name implies—a redolent profusion of lotions, emollients, soaps, oils and other cosmetics and body-care products. It's an outpost of a popular European chain; all its products are natural and fresh. ~ 100-1025 Robson Street; 604-687-5874.

Vancouver's trendiest shopping area is **Robsonstrasse**, a Germanization of Robson Street that reflects the influx of European luxury shops, designer outlets and see-and-be-seen sidewalk cafés in recent years. The heart of Robsonstrasse is a six-square-block area along Robson bounded by Burrard, Haro, Jervis and Alberni streets, northwest of Robson Square. Along this fashionable strip you'll find famous-name stores like Armani, Benetton, Body Shop, Club Monaco and Saatchi side-by-side with little specialty shops selling handcrafted jewelry, clog shoes, Belgian chocolate and art glass. You'll find a wide selection of handmade regional gift items at **Canadian Crafts**. ~ 1045 Robson Street; 604-684-6629. **Northern Art Company** specializes in British Columbia jade, native American masks, and other Canadiana. ~ 1026 Robson Street; 604-683-3773. The **Silver Gallery** offers contemporary native American jewelry handcrafted in British Columbia. ~ 1226 Robson Street; 604-681-6884; www.silvertalks.com, e-mail mail@silvertalks.com.

Robson Fashion Park has a number of boutiques selling high fashion. ~ 1131 Robson Street. There are also several souvenir shops scattered along the strip in addition to some fun places such as the **Robson Public Market**, with over two dozen retail stores. ~ 1610 Robson Street; 604-682-2733, fax 604-682-2776; www.robsonpublicmarket.com, e-mail info@robsonpublicmarket.com.

Vancouver is a chocoholic's paradise, with an unusual number of fine chocolate shops throughout the city. A favorite is **Daniel's Le Chocolat Belge**, which uses top-quality Belgian choco-

VANCOUVER'S VERSATILE STADIUM

Since its completion in 1982, **B.C. Place**, the ten-acre stadium in the heart of downtown, is the home playing field of the B.C. Lions pro football team and the largest air-supported stadium in North America. In addition, it hosts trade shows, religious events, royal visits and rock concerts by the likes of David Bowie, the Beach Boys and the Rolling Stones. The domed roof is made of two layers of fiberglass-woven fabric, each only 1/30 inch thick and stronger than steel. Sixteen huge electric fans keep the air pressure inside the stadium higher than outside, holding the roof up without support beams. The removable synthetic turf floor used for sporting events is made of 32 rolls of nylon turf, weighing 72 tons and held together by zippers. Weekly summer tours sometimes available. ~ 777 Pacific Boulevard; 604-669-2300; www.bcplacestadium.com.

late to create truffles and other confections. ~ 4447 West 10th Avenue; 604-224-3361; www.danielchocolates.com.

A high-style boutique on the west side of town, **Boboli** features imported European clothing for men and women. ~ 2776 Granville Street; 604-736-3458.

The **Vancouver Opera Association** (604-682-2871; www.van couveropera.ca, e-mail tickets@vancouveropera.ca) stages productions several times a year at the Queen Elizabeth Theatre and Playhouse, also home to **Ballet British Columbia** (604-732-5003; www.balletbc.com) as well as major theater productions and visiting musicals. ~ Theatre and Playhouse: Hamilton Street between Georgia and Dunsmuir streets; 604-665-3050.

NIGHTLIFE

The **Vancouver Symphony Orchestra** (604-876-3434, fax 604-684-9264; www.vancouversymphony.ca, e-mail customer service@vancouversymphony.com) provides first-rate entertainment at The Orpheum, a multilevel vaudeville theater built in the mid-1920s that's worth a visit in itself. ~ Orpheum: 884 Granville Street.

There are hundreds of clubs, discos, cabarets, lounges, pubs and taverns in Vancouver; we touch on only a few popular selections here. A complete listing of all the acts at all the clubs, bars and taverns appears every Thursday in the *Georgia Straight* (www.straight.com). **Richard's on Richards**, with its refined wood, brass and stained-glass decor, has live music on weekdays and deejays on weekends, attracts a mixed crowd, predominantly upscale businesspeople. ~ 1036 Richards Street; 604-687-6794; www.richardsonrichards.com, e-mail info@richardson richards.com.

If you don't like hockey, don't venture into the **Shark Club**, where dozens of TV monitors are tuned to Canada's national madness. During hockey interregnums, other sports manifest themselves. As sports bars go, this one is a bit more refined than most. ~ 180 West Georgia Street; 604-687-4275; www.sharkclubs.com.

For an unhurried drink and quiet conversation, your best bet is the **Gérard Lounge**, a genteel gentlemen's-style club; this is the place to spot visiting celebrities as well. ~ Sutton Place Hotel, 845 Burrard Street; 604-682-5511.

The **Coastal Jazz and Blues Society Hotline** lists what's going on in the numerous jazz clubs around town. ~ 604-872-5200; www.coastaljazz.ca.

Of the local gay haunts, **Celebrities Night Club** is open to both men and women. ~ 1022 Davie Street; 604-689-6180; www.cele britiesnightclub.com.

The **Lotus Sound Lounge** offers Top-40 music played by a deejay. A mixed gay and lesbian crowd frequents the dancefloor at this contemporary lounge. ~ The Lotus Hotel, 455 Abbott Street; 604-685-7777.

Casino gambling is legal here, with half the profits going to local charities; for a little roulette, sic bo or blackjack action, try the **Great Canadian Casino.** ~ 709 West Broadway; 604-872-5543.

BEACHES & PARKS

ENGLISH BAY BEACHES (NORTHERN SHORE) 🏊 Connected by Stanley Park's seawall promenade, silky English Bay Beach and broad Sunset Beach Park are prime candidates for a long sunset stroll. Within walking distance of the city center, they are a favorite of businesspeople out for a lunch break or there to catch the last rays after work during the week. There are restrooms, as well as changing rooms and intermittent food stalls in summer. ~ Off Beach Avenue on the southwest side of town; 604-257-8400, fax 604-257-8427; www.vancouverparks.ca.

STANLEY PARK 🏃 🚵 🏊 Beautiful Stanley Park is a green oasis in downtown Vancouver. Highlights include the aquarium, children's farmyard, seawall promenade, children's water park, a miniature railway, scenic lighthouses, totem poles and statues, pitch-and-putt golf, tennis courts, an evening gun salute (each day at 9 p.m.), open-air theater, a swan-filled lagoon, nature house and miles of trails through thick coniferous forest. Second and Third bathing beaches are extremely popular among sun lovers and water enthusiasts. Second Beach boasts a heated outdoor pool. Facilities include restaurants and concession stands, restrooms, showers and picnic facilities. ~ Follow Georgia Street heading west through downtown to the park entrance; 604-257-8400, fax 604-257-8427; www.vancouverparks.ca.

▼▼▼▼▼▼▼▼▼▼
North Shore

One of Vancouver's best features is its proximity to nature. Just a few minutes from the heart of town is this lush, green slope with scenic beaches, ecology centers and campgrounds. Easily reached by transit, this area also offers a great bird's-eye view of the metropolitan district.

SIGHTS

There are several sights of interest on the North Shore, beginning with **Capilano Suspension Bridge and Park**, a swaying footbridge stretched over the chasm 230 feet above the Capilano River; you will pass through a park complete with totem poles and souvenir-filled trading post to reach the bridge. The Treetops attraction takes visitors through the rainforest canopy on rope bridges. Admission. ~ 3735 Capilano Road, North Vancouver; 604-985-7474, fax 604-872-3055; www.capbridge.com.

Up the road a bit is the **Capilano Salmon Hatchery**, where the public can take a self-guided tour and learn about the life cycle of this important fish. ~ 4500 Capilano Park Road, North Vancouver; 604-666-1790, fax 604-666-1949; e-mail capilano@pac. dfo-mpo.gc.ca.

Up farther still is **Grouse Mountain,** the top of Vancouver, where visitors catch the Skyride gondola to the mountain peak complex to ski, hike, snowshoe, see the incredible high-tech mythology and history presentation about Vancouver in "The Theatre in the Sky" or settle in for a meal at one of the restaurants. Admission. ~ 6400 Nancy Greene Way, North Vancouver; 604-984-0661, fax 604-984-6360; www.grousemountain.com, e-mail info@grousemountain.com.

LODGING

Since 1985, the **Inn Penzance** has been a breath of fresh air in North Vancouver, offering welcome respite for weary travelers. There are three posh, deluxe-priced guest rooms (each with private bath) within the elegant, antique- and art-filled main house. Of the two ultra-deluxe housekeeping cottages on the grounds, the larger has an extra sleeping loft making it suitable for families. The smaller, nestled in the prim English garden, is designed for romance. Newly remodeled with a pirate theme, the Inn offers ever-changing and ever-delicious breakfasts. ~ 1388 Terrace Avenue, North Vancouver; 604-681-2889, 888-546-3327, fax 604-688-8812; www.innpenzance.com; e-mail info@innpenzance.com. DELUXE TO ULTRA-DELUXE

The **Grouse Inn,** near the north end of the Lions Gate Bridge not far from shopping, dining and sightseeing spots, offers 80 tidy but plain, motel-style rooms decorated in earth tones. Standard rooms have the basics—full bath, queen bed, cable television, small table and chairs—though a few are set up as family suites and others are equipped with kitchenettes. There's a playground and heated pool. Continental breakfast included. ~ 1633 Capilano Road, North Vancouver; 604-988-7101, 800-779-7888, fax 604-988-7102; www.grouseinn.com, e-mail stay@grouseinn.com. MODERATE TO DELUXE.

If you're looking for quiet, **Bay View B&B's** perch in an exclusive residential neighborhood above West Vancouver is the place. A spacious, neat home at the end of a little-traveled cul-de-

UNDER THE BRIDGE

Located under the north end of Lions Gate Bridge, **Capilano RV Park** is the closest camping option you will find. While it's primarily set up for recreational vehicles, there are eight grassy tent sites; reservations can be made for 125 hookup sites only, and are essential during the busy summer months. There are restrooms, showers, picnic tables, a playground, a lounge, laundry facilities, a pool and a whirlpool. ~ In North Vancouver at 295 Tomahawk Avenue; 604-987-4722, fax 604-987-2015; www.capilanorvpark.com, e-mail info@capilanorvpark.com. BUDGET.

sac, Bay View has a four-room suite on the main floor and two three-room suites upstairs. Canadian art and European antiques adorn the rooms. All offer panoramic views of English Bay, Stanley Park, the city skyline and the Lion's Gate Bridge. Guests are greeted with a plate of steaming fresh cookies and a scrumptious four-course breakfast is served. It's grounds are equally stunning, with beautifully landscaped gardens and a quaint gazebo. Despite its bucolic locale, it's just 15 minutes from downtown Vancouver. ~ 1270 Netley Place, West Vancouver; 604-926-3218, 800-208-2204, fax 604-926-3216; www.bayview-bb.com, e-mail bayview@bayview-bb.com. DELUXE TO ULTRA-DELUXE.

DINING   Neighborhood pubs are a much-loved part of life in Canada, and the **Black Bear** is the most popular in North Vancouver. Housed in a handsome Craftsman building, the restaurant offers a good selection of ale and beer, as well as an outstanding menu you'll be hard-pressed to find in any other pub: peppercorn steak with an Irish whiskey sauce, pulled-pork sandwiches, chicken *roti*, Indonesian curry pasta. There are also burgers but you can opt for chicken, ostrich or salmon instead of ho-hum beef. Closed Monday. ~ 1177 Lynn Valley Road, North Vancouver; 604-990-8880, fax 604-990-8860; www.blackbearpub.com, e-mail steve@blackbearpub.com. MODERATE.

For that million-dollar view of the city and outstanding seafood to match, **The Salmon House**, perched on a West Vancouver hill, fits the bill. The specialty here is fresh Alder salmon grilled over alderwood, but the prawns and scallop brochettes and rack of lamb are also worth trying. Lunch, dinner and Sunday brunch; reservations recommended. ~ 2229 Folkestone Way, West Vancouver; 604-926-3212, fax 604-926-8539; www.salmonhouse. com, e-mail dinner@salmonhouse.com. MODERATE TO DELUXE.

HIDDEN ►   **Village Fish** is a traditional seafood store much favored by locals. There's fresh crab, prawns and salmon among the many se-

AUTHENTIC EATING

Packed to the gills with Northwest Indian artifacts, **The Tomahawk** is more than a small diner-style eatery pleasing locals since 1926. It's an archaeological treat, one that came to be when the original owner allowed the exchange of knickknacks for food during the Depression. Nowadays, you'll have to pay for your meal: egg dishes, french toast and pancakes at breakfast, sandwiches and burgers at lunch, and steak, meatloaf and chicken pot pie at dinner. If you can, save room for homemade pie. ~ 1550 Philip Avenue, North Vancouver; 604-988-2612, fax 604-988-5262; www.tomahawkrestaurant. com, e-mail info@tomahawkrestaurant.com. BUDGET TO MODERATE.

lections. Ask for some Indian candy (honey-cured salmon) to take with you as you leave. ~ 1482 Marine Drive, West Vancouver; 604-922-4332. BUDGET.

Right across the street from Savary Island Pie Shoppe, **Bean Around the World** offers much better coffee—roasted on-site—and friendlier service. The adjacent bakery turns out a rich selection of muffins, breads and pastries every morning; it's hard to find a seat here around 8 a.m. but worth a few minutes' wait. Breakfast and lunch only. ~ 1522 Marine Drive, West Vancouver; 604-925-9600. BUDGET.

SHOPPING

Across Burrard Inlet in North Vancouver, **Lonsdale Quay Market** is a tri-level atrium mall on the waterfront. In addition to postcard views of the Vancouver skyline, this bustling shopping center combines hotel rooms, trendy stores and a fresh fish market. A great place to spend money, people watch and survey the shoreline. ~ 123 Carrie Cates Court, end of Lonsdale Avenue; 604-985-6261; www.lonsdalequay.com, e-mail information@lons dalequay.com.

BEACHES & PARKS

LYNN CANYON PARK 🏃 🛶 ⛵ Though it's much shorter but slightly higher than the Capilano Suspension Bridge, there is no charge to venture out onto Lynn Canyon Suspension Bridge, stretched 240 feet above the rapids of Lynn Canyon. There is also a fine ecology center in this pretty, 617-acre park. Facilities include restrooms, picnic facilities, nature trails, a concession stand and an ecology center. Please heed the signs warning of the dangers on nearby cliffs. Admission. ~ In North Vancouver at the end of Peters Road; 604-981-3103.

Whistler

One of Vancouver's best day trips leads to Whistler, a resort area famous for its skiing and après-ski life. Snow lovers are drawn to the region's crystalline lakes and lofty mountains as well as its alpine trails and cosmopolitan ski village. Located 79 miles northeast of Vancouver, the Whistler area has a number of British Columbia's best-known provincial parks that make the area ideal for fishing, windsurfing, swimming and, of course, loafing.

SIGHTS

On your way up to Whistler, stop for a tour underground through the **B.C. Museum of Mining**, which takes you deep into the workings of what was once the highest-yielding copper mine in the British Empire. The kids will enjoy panning for gold and exploring the large museum area. Closed most of December and January. Admission. ~ Route 99, Britannia Beach; 604-896-2233, 800-896-4044; www.bcmuseumofmining.org, e-mail general@bcmuseumofmining.org.

As you're cruising farther up the Sea to Coast Highway, you'll pass a couple of sights worth a detour near the town of Squamish. First will be **Shannon Falls**, a high, shimmering ribbon of tumbling water immediately off the highway. Next you'll come to the **Stawasmus Chief**, often called, incorrectly, the second-largest monolith in the world after the Rock of Gibraltar. At 1900 feet, it's actually the second-largest in the British commonwealth. On a fine day there will be climbers dangling all about the face of this mountaineer's dream.

One of the more interesting heritage sites in Whistler is at **Rainbow Park**, the site of the area's first vacation retreat and now a day-use park. This is also the best spot for a view of the valley and the Blackcomb and Whistler mountains. ~ Alta Lake Road.

For an in-depth look at the history of the area, visit the **Whistler Museum and Archives Society**, a quaint museum next to the public library in Whistler Village that houses relics, artifacts, documentary videos and an interesting slide presentation (which must be booked for viewing). Call ahead for hours. Admission. ~ 4329 Main Street; 604-932-2019, fax 604-932-2077; www.whist lermuseum.org, e-mail info@whistlermuseum.org.

HIDDEN ►   North of Whistler past the logging and farming town of Pemberton is **Meager Creek Hot Springs**, a series of pools, each varying in temperature, set in a pristine grove of evergreens. To get there, take Route 99 to the Pemberton Meadows Road and follow it north to Hurley River Road. After 45 minutes on this logging road, you'll come to the springs. If the road's not washed out (and it often is), it's possible to drive all the way through in summer, but a snowmobile trip is required to reach it during winter. Call ahead for road conditions. ~ 604-898-2100, fax 604-898-2191.

LODGING   **Hostelling International—Whistler** is located on Lake Alta, ten minutes from Whistler Village. Accommodations are basic here, with men's and women's dorms and a private room upstairs, and a kitchen, dining room and game room downstairs overlooking the lake. There's also a sauna. ~ 5768 Alta Lake Road; 604-932-5492, fax 604-932-4687; www.hihostels.ca, e-mail whistler@hihostels.ca. BUDGET.

A nicer alternative is the UBC **Whistler Lodge.** You still need to provide your own food and bedding and will share cubicles with other hostelers, but this rustic lodge set above a quiet residential section offers lots of pleasant extras like a sauna and jacuzzi, barbecue and fire pit off the large deck, ski-equipment/bike storage locker, kitchen, laundry, game lounge, separate television room and internet access. Bedding can be rented for a nominal fee. Book well in advance for ski season. ~ 2124 Nordic Drive; 604-822-5851 or 604-932-6604, fax 604-822-4711; www.ubc whistlerlodge.com, e-mail whistler@ams.ubc.ca. BUDGET.

Its location in a quiet residential area places **Lorimer Ridge Pension** pleasantly apart from Whistler's bustle; but the main village and lifts are just a few minutes' walk. Rooms are spacious and handsomly appointed, with duvets and private baths; some have balconies and fireplaces. There's a billiards room, too. ~ 6231 Piccolo Drive, Whistler; 604-290-5833, 888-988-9002, fax 604-938-9155; www.lorimerridge.com, e-mail lorimerridge@telus.net. MODERATE.

The Coast Whistler Hotel is farther from the lifts but has resort amenities like a dining room, pub, fitness room, sauna, jacuzzi, shiatsu massage clinic and a heated pool. Rooms are boxy, with basic, light-wood furniture, mini-fridges and cramped bathrooms; some have built-in window seats to take advantage of the views. Request a corner unit or one with vaulted ceilings, which seem to be roomier and are the same price. ~ 4005 Whistler Way; 604-932-2522, 800-663-5644, fax 604-932-6711; www.coastwhistlerhotel.com, e-mail reserve@coastwhistlerhotel.com. DELUXE.

"Lifestyles of the Rich and Famous" dubbed the **Fairmont Château Whistler**, located at the base of Blackcomb Mountain, "Whistler's premier address" with good reason. The property is strikingly elegant and brimming with Old World charm. Guests enjoy inspiring alpine views from more than 500 rooms, all smartly furnished with country-style wood furniture, queen or king beds, mini-bars and large bathrooms. They also have an 18-hole golf course designed by Robert Trent Jones, Jr. ~ 4599 Château Boulevard; 604-938-8000, 800-257-7544, fax 604-938-

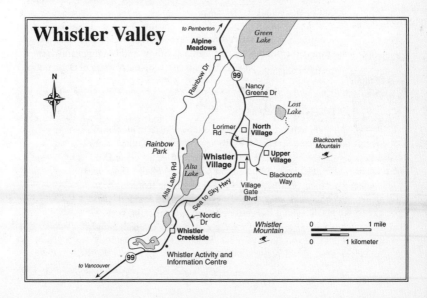

2055; www.fairmont.com/whistler, e-mail chateauwhistlerresort@ fairmont.com. ULTRA-DELUXE.

Le Chamois, a full-service luxury hotel, shares the same prime ski-in, ski-out location at the base of the Blackcomb runs. However, its smaller proportions (only 50 rooms) allow for a high degree of personal attention. The guest rooms are spacious, with big bathrooms, kitchenettes and designer touches evident throughout the decor; some of the studio rooms are especially wonderful, with two-person jacuzzi tubs in the living room area set before bay windows overlooking the slopes and lifts. ~ 4557 Blackcomb Way; 604-932-8700, 888-560-9453, fax 604-932-4486; www.leschamoiswhistlerhotel.com, e-mail res@wildflower lodge.com. ULTRA-DELUXE.

DINING

The abundance of fresh seafood at the **Crab Shack** is complemented by nautical decor and an oyster bar. You can also order pasta, steak or chicken while cracking jokes with the entertaining waitstaff. There's occasional live music in the bar. ~ 4005 Whistler Way; 604-932-4451, fax 604-938-0118; www.whistlercrab-shack.com, e-mail crabshack@telus.net. DELUXE TO ULTRA-DELUXE.

Araxi's Restaurant and Bar, a bright and airy restaurant with congenial staff, has been a dependable favorite in town since its beginning. The menu features creative Italian cuisine. Breads, sausages and pasta are all house-made. The dining room is often overflowing with customers, while the bar is best for a rousing drink with your friends. ~ 4222 Whistler Village Square; 604-932-4540, fax 604-932-3348; www.araxi.com, e-mail info@araxi. com. MODERATE TO DELUXE.

HIDDEN ►

At **Ingrid's Village Café** the tradition of savory home cooking continues in this family-owned tiny bistro on the village plaza a few minutes from the central lift base. Soups and bulging sandwiches are fresh-made daily; breakfasts are heaping platters of eggs, pota-

AUTHOR FAVORITE

When I want to escape from the bustling activities of the central village, I book a table at **The Wildflower**, a perfect destination for a romantic dinner. This elegant restaurant is decorated to echo the Old World charm of its setting in the Fairmont Château Whistler. The award-winning chef focuses on fresh Pacific Northwest cuisine featuring organically grown regional herbs, veggies, fruits, eggs and meat. Seafood is also a specialty of the house, with a featured buffet on Tuesday night. The Sunday brunch is a bargain, considering the quality, as is the daily breakfast buffet. ~ 4599 Château Boulevard; 604-938-2033, fax 604-938-2020; www.fairmont.com/whistler. ULTRA-DELUXE.

toes, toast and sausage. It's hard to find a better value in Whistler. ~ 4305 Skiers Approach #102, Whistler; 604-932-7000, fax 604-932-2930. BUDGET.

Amazingly, there are five Japanese restaurants in little Whistler Village, and of those five, **Sushi Village** is the one the locals most often visit. This place is busy, so service can be slow to a fault, but the atmosphere is serene, the decor clean-cut and the food quite good, especially the tasty tempura and à la carte sushi items. ~ 4272 Mountain Square; 604-932-3330, fax 604-932-2594; www.sushivillage.com, e-mail info@sushivillage.com. MODERATE TO DELUXE.

Caramba! sounds Mexican, but it's really not. It's comfort food—black-bean soup, roast chicken, grilled salmon, pizzas from an alder wood–fired oven. Yes, there's even macaroni and cheese. ~ 4314 Main Street #12; 604-938-1879, fax 604-938-1856. BUDGET TO MODERATE.

SHOPPING

Most of the great shopping in Whistler is done in the Town Plaza, at shops like **Escents Aromatherapy of Whistler.** It offers a variety of essential oils—rosemary, lavender and such—as well as a dizzying array of lotions, oils, soaps, scents, potions and emollients. ~ Town Plaza, 4314 Main Street #20, Whistler; 604-905-2955. **The Plaza Galleries** have a unique distinction: among their artists are celebrities such as Tony Curtis and the late Anthony Quinn. Keep your eyes open for the occasional Rembrandt or Picasso, too. It's all very ritzy. ~ 4314 Main Street #22, Whistler; 604-938-6233. Chocoholics will be in seventh heaven at the **Rocky Mountain Chocolate Factory.** ~ 4292 Mountain Square #214; 604-932-4100.

NIGHTLIFE

You'll find a good selection of lounges, taverns and discos in Whistler Village (not surprising for a resort destination). The après-ski scene is big everywhere, though one of the most popular spots is the **Longhorn Saloon,** with a deejay nightly and one of Whistler's largest dancefloors. ~ 4284 Mountain Square; 604-932-5999, fax 604-932-6124; www.longhornsaloon.ca.

Rustic and rowdy **Garfinkel's** offers a wide variety of music, including reggae and rock. Cover on weekends. ~ 4308 Main Street #1; 604-932-2323; www.garfswhistler.com, e-mail info@garfswhistler.com. The glitzier **Savage Beagle** has an eclectic mix of sounds: hip-hop, house, classic rock and salsa can be found in its upstairs lounge and the danceclub down below. ~ 4222 Village Square; 604-938-3337; e-mail info@savagebeagle.com.

The refined **Mallard Lounge,** with a large fireplace, soft piano music and expansive views of the Blackcomb Mountain base, is infinitely suitable for a quiet drink with friends. ~ Fairmont Château Whistler, 4599 Château Boulevard; 604-938-8000.

BEACHES & PARKS

PORTEAU COVE PROVINCIAL PARK This is a favorite among scuba enthusiasts because of its sunken ships and concrete reefs full of marine life located not far off the rocky beach. Porteau Cove is a long, narrow park stretched along the B.C. Rail tracks on the east shore of picturesque Howe Sound. Swimmers and kayakers are also welcome. Restrooms, showers, picnic facilities, an amphitheater, and a divers' changing room are available. Parking fee, $5. ~ Located off Sea to Sky Highway 15 miles north of Horseshoe Bay; 604-986-9371; www.seatoskyparks.com, e-mail info@seatoskyparks.com.

▲ There are 44 developed tent/RV sites (no hookups); C$22 per night; and 16 walk-in sites; C$10 per night. Very popular, reservations recommended (800-689-9025; www.discovercamping.ca).

GARIBALDI PROVINCIAL PARK Named for Mt. Garibaldi, its crowning point, this awe-inspiring park is made up of 480,000 acres of intriguing lavaland, glaciers, high alpine fields, lakes and dense forests of fir, cedar, hemlock, birch and pine. Thirty-six miles of developed trails lead into the five most popular spots—Black Tusk/Garibaldi Lake, Diamond Head, Singing Pass, Cheakamus and Wedgemont Lake. You can try for rainbow trout in Mamquam Lake (Diamond Head area), but swimming is very cold throughout the park. You'll find restrooms, picnic tables, shelters and nature, bike and cross-country ski trails (biking is restricted to the Cheakamus area). Parking fee, $3. ~ Located 40 miles north of Vancouver off the Sea to Sky Highway (Route 99), north of Squamish; 604-898-3678, fax 604-898-4171.

▲ There is a hike-in shelter with propane stoves (seven-mile hike) at Diamond Head; you must bring your own gear, including toilet paper; C$10 per night. There are two hike-in campgrounds at Garibaldi Lake (six-mile hike) with propane stoves; C$5 per night. Elfin Lakes has a shelter with bunks for 33 people; C$10 per night or C$25 per family.

BRANDYWINE FALLS PROVINCIAL PARK The highlight of this small park is its 230-foot waterfall; winding nature trails are also close at hand. Perched alongside the highway, the sparsely wooded campsites can be a bit noisy at high-traffic times (weekends). There are restrooms, picnic facilities, fire pits and nature and hiking trails. Day use only. Parking fee, $3. ~ Located approximately 60 miles north of Vancouver on the Sea to Sky Highway (Route 99); 604-986-9371; www.seatoskyparks.com, e-mail info@seatoskyparks.com.

Sunshine Coast

With a 100-mile shoreline that stretches along the northeast side of the strait of Georgia, the Sunshine Coast is bordered by sandy beaches, secluded bays and rugged headlands. It reaches from Howe Sound in the south to Desolation Sound in the north. This area is rustic, even a bit worn around the edges, but don't let that stop you. There are pleasant sites, plus a good number of artists in residence whose work is worth checking out.

SIGHTS

As you leave the ferry at Langdale and begin to wind your way up the Sunshine Coast along Route 101, one of the first areas of interest is the port town of **Gibsons**. Be sure to stop at **Molly's Reach** on Route 101, for years the setting for a popular Canadian television series, "The Beachcombers," and still a restaurant. ~ 604-886-9710.

The **Sunshine Coast Museum and Archives** maps the history of the area. The first floor exhibits cover the region's maritime history, while the second floor displays explore the First Nations and early European pioneers, along with the area's natural and industrial history. Closed Sunday and Monday. ~ 716 Winn Road, Gibsons; 604-886-8232; www.sunshinecoastmuseum.ca, e-mail curator@sunshinecoastmuseum.ca

Next stop on the lower coast is the **House of Héwhîwus**, or House of Chiefs, the center of government, education and entertainment for the self-governing Sechelt Indian band. Photographs and artifacts relating the history of the tribe are on display in the **Tems Swîya Museum** (604-885-6012). Ask for directions to the totems and grouping of carved figures behind the complex. Closed some Sundays (call ahead). ~ 5555 Route 101, Sechelt; 604-885-2273, fax 604-885-3490.

If you have an interest in archaeology, rent a boat and head north up the inlet from Porpoise Bay to view ancient Indian **pictographs** on the faces of the cliff walls looming above the water. The pictographs are very difficult to see; local guidance is essential.

◀ *HIDDEN*

From the trailhead near the town of Egmont, it takes approximately an hour to stroll the well-posted trail in to see **Skookumchuk Narrows**, a natural phenomenon of rapids, whirlpools and

PULP-FACTION

During the months of June, July and August you can take a free two-hour tour of the Norsk Canada pulp and **paper mill**, the lifeblood of Powell River. The tour gives you an inside view on the process of turning logs into lumber and paper products, from water blasting the bark off through forming pulp sheets to rolling the finished newsprint, and Pacifica is justifiably proud of the efforts it has made to reduce pollution from the mill. No children under 12 permitted. Closed weekends during winter. ~ For information and reservations, contact the Powell River Info Centre; 604-485-4701, 877-817-8669; e-mail info@discoverpowellriver.com.

roiling eddies created by massive tidal changes pushed through the narrow inlet. If you arrive at low tide you can view the fascinating marine life trapped in tidal pools near Roland Point.

HIDDEN ▶ Taking the next ferry hop, from Earls Cove to Saltery Bay, brings you to the **Lang Creek Salmon Spawning Channel** about midway to Powell River. During the peak spawning season (September to November) you can get a close look at pink or chum salmon making the arduous journey upstream. ~ Route 101.

The **Powell River Historical Museum**, an octagonal building just across from Willingdon Beach, houses a fine collection of regional memorabilia including furniture, utensils and hand tools of pioneers and indigenous people along with a photo and print archive with material dating back to 1910. Closed weekends September to mid-June. Admission. ~ 4800 Marine Avenue, Powell River; 604-485-2222, fax 604-485-2327; www.armour tech.com/museum, e-mail museum@aisl.bc.ca.

For a further lesson in the history of the area, take the **heritage walk** through the Powell River Townsite to view the early-1900s homes, churches and municipal buildings of this old company town. Maps are available from the **Powell River Info Centre**. Closed weekends in winter. ~ Joyce Avenue, Powell River; 604-485-4701; www.discoverpowellriver.com, e-mail info@discoverpowellriver.com.

There's a great hilltop view of the "Hulks," a half-moon breakwater of ten cement ships protecting the floating logs waiting to be processed in the mill, at the **Mill Viewpoint** on Route 101. Interpretive signs give a bit of history about the ships and the mill.

LODGING   There are no big resorts or major chain hotels yet. Motels, inns and lodges are sometimes a shade worn but generally are friendly and inexpensive—part of the coast's unique charm.

AUTHOR FAVORITE

A bed and breakfast since 1922, **Bonniebrook Lodge** is a charming yellow clapboard house overlooking the Strait of Georgia. There are four guest suites inside the house featuring Victorian-style furnishings, jacuzzi tubs and fireplaces. Three suites in a new building have the same amenities, along with their own private patios. Forty campsites for tents and RVs (half of the sites have hookups) are also available on the grounds behind the house. ~ 1532 Ocean Beach Esplanade, Gibsons; 604-886-2887, 877-290-9916, fax 604-886-8853; www.bonniebrook.com, e-mail info@ bonniebrook.com. BUDGET TO DELUXE.

The **Royal Reach Motel and Marina** offers clean, basic accommodations in 32 simple rooms that are pretty much the same. Nondescript furnishings include one or two double beds, a long desk/TV stand, plain bedside table and lamps, a mini-fridge, electric kettle and a small bathroom. Ask for one of the waterfront rooms that looks out over the marina and Sechelt Inlet. You can also book a bay cruise, on a sailboat or powerboat, with the proprietors. Rowboats and paddle boats also for rent. ~ 5758 Wharf Road, Sechelt; 604-885-7844, fax 604-885-5969. MODERATE.

The **Beach Gardens Motel and Marina** recently underwent a $15 million renovation, adding 48 oceanfront rooms with private decks. There are also cabins and kitchenette units available. Extra amenities include the private marina, dining room and weight room. ~ 7074 Westminster Avenue, Powell River; 604-485-6267, 800-663-7070, fax 604-485-2343; www.beachgardens.com, e-mail beachgardens@shaw.ca. MODERATE TO DELUXE.

Within moments of arriving at the charming **Beacon B&B and Spa** and getting settled into one of the two inviting upstairs bedrooms or roomy downstairs suite, you'll begin to unwind and feel right at home. It's hard to tell whether to attribute this to the genuine hospitality or the cozy, down-home decor. Whatever the case, the congenial hosts, large hot tub, great ocean view, proximity to the beach and thoughtful touches like on-site massage and scrumptious breakfasts make this one of the most delightful lodging options in the region. ~ 3750 Marine Avenue, Powell River; 604-485-5563, 877-485-5563, fax 604-485-9450; www.beaconbb.com, e-mail stay@beaconbb.com. MODERATE TO DELUXE.

Powell River's **Old Courthouse Inn** is in the middle of the historic townsite, not far from the lower end of Powell Lake and its popular canoe route. The heritage building, handsomely refurbished, holds very comfy dorm-style and private rooms, with an on-site café, cable TV and ready access to outdoor activities. The inn is nonsmoking. ~ 6243 Walnut Street, Powell River; 604-483-4000, 877-483-4777; www.pacificspirit.org/oldcourthouse, e-mail oldcourt@telus.net. BUDGET TO MODERATE.

DINING

◄ HIDDEN

Gibsons Fish Market, a smallish outlet on the main drag above the landing, does a booming business with tasty takeout fish-and-chips. It may not look like much, but there's usually a crowd lined up on the front sidewalk. Closed Sunday. ~ 294 Gower Point Road, Gibsons; 604-886-8363. BUDGET.

The **Blue Heron Inn**, a delightful waterfront home-turned-restaurant on picturesque Porpoise Bay, is home to masterful creations. The daily menu uses fresh regional produce and seafood in the dishes. Reservations are recommended. Dinner only. Closed Monday and Tuesday. ~ Porpoise Bay Road, Sechelt; 604-885-3847, 800-818-8977; www.bigpacific.com. DELUXE.

Stop by the **Royal Canadian Legion Hall Branch 112** for a super-cheap supper of chicken and chips, Salisbury steak or juicy burgers. This is actually one of the nicest (and only) places in town to get a meal. The salt-of-the-earth folks here might even let you in on a hand of cribbage or a fevered dart game. Closed Sunday. ~ 12829 Lily Lake Road, Madeira Park; 604-883-0055, fax 604-883-2005. BUDGET.

For homemade Mediterranean and Greek cuisine, try **The Sea House**. Entrées include seafood, souvlaki, steak, focaccia and brick-oven pizza. No lunch on Saturday or Sunday. ~ 4448 Marine Avenue, Powell River; 604-485-5163. MODERATE.

The **Shingle Mill Bistro and Pub**, situated at the tip of Powell Lake, has large windows on three sides so the views of this beautiful, pine-trimmed lake are enjoyed. It's no surprise that they serve grilled B.C. salmon in this waterfront eatery, but the steak *au poivre*, chicken in puff pastry, and fusilli primavera are unexpectedly good. Items from the dinner menu are available in the relaxed bistro. ~ 6233 Powell Place, Powell River; 604-483-2001, fax 604-483-9413. MODERATE TO DELUXE.

SHOPPING   There is an abundance of artists living in small communities all along the Sunshine Coast, many willing to open their studios to tours. Brochures are available through the **Sunshine Coast Arts Council**. Closed Monday and Tuesday. ~ Corner of Trail and Medusa streets, Sechelt; 604-885-5412; www.suncoastarts.com.

For arts and crafts of Northwest First Nations including masks, drums, totems and baskets, visit the Sechelt Indian Band's **Cultural Center Gift Shop**. Closed some Sundays (call ahead). ~ 5555 Route 101, Sechelt; 604-885-4592.

You'll find fine representations of local art (serigraphs, pottery, woodwork, watercolors, jewelry, sculpture) at Gibsons' **Westwind Gallery**. Closed Sunday. ~ 292 Gower Point Road, #14, Gibsons; 604-886-9213; www.westwindgallery.net.

HIDDEN ►   **Cranberry Pottery**, a working studio, offers functional and affordable handmade stoneware in varying designs and glazes. Closed Sunday. ~ 6729 Cranberry Street, Powell River; 604-483-4622; www.cranberrypottery.bc.ca.

NIGHTLIFE   Along the Sunshine Coast you'll find slimmer after-hours pickings, limited primarily to friendly, no-airs local taverns and pubs that occasionally have a dance space, live music and great water views.

A popular neighborhood hangout, **The Blackfish Pub** has very occasional live music. ~ 966 Venture Way, Gibsons; 604-886-6682.

Powell River has an amiable establishment in which to spend a comfortable evening after canoeing the lakes. Kick back with a brew and a view overlooking Powell Lake at the **Shingle Mill Bistro and Pub**. ~ 6233 Powell Place, Powell River; 604-483-2001.

PORPOISE BAY PROVINCIAL PARK 🏃 🛶 🚣 ⛴ One of the prettiest parks along the coast, Porpoise Bay has a broad, sandy beach anchored by grass fields and fragrant cedar groves. This is a favorite base for canoeists who come to explore the waterways of the Sechelt Inlets Marine Recreation Area. You'll also find excellent sportfishing. The park has restrooms, showers, picnic tables, an adventure playground, an amphitheater, nature trails, visitor programs and a fall salmon run. Parking fee, $3. ~ Located northeast of Sechelt off Porpoise Bay Road; 604-898-3678, fax 604-898-4171.

BEACHES & PARKS

> Scuba divers flock to Saltery Bay Provincial Park to visit the nine-foot bronze mermaid resting in 60 feet of water not far offshore from the evergreen-shrouded campground.

▲ There are 84 tent/RV sites (no hookups); C$20 per night. They also have cyclist campsites with showers; C$10 per night.

SALTERY BAY PROVINCIAL PARK 🛶 🎣 🚣 🛥 ⛴ Named for the Japanese fish-saltery settlement located in this area during the early 1900s, this lovely oceanside park with twin sandy beaches enjoys grand views of Jervis Inlet, where sharp-eyed visitors often catch glimpses of porpoises, whales, sea lions and seals. Swimming and offshore salmon fishing are excellent. There are restrooms, picnic sites, fire pits and disabled diving facilities. ~ Located off Sunshine Coast Highway 17 miles south of Powell River; 604-898-3678, fax 604-898-4171.

▲ There are 42 developed tent/RV sites (no hookups); C$14 per night.

POWELL FOREST CANOE ROUTE 🏃 🚣 ⛴ There are 8 fjord-like lakes interconnected by rivers, streams and miles of hiking trails making it possible to make portage canoe trips of anywhere from three days to a week in this beautiful Northern Sunshine Coast recreational area. There are over 200 miles of hiking trails around Powell River. Best time to make the trip is between March and November; lakes at upper elevations tend to freeze, and roads are inaccessible during winter months. Facilities include outhouses, picnic tables and hiking trails (the Inland Lake trail is wheelchair accessible). Closed weekends. ~ Jumpoff point for the canoe route is Lois Lake, accessed by the Canoe Mainline; 604-485-4701, 877-817-8669, fax 604-485-2822; www.discover powellriver.com, e-mail info@discoverpowellriver.com.

◀ HIDDEN

▲ Permitted at any of the 12 recreation sites. Prices vary from free (at forestry-run campgrounds) to C$20 at some of the municipal and provincial campsites around the area.

WILLINGDON BEACH MUNICIPAL CAMPSITE 🏃 🛶 The sandy, log-strewn, crescent beach bordered by wooded acres of campsites draws a big summertime crowd to this comfortable municipal site in Powell River. Some of the campsites are right up on the beach, while others in a grove of cedar are more secluded. The site has great, though unsupervised, swimming. You'll find restrooms, showers, a laundry, a barbecue area, playgrounds, a nature trail and a seasonal food stall. ~ Located immediately off of Marine Avenue in the Westview section of Powell River; 604-485-2242; www.willingdonbeach.ca.

▲ There are 81 sites, half with full hookups; C$16.50 to C$23 per night. Monthly winter rates are available.

DESOLATION SOUND MARINE PARK This park is made up of 37 miles of shoreline and several islands. The waters here are very warm and teem with diverse marine life, making the area ideal for fishing (excellent for cod or salmon), swimming, boating and scuba diving. The park is wild and undeveloped, with magnificent scenery at every turn. There are a few onshore outhouses and numerous safe anchorages. ~ Boat access only from the coastal towns. Easiest access is from Powell River; 604-898-3678, fax 604-898-4171.

▲ There are several walk-in wilderness campsites; no charge.

White Rock

Perhaps because it is so close to the border that they whiz right on by, U.S. travelers overlook White Rock, a peaceful seaside town about 40 minutes from downtown Vancouver that claims Canada's best climate—and has a couple of palm trees growing right along the main drag for proof. Canadians and European visitors to Canada flock to White Rock's small inns, motels and B&Bs; on summer weekend afternoons the town is astir with people using the beachside promenade, or strolling the avenue of small shops, cafés and restaurants behind it.

There isn't anything particularly glamorous about White Rock. In fact, it seems ever so much like the small British beach towns from which it drew its inspiration. That's what makes it charming—no big resorts, no famed sights, no fancy shops. Facing south into the sun, with a Mediterranean cast to the houses climbing the slope that fends off northerly storms, it does offer a balmier clime than most of the rest of B.C. Innumerable places offer fish and chips, and lots of happy couples stroll hand in hand along the promenade. For a tourist destination, it's charmingly low-key.

SIGHTS

Built in 1986 with assistance from the national and provincial governments, the **White Rock Promenade** spans one and a quarter miles of the town's gray-sand beach. Paved in brick, with numerous benches, it's a great place for a walk or a run; the sun keeps it warm, but the harbor breeze prevents excess warmth. When the tide's out, a truly vast expanse of gray sand beach lies exposed, attracting many sandcastle builders young and old. A pier leads a quarter-mile out into deeper water; you can toss crab pots in the water here if you're interested in hand-caught seafood. Not far south of the pier, the White Rock that lent the city its name sits on the slope above the beach. At 486 tons, it's staying put. If it was not truly white historically, liberal coats of paint ensure that it is now. ~ Along Marine Drive in downtown White Rock. Please note that White Rock's parking meters are in force until midnight along the promenade.

Built into the handsome, restored 1912 railroad depot, the **White Rock Museum and Archives** offers revolving exhibits focused on regional cultural and natural history. There's an on-site gift shop and a visitor information booth located just east of the depot. Admission. ~ 14970 Marine Drive; 604-541-2222, fax 604-541-2223; www.whiterock.museum.bc.ca, e-mail whiterockmuseum@telus.net.

LODGING

Seasoned travelers ordinarily avoid airport hotels, but the **Fairmont Vancouver Airport** is a remarkable property that's worth a stop if you're heading out of Vancouver on a morning flight. Built right in the terminal's east end, the hotel is a high-tech marvel with computerized gadgets galore—lights flick on automatically when you enter a room. The room decor is discreetly luxurious, with plum fabrics and maple-burl desks, and vast baths that include tiled showers and a soaking tub. Substantial insulation keeps jet noise to a minimum (not zero, though), and the reception area has an intriguing space-age look (hotel staffers stand at solo terminals). Prices are deluxe, but off-season the hotel offers some remarkable bargain packages. ~ Vancouver International Airport; 604-207-5200, 800-257-7544, fax 604-248-3219; www.fairmont.com. DELUXE TO ULTRA-DELUXE.

DINING

Tapas are the fare at **Cielo,** one of the Mediterranean-style eateries on Marine Drive, White Rock's main drag. But the restaurant's chefs have expanded the menu to also include a raw bar. Three

TRADING PLACES

It seems as if most of British Columbia's historic figures came from the United States. They include founding father Simon Fraser (New York), eight-term Vancouver mayor L. D. Taylor (Michigan), timber tycoon Sewell Moody (Maine), B.C. Sugar Refinery founder Benjamin Tingley Rogers (Pennsylvania), and Canadian Pacific Railway builder William Cornelius Van Horne (Illinois), who gave the city of Vancouver its present-day name. British Columbia, in turn, has provided more than its share of American movie and TV stars—among them Raymond Burr, Michael J. Fox, Pamela Anderson, Jason Priestley, Jennifer Tilly and James Doohan (Scotty from the original Star Trek).

plates is an ample amount for two, and the atmosphere is a bit more elegant than the typical pub eatery found on Marine. ~ 15069 Marine Drive; 604-538-8152; www.cielosrestaurant.com, e-mail info@cielosrestaurant.com. MODERATE TO DELUXE.

If it's a full-scale breakfast you're after, you want "The Big One" at **Holly's Poultry in Motion**. The plate comes piled high with eggs, hash browns, toast and ham or bacon. Lunch entrées, sandwiches and burgers are similarly generous. ~ 15491 Marine Drive; 604-538-8084. BUDGET.

As a quasi-beach resort, White Rock has at least a dozen ice cream stands along its waterfront drive. The best of them all is undoubtedly **White Mountain Ice Cream**, where they advertise homemade product, and deliver the best you can imagine. The acid test is vanilla—it's practically perfect at White Mountain. In fact, it's almost cause to visit the town just for the ice cream. ~ 14909 Marine Drive; 604-538-0030. BUDGET.

Outdoor Adventures

WATER-SPORTS

With 5000 miles of sheltered water within easy reach, Vancouver and southwestern British Columbia afford many opportunities to get out on the water. You can rent a powerboat or a sailboat and head north to the Sunshine Coast, where Desolation Sound has the warmest waters north of Mexico, or you can hop into an inflatable raft and paddle the Chilliwack River whitewater.

DOWNTOWN VANCOUVER   Although Canada does not require a license to operate either a powerboat or a sailboat, **Blue Pacific** requires that you prove your expertise before you rent one of its vessels. Otherwise, Blue Pacific will set you up for a three- to five-day skippered cruise; you can learn sailing basics or laze around on the deck. ~ 1519 Foreshore Walk, Granville Island; 604-682-2161, 800-237-232; www.bluepacificcharters.com, e-mail info@bluepacificcharters.com.

HELI-ADVENTURES

Quick trips to the backcountry for hiking, fishing, skiing or other activities are possible via helicopters. **Whistler Heli-Skiing**. will arrange skiing trips to the Sea-to-Sky Corridor near Whistler. ~ 604-932-4105, 888-435-4754; www.whistlerheliskiing.com. **Blackcomb Helicopters** arranges fishing and hiking trips during the summer. ~ 604-938-1700, 800-330-4354; www.blackcombhelicopters.com. **Helijet** specializes in drop-off service to the Tantalus Range, a rugged area with glaciers, lakes and the highest concentration of bald eagles in North America. ~ 604-270-1484; www.helijet.com.

NORTH VANCOUVER Canadian Outback Adventures also offers five-day guided kayak trips into Desolation Sound. ~ 657 Marine Drive #100, West Vancouver; 604-921-7250, 800-565-8735.

WHISTLER Canoeing and kayaking are very popular on Whistler's five beautiful lakes. Rentals and tours are available through **Whistler Outdoor Experience Co.** from mid-May to mid-October. Rent a canoe or kayak and take a self-guided tour of the Serene River of Golden Dreams, where you'll see plenty of wildlife. ~ 8841 Highway 99; 604-932-3389, 877-386-1888; www.whistler outdoor.com.

SUNSHINE COAST Desolation Sound Marine Park and the 50-mile **Powell Forest Canoe Route**, which includes eight breathtaking lakes and lush, interconnecting forests, are ideal spots for canoeing and swimming. "Powell Forest Canoe Route is as beautiful as the more popular Bowron Lake Route in northern British Columbia, but it's less populated by people in canoes," explains a local outfitter. ~ www.env.gov.bc.ca/parks.

To rent a canoe for one or eight days, contact **Mitchell's Canoe, Kayak and Snowshoe** in Powell River. They also rent kayaks and provide transportation to Desolation Sound. ~ 8690 Route 101, Powell River; 604-487-1609; www.canoeingbc.com. Experienced kayakers can rent craft for the day from **Sunshine Kayaking Ltd.** in Gibsons, on Howe Sound. Longer tours and kayaking classes are also offered. ~ Molly's Lane, Gibsons, BC V0N 1V0; 604-886-9760; www.sunshinekayaking.com.

Scenic floats and whitewater rafting are also immensely popular around Vancouver, especially on the Chilliwack River, 65 miles east of the city. Near Whistler, the Green and Birkenhead rivers are popular, as are the Thompson, Squamish and Elaho rivers.

RIVER RUNNING

GREATER VANCOUVER Hyak Wilderness Adventures runs guided whitewater-rafting trips on the Chilliwack River in the spring, when snow still caps surrounding mountains. By summer, focus shifts to the Thompson River, with its desert scenery. Rapids along these rivers range from Class II to Class V. You can actively participate by paddling or go the lazy route and let the guides do the work. ~ 3823 Henning Drive #203, Burnaby; 604-734-8622, 800-663-7238; www.hyak.com.

WHISTLER There are mountains, glaciers and waterfalls to observe on guided raft trips on several local rivers, including the Green and Squamish. Jet boat trips (on the Green and Lillooet rivers) and guided fishing trips are also arranged by **Whistler River Adventures** from late May to September. ~ P.O. Box 202, Whistler, BC V0N 1B0; 604-932-3532, 888-932-3532, fax 604-932-3559; www.whistlerriver.com.

SPORT-FISHING

The tremendous variety of fish in southwestern British Columbia waterways affords an array of exciting challenges for the angler. In the mountain country, you can flyfish or spin-cast in high alpine lakes and streams for rainbow trout, Dolly Varden, steelhead or kokanee salmon. On the coast, you'll find chinook, coho, chum, pink and sockeye salmon and bottom-dwelling halibut, sole and rockfish. Licenses for both fresh- and saltwater fishing are required (charter operators usually can provide them); regulations change frequently. **Saltwater licenses** are issued by the federal government's Pacific Fishery Licence Unit. Closed Saturday and Sunday. ~ Department of Fisheries and Oceans, 401 Burrard Street, Vancouver, BC V6C 354; 604-666-0566, 800-663-1660, fax 604-666-5835; www.pac.dfo-mpo.gc.ca.

Freshwater licenses are issued through the provincial government and can be bought at most sporting goods stores. **The Ministry of Environment, Lands and Parks (B.C. Environment)** maintains a list of licensed **freshwater fishing guides**. For a copy, call 604-582-5200.

SCUBA DIVING

A thick soup of microscopic plant and animal life attracts and feeds an abundance of marine life that in turn attracts divers in numbers that continue to grow. This area is home to the largest artificial reef in North America, a 366-foot destroyer that sank and is now a diver's paradise. Add to this the array of wrecks and underwater sights (such as a nine-foot bronze mermaid in the Powell River) and it's easy to understand the popularity of scuba diving around Vancouver and the Sunshine Coast.

Dive charters to local waters, the Gulf Islands and Howe Sound are arranged by **Great Pacific Diving**. Rentals and lessons are also available. ~ 1236 Marine Drive, North Vancouver; 604-986-0302; www.greatpacific.net.

SKIING

NORTH SHORE   The majestic range crowning Vancouver's North Shore offers three fine ski areas within minutes of the city. **Cypress Mountain**, with 35 runs on two lift-serviced mountains, boasts the longest vertical run of the local Vancouver resorts. Snowboarders share the runs with downhills skiers. A third area features 10 miles of groomed cross-country trails tracked for both classic and skate skis. Night skiing and backcountry skiing trails are available in the provincial park. ~ 604-926-5612; www.cypressmountain.com.

The glittering string of lights visible each night on the North Shore across the inlet from downtown Vancouver marks the arc-lit runs of **Grouse Mountain**, where residents head after work to get in some slope time. The resort has 25 runs, a variety of lifts, a snowboard park and a snowshoeing park. There's also outdoor skating on a pond. ~ 6400 Nancy Greene Way, North Vancouver; 604-984-0661; www.grousemountain.com.

On a clear, fogless day, Burnaby and Richmond are visible from the 21 ski runs at **Mt. Seymour.** Good novice runs make this a best bet for beginners or those who want to avoid hot doggers. Downhill runs are serviced by a network of chairlifts and tows and are open for night skiing. Though the skiing here is mainly beginning and intermediate (80 percent of the runs), Mt. Seymour attracts international professional snowboarders who come for the natural terrain in its three parks. Hilly cross-country trails run through the adjacent Mt. Seymour Provincial Park. ~ 1700 Mt. Seymour Road, North Vancouver; 604-986-2261; www.mountseymour.com.

Vancouver's waterfront path links up with interior paths in Stanley Park and Pacific Spirit Park, where bikers will find hills and solitude.

WHISTLER Whistler is considered by many to be one of North America's top ski areas. **Whistler-Blackcomb,** located 75 winding miles northeast of Vancouver at the base of Whistler and Blackcomb mountains, is a world-class resort and one of the top ski destinations in the world. The resort offers over 200 marked runs and the longest lift-serviced ski runs in North America, with a drop of one vertical mile. The official season runs from late November to late May, then starts again for glacier skiing in mid-June. ~ 4545 Blackcomb Way, Whistler; 604-904-7060, 888-403-4727; www.whistler-blackcomb.com.

RIDING STABLES

WHISTLER **Whistler Outdoor Experience Co.** leads guided rides in the summer through the Pemberton Meadows and along Ryan Creek and the Lillooet River. Winter sleigh rides provide views of glacier-fed Green Lake and a ring of mountains. ~ 8841 Route 99; 604-932-3389, 877-386-1888; www.whistleroutdoor.com.

GOLF

Golf in Vancouver is bound to involve water in some way. Even if there isn't much of it on the course, the location or the view will likely encompass a body of water—English Bay, the Strait of Georgia, one of the rivers.

DOWNTOWN VANCOUVER There are dozens of golf courses and practice facilities in and around Vancouver and Richmond. Near the Fraser River, **Fraserview Golf Course** is a par-72, 18-hole public course. ~ 7800 Vivian Street, Vancouver; 604-257-6923; www.frasierviewgolf.ca. The semiprivate **Mayfair Lakes Golf and Country Club** has lots of water—14 out of 18 holes have water, including the heavily bunkered 18th with water right up to the green. ~ 5460 Number 7 Road, Richmond; 604-276-0505; www.golfbc.com.

WHISTLER In Whistler you can tee off amid the splendid terrain at the **Whistler Golf Course,** an 18-hole public course. ~ 4001 Whistler Way; 604-932-3280, 800-376-1777; www.whistlergolf.com. Or you can swing and putt at the 18-hole **Château**

Whistler Golf Club. This narrow mountainous course is surrounded by trees and has scenic views of Blackcomb and Whistler mountains. ~ 4612 Blackcomb Way; 604-938-2097.

SUNSHINE COAST Open year-round, the 18-hole **Myrtle Point Golf Club** also has splendid views of Texada and Vancouver islands. ~ C-5 McCausland Road, RR #1, Powell River; 604-487-4653; www.myrtlepointgolfclub.com. **Pender Harbor Golf Club** has nine holes, surrounded by lush vegetation and breathtaking scenery. ~ Sunshine Coast Highway, Pender Harbor; 604-883-9541. The **Sunshine Coast Golf and Country Club** is an 18-hole semiprivate course. With challenging greens, the tree-lined par-71 course isn't too long and is good for the average golfer. ~ 3206 Sunshine Coast Highway, Roberts Creek; 604-885-9212, 800-667-5022; www.sunshinecoastgolf.com.

TENNIS

There are over 80 locations in the Vancouver area with tennis courts: most are free and first-come, first-served; all are open for play year-round, weather permitting. Call the Park Board (604-257-8400) for a list of locations other than those listed here. Of course, many of the area's resorts provide tennis facilities for guests as well.

WEST SIDE/GRANVILLE ISLAND **Kitsilano Beach Park** has ten public courts charging minimal fees (only during warm weather months). ~ Cornwall Avenue and Arbutus Street. Other parks with courts include **Queen Elizabeth Park,** just off Cambie Street, and **Jericho Beach Park,** off Northwest Marine Drive.

DOWNTOWN VANCOUVER Of the 21 courts in **Stanley Park,** six charge minimal fees for reserved playing times; the rest are free.

BIKING

WEST SIDE/GRANVILLE ISLAND To avoid busy streets, try the shoreside paths at **Jericho Beach** and **English Bay** and the pathways that parallel Chancellor and University boulevards and 15th Avenue on the scenic campus of the **University of British Columbia.**

DOWNTOWN VANCOUVER Because of heavy traffic in Vancouver, cyclists are better off sticking to the protected 5.5-mile seawall path around the perimeter of **Stanley Park.**

WHISTLER Biking is popular in Whistler, especially mountain biking on rough alpine trails or paved trails around **Lost Lake** and along the **Valley Trail,** which connects the village with the nearby residential areas, parks and lakes. Daredevils go for the **mountain descents,** often taking a helicopter or gondola to the peaks so that they don't expend the energy needed for zooming down the dry ski runs. At ungodly speeds they follow an experienced trail leader who knows how to run the slopes safely.

Whistler Outdoor Experience Co. offers a guided descent on Blackcomb Mountain as well as slower-paced bike tours of parks and lakes. ~ 8841 Highway 99; 604-932-3389, 877-386-1888; www.whistleroutdoor.com.

For a "heli-biking" adventure (a helicopter will fly you into a wilderness area for single-track mountain biking), contact **Whistler Backroads Mountain Bike Adventures.** ~ P.O. Box 643, Whistler, BC V0N 1B0; 604-932-3111; www.backroadswhistler.com.

SUNSHINE COAST There is no protected bike path along **Route 101**, the main artery of the Sunshine Coast, and the rocky shoulder drops off entirely at times, forcing bikers onto the highway. However, the moderately challenging trip from Langsdale to Earls Cove is popular nonetheless. The backcountry of the entire coast is laced with marked and unmarked **logging trails** leading off Route 101 just waiting to be explored by intrepid mountain bikers; a detailed map of the trails between Jervis Inlet and Lund is available from the Powell River Travel InfoCentre (604-485-4701; e-mail info@discoverpowellriver.com).

> The Soames Hill Mountain Trail is also known as "The Knob" because of its appearance to passengers on ferries approaching Langdale.

Bike Rentals & Tours **Spokes Bicycle Rentals** has a large selection of bike rentals; they arrange group tours to nearby Stanley Park. ~ 1798 West Georgia Street, Vancouver; 604-688-5141, fax 604-681-5581; www.vancouverbikerental.com. **Whistler Backroads Mountain Bike Adventures** also rents during the warm months. ~ Westbrook Hotel Base; 604-932-3111; www.backroadswhistler.com. On the Sunshine Coast, rent bikes at **Taws Cycle and Sports.** ~ 4597 Marine Avenue, Powell River; 604-485-2555, 877-481-2555; www.tawsonline.com.

All distances listed for trails are one way unless otherwise noted.

HIKING

◀ *HIDDEN*

WEST SIDE/GRANVILLE ISLAND **Pacific Spirit Regional Park** (30 miles) crisscrosses 1000 acres of parkland on Point Grey Peninsula, offering easy-to-moderate hikes of varying length through this largely unmarked ecological reserve. Here you're more likely to run into a blacktail deer or bald eagle than another hiker. A map is available from the Greater Vancouver Regional Parks office (604-432-6350).

DOWNTOWN VANCOUVER **Stanley Park Seawall Path** (5.5 miles), carefully divided to accommodate both cyclists and pedestrians, is easily the most popular hike in town. There are also numerous paths that plunge into the thickly forested acres of the park.

NORTH SHORE **Capilano Pacific Trail** (4.5 miles), in North Vancouver's Capilano River Regional Park, passes from massive Cleveland Dam to Ambleside Park through sections of coastal rainforest and offers great views of the Lions, the twin mountain peaks soaring majestically above the dam.

Norvan Falls (9.5 miles) offers a more rugged backcountry trek for the experienced hiker through the wilderness areas of Lynn Headwaters Regional Park. The shorter **Lynn Loop Trail** (3 miles) affords views of Lynn Valley and passes an abandoned cabin. Call 604-985-1690 for trail conditions.

WHISTLER   There are trails in Whistler for all levels. **Valley Trail** (15 miles roundtrip) is a bustling paved walkway/bike path/cross-country ski trail that winds through town, connecting Alpha, Nita, Alta, Lost and Green lakes, the village and the various residential areas.

Lost Lake Trails (9 miles, all together) serve as cross-country ski trails during the winter and make for fairly level summer hiking paths (with some paved areas) through the forested area between Lost and Green lakes.

Singing Pass-Russet Lake (6.75 miles), an alpine hiking trail just behind Whistler Village, and the graded **Garibaldi Lake Trail** (5.5 miles), located off Route 99 south of town, are prime options for experienced hikers interested in heading into the steep fringes of incredible Garibaldi Park.

SUNSHINE COAST   The **Soames Hill Mountain Trail** (1.5 miles) is a brisk stair climb to an elevation of 800 feet followed by expansive views of Howe Sound, the surrounding mountains and villages.

Smuggler's Cove Marine Park Trail (.5 mile) is an easy walk leading from the parking lot off Brooks Road approximately six miles north of Sechelt to the cove once used to smuggle in Chinese immigrants and other contraband and now home to an array of seabirds.

Mt. Valentine Trail (approximately 1 mile) offers a short walk up a gravel path followed by a steep climb up a stone staircase leading to panoramic views of Malaspina and Georgia straits, Vancouver Island and the surrounding town of Powell Lake.

Inland Lake Trail (8 miles), just north of Powell River, offers a longer hike over a well-maintained circuit of boardwalks and bridges through scenic swamp areas and skirting lovely Inland Lake. The entire trail is wheelchair accessible, and several handicap shelters and fishing wharfs are along the way.

▼ ▼ ▼ ▼ ▼ ▼ ▼ ▼ ▼
Transportation

CAR

From the West Coast of the United States, **Route 5** turns into **Route 99** after crossing the Canadian border at Blaine and proceeds northwest through Vancouver's suburbs and into the city core where the name changes once again, this time to **Granville Street**. The **Trans-Canada Highway (Route 1)** connects Vancouver with points east in Canada.

Route 99, referred to as the **Sea to Sky Highway** from Horseshoe Bay northward, picks up again in North Vancouver, hugs the rugged coastline and continues north into the mountains to Whistler.

Route 101, the only major thoroughfare through the Sunshine Coast, connects Langdale to Earls Cove and Saltery Bay to Lund, the northernmost point of this long, transcontinental highway with southern terminus in Chile.

AIR

Vancouver International Airport services domestic charters and flights by Harbour Air and Whistler Air Service. International airlines include Air Canada, Air China, Air New Zealand, Alaska Airlines, American Airlines, British Airways, Cathay Pacific Airways, Continental Airlines, Delta Air Lines, Horizon Air, Japan Airlines, KLM, Korean Air, Lufthansa, Northwest Airlines, Qantas, Singapore Airlines and United Airlines. ~ www.yvr.ca.

Airport express buses operated by **The Airporter** depart every 20 to 30 minutes or so from the arrivals level of the Main Terminal building and stop at the bus station and most major hotels in downtown Vancouver. ~ 604-946-8866, 800-668-3141; www.yvairporter.com. **Translink** buses also serve the airport; catch #424 from the airport and then transfer to #98 at Airport Station, which will take you right into downtown Vancouver. ~ 604-953-3333; www.translink.bc.ca.

BOAT

Between May and October, cruise ships call regularly at the terminal at **Canada Place**, an architectural stunner under Teflon-coated white "sails." ~ 999 Canada Place, Vancouver; 604-775-7200; www.canadaplace.ca.

BUS

Greyhound Bus Lines offers service to and from the United States. ~ 1150 Station Street, Vancouver; 800-231-2222 from the U.S., 800-661-8747 from Canada; www.greyhound.com.

TRAIN

Via Rail Canada (800-561-8630, within Canada; www.viarail.com) at 1150 Station Street in Vancouver provides rail service throughout Canada and connects with **Amtrak** (800-872-7245; www.amtrak.com) to points within the United States.

CAR RENTALS

Rental agencies at Vancouver International Airport include **Alamo Rent A Car** (800-462-5262), **Avis Rent A Car** (800-879-2847), **Budget Rent A Car** (800-299-3199), **Dollar Rent A Car** (800-800-3665), **Hertz Rent A Car** (800-263-0600), **Thrifty Car Rental** (800-847-4389).

Discount Car Rentals (604-207-8180) has an office in the neighboring suburb of Richmond and offers free airport pickup.

PUBLIC TRANSIT

Translink governs Vancouver's expansive transit system, with buses, the SkyTrain and the SeaBus, covering all the main arteries within the city and fanning out into the suburbs. Running on a 16-mile, mostly elevated track between Canada Place downtown and the suburb of Surrey, the SkyTrain is a good way to see some of the major sights of the city. You can also get a great view of the skyline from the water aboard the SeaBuses that cross Burrard Inlet between downtown and the North Shore. The handy "Transportation Services Guide for Greater Vancouver" tour guide, day passes and timetables are available from Travel Info Centres. ~ 604-953-3333; www.translink.bc.ca.

Whistler Transit (604-932-4020), the local operator for B. C. Transit, runs buses connecting Whistler Creek and Whistler Village every fifteen minutes. Translink is also responsible for transit service along the Sunshine Coast; for more information dial 604-953-3333.

TAXIS

Cab companies serving the airport include **Black Top and Checker Cabs** (604-731-1111), **Vancouver Taxi** (604-255-5111) and **Yellow Cab** (604-681-1111).

TWELVE

Victoria and
Southern Vancouver Island

I say, do you want a taste of veddy proper Britain without having to fly across the Atlantic? Then step into Victoria, a city of stately government buildings, picture-perfect lawns and fascinating glimpses of the British influence. Shorn, manicured and embellished, Victoria is called more British than Britain itself.

But have no fear: This is not stiff-upper-lip territory. Travel out of Victoria and you will find the rest of Vancouver Island an untamed land. Stretching 280 miles along the rugged Pacific coastline of Canada and the United States, it occupies some 12,400 square miles. Most of this mass protects the lower mainland of British Columbia from torrential rains and gale-force winds of the open ocean. However, the island does cross the 49th parallel, the general boundary between the United States and Canada, and its southern one-fifth, including the city of Victoria, is on the same latitude as parts of Washington State.

Much of the island lies in its natural state with beaches, forests, mountains and meadows. Rains nurture thick, sometimes ancient forests, and over centuries the ocean has carved out sandy beaches. The area is a stunning contrast of the rugged, mountainous and relatively uninhabited west coast to sleepy seaside villages, farms and provincial islands on the southeastern shore. Not all of Vancouver Island is so bucolic. The west coast is rugged with craggy mountains, a rugged coastline and often dramatic weather. Starting in September, the winter rains start to pour, and blustery winds are not uncommon. On the west coast, winds and rains can be brutal. Mountains drop right into a raging Pacific Ocean. Many remote settlements or camps—too small even to be called villages—have scant road access and rely on freighters, boats or float planes to deliver everything from apples to asphalt.

Geography and the elements have conspired to make the southern part of the island a relative haven where farming, tourism and commerce thrive. A number of picturesque villages and towns are perched on the coast. The Malahat Drive offers fabulous views of Washington's Olympic Mountains, the Gulf Islands and the Saanich Peninsula, which is dotted with small farms, orchards and gardens.

For the most part, the island's climate is gentle, thanks to the warmth from the Japanese current. A majestic range of mountains divides the island into a dense rainforest on the west coast and the drier lowlands on the east coast. The eastern summers can be blissful with long, sunny days. The climate of Victoria and the southeastern part of the island is akin to that of the Mediterranean—dry, cool summers and mild winters. It is no accident that many Canadians choose to retire there.

In contrast to the rugged side of Vancouver Island, Victoria emerges gracious and genteel. On the island's southern shore, this is the seat of the provincial government, but there is also a cozy and quaint look to the place. It overflows with flowers, the lawns graced with tulips, rhododendrons and roses, the window boxes and hanging planters filled with geraniums and lobelia. Victoria's economy rests on the shoulders of government and tourism. Although heightened in summer, tourism is a year-round activity in this city.

Unfortunately, the Victoria area's development has not come without some cost. The Saanich Peninsula once held large tracts of an ecosystem known as oak savannah, very similar to terrain a thousand miles south in California. Today the savannah, the rarest ecosystem in Canada, is almost gone, replaced by housing and farms. (You can see hints of what it looked like on Rockland Hill east of downtown Victoria, where a number of beautiful old oaks remain, and in Beacon Hill Park.)

Prior to settlement by white explorers, the island's people lived in harmony with nature. Natives lived in bands of the Nootka or Nuu-chah-nulth on the west, the Coast Salish to the south and east and the Southern Kwakiutl to the north. These people lived off the bounty of the land, principally the salmon, cedar and wild berries. Spanish explorers first came to the island in 1592, followed by Captain James Cook in 1778. Vancouver Island is the namesake of George Vancouver, British naval captain, who negotiated the island away from Spain in 1795.

In 1843 James Douglas, a representative of the Hudson's Bay Company and an explorer (the Douglas fir was named for him), established a fort. He named it after the British queen, Victoria, where Bastion Square sits on Wharf Street today, just above the Inner Harbour, an admirably protected anchorage. Coal mining, fishing, logging and fur trading brought settlers to other parts of the island.

Fortunately, the island's wealth of wildlife has not all been hunted away. Home to several species of salmon, the waters surrounding the island make for excellent fishing and offer a supply of natural food for orcas or killer whales, sea lions and seals. These waters also contain a wide variety of seabirds. The mountains and highlands contain Roosevelt elk, black bears, black tail deer, marmots, wolves and cougars.

It's all waiting for you. Ta-ta!

Downtown Victoria

The City of Gardens combines a rich, British heritage with a relaxed lifestyle and climate of the North American West Coast. Winsome, gracious and colorful, the city comes alive with sights that illustrate its history, customs and ties with the sea. Sightseeing in Victoria veers in the direction of its British influence, its natural history and the residents' passion for gardening.

The place to get information is the **Tourism Victoria Visitor Centre**, on the Inner Harbour. ~ 812 Wharf Street; 250-953-2033, 800-663-3883; www.tourismvictoria.com, e-mail info@tourismvictoria.com.

The **scenic marine drive** along the coast is the best route to see views of the water, the coast, the Olympic Mountains and some of Victoria's most elegant homes. Starting at Mile 0, the end of the Trans-Canada Highway, (at the intersection of Dallas Road and Douglas Street), follow the signs as the drive winds along the coast. You pass through Oak Bay, around part of Cadboro Bay, to Mount Douglas Park and the Saanich Peninsula. At Elk Lake, you can turn left onto Route 17 to head back to Victoria.

Visitors get a good overview of the city by taking a horse-drawn tour with **Tally-Ho Sight Seeing**, whose steeds have been clip-clopping their way through the streets since 1903. ~ Inner Harbour; 250-383-5067, 866-383-5067, fax 250-652-0143; www.tallyhotours.com. Another tour company offering horse-drawn outings is **Victoria Carriage Tours**. ~ Tours leave from the corner of Belleville and Menzies streets; 250-383-2207, 877-663-2207, fax 250-383-2097; www.victoriacarriage.com.

SIGHTS

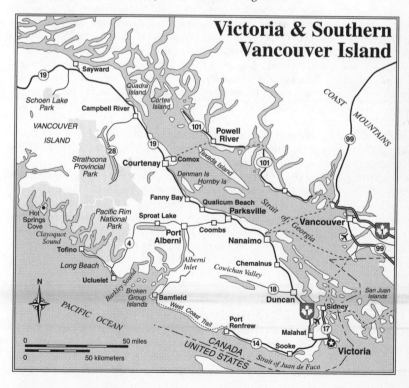

Victoria & Southern Vancouver Island

The **Fairmont Empress** is Victoria's unofficial central landmark and faces the Inner Harbour. Opened in 1908, it reflects the gentility of an earlier time. The Palm Court, with its magnificent stained-glass dome, is renowned for its afternoon teas and tropical plants. ~ 721 Government Street; 250-384-8111, fax 250-389-2747; www.fairmont.com/empress, e-mail theempress@fairmont.com.

On the ground floor of the Empress hotel, you will find **Miniature World**, with more than 80 miniaturized illustrations of history and fantasy. Miniature World includes the world's smallest operational sawmill, two of the world's largest dollhouses and one of the world's largest model railways. Admission. ~ 649 Humboldt Street; 250-385-9731, fax 250-385-2835; www.miniatureworld.com, e-mail info@miniatureworld.com.

Walk across Belleville Street, just south of the Fairmont Empress, to a complex anchored by the **Royal British Columbia Museum**. One of the best on the continent, the museum focuses on the history of British Columbia—its land and people from prehistoric times to the present—in a personal and evocative way. Visitors sit among totem poles, walk inside a longhouse and learn stories of native people and the changes they encountered once white settlers arrived. The museum's spectacular collection of First Nations ceremonial masks is probably the finest in the world. Museum guests also can stroll down the streets of Old Town, plunge into the bowels of a coal mine and walk through the *Discovery*, a replica of the ship used by Captain Vancouver. In the Ocean Station exhibit you can peer through portholes and a periscope at kelp beds, fishes, sea stars, sea urchins and other B.C. ocean life in a 95-gallon aquarium. There is also an IMAX theater on site. Admission. ~ 675 Belleville Street; 250-356-7226, 888-447-7977, fax 250-387-5674; www.royalbcmuseum.bc.ca.

Part of the complex is **Thunderbird Park**, a postage stamp–sized park covering only a quarter of the block. The park is the site of ten or so magnificent totem poles and a longhouse in which natives demonstrate the crafts of carving and beading during the summer. ~ Belleville and Douglas streets.

Just behind the park and adjacent to the museum is **Helmcken House**, built in 1852 for pioneer doctor J. S. Helmcken. This is British Columbia's oldest residence on its original site. Rooms decorated in the style of the period are furnished with pieces brought around Cape Horn from England by Victoria's founding families. The library includes Dr. Helmcken's medicine chest and medical instruments. Call for winter hours. Admission. ~ 10 Elliott Street beside the Royal British Columbia Museum; 250-356-7226; www.royalbcmuseum.bc.ca, e-mail reception@royalbcmuseum.bc.ca.

From here you can take a detour (just a couple blocks south) to a Victorian Italianate cottage known as **Emily Carr House**, where Canada's most famous female artist, British Columbia landscape painter Emily Carr, was born in 1871 and lived her girlhood years. Carr was a contemporary of Georgia O'Keeffe in the U.S. and Frida Kahlo in Mexico. Historians have restored the home with period wall coverings and furnishings to look as it did when she lived there. Carr was also an author, and her gardens have been re-created from her books, excerpts of which are inscribed on plaques among the vegetation. Closed October to June, except the month of December. Admission. ~ 207 Government Street; 250-383-5843; www.emilycarr.com.

The **Parliament Buildings** are in the next block west of the Royal British Columbia Museum. The legislative buildings are

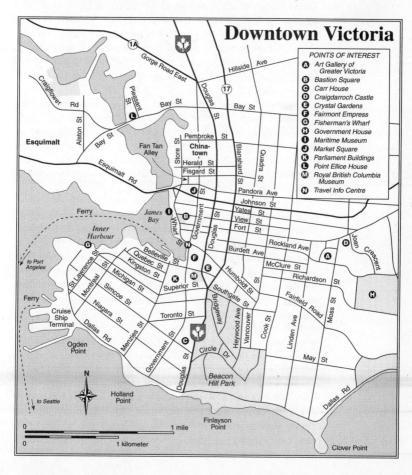

Downtown Victoria

POINTS OF INTEREST

- **A** Art Gallery of Greater Victoria
- **B** Bastion Square
- **C** Carr House
- **D** Craigdarroch Castle
- **E** Crystal Gardens
- **F** Fairmont Empress
- **G** Fisherman's Wharf
- **H** Government House
- **I** Maritime Museum
- **J** Market Square
- **K** Parliament Buildings
- **L** Point Ellice House
- **M** Royal British Columbia Museum
- **N** Travel Info Centre

Francis Rattenbury's creation, dating back to 1898, and feature 33 copper domes. At night they are outlined with more than 3000 twinkling lights. A statue of Queen Victoria stands in front of the buildings, and many others are located in the buildings themselves. Guided tours explain historic features and the workings of the provincial government. Closed weekends between Labor Day and early June. ~ 501 Belleville Street; 250-387-3046, fax 250-356-5876.

> More Canadians retire to Greater Victoria than anywhere else in the country, thanks to its relatively mild climate and fairytale Olde English character.

Across the street is the **Royal London Wax Museum**, also designed by Rattenbury as the Victoria terminal for the Canadian Pacific Steamships. The Acropolis-style building now contains wax sculptures of the Princess of Wales, President George W. Bush and some 300 other Josephine Tussaud figures. The likenesses of the American figures are lacking, but the Royal Family is very lifelike. You will want to keep young children out of the Horror Chamber with its gruesome depictions of decapitations and other methods of torture, but adolescents love it. Admission. ~ 470 Belleville Street; 250-388-4461, 877-929-3228, fax 250-388-4493; www.waxworld.com, e-mail khl@pinc.com.

On the water side of the Wax Museum is the **Pacific Undersea Gardens**, a salute to British Columbia life below water. At regularly scheduled intervals, divers swim behind huge windows in the enclosed aquarium tanks to show and tell visitors information about sea creatures within the province. Admission. ~ 490 Belleville Street; 250-382-5717, fax 250-382-5210; www.pacific underseagardens.com, e-mail pug@obmg.com.

You can continue out Belleville Street by car, cab, bus or bicycle to picturesque **Fisherman's Wharf**, a working fishing pier. Moorage allows for up to 400 boats, but the little bay often is jammed with many more, tied up to one another. If the fishing fleet is in, visitors can buy fresh fish from the docks. ~ Corner of Dallas Road and Erie Street. A walk in the **James Bay neighborhood,** one of the city's more fashionable areas, takes you past several restored Victorian and Edwardian homes.

Continue back around the Inner Harbour past the Empress and the Travel Info Centre heading north on Wharf Street to **Bastion Square**. In 1843–44, James Douglas established Fort Victoria here, but the buildings there now, including warehouses, offices, saloons and waterfront hotels, were constructed in the late 1800s, the city's boom period. The buildings, many of them red brick, have been restored and now house restaurants, shops and art galleries. The square itself is home to a couple dozen craft and gift booths during good weather. ~ Off Wharf Street between Fort and Yates streets.

The **Maritime Museum of British Columbia** is housed in a large, turreted building that was originally the Provincial Court House. The museum depicts British Columbia's maritime history from its early days to the present. It includes nautical charts, an extensive model ship collection, brassware from old ships, Navy uniforms and an incredible vessel—*Tilikum*, a 38-foot dugout canoe that sailed from Victoria to England at the turn of the 20th century. The museum's lighthouse includes both old and new apparatus, along with the history of the characters who ran the equipment. Admission. ~ 28 Bastion Square; 250-385-4222, fax 250-382-2869; www.mmbc.bc.ca, e-mail info@mmbc.bc.ca.

Walk over to Government Street and continue north to Johnson Street. Here you will find **Market Square**. Market Square incorporates the original Occidental Hotel, the choice of many Klondike gold miners in 1898, now a favorite area for shopping and dining. ~ Government and Johnson streets.

Take Fan Tan Alley north another block to **Chinatown** at Government and Herald streets. In the late 19th century, Victoria's Chinatown was second largest on the continent, only trailing that of San Francisco. The Chinese immigrants headed to British Columbia to work on the railroad and to mine for coal and gold. Approaching Chinatown from Government Street, you see the ceramic-tiled Gate of Harmonious Interest with two hand-carved stone lions standing guard. Fan Tan Alley, dubbed Canada's narrowest street, contains boutiques and artists' studios.

LODGING

The problem with lodging in Victoria is the same as elsewhere in popular cities—it's expensive. Several luxurious hotels line the Inner Harbour. Several others charge luxurious prices for mediocre to shoddy rooms. Budget prices can be found, but those accommodations are often farther from downtown.

Like Vancouver's, Victoria's high season is the end of June to October. And like Vancouver's, the city's hotels offer superlative off-season lodging packages that often bring room rates down to near 50 percent of the summer tariff. The weather isn't as dependable, but the streets aren't thronged with crowds of bus-borne tourists. For more information, call **Tourism Victoria**, whose accommodation line provides travelers with current rates and availability at a full range of places. ~ 812 Wharf Street; 800-663-3883, fax 250-382-6539; www.tourismvictoria.com, e-mail info@tourismvictoria.com.

Located in an ideal location downtown, across from Victoria Bay Centre, is the **Bedford Regency Hotel**. The large open lobby is furnished with traditional pieces. Invoking the charm of early Victoria, the hotel's 40 individually decorated guest rooms feature comfortable beds complete with down comforters and pillows, cotton sheets, window boxes overflowing with colorful flowers; some have marble fireplaces. A full breakfast is served in the hotel's Belingo 1140 Lounge and fresh coffee or tea is placed outside each room in the morning. ~ 1140 Government Street; 250-384-6835, 800-665-6500, fax 250-386-8930; www. bedfordregency.com, e-mail bedford@victoriabc.com. DELUXE TO ULTRA-DELUXE.

The dominant sight in Victoria's Inner Harbour is the stately, neo-Gothic **Fairmont Empress**. Canadian Pacific Railways commissioned architect Francis Rattenbury to design this magnificent hotel. Amenities include a swimming pool, sauna, health club, spa, lobby and lovely grounds. This grande-dame hotel with 477 guest rooms is known throughout the world for its British-style elegance and wonderful afternoon teas. Make reservations one to two weeks in advance. ~ 721 Government Street; 250-384-8111, 800-441-1414, fax 250-389-2747; www.fairmont.com/empress, e-mail theempress@fairmont.com. ULTRA-DELUXE.

Even after renovating its 45 rooms, the **James Bay Inn** still fills the bill for price-minded travelers. It is located in a residential area among heritage homes and small cafés but is pretty convenient to downtown. The hotel, which opened in 1911, features light-oak paneling and period furnishings in the lobby. Guest rooms are small but have been updated with new paint, carpet and linens. Pub and restaurant are on the premises. A few travelers have found the service here a bit gruff. ~ 270 Government Street; 250-384-7151, 800-836-2649, fax 250-385-2311; www.james bayinn.com, e-mail info@jamesbayinn.bc.ca. MODERATE.

For luxury accommodations along the Inner Harbour near the Parliament Buildings, **Hotel Grand Pacific** is one of the city's finest. The lobby and other public areas are airy and lavish affairs.

AUTHOR FAVORITE

Abigail's is just four blocks east of downtown. This Tudor inn has a European ambience with colorful, well-kept gardens and a light, bright interior. The foyer features marble floors and an open oak staircase to the guest rooms. The sitting room is luxurious with hardwood floors, leather sofa, fireplace and fresh flowers. Each of the 23 rooms and suites features down comforters and antiques, and some have whirlpool baths, fireplaces and vaulted ceilings. In a new spa treatment room, guests can receive a massage, manicure or facial. Included in the room rate are evening hors d'oeuvres in the library and a gourmet breakfast served in the dining room. Free parking. ~ 906 McClure Street; 250-388-5363, 800-561-6565, fax 250-388-7787; www.abigailshotel.com, e-mail innkeeper@abigailshotel.com. DELUXE TO ULTRA-DELUXE.

The rooms and suites offer views of the harbor or downtown, as well as private balconies; the west wing offers one of the city's best views of the Inner Harbour. Amenities include an indoor swimming pool, sauna, whirlpool, health and fitness facilities, a European-style spa, restaurants and a lounge. ~ 463 Belleville Street; 250-386-0450, 800-663-7550, fax 250-380-4475; www. hotelgrandpacific.com, e-mail reserve@hotelgrandpacific.com. ULTRA-DELUXE.

Just a brisk walk, shuttle or ferry ride from the downtown attractions, the **Coast Harbourside Hotel & Marina** faces a 42-slip marina. Marine colors of teal blue, dark mahogany, original art and watery motifs are found throughout the hotel. The 132 rooms and suites, each with private balcony, come with all the amenities of a top-rate hotel, including a bar and computer hookups. Pick your view: the harbor or the Olympic Mountains. The hotel features an indoor/outdoor pool and deck, with whirlpool, sauna and exercise room. They also offer free parking and a courtesy van to downtown. ~ 146 Kingston Street; 250-360-1211, 800-716-6199, fax 250-360-1418; www.coasthotels.com, e-mail info harbourside@coasthotels.com. DELUXE TO ULTRA-DELUXE.

The place for basic accommodations is the **Victoria Hostel**, sandwiched between historic buildings and offices downtown. The hostel features two kitchens, a game room, a lounge, an eating area, a library, a bicycle-storage area, laundry facilities and hot showers. There are 108 beds, dormitory-style, and five small family rooms. Private double-occupancy rooms are available with reservation. ~ 516 Yates Street; 250-385-4511, 888-883-0099, fax 250-385-3232; www.hihostels.ca, e-mail info@hihostels.ca. BUDGET.

Ocean Island Backpackers Inn is a funky but very economical property in the west end of downtown Victoria, near Chinatown. Facilities include a licensed pub, kitchen, internet access, storage and parking. The 200 beds include some private rooms, and there is no curfew. Rates start as low as C$18.95 (US$12). ~ 791 Pandora Avenue; 250-382-1788, 888-888-4180, fax 250-385-1780; www.oceanisland.com, e-mail get-it@oceanisland.com. BUDGET TO MODERATE.

Swans Suite Hotel is a small, 29-suite hotel in a restored brick heritage building along the harbor in downtown Victoria offering a colorful pub and restaurant. Each contemporary unit, ranging from studios to two-bedroom suites, features designer decor and includes a full kitchen, dining area and original art on the walls. ~ 506 Pandora Avenue; 250-361-3310, 800-668-7926, fax 250-361-3491; www.swanshotel.com, e-mail info@swans hotel.com. MODERATE TO DELUXE.

A truly hidden discovery for couples seeking a romantic getaway is **Humboldt House Bed & Breakfast**, which looks like a   ◀ *HIDDEN* private residence. A Victorian home built in 1895 and renovated in 1988, it includes six suites. The library offers walls full of books and a fireplace. Guests are served champagne and truffles on arrival. The rooms are individually decorated with stained glass and have jacuzzis and fireplaces. Guests have breakfast delivered to their room via a two-way compartment. ~ 867 Humboldt Street; 250-383-0152, 888-383-0327, fax 250-383-6402; www.humboldthouse.com, e-mail rooms@humboldt house.com. ULTRA-DELUXE.

A large, 1905 Edwardian-style home, the **Beaconsfield Inn** has an early 1900s ambience with antique pieces, stained glass, oak fireplace, 14-foot beamed ceiling and the original, dark paneling. Millionaire R. P. Rithet built it in 1905 as a wedding present for his daughter, Gertrude. The nine guest rooms vary in charm, but all include down comforters and antiques. Many feature canopy beds, jacuzzis and fireplaces. Guests also can enjoy afternoon tea, sherry hour in the library and a full gourmet breakfast in the original dining room or sunroom, all included in the room rate. ~ 998 Humboldt Street; 250-384-4044, 888-884-4044, fax 250-384-4052; www.beaconsfieldinn.com, e-mail info@beaconsfieldinn.com. DELUXE TO ULTRA-DELUXE.

Dashwood Manor Bed and Breakfast, a gracious Tudor mansion built in 1912, sits next to Beacon Hill Park and offers unobstructed views of the Strait of Juan de Fuca and the Olympic Mountains. Breakfast is make-it-yourself with ingredients provided in the kitchenettes in each of the guest rooms. Three of the 14 rooms have fireplaces and four have jacuzzis. Complimentary wine and cheese are served in the late afternoon. The grounds are impeccable and the rooms are clean. ~ 1 Cook Street; 250-385-5517, 800-667-5517, fax 250-383-1760; www.dashwood manor.com, e-mail frontdesk@dashwoodmanor.com. DELUXE TO ULTRA-DELUXE.

DINING

HIDDEN ►

How can anything at the Fairmont Empress be hidden? Easy: So much attention focuses on the hotel's lobby, tea service and upscale shops that visitors overlook the **Bengal Lounge**, a curry bar par excellence. Once the hotel's library, the lounge is decorated with curios reflecting the British Empire's colonial era—a tiger-skin wall hanging, Indian ceiling fans. The curry is served buffet-style at lunch and dinner; a death-by-chocolate dessert bar is available Friday and Saturday nights. A word to the wise: The Bengal Lounge serves an all-day à la carte menu. If you want to experience tea at the Empress, but haven't made a reservation, you can order tea and scones here. It's a welcome contrast to the monotony of British pub fare that tends to overwhelm Victoria dining. ~ Fairmont Empress, 721 Government Street; 250-384-8111, fax 250-389-2747; e-mail theempress@fairmont.com. DELUXE.

James Bay Tea Room and Restaurant is a homey place with photographs of English royalty overlooking tables set close together with hand-crocheted tea cozies insulating every teapot. This place is popular with the older set and families. Breakfast, lunch and tea service available all day. ~ 332 Menzies Street; 250-382-8282, fax 250-389-1716; www.jamesbaytearoomand restaurant.com, e-mail jamesbaytearoom@shaw.ca. BUDGET.

A charming and graceful Japanese restaurant is **Yokohama**. Its large sushi bar with an extensive menu is deemed the best place in town for such fare. The restaurant features authentic Japanese entrées as well as familiar favorites of tempura, sukiyaki and ginger pork in the main dining area or in private tatami rooms. ~ 980 Blanshard Street; 250-384-5433, fax 250-384-5438. MODERATE.

The Keg Steakhouse and Bar is an informal restaurant, one of the most popular, reasonably priced places downtown. Its dining room offers great views of the Inner Harbour. Entrées include prime rib and grilled shrimp. Try the Classic Meal, a sirloin or New York steak served with seasonal vegetables and caesar salad. Dinner only. ~ 500 Fort Street; 250-386-7789, fax 250-386-5201; www.kegsteakhouse.com. MODERATE TO DELUXE.

Delicious Greek food, including moussaka, souvlaki and spanakopita, along with standard steaks and seafood are served at **Periklis**, a convivial, *taverna*-style restaurant with dining areas on three levels and Greek posters on the walls. Greek and belly dancing draws big crowds on the weekends in winter and seven nights a week during the summer. Dinner only. ~ 531 Yates Street; 250-386-3313, fax 250-386-5531. MODERATE TO DELUXE.

Thai Siam serves up some of the best Thai food in Victoria. The atmosphere is dark and quiet, with soft lighting lending a bit of mystery to this ethnic eatery. Only fresh ingredients are used in the entrées, such as *larp gai*, diced chicken in spicy lime juice,

AUTHOR FAVORITE

Historic Bastion Square is home to one of Victoria's best restaurants. **Camille's Restaurant** is romantic and elegant with brick walls, balloon curtains and linen tablecloths. This intimate restaurant prepares delicious West Coast and Pacific Rim cuisine, such as local Muscovy duck with orange and lavender demiglace, and spice-crusted venison on beet and barley risotto. The breads and desserts are heavenly. Camille's also has an extensive wine cellar. Dinner only. Closed Sunday and Monday. ~ 45 Bastion Square; 250-381-3433, fax 250-381-3403; www.camilles restaurant.com, e-mail info@camillesrestaurant.com. DELUXE.

onions and vegetables, or *kung phad prik paow*, sautéed prawns with green-red peppers, onions, mushrooms and chili paste. ~ 512 Fort Street; 250-383-9911, fax 250-380-2220. MODERATE.

HIDDEN ►

Crowds line up outside the **Blue Fox** on weekend mornings to get in this small Fort Street café. They've come for heaping platters of breakfast—huge omelettes, piles of hash browns and toast, or redolent huevos rancheros—and equally filling lunch, including that endangered rarity: handmade hamburgers. Breakfast is available all day, of course. ~ 919 Fort Street; 250-380-1683. BUDGET.

Bean Around the World is a cozy, friendly and top-quality coffee shop in Chinatown. The coffee is custom roasted, and the muffins and pastries are fresh and filling. It also serves light lunches. ~ 533 Fisgard Street; 250-386-7115; www.cowboy coffee.ca. BUDGET.

A traditional Chinese restaurant in the heart of Chinatown is **Don Mee**. Go through the door under the neon sign and walk up a long, burgundy-carpeted staircase to the large dining area. The food here is good, portions are ample and the presentation is upscale. People come for the Cantonese-style seafood dishes like lobster in ginger sauce or crab with black beans. Favorites include Szechuan chicken and fresh vegetable dishes. The dim sum, served for lunch daily, is especially good. ~ 538 Fisgard Street; 250-383-1032, fax 250-383-8387; www.donmee.com. MODERATE.

Outdoor dining made warm and cozy by fireplaces and overhead heaters is offered by **Il Terrazzo**. Here they serve sophisticated Northern Italian cuisine on a brick plant-filled terrace off Waddington Alley. Daily specials yield such possibilities as grilled lamb chops seasoned with garlic and fresh mint or baked halibut with fresh raspberry sauce No lunch on weekends in winter. ~ 555 Johnson Street; 250-361-0028, fax 250-360-2594; www.il terrazzo.com. MODERATE TO DELUXE.

SHOPPING

Victoria's downtown is chock full of fascinating shops. Best buys are locally made candies, Indian-made sweaters, carvings and silver, British Columbia jade, weavings and pottery, books on Canada and goods imported from Britain. Shopping starts with tiny shops in the Empress Hotel and extends north on Government Street.

Even if you brought all your reading with you, stop at **Munro's Books** to see this neoclassical heritage building with high ceilings and carved details, formerly the head office of the Royal Bank. It is one of the finest bookshops in western Canada. The shop holds more than 50,000 titles of Canadian, British and American works. ~ 1108 Government Street; 250-382-2464, 888-243-2464, fax 250-382-2832; www.munrobooks.com, e-mail service@ munrobooks.com.

The purveyor of fine teas and coffees is **Murchies**, where you can also pick up some delectable pastries and enjoy lunch or afternoon tea. ~ 1110 Government Street; 250-383-3112, fax 250-383-3255; www.murchies.com.

For Irish linen tablecloths, fine handkerchieves, linen blouses and embroideries, visit the **Irish Linen Store**. ~ 1019 Government Street; 250-383-6812; www.irishlinenvictoria.com.

The Bay Centre, a multilevel shopping mall located in the heart of Victoria, has more than 90 shops and opens to an interior courtyard under skylights and arches. Bay Centre offers goods from all over the Commonwealth, especially china and woolen products. ~ Government and Fort streets; 250-952-5690, fax 250-381-5285; www.baycentre.ca.

Located within Bay Centre, the **Hudson's Bay Company** is the Canadian company that pioneered settlement of the West. It still carries the famous Hudson's Bay point blankets and top brands of English china and woolens. It also houses a gallery featuring bay history art. ~ 1150 Douglas Street; 250-385-1311, fax 250-385-9247; www.hbc.com.

Fort Street between Blanshard and Cook streets is known as **Antique Row**, with stores offering antique maps, stamps, coins, estate jewelry, rare books, crystal, china, furniture and paintings.

NIGHTLIFE

In the Fairmont Empress, the **Bengal Lounge**, with its high ceilings, potted plants and rattan furnishings, is fit for the raj. It is a comfortable, old-money place for a drink. ~ 721 Government Street; 250-384-8111.

Hush, a gay-friendly danceclub, features house music. Deejays provide music Wednesday through Sunday until 2 a.m. Cover. ~ 1325 Government Street; 250-385-0566.

AUTHOR FAVORITE

Roger's Chocolates is the place for connoisseurs of fine chocolates. Roger's started offering chocolates to Victorians in 1885, and ever since then fans have been returning for the hugely popular "Victoria Creams." Housed in a 1903 building with a tiled floor, dark-oak paneling and oak-and-glass display cases, the shop is full of Dickensian charm. Some of the sinfully luscious confections include Empress Squares (caramel and roasted almonds in semisweet chocolate), classic truffles (filled with orange, raspberry, mocha and coconut) and traditional chocolate almond brittle. ~ 913 Government Street; 250-384-7021, 800-663-2220, fax 250-384-5750; www.rogerschocolates.com, e-mail info@rogers chocolates.com.

For a more cultured evening, Victoria offers several options. The well-respected **Pacific Opera Victoria** performs at the **Royal Theatre**. ~ Theatre: 805 Broughton Street; 250-385-0222, 250-386-6121; www.pov.bc.ca, e-mail boxoffice@pov.bc.ca.

The **Victoria Symphony** offers concerts featuring international conductors and artists. On the first weekend in August it holds the celebrated "Symphony Splash," a free, open-air concert where the orchestra plays from a barge in the harbor. ~ 846 Broughton Street; information 250-385-9771, tickets 250-385-6515, fax 250-385-7767; www.victoriasymphony.bc.ca, e-mail box.office@victoriasymphony.bc.ca.

Victoria's pubs offer an alternative to the expensive price of having a drink in the hotel lounges. Some of these pubs feature beers made on the premises, while others stock a wide variety of local and imported beers and ales. Whether in historic buildings or cottage breweries, you also are apt to find a game of darts and a number of skilled competitors. One of the liveliest pub crowds is found at the **Swans Suite Hotel**, where you can hear great live music every night and see a changing and colorful collection of local and international art. ~ 506 Pandora Avenue; 250-361-3310, 800-668-7926; www.swanshotel.com.

Centennial Square arts center includes the original City Hall (1878) and the **McPherson Playhouse**. The playhouse is a restored baroque and Edwardian-style theater seating 818. It hosts stage plays, classical and pops concerts, dance performances, films and touring lectures. **The Gallery at the** MAC, located in the lobby, showcases local visual artists. ~ Government and Pandora streets; 250-386-6121; www.rmts.bc.ca, e-mail marketing@rmts.bc.ca.

Darcy's Wharfside Pub is a comfy old-style pub with pool tables, a patio and live music on weekends. Cover. ~ 1127 Wharf Street; 250-380-1322; www.darcyspub.ca.

A favorite spot for karaoke singalongs is **Sopranos Karaoke Club**. ~ 730 Caledonia Street; 250-382-5853; www.sopranos karaoke.com.

PARKS

BEACON HILL PARK   This sedate park near downtown, founded in 1882, contains forest, open grassy areas, ponds and Goodacre Lake, a wildfowl sanctuary. Among gardens blooming nearly year-round, you also will find one of the tallest totem poles in the world, lawn bowling, an 1850s cricket pitch, the Mile 0 marker of the Trans-Canada Highway and a children's petting zoo in the summer, all at the southwestern corner where Dallas Road and Douglas Street meet. Facilities include restrooms, picnic areas, tennis courts, playground, lawn bowling, baseball and soccer fields, a children's wading pool and water play area. ~ Along Douglas Street, only a ten-minute walk from the Empress hotel; 250-361-0600, fax 250-361-0615.

Beyond the heart of Victoria are some of the city's most important landmarks including a castle fit for a queen and the

Victoria Neighborhoods

house where Her Majesty actually stays on her visits. Your itinerary also features Victoria's major art gallery and a leading museum of Victoriana. If you have half a day at your disposal, just follow our lead.

You'll need your own or public transportation to head out east on Fort Street to **Craigdarroch Castle**. Robert Dunsmuir had the house built for his family after he made his fortune mining coal on Vancouver Island in the mid-1800s, making him one of the richest men in British Columbia. Sadly, Dunsmuir himself died before the castle was completed in 1890. Today, visitors can tour Craigdarroch, furnished in turn-of-the-20th-century style featuring 22,000 square feet on five floors with stained-glass windows, intricate woodwork, period furniture and turrets. Exploring the castle requires some agility; there is no elevator and there are 87 steps throughout the self-guided tour. Admission. ~ 1050 Joan Crescent; 250-592-5323, fax 250-592-1099; www.thecastle.ca, e-mail info@thecastle.ca.

SIGHTS

Just a couple of blocks southwest of the castle is the **Art Gallery of Greater Victoria**. One of Canada's finest art museums, this gallery features Canadian art, European pieces from the 15th through 20th centuries and the only authentic Shinto shrine outside Japan, plus a large Asian art collection. A portion of the gallery is housed in Spencer Mansion, built in 1890, which features a dramatic staircase, a Jacobean ceiling and a dollhouse with many intricate details. Admission. ~ 1040 Moss Street; 250-384-4101, fax 250-361-3995; aggv.bc.ca.

VANCOUVER ISLAND'S VICTORIAN FORT

Swing west of Victoria along Esquimalt Harbour to visit one of the region's most important landmarks, **Fort Rodd Hill National Historic Site**, a 44-acre park of rolling hills; an open, parade-grounds area; woods; and beach. The fort was built in 1895 to protect the entrance to the Royal Navy Yards in Esquimalt Harbor. It became a park in 1962. Visitors can see restored gun batteries and the restored Fisgard Lighthouse, the oldest lighthouse on the Pacific Coast, which features exhibits on shipwrecks and navigation. A film is shown at the entrance of both sites. Admission. ~ Ocean Boulevard off the Old Island Highway, Esquimalt; 250-478-5849, fax 250-478-2816; www.pc.gc.ca/fortroddhill, e-mail fort.rodd@pc.gc.ca.

A few blocks southeast is **Government House,** where the Queen of England and her family stay when they visit Victoria. It is the official residence of the Lieutenant Governor, the Queen's representative in British Columbia. When royalty is not visiting, the public can stroll through the formal lawns and gardens, complete with a lily pond, waterfall and extensive collection of roses. It's a pleasant, uncrowded (and free) contrast to the frenzy of Butchart Gardens. ~ 1401 Rockland Avenue; 250-387-2080, fax 250-387-2078; www.ltgov.bc.ca.

Take a few minutes to explore **Rockland Avenue,** home of many mansions, ranging from late Victorian to Craftsman style, built during the 1880s and 1890s.

If you enjoy Victorian furnishings, you will want to see **Point Ellice House,** which contains British Columbia's most comprehensive collection of Victorian furnishings and art in its original setting. The house was built around 1862. Visitors also can stroll through a wonderful 19th-century garden where afternoon tea is served daily (reservations required) throughout the summer. The house can be reached by a ten-minute ferry ride from Victoria's Inner Harbour (ferry information, 250-708-0201). Limited hours; call ahead. Admission. ~ 2616 Pleasant Street off Bay Street; 250-380-6506; www.pointellicehouse.ca.

LODGING

Ifanwen Bed and Breakfast is in the quiet residential area of James Bay, but downtown shopping and attractions are only a leisurely stroll away. The full breakfast is cooked to order and guests can enjoy the sundeck or the secluded garden, depending upon the weather. Gay-friendly. ~ 44 Simcoe Street; 250-384-3717; www.ifanwen.com, e-mail ifanwen@telus.net. MODERATE.

Many of the furnishings in **Amethyst Inn** were shipped around Cape Horn in barrels of protective molasses—they and this exquisite 1885 Victorian mansion remain in pristine condition today. The decorative frieze girdling the high walls of the public rooms is incredibly intricate, and the European tilework on the fireplaces is priceless. Every room has a soaker tub, spa or antique clawfoot tub. ~ 1501 Fort Street; 888-265-6499, fax 250-595-2054; www.amethyst-inn.com, e-mail innkeeper@amethyst-inn.com. DELUXE TO ULTRA-DELUXE.

Oak Bay Bed and Breakfast Guest House is a 1912 B&B furnished with period antiques. The 11 rooms offer garden views and private baths, some with clawfoot tubs. Relax by the living-room fireplace or enjoy a book in the sunroom. Gay-friendly. ~ 1052 Newport Avenue, Oak Bay; 250-598-3812, 800-575-3812, fax 250-598-0369; www.oakbayguesthouse.com, e-mail stay@oakbayguesthouse.com. MODERATE.

If you don't mind student housing without frills, the **University of Victoria Housing Services,** 20 minutes north of downtown,

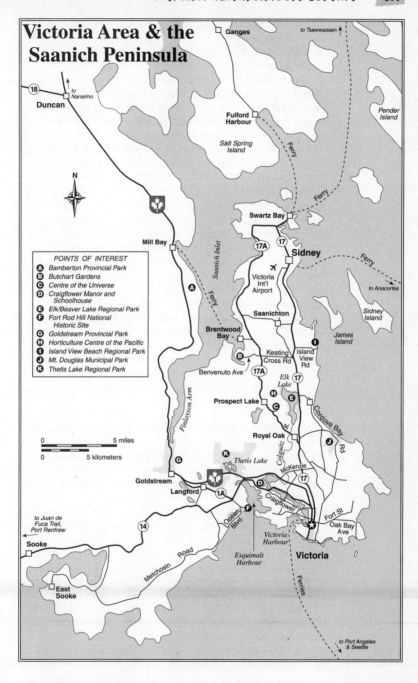

Victoria Area & the Saanich Peninsula

to Tsawwassen

Ganges

to Nanaimo

18

Duncan

Fulford
Harbour

Pender
Island

Salt Spring
Island

Ferry

N

Mill Bay

Swartz Bay

Ferry

17A   17

Sidney

Ferry

Victoria
Int'l
Airport

to Anacortes

Saanichton

Sidney
Island

POINTS OF INTEREST

A Bamberton Provincial Park
B Butchart Gardens
C Centre of the Universe
D Craigflower Manor and
    Schoolhouse
E Elk/Beaver Lake Regional Park
F Fort Rod Hill National
    Historic Site
G Goldstream Provincial Park
H Horticulture Centre of the Pacific
I Island View Beach Regional Park
J Mt. Douglas Municipal Park
K Thetis Lake Regional Park

Brentwood
Bay

Keating
Cross Rd

Island
View
Rd

James
Island

Benvenuto Ave

17A

Elk
Lake

17

Prospect Lake

Cordova Bay Rd

0   5 miles

0   5 kilometers

Royal Oak

Colquitz Rd

Thetis Lake

McKenzie

17

Goldstream

Langford

1A

to Juan de
Fuca Trail,
Port Renfrew

14

Ocean Blvd

Craigflower

Fort St

Oak Bay
Ave

Sooke

Metchosin Road

Victoria
Harbour

Victoria

East
Sooke

Esquimalt
Harbour

Ferries

to Port Angeles
& Seattle

offers over 800 rooms, including breakfast in the residence dining room, from May 1 to August 30. ~ P.O. Box 1700, Sinclair Road, Victoria, BC V8W 2Y2; 250-721-8395, fax 250-721-8930; housing.uvic.ca, e-mail keene@uvvm.uvic.ca. BUDGET.

The Gorge Waterway extends northwest from the Inner Harbour. Here you will find a number of less expensive motels. Hidden among the many motels lining Gorge Road, the **Travelodge** is one that offers the most quality and service for your money. The hotel appeals to families because of its indoor pool, twin saunas, full-service restaurant and lounge. Just a few minutes drive from downtown, the motel has 73 newly renovated guest rooms that are clean, are decorated in cool colors and feature oak trim. Some rooms and 12 one-bedroom suites feature kitchenettes. ~ 229 Gorge Road East; 800-565-3777 or 800-578-7878, fax 250-388-4153; www.travelodgevictoria.com, e-mail info@travelodgevictoria.com. DELUXE.

The Aerie resort is one of Canada's most conspicuous inns, an over-the-top Mediterranean-style complex resting astride Malahat Mountain. With a dizzying array of levels, angles and perspectives, it sprawls along the hill like a Greek resort; but inside the decor and ambience aim for Roman Empire opulence, with columns and canopy-draped beds, whispering baths and neoclassic statuary. The air of sensuous decadence is bolstered by the restaurant's legendary multicourse dinners (see "Dining" below). Closed for two weeks in January. ~ 600 Ebedora Lane, Malahat; 250-743-7115, 800-518-1933, fax 250-743-4766; www.aerie.bc.ca, e-mail resort@aerie.bc.ca. ULTRA-DELUXE.

DINING   A warm contemporary room with local artwork on the walls forms the interior of the **Paprika Bistro**. George and Linda Szasz pay homage to generations of recipes with classic bistro fare. The tiger prawn curry and the half-roasted duckling with sour cherry and ginger sauce show off the kitchen's varied talents. Desserts include homemade ice cream and sorbet. Dinner only. Closed Sunday. ~ 2522 Estevan Avenue; 250-592-7424, fax 250-592-7425. DELUXE TO ULTRA-DELUXE.

For a truly English dinner or afternoon tea, meander out to Oak Bay to the **Blethering Place**. There you will find the silver-haired set gossiping over hours-long tea, and families stopping by for supper. The fare includes crumpets, tarts, scones, Welsh rarebit, bangers, steak-and-kidney pie and decadent desserts. You'll find live music and entertainment on weekends. ~ 2250 Oak Bay Avenue, Oak Bay; 250-598-1413, fax 250-592-9052; www.thebletheringplace.com, e-mail tearoom@theblethering place.com. BUDGET TO MODERATE.

The **Marina Restaurant** not only has a smashing view of Oak Bay and the Lower Mainland in the distance, it also offers excellent seafood and pastas, along with house-made breads. There's also a fine sushi bar making good use of local fish and shellfish. It's extremely popular with residents. ~ 1327 Beach Street; 250-598-8555, fax 250-598-3014; www.marinarestaurant.com. DELUXE TO ULTRA-DELUXE.

The **Beacon Drive-in** is a Victoria institution, offering all the usual drive-in items—hamburgers, fries, shakes, ice cream and hearty breakfasts—made the old-fashioned way. Be sure to try an island favorite, the oyster burger. ~ 126 Douglas Street; 250-385-7521. BUDGET.

The **Aerie** is one of Victoria's most elegant restaurants, sitting atop the Malahat summit. Located outside greater Victoria on the way to Duncan, this eatery's dining room has a 23-carat-gold-leaf ceiling, with panoramic views stretching from the Gulf Islands to the Olympic Mountains. The menu changes, depending on availability of the very freshest local ingredients. Entrées such as seaweed-wrapped Salt Spring Island lamb or roasted venison loin with a matsutake mushroom sauce attract enough high-flying guests that a helicopter pad was added to the restaurant and 35-room guesthouse. ~ 600 Ebedora Lane, Malahat; 250-743-7115, 800-518-1933, fax 250-743-4766; www.aerie.bc.ca, e-mail resort@aerie.bc.ca. ULTRA-DELUXE.

SHOPPING

The municipality of Oak Bay offers an array of boutiques and specialty stores on Oak Bay Avenue featuring designer clothing, English toffees, New Age toys and games, crafts and jewelry. **Avenue China & Chintz** typifies the district, with a pleasing and eclectic array of elegant housewares and decor items. Closed Sunday. ~ 2225 Oak Bay Avenue; 250-595-1880.

Mayfair Shopping Center is one of the largest and most up-scale shopping centers on the island. It contains more than 120

AUTHOR FAVORITE

To experience an off-the-beaten-path aspect of Victoria's unique merry olde England character, I head out to an 1855 carriagehouse six miles from downtown, one of the oldest buildings in the Pacific Northwest. **Six Mile Pub** is the picture of an old English pub with hanging lamps, oak moldings, dartboards, pool and poker tables, and stained-glass windows. At lunch expect traditional pub fare such as fish and chips or steak-and-mushroom pie. Changing specials at dinner may include charbroiled salmon or New York steak. ~ 494 Island Highway; 250-478-3121, fax 250-478-8765; www.sixmilepub.com, e-mail info@sixmilepub.com. MODERATE TO DELUXE.

shops specializing in men's and women's fashions. ~ A mile from downtown near Douglas Street and Finlayson Avenue; 250-383-0541, fax 250-361-9226; www.mayfairshoppingcentre.com.

NIGHTLIFE In Oak Bay, east of downtown Victoria, **The Snug Pub** at the Oak Bay Beach Hotel attracts locals and visitors alike. It has a warm, British atmosphere with plaster walls, dark-wood beams, a large bar and fireplace. During the summertime, the balcony overlooking the ocean is popular. ~ 1175 Beach Street, Oak Bay; 250-598-4556, fax 250-598-6180; e-mail sales@oakbaybeach hotel.bc.ca.

BEACHES **THETIS LAKE REGIONAL PARK** 🏃 🚵 🐴 🏊 🚤 ⛵ Just five
& PARKS miles from the city center, this park offers opportunities for walking, hiking and solitude on more than 1900 acres of rolling hills, fir and cedar forest and lake frontage. You can swim in the lake during the summer. There are picnic areas and restrooms. ~ Off Route 1, about five miles northwest of downtown Victoria; 250-478-3344, fax 250-478-5416.

MOUNT DOUGLAS MUNICIPAL PARK 🏃 🏊 On the east side of the Saanich Peninsula is this 500-acre park with forests of arbutus, fir and cedar, a beach and Mount Douglas peak. Visitors can drive a one-and-a-half-mile paved route to a parking area and then hike a short distance to the peak where the view stretches in all directions. You can swim here in summer. You'll find picnic areas and restrooms. ~ Located about five miles northeast of downtown Victoria off Route 17 and Royal Oak/Cordova Bay Road; 250-475-5522.

▾▾▾▾▾▾▾▾▾▾▾▾▾
Saanich Peninsula One of Vancouver Island's leading tourist attractions, Butchart Gardens, is the Saanich Peninsula's primary draw. This area also offers a host of other garden retreats featuring exotic fauna from all over the world.

SIGHTS Traveling north on Route 17 from Victoria toward Sidney, signs direct you to **Butchart Gardens**. Dating back to 1904, the industrious wife of a manufacturer of Portland cement turned a quarry pit created by her husband into a fabulous sunken garden. Today, Jennie Butchart's project (still run by the Butchart family) is a 55-acre display garden, which includes the Rose Garden, the Italian Garden, the Japanese Garden, the Star Pond and the Ross Fountain. The gardens are now a National Historic Site of Canada. Joined by a series of walkways, the gardens display masses of color and rare and exotic plants, although critics find the overall impression a bit too artificial. See fantastic fireworks displays every Saturday night in July and August. In summer the bus-borne crowds can be a bit much (some of the paths are rather narrow) so it's a good idea to come early in the day. Christmastime features an extensive lighting display and open-air ice skating rink. Admission. ~ 800 Benvenuto Drive; 250-652-5256, 866-652-4422, fax 250-652-3883; www.butchart gardens.com, e-mail email@butchartgardens.com.

Near the entrance to Butchart Gardens, **Victoria Butterfly Gardens** is one of the largest butterfly conservatories in Canada. Its indoor rainforest habitat is designed for the breeding of tropical species imported from throughout the world. Thirty-five rare species are bred, hatched and raised here—including the Atlas moth, the world's largest moth—with roughly 2000 butterflies taking wing among the banana trees, hibiscus, bougainvillea and coconut palms. Flamingos, South African turacos, koi and tropical ducks also grace the gardens. There's also an orchid display and restaurant on the premises. Closed November through February. Admission. ~ West Saanich Road at Keating Cross Road, Brentwood Bay; 250-652-3822, 877-722-0272, fax 250-652-4683; www.butterflygardens.com.

The **Sidney Historical Museum**, in what was once a ferry customs building, offers a glimpse of turn-of-the-20th-century Saanich Peninsula through photographs, dioramas and even a fully re-created Depression-era kitchen. Admission. ~ 2423 Beacon Avenue, Sidney; 250-655-6355; www.sidneymuseum.ca, e-mail info@sidneymuseum.ca.

Whale fans will be lining up to tour the state-of-the-art **New Marine Centre** when it opens in spring 2008. Conceptualized in cooperation with the Vancouver Aquarium, the New Marine Centre will offer visitors an undersea tour of the nearby gulf, from its depths to its beaches, along with tide-touch pools and a killer whale skeleton that seems to come to life. Admission. ~ In the Pier Building on Seaport Place, Sidney; 250-858-4427; www.newmarinecentre.ca.

Returning south on Route 17, you can stop at the **Glendale Gardens and Woodland**, where displays are cultivated year-round. You walk on forest paths to see a fabulous display of Asian lilies, a creek flanked with ferns and hostas and a rhododendron

AUTHOR FAVORITE

sights   **Butchart Gardens** is a must-see for anyone who has ever dreamed of having a green thumb. This world-famous horticultural display features a series of neatly landscaped gardens so perfect you have to see it to believe it. This is a hugely popular destination, so come early to avoid the masses of tourists who arrive by bus. See page 582 for more information.

vale. They have a winter garden of fruit trees and a fuchsia arbor, giving the center flowers year-round. Admission. ~ 505 Quayle Road; 250-479-6162, fax 250-479-6047; www.hcp.bc.ca, e-mail info@hcp.bc.ca.

Farther south on Route 17, on a hilltop overlooking Elk Lake, stands a white dome. Here **Centre of the Universe** houses what in 1918 was the largest telescope in the world, a 65-inch optical masterpiece that still offers a stunning view of the heavens—tour visitors get to turn the massive instrument. On Saturday night, visitors can hear nontechnical talks about astronomy. The nearby interpretive center offers exhibits on Canadian contributions to space exploration, and lots of interactive displays for kids. Closed Sunday and Monday from November through March. ~ Little Saanich Mountain, 5071 West Saanich Road, Victoria; 250-363-8262; www.hia.nrc.ca/cu.

When Route 17 intersects with Route 1, head west on Route 1 and follow the signs to **Craigflower Manor and Schoolhouse.** Craigflower grew out of the requirement that in order to have a lease on Vancouver Island, the Hudson's Bay Company had to colonize it. Craigflower is one of four farms planned by the company. Some 25 families arrived from Scotland in 1853 to live on and work the farm. Visitors can tour the Georgian-style farmhouse built for bailiff Kenneth McKenzie in 1856, which contains furnishings and articles brought from Scotland. Craigflower Schoolhouse is the oldest school building in western Canada. There is also a heritage garden with heirloom plants and farm animals. Open Wednesday through Sunday. Closed mid-September to mid-May. Admission. ~ 110 Island Highway, corner of Craigflower and Admirals roads; 250-479-8067, fax 250-744-2251.

LODGING   Near Butchart Gardens, ferries and the airport, the **Best Western Emerald Isle Motor Inn** appeals to families because it is convenient and rooms have kitchenettes. No decorator interiors here, but the decor is functional. The 63 rooms (including 12 two-room suites), some of which are nonsmoking, are clean. Amenities include a restaurant, whirlpool baths, a sauna and laundry facili-

TEA TIME

What is the difference between afternoon tea and high tea? Afternoon tea consists of a pot of tea and a selection of delicate finger sandwiches, scones, cakes, fruit, cookies or petit fours served anytime after noon, while high tea is more substantial, served in the early evening in place of dinner.

ties. ~ 2306 Beacon Avenue, Sidney; 250-656-4441, 800-315-3377, fax 250-655-1351; www.bwemeraldisle.com, e-mail best westernemeraldisle@shaw.ca. MODERATE TO DELUXE.

The three cabins at the **Compass Rose Cabins & Marina** are not only waterfront: They are over the water on pilings, facing south on Brentwood Bay just north of Butchart Gardens. Each cabin is a clean, light and airy space with a loft bedroom, and sitting, dining and cooking areas downstairs. Full meal service is available at an adjoining restaurant. Guests can rent canoes and kayaks on-site, either for a leisurely cruise on the bay or a crowd-free quick trip to the back entrance at Butchart Gardens. ~ 799 Verdier Avenue, Brentwood Bay; 250-544-1441, fax 250-544-1015; www.compassrosecabins.com, e-mail compassrosecabins@shaw.ca. DELUXE.

DINING

Seahorses Café is right on the water next to the Brentwood Bay ferry dock—a suitably marine environment for this lovely little seafood bistro. Shellfish, prawns and fish dishes dominate, with the fresh sheet menu the best choice. A variety of salads, sandwiches and pasta dishes are also available. The outdoor deck is a great choice in nice weather. ~ 799 Verdier Avenue, Brentwood Bay; 250-544-1565. MODERATE.

BEACHES & PARKS

ISLAND VIEW BEACH REGIONAL PARK On the eastern shore of the Saanich Peninsula, the weather has molded this relatively flat park with rolling sand dunes at the north end and a long, accretion beach at the water's edge. The beach, full of fine, white sand, is strewn with sculpture-like driftwood. The water, however, is cold, although some do swim in it. The park offers views of Mt. Baker, Haro Strait and the San Juan and Gulf islands. Facilities include picnic areas, hiking and restrooms. ~ Located northeast of Victoria on the Saanich Peninsula off Route 17 and Island View Road; 250-478-3344, fax 250-478-5416, e-mail crdparks@crd.bc.ca.

ELK/BEAVER LAKE REGIONAL PARK Lush wetlands, tranquil forests and hilltop vistas surrounding Elk and Beaver lakes (good trout and bass fishing) provide more than 1000 acres of habitat at this regional park for many birds, including owls, woodpeckers and ducks. There are picnic areas and restrooms. ~ Located north of Victoria off Route 17 and Beaver Lake Road; 250-478-3344, fax 250-478-5416; e-mail crdparks@crd.bc.ca.

GOLDSTREAM PROVINCIAL PARK This park provides two distinct vegetation zones—dry ridges with dogwood, lodgepole pine and arbutus, and wetter areas with 600-year-old Douglas fir, western red cedar, western hemlock, western yew, black cottonwood and big-leaf maple, as well as many wildflowers. A salt marsh, where the Goldstream River flows into Finlayson Arm, contains many salt-tolerant plants such as sea asparagus and gumweed. Each November, the river draws thousands of salmon returning to spawn. The river got its name after gold was discovered there, but the find was a small one. You'll find picnic areas, restrooms and a visitor center that provides information about the area's natural history. ~ Off Route 1, ten miles northwest of Victoria; 250-474-1336, fax 250-478-0376.

▲ There are 173 sites for tents and RVs (no hookups available); C$22 per night. Reservations: 800-689-9025.

Southeast Island

▼ ▼ ▼ ▼ ▼ ▼ ▼ ▼ ▼ ▼ Vancouver Island's southeast region is a great place to learn about the area's native heritage and logging industry as well as swim at surprisingly warm beaches such as those on Qualicum Bay.

SIGHTS

The towns on the island's protected southeastern shore tend to be more low key than the proper British Victoria. The town of **Duncan** is the site of a collection of some 60 totem poles, ten of which are along the highway and the others scattered about town.

This logging community is the site of the **British Columbia Forest Discovery Centre**, where you ride the rails on a steam locomotive or a gas-powered train through a typical Northwest forest, across a trestle over Somenos Lake to the train station. Once there you can walk around the 100-acre park to see early logging equipment, the Log Museum exhibiting logging artifacts and dioramas explaining the history of logging. There's also a picnic area and playground. Closed mid-October through March. Admission. ~ 2892 Drinkwater Road, Duncan; 250-715-1113, 866-715-1113, fax 250-715-1170; www.discoveryforest.com, e-mail info.bcfdc@shawlink.ca.

Visitors have an opportunity to experience authentic traditions of the Cowichan people at the **Quw'utsun' Cultural and Conference Centre** in Duncan. Today, the Cowichan Band, with about 3300 members, is the largest group of native peoples in

PICTURES OF THE PAST

Chemainus is known as the little town that did. Instead of allowing unemployment to turn Chemainus into a ghost town when the local mill closed, residents hired well-known artists to paint murals all over the town. Yellow footprints on the sidewalks direct visitors past images of native chiefs, loggers felling huge trees and locomotives hauling logs through the forest. The murals have drawn tourists from around the world, creating a new industry there.

British Columbia. During the summer you can see carvers at work and watch women as they spin and knit authentic Cowichan sweaters. Call to make a reservation for the midday salmon barbecue with two shows of interpretive dancing. Guided tours are available and an audiovisual presentation gives a sense of the Cowichan spiritual traditions so closely tied with the earth and nature. The center also includes a fine-art gallery and a smaller gift shop. Admission. ~ 200 Cowichan Way, Duncan; 250-746-8119, 877-746-8119, fax 250-746-4143; www.quwutsun.ca, e-mail shelia@quwutsun.ca.

Nanaimo, population 75,000, is a hidden destination right ◄ *HIDDEN* under the noses of visitors who pass through it on their way from the ferry landing. The city's name grew out of its native title, "Snenymo," meaning both "great and mighty people" and "gathering place." White pioneers came to the area after large deposits of coal were discovered in 1851. The city was incorporated in 1874, and today its economy rests on fishing, forestry, port business and tourism.

The **Nanaimo District Museum** gives visitors an experience of the city's past by taking them through a coal-mining tunnel, a blacksmith's shop, a general store, and a barbershop in a turn-of-the-20th-century town; a restored miner's cottage; dioramas depicting the history and culture of the Nanaimo First Nations people; and an area focusing on Chinatown. Closed Sunday and Monday during the winter. Admission. ~ 100 Cameron Road, Nanaimo; 250-753-1821, fax 250-740-0125; www.nanaimo museum.ca, e-mail info@nanaimomuseum.ca.

There's a self-guided, historical walking tour of Nanaimo detailed in a map available at the **Tourism Nanaimo Info Centre**. ~ 2290 Bowen Road, Nanaimo; 250-756-0106, 800-663-7337, fax 250-756-0075; www.tourismnanaimo.com, e-mail info@ tourismnanaimo.com.

The **Hudson's Bay Bastion**, a 30-foot-tall building, was built on the waterfront in 1852, ostensibly to protect white settlers from the natives. But because the Indians proved to be peaceful, the fort really didn't protect anything. Since 1910 it has been a museum depicting Nanaimo's heritage. ~ Just south of the Seaplane Terminal along the harbor.

In the Parksville–Qualicum area, you can visit **St. Anne's Anglican Church**, one of the oldest churches on the island. A group of 45 farmers in the area used oxen to haul the logs for building it. The log church features stained-glass windows. Closed weekends. ~ 407 Wembley Street at Church Road, Parksville; 250-248-3114, fax 250-248-3295; e-mail pelican407@ shaw.ca.

The **Craig Heritage Park and Museum** displays artifacts from the local area, including an old schoolhouse, fire engine and period cottages. Very limited winter hours; call ahead. ~ 1245 East Island Highway, Parksville; 250-248-6966.

If you visit the **Big Qualicum Fish Hatchery** during the fall spawning season, you can watch the salmon thrashing their way upstream to lay their eggs. After the staff "milk" the salmon eggs, they are placed under controlled conditions for hatching. There are hiking trails and a picnic area on the grounds. ~ Off the East Island Highway north of Qualicum Bay; 250-757-8412, fax 250-757-8741; e-mail dunsmoreb@pac.dfo-mpo.gc.ca.

Located just a few miles west of Parksville is the little town of **Coombs** with its Old West look of boardwalks and hitching posts. In the summer, goats graze on the thatched roofs of some of the shops.

West of Coombs is **Butterfly World**, where visitors can see all stages of butterfly life, including egg laying and caterpillar rearing. The most colorful area is the tropical indoor garden where butterflies sip nectar, court and flit among colorful blossoms. Also check out the aviary, koi pond and gift shops. Closed November to mid-March. Admission. ~ Route 4A; 250-248-7026, fax 250-752-1091; www.butterflyworld.info.

LODGING

The Victorian **Pacific Shores Inn** offers three suites (sleeping two to four people) with kitchens and private entrances. Two of the suites feature washers and dryers, making them ideal choices for families. For a romantic getaway, rent the Fairy Tale Cottage with its unique stonework and wood detailing, fireplace and private deck and yard. ~ 9847 Willow Street, Chemainus; 250-246-4987, fax 250-246-1051; e-mail pacificshoresinn@shaw.ca. MODERATE TO DELUXE.

The **Coast Bastion Inn** is one of the most luxurious hotels in the area with 177 air-conditioned rooms whose balconies offer views of the harbor. The inn has a sauna, whirlpool and exercise room, restaurant, café and lounge. ~ 11 Bastion Street, Nanaimo; 250-753-6601, 800-663-1144, fax 250-753-4155; www.coasthotels.com, e-mail coastbastion@coasthotels.com. MODERATE TO DELUXE.

The **Best Western Dorchester Hotel** offers oceanfront views from most of its 70 Victorian-themed guest rooms. Built on the former site of the old Windsor Hotel and Opera House near the Bastion, the hotel also has a restaurant, lounge, rooftop garden and library. ~ 70 Church Street, Nanaimo; 250-754-6835, 866-473-9842, fax 250-754-2638; www.dorchesternanaimo.com, e-mail info@dorchesternanaimo.com. DELUXE.

Surrounded by woods on three sides, **Beach Acres Resort** opens onto a large, secluded beach. The 55 beachfront or forest cottages or oceanview condominiums with kitchens are clean, comfortably furnished and all feature fireplaces. Amenities here include an indoor pool, whirlpool, sauna, tennis courts, a playground, laundry and a restaurant. ~ 1051 Resort Drive, Parksville; 250-248-3424, 800-663-7309, fax 250-248-6145; www.beachacresresort.com, e-mail reservations@beachacresresort.com. ULTRA-DELUXE.

The original Duncan post office, built in 1913, is now the town's city hall.

Wood paneling, plush carpets and water views mark the 43 rooms at the **Parksville Beach Resort**, right on the beach in this sunny resort town north of Nanaimo. Rooms have either two queen or two double beds, and some include kitchenettes. The resort itself has two beach volleyball courts, a whirlpool and sauna, an indoor pool, horseshoe pits and tennis courts. A playground and water park are next door. Closed in winter. ~ 161 West Island Highway, Parksville; 250-248-6789, 888-248-6789, fax 250-248-4789; www.parksvillebeachmotel.com, e-mail info@parks villebeachmotel.com. MODERATE TO ULTRA-DELUXE.

Once a private boys' school, the old-English, Tudor-style **Qualicum Heritage Inn** sits on three acres overlooking Georgia Strait. Half the inn's 70 attractive rooms have water views, and some include fireplaces. Amenities include six nearby golf courses, a lounge, dining room, neighborhood pub and beach access. ~ 427 College Road, Qualicum; 250-752-9262, 800-663-7306, fax 250-752-5144; www.qualicumheritageinn.com, e-mail info@qualicumheritageinn.com. MODERATE.

DINING

The **Lighthouse Bistro and Pub** is designed to look like a lighthouse built into a white, Cape Cod–style building with light blue trim. The restaurant offers a great view of the harbor, especially from the tables on their large deck, and a menu that changes with the local fish in season, such as wild salmon. The pub upstairs serves a different menu, featuring pub fare, for example the popular smoked salmon corn chowder. ~ 50 Anchor Way at the Seaplane Terminal, Nanaimo; 250-754-3212, fax 250-753-1299; www.lighthousebistro.ca, e-mail lighthousebistro@telus.net. MODERATE TO DELUXE.

In Parksville, visit **Kalvas**, a large, log-beam building, for fine French and German fare. You can feast on East Coast lobster, fresh local crab and oysters. Dinner only. ~ 180 Moilliet Street, Parksville; 250-248-6933, fax 250-248-2154. DELUXE TO ULTRA-DELUXE.

For English-style fish and chips, try **Spinnaker Seafood House**. The comfortable restaurant features a nautical theme, and the eclectic menu includes fresh seafood, pizza, hamburgers and salads for eating in or taking out. ~ 625 East Island Highway, Parksville; 250-248-5532. BUDGET TO MODERATE.

SHOPPING

In Duncan, the **Quamichan House** at the Quw'utsun' Cultural and Conference Centre offers one of the largest selections of authentic native arts and crafts on the island, including original paintings, jewelry, carvings, masks, rattles, drums, Cowichan knitted items and books on the culture and art of native Northwest coastal peoples. Closed Saturday and Sunday October to April. ~ 200 Cowichan Way, Duncan; 250-746-8119, fax 250-746-4143; www.quwutsun.ca, e-mail askme@quwutsun.ca.

Hill's Native Art features Cowichan sweaters, hand-carved totem poles of all sizes, carvings, jewelry and prints. ~ 76 Bastion Street, Nanaimo; phone/fax 250-755-7873; www.hillsnative art.com, e-mail info@hillsnativeart.com.

NIGHTLIFE Nightlife isn't plentiful outside Victoria, but that doesn't mean you can't have an enjoyable time in some of the island's southeastern communities. Try Nanaimo's **Dinghy Dock Pub**, reached by a ten-minute ferry ride (ferry information 250-753-8244, fax 250-741-8244). The pub offers locally brewed beers and other spirits and spectacular views of Nanaimo, its harbor and Newcastle Island. ~ 8 Pirate's Lane, Protection Island; 250-753-2373, fax 250-741-8244; www.dinghydockpub.com.

Nanaimo also has a handful of **theater companies**, including the Nanaimo Theatre Group, Yellow Point Drama Group and Malispina College Drama Group. For information on all groups, call the Tourism Nanaimo Info Centre at 250-756-0106.

BEACHES & PARKS

BAMBERTON PROVINCIAL PARK 🚶 ⛵ 🦅 ⛵ ⛵ ⛵ The warm waters of the Saanich Inlet make this park, with a 750-foot sandy beach, attractive to swimmers. The park contains many arbutus trees in a second-growth forest. The Saanich Peninsula, Mt. Baker and the Gulf Islands form the backdrop to water and mountain views from this park. Picnic areas and restrooms are the only facilities. ~ Located northwest of Victoria off Route 1 at the northern foot of Malahat Drive; 250-474-1336, fax 250-478-0376; www.env.gov.bc.ca/bcparks.

▲ There are 50 tent/RV sites (no hookups); C$14 per night. Reservations: 800-689-9025.

NEWCASTLE ISLAND PROVINCIAL MARINE PARK 🚶 🚲 ⛵ 🦅 ⛵ ⛵ ⛵ ⛵ Over 750 acres of woods and sandy beaches on an island in Nanaimo Harbor afford views of Vancouver Island and the mainland's Coast Mountains. The park features sandstone ledges and sandy, gravel beaches. The area was a site for coal mining and sandstone mining in the mid- to late 1800s. Cast a rod for salmon. There are picnic areas, a playground, restrooms, over 130 feet of docks, a visitors center and a snack bar in the summer. ~ In summer, scheduled foot passenger ferry service departs from behind the Nanaimo Civic Arena off Route 1, north of downtown. Cars are not allowed; 250-754-

7893, fax 250-754-7894; www.newcastleisland.ca, e-mail admin@newcastleisland.ca.

▲ There are 18 tent sites available on a first-come, first-served basis; C$14 per night.

RATHTREVOR BEACH PROVINCIAL PARK 🏃 🚲 ⛵ 🍴 🛶 ⛴

⌄ Located between Nanaimo and Parksville, this park's popularity lies within its sandy beach. There are also a wooded upland area, excellent birdwatching during the spring herring spawn and views of Georgia Strait. There are picnic areas, restrooms and showers. Parking fee, C$5. ~ It's about two miles south of Parksville off Route 19; 250-474-1336, fax 250-478-0376; www.vislandcamping.com.

> The name of Qualicum is derived from a native word that means "where the dog salmon run."

▲ There are 174 tent/RV sites (no hookups), C$22 per night; and 24 walk-in sites, C$14 per night. Reservations (mandatory in July and August): 604-689-9025, 800-689-9025; www.discovercamping.ca.

ENGLISHMAN RIVER FALLS PROVINCIAL PARK 🏃 🚲 ⛵ 🎣

⌄ Forests of huge cedar trees surround two large, crashing waterfalls in this lush 97-hectare park. Large groves of hemlock and fir also can be found in the park. A good time to visit is in autumn when the maple trees offer a colorful contrast to the evergreens. You'll find picnic areas and restrooms. Parking fee, C$3. ~ Located west of Parksville off Route 4; 250-474-1336, 250-478-0376; www.vislandcamping.com.

▲ There are 103 tent/RV sites (no hookups); C$17 per night. Reservations: 604-689-9025, 800-689-9025.

LITTLE QUALICUM FALLS PROVINCIAL PARK 🏃 ⛵ ⌄

Although a neighbor to Englishman River Falls Park, this park is much drier. Consequently, visitors see more pine, Douglas fir and arbutus trees in this park that straddles the Little Qualicum River. A must-see are the impressive waterfalls splashing down a rocky gorge. Fish for salmon and take a dip in Cameron Lake. Picnic areas and restrooms are the only facilities. Parking fee, C$3. ~ Located 11 miles west of Parksville off Route 4; 250-474-1336, fax 250-478-0376; www.vislandcamping.com.

▲ There are 91 tent/RV sites (no hookups); C$17 per night. Reservations: 604-689-9025, 800-689-9025; www.discover camping.ca.

STRATHCONA PROVINCIAL PARK 🏃 ⛵ ⌄ This is British Co-

◄ HIDDEN

lumbia's oldest provincial park, a half-million-acre enclave in the middle of Vancouver Island four hours north of Victoria. It offers popular day hikes from Paradise Meadows on the Forbidden Plateau and Buttle Lake; both can also serve as the starting point for extensive backcountry pack trips. Intrepid hikers might want to try for 1443-foot Della Falls, one of the ten highest waterfalls in the world, accessible only by boat and foot on the Port Albani side of the park. Less determined visitors can just relax in the Buttle Lake campground. ~ The park is 40 minutes west of Campbell River on provincial Route 28; 250-337-2400, fax 250-337-5695; www.strathcona.bc.ca.

▲ Campsites at Buttle Lake (86 sites) or Ralph River (60 sites) are on a first-come, first-served basis; C\$12 and C\$15 per night from Memorial Day through September, free the rest of the year. The nearby Strathcona Park Lodge (250-286-3122, fax 250-286-6010) offers simple rooms (MODERATE TO DELUXE) and cabins (DELUXE).

▼▼▼▼▼▼▼▼▼▼▼▼▼
Southwest Island

Whether you come by land or sea, southwest Vancouver Island is one of the Pacific Northwest's most accessible wilderness regions. With its national parks, wildlife and snow-capped peaks, this is a favorite getaway.

SIGHTS

Board the **M. V. Lady Rose** for a unique experience traveling the Alberni Inlet aboard a freighter, the likes of which have served the hidden, remote communities on the island's west coast for over 50 years. Passengers on the day-long trips can see deliveries of fish food to commercial fish farms, asphalt shingles to individuals re-roofing their homes and mail to residents of communities such as Bamfield and Kildonan. Kayakers can be dropped off at the Broken Group Islands. Tourists should be forewarned that the boat is primarily a freighter, so don't expect a naturalist or interpretive guide with fascinating commentary. ~ Argyle Pier; 250-723-8313, 800-663-7192, fax 250-723-8314; www.ladyrosemarine.com.

HIDDEN ►

Just outside Port Alberni at Sproat Lake, take the time to view a hidden attraction, the **Flying Tankers Inc.**, a private fire protection service. Although not regularly scheduled, and certainly not developed for tourists, the sight of the largest firefighting aircraft in the world dropping 7200 gallons of water on the lake in a test run is almost too impressive for words. ~ 9350 Bomber Base Road, off Lakeshore Road; www.martinmars.com.

Pacific Rim National Park, comprising three units, protects the windswept and jagged west coast of Vancouver Island. The three parts of the park are distinctly different. The West Coast Trail should be traveled only by experienced hikers. The Broken Group Islands unit can be reached by boat, canoe or kayak. The Long Beach unit, the most accessible, includes a six-mile-long sandy beach. There, between Ucluelet and Tofino, you will find the Wickaninnish Centre, an interpretive center that displays exhibits on Pacific Ocean history. Here visitors can see powerful waves rolling up on the beach, watch nature presentations, participate in day hikes and view whales, seals and sea lions. There's also a restaurant with views of the surf and spectacular sunsets. The center is closed from October to mid-March. ~ 250-726-7721, fax 250-726-4720; www.parkscanada.gc.ca/pacificrim, e-mail pacrim.info@pc.gc.ca.

Most of the park includes a rocky shoreline that supports tidepools with barnacles, mussels, starfish, hermit crabs and anemones. Sitka spruce thrive just behind the pockets of sandy beaches and the rocky outcroppings. Farther inland are cedar, hemlock, fir and areas of bog and muskeg with pine and laurel. The forest floor is redolent with moss, ferns, huckleberry and salmonberry. The park also offers sightings of sea lions, harbor seals, river otter, mink and a vast array of resident and migrating birds (see "Beaches & Parks" below for more information).

> Canada's $1 coin, which bears an image of a loon, is called a "loonie"; there's also a $2 coin, sometimes called a "toonie."

The **Eagle Aerie Gallery** is as much a cultural experience as it is an art gallery. The building was designed and constructed by native artist Roy Henry Vickers and his brother Arthur. The gallery is built in the longhouse style with adzed cedar paneling and massive totem houseposts. Effective lighting, evocative subject material and background music of taped native chanting and flute playing inspire a spirit of reverence unlike almost any other place. The gallery represents Vickers' art only. ~ 350 Campbell Street, Tofino; 250-725-3235, 800-663-0669, fax 250-725-4466; www.royhenryvickers.com, e-mail tofino@royhenryvickers.com.

LODGING

A bed and breakfast that started as a 1940s log cabin and grew to include a cedar addition with nine guest rooms, **Ocean Wilderness** offers travelers a secluded seaside retreat. Set on five oceanfront acres just outside Sooke, the original log cabin is now the inn's breakfast area, and accommodations in the addition are adorned with romantic canopy beds and eclectic antiques. Decks overlook the water or garden. The inn offers massage, mud and seaweed treatments and clay facials. ~ 9171 West Coast Road, Sooke; 250-646-2116, 800-323-2116, fax 250-646-2317; www.oceanwildernessinn.com, e-mail info@oceanwildernessinn.com. MODERATE TO DELUXE.

The **Best Western Barclay Hotel** with 86 rooms is the largest hotel in town. It features an attractive lobby, a coffee shop, dining room, sports bar and lounge. Accommodations are clean, fairly standard rooms and suites. Amenities include a heated outdoor pool, whirlpool, fitness center, and sauna. ~ 4277 Stamp Avenue, Port Alberni; 250-724-7171, 800-563-6590, fax 250-724-9691; www.bestwesternbarclay.com, e-mail info@bestwesternbarclay.com. DELUXE.

The **Hospitality Inn** has recently become an independently owned hotel, and was remodeled, renovating all bathrooms and adding a swimming pool and exercise room. The lobby features comfortable seating in front of a fireplace. The inn offers 49 rooms in soft, attractive colors with firm beds and standard motel furniture. Exercise room onsite. ~ 3835 Redford Street, Port Alberni; 250-723-8111, 877-723-8111, fax 250-723-0088; www.hospitalityinnportalberni.com, e-mail info@hospitalityinn portalberni.com. DELUXE.

The **Canadian Princess Resort** is unique in that 30 of its 76 rooms are aboard the ship of the same name (which serviced from 1932 to 1975 as a hydrographic survey vessel). Consequently, these moderately priced staterooms are small, and many share a bath. Three buildings contain 46 spacious, contemporary rooms and loft suites with fireplaces, decks and views of the ship and the harbor. The resort also includes ten fishing boats and a nautical-themed restaurant and lounge for guests. Closed mid-September to April. ~ Ucluelet Harbor, Ucluelet; 250-726-7771, 800-663-7090, fax 250-726-7121; www.canadianprincess.com, e-mail info@ obmg.com. MODERATE TO ULTRA-DELUXE.

Just a block from the Ucluelet marina is the **Thornton Motel** with 19 rooms and suites with standard furnishings, some with kitchenettes. It is popular with the fishing crowd. ~ 1861 Peninsula Road, Ucluelet; 250-726-7725, fax 250-726-2099; www. thorntonmotel.com, e-mail thorntonmotel@yahoo.ca. MODERATE TO DELUXE.

At the **West Coast Motel,** views of the harbor from some of the 21 rooms make up for the rather standard motel decor. Non-smoking rooms are available. Added advantages are an indoor swimming pool, gym, sauna and tanning salon. The dining room (open summer only) overlooks the harbor. ~ 247 Hemlock Street, Ucluelet; 250-726-7732, fax 250-726-4662; www.westcoastmo-tel.com. MODERATE TO DELUXE.

If you want a more personal experience, try **Chesterman Beach Bed and Breakfast,** which offers three private units with

AUTHOR FAVORITE

When I feel the need to *really* get away from it all, my favorite writer's hide-away in all of Canada is a shorefront suite at the **Pacific Sands Beach Resort**, adjoining the Long Beach section of Pacific Rim National Park. Located on Cox Bay, it's one of the best resorts on the West Coast, offer-ing 54 housekeeping suites with contemporary furnishings, fireplaces and views of the beach and the ocean, as well as 22 new beachfront villas. Three of the suites have hot tubs. ~ 1421 Pacific Rim Highway, Tofino; 250-725-3322, 800-565-2322, fax 250-725-3155; www.pacificsands.com, e-mail info@pacificsands.com. ULTRA-DELUXE.

fireplaces and oceanfront decks, including a charming cottage, a spacious suite and a cozy honeymooner's room, on the beach by the same name. Kayaks and bikes are available for guests' use. After a visit to the island's west coast, owners Todd and Lynda fell in love with the place. Their hospitality and tasty breakfasts match their enthusiasm. ~ P.O. Box 72, Tofino, BC V0R 2Z0; 250-725-3726; www.chestermanbeach.net, e-mail surfsand@island.net. ULTRA-DELUXE.

The best thing about **Duffin Cove Resort** is that it offers views of the ocean from a bluff a block away from downtown. Eleven suites and kitchen units and two cottages with fireplaces on the beach are a winter storm-watcher's delight. ~ 215 Campbell Street, Tofino; 250-725-3448, 888-629-2903, fax 250-725-2390; www.duffin-cove-resort.com, e-mail duffin@island.net. DELUXE TO ULTRA-DELUXE.

Ocean Village Beach Resort is a nest of 51 comfortably rustic duplex and single cedar chalets on McKenzie Beach, a quarter-mile of safe, sandy beach facing the Pacific Ocean. The units feature an eating area with table and benches, sitting area and a sleeping area or separate bedroom and bath. The resort also includes an indoor swimming pool, hot tub, laundromat and wireless internet. ~ 555 Hellesen Drive, Tofino; 250-725-3755, fax 250-725-4494; www.oceanvillageresort.com, e-mail info@oceanvillageresort.com. MODERATE TO DELUXE.

Perched on a rocky point thrusting out into the Pacific, not far from Pacific Rim National Park and Clayoquot Sound, the **Wickaninnish Inn** has a spectacular setting under any circumstances. During the West Coast's sometimes phenomenal winter storms, it's an unparalleled natural experience. Each of the 76 spacious rooms faces the ocean, and includes a soaking tub, large-screen television, refrigerator, fireplace, and furniture made from recycled old-growth fir, cedar and driftwood. A spa at the inn offers massage and other treatments. Full communications technology, including high-speed dual-line phones, makes it possible to use the inn as an executive retreat. ~ Osprey Lane at Chesterman Beach, Tofino; 250-725-3100, 800-333-4604, fax 250-725-3129; www.wickinn.com, e-mail info@wickinn.com. ULTRA-DELUXE.

DINING

Some of the finest dining in British Columbia is offered by **Sooke Harbour House,** a white clapboard inn surrounded by colorful, organic gardens on a bluff above Sooke Harbour's Whiffen Spit. In a setting of handsomely refinished pine and maple furnishings with whimsical folk art accents, the dining room offers a changing menu. There's an emphasis on fresh seasonal ingredients and local seafood that might include such unusual delicacies as sea urchin roe or fresh skate served with cranberry vinegar. Suckling kid, duck and rabbit are among the possible meat choices. Winter closures, call ahead. ~ 1528 Whiffen Spit Road, Sooke; 250-642-3421, 800-889-9688, fax 250-642-6988; www.sookeharborhouse.com, e-mail info@sookeharborhouse.com. ULTRA-DELUXE.

It would be hard to leave hungry after a meal at **Little Bavaria**, which seduces local appetites with huge plates of traditional German favorites such as schnitzel, homemade bratwurst and a variety of seafood dishes. The Bavarian Platter offers meat, sausage, potatoes, noodles, bread and vegetables for two at about $35. No lunch on weekends. ~ 3035 4th Avenue, Port Alberni; phone/fax 250-724-4242, 800-704-2744; www.little bavariarestaurant.com. MODERATE.

Perched on a knoll above the harbor, the **Schooner Restaurant** is a cozy place with a loyal local following and a slate of excellent food. Cedar plank walls and intimate candle-lit tables are the backdrop to an array of entrées such as bouillabaisse, roast duck, ribs, salads and seafood, all carefully prepared from local produce and the freshest seafood, delivered daily. The upstairs dining area and lounge are open in the spring and offer harbor views over Clayoquot Sound. Closed over Christmas. ~ 331 Campbell Street, Tofino; 250-725-3444, fax 250-725-2100; www.schoonerrestaurant.com, e-mail schooner restaurant@seaviewcable.net. MODERATE.

In the early 19th century, during the era of sailing ships, the West Coast of Vancouver Island was dubbed "Graveyard of the Pacific" for the number of shipwrecks that occurred there.

Everybody needs a cup of coffee and a muffin in the morning. The best place to get them in Tofino is the **Common Loaf Bake Shop**, where the espresso makers are capable and the baked goods are filling. You'll also find calzones, pizzas and curries. The bulletin board is also the news center for the counterculture community in Clayoquot Sound, if you want to find out who's protesting what this month. ~ 180 1st Street, Tofino; 250-725-3915. BUDGET.

SHOPPING   In Tofino, the **House of Himwitsa** gallery offers a good selection of native art including limited-edition prints, silver jewelry, weavings, carvings, beaded items and pottery. ~ 300 Main Street, Tofino; 250-725-2017, fax 250-725-2361; www.himwitsa.com, e-mail tofino@himwitsa.com.

Wildside Booksellers is fairly small, but as the name implies it has an excellent selection of natural history and outdoor recreation books geared toward the West Coast. Summer reading selections and social activism books round out the book fare. ~ 320 Main Street, Tofino; 250-725-4222.

Nearby, the **Eagle Aerie Gallery** features works by Roy Henry Vickers, a native artist who has found international acclaim for his works that integrate the contemporary and traditional. ~ 350 Campbell Street, Tofino; 250-725-3235.

You won't find nightclubs on the rugged West Coast. Some bars and lounges offer sunset views. **Shelter Restaurant** has an extensive wine list designed to complement its organic and locally grown appetizers and entrées, such as Cortez Island mussels and Tofino Dungeness crab. ~ 601 Campbell Street, Tofino, 250-725-3353; www.shelterrestaurant.com.

NIGHTLIFE

A note about using parks and beaches in the Sooke area: Do not leave valuables in your car, as the region has been plagued by gangs of thieves that prowl the trailhead and picnic area parking lots. It's best to leave valuable items in your hotel room, but if you can do nothing else, make sure they're locked in the trunk.

BEACHES & PARKS

EAST SOOKE REGIONAL PARK This regional park is where the west coast begins. The 3500-acre park encompasses beautiful arbutus trees clinging to the windswept coast. You'll find small pocket beaches, rocky bays and islets for beachcombing and tidepooling. It features six miles of rugged coast trails and 30 miles of trails through forest, marsh and field with opportunities to view orca whales, sea lions, harbor seals, Columbian black-tailed deer and cougar. In September, check out the large number of bald eagles, hawks and other raptors that stop here during their migration. The park has views of the Strait of Juan de Fuca and the Olympic Mountains. You'll find picnic areas and restrooms. ~ Located about 25 miles southwest of Victoria off East Sooke Road on Becher Bay Road; 250-478-3344, fax 250-478-5416.

FRENCH BEACH PROVINCIAL PARK Visitors have the opportunity to see whales in the spring from this mile-long, sand-and-gravel beach on the Strait of Juan de Fuca. The park also contains second-growth forest. There are picnic areas and restrooms. ~ Located west of Sooke off Route 14 near Jordan River; 250-474-1336, fax 250-478-0376; wlap www.env.gov.bc.ca/bcparks.

▲ There are 69 tent/RV sites (no hookups); C$14 per night. Reservations: 800-689-9025; www.discovercamping.ca.

PACIFIC RIM NATIONAL PARK Cliffs, islands, bog and beach are just some of the topography visitors discover at this vast, 158,400-acre park. The reserve is divided into three units: Long Beach, the Broken Group Islands and the West Coast Trail. During the park's low season, from mid-October to mid-March, expect most park facilities to be closed. Fee. ~ 250-726-7721, fax 250-726-4720; www.pc.gc.ca/pacrim, e-mail pacrim.info@pc.gc.ca.

Long Beach The most accessible section of the reserve, Long Beach is a six-mile stretch of

Text continued on page 600.

The Gulf Islands

Ready for some island-hopping? Whether you're into beaches, arts and crafts, birdwatching, dining or just plain looking around, there is something here for everyone. The Gulf Islands provide plenty of activities—swimming, windsurfing, scuba diving, beachcombing, boating, bicycling, hiking and horseback riding—to suit families and outdoor enthusiasts of all abilities.

These islands are isolated places where residents enjoy a bucolic lifestyle. At sunset, basking like a group of sea turtles in the water, the islands appear like shadows, amorphous shapes in muted shades of blue, mauve and gray stacked up behind one another. The islands, sisters of the San Juan Islands in Washington State, include mountain peaks, sandy beaches, and pastoral farms. The climate is Mediterranean-like—mild and dry. The archipelago includes almost 200 islands, but only five have a population of more than 250—Salt Spring, Pender, Galiano, Mayne and Saturna. **B.C. Ferries** plies the waterways between Tsawwassen, just south of Vancouver, and the Gulf Islands and Vancouver Island's Swartz Bay and the islands. ~ 250-386-3431, 888-223-3779, fax 250-381-5452; www.bcferries.com. **Harbour Air** also provides scheduled floatplane service to several of the islands from Vancouver. ~ 250-537-5525, 800-665-0212.

Salt Spring Island, named for a series of briny springs at the island's north end, is the largest, with a population of about 9500. The first nonnative settlers were blacks escaping slavery in the United States in 1859. Once supported by an agrarian economy, the island now thrives on tourism and the arts. In fact, the Gulf Islands are believed to be home to more artists per capita than most other regions in Canada.

The largest village on Salt Spring is Ganges, a pedestrian-oriented, seaside hamlet, where visitors flock to a summer-long arts-and-crafts fair, art galleries and the Saturday morning market. Mid-June to mid-September, a dozen of the galleries stay open late Friday evenings for visitors to browse.

Another attraction is Cusheon Lake, a popular, freshwater lake with a large swimming area—and the water is warm. The island also offers popular oceanside beaches; Vesuvius and Bader's beaches on the island's west side have the warmest water. Because it sits at the edge of the forest, Bader offers much more privacy, but the sandy beach is small.

Pender Island, population 1500, is really two islands connected by a narrow, wooden bridge that affords splendid views of Browning and Bedwell harbours. Medicine Beach in Bedwell Harbour and Hamilton Beach in Browning Harbour are popular picnic spots. The Driftwood Centre and Port Washington are locations of several galleries.

Birdwatching is a prime activity on the Gulf Islands. Cormorants, harlequin ducks, gulls, oyster catchers, turkey vultures, ravens and bald eagles are commonly seen. Other birds include tanagers, juncos, bluebirds, flycatchers, blackbirds and sparrows. Many of these birds can be seen in the island's parks.

Mouat Provincial Park (Seaview Avenue, Ganges) on Salt Spring Island is a pleasant, wooded park with camping and picnicking facilities. **Prior Centennial Provincial Park** is near Bedwell Harbour on Pender Island. It features good fishing, swimming, a boat launch, picnic areas and restrooms. The islands also are sites of several marine parks. One of the largest is **Beaumon Marine Park** on South Pender Island and sheltered by Bedwell Harbour. It includes upland forest, picnic areas, campsites and hiking trails.

If you are a diver, the Gulf Islands provide a number of good locations. Divers often see octopi, wolf eels, sea cucumbers, sea stars, sea urchins and sea pens. Shore dives include Vesuvius Bay on Salt Spring Island for sighting octopus and ling cod; Fulford Harbour opposite the ferry terminal with a shallow area perfect for seeing crabs and starfish; and Tilley Point on North Pender Island for viewing interesting kelp beds. Near Thetis Island, the *Miami*, a steel- and coal-carrying freighter that sunk in 1900, is covered with interesting vegetation and marine life. The *Del Norte*, a 190-foot side-wheel passenger steamship that sank in 1868, is between Valdez and Galiano islands and appropriate only for more advanced divers.

Visitors can find a variety of accommodations on Salt Spring and Pender islands. **The Inn on Pender Island**, with nine rooms, three cabins and a hot tub, sits on seven acres of wooded tranquility near Prior Centennial Provincial Park, where hiking, bicycling and beachcombing are in abundance. Breakfast is included in the price. ~ 4709 Canal Road; 250-629-3353, 800-550-0172, fax 250-629-3167; www.innonpender.com. MODERATE TO DELUXE.

Cusheon Lake Resort has fully equipped log and A-frame chalets, all with kitchens and water views, some with fireplaces, and an outdoor jacuzzi. Fishing, swimming and boating are available. ~ 171 Natalie Lane, Salt Spring Island; phone/fax 250-537-9692, 866-899-0017; www.cusheonlake.com, e-mail resort@cusheonlake.com. DELUXE TO ULTRA-DELUXE.

sand and surf between rocky outcroppings. Beach hiking is excellent. Nine marked trails traverse old-growth rainforest. Facilities include picnic areas, restrooms and a restaurant. Parking fee, C$10. ~ Route 4 (Pacific Rim Highway), 62 miles west of Port Alberni; 250-726-7721.

▲ Green Point Campground has 18 primitive walk-in sites above the beach and 94 inland tent/RV sites with beach access; C$16.80 to C$22.75 per night. Closed November to mid-March. To reserve a drive-in site, call 800-689-9025.

Broken Group Islands 🏃 🛶 🛥 🚣 🛥 🛶 With more than a hundred islands and islets in Barkley Sound, this is kayak and sailboat territory. Accessible only by boat, these remote islands offer up wildlife ranging from sea lions to eagles; diving is excellent. Composting toilets are available in the camping areas. ~ The M. V. *Lady Rose*, a mail boat that also takes passengers and kayaks, makes trips to Bamfield, Sechart Lodge at Sechart Bay and Ucluelet; 250-723-8313, 800-663-7192.

▲ There are primitive campsites on eight of the islands; C$9.90 per night, per adult.

West Coast Trail 🏃 This demanding 47-mile stretch between Bamfield and Port Renfrew follows a turn-of-the-20th-century trail constructed to aid shipwrecked mariners. Only experienced backpackers should undertake this grueling five- to eight-day trek. Expect to see coastal rainforests, the remains of early settlements, shipwrecks and a plethora of marine life. The number of hikers on the trail is regulated. Reservations and permits are required. Closed October through April. ~ Land access to the Bamfield and Port Renfrew trailheads is by logging roads only. The M. V. *Lady Rose* (250-723-8313, 800-663-7192) drops hikers at Bamfield. For reservations and permits, call 800-663-6000.

The Douglas firs at MacMillan Provincial Park are believed to have survived a fire some 300 years ago because of their fire-resistant bark, nearly a foot thick on some of the trees now.

MACMILLAN PROVINCIAL PARK 🏃 On the shores of Cameron Lake, this 336-acre park, available for day-use only, provides access to Cathedral Grove, a large stand of giant, old-growth Douglas fir. Some of the trees are 800 years old, and the largest are nearly 250 feet tall and nearly ten feet in diameter. Walking through this ancient forest can be a spiritual experience, but the area is so popular it is being "loved to death" by tourists. Parking fee, C$3. ~ Located west of Parksville, about 11 miles east of Port Alberni off Route 4; 250-474-1336, fax 250-478-0376; www.vislandcamping.com.

SPROAT LAKE PROVINCIAL PARK 🏃 🛶 ⛴ 🚣 🛥 🛥 🛶 On the north shore of Sproat Lake just west of Port Alberni, this park is a water enthusiast's paradise. The lake is warm and sunny, perfect for summer swimming. Fishing is excellent for steelhead, trout and salmon. Visitors can walk a short distance through the woods to see prehistoric petroglyphs. Facilities are limited to picnic areas and pit toilets. Parking fee, C$3. ~ Eight miles northwest of Port Alberni off Route 4; 250-474-1336, fax 250-478-0376; www.vislandcamping.com.

▲ There are 59 tent/RV sites (no hookups); C$17 to C$20 per night. Reservations: 604-689-9025, 800-689-9025; www.dis covercamping.ca.

STAMP FALLS PROVINCIAL PARK 🕴 🛶 🛶 ⬝ This park offers pleasant walks among the stands of cedar and fir, and an area for contemplation near the waterfall. Visitors can view salmon jumping up the fish ladders in summer and fall. Steelhead and cutthroat trout also invite anglers. Picnic areas are the only facilities. ~ Located about eight and a half miles north of Port Alberni off Route 4 on Beaver Creek Road; 250-474-1336, fax 250-478-0376; www.vislandcamping.com.

▲ There are 23 tent/RV sites (no hookups); C$14 per night. Reservations: 604-689-9025, 800-689-9025; www.discover camping.ca.

Outdoor Adventures

FISHING

Victoria has incredible sportfishing for salmon, primarily, but also for bottom fish like rock cod and red snapper and the occasional halibut. Besides the great angling possibilities, there's the unsurpassable natural backdrop of scenery and wildlife: snowcapped mountains, old lighthouses, sea lions, whales, bald eagles, herons and other water birds. **Saltwater licenses** are issued by the federal government. Charter operators will usually sell the license to you. ~ Information: Department of Fisheries and Oceans, 555 West Hastings Street, Vancouver, BC V6B 5G3; 604-666-2074; e-mail info@dfo-mpo.gc.ca. **Freshwater licenses** are issued through the provincial government and can be bought at most sporting goods stores. The Ministry of Environment, Lands and Parks (B.C. Environment) maintains a list of licensed **freshwater fishing guides**. For a copy, call 604-582-5200.

DOWNTOWN VICTORIA It's just a few minutes' drive from downtown Victoria to the marinas where charter outfits operate saltwater fishing trips. **Oak Bay Charters** provides bait and tackle for up to five people on charter trips into the protected waters around Victoria. Charter sightseeing excursions are also available. ~ Oak Bay Marina, 2141 Newton Street; 250-598-1061, 800-413-1061; www.oakbaycharters.com, e-mail sunbeam@shaw.ca. **Adam's Fishing Charters** has a standard charter package for a minimum of four hours for up to four people, as well as more customized trips. ~ Inner Harbour; 250-370-2326; www.adamsfishingcharters.com, e-mail gethooked@shaw.ca.

SOUTHWEST ISLAND   As you angle along the west coast of the island, you might even see an occasional bear walking along the coast. Located right next to the Pacific Rim National Park, **Day's Inn Weigh West Marine Resort** offers charters for fishing trips and whale watching. ~ 634 Campbell Street, Tofino; 250-725-3277, 800-665-8922.

WHALE WATCHING   The southern part of Vancouver Island is known for orca (or killer) whales, porpoises, harbor seals, sea lions, bald eagles and many species of marine birds. Watch also for the occasional minke whale, gray whale or elephant seal. Whale-watching season extends from April through September. June is the best time to see the orcas. By July and August, cruise operators are very busy, so try to call a day or two ahead for reservations.

DOWNTOWN VICTORIA   Look for little black-and-white Dall's porpoises that play off the bow or follow behind in the wake when you're out on one of these whale-watching excursions. **Seacoast Expeditions** can accommodate 12 people per boat (for a total of up to 36 people) on its whale-watching cruises, which begin in April. The cruises last about three hours. ~ Coast Victoria Harbourside Hotel, 146 Kingston Street; 250-383-2254, 800-386-1525; www.seacoastexpeditions.com.

The most popular wildlife of Pacific Rim National Park is the Pacific gray whale, seen during spring migration between mid-March and mid-April.

Five-star Whale Watching offers three-hour cruises with trained naturalists, departing from the Inner Harbour. ~ 706 Douglas Street; 250-388-7223, 800-634-9617; www.5starwhales.com.

SEA KAYAKING   Kayaking is an up-close way to explore the coastal inlets of Vancouver Island, where there's plenty of sea mammals, birds and other wildlife to keep you company.

DOWNTOWN VICTORIA   **Ocean River Sports** will rent single or double kayaks to individuals, but only to those with kayaking experience. During the summer the store offers a three-hour "get your feet wet" introductory class for people who want to find out more about kayaking. Experienced kayakers can join one of the scheduled two- to three-day trips to the southern Gulf Islands or inquire about customized trips to other locales. ~ 1824 Store Street; 250-381-4233, 800-909-4233; www.oceanriver.com.

SOUTHWEST ISLAND   No experience is necessary to join one of the guided day trips or overnight excursions into Clayoquot Sound, along the island's west coast offered by **Tofino Sea Kayaking Co.** Longer excursions, lasting six days, head farther into Clayoquot Sound. ~ 320 Main Street, Tofino; 250-725-4222, 800-863-4664; www.tofino-kayaking.com.

There are several popular and worthwhile dive spots around Victoria and Sidney. Easily accessible from downtown Victoria, **Ogden Point Breakwater** on Dallas Road is a marine park where diving depths range from 20 to 100 feet. Not the best dive spot, but one that's great for snorkeling and exploring tidepools is **East Sooke Park**, between Victoria and Sooke. For advanced deep-sea diving, try **Race Rocks**, also a marine park, where high-current activity stirs up much marine life.

Between Victoria and Sidney, on the Saanich Peninsula, there's good shore access at **10-Mile Point**, the ecological reserve, although it has strong currents and is not for beginners. **Saanich Inlet** is several hundred feet deep with a sharp 200-foot drop and little tidal exchange, so there's no current.

DOWNTOWN VICTORIA   **Frank White's Dive Store** rents equipment and can provide information and directions for you and your diving buddy or buddies. The shop sponsors group shore dives every Saturday at 10 a.m. and monthly night dives on every second Thursday. You can also arrange a private dive trip with a dive master. ~ 1602 Blanshard Street, Victoria; 250-385-4713, 800-606-3977; www.frankwhites.com. **Great Ocean Adventures** rents gear and runs full-day trips to the lower Gulf Islands, Race Rocks and wreck dives along the artificial reefs off Sidney. ~ 1636 Cedar Hill Crossroad, Victoria; 250-475-2202, 800-414-2202; www.greatoceanadventures.com.

SCUBA DIVING

Boating and sailing are popular all around Victoria, the southeastern side of Vancouver Island and in the waters surrounding the Gulf Islands. The waters off the west coast are often too rough for relaxed boating, but some pleasure charters are available.

BOATING

SAANICH PENINSULA   For bareboating rentals (without a guide) of sailboats or powerboats, contact **Bosun's Charters Ltd**. Closed weekends in the winter. ~ Bosun's Landing, Sidney; 250-656-6644, 800-226-3694; www.bosuns.bc.ca.

Golf is very popular in Canada, and Vancouver Island is no exception.

GOLF

DOWNTOWN VICTORIA   There's a "mean" 16th hole at **Cedar Hill Municipal Golf Course**. It's a par-four downhill, with a two-tiered elevated green. ~ 1400 Derby Road; 250-595-3103. The nine-hole par-three **Henderson Park Golf Course** is fun for beginners. You'll only need three clubs to play this course, and you can rent them there. Closed in winter. ~ 2291 Cedar Hill Road; 250-370-7200. Just as the name suggests, **Olympic View Golf Club** offers views of the Olympic Peninsula from its 18 holes. It's cut right out of the wilderness, situated about 25 minutes from Victoria. ~ 643 Latoria Road; 250-474-3673. The nine-hole

Prospect Lake Golf Club is a challenging course set on the shore of Prospect Lake. ~ 4633 Prospect Lake Road; 250-479-2688; www.golfprospect.com. The executive nine-hole **Royal Oak Golf Course** is just minutes from the ferry. ~ 540 Marsett Place; 250-658-1433.

Vancouver Island, 275 miles long, is North America's largest Pacific island.

SAANICH PENINSULA Glen Meadows Golf and Country Club is a semiprivate 18-hole championship course that has hosted the World Lefthanders Golf Tournament. Also available are three tennis courts and a curling rink. ~ 1050 McTavish Road, Sidney; 250-656-3136; www.glenmeadows.bc.ca.

SOUTHEAST ISLAND For some beautiful views of southeast Vancouver Island, try the 18-hole **Eaglecrest Golf Club** in the Parksville-Qualicum neighborhood. ~ 2035 Island Highway West, Qualicum Beach; 250-752-9744, 800-567-1320. **Morningstar International Golf Course** hosts one of the events on Canada's professional golf tour. The holes have four sets of tees, so this course can provide a challenge to most golfers. ~ 525 Lowry's Road, Parksville; 250-248-2244, 800-567-1320.

BIKING

DOWNTOWN VICTORIA Although Victoria's terrain is perfect for cycling, the city's streets and walkways are often very crowded; there are no official bike paths, and many walking paths prohibit bicycles. One of the best bets for great views of the water and the Olympic Mountains is Victoria's **Beach Drive**, a six-mile route that passes through lovely Victorian neighborhoods near the ocean. It's an easy ride, with only a few low hills. But use caution on Beach Drive; it is winding and there is often considerable motor traffic. The **Galloping Goose Trail** is a multi-use section of the Trans-Canada Trail. You can pick it up in downtown Victoria and head west toward Sooke and beyond into the mountains. ~ Capital District Regional Parks; 250-478-3344.

For a map of bike routes in the area, contact the **Greater Victoria Cycling Coalition**. ~ 12 Centennial Square; 250-480-5155; www.gvcc.bc.ca.

Bike Rentals **Sports Rent** rents bikes and inline skates, as well as equipment for camping and water sports. ~ 1950 Government Street #3; 250-385-7368; www.sportsrentbc.com. **Cycle BC Rentals** has several locations that rent bikes and scooters. ~ 747 Douglas Street, 250-380-2453, 866-380-2453; 950 Wharf Street, 250-380-2453; www.cyclebc.ca.

HIKING

All distances listed for hiking trails are one way unless otherwise noted.

DOWNTOWN VICTORIA A good hiking resource is the **Capital Regional District**, with helpful information about trails in Victoria (see below). ~ 490 Atkins Avenue, Victoria, BC V9B

2Z8; 250-478-3344; www.crd.bc.ca/parks. For information on trails outside the Greater Victoria area, call B.C. Parks at 250-391-2300; www.env.gov.bc.ca/bcparks.

For an easy stroll (just over 2 miles) around the Inner Harbour take the **Westsong Way Walk**. From there you can watch all kinds of water vessels, including float planes, passenger catamarans, fishing boats and yachts.

VICTORIA NEIGHBORHOODS There is a maze of trails in **Thetis Lake Park**. Trails loop around Upper Thetis and Lower Thetis lakes and along Craigflower Creek.

The **Norn Trail** (less than 1 mile) at Mount Douglas Municipal Park is an easy walk on a well-marked route with plenty of trees. It joins the **Irvine Trail** to reach the summit of Mount Douglas. Hikers can access the Norn Trail from the parking lot at the intersection of Cordova Bay Road and Ash Road.

SAANICH PENINSULA On the **Island View Beach Regional Park Loop** (1.5 mile roundtrip), visitors can take an easy hike from the parking lot at Island View Park that loops through fragile sand dunes and provides views of the beach and Haro Strait.

The **Lakeside Route** (6.3 miles) located at Elk/Beaver Lake Regional Park is a shaded and well-groomed trail of wood chips and wooden bridges through the beaches surrounding Elk and Beaver lakes.

The trail system within **John Dean Provincial Park** (total of 6 miles of trails) provides views of Saanich Inlet, fertile farmland and orchards. Take East Saanich Road to Dean Park Road.

The **Goldmine Trail** (1 mile) at Goldstream Provincial Park is a dirt pathway that travels past a miner's spring and out to Squally Reach Lookout.

SOUTHEAST ISLAND For an easy walk in Nanaimo, take the **Harbourside Walkway** (2.5 miles) around the harbor with views of Protection Island and the Coast Mountains.

The **Galloping Goose Regional Trail** (37 miles) is a popular multi-use path. Favored by hikers, bicyclists and horses, it begins in downtown Victoria, winds through farmland of Metchosin, then into the semi-wilderness of the Sooke River Valley and up the hills providing ocean views. As a former railroad bed, most of it's perfect for long bike rides but a bit monotonous for walking.

SOUTHWEST ISLAND **Gold Mine Trail** (approximately 1 mile) begins just west of the Pacific Rim National Park information center on Route 4 for a nonstrenuous hike through a forest of amambilis fir, red cedar, hemlock, Douglas fir and red alder.

South Beach Trail (approximately .5 mile) starts behind the Wickaninnish Centre and winds through a stand of Sitka spruce. Side trails lead to rocky or sandy coves surrounded by headlands. At the far end of Lismer Beach, a boardwalk climbs over a bluff to South Beach. At the top of this bluff, the Wickaninnish Trail leads to the left, but continuing to the right takes hikers past groves of moss-enshrouded Sitka spruce and western hemlock.

The **Wickaninnish Trail** (1.5 miles) links Long Beach to Florencia Bay. The trail is a part of the early Tofino-Ucluelet land route that used beaches, forest trails and sheltered inlets to link the two towns before a road was built farther inland. Hikers have access via the South Beach Trail or from the Florencia Bay parking lot.

The most arduous trek on Vancouver Island is the **West Coast Trail** (47 miles), stretching along the west coast. Hikers need to be prepared for five to eight days traveling on an irregular slippery trail. There are tidepools, fjordlike cliffs, opportunities to see Pacific gray whales, sea lions, harbor seals, shorebirds and seabirds. Access to the southern trailhead is at Port Renfrew. The northern trailhead access is at Bamfield.

Transportation

CAR

Vancouver Island lies across the Strait of Juan de Fuca from the state of Washington and west of mainland British Columbia. Victoria and the southeastern communities are accessible from either. **Route 14** runs from Victoria through Sooke to Port Renfrew on the west coast. The **Trans-Canada Highway (Route 1)** goes from Victoria to Nanaimo. **Route 4** goes from the Parksville-Qualicum area west to Port Alberni, leading to the west coast communities of Ucluelet and Tofino.

AIR

The **Victoria International Airport** is 20 minutes from Victoria in Sidney. Carriers include Air Canada, Horizon Air, Pacific Coastal Airlines and WestJet. ~ www.victoriaairport.com.

Airport bus service between downtown Victoria and the Victoria International Airport is provided by **AKAL Airport Shuttle Bus**. ~ 250-386-2525.

Helijet Airways has helicopter service into downtown Victoria from downtown Vancouver, and from Victoria Harbour to Vancouver Airport. ~ 250-382-6222, 800-665-4354; www.helijet.com.

Nanaimo Airport is served by Air Canada and Canadian Western Airlines. ~ www.nanaimoairport.com.

Floatplanes offer a unique experience as they take off on the water and land directly in Victoria's Inner Harbour. **Kenmore Air Harbor** has a daily schedule to Victoria and the San Juan Islands from the Seattle area and also goes to Nanaimo in the summer. ~ 425-486-1257, 866-435-9524; www.kenmoreair.com. **Harbour Air**, the B.C. coast's major operator, flies from Victoria to the Gulf Islands, Vancouver and other coastal destinations. ~ 604-274-1277, 800-665-0212; www.harbour-air.com.

FERRY

Ferries provide daily, year-round sailings to Victoria and Nanaimo. The number of sailings daily usually increases in the summer, but it is advisable to call for up-to-date schedules and rates.

Travelers wishing to depart from the U.S. can take Black Ball Transport, Washington State Ferries or Victoria Clipper to Victoria. **Black Ball Transport** takes vehicles and foot passengers from Port Angeles to Victoria's Inner Harbour. ~ 101 East Railroad Avenue, Port Angeles, WA, 360-457-4491; 430 Belleville Street, Victoria, BC, 250-386-2202; www.cohoferry.com. **Washington State Ferries** takes vehicles and foot passengers on a scenic route through Washington's San Juan Islands between Anacortes, WA, and Sidney, BC, and buses take foot passengers to downtown Victoria from Sidney. ~ Seattle, WA, 206-464-6400; www.wsdot.gov/ferries. The **Victoria Clipper** ships are 300-passenger, high-speed catamarans that run year-round between Seattle's Pier 69 and Victoria's Inner Harbour with separate trips to the San Juan Islands from May through September. ~ U.S., 800-888-2535; Seattle, WA 206-448-5000; Victoria, BC, 250-382-8100; www.victoriaclipper.com.

B.C. Ferries travels year-round from Tsawwassen, just south of Vancouver, to Swartz Bay, a scenic, half-hour drive by car or bus from Victoria. Long, long lines in summer suggest trying out B.C.'s ferry reservations system; call the main ferries number. You can also sail from Tsawwassen or Horseshoe Bay to Nanaimo. ~ Victoria, BC, 250-386-3431; within B.C., 888-223-3779; www. bcferries.com.

VIA Rail provides Vancouver Island rail service between Victoria and Courtenay, with stops at Nanaimo. ~ 888-842-7245; www. viarail.ca.

TRAIN

Agencies in downtown Victoria and at the Victoria airport include **Avis Rent A Car** (800-331-1084), **Budget Rent A Car** (800-268-8900), **Hertz Rent A Car** (within the U.S., 800-654-3001; within Canada, 800-263-0600), **Island Rent A Car** (250-384-4881), **National Car Rental** (800-328-4567).

CAR RENTALS

Island Coach Lines (250-385-4411) has bus service between Victoria and other points on Vancouver Island, connecting with B.C. Ferries routes as well. **B.C. Transit** (250-382-6161) provides local bus service throughout the greater Victoria area. B.C. Transit and Victoria Regional Transit Commission offer public transit service to the disabled called **Handy DART** (250-727-7811).

PUBLIC TRANSIT

In the Victoria area, you will find **Bluebird Cabs** (250-382-4235, 800-665-7055), **Empress Taxi/Yellow Cabs** (250-381-2222, 800-808-6881) and **Victoria Taxi** (250-383-7111, 888-842-7111).

TAXIS

Index

608

Lodging Index

Dining Index

HIDDEN GUIDES

Adventure travel or a relaxing vacation?—"Hidden" guidebooks are the only travel books in the business to provide detailed information on both. Aimed at environmentally aware travelers, our motto is "Where Vacations Meet Adventures." These books combine details on unique hotels, restaurants and sightseeing with information on camping, sports and hiking for the outdoor enthusiast.

THE NEW KEY GUIDES

Based on the concept of ecotourism, The New Key Guides are dedicated to the preservation of Central America's rare and endangered species, architecture and archaeology. Filled with helpful tips, they give travelers everything they need to know about these exotic destinations.

PARADISE FAMILY GUIDES

Ideal for families traveling with kids of any age—toddlers to teenagers—Paradise Family Guides offer a blend of travel information unlike any other guides to the Hawaiian islands. With vacation ideas and tropical adventures that are sure to satisfy both action-hungry youngsters and relaxation-seeking parents, these guides meet the specific needs of each and every family member.

Ulysses Press books are available at bookstores everywhere. If any of the following titles are unavailable at your local bookstore, ask the bookseller to order them.

You can also order books directly from Ulysses Press
P.O. Box 3440, Berkeley, CA 94703
800-377-2542 or 510-601-8301
fax: 510-601-8307
www.ulyssespress.com
e-mail: ulysses@ulyssespress.com

HIDDEN GUIDEBOOKS

____ Hidden Arizona, $16.95
____ Hidden Baja, $14.95
____ Hidden Belize, $15.95
____ Hidden Big Island of Hawaii, $13.95
____ Hidden Boston & Cape Cod, $14.95
____ Hidden British Columbia, $18.95
____ Hidden Cancún & the Yucatán, $16.95
____ Hidden Carolinas, $17.95
____ Hidden Coast of California, $18.95
____ Hidden Colorado, $15.95
____ Hidden Disneyland, $13.95
____ Hidden Florida, $19.95
____ Hidden Florida Keys & Everglades, $13.95
____ Hidden Georgia, $16.95
____ Hidden Hawaii, $19.95
____ Hidden Idaho, $14.95
____ Hidden Kauai, $13.95
____ Hidden Los Angeles, $14.95
____ Hidden Maine, $15.95
____ Hidden Maui, $14.95
____ Hidden Miami, $14.95

____ Hidden Montana, $15.95
____ Hidden New England, $19.95
____ Hidden New Mexico, $15.95
____ Hidden Oahu, $14.95
____ Hidden Oregon, $15.95
____ Hidden Pacific Northwest, $18.95
____ Hidden Philadelphia, $14.95
____ Hidden Puerto Vallarta, $14.95
____ Hidden Salt Lake City, $14.95
____ Hidden San Diego, $14.95
____ Hidden San Francisco & Northern California, $19.95
____ Hidden Seattle, $14.95
____ Hidden Southern California, $19.95
____ Hidden Southwest, $19.95
____ Hidden Tahiti, $18.95
____ Hidden Tennessee, $16.95
____ Hidden Utah, $16.95
____ Hidden Walt Disney World, $13.95
____ Hidden Washington, $15.95
____ Hidden Wine Country, $14.95
____ Hidden Wyoming, $15.95

PARADISE FAMILY GUIDES

____ Paradise Family Guides: Kaua'i, $17.95
____ Paradise Family Guides: Maui, $17.95
____ Paradise Family Guides: Big Island of Hawai'i, $17.95

Mark the book(s) you're ordering and enter the total cost here ⇨ [   ]

California residents add 8.75% sales tax here ⇨ [   ]

Shipping, check box for your preferred method and enter cost here ⇨ [   ]

❏ BOOK RATE   **FREE! FREE! FREE!**

❏ PRIORITY MAIL/UPS GROUND   cost of postage

❏ UPS OVERNIGHT OR 2-DAY AIR   cost of postage   [   ]

Billing, enter total amount due here and check method of payment ⇨

❏ CHECK   ❏ MONEY ORDER

❏ VISA/MASTERCARD _____ EXP. DATE _____

NAME _____ PHONE _____

ADDRESS _____

CITY _____ STATE _____ ZIP _____

MONEY-BACK GUARANTEE ON DIRECT ORDERS PLACED THROUGH ULYSSES PRESS.

ABOUT THE AUTHORS

NICKY LEACH, the update author for this edition, is a Santa Fe–based author specializing in writing books on the natural and cultural history of the American West. She has written over 40 guidebooks, including several award-winning visitor guides to national parks. Nicky lives in a historic artist's home off the Santa Fe Trail with her tabby cat Molly.

JOHN GOTTBERG has traveled and worked all over the world. The former chief editor of the Insight Guide series and the travel news and graphics editor for the *Los Angeles Times*, he has written eight travel guides, including *Hidden Seattle* and *Hidden Montana*, and been published in *Travel & Leisure* and *Island* magazines. He lives in Seattle, WA.

ERIC LUCAS is a freelance writer and editor who has been a newspaper editorial columnist, travel writer, magazine editor and business journalist. Author of Ulysses Press' *Hidden British Columbia*, he is also an avid gardener, fisherman, backpacker and runner.

STEPHEN DOLAINSKI, a regular contributor to *Westways* and *Avenues*, is a freelance travel editor and writer living in Southern California. He has written about travel and business for magazines, and has contributed to several travel guidebooks, including *Hidden Southern California*.

RICHARD HARRIS has written or co-written 20 other guidebooks including *Hidden Colorado*, *Hidden Bahamas* and *Hidden Guatemala*. He has also served as contributing editor on guides for John Muir Publications, Fodor's, Birnbaum and Access guides and has written for numerous magazines.